Circles and Settings

SUNY Series in Gender and Society
Cornelia Butler Flora, Editor

Circles
and *Role Changes of American Women*
Settings

Helena Znaniecka Lopata

State University of New York Press

Published by
State University of New York Press, Albany

© 1994 State University of New Y ork

For information, address the State University of New York Press,
State University Plaza, Albany, NY 12246

Production by Bernadine Dawes
Marketing by Dana Yanulavich

Library of Congress Cataloging-in-Publication Data

Lopata, Helena Znaniecka, 1925–
    Circles and settings : role changes of American women / Helena
Znaniecka Lopata.
       p. cm. — (SUNY series in gender and society)
    Includes bibliographical references and index.
    ISBN 0-7914-1767-0 (hardcover : alk. paper) — ISBN
0-7914-1768-9 (pbk. : alk. paper)
      1. Sex role—United States—History. 2. Woman—United States—
Social conditions. 3. Woman—United States—Psychology.
I. Title. II. Series.
HQ1075.5.U6L66   1994
305.42'0973—dc20   93-14927
                                         CIP

1 2 3 4 5 6 7 8 9 10

Dedicated to
Allisa Menasco
Caitlin Eileen Lopata
Colleen Elizabeth Lopata

Contents

Preface

The role involvements of Americans have changed considerably since the 1950s when I was a foreigner to America. I first became fascinated by the gap between how its women were self- and other-defined and the contributions they were actually making to the society. Upon the birth of our daughter, and while I finished my Ph.D. at the University of Chicago, my husband and I moved from Hyde Park to suburban Skokie. We were convinced that this move was "best for the children," even though I was leery about leaving the academic community to dwell among American housewives in the "wilderness," which was described so negatively by many observers.

To my surprise and pleasure, I found suburbia and its women very different from the stereotypes. Armed with Znaniecki's dynamic theory of social roles as sets of social relations, and the methodology of symbolic interactionism, which I acquired from many theoretical ancestors through Herbert Blumer, I decided to study this gap between the American portrayal of women (as believed by the women themselves) and the actual behavior of the women I observed around me. Howie Becker's concept of "becoming" (from "becoming a marijuana user"), and the concepts of "life space" and "life cycle" from the Chicago School of Human Development, enabled me to develop a social role definition for the American "housewife." I interviewed many suburban and urban housewives as well as women with paying jobs. My questions focused on women's conceptions of their major roles, how these roles changed from their grandmother's time, and how they expected them to change by the time their own daughters reached adulthood. I also asked them about their perceptions of past and future changes in the roles of men. I learned what the home, neighboring; couple companionate interaction and friendship, as well as community involvement, meant to these respondents.

Over the years, my interest in the involvements, self-concepts, and life spaces of American adult women became evident through numerous studies and efforts to develop middle-range concepts and theories that would help answer some of the sociological questions. The studies focused on the congruity of constructed reality, commitments, and changes over the life course, including role modifications produced by the death of a husband, and the effect of support systems on widows. Remembering Everett Hughes, I continued to be interested in the occupations and professions, the meaning of different kinds of jobs, and how people pull roles together into role clusters. Using the symbolic interactionist framework, I continued to turn to women for the answers. I even managed, while studying Polonia, to look at the roles of women in the Polish American community. References to these studies are made throughout this book.

I finally decided to combine as much of this knowledge as possible into a single volume on role involvements, as seen from the perspective of a feminist symbolic interactionist. The venture has been an exciting one, assisted by the contributions of an overwhelming variety of scholars. There is an abundant body of knowledge concerning American women, not only as a result of the feminist revival, but also as a response to the dramatic changes in the roles and life spaces of all people. In addition, symbolic interactionism has progressed in many directions from its original founding fathers, and I have drawn freely on the work of such scholars as Goffman, Becker, Turner, Rosenberg, Stone, Daniels, Denzin, Maines, Strauss, Gusfield and others. In recent years there has also been an increasing number of women combining feminist and interactionist perspectives in their research.

It is impossible to thank individually the many persons and formal groups with whom I have interacted and who have helped me in the various ventures, but some need special recognition. Let me first list my funding sources: The Midwest Council for Social Research on Aging, Roosevelt and Loyola Universities, the Administration on Aging, and the Social Security Administration. Hank Brehm of the Social Security Administration also provided invaluable assistance in dealing with vast quantities of data needed by a qualitatively trained sociologist. The National Opinion Research Center of the University of Chicago and the Survey Research Laboratory of the University of Illinois, Chicago, conducted the interviews of the larger studies.

I can't help thinking back over my own role as a student, especially now that so much biographical data about our cohort at the University of Chicago are coming out. I was fortunate in having Blumer, Hughes and Wirth on my dissertation committee, and some great colleagues in my study groups. The University of Illinois provided me with a wonderful background, thanks to E. T. Hiller, William Albig and Donald Taft. Obviously, my debt to my father, Florian Witold Znaniecki, and my mother, Eileen Markley Znaniecki, is enormous, not only for sociological imagination, but also for having created such an exciting home atmosphere on both continents.

The major research of the last twenty-plus years has been carried forth from the Center for the Comparative Study of Social Roles at Loyola University of Chicago. Many people have taken part in these projects. The main contributors to the various studies in which women are featured include: Kathleen Fordham Norr, Cheryl Allyn Miller, Debra Barnewolt, Frank Steinhart, Sister Kim, and Monica Shoemaker. Ligaya McGovern, Rebecca Morrow-Nye, Kandace Pearson and Colleen Carpenter have been involved with the recent studies.

I have spent many hours of informal discussion with colleagues at meetings of the Society for the Study of Social Interaction, Sociologists for Women in Society, and the Society for the Study of Social Problems. I also happen to be a person who has gained much from the American Sociological Association (more in recent years than during some of the more formal, male-dominated eras of the past). I have become increasingly involved in comparative research and international events—which I enjoy tremendously—with the help of Jan Trost, Irene Levin, Lea Shamgar-Handleman, Stella Quah and James Beckford. Judith Levy, Nona Glazer, Joe Pleck, Warren Peterson, Beth Hess, Millie Seltzer, Lillian Troll, Robert Atchley, Rhoda Blumberg, David Maines and many others have my gratitude for all the ideas and idea testing related to *Circles and Settings*.

I am very fortunate in the colleagues I have had at Loyola University of Chicago. Ideas have been formulated in discussions with Judith Wittner (she has an enormous fund of knowledge as to the roles of women), Kathy McCourt, Peter Whalley, Kirsten Gronbjerg, and Phil Nyden of our very companionate department of sociology. I would have been stuck many a time with the (now greatly appreciated) PC had it not been for Richard Block, Ken Johnson, Anne Figert, Fred Kniss and Chris Fry.

As before, I have looked to my nonsociological friends for discussion and have even asked them to review manuscripts to see if they think the ideas reflect life as they see it. This includes Teddy Lopata Menasco, Dennis Menasco, Stefan Lopata, and Peggy Lopata, Dick Lopata, Helen Janus Lopata Burns, Cele Shure, Pat Benoliel, Carol Hanke, Juliet McNamara, and recently, Jule Grady Barry, Joan Sullivan and Jeanne Goulet. Literally thousands of women have contributed directly to my research, or to the research of scholars whose studies I have used here. I hope that they get a chance to read the results and that they enjoy them.

Very direct editorial help with this book has been provided by Michael Ames, Judith Levy, Ronnie Steinberg, Catherine Surra, Rose Coser, Judith Wittner, and an anonymous reviewer. I am especially grateful to Wendy Nelson, an outstanding and imaginative copyeditor. It is hard to write alone and see alternative ways of organizing and explaining ideas. The staff of the sociology department at Loyola University of Chicago has been extremely cooperative. This has included, over all the years, Peggy Cusick, Maureen Abraham, Dorothy Blumental, Tracy Wood, Karen Chase, and Mary Ellen Folk.

1

Social Roles of American Women

Enormous changes have occurred in the lives and role involvements of American women in the past century and a half. Our grandmothers led lives different from those of our mothers, who, in turn, experienced different lives from our own. How can we understand these differences and any abiding similarities?

This book examines some of the ways American women have been modifying their social roles. It is guided by the idea that the historically recent processes of modernization or social development affected men and women, urban and rural residents, upper and lower classes differently, but that in general there has been a movement toward greater societal and individual complexity and autonomy (Inkeles and Smith 1974; Inkeles 1983).[1] These processes involve three ideal-typical periods: the traditional, the transitional, and the modern. Ideal type analysis accentuates the differentiating characteristics of the phenomena (Weber 1949). The fact that we can trace these periods in the history of American women does not mean that all women currently living in this society are involved in modern

1

type roles. Modernization has affected women in different settings differently, as stated above. In fact, most American women are involved in transitional forms or types of family roles, and many even remain in traditional roles of, for example, wife and mother. The complexity of the society and the mobility of world populations insure the presence of all three types in even as modern a society as the American one. The vast majority of the world is still situated in traditional times, as far as women's roles are concerned.

Traditional, preindustrial society embedded women and men in an extended family system, organized usually along patrilineal lines, with patriarchal authority and patrilocal residence. Women's roles were formalized and established in this familistic intergenerational structure. According to Aries (1965), most European men and women were living in one of two worlds prior to the eighteenth century: that of the manor house or that of the village. Within each world each person was involved in a complexity of social roles. Life was public, which meant that each person had multiple obligations to many others and enjoyed multiple rights in relations with them. Mothers were assisted in child care and rearing by extended families, all the residents of households, and even communities. Children moved among adults and other youths with relative freedom but simultaneously were active in contributing to the economic maintenance of the social units. The role of wife was equally complicated by the multiplicity of people with whom she interacted precisely because she was the wife. These roles were embedded in an extended kinship network. The role of homemaker was equally complex— many women managed large households, whether in a village or in a manor. Aries (1965) found manor homes to contain as many as two hundred persons living inside or nearby who operated as a household, with many more coming and going for different reasons. The roles of neighbor and friend, of community and societal member, certainly varied by social classes and by age as well as gender, yet there appears to have been a relative similarity in the life spaces of men and women within each class. Upper-class daughters were educated by the same tutors as were their brothers, since they had to become knowledgeable about managing complex social units. However, formal public education (as in universities) excluded women until relatively recent centuries. Women ruled households and principalities in the absence of men, or in their own right. Each person operated within his or her *okolica,* as the authors of *The Polish Peasant in Europe and America* (Thomas and Znaniecki 1918–

20) called the territory within which a person's reputation was contained. Among the upper classes, this could include a vast territory with the help of communication and transportation networks. Among the peasants, emergencies and daily life necessitated a tight interdependence of more localized people.

The transitional period of social development, which lasted since the middle of the eighteenth century and even up to recent years in some parts of Europe and America, started to introduce dramatic changes in women's roles (Lerner 1958). Industrialization and urbanization disorganized the ascribed, i.e. assigned, familial and community roles. Mass education and mobility diminished the power of these social units. The combination organized increasing segments of work into jobs away from the ongoing life, and specialized roles emerged in other institutions. The effects of increasing societal complexity first affected middle-class urban men, freeing them from dependence upon the male family line and the local community. The public world of economic and political life, judged to be of primary importance by the blooming American society, became dominated by men. The home lost much of its centrality, and the settings and social circles of women narrowed considerably into a "woman's sphere" (Ehrenreich and English 1979; Sicherman 1975). Although women were freed from the control of the male kin network, they were transformed into personal dependents of their fathers and husbands (Eichler 1973).

This artificial division of the world into two spheres, one much smaller than, and judged inferior to, the other, became difficult to maintain in rapidly developing, complex societies. As the transitional period moved closer to modernization in the last few decades, women started revolting over the restrictions on them and increasingly ventured into male-dominated public arenas. However, the separation of women's and men's interests and developed abilities was so embedded in American society that change was very, very difficult for these pioneers. Structural and sociopsychological barriers often made it necessary for women to focus either on the private domain, centered in the home and family, or on the public, in the form of occupations, careers, and organizational involvements.

Increasing modernization allegedly has made it necessary for all members of a society to share the complexity of its life. Mass education, the demands of democracy, and ideological reconstructions of reality by various social movements, especially that of women, are increasingly individuating people's self-concepts and patterns of behavior. Women, and in some relations men, are creating or entering negotiated, rather than formalized, social roles.

The uneven rate of social development means that no matter how "modern" or developed a society is considered to be by those labeling social change, many traditional or transitional aspects of major institutions exist side by side with new technology and occupations. This means that not all women have as yet benefited from these changes (if we can call these changes "benefits")—far from it. Poverty, lack of education, discrimination, sexism, and racism keep the majority of women from exercising free choices in their role involvements and limit their rights of negotiation with circle members of many roles. In fact, most men have not benefited fully from social development. Many are stuck in the transitional stage of rigid settings, roles, and schedules. Both men and women are carrying the double burden of traditional and modern role involvements, and are feeling the strain and conflicts. We must acknowledge that even American society has not become fully "modern," if by that we mean providing equal opportunity for the development of human potential. But increasing proportions of Americans are living within, and enjoying, a complex, flexible, and negotiated social life space.

We will examine the changing roles of American women through the perspective of a symbolic interactionist form of social role theory.

Social Role as a Set of Social Relations

A *social role* is a set of patterned, mutually interdependent relations between a social person and a social circle, involving negotiated duties and personal rights (Znaniecki 1965; see also Lopata 1966, 1969b, 1971b, and 1991a).[2] The *social person* is that "package" of characteristics with which an individual enters a specific role. The *social circle* contains all those persons with whom the person interacts in the performance of *duties or obligations* and from whom she or he receives *personal rights*.[3] These definitions and the analyses that stem from them are based on a symbolic interactionist perspective.[4]

The *social person* carries the title of the social role, although it is only in relationship with circle members that the role actually exists. A social person is that package of characteristics that an individual pulls together to enter and carry forth her or his part of the role. The total individual has many characteristics, consisting of a constructed reality, sentiments, and emotions, as well as behavior, that are not called for or needed in each social role. Human beings live in a symbolic world whose meaning or reality they construct (Blumer 1969). The person of a student is quite different from that of a girlfriend, daughter, or waitress. Thus, a woman wishing to enter a specific social role prepares herself through anticipatory socialization—the process of learning necessary behavior and visualizing the self in the role. She becomes a candidate and, upon acceptance by the social circle, carries forth the duties, and receives the rights of that role. Or she can pull together a social circle and assign duties and rights, as in the role of homemaker.

The title of a role contains the typified, categorical identification, or the ideal image, of how a person is expected to fulfill the role's basic purpose (see Gerhardt's 1980 discussion of Simmel, Weber, and Schutz). A mother must give birth or adopt a child and take on the role in cooperation with others. If she is judged unfit, the child may be taken away from her. She must have the characteristics that will guarantee cooperation from all circle members besides the child, since she cannot take care of the child herself.[5] The social circle can include the father, relatives on either side, pediatricians, teachers, representatives of the state, and so forth. The title of mother is carried by her into interactional situations (Simmel 1971). It serves as a label, an anticipation of behavior by potential circle members, and as a means of evaluating her as a social person. The title, however, is not the social role itself, since that requires continued relationships between the social person and the social circle.

The whole process by which an existing social circle such as an employing organization selects a social person is indicative of the qualifications deemed necessary for the role. Often latent criteria are evident only in the characteristics of the persons who are rejected. The Catholic church is convinced that women cannot be good priests. Management consulting or law firms have frequently argued (allegedly only in the past) that they would love to hire a black or a woman consultant or lawyer, but that their clients would not accept persons with those identities.

The social person must have the sort of personality that is assumed to be necessary for meeting the purposes of the relations and for interaction with circle members, and must be able to "take the role of the other," as George Herbert Mead (1934) called the process of empathetically understanding other human beings. Physical characteristics such as sight or hearing and locomotion are often demanded of the social person, unless she or he can prove she or he has the ability to function in the negotiated manner without them.

The *social circle* of a role contains all those people toward whom the social person has duties and who have obligations toward him or her that are that social person's rights that enable him or her to carry forth the role in the agreed-upon manner. The social person's relationships with each segment of the social circle are negotiated, unless enforced by other segments or outside powers. No matter how clearly each contributor to the role has defined it prior to involvement, the actual set of relations always requires flexibility of interaction that must be negotiated. The social circle can best be literally visualized as a circle, as in figure 1. At its center is the social person, with duties and rights of self-maintenance necessary to carry forth other duties.

All social circles contain "clients" or beneficiaries, who in turn have duties toward the social person that are part of her or his rights. These rights may simply be the permission to the social person to perform her or his duties. The title of a role often contains a presupposition as to the beneficiary. University professors profess to students, judges judge defendants, architects design buildings for clients. Social roles tend to contain assisting segments of the social circle, which vary enormously in the amount of work they contribute and the duties that must be directed toward them. Each member of the assisting segments must be related to the beneficiary, with duties and rights connected to what they do for him or her. In fact, the beneficiaries do not necessarily receive the greatest amount of direct attention by the social person, as in the case of patients of physicians who have a large staff of receptionists, nurses, laboratory technicians, medical specialists, and hospital personnel who serve as intermediaries. In modern times the doctor often spends more time with these circle members than with the patient for whom all the activity is carried forth.

Many roles contain a "colleague" segment—people carrying forth the same role in the same organization—with whom cooperation is often necessary and without whom there would be no role for the social person. A saleswoman needs others selling goods in a large store. The segment containing suppliers includes anyone whose objects or services make possible the person's performance of her duties.

A social person may have rights to include or exclude members of a preexisting social circle. If she creates her own circle, she will

Fig. 1.

THE SOCIAL ROLE OF HOMEMAKER*

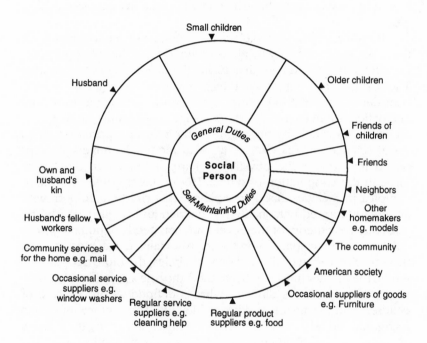

Beneficiaries

Small children

Older children

Husband

Friends of children

Friends

General Duties

Own and husband's kin

Social Person

Self-Maintaining Duties

Neighbors

Husband's fellow workers

Other homemakers e.g. models

Community services for the home e.g. mail

The community

American society

Occasional service suppliers e.g. window washers

Occasional suppliers of goods e.g. Furniture

Regular service suppliers e.g. cleaning help

Regular product suppliers e.g. food

Suppliers and Assistants

* The size of the area represents its relative significance to the role, performed at a complex level. Modified from Helena Znaniecka Lopata, *Occupation: Housewife.* (New York: Oxford University Press, 1971), 138.

include those she thinks necessary for the carrying forth of her duties, or those whom she may not be able to avoid. A wife may have to relate with the in-laws who come into her circle with the husband. The social circles of different persons in the same type of role can vary considerably due to the influences of size, setting, the number and social class of beneficiaries. Hillary Clinton, as the manager of the household of the president of the United States, has a different social circle than she had when she lived a more private life.

The *duties* of a social role's central person are of two major sorts: those deemed necessary by all involved to meet the role's purpose, and the relational duties that make the whole process possible. These duties are not necessarily determined by what we would consider logical methods, since they tend to be lodged in history and beliefs about life held by the participants. Certainly, some duties are made inevitable by the nature of the role's purposes. As far as social science has discovered, a social mother is universally supposed to care for the physical welfare of her child, directly or through the cooperation of others. Her duties become even more complex in societies that do not believe that children are born with an already formed personality (Ehrenreich and English 1979). The relatively new theory of the developmental needs of human potential places a heavy burden on the main socializer. The more people that are involved in each child's social circles, the more people with whom the mother must interact to meet the role's purposes. Cultures and even subcultures differ in what is defined as proper care of children and the means used to achieve it. The mother must also recognize and relate to all the circle members, accepting their duties as her rights and giving them the resources they need to help her.

The *personal rights* of a social role include all those resources that must be supplied to the social person so that she can perform her duties as negotiated with circle members. Her rights also include circle members' obligations toward her. The personal rights of a social role must contain the permission to carry forth the duties. As Hughes (1971) and other sociologists of work point out, many roles cannot be carried out without the person's learning "guilty knowledge" about circle members. Priests, psychiatrists, physicians, and newspaper reporters claim and usually receive the right to gain, and not to divulge, confidential knowledge about people with whom they work, no matter how important that information is to others. The right to safety, unless waived by the social person—as in the case of military personnel in time of war—is an important right, as is the right to be recognized and to have one's performance of one's duties acknowledged. Rights in roles with similar functions vary by societal norms regarding what is necessary to the person.

Cooperation from circle members must be built into personal rights, because duties cannot be carried forth otherwise. The rights and duties of a role are often paired. The duty to exert authority must be accompanied by the right to obedience. If initiating behavior is not required, then someone else must direct the person. All roles are located in one or more social settings, such as houses, factories, or streets, with specific rights and duties of access and management of the space and objects.

Role Strain

The fact that social circles can be large and complicated may result in a great deal of role strain. One of the sources of strain is *role overload,* which occurs when there is too much to do in general, or when too many circle members make too many demands, each considering his or hers as most important (Goode 1960). The social person may be deeply committed to her role and frustrated by obstacles or barriers to adequate performance, such as the lack of cooperation from others. Role strain also arises when members of the social circle make conflicting or inconsistent demands. Fathers and children sometimes demand contradictory behavior from the mother. Strain also occurs when a circle member makes conflicting demands, creating a double-bind situation. Problems can also arise when the role demands behavior that the person considers to be objectionable or incompatible with her or his abilities and desires (Turner 1978 and 1981).

The social person can handle role strain in several ways, such as compartmentalization (dealing with each demand separately), delegation of duties, or negotiation. She or he can ignore a troublesome member of the circle. And, if things are too bad and there are alternatives, she or he can leave the role or that role relationship. Divorce is an established way out of a marriage, and jobs may be quit. All kinds of culturally approved explanations are available to people who fail to meet some role expectations, while barriers against intrusion can prevent circle members from claiming rights (Becker 1951; Scott and Lyman 1968). Some people, of course,

thrive in roles that require constant negotiation and flexibility, preferring these to roles in which all relational problems are allegedly
minimized.

Social circles, especially organized groups, can be aware of
problems built into their roles and may introduce strain-reducing
mechanisms (Goode 1960). Roles can be shifted in the structure;
third parties (such as therapists) may be brought in to mediate
conflict; norms of adequacy of role performance can be redefined;
and people of "the right persuasion" or the "right" color or other
characteristics can be hired to produce greater trust among circle
members. Kanter (1977) found corporation men unwilling to admit
women to their circle because they did not trust them.

The Role Cluster and Social Life Space

Each human being is involved in numerous social roles, at any time
and throughout the life course. The *role cluster* changes over time,
as some roles are exited, new ones are added, modifications are
introduced to current ones, and hierarchies are adjusted. In order to
explore the connections among roles in an individual's cluster, I
have developed the concept of "social life space" (Lopata 1969b and
1987e), adapted from the work of Kurt Lewin (see Deutsch 1954),
who used the term *life space* to refer to a field or total situation of
action containing the actor.[6] My housewife interviews (Lopata 1971b
and 1987e) indicated a very logical way of organizing the social life
space: We can look at roles within the same institutional dimension
as sharing a similar cultural base and so as enabling more effective
negotiation than do roles in different institutions.

People vary in the *dimensional richness* of their social roles, that
is, in the number of roles in which they are involved within a single
institution and also in the relative importance assigned each role.
Sociologists refer to an institution as a set of patterned procedures
by which a major area of societal life is carried forth. We can thus
compare different women within the same society, or cross-cultur-
ally, or women to men, in terms of the richness of their involvement
in any of the major institutions, such as educational, family, political,
economic, religious, and recreational institutions. People also vary
in the complexity or multidimensionality of their social life spaces,
in that they undertake roles in different institutions (see figure 2).

This perspective is central to my analysis of the changing roles

Fig. 2.

A MULTIDIMENSIONAL LIFE SPACE WITH VARIED "RICHNESS" OF INSTITUTIONAL DIMENSIONS

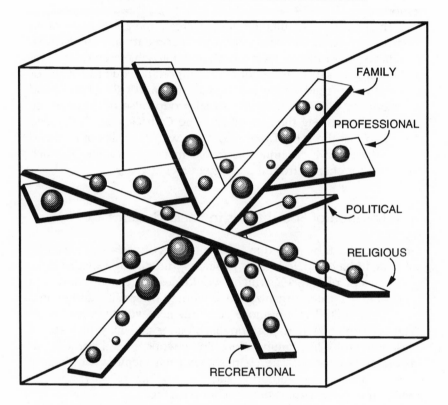

FAMILY

PROFESSIONAL

POLITICAL

RELIGIOUS

RECREATIONAL

Modified from Helena Znaniecka Lopata, "Women's Family Roles in Life Course Perspective." Pp. 381–407 in *Analyzing Gender: A Handbook of Social Science Research,* edited by Beth B. Hess and Myra Marx Ferree (Newbury Park, Calif.: Sage, 1987), p. 384.

of American women. The process of modernization appears to proceed first from the destruction of a full life space within a traditional community, flattening women's life spaces into the domestic/ family sphere, and men's into the public sphere, during the transitional period. Only gradually does modern society provide opportunities for socialization and education to expand people's life spaces again to new multidimensionality, this time within a greater scale of complexity. Modern life requires the presence of many multidimensional people, able to manage roles in most institutions and even roles bridging two or more institutions. However, not all members of even modern societies have such complexity of self. Most people still exist in relatively "flat" social life spaces, focusing on one institution.

The presence of multiple roles can create *role conflict,* similar in sources to role strain. One of the ways people try to diminish role conflict is by organizing their role clusters into a hierarchical system, either temporarily, as roles surface in importance due to events, or in more or less rigid structures (Lopata 1969b and 1987e; Lopata and Barnewolt 1984; Stryker 1980). Social groups also try to decrease role conflict among their members. The Catholic church decided long ago that the role of priest conflicts with the roles of husband and father, and it continues to forbid marriage in spite of much pressure for change from the clergy in recent years.

The Location of Social Roles in Social Systems

Social roles can be placed in different types of social systems, one of which I have labeled "chart positions," modifying Davis's (1966, 68) concept of "office," which "would designate a position in a deliberately created organization, governed by specific and limited rules in a limited group, more generally achieved than ascribed." The concept of "chart position" is broader and may be used in describing roles in a family, a kinship network, a neighborhood, or a formal association. The chart shows each member the lines of communication and authority, and the province of activity within which the role is connected to other social roles.

Another system within which social roles can be positioned is that of prestige, often accompanied by power or its legitimated version of authority. In American society, men are located at a higher-status position in the gender stratification system than are women. Such a location has very important consequences for the status of other roles available to men and permeates the availability of choices of many objects, such as kitchens or airplanes, within the culture.

People entering social roles as social persons or members of social circles usually have a fairly good idea of what to expect, because models of roles are contained in cultures. Most roles have a historical base and are performed by more than one person at any given time. The models are more or less visible parts of the culture, learned at home and in other primary and secondary groups such as neighborhoods and schools. Established roles vary by specialized function, alternative ways of meeting purposes, and relationships of members. Thus, there are two ways in which social roles influence societies and their members: as actual sets of relations (e.g., waitresses at a Four Seasons restaurant) and as cultural models of relations (e.g., our image of waitresses in general).

The Life Course of Role Involvements of American Women

The presence of cultural models of roles does not guarantee the match between social persons and the social circles that makes the life of the society possible. In order for the whole thing to work, new societal members must be socialized into "humanness" and the necessary knowledge, identities, and motivations to become involved in all kinds of interactions and social roles. Social groups develop whole socialization and educational systems to guarantee that enough people want to, and are able to, carry forth needed roles.

One important form of socialization is into pervasive identities that are deemed appropriate to different roles, and one of these identities is gender. Every society identifies each newborn as male or female on the basis of its visible genitals. The implications of such classification, however, vary considerably the world over, because it contains assumptions as to personality and potentials for action throughout childhood and adulthood. Socialization insures that each individual develops the appropriate *gender personal identity*, which is carried everywhere and is more or less intrusive in all social roles.

One of the problems with discussions of gender identity has been the recent introduction into the social sciences of the theoretically and actually inappropriate concept of "sex roles." There are, simply, no sex roles in America any more than there are race or class roles (Lopata and Thorne 1978; see also Thorne 1982). There is no set of relationships of social persons with social circles whose main function is gender identity (Lopata, Miller, and Barnewolt 1984).

There are only gender or racial identities—and probably class identities at the self-conscious extremes of the class structure.

In order that sexual identification of people by others and socialization into gender identity be possible, the culture must contain images of "typical" girls (and boys), and young, middle-aged, and old women (and men). In order for the self and the others to include gender in their consideration of selection and interaction in roles, they must have indicators of such identity. Girls and boys have traditionally worn divergent hair and clothes styles, enabling easy identification. Visitors entering a home usually receive multiple clues as to the gender of a child, and adult roles often utilize uniforms as aids to classification. Changes in visual cues that occurred when the Catholic church allowed nuns to remove their identifying and isolating clothing made it easier for nuns to leave their orders. One of the major functions of the habit is to camouflage those aspects of gender identity that were traditionally associated with the roles of wife and mother, roles considered more normal for women in American society.

Language also contains clues as to gender identity. Girls must learn to talk like girls, and women allegedly share a universe of discourse apart from that of males.[7] In fact, Jessie Bernard (1981) developed a complex analysis of this in *The Female World*. Dale Spender (1980) devotes a whole volume to the analysis of "man-made language," pointing out, for example, that *master* and *mistress* have different meanings. M. Johnson (1988, 5) noted the same variation in the phrases *mothering a child* and *fathering a child* (see also Thorne, Kramarae, and Henley 1983). The world of discourse of different areas of life can keep unwanted people out of a role or group. There is much documentation of the difficulties faced by women trying to function in male-dominated occupations (Lopata, Miller, and Barnewolt 1986; Walshok 1981). Even the idea of high levels of achievement in competitive fields assumed to be masculine can lead young women into "fear of success," according to Matina Horner (1972). The initial popularity of that concept indicates that it must have some relevance even in modern America.

Children gradually develop their self-concepts, going through the stages G. H. Mead so carefully analyzed: awareness of the physical self, *playing at a role,* and *game playing* leading to the incorporation of a *generalized other* (Mead 1934). As a girl grows, she becomes increasingly conscious of how she looks in the eyes of others, not just physically, but as an actor in social roles. She learns to apply to herself the standards others seem to be applying to her, and to feel certain sentiments, such as pride or mortification, in response (Cooley [1902] 1922). She can try to change these responses, if she wishes. Unfortunately, life is not that simple. She learns that she frequently cannot fully control her environment, especially others within it.

It is obvious that people do not remain in the same social roles all their lives, and that involvement in any one social role changes over time (C. A. Miller, 1981). In order for a woman to enter a social role she must be aware of its existence and must take the necessary steps to enter its social circle—unless she pulls together a new one. For example, let us say that a woman wants to take on her first full-time job. First, she must choose one or more occupations, out of the welter available to women nowadays, that she thinks she might like and for which she feels probably qualified. There are special agencies that can help her at this stage, including career counselors at schools and employment agencies. She will probably place some other limitations on her search—territorial, geographical, or social (e.g., she may be unwilling to move out of state or to venture into a very large corporation). Next, she must learn from newspaper advertisements, or other search agents about the various organizations that can provide the circle within which her role can be carried forth. She must learn the potential employer's hiring criteria and eliminate those potential employers that she knows will never accept her, or take the time to better prepare herself to meet their standards. She then selects the one (or ones, in case she does not get her first choice) she prefers and goes through a process of application. After testing, which usually includes personal interviews by people trained to fit workers into slots, she may get the job. She must follow the same procedures, with more or less complexity, any time she enters a new social role in an established organization. Of course, not every woman goes through such calculated procedures to find a new job. Some simply hear of one through a friend or go to a place that is likely to hire persons of their capabilities.

That is not, however, the end of the entrance stage of involvement in a social role. Regardless of prior formal preparation, the person must learn the rules of the game in that particular circle. Anticipatory socialization is a process by which she learns by anticipating what she might need to know. Some schools or job training programs may provide opportunities to role-play the future occupation, with other trainees enacting the duties and rights of circle members. Reading about the job, even in fiction, may enable the applicant to go through dress rehearsals for her own performance. Talking to others in the same or a similar role can also provide clues, as does the simple process of asking people about their jobs.

Entering a social role requires forming relationships with all circle members, which is a gradual process, since the person usually does not come into contact with all at the same time. Involvement in a social role important to the woman requires, in greater or lesser degree, "becoming" the title bearer (a mother) (a wife) (see Becker 1953; Lopata 1971b). This is a process of placing oneself within the role, seeing oneself as a "natural" center of the circle and the role as part of one's role cluster and self-concept. Gradually, the person quits being a novice and enters the regular performer stage. Relationships are established and modified only by events in the lives of partners, or by the exits and entrances of circle members. Role strain has been decreased by negotiations, or the person has learned to live with it. Duties become standardized, sometimes to the level of boredom. Several paths can lead from this stage. The person can be fired for losing enthusiasm and the ability to innovate; she can be retained in a dead-end position until the phase-out stage (Kanter 1977); or she can start to again socialize herself anticipatorily into another role—one of higher status in the hierarchy or in another organization, or of a completely different type. Effective preparation can lead to promotion, until the person is no longer willing or able to socialize herself to the new role. The process of phasing oneself out of one role is influenced by one's stages of involvement in other roles.

The concept of *life course involvements* can be applied not only to roles but also to the individual's total life. A life course is usually defined in terms of stages; transitions are bounded by cultural norms of timing and the consequences of being "off time" or not at the typical time of life. Some social roles cannot be entered until certain age-related criteria are met. The biological system refuses to allow a woman to become impregnated and carry a child to birth until a certain stage of development. Most societies have motherhood norms related to schooling, official adulthood, or marriage age. At the other end of the life course, some roles must be left. Women cannot bear children after a certain age; retirement policies force or encourage the dropping of major occupational roles. Some circles put definite age parameters on candidates because of assumptions about age-related abilities. In traditional societies, it was impossible to be an "expert" in most social roles until at least adult age. One of the problems of modern society, based as it is upon traditional but rapidly changing culture, is that young people are learning the new technology required in many roles faster, earlier, and more exclusively than are their elders, which often lands them in positions of authority over their seniors.

Social Psychological Aspects of Role Involvement

A person's involvement in a particular social role can be conceptualized as including nine sociopsychological aspects. The first set consists of the *hierarchical importance of the roles* in the role cluster, the *richness of each institutional dimension* in which the roles are located, and the *multidimensionality of the social life space* (Lopata 1969b).

As mentioned above, women tend to diminish role conflict by developing, more or less consciously, a hierarchy within the cluster of roles they are performing at any one time. The role order changes with the introduction of important new roles to the cluster. For the most part, occupationally committed American women do not face competition from the two roles considered most important to their gender—wife and mother (Lopata and Barnewolt 1984). Once these roles are added, the whole cluster changes. The role of mother was generally considered most important for women with young children, even more so than the role of wife, if both are active in the role cluster (Barnewolt 1986). More-educated husbands in higher status jobs often rank higher for these women than their children do, but then the duties of these wives are often more complex than those of wives of men in less "greedy" jobs (L. Coser 1974; Lopata 1971b; see also the discussion in chapter 2 on the role of wife). Some women see life-course changes in their role hierarchies, explaining that they now have to focus on being mothers, because of the needs of small children, but that they will return to a focus on wifehood in the future (Lopata and Barnewolt 1984).

We can assume that involvement in a social role is also influenced by the richness of the dimension in which it is located. On the one hand we can predict that a woman with multiple roles in one institution will receive much support in each role from circle members in other roles in that institution. A mother can count on support with minimum conflict from her other roles in the family institution. On the other hand, members of the circles of her roles of wife, daughter, granddaughter, sibling, aunt and cousin may compete for her attention and complicate her life. Having to be a daughter-in-law may make life miserable for her in her role of mother.

The complexity or multidimensionality of the social life space is also important. Social roles in other dimensions can compete severely with roles in the family dimension, and vice versa. Although a mother may understand the priority her daughter gives to her children, the daughter's boss may not.

The next three aspects of role involvement deal with the role itself. People vary in their *assignment of importance to the different segments of the social circle,* in the extent to which they are *task-* versus *relations-oriented,* and in whether they see the duties as a set *of unrelated actions or processes* or in terms of *product* (Lopata 1969b, 290–92). Mothers may be more concerned with how their in-laws view their child rearing than with how the child is affected. Women differ in their perceptions of the duties of any role, seeing them variously as a series of disjointed incidents or events, as a set of processes, or in terms of product alone (Lopata 1969b, 291). Many homemakers are so overwhelmed by daily existence that they move from one task to another without seeing patterns or end results. Others plan the sequence of processes, with a rhythm of start, work, and finish, moving from one sequence to the next. Finally, there are many women who, for example, do not concentrate on what they do, but concentrate only on maintaining or restoring things to their proper state. Their work is done when the house is clean or the laundry finished.

The final set of aspects of role involvement are those of "style" or of being the self in the role. People can vary along the continuum of *passive-reactive-initiating approaches,* the type of *sentiments* experienced as a result of being in that role, and the *judgments of the self* in it (Lopata 1969b, 292–96). Both the passive and the reactive person in a role are noninitiating, but the first responds only to outside pressure without thinking about it or preparing herself for the onslaught of demands. The reactive person knows that she must respond and is prepared to do so, seeing that as the function of the role rather than as a natural response on her part. People can carry forth all three stances, usually in separate roles but often in relation to different segments of the same role. A mother can wait passively for the children to come home from school and make demands on her, she can prepare hygienic lunches for them because she knows what the school demands, and she can arrange a birthday party, inviting grandparents. The historical past of many societies demanded either passive or reactive stances toward the public sphere by the vast majority of their members. This is not desired, or possible, in a democratic society. The changes accompanying modernization and the feminist movement in America, at all stages, have pushed toward the self- and other-definition of women as initiators in their role selection and behavior. Education and the ability to see the wider scene within which one's role is located enable people to make such decisions and know where to push for rights. Conflict occurs when circle members do not respond to a person's changes of approach. Families may object to a wife/mother's refusal to be passive or reactive to their demands.

People differ in the sentiments they feel about various aspects of their roles. Women may hate the role of homemaker in which they feel they must be involved; they may dislike certain duties, or feel antagonistic to some segments of the circle that benefit from their work (such as in-laws). The same task may be greeted neutrally, or even with pleasure, by others. The concept of sentiments, merged by symbolic interactionists with that of emotion, is very important for the understanding of role relations.

Finally, women can vary in how they see themselves in each role or parts of it. They judge how well they are doing, aware that others are also judging them, and they feel certain ways in response to these judgments. "I am very good with the children, I read and play with them, but I can't follow a tight schedule. They get to bed when I get them to bed—this irritates their father," a woman once stated in an interview.

Thus, there are many ways in which people differ in their involvement in any role. This is not surprising, since each individual gradually builds her own social self or adjusts to the characteristics needed to enter social roles. She learns from the past, practices anticipatory socialization, interacts with circle members, and experiences the various aspects of involvement discussed here.

Commitment

The end result of the social psychological aspects of role involvement is role commitment (Lopata 1992d). People differ in which role they are most committed to, the degree of commitment they have to any role, and the kinds of "side bets" they have placed in order to insure continued participation and success (Becker 1960). Side bets include investment in education and job training, the search for and performance in an appropriate role, and the selection and arrangement of other roles so that they do not conflict or interfere with the commitment role.

The shift in women's ideology from total commitment to family roles to involvement in broader life choices accompanying modernization has moved women toward direct involvement in the public sphere. Simultaneously, it has reaffirmed the commitment of some women to motherhood and wifehood (Lopata, 1987). Some of these women have little choice, and their commitment is quite defensive; but many of them are relatively young, highly educated mothers who experienced success in occupations and then decided to stay home. They, however, unlike women in traditional or transitional times, consider such commitment to be temporary, to be followed by a return to commitment to an outside career (see also Lopata, Barnewolt, and Miller 1985).

Summary

We have now examined the basic theoretical framework guiding our analysis of the changes in social roles and life spaces of American women and some of the basic concepts to be used throughout this book.[8] The framework applies social development or modernization theory to such women. The conceptual model hinges upon the definition of social role as a set of patterned, mutually interdependent social relations between a social person and a social circle, involving task and relational duties and personal rights.

Social roles are located in the role clusters and social life spaces of individual members of the society, either within a single institutional dimension or multidimensionally in several separate institutions. Involvement in social roles influences not only the life spaces but also the identities of human beings. The models for such sets of relations are contained in a society's cultural base, while actual, situated roles are located in several social systems, organizational charts, or status structures.

Socialization into feminine gender identity and appropriate behavior begins as soon as the baby is identified as female. Girls are assigned relevant roles, or they are so heavily encouraged to antici-patorily socialize themselves in those directions that purposeful deviation is hard to accomplish. This female identity is carried through-out life, entering more or less intrusively into all other social roles. The social structure of a society constantly reminds people of their pervasive identities, which can block or open opportunities for role involvements.

Social roles have their own life courses, and each individual fits them into her total life course. Social psychological aspects of in-volvement in any particular role include the role's rank order of importance and the individual's stances vis-à-vis its various compo-nents. The complexity of the social life space influences not only the breadth of perspective with which life is constructed, but also the manner in which role conflict is resolved.

We now turn to the examination of the social roles of American women in their traditional, transitional, and modern variations.

2

The Role of Wife

All societies known to us have some institutionalized arrangement for mate selection and for the formation, continuation and dissolution of the roles of wife and husband. The complexities and changes in the role of wife over the past few generations and in comparison to other societies are too extensive to develop in detail. Therefore, I will provide only a brief analysis of the traditional role of wife that is still much in evidence in other parts of the world. I will concentrate, however, on the changing role of wife in America: from one dependent upon the traditional patriarchal family, through the "personal dependent" of the transitional type, to the emerging "modern" one. In traditional families, and especially in other parts of the world, the role of wife was basically controlled by the husband's family, in transitional times, by the husband, and in modern times it is negotiated with flexibility between the husband and wife. The role variations in transitional times, which stretch from the period of extensive industrialization and increasing societal complexity to all but recent decades, is of itself so complicated that I have broken it down by social class, with some attention to racial and ethnic variations.

Traditional Times, Traditional Places

In traditional families of the world and in America's traditional past, a girl was selected to become a wife by the two families, hers and the potential husband's. The qualities for which a future wife was chosen depended upon the culture, with strong class restrictions and in some societies caste restrictions. Three sets of criteria were considered. The most important was the match in social status of the families. Family alliances brought about by marriages of the young have been socially important. They have been used to prevent wars (or initiate them), provide for economic exchanges, and insure other privileges. In turn, the status of each family was influenced by the excellence of the match, verified by the amount of dowry or bride-price. A second set of criteria was provided by cultural norms. Among many contemporary traditional Asian families (and some American, if we are to believe the *National Enquirer*), soothsayers are also consulted to determine whether the match will be auspicious.

The social person characteristics of the future wife, which became the third layer of consideration, counted in the balance of negotiation, after the major family-matching considerations were taken care of. In societies deeply concerned over "bloodline purity" of each offspring, an important criterion was the bride's virginity. Families went to great lengths to insure this, creating Purdah-like isolation of girls from any contact with non-family males (Papanek and Minault, 1982). Other societies were more concerned with the woman's ability to bear children, even if biologically fathered by other men, although pregnancy by the future husband could be favored. Families in such cases provided opportunities for impregnation of their daughters. Other social person characteristics of the potential wife included proper appearance and such abilities as were deemed important by the social class of the families. The personal preferences of the man or woman, if known or allowed, were often overridden for benefit of the families. As Westernization spread the world over, these preferences were taken into consideration with increasing frequency; today the parents are simply asked for their consent and marriages even take place without their approval.

The husband's family formed a major segment of the social circle of, and had the greatest influence upon, the role of wife in traditional families. In many situations, the wife's duties toward, and rights from, her family of orientation into which she was born, decreased dramatically upon marriage. Her duties to the husband varied considerably from place to place, ranging from the minimal one of allowing sexual access and contributing to the family work group to being almost his and his family's servant. The demands considered appropriate within the norms of the male group could be extreme, even to the point of causing her death. The wife's right to safety has not been universal. Companionship and empathetic understanding have also not been common to marital roles.

Bohannan (1963) concluded his comparative analysis of marriage in traditional families with four sets of rights that men acquired in women upon marriage: rights to sharing a domicile, rights to sexual access, *in genetricem* rights of filiation of the children with their male line, and economic rights, including rights to goods she brought with her in marriage, goods they produced together, and sometimes even those she produced alone. In the extreme situation of a patriarchal, patrilineal, and patrilocal system, the wife had no rights over any economic goods, and her children remained behind if she decided to quit the marriage. In return, the remaining wife had the rights to a domicile, the product of sexual access (which is usually not pleasure but offspring), and maintenance till death. The woman who produced sons for the family was guaranteed their care, inheritance and other privileges of membership in the male line.

In general, the higher the evaluation of the wife's contribution to the husband's family, the higher is her status, although this does not translate automatically into freedom of action. As Goode (1963) and Ward (1963) point out, a woman's power in a family system is often influenced by her control over economic goods.

Wives in ancient Europe did not fare well, as far as their legal and personal rights were concerned. The British system, upon which much of American legal policies and culture were based, operated by "common law" by which the husband and wife formed a single legal unity, of which he was the representative. Common law disenfranchised wives, who were legally minors and had few legal rights until relatively recently (Chapman and Gates 1977). However, it also laid on the husband the duty of supplying the wife with what the lawyers called "necessities," that is, with those things that seemed essential for her existence, and such other things as accorded with the standard of life he was able to maintain (Abbott 1938, 600).

The rights to legal guardianship of the family meant that "in the nineteenth century females were not allowed to testify in court, hold title to property, establish business, or sign papers as witnesses" (Chafe 1972, 5). Other men were even appointed guardians in the absence of a husband/father, holding property until a male child reached adulthood. These policies did not mean that the wife was completely powerless in intrafamily relations, as the husband was also economically dependent upon her work in agriculture, in the informal urban marketplace, or, by the eighteenth century, in the cottage industry.

The Transitional Form of the Role of Wife

The traditional forms of economic interdependence of husbands and wives began to modify with the increasing complexity or scale of the societies within which families were located. Many technological and ideational changes contributed to this complexity in Western Europe and America, including industrialization and the increasing influence of a money economy. According to Weber ([1904] 1958), the Protestant ethic provided justification for a man to concentrate his energy upon economic activity, confirming his heavenly predestination through earthly success, rather than passively waiting for a better life in the afterlife.

Families were transformed through these changes in a two-step fashion, freeing the nuclear unit from the power of the male line. The first step freed the man, the second his wife and children. Sons could obtain formal education and job training away from the family of orientation, marketing their abilities for an income to maintain themselves in varying levels of comfort. Their success was to be won individualistically, without dependence on the family of orientation—although it could provide a foundation.

In fact, the cultures of much of Europe and subsequently America, influenced by this Protestant ethic, focusing upon the economic institution, pushed the values and reference groups of other institutions into the background. One of the major functions of the family became the support of the male earner and the reproduction of future earners. The educational institution became limited to preparing men for their participation in the economic sphere. The religious institution and the state were allowed to interfere with economic freedom only minimally.

This dramatic push toward the economic institution was accompanied by the removal of women from direct participation in its formal, public life, through very convoluted ideological and behavioral changes. When paid work first entered the economy, women and children followed (Kessler-Harris 1982; Oakley 1974b). However, as P. Laslett (1971) explains:

> The factory won its victory by outproducing the working family, taking away the market for the product of hand labour and cutting prices to the point where the craftsman had either to starve or take a job under factory discipline himself. (P. 18)

Men became increasingly interested in paid employment, and their wives and children ended up as "personal dependents" upon the men's earnings as sources for their independent income dried up (Eichler 1973). As the public domain of life grew in size and importance with all the societal changes, men developed or tightened their masculine, homosocial monopoly over it, squeezing women out (Lipman-Blumen 1976b).

The removal of women from paid employment in all but a few occupations was accompanied, in chicken-or-egg sequence, by ideological shifts. There were several components to the ideology. One was protective legislation that redefined women (who were previously considered able to do heavy work in agriculture, mines, or elsewhere) as persons of weak physique and disposition. (Actually, the reformers were more interested in the welfare of children these women could produce than of the women themselves). "Protective" legislation of the 1800s in England, and later in America, changed conditions under which women could work in industry, with an unanticipated result of making them less attractive to employers.

The Victorian upper-class image of women's delicacy and refinement also began filtering to the new middle classes and as far down the social structure as husbands could afford to keep their wives protected from work in the new competitive world. As Bernard (1981, chapter 9) concluded, a wife was stripped to a considerable extent of her access to cash-mediated markets, and left without legal rights and her own source of income. She could not be economically self-sufficient or visibly contributing a major share to the economic welfare of the family unit. Obviously, her contributions as a homemaker could be evaluated as equal to those of the man only if what each does is measured as equally important (Krauskopf 1977, 105–6). Working for money was more prestigeful than other economic activity and by law wives were kept from taking on roles that would make them economically independent.

The importance assigned to the public sphere of life led to an ideological division of the world into two spheres, accompanied by a stereotyping of personalities of each gender. According to the two-sphere sociopsychological perspectives, men are best suited to the highly competitive public sphere. They are so aggressive, controlled in their emotions, instrumentally oriented, and involved in being "the good provider" (Bernard 1983) that they do not have the interest, time, or energy to devote to other aspects of life, such as the family. Women, in this imagery, are nurturing, they care for husbands, small children, and animals, and they are passive and patient. They are expected to be weak in abilities required for the public world, such as mechanical skills, logic, mathematics, and long-range complex thinking. The ideal situation was for the husband and wife to function cooperatively out of their own spheres, meeting both instrumental and expressive functions through specialization by person rather than by activity (Parsons and Bales 1955).

The result of all these changes made the woman who became a wife in transitional times economically dependent upon the husband; she had lower status than the man and little recognition of her contribution to the unit. Rosaldo (1974), comparing many societies, developed the following structural model:

> women's status will be lowest in those societies where there is a firm differentiation between domestic and public spheres of activity and where women are isolated from one another and placed under a single man's authority, in the home. (P. 36)

Class Differences

The transitional role of wife in American society is not woven of a single fabric. It varies especially by social class. In different classes the ideal characteristics desired of a wife, and her duties and rights, can be quite different, and the social circle can vary considerably. It may contain multiple assistants and suppliers, as well as associates of the husband, or a simple set of co-workers. The social psychological aspects of role involvement vary likewise.

Working-Class Wives. Much of the literature on the role of wife in the socioeconomically lower classes in America is closely related to ethnicity—which is not surprising, since the majority of America's large-wave immigrations were composed of members of those classes. People doing well elsewhere generally stayed, unless pushed out by political or religious problems. Although the immigrants have come at different times, and from highly divergent cultures, most have shared certain characteristics (see Mindel, Habenstein, and Wright 1988). Generally speaking, their societies have been highly patriarchal, and the role of wife has been dependent upon male-defined rights and duties. For example, Kourvetaris (1988) found many vestiges of patriarchal power among first-generation Greek Americans. Cultural norms are still constantly reinforced among Puerto Rican immigrants (Sanchez-Ayendez 1988) and Mexican immigrants (Becerra 1988) by the frequent movement back and forth to the homeland, delaying the "Americanization process." However, the very process of migration increased the power of wives, compared to their traditional situations in the home countries, as found by Wrobel (1979) and myself (Lopata 1976b and 1994) in the Polish American community. They could establish their own homes, if the husband's family did not come over and thus could not back up his demands. The husband was much more dependent upon his marital partner than was true of village situations in Poland. The first generation of immigrants tried to preserve patriarchal family traditions, but rights of husbands (e.g., duties of wives) became more flexible by the second generation, much to the frustration of the elders. That does not mean that the newly emerging middle-class American ideal of wife-husband egalitarianism has permeated down through lower social classes or outward into ethnic groups socialized into different norms. As Schooler (1984) argues, "serfdom's legacy" continues into the ethnic world in America. The newer, or newly expanding, immigrant groups from Asia also bring with them the ideal of submissiveness of women, as found among the Chinese and Japanese by Sue and Morishima (1982).

The gender-segregated lives of working-class wives are found to continue across generations of Italian Americans (Whyte 1956 and Gans 1962), even into the third and later generations, according to Johnson (1985). Komarovsky (1962), Rainwater and his associates (1959) and Rubin (1976) describe the role of the wife in such groups as very difficult. The women marry young, hoping for a better life and often in order to escape unpleasant situations in their parents' homes (Rubin 1976). Their romanticized expectations of married life are obtained from the mass media, rather than from their families' problematic relations (Rainwater, Coleman, and Handel 1959). The stage of becoming a wife is full of frustration, and later years bring passive acceptance rather than positive change. The husband is unable to provide the emotional support both wish for, and both are disappointed in themselves and in each other. The man dominates, sometimes becoming violent under the influence of alcohol or in response to his own problems and insecurities (Rubin 1976, 1983). Sexual difficulties combine with those of finances and child rearing to create an oppressive environment (see Komarovsky 1962).

The wife's problems can be so disabling that they push her into "hysterical" behavior, which the husband handles by trying to maintain a "logical" (i.e. distant) stance (Warren 1987). For marriages like this in the 1950s, when the whole culture was inundated with what Friedan (1963) called the "feminine mystique" demanding passive stances by women, personal emotional problems were often defined in psychiatric terms (Warren 1987). A woman depressed by the restrictions of "true womanhood" could become classified as a "madwife" and subjected to hospitalization and even to shock or electroconvulsive therapy (Warren 1987). Her social circle in the role of wife did not come to her defense, since she deviated from what its members considered necessary behavior. She was declared cured of her madness when she acquiesced in her roles.

According to Rainwater, Coleman, and Handel (1959, 58–66), the workingman's wife lacks the ability to change her roles because of several characteristics of her construction of reality. She accepts things as given, has little interest, energy, or skill to explore things for herself, lacks faith in her personal efficacy, experiences limitations on self-command due to strong and volatile emotions, and is oriented toward the present and her immediate surroundings rather than the future and planning.

Much of what is known about the working-class wife comes from research of decades ago, although more recent studies support these basic theses (Langman 1987). The transitional aspect of such a woman's role of wife is the role's location in a traditional, male-dominated, often violent circle, combined with dreams of intimacy, mutual self-disclosure, companionship, and sharing that are contained in new images of husband-wife relationships (Rubin 1976, 120). Her relationship with the husband is strained by the fact that he does not share the dream, wishing her to simply be like his mother, without these "crazy ideas" that require from him acts that he is incapable of undertaking. He openly resents giving up any of his traditional masculine rights—such as his right to sexual access when he wants it and not in negotiation with the wife. Such a man has no models for behavior that expresses feelings and meets some of the woman's needs. He thus often has extreme reactions to any demands that he change, whether by considering the wife's sexual desires or "helping" her with the roles of mother or homemaker. He does not discuss his world, including his job, with her, considering it too technical for women, and he thinks that talking about frustrations is too much like "griping," which men should not do. He wants work and home to be kept separate, not wishing to hear the wife's side of life (Komarovsky 1962, 152–55). Cross-gender communication requires a different socialization and educational background than has been true of blue-collar couples.

The life cycle of the role of wife appears to have changed less from traditional to transitional times among working-class families than among middle-class ones. The birth of children creates a common bond between husband and wife, unless their presence is fraught with problems, as in cases of unwanted or difficult offspring. Few other subjects form a bridge between the worlds of men and women. Money, friendships, and in-laws are all possible sources of strain. Desertion and divorce are fairly frequent, with the wife gaining little power or benefit from such action. Working-class women are generally distrustful of governmental or other formal agencies and do not have the resources to demand their rights. Social security or welfare can help, especially if it brings steady income compared to a husband's irregular employment or contribution to the family maintenance (Lopata 1979).

The general picture of the social psychology of role involvement presents the women as focused on the role of mother, hoping that all will go well—or at least not too badly—in marriage. They tend to be passive or reactive, meeting demands as they are made, and do not consider themselves as especially good wives or persons. They fear sexual temptation from outside of marriage and tend to be impulsive in most of their actions (Rainwater, Coleman, and Handel 1959). Such women settle into their marriages as the years go by, still within the gender-segregated home and relations with others.

Middle-Class Wives. Transitional middle-class families in America have also varied considerably, mainly by the degree of crystallization of their life-styles and closeness to either their lower- or their upper-class counterparts (Langman 1987, 226–29). Mate selection has increasingly become a matter of personal choice, preceded by dating rituals but not frequently by the cohabitation more typical of modern times. Dating and the honeymoon allegedly provide opportunities for self-disclosure and learning about the other. The social circle of the wife is relatively free of control by the families, and though in-laws are generally recognized and interacted with. The circle is now more likely to contain couple-companionate relations and the husband's work associates. Middle-class couples in transitional marriages tend to communicate more with each other than do transitional couples of lower status. Berger and Kellner (1970) found such couples, especially the wives, active in reconstructing reality upon marriage. The change of name and of relationships with others by the woman is accompanied by frequent modifications of the past in memory and of her anticipated future through shared communication with the husband.

Actually, marriage often does not change life dramatically unless each partner has to cease, or restrict, prior outside activities. Both the man and the woman tend to continue their main occupational or educational activities. The greatest amount of change in the role of wife usually accompanies the birth of the first child, specially if the mother quits her job to take care of the offspring, as she tends to do in transitional families. This shift is a major component of what researchers have labeled the "crisis" in the role of wife due to early parenthood. The wife is often too tired to pay attention to the husband, appears more interested in the baby than in him, and is prohibited from, or uninterested in, sexual interaction. The couple's finances are stretched by the loss of her earnings and the cost of the pregnancy, birth, and the child, and leisure is either interrupted or requires advance preparation and added expenditure. The wife often feels like, and appears to the husband to be, a different woman from the one he married. The multidimensional world they shared in the past has become for her a single-dimensional one, focused on the home and motherhood.

On the other hand, the lives of many middle-class transitional wives are shaped to a considerable degree by their husband's occupations and their couple-companionate activities.

The Two-Person Single Career. A wife in a transitional middle-class marriage can, and is expected to, do much to help her professional, entrepreneurial, or corporate-management husband in his career. Many men are in jobs or organizations defined by L. Coser (1974) as "greedy institutions." These require total commitment and heroic effort, not only on the part of the man, but also by his wife. In transitional families she is not expected to have a career of her own or any serious involvements that might interfere with her contribution to the husband's career. Papanek (1973) described this situation as a two-person single career in which the man holds the occupational or office title and receives the rewards directly, while the wife is the backup person and benefits vicariously. The role of a wife is influenced in two major ways by her husband's position or occupation, as summarized by Finch (1983) from a large literature on this subject. First, the husband's job structures the wife's life through income, time, space, and social relationships. Characteristics of his job also impinge on what she can do in other roles. Second, his job can require contributions from her in the form of supportive work as well as family-status-production work that "affects the family's relation with others in the community or reference group" (Papanek 1979, 775).

When a husband's earnings constitute the total family income, the effect upon the role of wife is easily discernible. The amount he earns, whether his income is dependable, the method of payment, the additional perquisites, and his uncompensated work-related expenditures—all influence the life she can create for the family. Although the earnings provide resources, a woman's lack of control over their characteristics and the way they reach her is a major problem. Even when the wife contributes to the family income, she usually contributes a smaller proportion than he does, and her earnings are not formally recognized by the husband. Bird (1979) classified the attitudes of transitional families toward the wife's earnings into four categories. The portion of her earnings identified as "pin money" is kept out of sight, for her to spend as she wishes:

> The object is not to give her independence to flout his wishes—but to save him from the pain of seeing it. . . . Earmarker Couples are neo-traditionalists. They deal with the threat of her money by building a Chinese wall around it to show that the family is "really" living on his pay alone. . . . Pooler Couples deal with the threat of her money by insisting that it doesn't matter where it comes from. . . it becomes "our money." . . . Bargainer Couples are radicals. They look the threat of her money full in the face and accept it at full value. (Pp. 130–35)

In all such marriages, the wife is expected to carry out her job, if she is able to hold one despite complications, without neglecting the role of homemaker and all her husband-supportive work. The time schedule of the husband's job obviously impinges on the social life space of the wife, especially if she is also a home manager and mother. She must synchronize the activities of all family members around those of her husband and prevent interference with the timing of his work. Irregularity or unusual scheduling of the husband's job may preclude the wife's seeking a job of her own. Some jobs, such as those of consultant or traveling salesman, require absence from home for extended periods of time, consigning total family management to the wife and complicating her relations with other circle members and in her other social roles.

A major complaint of wives of entrepreneurs, professionals, or corporation workers is the "spillover" of concerns and even work into home time. Many middle-class workers are unable to leave the work behind, carrying it home at least in their heads and often physically. The family must compete with it, often feeling neglected and insignificant in comparison to the job.

The wife's life is also affected by the spatial elements of the husband's job. This is obvious in the case of the geographically mobile husband. The migration of men in search of a livelihood helped populate America and other lands, but it can cause family strain. Wives left behind must wait for their husbands to send back money for their journey to join them, or wait for them to return and fetch them. Corporations with branches all over the world often shift members of management as needed, regardless of family needs. The loneliness of the transferred wife can be a major problem, especially for women lacking the social skills to make new friends and enter new roles. The man's organization provides his incorporation and transfers his personal credentials, while the wife must do this on her own. Again, one of the obvious problems with the geographical mobility of a husband is the wife's lack of control over the location and timing of any particular move. Frequent moves make it unlikely that the wife will be able to find a job. A wife's refusal to give up her own life inevitably hurts the husband's career.

The spatial impingement of the husband's work on the life of the wife points to the artificiality of the division of the world into private and public spheres. This is especially evident when the husband works out of the home. Lawyers and other professionals may have their only offices in their homes. Husbands may also carry forth work activities from the home without an isolated work space, thus penetrating all areas. Others do some of the work at home, even when based elsewhere, using it as a branch office. Although having the freedom to use the home is an advantage to the employee or self-employed man, it plays havoc with "normal" households. Family routines must be organized around the worker, and activities of importance to other members are often curtailed. Apprentices or other assistants might actually live in the home, and they have to be supplied with services by the homemaker simply because her role of wife includes obligations to the husband's work circle. Spatial proximity of the husband's work can also introduce clients, customers, or representatives of a variety of organizations to the home.

A special case of interweave between the husband's job space and the wife's space in all her roles exists if the couple lives in territory provided by the employer. The clergy, officers of corporations, universities, or prisons, domestic workers, farm laborers, and many others sometimes have the right to homes owned and controlled by the organization to which the husband is attached. Although the employee receives benefits from such arrangements, in terms of closeness to work, free or adjusted rent, and services, the main beneficiary is the employer because of his or her control over the situation. The wife benefits from these rights of the husband, but faces many restrictions on her life. The uncertainty of housing also hangs over her, as she can lose her home if they divorce or the husband leaves the job or dies.

An even stronger spatial impingement on the wife occurs in institutional settings. The military can place families on bases in which they can "shop, drink, dance, attend movies, parties and planned trips at all times and at lower costs" than do others (Dobrofsky and Patterson 1977). The same is true of faculty at military schools or workers in company-owned communities. In such a total institution, much of the wife's life is controlled by the organization. Such a woman is incorporated into the hierarchy, in a peripheral and vicarious manner. She carries her husband's rank with her, in terms of her appearance, deference, and demeanor, at all times in which she is known as, for instance, "the captain's wife."

In addition to the "spillover" effect, a job can force or prevent relationships with others. Police wives, whether the husband is hired by the community or by private employers, complain that there are restrictions on whom they can develop friendships with (Young 1984). Army officers' wives are not allowed to fraternize with women whose husbands are mere enlisted men, while wives following husbands to foreign stations must formalize all relations with natives. The literature and films on the colonial wife in India or Africa document the constraints placed on her behavior (see Callan and Ardener 1984). On the other hand, relationships with superiors, work colleagues, or clients of the husband are often forced upon the wife. The wives of public figures are embedded in the community, which can be as large as a nation, with "contamination" of the private person by the occupation (Finch 1983, 36).

The contributions of the wife in a two-person career of the husband fall into four major areas: maintaining the husband's physical and psychological environment, "stroking," direct involvement in the social circle of the husband's job, and "status production" (Bernard 1973; Papanek 1979). The first area overlaps the role of homemaker. Although it is possible for a wife not to be a homemaker, most women combine the two roles. The duties of maintaining the husband physically so that he can successfully perform his job include caring for his clothes, maintaining a functioning household, preparing food, and locating needed objects. It also means protecting his "recreation" time, during which he recuperates from the strain of the job and prepares for the next stint. Domestic labor can be seen as economically productive when it contributes to the productivity of the male worker. His time, money, and energy are preserved by the work of the wife, who "oils the wheels of production" (Finch 1983, 79). Her activities can enable him to entertain at home and provide the required family appearance both inside the home and away from it. These backup services may be required consistently, as in the case of the First Lady or the wife of the president of an organization, or in emergency times only. Even if she does not do the work itself, she is responsible for seeing that it is done, when and where needed.

The provision of "moral support" is also an extremely important part of the role of wife, even to workers who do not need much direct contribution to their careers. Bernard (1973) calls this the "stroking" function. It consists of "showing solidarity, giving help, rewarding, agreeing, understanding and passively accepting" (Ostrander 1984, 39). It usually does not mean giving advice.

Participation in a two-person single career can entail even more direct, although still peripheral, duties on the part of the wife—answering the telephone or being active in wives' organizations such as the Women's Auxiliary of the American Medical Association

(Fowlkes 1980). The trips that the U.S. president's wife makes with him, especially abroad, require a great deal of preparation, including knowledge of the cultures and societies involved. Such preparation can be an awesome obligation, with possibilities for many a faux pas. In fact, it can take up most of a wife's time, even with briefing from the husband's other assistants.

Another set of activities that involve the wife directly in the job of the husband Finch (1983, 94) calls "back-up services." These are typical for wives of male academics or other male researchers and writers, as attested to by their acknowledgments: "could not have done this without the help of my wife, who found references, edited and typed the manuscript . . ." The advantage for the worker of having his wife provide such help is that she is "always on the spot" (Finch 1983, 96).

The wife can serve as an assistant in the husband's social circle to such an extent that she is an additional worker whom the organization gets for free. Sometimes referred to as part of a team, such a worker is nevertheless seen by others as peripheral to the main actors.

The combination of all these activities can involve what Papanek (1979) defines as "family status production" work, which has two main levels. For wives of upwardly mobile husbands it involves the production of status, and for already established families it consists of status-maintenance activity. It encompasses not only the role of wife, but the woman's whole role complex. While supportive effort is expected of the wife in a two-person career throughout the husband's career life, the higher his actual or potential status is, the more important is her status-productive work. Papanek (1979) places its peak mainly at midlife, when income and aspiration are still rising and there is enough discretionary income to allow the wife a wide range of activities.

The constraints and contributions connected with the role of wife in a two-person single career can be overwhelming. Role conflict can be avoided only by placing the role of wife in the top position in the role cluster, stripping away or pushing into the background social roles that are not compatible. Few such wives can devote considerable time to the role of daughter to ailing elderly parents, or even sometimes to the role of mother. Friendships are hung on the activities of the husband, as many a woman has found when dropped by erstwhile friends after her husband's death or demotion.

Wives of public figures are particularly vulnerable to the strain of trying to balance privacy with the obligation to be visible to people who feel they have the right to treat them personally. The strategies available to wives in such situations of vicarious contamination of sentiments directed to the husband are limited, and must be learned, often painfully, as a number of biographies and autobiographies of such women attest (see the various write-ups of Kitty Dukakis during and since her husband's bid for the American presidency).

All in all, however, a wife can be a major contributor to her husband's career, even if she is seldom acknowledged as such or given only honorary rewards. Outside observers may feel that she receives sufficient benefits, basking in her husband's fame and sharing more tangible privileges. The suspicion that such rewards might draw a woman into a marriage is often mentioned by the mass media when an attractive young woman attaches herself to a very successful but physically unappealing older man. Each of the two obtains what she or he considers desirable, reflecting the gender-specific values of our culture. A major problem with a wife's rights and privileges is their vicarious nature, which women in the role of wife in "modern" marriages find objectionable.

The historical facts of the focus, in the Protestant ethic, on men's occupational success, and of the feminine mystique ideology directed toward women, have been recognized by many observers. Even before World War II, a series of books by Nancy Shae, such as *The Army Wife* (1941) trained into proper behavior women married to officers of the U.S. armed services. William H. Whyte, Jr.'s *Organization Man* (1956) and subsequent articles discussed the "wife problem" of business executives. What to do with these women, since the corporation was internally organized with no place for external appendices? In addition, some wives were uncooperative and even hurt their husbands' careers and the success of the organization. Fowlkes (1980) studied the wives of men in medicine and academia in *Behind Every Successful Man,* finding the older ones fully accepting the adjunct role, while Vandervelde wrote in *The Changing Life of the Corporate Wife* (1979) about wives who refused to fit into the mold. Kanter's classic *Men and Women of the Corporation* (1977) devoted a whole chapter to wives, their duties and rights. Actually, the wives had few rights, since they were seen as external to the system and partially replaced by the "office wife," or secretary, who meets many of the needs of the managers. Margolis

(1979) reported many contributions of wives in *The Managers*. Helen Hughes (1977) described her personal experiences as a Ph.D. sociologist married to a member of the University of Chicago faculty during years when nepotism rules were used by organizations to prevent the employment of more than one member of a family. Chapters in the Callan and Ardener (1984) volume *The Incorporated Wife* cover similar situations of wives within academia, the police, the armed services, overseas branches of corporations, settler families in Northern Rhodesia, and several colonial locations.

Situations in which the wife has a powerful public position while the husband must perform the backup duties, as in the case of the former prime minister of Britain, make people most uncomfortable. Interestingly enough, males accompanying public women are often referred to as "escorts," even when they perform much more important functions directly contributing to the job. When two independent persons "escort" each other in a modern marriage, but the husband's only function is to insure that his wife can perform her important duties as effortlessly as possible, that is another matter. Having the wife as the major partner in a two-person career goes against two cultural norms: that the wife should be the supporting partner who adjusts to the husband's needs, and that the husband should not be in the subordinate position of the backup person.

It is probably not surprising that many women in public roles either do not have husbands or are married to men with independent careers.

Of course, many of the impingements of the husband's job upon the wife's social life space and the contributions she makes to his career are also experienced by working-class wives, and, especially, upper-class wives.

Middle-Class Black Wives. The situation of middle-class black families appears to be similar to that of their white counterparts, but there are important variations. The black community has long encouraged and rewarded educational and economic involvement by its married women, as a natural outgrowth of the fact that whites discriminated much less against them than against black men. Families often had to depend on the earnings of the wife, who was more likely than her husband to have a steady white-collar job.

The interviews in *Occupation: Housewife* (Lopata 1971b, 122–35) from the 1950s and 1960s showed the middle-class black wives to be very supportive of their husbands. One of the full-time homemakers, aged twenty-three, explained the complexity of her role as wife as including

> dividing each thing into its proper place and trying to be able to give your man the type of warmth or consolation he needs when he feels that he is not being treated fairly outside of the home. (P. 133)

The need to be emotionally supportive of the middle-class man who is facing discrimination from the white world is expressed over and over in these and later interviews. Most of the middle-class black respondents who are employed fall easily into the role of the wife in the "modern marriage" category. The same conclusion was reached by Willie and Greenblatt (1978) from a review of four "classic" studies of power relationships. In fact, they, as well as Staples (1988, 312), point to the fact that middle-class black women have been virtually absent from the women's movement in America, mainly because their concerns are economic and less oriented against sexism than against racism. Awareness of the depth of prejudice and discrimination facing the black man in the middle-class world, the shortage of men in the black community, and the problems of "finding and keeping a mate" (Staples 1988, 313) decrease the probability of anti-male stances on the part of these women. Middle-class married couples of other racial and ethnic minorities in America also resemble their dominant-group counterparts.

Upper-Class Wives. Ostrander (1984) defines upper-class families as being in that position because of unique characteristics in addition to income, occupation, and education, which are used to classify other families.

> In conceptual terms then, "upper class" is defined here as that portion of the population that owns the major share of corporate and personal wealth, exercises dominant power in economic and political affairs, and comprises exclusive social networks and organizations open only to persons born into or selected by this class. (P. 5)

The mate selection process of the upper classes in American society has been of special interest to sociologists as well as to the mass media (see Rosen and Bell 1966). Social Register families insure appropriate partners for their offspring by structuring the environment, sending the young to the proper schools, joining clubs, and arranging opportunities for contact at a geographical and social distance from members of lower classes.

Women who enter the role of wife in this social class are well aware of the enormity of their responsibility. Their husbands run the economic and political life of the society, and definitely of the community within which they reside. The wives realize that this will not be an egalitarian marriage. Even those who inherit wealth in their own right tend to turn it over to the husband to manage (Ostrander 1984). This is one of the extreme cases of patriarchal control and personal dependency, even though it is not the husband's oldest male relative, but the husband himself, who has all the power. Both in-law families influence their lives, opening doors to major social clubs and supporting the wife's status-maintenance activities. Most of these women do not have status-production duties, since the families are already established. Theirs are the status-maintaining obligations, and their rights include having funds available for such activities. They conduct their lives to maintain the general standard of family position, rather than to influence the husband's job.

These are the women who always place the role of wife first in line of importance, even over that of mother; in this they are quite different from working-class wives, who almost invariably focus on the children, or middle-class transitional wives, who tend to have life-course commitments (Lopata and Barnewolt 1984). Upper-class wives have to be always available to fulfill duties in the role of wife, even if it means shifting obligations to others. They know they cannot take a full-time job, although the husbands worry that they may wish to do so. Even voluntary-organization activities, necessary for status maintenance, must never appear to be more important than actions directly in response to the husband. The marital relationships described by Ostrander (1984) do not appear close, warm, or empathetic.

Actually, we know less about the role of wife in this class than in others, as there are so few women in it and they have complex means of protecting their privacy. They are conscious of the importance of reputation, transmitting only such information about themselves as they wish to publicize. They have both the space and the social distance to keep away strangers. Servants intercept even social scientists, and participant observation is difficult when entrance into interaction centers is restricted.

The Modern Form of the Role of Wife

It is actually hard to determine the characteristics of the role of wife
in modern marriages, since we have not, for the most part, moved
far from the transitional female-male relationships of this type. If we
follow Inkeles (1981; see also Inkeles and Smith 1974), "modern"
people are highly individuated and competent to function in a
complex, industrialized society. Even in transitional phases of social
development—maybe particularly then—marriage certainly did not
involve two independent persons in a relationship in which they
were cooperative and interdependent but equal in power and status. There is evidence of change, however, even if we are not quite
sure where it will lead.

Indices of Change

One of the dramatic indices of change in the relations between
women and men has been sexual. Allegedly, the double standard of
sexual "freedom," which has a long history and allows the man other
relationships while the woman is supposed to stay a virgin and then
a "chaste" wife, is in the process of vanishing (Reiss and Lee 1988).
The whole subject of what is still called "premarital" sexual permissiveness is complex, and it is uncertain how it influences the role of
wife. An important aspect of the changes, however, is cohabitation
of unmarried couples. Trost (1979) defines cohabitation as "sharing
a bedroom during at least four nights per week during at least three
consecutive months with someone of the opposite sex" (p. 13).

Initial conclusions of research on cohabitation in the United
States showed differences in the attitudes of women and men. The
women saw cohabitation as a trial marriage or a step toward wifehood. Men allegedly spoke of many conveniences without strong
marital commitment (Ehrenreich 1983). Defining it simply as an
"expanding dimension of the courtship process" (Henze and Hudson
1974, 725) implies increasing commitment during dating but includes
the possibility of impermanence. But then, even marriage now no
longer means lifelong involvement.

The current interest of women in developing their own careers
and feelings of personhood prior to marriage, combined with increasing sexual permissiveness, makes cohabitation unsurprising. Such
heterosexual couples face many of the same problems experienced

by married couples, except that it is harder for them to build trust in each other concerning money, work, or sexual matters (Blumstein and Schwartz 1983). Power still accrues to the one with the higher paycheck and the person who has least to lose if the relationship dissolves.

Whether seen by participants as a trial marriage, a nonpermanent relationship, or just a convenience, cohabitation provides a certain amount of preparation, socialization, and task learning that can be useful for entrance into the role of wife. This includes decisions as to location, furnishings, financial obligations, friendships, and so forth. However, our definition of social roles disqualifies this relation from being that of wife-husband, for various legal and social-circle reasons and because the participants appear to be "playing at the roles" rather than actually involved in them. Trost (1979) asks, Why do cohabiting couples, or any couples for that matter, marry? The reasons include the wish to have "legalized" children, security and safety, freedom from outside criticism, and the belief that marriage is morally better.

The modern wedding is apt to be planned fully by the couple (rather than by the woman's parents as in the past) to the extent that they define its rituals and even pay many of the costs. This frees them from dependence upon their families of orientation and allegedly provides each partner with equal power for the future.

The modern woman is inevitably involved in a multidimensional life prior to, and at the early stages of, marriage, being more educated and middle-class in her life-style and aspirations than were her grandmother or mother. Even the 1956 suburbanites of the *Occupation: Housewife* study claimed that "modern woman" has many more rights than her grandmother had, although many added that she has many more responsibilities (Lopata 1971b). The modern woman is able to pull together her own social circle within the role of wife, being freed from many family- imposed and societal restrictions. She can even ignore her in-laws, if that is what she and her husband have negotiated.

The 1989 respondents saw modern women as having much more choice, and they expressed fewer worries and concerns than bothered the feminine mystique wives. The answers had a much freer feeling than those in the 1950s.

The woman of modern times has been influenced by revised feminism, whether she is conscious of it or not. She tends to have planned her life course in addition to and beyond marriage, if she considers marriage at all. Whether young or rethinking her involvements, she intends to work in a relatively demanding job and to have a "career." Although this latter aspect of life is vaguely conceptualized, the woman is likely to prepare for a specific occupation much more often than did her mother, and she intends to "have it all" in terms of success in the roles of wife, mother, and career woman. She does not count on marriage as a solution to all problems, and she expects to have to support herself if it breaks up. Thus the role of wife is not seen as the major commitment of the future.

It is interesting to note here that students in my sociology classes, and in those of other professors with whom I have talked, are quite split in their view of marriage: The women expect to continue in their interesting jobs with the help of a "sharing" husband, while the men want wives who will support them in the two-person single career style. They had better not marry each other!

In *The Marriage Contract* (1981) Weitzman studied a phenomenon that appears to have gained popularity in modern times. A marriage contract establishes the rights and duties of the husband and wife regarding each other and often regarding other members of their social circles and even their commitments to other social roles. Whether they formalize them to this extent or not, many more couples than in the past discuss their future expectations and negotiate major subjects over which they anticipate problems.

Another subject recently drawing both public and social science attention is that of intermarriage. One of the historical, though not common, trends in the African American community has been marriage of successful black men to white women, thereby decreasing even more the pool of eligible black males for black women (Staples 1988, 315). Interestingly enough, three of the five couples featured in a recent *Chicago Tribune Magazine* section devoted to intermarriage included a black spouse, but in two cases the African American was the woman, not the man (Emmerman 1990). Intermarriage appears to be increasing in recent years, as ethnic and racial enclaves and subcultures have loosened their hold on people, and educational or occupational interests have brought previously separated individuals together (see Stephan and Stephan 1989 for this trend in Hawaii and the American Southwest, and Kitano and associates 1984 for both Los Angeles and Hawaii).

The Negotiated Marriage: Rights and Duties

One of the major characteristics of the role of wife in modern marriages is its flexibility in consequence of negotiation with not only the husband but the whole social circle. The negotiations and the resources available to each partner to work out the relationship they want focus around three major areas of life. Gone are the chattel, senior-junior partner, and other marital combinations described by Scanzoni and Scanzoni (1981), and the sub rosa games involved in prior relationships.

One subject of negotiation that is a dramatic break from the past is the right of equality in sexual behavior and satisfaction. There still appears to be a difference between women and men in styles of lovemaking since women are reportedly still trying to get men to broaden the interaction beyond sexual intercourse to include tenderness and affection (Cancian 1987). Alternatives to a particular sexual partner are much more easily available to modern wives, now that they are able to continue or resume a multidimensional life at any stage of the life course. Homosexual relationships have either expanded in frequency or simply become more visible. Sexual interaction is one of the three major subjects of constant negotiation among all couples, whether heterosexual cohabiting, married, lesbian or gay (Blumstein and Schwartz 1983). The fact that it remains a subject that has to be negotiated shows that it remains a problem. Various experiments, such as an "open marriage" that allows each partner full freedom in extramarital relationships, "swinging," or various forms of group marriage, have not worked out for people who, after all, were not socialized into such rights (Reiss and Lee 1988, 259). Although there appears to be a trend in recent years back to strictly monogamous sexual interaction, this time adhered to by both husbands and wives, Reiss and Lee (1988) hypothesize: "What many in America are seeking today is a combination of a deep love relationship in marriage and some lesser level of intimacy outside of marriage" (p. 279). Of course, fear of AIDS is encroaching with apparent speed upon sexual promiscuity, and even more limited sexual exploration, in very recent years.

A second major subject for negotiation in modern marriages is money. It is not that marital financial problems had been absent in previous centuries, but that the base has shifted with the growing economic independence of the wife. Women entered traditional marriages with a dowry or a hope chest that was their economic contribution. With the spread of a money economy, many wives also worked in paying jobs. However, their contributions were discounted, especially when they had no legal power over family property.

The restructuring of the American economic system and changing ideologies are creating an environment that supports women's outside employment. Many couples realize that they cannot maintain a desired standard of living unless the wife brings in earnings. Although the modern wife still does not contribute 50 percent to the family income, she has a stronger base for negotiation than when her earnings were not considered important because the man was the main breadwinner. In addition, financial negotiations can focus not only on how the money is spent, but also on how the couple should invest in each other's careers. No longer is the total investment in the husband.

This brings us to the third subject of negotiation among marital partners of modern, and future, times: commitment to work, not only within the family, but also in jobs. The modern wife is negotiating for rights unusual in past marriages, such as the right to decide when and where to have a job, and to have it influence family time and space, including where they live and couple relationships. Equally on the table is her need for supportive behavior from her husband, similar to, if not as extreme, as what wives have provided to husbands in two-person careers. Bird wrote already in 1979 in *The Two-Paycheck Marriage* that a daunting problem faced by "revolutionary" couples of modern times is the "two-career collision course." Both ordinary daily routines and crisis situations are affected by a person's "greedy" occupation, but when both spouses have such occupations, this creates possibilities for serious conflict. Whose career must be put on hold while the partner meets a new challenge? Who meets emergencies in shared roles without bothering the other? In other words, whose career is most important and should be placed first when its demands appear on the scene? Who gives up a job to follow the spouse in situations of transfer? Thus far, most research points to a failure of wives and husbands to reach a "modern" arrangement with equal treatment of the demands of jobs in two greedy organizations. Underneath it all is the usual lurking suspicion that the family could not exist on the earnings of the wife and that the possibility of parenthood would throw it into dependency on the husband's paycheck. Bird (1979) points to a few examples of "the cool supercouples," but the mass media are full of stories of the women Harvard M.B.A.s who drop out of the corporate structure when they reach the "baby panic" years of life, or after trying to be "supermoms." It is interesting that they are not referred to as "superwives," possibly because the fight on that front has already been won. This would mean that the wives have negotiated a refusal to function in two-person careers of a husband. The reverse will probably never develop, but limited involvement of each partner in the other's job appears to be emerging.

The topic of shared home management and parenting has not as yet progressed beyond discussion level. As Hochschild (1989) and many other social scientists have documented, the declared necessity for a second paycheck has not resulted in shared "second shifts" of work and responsibility at home and with children in more than a very few families. Part of this delay of responsiveness to perceived economic need for the wife's employment is due to the ever-threatening career-scheduling system that punishes women and, it is feared, will punish men if adjustments are made to the two-career family.

There are other aspects of the role of wife that have been, or are being, modified in modern families. The decrease of significance of the husband's associates in the wife's social circle may increase his involvement in her job's circle. The couple can negotiate kinship involvement; the wife is no longer forced to associate with his male line. Dramatic changes are occurring in all American institutions that will reflect back and forth on changes in the role of wife. Observers of the occupational structure point to increasing flexibility of employers in response to the needs of families. Modifications are occurring in the ideological, political, educational, and religious realms of our lives. All these shifts reflect back on the resources and wishes brought by women into marital negotiations. Sources of strain remaining in marriages are partly vestiges of problems embedded in traditional or transitional ones. As Settles concludes in "A Perspective on Tomorrow's Families" in the massive *Handbook on Marriage and the Family* (Sussman and Steinmetz 1987), adjustments to all these shifts will be made primarily by the woman, indirectly affecting the role of husband. And Goode (1982) reminds us that men resist the changes demanded of them because they signal, and actually involve, a loss of power.

In view of all the uncertainties as to what the role of wife will be in a "modern" marriage, we are safe in simply hypothesizing great

variations and life-course flexibility, and not just along societal subgroup lines, such as social class.

The Life Course of the Role of Wife

A woman takes on the role of wife through a series of stages. Contact
must be established between herself and those representatives of
the social circle who are involved in the selection process. In modern times and places, a woman focuses first on the potential husband (and vice versa), and then gains or selects most of the other
circle members. Of course, it is usually difficult to ignore people to
whom the selected husband is already attached, and in-laws can
become an unavoidable addition to the role of wife. A second stage
in becoming a wife involves mutual testing of partners, whether by
families or in dating situations. The characteristics for which the
testing takes place depend upon the perception by the tester as to
future duties and rights of the role, which is sometimes, although not
often, seen in life-course perspective. The sequence of announcements of the decision to enter the role of wife is the third stage. Each
segment of the future circle is informed in acceptable sequence.
People who will not be involved, such as former boyfriends or
associates with whom relations must be cut off because of the
woman's becoming a wife and the man's becoming a husband, must
also be told. In past times in this society, employers were to be
informed, and employment terminated upon marriage.

The procedures of entrance into the role of wife are often very
elaborate, depending not just on the wishes of the marital unit, but
also on those of the circle influenced by its social importance.
Weddings are traditional events carried forth into modern times,
although with innumerable variations. The final stage of becoming
a wife involves the incorporation of that identity into the woman's
self-concept and the reconstruction of reality to fit the marriage and
her marital status. The depth of the changes in her self-concepts and
construction of reality is allegedly greater for traditional and transitional women than for men, and it definitely varies among women
depending on the other sociopsychological aspects of role involvement. Bernard (1973, 42) refers to the "shock theory of marriage" for
women; that marriage involves "dwindling into a wife." The woman
leaves behind her birth name and becomes Mrs. John Doe. Most

observers claim that major legislative reforms are needed before full partnership becomes possible in marriage.

Over the life course a wife's social relationships vary considerably in the content of the circle and of interaction. Any changes in the life of the woman and the lives of the other family members can modify this role. Parents who must be cared for, the movement of the husband up the patriarchal family line in seniority, promotion of the husband or the wife in modern times, addition of the role of mother, health problems, and aging, for example, can have consequences upon relations with the husband and others in the circle. Changes in the husband's job, especially when they involve geographical mobility, can add or remove people from the wife's social circle. Of course, divorce, desertion, and the death of the husband modify the role of wife.

The husband-wife relationship can change from its own dynamics. Sexual interaction may recede in importance as years go by. Conflict over children may diminish as the children grow up. Some couples drift onto different paths, becoming less frequently joined. In fact, Pineo (1966) claims that the later years of marriage bring "disenchantment." Wives and husbands who have taken each other for granted while pursuing their own interests may come to find competing roles less engrossing and wish for more satisfaction from the marriage. However, by that point they have little in common. Levinson (1978) and associates found middle-aged men in a "midlife crisis," worrying about death and feeling they missed many good years by concentrating so hard on financial success. They wish to "modify their life structures," leave their wives for younger women, and start new families. The wives, even those who have not divorced but who find no vitality in the marriage, ask themselves, according to Rubin (1979), "What do I do with the rest of my life?" On the other hand, some studies find that, as the spouses decrease involvement in other roles, each may turn to the other for companionship and more leisure-time activity, revitalizing the marriage (Deutscher 1964).

The Social Psychology of Role Involvement

Not all wives grant the role of wife first importance in the hierarchical arrangement of their role clusters. The rank also varies in relation to the other roles in the family dimension and the multidimension-ality of the life space. The richer the dimension, in terms of the number of family roles within it and the importance assigned each, and the more complex the life space, the less significant or all-encompassing is the identity of wife. In addition, women can vary the importance they assign to the duties and rights connected with the husband, in comparison to those involving other members of the social circle. For example, a wife in a highly patriarchal family may feel, or may have to express, greater allegiance to the parents of the husband than to the husband. Many a wife is more task- than relation-oriented in her interactions with her husband, feeling that physical duties of providing for his comfort are more important than empathetic ones. She can also see herself as simply responding to his demands, rather than anticipating his needs and or considering their mutual needs. Thus, her stance of responsiveness can be passive or reactive, without necessarily including deep sentiments of love or a view of herself as a loving wife. In fact, such an involvement in the role of wife is true of many lower-class women, according to research regarding many countries and times. Middle-class women with more education and more comfortable living styles tend to be more empathetically involved in this role.

Those who study marital happiness and its effect on life satisfac-tion face the problems of both defining these sentiments and form-ing methodologies for their research. Americans generally declare their marriages to be happy, although there has been a decrease in such statements by wives in recent years. Increases in divorce do not prove rejection of marriage itself, as evidenced by the frequency with which women reenter this relationship.

> In the middle and late 1970s, when many journalists and lay persons believed that the soaring divorce rate meant that the institution of marriage was declining if not disintegrating, many family social scien-tists, including us, took the position that marriage was just as impor-tant to Americans as ever, and that the increase in divorce partly reflected the fact that marriage was so important to people that they were becoming less willing to tolerate unsatisfactory marriage rela-tionships. (Glenn and Weaver 1988, 317)

So, with decreased economic dependence of wives on husbands and the increased ease and acceptability of divorce, observers assume that women who remain married are satisfied with this relationship.

One problem with that argument is the frequency with which abused wives remain in their marriages. As Wittner (1990) reports in her study of the domestic violence court, the whole structure of the society and its system of protecting people from violence is so complicated and ineffectual as to make a wife's efforts to leave an abusive marriage extremely difficult. And reports of violence and psychological abuse have abounded in recent years, though so have the number and variety of self-help and other groups attempting to deal with such marital problems.

The role of wife is affected by the retirement of the husband; he is no longer absent during the working day, making constant contact inevitable or providing time for leisure-time activity. The wife may demand greater cooperation in her role of homemaker. Reduced finances can be a consequence, but so can reduced costs. Of course, the wife's adjustment to changes in the husband's social circle depends also upon her involvements outside of the home. Employed wives are less satisfied with their marriages than are full-time homemakers, though the latter are more frequently depressed (Shehan and Rexroat 1986).

The Ex-Wife or Widow

In highly patriarchal families, a woman often did not have the right to divorce, nor could she continue to live with the husband's family if he divorced her, which left her with few choices. In some situations she could return to her family of orientation, but she could not take the children with her, because they belonged to the husband's line. Divorce has been forbidden by the Catholic church and is against the norms of many societies. Until very recent times, divorcées were ostracized, a reflection of the status of women. Situations in which whole families are involved in arranging the marriage, especially when economic goods are exchanged, usually discourage divorce, since it complicates the lives of so many. The modern increase in divorce can be partly accounted for by the independence of the marital unit from external pressures, such as powerful families or communities from which the partners could not escape.

The subject of divorce has attracted a great deal of attention in America in recent times simply because of its frequency, in face of the traditional assumption, written into most religious ceremonies, that marriage is "till death does us part." Wives traditionally were not expected to leave this role except in dire circumstances defined by law, religion, or custom (Halem 1982). As mentioned above, the importance of the patriarchal system and the concern over patrilineal inheritance insured that men could more easily substitute wives than women could substitute husbands. Of recent times, divorce has been of special concern to the husband's family, since the woman has the right to remove the children from contact with it. Thus, two sets of social groups have been threatened by women's ability to obtain divorce: those who consider marriage a permanent relationship and those concerned with patrilineal continuity. Of course, in many societies the woman who has wished to leave a marriage has had no place to go, since there have been so few alternative ways in which she could maintain herself and no groups that would accept her.

The loss of the role of wife through divorce or widowhood can be a major life-disrupting event even in modern times, since it affects not only the marriage, but also other of the woman's roles. Although these two means of exiting the major aspects of the role of wife are very different, there are some similarities. Many factors influence the degree of disorganization of self, social roles, and life-style produced by divorce or the death of the husband. Of signal importance is the degree of psychological, social, and economic dependence of the wife upon the husband and upon being married. Some women never develop strong emotional ties with the husband and live quite independently from him and other members of the social circle. Others build their identities upon the husband and live vicariously through him. He can serve as their connecting link to the world outside of the household. The amount of distress felt by the wife at these events is influenced by the circumstances surrounding them: when in the life course it occurs, its degree of suddenness, the presence or absence of alternative supports and relations, and the status loss or amount of stigma in the role of ex-wife. The process of getting a divorce can be traumatic even for women at lower levels of marital integration, especially in times when such action was disapproved by the community and significant others, and when the legal procedures were demeaning. Although widows, unlike divorcees, had no choice in losing the role of wife, both can feel some blame. Women in America are expected to provide the emotional glue to the marriage. Asian Indian families of the deceased have been known to directly blame the wife for not properly taking care of the husband or not fulfilling other duties that could have prevented the death (Lopata 1972, 1987a, and 1987c).

There can be other unpleasant consequences of divorce or widowhood. Economic repercussions can be traumatic. Weitzman (1985) found that, in states with no-fault divorce, women and children were being pushed into poverty while men gained in discretionary income. A widow lacking other sources of economic support can also be impoverished, especially if she is ineligible for social security. A decrease in income can result in a need to sell the house and move into a less desirable neighborhood, breaking ties with the former community of residence. Problems arise in child rearing. Friendships can be weakened if the woman's funds are inadequate to retain her former round of activity, or because the absence of a partner makes couple-companionate "fun" awkward. In-law relations can also wither—a positive consequence if she wants independence, but negative if it means a loss of support. Social group memberships often drop, and existing roles must be modified to a varying extent. If reconstruction of reality, including of the self, occurred in the process of becoming a wife, it must again take place when the woman is no longer in that role.

There are major differences, however, between the effects of widowhood and the effects of divorce upon the former wife: The vestiges of the roles are not comparable, nor are many of the forms of resultant loneliness (Kitson et al. 1980). In the case of divorce, there is the problem of the continued existence of the ex-husband, and vestiges of the role of being his wife remain, often painfully (Ebaugh 1988). Conflict with the ex-husband over children or financial arrangements can create a life of tension and anger. So can jealousy over the ex-mate's social, sexual, and emotional life. Some wives wish to return to the marriage, others are lonely for many aspects of the prior life but don't want their husbands back. In any case, there are many emotional "hang-ups" associated with divorce, even in modern times when divorce is allegedly so easy.

There are some problems unique to widowhood. Caring for an ill husband for years can be debilitating, while sudden death can leave a lot of "unfinished business." In either case, the woman feels powerless. A widow often feels obligated to continue the social existence of her late husband, sometimes even to the point of sanctifying his memory, a process which interferes with her social relations (Lopata 1981b). She is also expected to insure that the children remember their father positively. Often she is older and does not have the personal resources to reengage in a new support network or modify the existing ones after the period of grief is over. A voluntaristic society demands knowledge of its resources and initiative in social integration, characteristics that are often absent among women brought up to depend on the family and the domestic sphere of life. The loss of traditional support systems leaves many an urban American widow in a relatively restricted social life space (Lopata 1973c and 1979; see also chapters in Lopata 1987c and 1987e).

A major problem in widowhood, experienced in somewhat different ways following divorce, is loneliness. A widow can experience any or all of these forms of loneliness: loneliness for that particular man, for having a love object, for being a love object, for a sexual and physically intimate partner, for a companion, for an escort to public places, for a partner in couple-companionate interaction, for someone around whom to organize time and work, for another presence in the home. She can be lonely for the social life she used to enjoy when married. Friendships with married friends need to be dropped and auxiliary memberships in groups made inoperative; activities connected with the husband's occupation and person no longer are demanded or possible. Widows even miss some of the duties their role of wife required, and the rewards that came from their performance. Thus, the whole life-style can be affected by the death of the husband, to the extent that his presence or other forms of contribution are needed for its continuance (Lopata 1969a). The Widow-to-Widow programs, existing in many communities on the model developed by Silverman (1987) at Harvard Medical School, aim to help widows solve some of these problems by serving as emotional supports and as providers of resource information. The emotional supports include an opportunity to talk about the deceased and the circumstances of death as well as current problems. Other associates often do not want to hear the story again. Widows report that other widows "really understand," having gone through the same experience themselves.

On the other hand, divorce or the husband's death can remove many restrictions in life and self-concept. Divorcées and some widows report that, after the period of grief for the husband or the marriage is mainly over, they blossom. Many others report feelings of independence, a fuller self-concept, and an interesting life. Among widows, however, the vestiges of the prior role usually contain the obligation to remember the deceased and to insure that his children and others with whom he had important relationships keep him socially alive—that is, alive in their memories. Segments of the social circle of the role of wife may still remain in interaction with her.

Reentry into the Role of Wife

Remarriage, or reentry into the role of wife, has its own dynamism. After all, there are still the vestiges of the prior marriage, often in the form of children, and a socioeconomic life-style produced by the marital team working together. The former or late husband is still around, in consciousness if not physically. Some women are simply unwilling to remarry, because they enjoy their independence and do not wish to invest in that role again. Divorcées may not wish to go through another failure; widows may feel that no one can replace the deceased or that they do not want to care for an ill man again (Lopata 1979 and 1988b). Others report that children fear loss of inheritance if they remarry, or resent anyone taking their father's place. On the other hand, remarriage can solve the problems of loneliness and emotional and financial insecurity.

Of course, the older the woman, the less the probability of finding a new mate, in view of the statistical shortage of eligible men. Divorcées are more apt to remarry than widows but not as likely as divorced men (Cherlin 1981, 29). Younger women are more apt to enter that relationship than are older ones. Remarriage is, of course, dependent upon the ability to go through all the stages of meeting an appropriate candidate for husband, developing a relationship, and "becoming" a wife. There appears to be a higher-than-by-coincidence probability that a widow will marry someone she knows from the past, often a widower from a prior network. Groups such as Parents Without Partners or Spares provide opportunities for cross-gender contact, and the mass media are full of advertisements for mates and for "singles" events. Contact can also be established through special-interest groups that draw both men and women of the appropriate age, racial, or other qualifying characteristics.

The woman who reenters the role of wife has added not only a husband but a whole new social circle, in addition to the one that remains from her prior marriage. A factor affecting her success with the new role is her ability to keep it separated, psychologically and socially, from the vestiges of the old one. Her new husband's marital history must also be dealt with in the reconstruction of reality this time around. The quality of relationships in remarriage varies by the same factors as in the initial marriage, with some modifications due mainly to past experiences (Furstenberg and Spanier 1984). Complications result in an even higher chance of divorce than in first marriages, but McKain (1969) found that people entering older, retirement marriages were quite realistic in their requirements and expectations.

Summary

Both modifications in American society and new constructions of reality by women have introduced many changes into the relations of the wife with all circle members of that role, within relatively recent times. Social class differences complicate the movement from traditional to modern role of wife; the least change is experienced by the extremes of the lower and upper classes. The role of wife in traditional times was heavily controlled by the husband's family and by strict norms of behavior. Transitional marriages combined vestiges of the patriarchal dependency system, in which the man is head of the household and major decision maker, but with relative independence of the nuclear family from the male line. The wife becomes the personal dependent of the husband, since his job and earnings provide the basis of their life-style. Her social circle, duties, and rights are tied into the husband's involvement in an occupational role. It is in the expanding middle class that two-person single-career demands have most affected the transitional wife. As a man's job became defined as requiring total commitment, it acquired the right to impinge upon the life of the wife and to demand extreme support. Assisted by the feminine mystique, which assigned women total responsibility for the home and the family, this system functioned within the two-sphere world.

The role of wife in modern marriage is still in the process of emerging, but it will undoubtedly have two main characteristics: variation along many self-defined and negotiated lines, and great flexibility. As both men and women decrystallize the traditional life course, dependent upon life chances of family background through repeated entrances and exits in education, occupation, and other role involvements, their marital roles will of necessity become more flexible. Entrances into and exits from the role of wife will become more attuned to events in the whole role cluster. Already many women are foregoing marriage or marrying at a later date. Divorce at a later stage of life does not preclude reentry into this role. Negotiated sexual, emotional, occupational, and general supports are subject to renegotiation as self- and other-defined needs change. As of now, this flexibility and variability are most evident in the role of wife, but it is quite possible that these characteristics will become more visible in the role of husband. In the meantime, greater pressure from all kinds of people upon the established institutions may make marriage less repercussively dependent upon changes in the rest of the world.

3

The Role of Mother

The role of mother is universal. The norms surrounding it depend to a great extent on assumptions within the culture as to the needs of social mothers and of the offspring throughout their life courses. The role also depends upon other members of the social circle and how deeply they are involved in monitoring, contributing to, and benefiting from it. No woman has been able to carry out the role of mother without the cooperation of many other people. In past times in America, and currently in most places in the world, responsibility for the child was shared not only by the social father, but also by the extended kin.

A woman enters the social role of mother when she accepts that role in relation to a particular child, or children, and is accepted as such by the social circle she pulls together, more or less voluntarily. Throughout history, the biological mother did not necessarily enter the role of social mother, since the newborn could die, with or without the help of those involved, or she could give it to someone else, usually a woman. In the same vein, the social mother did not necessarily give birth to the child, being able to acquire it in other ways. In modern societies her announcement that she will mother the child has to be legally approved by representatives of the state, such as school personnel, treating her as the mother. Birth certificates assume that the birth mother will undertake social motherhood, while adoption papers recognize the separation of the two forms of motherhood. Women, and even men, can be called "mother" and may even perform many of the duties and receive many rights of that role without being granted its full identity, if they are considered substitutes.

> There are several widespread institutions that involve shifting children between domestic groups. The first is wet-nursing, which is essentially a service institution and may consist of bringing in a servant rather than sending out an infant. The second is fostering, which is often reciprocal between kin though it too may have a service component, for it is a practice that is related to the in-house nursing (nannying) of older children, to servanthood, and to apprenticeship. The third is adoption, a practice associated with the problem of heirship. (Goody 1983, 68)

This role, like that of wife, has gone through three major changes in the last century or so. In traditional families the main burden of mothering fell on the mother's shoulders. The emerging modern era is moving toward a wider circle of shared, negotiated parenting, involving the father and various nonrelated persons or groups of the community. Before analyzing these variations in the role of mother in American society, we must look at the social person characteristics of women who can or cannot enter this role.

Preventing or Insuring the Role of Mother

Decisions as to who enters, and who does not enter, the role of mother go beyond biology and have been very important in the history of humankind. There has been an interesting movement back and forth as to the rights of decision making in cases in which entrance into the role was not ascribed by biology alone.

Societies have had ambivalent feelings about children, giving varying freedom of choice to potential mothers. These feelings have been converted into ideologies, cultural norms, official policies, and even laws. Some societies at some times have not wanted some of its women, or some segments of the population, to reproduce. This was and is particularly true of societies concerned about children as a "national asset" and the "physical deterioration of the population" (Oakley 1981, 212). Sterilization of people judged mentally or physically inferior, or of those who already have children, has been state policy for centuries in India and other countries and was the policy of Nazi Germany. America's history contains references to this form of control of population "quality":

> Paul Popenoe, a leading eugenics spokesman, estimated that 10 million Americans should be sterilized on the basis of IQ testimony. By 1932 compulsory sterilization laws for the feeble-minded, insane, criminal and physically defective had been enacted by twenty-seven states. (Hartmann 1987, 96–97)

Official policies influencing motherhood have included economic rewards or punishment, sex education, funding and dispersal of birth control technologies, health care for the mother and children, and other supports or barriers. Laws define incest and intermarriage. Underlying these are the cultural milieu, the way the society is organized around gender identity, the value given to the role of mother in competition with other roles, and the socialization of children for the future. Judith Blake (1974) found America of the 1970s to be characterized by strong pronatalism, encouragement of marriage for women, high gender-role differentiation, a negative attitude toward careers for women, emphasis in higher education on fields of specialization appropriate to future family roles, an assumption of the naturalness of the desire to have children, and personality socialization into polarized social roles. Blake, as well as Betty Friedan (1963), documented the contributions of psychoanalysis and sociology to the coercive pronatalism imposed on women. On the other hand, Huber (1980) concluded that American society is antinatalistic in that it does not help families after children are born. The Reagan and Bush administrations opposed sex education in schools, the dispensing of contraceptives, and abortion, while cutting back on prenatal and child health care. These administrations claimed to be shocked by reported child abuse, yet did not wish to spend money to prevent it. No serious efforts were made to encourage employers to provide parental leave at birth or adoption, or to insure child support payments by fathers.

In times and places in which birth control has not been frequently practiced and multiple pregnancies have been desired even
by women drained by their frequency, the period of childbearing
has extended from puberty till menopause or death. The high death
rate of the young, and the contributions of children to the economic,
emotional, and old-age support of parents, as well as ancestor
worship insuring an afterlife, made frequent birthing a necessity.

In spite of the current assumption that women have a biologically determined "mothering" propensity, some mothers have killed
their children or allowed their children to be killed, sometimes even
after several years of mothering. Only occasionally have mothers
protested against their children's being sent to probable death in
wars. Infanticide has been practiced for a variety of reasons, including sacrifice to gods, deformity, illness, sex, birth order, and illegiti-
macy (Bennett, 1983, Sommerville 1982). Even European families of
the Middle Ages did not have the sentimental views about children
that developed later, but accepted as necessary the probably pre-
ventable deaths of many newborns and young babies. It must be
remembered that the strongly patriarchal systems of most of Europe
did not give mothers many rights over their children, so that they did
not have the power to prevent child abuse, even in situations in
which their attachment went against the cultural norm of indifference to, or even neglect of, sickly infants.

Modern technological advances have increased at two extremes
women's choices about whether to enter the role of mother: voluntary rejection of the role, and help for those having difficulties in
bearing children. In traditional societies of the past and present, and
in much of America, abortion was often the only way a woman
could prevent unwanted children. Russian women have allegedly
resorted to it frequently during their childbearing years. There are
thus many ways in which a woman can reject entering the role of
mother, ranging from celibacy, contraception, infanticide, to giving
the child to someone else to mother.

Voluntary childlessness was defined as a form of deviant behavior in America's allegedly pronatalistic past (Veevers 1980). Although
the reported rate of expected childlessness has varied little over
studied time in America, there appears to be a change from unwanted, as compared to chosen, childlessness. Also, it is only recently that we have a record of reasons women give for rejecting the
role of mother. Many estimate the costs to outweigh the benefits
(Houseknecht 1987). The economic costs of raising children have

become increasingly high, especially since children contribute little, if anything, to family income, and when a loss of earnings by a stay-at-home mother is included in the calculations. Sociopsychological costs can include loss of freedom, heavy responsibility accompanied by worry and anxiety, negative consequences on marriage, and interference with careers and other roles and relationships (Miller 1987, 584).[1] Some also report a general dislike of children, concern over population growth, troubled early life experiences, or the wish not to lose control over their bodies and future. Care of children can be seen as arduous and complex. Comfortable routines, self-fulfillment, and marital harmony can be seen as destroyed by the addition of motherhood to the existing role cluster. The decision can involve another person, usually the potential father, and difficulties arise if the two are not in complete agreement. It also appears that early decisions not to enter into the role of mother are sometimes questioned as the couple nears the age when pregnancy is no longer advisable or possible. The reported benefits of motherhood include primary ties and affection, stimulation and fun, expansion of self, adult status and identity, achievement and creativity, and becoming a wanted and "better" person. The Chicago women I studied also added under benefits the pleasure of "watching them grow" and "the sense of family" (Lopata 1971b). To these we can add avoiding the stigma of not being a "normal woman" (Oakley 1981, 226). These values hold for America; in other times and places, economic and religious benefits, plus care in old age, have been primary.

The technological means available to women who want to avoid becoming mothers have multiplied considerably, although American society has mixed feelings about their use. Rothman has raised a new concern in *The Tentative Pregnancy: Prenatal Diagnosis and the Future of Motherhood* (1986). Medical technology in the form of amniocentesis or ultrasound now makes it possible for women to determine early on, even before others know they are pregnant, whether they wish to accept a problem fetus, or even one of the "wrong" gender. The long-range consequences of these technologies have not been fully thought out in America, or elsewhere for that matter.

Entering the role of mother can be quite unplanned, a consequence of sexual intercourse without thought of such consequences. Accidental, or "mistimed," pregnancies can be met by the future mother with several emotional responses, depending on many factors. The circumstances of the pregnancy, such as the absence of a husband to give the child patriarchal legitimacy or a social father to share its care, or its occurrence when other roles make heavy demands, can create negative feelings. The experiences of pregnancy, including bodily changes and emotional responses of others, are important factors.

One of the situations that most Americans find "unnatural" is that of ex-mothers or "absentee mothers" (Paskowicz 1982) who accepted the role, related with the child, usually for several years, and then left or gave up custody, and thus the major duties and rights, to someone else, usually the father. Like people who give up other important roles, such women appear to go through several stages: experiencing doubts, seeking alternatives, facing a turning point, and finally creating what Ebaugh (1988) calls an "ex-role." Being an ex-mother is one of the hardest of ex-roles. Women who choose to relinquish custody usually feel incapable of performing the role adequately and consider other people and their life situations better for the child. Others lose custody in courts or through the decision of the children. The state still takes children away from mothers judged to be abusive or neglectful (Wittner 1977).

Women who cannot get pregnant although they wish to do so face a different set of problems, especially when adoption of babies judged by them and intermediaries to be appropriate is difficult. Some couples are determined to parent their own biological children. Infertility can lead to a sense of failure, marital problems or prolonged and expensive medical experimentation. New reproductive technologies are often painful and leave the woman feeling a complete loss of control over her body. In fact, Lauritzen (1990) calls the new developments a "tyranny of technology." He says such technology as artificial insemination or surrogate parenting constitutes a "dismemberment of motherhood"—in that three women, the genetic, gestational, and social mothers can be involved in the process—and calls the process a "commodification of reproduction." Social scientists have been trying hard to imagine consequences of recent reproductive technology, as evidenced by some recent titles (Rapping 1990): *The Mother Machine: Reproductive Technologies from Artificial Insemination to Artificial Wombs, Once upon a Future: The Women's Guide to Tomorrow's Technology, Made to Order: The Myth of Reproductive Progress, Test-Tube Women: What Future for Motherhood?*

Despite the critiques, reports by women who entered the role of mother with the help of the new procedures, such as surrogate motherhood, are very positive (Overbold 1988). The major problems here can be the failure of the biological mother to give up the child, and the complications of all the procedures, which involve legal and medical intermediaries. It will take time before the situation is sufficiently institutionalized to resolve its technical and ethical problems. The combined technology, including genetic experimentation, and societal redefinitions of what is "natural" may decrease the frequency of infertility and the fear of transmitting genetic problems (Rothman 1986, 67). Some women are using the technologies to become mothers, biologically and socially, without there being an acknowledged father of the child.

Traditional Times, Traditional Places

Patriarchal families controlled who could father the child to which the woman gave birth, and insisted on having sons, which was seen as the responsibility of the woman, even when people knew that the male sperm determined the gender of the child. Since the mothers were usually also responsible for managing the household, and they continued having children, they had little time for the actual care of the offspring. The kinship group, older children, or servants, among those who could force or hire others to provide such assistance, did most of the physical care and the socialization of new family members. British common law, copied by early American society, gave the "absolute right to the custody of their minor children to the father" (Lindgren and Taub 1988, 332–33). The main responsibility for the children lay with the father's family, especially in the case of male children. Girls stayed with the mother and other female members of the family, their lives controlled by the family's concerns over the possibility of their becoming impregnated at an inauspicious time.

Transitional and Modern Forms of the Role of Mother

The main characteristic of transitional families in America has been the placement of the total responsibility for the care and socialization of children upon the social mother. Aries (1965) dates from the eighteenth century the idealization of childhood as a distinctive stage of human life and of the mother as the caregiver of children.

Of course, the romanticization of children did not prevent their continued economic exploitation in early industrialization (see Sommerville's *The Rise and Fall of Childhood,* 1982). Families also fought child labor laws, considering their offspring to be necessary to their economic support. Care of the young by mothers, assisted by the role's circle, often included what would now be considered child abuse. The Puritans believed in physical punishment—that "sparing the rod" resulted in problem youth.

The reversal of the position of the child from being expendable to being a "precious" member of the family had become so strong by the mid-1900s that several authors labeled the recent past "the century of the child" (see Ehrenreich and English 1979). The increased emphasis on child protection and the importance of motherhood for the socialization of the young had a backlash effect on women in the midtwentieth century. Women had to live with "the fantasy of the perfect mother" (Chodorow and Contratto 1982). The emphasis on this role, which was less apparent in Europe, was due to American society's refusal to take responsibility for its children, the growing difficulty of mothering in the absence of traditional formulas for rearing and controlling the young, the prevailing theories of human development, and the relative isolation of mothers from the extended family (Lopata 1971b, 182–88). The main contribution of the father was to provide the economic support for the family. His prior responsibility for what the children did was thus diminished, shifted to the mother. A look at the titles of books with widespread popularity in the 1950s indicates that some Americans were concerned about the total interdependence of mother and child in relative isolation from other socializers. Mothers became accused of living vicariously through their children, and of rearing them too "permissively." Wylie's *Generation of Vipers* (1955) is a good example of the extremely negative portrayal of American women during the "feminine mystique" years. The anti-Semitic stereotype of the overprotective Jewish mother is an example of extreme "mother bashing" (R. Coser, 1992). Bettelheim (1962) went so far as to advocate child care organized by the kibbutzim movement in Israel, which took the children away from the mother for most of the time, to be reared in peer groups by caregivers on eight-hour shifts. He defined American mothers as too protective of their children, whose moral development needed contact with peers in what Mead called the "game stage."

It is very difficult to differentiate the transitional from the modern role of mother in the United States, mainly because American society has not really moved beyond the idea that the mother is the only one responsible for the child. There is a great deal of public commentary and outcry over the failure of other people to feel responsible for our youths, but little has been done to change either the ideology of perfect motherhood or the behavior of all involved. The problem of child care arose in transitional times as a result of the decreased availability of extended kin, older children, servants, and the community at large to care for the young and the organization of much work into jobs in organizations away from home, jobs entered into by individuals without arrangements for care of family members. The most recent trend of increased labor-force participation of mothers compounded the problem, because the fathers were already gone for most of the day.

Modern women who have moved into the multidimensional life space required by the complexity of social development find life complicated by the addition of the role of mother, with all its transitional characteristics (see Rossi 1968 and the discussion of role conflict in chapter 8). Employed mothers now seldom send children back to villages from which they migrated or to relatives in other locations, as they did in the past (Hareven 1978a, 1978b; Hareven and Langenbach 1978). Older children are in school and related activities, the extended family has dispersed, and its older female members, such as grandmothers, also hold jobs. Exceptions still exist in ethnic communities, in which kin care is institutionalized and/or the women live nearby and cannot get jobs.

Nonfamilial child care is expensive, servants either are no longer available or are prohibitive in cost, and out-of-home caregivers can be unreliable. American mass media are constantly reporting cases of physical, sexual, and psychological abuse by people hired to take care of the young. This does not mean that mothers themselves never abuse their children, but that caretakers paid for the service are forbidden from breaking established rules of care. These reports create great concern and guilt in employed mothers, who nevertheless need the money from their jobs (Kamerman 1980).

One solution is to allow older children to take care of themselves at home after school. Labeled "latchkey children" by the press, which has not presented this solution in a positive light, such children reportedly do not suffer any long-term social or cognitive developmental problems (Rodman 1990; Rodman and Pratto 1987). Cain and Hofferth (1989, 76) report that such self-care is usually for only short periods of time and carried out by older children of white, middle-class families who live in suburban or rural areas. Mothers are available by telephone, and some communities have developed volunteer hot-lines for troubled situations. There is little mention of fathers.

As of now, women are still held responsible for solving any problems arising out of the difficulty of being a mother in modern times and the dysfunctionality of transitional role relations. A perfect example of the double-bind situation of women is the constant public outcry over child care. It encompasses a complete refusal of the society to take on responsibility for its young, on the national or community level (see Grubb and Lazerson 1982).

Strong conflict between the role of mother of young children and the role of employee/worker/career woman is an American phenomenon. Other societies are still in traditional life patterns with extended-family and village involvement in their children or have found new ways in which the children are seen as part of the community, which shares their care (see Kamerman and Kahn 1989; Kahn and Kamerman 1975; Kamerman 1980, presents alternative responses from European countries). There are many ways in which employers, schools, community centers, organized sports, and other interest groups can contribute to the welfare of children so that the mother need not be present twenty-four hours a day. There is some evidence that American governmental and private employers are beginning to consider their responsibilities to their employees and that fathers are insisting on greater flexibility in their work schedules to enable active fathering. If these trends continue, the mother's social circle will take on much greater functions than just passive assistance to her.

The Life Course of the Role of Mother

Becoming a Mother

The process by which a woman enters the role of mother, even in adoption, takes time, during which she anticipatorily socializes herself and future circle members and is socialized by others (Rossi 1985). A mother's duties precede the child's birth, for they include self-care in order to insure the health of the newborn. Throughout human history the pregnancy and birth processes have been connected with fear, which is not surprising in view of how frequently mothers and children used to die during these processes (Miller 1987, 583). What are considered influences upon the physical and psychological welfare of the mother and the fetus vary considerably from society to society, and even among subgroups. "Experts" on childbirth abound, ranging from women already in that role, to midwives and people who will form the mother's social circle after the birth. Magical and religious rituals are performed even now to insure the protection of the fetus from all kinds of harm (Znaniecki 1965, 117). Whole books are devoted to prescriptions and proscriptions pregnant women should follow. In recent times, a large and successful profession has grown up around pregnancy, childbirth, and early childhood pediatrics (Halpern 1989). In fact, social scientists have labeled this the "medicalization," or professional regulation, of birth, taking decision making and even birth itself out of the "minds and hands" of the mother. The adopting mother can only hope that the biological mother took adequate precautions to insure that the baby she turns over is healthy.

Another duty of the future mother is to prepare in advance an adequate physical environment for the child, including clothing and related paraphernalia. Such preparations are aimed at insuring safety, health, and comfort. "Baby showers" provide many items judged necessary for the care and development of the newborn, or at least considered representative of his or her status. Complex social and religious ceremonies surround the birth and recognition of the newborn (Williams 1990).

Traumatic Events in Becoming a Mother

Of course, becoming pregnant does not guarantee entrance into or continuance in the role of mother. Demographers estimate that only about half of all infants ever born reach maturity (Miller 1987, 582). American mothers who are above the line of poverty, thus spared many of poverty's health complications, are much more likely to see their children grow into maturity than are mothers who live below that line.

An added complication to the role of mother has been the recent dramatic improvement in medical technology that enables intensive and extended care for newborns (see Guillemin and Holmstrom

1986, Frohock 1986). The technology available in the "closed world of the neonatal intensive care unit" (Guillemin and Holmstrom 1986, 141) raises important social and ethical issues. The medical staff tends to exclude the parents from the decision-making process, and the effect of this on the families is not always positive.

In spite of the modern technologies that save babies and older children, many mothers still experience the loss of a child. Research indicates that stillbirths, miscarriages, and even wanted abortions due to fetal abnormalities are highly traumatic to the woman who has already socialized herself into motherhood (Borg and Lasker 1988). Grief can be experienced even if the mother never had a chance to "bond" with the baby she carried. One would assume that it would be even harder if the child had already acquired human capacities and responsiveness. Knapp (1986) entitled her study *Beyond Endurance: When a Child Dies,* and teams of professional or volunteer assistants have recently emerged to help parents cope with caring for a dying child (Carlson 1984).

Being a Mother

Motherhood is a role for which many transitional American women feel unprepared, untrained, and inadequate. This was particularly true of the women influenced by the feminine mystique of the 1950s and 1960s (Lopata 1971a, 189). They, like mothers currently in the transitional stages of women's roles, were caught in a historical gap when traditional family child care became unavailable or rejected and before "modern" medical and social "experts" took over the responsibility of educating them into new knowledge. The proverbial postpartum depression is often analyzed as hormonal, but it is undoubtedly influenced by the enormity of responsibility suddenly thrust on the mother, especially in a society that gives so little of that responsibility to other members of the child's social circle, such as the father or kinfolk. The "parenthood as crisis" literature also points to the changes in life-style introduced into the homes of many a mother who had been in a multidimensional life space before. Such women experience a more dramatic shift in their lives with motherhood than with marriage, especially if they do not return to work or other full-time involvement after the birth.

Only in recent years have there been societal resources in the form of self-help groups or expert counselors for mothers, and even fathers, assisting with new parenthood. However, modern new mothers find themselves in a double-bind situation: resenting professional control yet anxious over their inability to meet all the demands of the role without it.

The consequences of becoming a mother are extensive in transitional and modern times. These include changes in the self, sometimes to the extent of identity crisis, or a feeling of being pushed into the background as an individual by the constant physical work and by social contacts being limited to mainly infants in a restricted life space. On the other hand, motherhood can be experienced as bringing an increase in maturity, capacities, and abilities (Lopata 1971b, 193). A third consequence is inevitably described as "being tied down." Previous freedom to come and go at will is gone. Elaborate arrangements, often expensive or involving unwanted dependencies, have to be made for child care. Mothers may face special problems in connection with the children, such as their handicaps or care for several children of different ages and with different needs. Changes in the relationship with the husband/new father are necessitated as the new role adds overlap dimensions to the one entered into before (Lerner and Spanier 1978). Lower-class women often report that becoming parents added a new tie to the marriage, while middle-class women tend to feel that it complicates and interferes with husband-wife interaction. Some families change residences after the addition of children, considering past locations less desirable for the children or for the parents (Lopata 1971b, 203; see also Rossi 1985). All in all, becoming a mother increases work and responsibility and decreases personal leisure to a level not anticipated before (Wearing 1990). These changes do not necessarily result in unhappiness, as they can be offset by the pleasure of having a child. This is particularly true of mothers who had planned not only for having a child, but also for its timing (see Michaels and Goldberg 1988).

Research of the past two decades, often undertaken on the assumption of changes in the roles of women and men due to the women's movement and other cultural modifications, invariably comes to the conclusion that responsibility for the child has remained with the mother since it became lodged there with social development or modernization (Backett 1982; Oakley 1974b). She continues to be responsible for the child's physical well-being, as were her grandmothers, but the growth of psychology and other social sciences has added the burden of also being responsible for the child's psychological development. In most of known history, personality inheritance or at least imprinting at conception or birth was taken for granted, so that the mother was not accountable for the results. Of course, the duties of a mother in insuring the psychological health of the child have varied considerably, depending on assumptions about human nature.

In addition, the mother must teach the child to be "a conscious partner in their relation" and a contributing member of present and future social circles (Znaniecki 1965, 121–22). The child must learn how to relate to other people, not just in general terms but within social roles. All societies contribute to the mother's duties and rights by adding experts in different areas of knowledge for the socialization and education of the child, be they mothers-in-law or physicians-cum-psychologists (Ehrenreich and English 1979). Some of these additions actually deprive the mother of her rights of socialization, implicitly or even quite openly informing her that she is not an adequate parent. This was the assumption behind the Head Start program in America, which is intended to insure that children not be disadvantaged in the educational system by the limitations of the "culture of poverty" (Berrueta-Clement 1984; Joffe 1977).[2] Part of the various programs of preschool or nursery care of children of immigrant or other lower-class families has been education of the parents, especially the mothers. "Friendly intruders" (Joffe 1977) have been teachers and others claiming professional license and mandate to intervene between mother and child, especially when the parent does not have the power to refuse such interference. In fact, our society's mistrust of the mother's ability to raise her children in the way the society wishes them raised has a long history.[3]

The mother can expect cooperation from the members of the social circle in her fulfillment of her duties in that role. The child has the duty of recognizing her as the mother and her demands as her rights. This usually means that the mother has the right to obedience from the child, within limits imposed by the society. Other people in the social circle of the mother can impose restrictions on her behavior, and on that of her child, to guarantee expected results. The mother's rights include the opportunity to be connected with other people, even outside of the family, especially as the child grows and becomes involved in the outside world. The decrease of embodiment in an extended family and neighborhood by women in the allegedly depersonalized and mobile urban environment increases the need for connecting links for the child, so that the mother must somehow serve as such a link to the outside world.

The growing child is expected to give the mother opportunities for vicarious experience, something that is desired especially, according to much social scientific literature, by the middle-class mother who gave up her personal ambition in taking on the role complex of wife/mother/homemaker. The mass media acknowledge this right by favoring pictures of proud mothers standing next to their famous sons (sometimes, daughters). Thus, the rights, like the duties, change over the life course of the role.

One must constantly keep in mind that the child is not just a passive lump of clay or *tabula rasa* upon which the mother simply "writes" the behavior she wants the child to exhibit, but a constantly interacting person (Mead 1934). The way the mother interacts with the child is thus deeply influenced by how the child relates to her, and by the surroundings within which all this takes place.

The social circle often, but not necessarily, includes the father of the child, especially if he is legally so recognized and is actively involved in the role. This father has specific duties and rights that can support, but sometimes interfere with, the rights of the mother. Each parent has a different involvement with the children, depending on their gender, birth order, and ages (Harris and Morgan 1990), which can create problems. For example, one parent might believe that the other is favoring or neglecting a child unfairly. Parents may disagree strongly over the best methods of socialization of the young. Arguments can be over a child's behavior—and reasons for discipline, the method of carrying it out, and the child's response to this. The mother thus must negotiate her mothering with the father. On the other hand, she is usually the only one present with the child for most of the time, especially if she is a full-time homemaker, so the father may have little input. The father's contribution to the role of mother varies considerably by social class in situations involving stepparenting or nonparental boyfriends of the mother (Jarrett 1990a, 1990b).

The circle may also include siblings of the child, i.e., other children of the mother, other relatives, on the mother's or father's side, who are interested in how the mother performs her role and in its consequences on the child (Kidwell 1981). Neighbors, school personnel, members of organized social groups to which the child belongs, the child's friends, teachers, even the community police may develop relationships with her because she is the mother of that child. These relationships can assist her in how she wants to function as a mother, but they often create role strain because of differences in values or means, or overload in demands. The paternal grandparents' ideas about how their grandchild should be reared to perpetuate the family status may differ greatly from those of the mother if she comes from a different background. The mother has duties to all these circle members, recognizing their contributions to—or interferences with—her role, making possible their access and actions in relation to the child. Variations in the composition of the social circle theme of transitional motherhood are now developing. For example, a Washington state judge has recently recognized two lesbians as a "two-mom family," the legal parents of a child. "Their daughter will now have a rare two-mother, no-father birth certificate" (Monagle 1989, 69). This legal decision made it possible for the adoptive mother to retain custody in case of the death of the biological mother, and to receive her life insurance and estate. "And if Lynn and Lisa should split, their daughter will be entitled to child support and visitation rights." Pepper Schwartz, sociologist and coauthor of *American Couples* (Blumstein and Schwartz 1983), testified in that case that "there is no discernible difference between children brought up in lesbian or heterosexual households" (Monagle 1989, 69).

The role of mother is also deeply influenced by how many children are involved. Even more than with other roles, the addition of each new child modifies the mother's relations with prior children and with other members of the circle.

The Older Mother

Both the satisfactions and the problems of the role of mother change during its life course, mainly in response to changes in the children and, in later years, in the mother. Changes are demanded of the mother by the growing child and the society, which wants the child to increasingly take on the responsibilities of full membership. These demands can be met in a variety of ways, often depending on the birth order of the child. The mother may be more protective of the firstborn child, who must fight for new rights, and the succeeding children benefit from their establishment. One of the benefits of motherhood may be learning new knowledge from the children, who keep the mothers up to date about the rapidly changing world.

The social circle of the mother changes as components of assisting segments come and go. Children develop their own social roles, more or less independent of the mother, with their own social person characteristics, duties, and rights within each social circle. Early studies of the "empty nest" stage of the life course of the role of mother concluded that it can be a source of depression. Bart (1971) studied Jewish women in California hospitalized with depression as a result of the last child's leaving home. Basing their feelings of self-worth mainly on being a mother, in traditional Jewish manner, they felt worthless once their mothering activities were severely diminished by the independence of geographically distant children. Recent analyses indicate, however, that women finally freed from most of the duties of in-house motherhood felt themselves expanding in social life space and personality (Baruch, Barnett, and Rivers 1983). This freedom may not last long. A new phenomenon is the return of children to the home after the parents have adjusted to the freedom provided by the empty nest (Schnaiberg and Goldenberg 1989). Unable to afford similar housing on their own, facing economic problems of unemployment or underemployment, married or divorced or in relationships that cannot sustain themselves, children come home, often bringing their husbands and children with them. Parents try to prevent their children's downward mobility by helping any way they can (Newman 1988). The role of mother does not necessarily decrease when the children leave home for allegedly independent lives.

Various factors contribute to intergenerational relations involving the older, often widowed mother, and her children, including the level of interdependence and personal resources of both. Mothers vary considerably in the extent to which they are dependent upon the children for economic, service, social, and emotional supports; many have other resources such as kinfolk, friends, neighbors, co-members of voluntary associations, and so forth (Lopata 1979). Middle-class American widows prefer not to live with married children, if at all possible. Not only independence of living style and rhythms, but also avoidance of conflict or irritation and housework or child-care work, encourages widowed mothers to live alone (Treas and Bengtson 1987). However, independent living is not possible for widows whose subcultures require or facilitate sharing of housing, or who cannot function in modern American cities. Some widows, such as many in lower-class black communities, take for granted continued intergenerational residence and mutual support systems (Bengtson and deTerre 1980). Independent residence can, but does not necessarily, mean social isolation or deprivation of supports. Shanas (1979a, 1979b) has repeatedly exploded the myth of the isolated older mother.

Motherhood in Retrospect

The fact that not every woman has enjoyed being in the role of mother may be partially indicated by a 1976 story by Ann Landers in *Good Housekeeping*. The article was featured on the front cover, under the headline "Why So Many Mothers Are Sorry They Had Children—a Shocking Report." Landers asked the magazine's readers, "If you had it to do over again—would you have children?" Seventy percent of ten thousand responses (80 percent from women) responded with no. Interestingly, most of those who so responded did not sign their names, while the positive responses included identification. The negative answers fell into three categories: parents of troubled teenagers, parents who stated that the children had ruined their marriage, and older people who felt unrepaid for their sacrifices. Of course, the respondents were not representative of American women, since the only selection criterion was that they were readers of that magazine, and since not all readers responded. The most likely to respond were people who were willing to openly express strong feelings on this subject. On the other hand, a 1990 Gallup poll, on a different kind of question, found that only about 4 percent of Americans are strongly antichildren: They don't have any, don't want any, or are glad they didn't have any (Gallup and Newport 1990, 3).

However women evaluate their lives as mothers, most experience a great deal of stress when their offspring encounter problems. After all, children do not just grow up and live happily ever after. Fifty-five percent of the mothers and 34 percent of the fathers studied by Greenberg and Becker (1988, 788), reported at least moderate levels of stress because of what was happening to their children or what the children themselves were doing. In order of frequency, these included problems with health, work, children (of adult child), emotions, and finances. Of special concern were problems with alcohol or marriages. In the order of the amount of stress experienced by the mother, marital, financial, emotional, and alcohol problems were the worst, while health problems created the least stress (E. Johnson 1981). The fathers felt the stress indirectly, in that the problems affected the wives first. The study concludes that the parents repeatedly act as resources to their children in spite of experiencing stress themselves. In fact, an increasing amount of research finds a downward flow of supports from the parents to their adult children for longer periods of time and in greater frequency than is true in the reverse direction. This means that parents are more often contributorsthan burdens to their children.

Social-Class Variations in the Role of Mother

Just like the role of wife, the role of mother varies by social class, which is not surprising since whole life-styles and provisions of life chances differ by social class.

Mothers of the Underclass

The American underclass, which is considered to be below the actual class system and isolated from its institutions, has become of concern to both social scientists and the mass media. Some of its characteristics are of recent origin, including the presence of many female-headed households containing children born to very young mothers and extreme poverty of a vicious-cycle nature. It consists mainly of descendants of slaves who have been deprived of their own heritage and consistently discriminated against, and who have ended up in those locales of the society from which most supportive institutions escaped. It also contains households headed by women of Puerto Rican and North American Indian background (John 1988; Sanchez-Ayendez 1988). The underclass is found in urban areas with extremely high unemployment, and its whole life-style is lodged in poverty. Corcoran, Duncan, and Hill (1988, 109) report from the Panel Study of Income Dynamics that 65 percent of persistently poor families are headed by women, and 70 percent of these are black. Seventy percent of black children are likely to have spent at least some of a ten-year period of their lives in poverty, and 30 percent were so disadvantaged for six out of the ten years. Of white children, only 30 percent were ever poor during the ten-year period, and only 2 percent spent over half of that time in poverty. One conclusion that comes from this study, supported by other research, is the temporary nature of poverty among white women, and the greater frequency of both poverty and long-lasting economic problems among African American women.

As stated above, a problem that is major and increasing for the underclass, although not limited to it, is entrance into the role of mother by teenagers, who are assumed to lack the maturity and support necessary to carry forth the role in the style deemed best by society. Wallis (1985, 82) estimated that, of the 163 pregnancies per 1,000 black teenage girls, 51 percent end in nonmarital births, 8 percent in marital births, and 41 percent in abortions. The comparable figures for whites are 83 pregnancies per 1,000 teenage girls, with 19 percent ending in nonmarital births, 35 percent in marital births, and 47 percent in abortions. Wallis's article appeared in a lead article of *Time* magazine entitled "Children Having Children: Teen Pregnancy in America." Its prominence indicates a serious American concern.

There are many reasons why girls become pregnant early in life. Most teens have limited knowledge of sexual matters, are suspicious of contraceptives, or use motherhood as a marker of adulthood. They see babies as sources of love and enjoy the idea of taking care of them. Their social circles of their own mothers and other kin and friends help them care for these babies, although not always in the best style (Furstenberg 1990).

> The centrality of the maternal role has been well documented in past literature on low-income black women. Motherhood is critical for female adult status, even when it occurs outside of marriage and particularly when other channels of mobility are locked. Within the community context, children are a symbol of womanhood. (Jarrett 1990b, 5)

These low-income black mothers have very traditional views; they wish they could marry a man with a good job but have little hope of doing so. As one explains, it would be "foolish" to have children just to get on welfare. Furstenberg, Gordis, and Markowitz (1969) found teenage girls to have very limited knowledge and much misinformation about contraception and to be very upset when they found out that they were pregnant. However, once they accepted the pregnancy and the baby, they appeared less worried about having another.

The consequences of early motherhood include reduced education, rapid subsequent childbearing and higher levels of fertility, economic deprivation and reduced asset accumulation relative to those who delay childbearing, and subsequent marital dissolution if married (Teachman, Polonko, and Scanzoni 1987, 17). As stated before, the Reagan and Bush administrations held inconsistent attitudes toward this problem. They discouraged sex education, the dispensing of contraceptives to young unmarrieds, and abortion, yet they did not adequately assist pregnant women and young mothers, or prevent the "feminization of poverty," and they promoted the punishment of mothers who, unable to control their frustrations, abused or neglected their children. The main solutions to these problems, provided through the Aid to Families with Dependent Children program, stigmatize the recipients. Critics of the program state that women take advantage of it by purposely becoming mothers. These critics do not realize the inadequacy of the support and the difficulties of caring for children and low-pay employment (Piven 1989).

Wilson's (1987) analysis of the underclass in the social structure of American society concluded that its situation is class- rather than race-based, but there is strong disagreement with that hypothesis among other social scientists, because it underestimates the consequences of racism. According to Wilson (1987), young men of the underclass cannot function as husbands and fathers, that is, cannot contribute actively to the raising of children they have fathered for mainly economic reasons. They cannot obtain adequate general and vocational education, and thus cannot find jobs in a market decreasingly needful of unskilled labor. Such unskilled jobs that remain have moved out of the American urban centers in which such men are ghettoized (Bluestone and Harrison 1982). The combination of frustrations facing such men alienate them from their families. Unable to support their children, they are unwilling to marry the mothers (see also Liebow 1967). Jarrett's (1990a, 1990b, and 1992) ethnographic study of these women finds many also choosing not to marry. Such mothers openly admit their powerlessness vis-à-vis the men and have developed a female support network of mothers and daughters (see also Omolade 1986). This does not mean that children grow up without male care or support. The separation of biological from social fatherhood, present in much of human history, makes it possible for many other men—brothers, grandfathers, boyfriends of the mother, and so forth—to be involved in parenting or other kin interactions. In many cases, the women understand the economic insecurity of the men and have fewer expectations of support than is true in middle-class families (Jarrett 1990a, 1990b).

Puerto Rican families on the mainland face similar problems. Only 46 percent of the married mothers have a husband present in the home, compared to 56 percent of Mexican Americans and 58 percent of Cuban Americans (Sanchez-Ayandez 1988). In fact, 46 percent of Puerto Rican women have children out of wedlock; feelings of responsibility on the part of these fathers reportedly are much weaker than those of legalized fathers. And, as the husband-absent figures indicate, even legal fathers may not undertake the role of social father.

On the other hand, recent research has pointed to the strength of the support systems surrounding solo black mothers and the temporary nature for many of dependence upon welfare (Jarrett 1990a, 1990b). De Anda and Becerra (1984) report the same among Hispanics, especially a close relationship between the adolescent mother and her own mother, although the father-daughter relations are weak. The mothers of the underclass have become relatively independent of long-lasting relationships with supportive adult men and solve their economic problems and child-rearing problems in a variety of other ways. One of these involves temporary relationships with limited support expectations. In fact, many do not want to be controlled by men who cannot provide the benefits of economic support due to their own economic marginality (Jarrett 1990a).

The most detailed description of such a life-style is presented by Carol Stack (1975) in *All Our Kin*. Mothers living at or below the poverty level, whose welfare benefits do not come close to meeting their needs, are quite flexible in sharing resources. Children are reared and socialized by an extended group of many real and fictive relations, mothers passing them back and forth to eat and sleep as resources become available to people. She also pointed to the separation of social from biological fatherhood. The sharing of funds, food, and all belongings has the advantage of meeting emergencies, but the interdependence and mutual obligations make it very difficult to move out of the cycle of poverty even if temporary "good fortune" comes along. The disadvantage to this support system is that all of its members are caught in the vicious cycle of poverty (Kriesberg 1970; Wilson 1987). The welfare program itself does not provide sufficient income to pull them out of poverty, but it does make the women subject to external interference with their life-style by "friendly intruders" who judge their fitness as mothers (Joffe 1977).

Thus, American society has not been able, or willing, to solve the problem of poverty. Concern with the future of the children has not extended to help in breaking poverty's vicious cycle in the underclass. Americans are embarrassed by the presence of poverty in their country, but predominant attitudes hark back to the Elizabethan poor laws of Britain, which "blame the victim" (Kriesberg 1970; Piven and Cloward 1977). Other industrial societies that provide more adequate assistance to families have decreased poverty, without detrimental effects upon the "character" of those being helped (Kahn and Kamerman 1975).

In spite of negative attitudes toward the poor, minorities, and especially women on welfare, a few efforts have been made by Americans to provide better support to pregnant adolescents. Some schools are allowing these girls to continue attendance and provide prenatal care and schedule modification. The most advanced have set up nurseries on school property to make it easier for these mothers to complete their education. Economic assistance by the state, with the help of a supportive network, allows the young mother to prepare for adult roles while she cares for the newborn.

Native American mothers have the additional problem of facing a different kind of prejudice and discrimination, which has included sterilization, child-placement programs that result in adoption by non-Indians, and missionary activity in schools that tries to remove traces of their culture (John 1988). Native American women are worried about cross-racial adoption, the loss of potential for masculine behavior of their men, and the refusal of their own communities and of the larger society to pay attention to their problems.

Working-Class Mothers

The families at the bottom of the social class ladder have usually been either members of racial minorities or voluntary immigrants of the European peasantry who brought with them a sustaining culture (Schooler 1984). The latter settled near each other and developed ethnic communities. People like the Poles built churches and schools and created multi-institutional frameworks within which mothers could rear their children (Lopata 1976b; Thomas and Znaniecki 1918–20). The Polonias (Lopata 1994), Little Italys (Gans 1962), Greektowns (Kourvetaris 1988), or Mexican American communities (Williams 1990) insured kin support in child rearing, and divorce was rare, community pressures favoring stability. Mothers generally did not hold jobs but obtained pay from boarders and lodgers, doing other people's laundry or exchanging services. Children assisted with that work or were even sent out to earn money on their own.

Whole families were sometimes employed by a single organization. Although usually able to live on a relatively stable income in good economic times, these families faced many uncertainties. The mothers reorganized their lives and budgets when hit by economic crisis, as during the Great Depression (Milkman 1979). Support networks and the ideology of upward mobility in a more or less democratic society helped create a full, if frequently uncomfortable, life. The children of the immigrants, facing cultural conflicts and the multiplicity of their parents' problems, disproportionally displayed delinquent behavior, which was frightening to the mothers, but most grew out of it and formed their own norm-following families. Although European immigrants faced some prejudice and discrimination in early culturally divergent years, they lacked the generationally transmitted physical differences that insured continued minority status, and thus they were able to melt into general society (Mindel, Habenstein, and Wright 1988).

The upwardly mobile European and, increasingly, Asian families have had the advantage of more frequent two-parent families, employed husbands and fathers and a lesser amount of long-lasting discrimination than has been true of the persistently poor (Jarrett 1990a).

Most working-class families stuck to strongly patriarchal and authoritarian norms of parent-child relationships (see Mindel, Habenstein, and Wright 1988, *Ethnic Families in America,* for details). Children were expected to be obedient and were punished physically for trespassing against the norms (Langman 1987). Rainwater, Coleman, and Handel portrayed the "workingman's wife" in 1959 as constantly worried about her children, hoping they would just sit still, not fight, not get dirty, and not get into trouble outside of the home. Although they contributed to a great deal of the mother's frustration, children also provided their mother with her major gratifications, life meaning, and evidence of personal worth. The mother spent many hours a day on their physical care but often felt that she could not understand them or influence their behavior. She wanted to teach them right from wrong, to become moral adults, but she did not even trust herself to do the same. Unlike the middle-class mother of that time, she could not, and did not, try to provide a varied back-ground of experience. Passivity and short-term satisfaction were her ideals for her children and for herself. Living in an environment that was limited both physically and in her construction of reality, she could not offer them anything else. She spent money on the children to provide them immediate pleasure rather than to achieve long-range goals.

> It is apparent that working-class mothers want to be needed and loved by their children in a way which middle-class women do not. (Rainwater, Coleman, and Handel 1950, 97)

The same orientation toward being a mother, socialization, and the future of children is found in many more recent studies, such as Rubin's *Worlds of Pain: Life in the Working-Class Family* (1976). Gender segregation of life, experienced by the mother, is translated into differences in relations with daughters and sons. There is no attempt by the mother to extend her children's adolescence by encouraging education, although most mothers wish for the continuance of early childhood years. A similar worldview has been found among the Polish Americans in Detroit (Wrobel 1979) and the Catholic Irish in America (Horgan 1988). It was also typical of the working-class Italian Americans of West End Boston:

> The West End family is an adult-centered one. Since children are not planned, but come naturally and regularly, they are not at the center of family life. Rather, they are raised in a household that is run to satisfy adult wishes first. As soon as they are weaned and toilet-trained, they are expected to behave themselves in ways pleasing with adults. . . . When girls reach the age of seven or eight, they start assisting the mother, and become miniature mothers. Boys are given more freedom to roam, and, in that sense, are treated just like their fathers. (Gans 1962, 56)

Several more-recent studies of Italian American families also point to the distance between fathers and small children, with the children's socialization and care being left to the mother (Johnson 1985; Squier and Quadagno 1988).

Some middle-class patterns of socialization of the young appear in ethnic communities as families become more affluent, but especially with increased education in the American system. Some working-class immigrants, such as Eastern European Jews, sacrificed for their children's education and have experienced strong intergenerational upward mobility (Farber, Mindel, and Lazerwitz 1988; Sklare 1971). The same pattern appears among Asian American families, such as the Chinese (Wong 1988), Japanese (Kitano 1988), and Korean (Min 1988). These groups have also displayed a high outmarriage rate, so that more of these children have a dual background and, presumably, either a more middle-class or a more conflict-ridden interaction with the mother, depending on whether she is of Asian or another culture.

Middle-Class Mothers

Mothers located in the various layers of the American middle-class are found to be much more involved in the long-range socialization of their children for success, anticipating satisfaction from their achievements as a right more than is true of mothers in lower social classes (Skolnick 1983). Motherhood involves duties of psychological development, of providing the child with tools toward self-expansion. These women have the background and current resources to link the child with the wider world.

Paid-for services are important to those middle-class families who are relatively isolated from the tight kinship support network available in some stable communities. Residence is influenced by jobs, and relatives tend to become socially diversified and distant. Upward mobility also makes many a mother unwilling to depend on her parents for child care, not wishing to reproduce their cultural patterns (Rapp 1982). Sue and Morishma's study *The Mental Health of Asian Americans* (1982) points to the refusal of younger mothers to conform in their child rearing to the strict, clearly defined roles of prior generations. These women are even drawn to intermarriage with men who allow more freedom in their mothering activities.

The American mass media have recently publicized an almost obsessive effort by more educated middle-class mothers to push their children toward very early achievement, with allegedly negative consequences of tension and anxiety. Such mothers are willing to expose their children to limited dangers, rather than constantly protect them from all threatening experiences.

Middle-class mothers in general control their children through threats of withdrawal of love, rather than through the physical punishment used by lower-class parents (Langman 1987). They try to involve the father in the socialization process and to discuss policies and actions with all circle members, including the children (Kohn 1977). Attempts at androgynous socialization are also reported, the mothers not wishing to restrict daughters or sons along traditional lines. This is particularly true of mothers of only, or a limited number of, children (Polit and Falbo 1987). However, such women are also more likely to be involved in jobs in "greedy institutions," presenting role conflict and a complexity of relations with the children, with the help of a variety of assistants (Epstein 1983; Lorber 1984). Such employment deprives many of the time and energy necessary for serving as connecting links to the community, making these mothers either more similar to working-class mothers or more dependent upon a complex social circle to accomplish this (O'Donnell and Stueve 1983). Their economic resources enable these mothers to use time- and energy-saving methods, such as using restaurants and cleaning services, and buying store-bought clothes for the children, if the mothers earn enough or have earning partners.

Mothers of the Upper Class

Upper-class mothers tend to relate to their children within a much broader world than that of their socioeconomically lower counterparts. Membership in the upper class is already established, and the task of the mothers is to have children and to ensure that they fit into the whole life-style of their position. Extended families, schools, and the other families of this social class assure that the children develop along the class lines. The children are socialized to follow the norms and control their behavior, since deviation brings notoriety harmful to the family status. They are surrounded with appropriate objects and persons, provided with boarding school and top-flight higher education, and isolated from interpersonal relations with "undesirable elements," that is, members of lower strata, unless on a status-maintaining level. Being in constant, equal power relationships with others of the same position is especially important when it comes to mate selection, mothers being very careful to provide close contact with children of eligible families. Upper-class women consider their role of mother to be of extreme importance, although subsidiary to the role of wife (Ostrander 1984). The threat of disinheritance, which would remove the child from a very nice life-style, appears sufficient to grant the mother rights of obedience. Money is also available to save the child from painful consequences of antisocial or even criminal behavior. Some amount of rebelliousness is allowed, possibly even expected, but long-range conformity is usually accomplished. Mothers, however, walk a tight line and create as many barriers to downward mobility as possible. Children whose parents fail to live up to the position within which the young were socialized often treat parents in a less-than-positive manner (Newman 1988).

Upper-class mothers participate in activities and organizations that insure continued family membership in their stratum, extending to the adulthood of their children (Daniels 1988, 7). The mothers' activities also insure the health, education, and welfare of the community in which they reside.

Other Variations in the Role of Mother

Raising Sons

There is an additional area of difficulty faced by mothers in this society: the raising of boys. The mother is expected to, and does, relate differently with sons than with daughters, with societal and subunit variations. British and American experts in psychology, medicine, social work, and mass media have been deeply influenced, especially in the past, by Freudian and neo-Freudian theories of child development (Oakley 1974b). These define boys as experiencing the oedipal complex of wanting to kill their fathers in order to sexually possess their mothers, and girls as experiencing penis envy for which there is no cure. Much of the psychological literature of recent years dealing with childhood socialization focuses on the boy's need to separate himself from a prior intense relationship with the mother, repressing tendencies toward emotional dependence and the need for close relationships (Chodorow 1978). This situation is very different from that in traditional India, where the son's tie with the mother was considered the most important (Lopata 1987e, 1991b). Less attention is paid in this literature to the actions of the mother to encourage such separation, and to the consequences upon her of this gradual, or sometimes sudden, alienation. In a society in which women have lower status than men, she obviously must encourage the son's growing awareness of her inferiority. The lower the status of the women, the more the mother must accept the fact, reinforced by others, that the son will end up seeing her as inferior to him. She must accept the change from being the child's focal point, as she is likely to be in early years, to being lumped together with other women as being of lesser status.

It is the duty of a mother to try to insure that the personalities of her daughters and sons develop gender-appropriate emotional, self-concept, world-construction, and behavioral packages. Traditional patriarchal societies insured this gender specific socialization by taking young boys away from the influence of mothers and kins-women to interact only with other boys and men. Transitional societies changed the base of human life, rearing children together in a relatively isolated household dominated by the mother, and then in the equally isolated classroom with female teachers. For this reason, members of society who are concerned with such things worry about the socialization of boys, providing toys, male role models, and many rights to insure that these women's influence will not prevent them from developing masculine identities.

The mother is thus encouraged to accept, even reward, behavior that runs counter to her view of the world. This is apparent when mothers who actively protest against wars allow, even buy, toy guns as gifts for their sons.

> Many tired, frustrated, or otherwise overwhelmed mothers of sons . . .
> encourage their sons to join the military because they believe there is
> no place else to turn. (Forcey 1987, 15)

The gender specialization of relations with the children continues into the mother's old age. American sons are not expected, even by their mothers, to be major support providers for their mothers. American society provides many ideological justifications to the adult son for not focusing on his mother's needs, primarily because he must function as the "good provider" for his own family of procreation (Bernard 1981). This society decided in the first third of the twentieth century that offspring should no longer be held responsible for the economic supports of old or disabled family members, mainly because it could not enforce rules of such responsibility. Thus, older mothers are provided for economically through social security, Medicare, and other support systems, rather than by their sons, with few residual expressions of blame or guilt (Lopata 1991b). The son's male identity excuses him from being the primary provider of emotional supports of the mother, while his employment excuses his absence from most service supports. However, he is not totally absent from the mother's support network, specializing in such gender-segregated activity as household repairs and help with decision making (Lopata 1979; O'Bryant 1987). Interestingly enough, some mothers most enjoy being with their sons, even if a daughter provides most of the supports.

The Role of Mother in Divorce and Widowhood

Many factors contribute to the degree of disorganization suffered in her role of mother when she and the father of the children divorce. Divorce can be especially stressful for children in contested cases, in which both parents fight in court for the custody, each one trying to prove the other unfit for such care (Solnit 1984). The process can bring in outsiders, in the form of representatives of the law who must decide what is "good for the children," thereby officially declaring what is not good for them. This can be devastating for the children caught in the middle, who hear the strong accusations on all sides. The fact that contested divorces often result in problems led some states to pass no-fault divorce laws. Weitzman (1985, 339) studied the new system in California and found the situation little improved for mothers and children because fathers failed to pay support even when ordered to do so by the courts. The nonsupport of children is in fact one of the two major law-breaking actions by American citizens, the other being evasion of taxes. Weitzman's study found that the majority of mothers and children of no-fault divorce have lost, on the average, 73 percent of their previous income, while the husbands/fathers gained 42 percent. Widowed mothers often experience less economic loss than do divorcees, thanks to the Social Security Act's amendment of 1939, which brought them benefits as mothers of dependent children of the deceased (Lopata and Brehm 1986).

The problems of rearing children without the help of a previously present father in a society organized around two-parent families are legion. To begin with, the father's leaving, through death or divorce, can be very traumatic for both the wife and the children. The Chicago-area widows who participated in two of my studies (Lopata 1973c and 1979) often expressed an inability to help their children with their grief because they were so immersed in their own feelings. Some even refused to acknowledge that the children were suffering from the death of the father, claiming they were too young or too old to be affected. Others worried particularly about the sons in the absence of a supportive male. The situation is more complicated for the mother in the case of divorce, because the father remains on the scene with rights to the children. The divorce itself is likely to create strong emotions with which the mother must deal when interacting with her children.

An additional problem of mothers without another adult in the home is the care for the children while they are away at a paying job. On the other hand, divorce can relieve the mother and children of a very tense, even hurtful, home situation, as when alcoholism or physical and sexual abuse were involved. All records indicate that the mother is less likely to be the perpetrator of sexual abuse, and in most cases children are considered better off with their mothers than with their fathers.

The absence of a father may have other benefits for the mother. In the *City Women* study (Lopata, Barnewolt, and Miller 1985), our interviews with full-time homemakers aged twenty-five to fifty-four were organized according to the complexity of the households they managed. We first placed single mothers at the high end; after all, they had to solve all problems themselves and lacked the help of a male parent. We found out quite early in the analysis that their roles were in fact simpler than those in father-present households. The man proved to create work and complexity more than to decrease these. Child rearing was easier with one person making the major decisions, preventing role strain from disagreements. In fact, a majority of respondents to a national survey of divorcées reported their relationships with their children actually improved after divorce (Genevie and Margolies 1987, 375). They had more time for them with less competition for attention from fathers, and experienced greater closeness and respect, while at the same time being more independent to make their own decisions.

Both the death of, and divorce from, the father affects the social circle of the mother. In-laws may drop out, except in cases in which inheritance is of great importance. Grandparents, aunts, and uncles may remove their contributions and even create problems for the mother. The courts may have rights over the way she raises the children. A drop in income may require a move to a less desirable location, resulting in her children's having less desirable associates. On the other hand, the mother's own family and friends may increase their supports.

Mothers-in-Law

Traditional patrilocal societies gave the mother considerable power over her son's wife. There are many recorded situations, as in pre-Communist China or even current rural India, in which the mother-in-law treated the young woman as a servant and made her life so unpleasant as to push her into suicide (Barnes 1987). Transitional

America has removed much of the rights of control by a mother-in-law, who is, anyway likely to be living at a distance from the younger marital unit. The stereotype of the mother-in-law and the frequency of mother-in-law jokes indicate that there are more sources of tension with this relationship than with other in-law interactions. The role is strongly influenced by the mother-son or -daughter relation to begin with, as well as by the other members of her social circle, such as the parents of the person her child married. Mother and daughter-in-law or son-in-law do not interact in a vacuum. Complications arise out of the fact that the woman can be simultaneously the mother, the mother-in-law, and the grandmother. A husband may feel that his wife's mother has too much influence over his wife, or the young woman that her husband is too much influenced by his mother. Or both may resent any suggestions, even offers of help, from the older generation. The classic study of in-law relationships by Evelyn Duvall (1954) discussed both the comparative freedom of choice and the complications of relationships in a society that did not force the daughter-in-law to live with, and provide supports to, the relatives of her husband. Her title, *In-Laws: Pro and Con,* is indicative of the transitional situation in which the mother-in-law is likely to have traditional attitudes toward the younger generation.

In general, the wife tends to mediate relations not only between her husband and her parents but also, and even more so once children are born, between her husband and his own mother. One source of intergenerational tension can be the mother's feeling that her son has obligations toward her care that only the daughter-in-law can meet. Mothers-in-law are more "likely to have strained relationships with daughters-in-law than with sons-in-law" (Fisher 1983, 190). However, they must establish some positive relations with the son's wife if they want to be involved with the grandchildren (Fisher 1986, 130). An interesting finding is that, although the birth of children makes a woman's relationship with her own mother closer, it increases "the ambiguity in the quasi-kin, quasi-maternal relationship between mothers-in-law and daughters-in-law" (Fisher 1983, 190; see also Fisher 1986). The awkwardness of the relationship is indicated by the fact that a mother-in-law tends to give the daughter-in-law things, while the mother is more likely to perform services for her (Fisher 1983, 191). The younger woman is apt to express ambivalence over help from the in-laws and ask her mother rather than her mother-in-law for advice. The fact that in-laws are a secondary relationship, added almost as an afterthought, to the primary one between a husband and a wife, through no choice by anyone, may account for part of the problem in their interactions. Another factor is the probability, especially in a society as heterogeneous as the American, that the spouses come from different backgrounds, accentuated in their parents' generation, which may clash over ritualistic or day-by-day routines. Of course, popular culture emphasizes the alleged feeling of all mothers that the person their son or daughter marries is never good enough.

We can assume that the role of mother-in-law in modern times will involve greater freedom of communication and negotiation with circle members.

Stepmothers and Foster Mothers

Many women carry out the role of mother who are not biologically or socially "real" mothers of the children they have taken under their care. There is a vast difference between stepmothers, who acquire that role with marriage to the children's father, and foster mothers, who are temporary substitutes when children are taken away from their biological parents. The frequency of divorce and of remarriage creates complex stepparenting relationships. Many factors affect the interaction between stepmother and stepchild, such as the reason for the absence of the previous mother (death, divorce, or desertion), where the children are living, who has custody over them, the ages of all involved, whether the woman has children of her own, especially if they live in the home, and the life circumstances in which all who are involved find themselves (Visher and Visher 1979). The presence of "reconstituted" or "melded" families is increasingly being recognized by social scientists and the mass media. *Newsweek* magazine's special issue "*The 21st-Century Family* "devoted a major segment to stepfamilies (Kantrowitz and Wingert 1989, 24), pointing to the fact that "half of all people entering first marriages in the 1970s and 1980s will eventually divorce" and that, since most will remarry, there will be more and more joint families in the future. Giles-Sims and Crosbie-Burnett (1989) pulled together much of the recent literature on the stepfamily for a special issue of the journal *Family Relations*. Glick (1989, 26) estimates that 40 percent of married couple families in 1987 would be stepfamilies before the youngest child became eighteen years old. Most stepfamilies require adjustment to a new father rather than a new mother, since most women retain custody over their children.

> Five residential stepfather families exist for every residential step-mother family, and 3% of remarried couple households include a stepfather and a stepmother. (Giles-Sims and Crosbie-Burnett. 1989, 20)

Even if the children of the new husband are not living full-time with the stepmother, they are apt to spend considerable time with her. The combination of mother and stepmother roles may be diffi-cult, with resentments over her attitudes and actions coming from both sets of children. Also, of course, she has to relate to the father of the stepchildren, as well as to their mother. The ages at the time the family blends together and the attitudes of the children toward their other parents may make the role of stepmother difficult, or a pleasure. Traditional women usually entered stepmothering as a result of the death of the mother. Transitional women are most strained by this role, because they tend not to have satisfactory models for dealing with the role complexities. Modern families try to work off the strains in the relationships openly and through negotiation.

The problems of foster mothers, who are paid to take children from problem families into the home to care for as substitutes for the biological and social mother, are also complex. The foster mother does not have all the rights and duties of a recognized mother and does not know how long the child will be in her care. Adjustments have to be made by the child, whose previous experiences with being mothered are likely to be negative, or whose mother is in a very difficult situation with which the child identifies. Adjustment must also be made by the foster mother, who did not contribute to the current personality and values of that child, and by all the circle members.

Other "variations on the theme," as *Newsweek* (Selingmann 1990) called gay and lesbian couples, and other domestic situations in-volving mothers proliferate in modern America.

Sociopsychological Aspects of Role Involvement

The role of mother has additional characteristics that, in combina-tion, make it unique among social roles. In the first place, it lasts a lifetime, unless the child dies, regardless of how involved the mother remains. It also changes throughout its course, especially during the first quarter or so of the child's life, when physical growth is accompanied by psychological maturation and constantly modifies the mother's duties and rights toward the child.

This role brings together multiple aspects of social psychological involvement. The birth of the first child is considered a major event of life. The role of mother is expected to be ranked as very important in the woman's role cluster. In fact, it competes with the role of wife; most women in the various Chicago-area studies gave it top priority (Lopata 1971b; Lopata and Barnewolt 1984). It frequently expands or activates other roles in the family dimension, including those of daughter, mother-in-law, and grandmother. In addition, it usually includes a great deal of emotional and sentimental, often contradictory, involvement. Although women allegedly depersonalize the role if there are "too many" children and they are too exhausted by childbearing and child rearing to differentiate among them, there is no substantial proof of such a tendency.

In American society, a mother is expected to demonstratively love her children and experience many other emotions and relational sentiments as she carries out the role, yet to control the level of these feelings. This combination can create person-role strain. Reared to control her emotions as "an adult," the mother faces the emotionally uncontrolled infant with trepidation and uncertainty. Reports of child abuse frequently point to the inability of the mother to stop the crying or anger of her child no matter what she does.

Problems of emotional involvement certainly do not end with the passing of infanthood, but they vary considerably from mother to mother and with each child. Some mothers feel possessive about their children, considering them extensions of themselves rather than persons in their own right. According to some critics (see Wylie 1955), such a woman lives vicariously through her offspring, hoping they will achieve and experience things she has visualized romantically for herself.

Most mothers experience a great deal of anxiety about child rearing and feelings of powerlessness over not being able to control the environment or the children. Often, knowing what they should do for the children does not solve the problem, in the absence of rights or resources. Some aspects of the role, such as the need to have patience, vicarious pain over children's troubles, or lack of privacy and time for herself, can be irksome to mothers. A child's problems of health or incapacity, such as in mental retardation, can be a perpetual drain upon the mother.

The duties of a mother are influenced by the attitudes and actions of other circle members, toward whom she may feel ambivalent. She has the duty to allow others to help in the socialization process of her children, and the right to be relieved of some of this work, although not of the responsibility for the result. The whole subject of child care is now receiving so much attention as to create strong guilt feelings and frustration among mothers who feel they must remain in or reenter the labor force and be away from home for many hours a day. The deeply ingrained American belief that only a mother can be an adequate caregiver for her child, and that all substitutes are of inferior quality, makes the psychological burden heavy. Forgotten are the centuries and the societies in which the socialization of children was turned over to others, often of a lower social class. The institutionalization of child care by the community, as in the kibbutz, does not apply here, where it is the private responsibility of each parent (that is, the mother) to make appropriate arrangements. It is not hard to predict, however, that public discussion of this subject will produce more community effort to help families, as is true in other societies within which the transition between traditional and modern support systems is occurring.

The weight of the ideology of motherhood contained in the concept of the "good" mother, and especially of the "ideal" mother, appears to transcend cultures, although variations exist by social class and other subunits. The characteristics of the ideal mother appear in descriptions given by women in transitional societies, especially in Westernized locales such as Sydney, Australia (Wearing 1990), as well as Chicago (Lopata 1971b) and elsewhere in America (Rainwater, Coleman, and Handel 1959). Such a mother "gives of herself," sacrificing her own needs in order to always be available and responsive to meet the needs of the children (Wearing 1990). Her role priorities place duties to the child above not only her duties in the role of wife and nonfamilial obligations, but also her duties to herself. Personal feelings, as well as such emotions as anger, must always be under control. Most women find the ideal impossible to achieve and always feel guilty for failing to meet it, for wanting time and space for themselves or for acting in "wrong" ways (Wearing 1990, 49). The image also offers many a woman the model by which she evaluates herself as less than good, with detrimental effects on her whole self-image since this is generally considered such an important role for women. This is particularly evident in cases in which the mother finally gives up the role, feeling that others can contribute to the welfare of her children more than she can.

The Chicago women's descriptions of the ideal mother reflected "passive-reacting-initiating" stances of sociopsychological involvement in interesting ways (Lopata 1971b, 219–23), reflecting their educational backgrounds. Traditional women with little formal education explain the ideal in self-sacrificing terms that reflect passivity. The mother caters to the needs of children without complaining. The reactive woman keeps up with the physical maintenance of the children, their clothes and food needs. The initiating one tries to teach them right from wrong. The less educated mothers focus on physical aspects of child care, the more educated see the ideal in psychological terms, responding to the emotional needs of the children or encouraging the children to venture and expand their horizons.

Warren (1987) found that the picture of the perfect mother that appears in the mass media, and often in stories told about other women, contributed to depression on the part of those labeled and treated as "madwifes." Chodorow and Contratto (1982) are highly critical not only of the mass media, but also of some feminist literature, for creating the "fantasy of the perfect mother" who is an all-powerful influence upon her offspring. How the children "turn out" becomes a major anxiety of mothers; the fact some turn out "OK" in adulthood is a major source of satisfaction for her, since she is given all the credit. The fact that for increasing periods of time the child is away from the home and the mother's sphere of influence leads to the mother's having feelings of powerlessness, especially in neighborhoods where drug and crime rates are high.

The image of the ideal mother as self-sacrificing can have repercussions in later life if the woman expects all those whom she has serviced to pay back past debts.

On the other hand, many mothers of the baby-boom cohort I studied simply dealt with the ideal as an unrealistic romanticization they did not need to deal with in reality. Others accepted aspects of it by which they defined themselves as good, disregarding aspects in which their performance was less than ideal. Most expressed great pleasure at "watching the children grow," seeing them healthy and happy, in spite of all the problems and frustrations. The satisfactions they reported are numerous, usually focused around love, the pleasure of providing a "good home," responsiveness by the children to their efforts, or even just enjoying the whole process of mothering, accepting the problems as part of life. The expressions of satisfaction covered wider spheres of life than did statements of problems or frustrations, which were quite specific (Lopata 1971b, 219).

Summary

These, then, are the major aspects of the role of mother, as developed in American society and contained in its cultural base. The role is lodged in the family institution, although it provides links to other institutions, such as education, religion, recreation, and the economic and even the political spheres, as when mothers function as family consumers or organize to fight for children's rights. The role, built upon a middle-class transitional-times model, assumes the presence of a rather complicated social circle, actively involving the father of the child, grandparents, and other kin in a bilateral fashion as assistants, physicians, service suppliers, and associates of the child. It assumes that these members will function cooperatively, helping the mother to care for the physical, psychological, and social welfare of the child, allowing her to be the center of her own role. The model takes it for granted that she can stay home full time and is willing and able to do everything to benefit the child, within a patriarchal structure of the family.

The model ignores two very important facts. One is that mothers seldom, if ever, have had all the resources to function at even the allegedly "average" level of role involvement. A major difficulty for most women is economic, forcing them often into a double-bind situation. The high incidence of divorce, desertion, and other reasons for the absence of a wage-earning father makes that source of income increasingly unavailable. If a mother cares for the children alone, she cannot earn money. If she takes a job, she is absent from the children and must find someone else to care for them during her work and transportation hours. The wage discrimination prevalent in this society results in her inability to earn enough to pay for child care and all the other household expenses (Steinberg 1982 and 1990; see also several chapters in Larwood, Stromberg, and Gutek 1985). The feminization of poverty is not just a mass-media creation.

But there is a much more basic problem with the role of mother at the present time: the rapid and dramatic structural and cultural changes in America have made many of the characteristics of the transitional family dysfunctional to the welfare of its members and the society as a whole. These changes are beyond the control of the family, yet family roles and their relations to other roles of its members have not been redefined. Such a reconstruction of reality and relationships would enable the parents (both the social mother and the social father) to serve as centers of organized family and community resources for the care and rearing of children. It would expand the social circle of the mother, with the help of numerous assistants all sharing not just the action but also the responsibility and emotional involvement. The transitional form of the role of mother is simply too artificial and harmful to all concerned. Those women who have expanded this role to include all sorts of circle members have actually duplicated some of the patterns of upper-class women of the past and present. They have been able to do so only because they can afford to pay for these resources in the absence of adequate assistance.

It is impossible to describe fully the role of mother in transitional and, especially, modern times without commenting on the decreasing contribution of men, in the role of father and as members of the social circle of the mother. Ehrenreich (1983) developed the argument in *The Hearts of Men: American Dreams and Flight from Commitment* that American men have been removing themselves from family responsibilities since the 1950s. Certainly the number of female-headed single-parent families, and the frequency with which male parents fail to cover child support, provide some backup to this argument (Weitzman 1985). Although the society at large, in its press and social scientific journals, expresses anger over the inadequacy of the responsibility taken for children by social and biological fathers, little is done about this situation, and the problems of female-headed households are somehow defined in terms of women alone. Maybe the recent male-consciousness movements will decrease the frequently expressed hostility of men concerning being "tied down" in marriage and fatherhood. On the other hand, contrasting macho movements appear to be moving in the opposite direction, valorizing the hero who faces the world alone.

In order for the role of mother to be brought into the modern world, there needs to be a complete change in America's attitudes toward its young. This society has either ignored family troubles brought about by its changes or, even when it turns these into recognized social problems, blamed the victims. Family members, especially mothers, are still seen as the source of problems they are helpless to control. According to many observers, and especially Kahn and Kamerman (1975; see also Kamerman and Kahn 1978; Kamerman 1977 and 1980), America does much less than other industrialized modern societies to assist families in daily life and crises. In fact, Huber (1980) calls this an "antinatalistic" society, and Grubb and Lazerson (1982) have focused the title of their book on public responsibility for children: *Broken Promises: How Americans Fail Their Children*. Other societies, and America of the future, we assume, can see the care of children as the responsibility not simply of the parents but of the community at large.

4

Social Roles in Kinship Networks

Most societies have been organized around kinship networks, which trace lines of descent and define roles for people united by marriage, birth, or adoption.[1] Roles in nonfamilial institutions have been dependent upon kinship roles. "These same kin groups may also be the property-owning units, the political units, the religious units, and so on" (Schneider 1989, vii). Transitional societies have weakened these bonds as other groups have taken on major aspects of such functions. Adams (1968) argues that the kindred form a network, not a social group, since there is frequently no organized structure within it. The networks consist of the one or both nuclear families of orientation and procreation plus other relatives in varying degrees of connection. A kin network can be differentiated from the biological grouping by the degree of actual involvement in interaction and social roles. Some societies refuse to consider the relatives of a wife coming into the husband's family as part of her children's kin. Persons who are part of the recognized family tree may be cut off from the network, or may fail to incorporate themselves into it

simply by not undertaking kin roles.[2] Conflict can break communication with, or even recognition of, a whole branch of the biological
family. Active involvement can be dissolved, as often happens in
America between in-laws once the connecting links die or are divorced. The high degree of choice in social relationships in modern
society carries over to the kin network.

World Revolution in Kinship Salience?

Traditional patrilineal and patriarchal family systems, the most common types of family systems among human beings, contain strong
norms of obligation to members, however the kinship boundaries
are demarcated. Patrilocal residence, with new family units of the
sons settling within or nearby the ancestral dwelling, helped insure
contact and control.

   Goode (1963) concluded from a survey of many societies that
the world revolution of modernization changed the basic family
structure from that of the extended family to that of the nuclear,
relatively isolated unit. He did find, however, that the elite segments
of both traditional and modern societies, even those in urban settings, maintained extended familism, while the masses usually did
not. His main conclusion about the unidirectional move from extended
to relatively isolated nuclear families, supporting that of Parsons
1943 and Parsons and Bales 1955, produced a strong reaction from
social scientists. Family sociology in the following years was full of
claims of continued involvement of the nuclear unit in the wider
extended network (reviewed by Sussman 1962; Adams 1968; Lee
1980; and Litwak 1965). Winch and Blumberg (1968) tested this and
related hypotheses and found a curvilineal relationship between
societal complexity and family organization, claiming that there are
independent familial systems, that is, small nuclear units, among
both the simpler, nomadic groups and in modern societies, while
sedentary, agricultural societies favor extended familism. The factors that lead to the separation of the smaller family unit from the
extended one include migration or mobility, independence from
stationary property such as land, and freedom from the family as a
unit of labor. Thus, they predicted that highly developed societies
will have "relatively low extended familism" (Winch and Blumberg
1968, 86). In addition, the decline of economic functionality of
extended familism in complex societies decreases men's interest in

that unit. This shifts the function of maintaining kin ties to the women, who are usually less geographically mobile due to the bearing and nursing of children.

The Transitional Form of Kin Networks

The kin network is traced in America bilaterally, that is, from both the woman's and the man's lines of ascent and down through both sons and daughters (Schneider 1980). This gives the woman much more importance as the connecting link between the families than is true of kinship groups that are traced unilaterally through the male line. The American system includes grandparents, aunts and uncles, plus cousins and all their spouses and children. Marriage adds the spouse's relatives, modified by the concept of "in-law." Grandchildren and even great-grandchildren may be active members of the network.

Americans differentiate the level of relation by what Schneider (1980, 22–23) calls "modifiers," some of which are restrictive, dividing blood relatives from those who are not, and some of which are unrestrictive, providing an unlimited range of relatives. Modifiers are also applied to degree of distance, as in "first cousin" versus "second cousin." The situation is complicated in this society by the fact that so many people come from cultures that contain other symbolic distinctions. For example, a niece in a Polish American community must differentiate in her language and behavior between her father's brother and uncles from other sources. In recent years the American kinship network has been made even more convoluted by the presence of ex-relatives with whom some duties/rights packages of interaction are maintained and new relatives that come along with new marriages (C. Johnson 1988).

Of course, all the effects of "the world revolution" upon the family emerge over time and have not reached many segments of even allegedly modern societies such as America. Kinship networks performed important economic functions among immigrant groups, as well as in subgroups of recent times (Bieder 1973). American ethnic communities still contain strong interdependencies among kinfolk (see Min 1988 for Korean; Glenn 1986 and Kitano 1988 for Japanese; Wong 1988 for Chinese; and C. Johnson 1985 for Italian American families). Patterns of chain migration and arrangements for housing and jobs are clearly documented in industrial Amoskeag (Hareven and Langenbach 1978, see also Hareven 1978). The Polish peasants from Europe crossed the ocean at the initiative of relatives, and then brought more of the family over (Thomas and Znaniecki 1918–20). Kinship groups shared housing, often taking shifts in beds, and all sorts of supports (Lopata 1976b and 1994). Immigrant women were even more dependent upon the kin network than the men, since they were culturally discouraged from seeking jobs alone (Lopata 1988a). The influence of kin and ethnic job-search support is evident in the clustering of immigrants in occupations and locales.

Patterns of kin support extend even into second and third generations of immigrants, and upward mobility of some members does not necessarily break ties (Winch, Greer, and Blumberg 1967). For example, uncles were known to help nephews in less fortunate family units attain a better education or economic position (Adams 1968). Winch, Greer and Blumberg (1967) summarized studies that found a higher level of extended familism among Polish Jews than among Polish Catholics in the United States. Their explanation for this interesting difference is that the Catholics came from peasant families with extended family systems of sedentary agricultural activity, which was disorganized in urban America. The Polish Jews, who had been traders in the home country, were able to reestablish entrepreneurial activity with extended family help after migration. The occupations in which they became concentrated under the influence of anti-Semitism, unlike bureaucratic occupations in large organizations, do not require much mobility and provide opportunity for supports of younger family members.

Another situation in which kindred relationships form an important part of life is among the underclass blacks in America. Stack's 1975 classic *All our Kin* documents the interaction among many layers of relatives in an urban community living at the poverty level. Kin members

> trade food stamps, rent money, a TV, hats, dice, a car, a nickel here, a cigarette there, food, milk, grits and even children. Thus networks of domestic co-operation come into being. The social and economic lives of men, women and children become so interwoven that failure to repay a debt might mean someone else's child will not eat. (Stack 1975, 195)

However, the extensive interaction reported by Stack, in which actual and fictive relatives provide multiple supports in crisis situations, such as illness or loss of a job, which occur almost daily, has some negative consequences. It drains the resources of the persons who are doing a little better, preventing movement out of the poverty cycle. The outlay of supports may prevent individualistic upward mobility. However, the members of the two lower-class extended black families followed by Martin and Martin (1978) through several stages of formation who reached middle-class status kept in touch without apparently hurting their social movement.

Ethnic communities are not similarly involved in kinship exchanges. For example, Polish Americans are much more involved in community-status competition and organizational life than are Italian Americans, who are much more family-oriented (Lopata 1988a; Squier and Quadagno 1988). Most research on kin relationships in England and the United States, building upon Bott's *Family and Social Network* (1957), stresses social class differences. African American mothers raising younger children alone appear to be receiving more kin help with child care, finances, and emotional support than they give, especially if they are poor (McAdoo 1980, 143). Life-course changes being what they generally are, the recipients will undoubtedly be the heavier givers as they grow older. Women of working-class families appear to be much more oriented toward all types of relatives than are their white-collar counterparts. This is also true of upper-class families that have benefited from the status attainment of prior generations (Ostrander 1985); however, these often neglect members who have not reached the appropriate position or who have experienced downward mobility (see Newman 1988). On the other hand, the extended family may replace friendships lost through a drop in social class. "Blood ties are often 'thick' enough to endure, even in the face of the downwardly mobile family's embarrassment" (Newman 1988, 125). Middle-class families appear to be less kinship-bound than the other classes.

Kin Member and Kin Keeper

One is born into, or adopted into, a family that is usually affiliated with a more or less organized kin network. However, the role of kin member exists only if the person develops sets of social relations with others identified as relatives. Many families also develop the role of kin keeper, who serves as the core keeping the spokes of the kin network together. The extensive discussion of kinship networks above accentuates the fact that families in transitional times placed most of the burdens, and benefits, of kin involvement upon women.

The roles of daughter and sister, wife and mother, are the most central to the kinship network, and the outer layers may be pooled together into a generalized set of relationships in the role of kin member by the kin keeper responsible for maintaining contact. Even the close relatives can be so generalized, or lumped together, by a woman who sees herself as a member of the network without being its center as a kin keeper. She can carry forth limited sets of duties, forming lines of contact within the larger unit, and can be treated by others as one of the connecting links. Such action can be a bridge to her role of daughter or sister, which pulls her side of the family into the larger network. An example of the networking behavior of people who do not take on the job of kin keeper for the whole network appears in Adams's 1968 study of cousin relationships in Greensboro, North Carolina. Cousins there were unlikely to be close to each other unless the two sets of parents interacted frequently or they lived nearby or shared a common interest. What is significant for our focus on women is the importance of sister closeness for cousin interaction.

> Relationship through the mother strongly predominates among the females from a blue-collar family, while a similar but less pronounced relationship holds for young white-collar background adults. (Adams 1968, 139)

These findings that the role of kin member is more salient to women than to men are reinforced by numerous other studies. In fact, although kinship roles appear to have somewhat atrophied in current-day America, the norms or expectations underlying them, including that they should be carried forth by women, continue.

Divorce or widowhood can deprive a woman of support exchanges with her husband's relatives, as numerous studies have indicated (Anspach 1976; Lopata 1973c and 1979). This break is easier to visualize in the case of divorce than in the case of death of the person who is the connecting link, since the man's family would be expected to place loyalties to him ahead of those of an in-law in conflict situations. The fact that such connection by marriage may never have been comfortable is indicated by the absence of the male kin in the support systems of widows in several studies. The Chicago-area widows whom I studied very seldom report any supports to themselves or even to their children from the late husband's kin (Lopata 1973c and 1979).

The role of kin keeper, rather than just kin member, or the relational outgrowth of "kin-keeping work," remains a familiar concept in America (Rosenthal 1985). Di Leonardo (1987), who studied Italian Americans, defines its duties as follows:

> By kin work I refer to the conception, maintenance, and ritual celebration of cross-household kin ties, including visits, letters, telephone calls, presents, and cards to kin; the organization of holiday gatherings; the creation and maintenance of quasi-kin relations; decisions to neglect or to intensify particular ties; the mental work of reflection about all these activities; and the creation and communication of altering images of family and kin vis-à-vis the images of others, both folk and mass media. (442)

Similar complexities of kin keeping are reported for other ethnic groups. Historians and social scientists find that it is usually a middle-aged or older woman of the kin network who has kept up with the desired kin members, knowing their locations and being the organizer of family gatherings and celebrations (Rosenthal 1985).

The person maintaining kin solidarity can also be the family historian, although these functions are not inevitably tied together. One of the interesting aspects of kin keeping is the transmission of the position through generations. It is "inherited" by another woman, although not necessarily by the daughter of the former facilitator. It has to be initiated by the social person, with cooperation from others. She must of necessity come from a family with numerous potential members of the network. The probability is high that she has economic resources to undertake this role. She must also have the personality to act as a bridge even between conflicting segments of the network, and she can easily experience role strain because of such conflict. Unfortunately, from the point of view of symbolic interactionists, too few studies of kin keepers have been conducted to determine how important this role is in the person's role cluster. We do know that the family dimension must be rich, but we do not know the form of multidimensionality of the life space. The woman must be an initiator of interaction, but she can undertake it out of either pleasure or a sense of duty. Being the center of the network requires not only time and interest but also power to enforce cooperation. The social circle of the kin keeper is created by the woman herself out of available members, but its maintenance requires a great deal of cooperative effort by others, not only in terms of work but also in terms of willingness to spend the time and often the cost of continued contact. As more and more women enter the labor force full time, one of the areas of life experiencing cutbacks is personal leisure activity. This definitely could include kin work.

Ethnic groups are not the only ones still concerned with kin keeping. More affluent and educated families are also interested in such interaction because of pride in the family's past or present accomplishments and the obvious advantages of continued contact (Bahr 1976). I found, for example, that widows kept their children in more frequent, and possibly closer, contact with their in-laws in cases of high-status families than if there were fewer advantages to such interaction (Lopata 1973c).

Of course, extensive involvement as kin keeper by a member of the nuclear family may create role conflict with a husband or children, who may resent the outlay of time, energy, and financial help, much as reported in cases of daughters' supports of parents. In fact, the modern emphasis on obligations to nuclear units may make assistance to the extended family less justifiable than before. This is particularly true in America, since kinship here does not form the major organizing principle of all social life, as it does in some other societies. Few bureaucratic organizations are now willing to hire a person simply on the recommendation of a family member, unless the latter has power in the system. Nephews of powerful men undoubtedly have an edge over anonymous candidates. There are few known cases of powerful women in public positions insuring their relatives an adequate position, but such women definitely exist and can be expected to increase in number.

The Modern Form of Kinship Networks

It is hard to predict what will happen to kinship roles when the family system becomes modernized. The trends toward individualization of social relations bode them little good. The revolution against ascribed roles, or those into which one is born or assigned without choice, had accentuated the perceived burdens of kinship roles and diminished the perceived benefits. It may be that this trend will continue with even greater speed in the future, so that selected collateral relatives are converted into "friends," and close contact is maintained with only those relatives who contribute actively to one's life. On the other hand, the broadening of the social circles of major roles, with the diffusion of obligations for primary relations to both genders and the community at large, may revitalize kinship roles. Women no longer burdened with almost exclusive responsibility for parenting, "daughtering," and maintaining social relationships in marriage and other partnerships, at work, and in the community may willingly enter negotiated kinship relations. So may men, who can negotiate to close the gap between themselves and all kinds of relatives.

Daughter

Children are born into a family of orientation, so called because it provides them with socialization necessary to orient the self into the world, which is already organized symbolically and in actuality by past generations and contemporary associates. The family of orientation includes parents, by birth or adoption, and siblings. The relationships of the daughter to various people in her social circle are modified dramatically over time as she matures and enters new roles or as circle members experience changes in their lives. A significant example of this is in the daughter-mother relationship, as discussed from the point of view of the mother in the previous chapter.

The Traditional Form of the Role of Daughter

The traditional patrilineal family incorporated the nuclear family as subservient to its needs. Often combined with patrilocal residence, it tied each marital and parental unit together. Children belonged to that unit and not to the mother. Males felt the strongest identification with their sons rather than their daughters. Sons were deemed necessary for family survival, continuity of identity, contributions to the male work group, care of elderly parents, inheritance rights, and, where applicable, ritualistic actions guaranteeing the afterlife of ancestors. The value assigned to daughters depended upon their contributions to the patriarchal family's welfare. The more costly their upkeep till they left in marriage, and the more their leaving cost through dowries, the less they were valued. Their work life was limited if marriage occurred early and if they were not allowed to perform necessary family and religious rituals.

In fact, as noted before, infanticide of girls has been historically more common than of boys (deMause 1974). Sons were often killed by enemies in battles, or as a means of genocide, but daughters were put to death or allowed to die by their own families. The devaluation of female newborns and babies has not vanished entirely in recent times, as evidenced by the neglect and infanticide of girls in areas of India and in China (B. Miller 1981; Mosher 1983). The current debate over the use of abortion to select the gender of offspring indicates the continued preference for male children.

It is not surprising that strong patriarchal systems, still present in societies such as Turkey (Heisel 1987), Korea (Koo 1987) and Iran (Touba 1987), encourage the mother to develop the closest possible relationship with the sons, particularly the son who is apt to inherit the property and therefore the responsibility for her care in old age and widowhood.

> Mother-son relations were most often stressed as being of love and affection more than any other, including husband and wife which were seldom mentioned and, when they were, were spoken of as entailing dislike and hatred as well as affection. (Ross 1961, 97)

Arranged marriages are not conducive to empathetic understanding between the son and his wife, so the mother-son tie can remain the son's closest throughout life. The mother gains power as she ages, either as the wife of the patriarch or as the mother of the inheriting son. The daughter-in-law then becomes the main service supplier to the household. Her lot in traditional China, for example, was reputedly so bad that it produced frequent suicides (Barnes 1987).

In such a system, in fact, the daughter had few rights, not being an important member of her family of orientation and relatively early in life becoming only a daughter-in-law.

Before modern times in America most families were dependent upon children for work and, when possible, for household finances. Children were expected to contribute to the family's subsistence along gender-specified lines, determined by the family's activities. A major set of duties of the role of daughter was to help care for younger children and assist the mother in age-appropriate tasks. Farm families often assigned the care of small animals to girls, while the boys helped the fathers in the fields. In preindustrial times and places, home-based work was complicated and hard, involving the making of basic family-maintenance goods. Some families or villages even produced goods for barter and, at a later stage of development, objects or services for sale. Girls were trained at a very young age to contribute to such activity (Boserup 1970, 140–41). The work was both a duty and a right, as it prepared them for increasingly complex participation in a family-based work team. The skill and knowledge made them valuable additions to their family of orientation and then to that of the husband. This direct contribution of children to family support continued even into the early years of industrialization, daughters often working in cottage industries (Oakley 1974b; Tilly and Scott 1978b). Children, even daughters, were also sent out of the home to earn money. Families at the turn of the century depended upon child workers:

> Children were employed in coal mines and steel mills; even five- and six-year-olds worked in seacoast fishing industries. In the city children shined shoes, sold newspapers, wrapped cigars in sweat shops and worked in stores. (Osborn and Osborn 1978, 28)

Many immigrant families built up their resources with the help of all members, including children. For example Polish Americans had definite ideas about what work for pay was appropriate for their daughters (Lopata 1976b and 1988a). Helping mothers maintain lodging and boarding homes or with take-in laundry was favored, because it taught domestic skills. Employment in the homes of others was a preferred alternative. Lower-class girls in general were kept from school on the assumption that they could learn all they needed in life in the home, while boys were more likely to be kept in school longer because of the assumption that they needed to learn how to survive in the outside world. Factory employment that would bring the girls into contact with men of other ethnic groups was heavily frowned upon. Immigrant women in this country developed their own monopolies over certain jobs, varied by location (Mindel, Habenstein, and Wright 1988).

The history of the role of daughter has had other complicating features as traditional support systems in American society have decreased. The transformation of work into jobs, and of economic support into dependence upon money to be earned by such jobs, made mothers and children into personal dependents of a husband/ father, as discussed in the last two chapters. In the process, the children, especially the daughters, lost many rights of support. The mother frequently could not support them. The absence of an in-come-earning man has either pushed children into poverty or re-sulted in society's taking over their support. The latter process has included either their economic support (usually at quite inadequate levels) within the home with the mother, or their removal from the home. American history abounds with cases in which children— daughters for moral reasons, sons for fear of delinquency—were taken away from their mothers and placed in alternative settings such as asylums, workhouses, and orphanages (Sutton 1983; Vandepol 1982). Abbott (1938) reprinted the conditions under which the state of Illinois allowed "female infants" to be placed in "industrial schools for girls":

> Every female infant who begs or receives alms while actually selling, or pretending to sell any article in public, or who frequents any street, alley or other place, for the purpose of begging or receiving alms; or, who having no permanent place of abode, proper parental care, or guardianship, or sufficient means of subsistence, or who for other cause is a wanderer through streets and alleys, and in other public places or, who lives with, or frequents the company of, or consorts with reputed thieves, or other vicious persons, or who is found in a house of ill-fame, or in a poor house. (P. 80)

One of the symbolic developments in American society centered around life insurance for children. While the value of children was measured in economic terms, as contributors to family maintenance, such insurance, whose popularity peaked in 1882, was seen as a protection against loss of their work through death. However, people were often accused of facilitating children's deaths in order to collect the monies, and such insurance became actively opposed by the national child-saving movement of that time. Rapid industrialization, combined with child labor laws, compulsory education, and the rejection of "baby farming," decreased children's economic value. Increased emphasis on the psychological value of children led then to the view that the insurance provided ready cash for mourning rituals. Finally, as children became considered expensive consumer items, its use has been publicized by insurance companies as an investment against that cost to parents, especially as a means of providing a proper education. That is the current use of child insurance (Zelizer 1981 and 1985).

The social circle of the daughter often contained, at least in the past, religious groups and personnel whose duties were to help the parents teach ideology and normative behavior. The duties of the child were to obey and learn. The same was true of the school system, to the extent that it contributed to the role of daughter.

The Transitional Form of the Role of Daughter

Gradual modernization is creating an extremely complicated world for a daughter. It increases her freedom of choice as to how she will live in it, but perpetuates her dependence on the resources and limitations of her family of orientation early in life, and of gender stratification throughout life.[3]

In the case of a baby born to an American urban family, the city is already there, with all its institutional resources, ready to be entered for various reasons at different stages of the life course. The family into which the girl is born lives in part of that city and participates in its life in limited ways depending on its own social life space. This family has constructed a view of the world that contains its beliefs of what is true and right, its emotions and sentiments concerning all component objects, and more or less integrated patterns of action. This worldview includes definitions of that baby as an object toward which patterned as well as idiosyncratic behavior is or will be directed. Once that baby is accepted into that family, mainly through the declaration by a woman that she is her mother—by birth or adoption—this unit will take responsibility for her till an age of societally defined adulthood when self-maintenance independent of the family is judged possible (Lopata 1984). In American society, the officially accepted baby is identified by sex, individual name, family, and any other relevant categories.

It is one of the functions of the significant others in the daughter's social circle to insure that these identifying categories become her pervasive identities.

The Life Course of the Role of Daughter

The birth of each child affects the social unit she joins. The influence the daughter's sex has upon her relations depends on how important it is for her future and that of her social circle. The circle consists of others besides the mother, and its size and complexity depends upon many factors. She may have an active father, one who accepts membership in that circle. The absence of the father from that circle, in a society that emphasizes his importance, may be very difficult for the daughter. This can be especially so if his absence is due to divorce (in years before the current tolerance of such action), desertion, or imprisonment. The death of either parent also affects children deeply. A complicating problem has been the effect of the father's absence upon the mother and other members of the circle. Siblings, as well as members of the extended family, are influenced in their duties by whether or not the daughter has an involved father. Research on families of divorce indicates that divorce may deprive daughters of their rights to an extended family on the father's side (Anspach 1976; Spicer and Hampe 1975). The social circle of the children may be quite asymmetrical if their mother fails to maintain contact with the grandparents and aunts and uncles on that side of the family (Farber 1966). On the other hand, the mother's remarriage may introduce a whole new segment to the daughter's circle, including a stepfather and stepsiblings.

The Dependent Daughter. A girl's position in the family structure is determined by the timing of her birth in its life cycle, its composition, and the surrounding circumstances, such as whether her mother is married, the ages and gender of the other children, the presence and availability of other family supports, and the family's socioeconomic position in the community and society. Her anticipated future as an adult is reflected in the complexity of the circle that helps her become one. Her circle provides the life chances upon which she builds the career of her various roles. There may be a nanny, other household servants or residents without assisting functions, babysitters, and pediatricians. If she is a daughter to the British royal family, she may have hundreds of people in her circle, of whom she becomes more or less individually aware as she grows biologically and socially. If she is born to a poor, relatively isolated farm family, the circle may be very small.

The perceived characteristics of the daughter influence how she is treated by the circle members. As discussed in chapter 1, her identification by sex leads to gender socialization by all, influenced by cultural definitions of girls, varied by social class and other subgroup membership. Her behavior—even as early as in the womb—and her appearance can lead people to make assumptions about her personality and future roles. Her family's social class is often a good predictor of which items of future personality are selected for encouragement in anticipation of her adulthood position. Circle members are constantly commenting on the baby, comparing her to others and predicting social person characteristics from "clues."

At this early stage the duties of the daughter are simply to survive the attention and care given by others and to respond positively to what is happening around her. Negative responses can result in negative reactions. Child abuse studies indicate that the victim can actually trigger abusive behavior on the part of emotionally disturbed mothers by crying or by looking or smelling "wrong" (Lamb 1987, 153–56). It does not take long before the baby's duty becomes to recognize major caregivers, with positive signs of pleasure at their contact. Sooner or later these signs are supposed to express love—especially to parents, in America, even if they are not the major caregivers. From then on, her duties to her circle keep expanding and becoming more complicated, often full of strain and, later, fraught with role conflict. In many if not most societies they include the duty to obedience, self-control along lines related to age and gender, pleasant appearance that makes family members "proud," and in general following the appropriate norms of behavior.

The rights of daughters actually precede the conscious duties and vary considerably from society to society and from subgroup to subgroup. Rights to physical and psychological care usually include the right not to be abandoned, although some groups allow the mother to "lend" or even "give" a daughter to others more in need of such a person or because the mother feels she cannot satisfactorily provide what the child has rights to. The right to receive care may mean that she can receive life- or pleasure-giving objects and actions on demand, or else training to fit the schedule of care determined by others. Considerable literature indicates that mothers give more attention to daughters than to sons, spend more time with them, and are involved in more extensive support exchanges with daughters throughout life (Losh-Hesselbart 1987; Peterson and Rollins 1987). The definition of care, and thus of neglect, varies, of course, by the definition of children's needs. Gilligan (1982) concludes that the standard definitions of human relationships are based on a male model of need. However, the definition of need in the case of girls appears to be shifting in America toward a more careful examination of the right to protection from harm, probably due to the public exposure by the feminist movement of the seriousness and frequency of the abuse they have suffered.

The subject of protection and the definition of abuse of children has had a convoluted history in American society, as conflicting demands have surfaced at different times (Pfohl 1978). These have included the right of the family to privacy and the right of both the society and the child to socialization for nondisruptive behavior. The right of a child to be socialized into becoming an acceptable member of society, and the duty of the parent to provide this socialization, may lead to harsh methods and punishments that endanger the child's physical safety, even fatally. Thus, the daughter's right to safety and empathetic care may clash with the right to be properly socialized by the parent into the family and the society. (E. Pleck, 1983). An example would be the treatment of children in Puritan America.

The right to safety can also include freedom from certain sexual or psychological actions by others, although the definition of, and emphasis upon, this area of life has also undergone change. Recent literature indicates that many, even very young, daughters have been sexually abused by their fathers, their stepfathers, and other family members. Runaways and prostitutes have been disproportionately victims of sexual abuse. The long-term effects of such experiences include traumatic sexualization, seeing sexuality as a commodity to be used for money, or its rejection, and feelings of betrayal, powerlessness, and stigmatization (Russell 1986, 167–70). Mothers are often aware of such impingement on the child's rights, but many mothers do not protect their children, especially if they feel powerless themselves and are afraid of the perpetrator. Sexual abuse by women family members, such as mothers or sisters, is very rare, supporting the conclusion that abuse is primarily a male phenomenon, accentuated by the patriarchal culture and sex stratification in which the woman is seen as inferior to the man.

The major duty of a daughter in a transitional family, as in the feminine mystique days, where the family no longer depends on her productive or income-earning activity, is to grow up without causing her parents problems, without shaming them in front of others, proving that they are good parents. More modern families are apt to give adolescent daughters greater rights to define their own needs, make their own decisions, and lead independent lives. The age at which restrictions are lessened, however, varies, and the negotiations involved are likely to bring problems. Kingsley Davis (1940) explained years ago the inevitability of conflict between parents and children because of their different rate of absorption of the culture, especially in rapidly changing societies. Parents socialized twenty-five to forty-five years ago have a construction of reality that is very different from that of their offspring. American parents, many of whom were immigrants or grew up in ethnic families and neighborhoods of a society very different from the one their children experience are unlikely to see the world from the vantage point of the younger generation. Traditional parents are also armed with the

"knowledge" that modern youths are not responsible, do not understand the realities of life, and so forth. Youths, on their part, have
great difficulty taking the role of the parent, whose value system
appears completely inadequate for life as it now is. This is true in
different ways for girls and for boys, although both feel the need to
establish themselves as independent people within their own worlds
(Chodorow 1978).

Daughter-parent conflict is often connected to the traditional
patriarchal concern over the daughter's sexual behavior. American
society defines delinquent girls in those terms, while people are less
concerned about heterosexual acts of boys, whose delinquency is
defined in terms of impingement upon property or personal rights
of mainly adults. At least this was true in the pre-AIDS days. Concerns about the virginity of their daughters, or at least over public
violation of sexual or motherhood norms, is still part of the culture
of many parents and conflicts with the modern girl's peer culture.
Regardless of the importance of friends, high school daughters are
highly dependent upon family approval for their self-estimation
(Eskilson and Wiley 1987). Chicano and Puerto Rican families still
worry about the daughter's reputation but are more tolerant of
deviation than are low-income white parents (Jarrett 1990a). Role-
straining mixed messages from the mother concerning independence, in what Fisher (1986) calls the "holding on and letting go"
double-bind syndrome, can permeate the whole relationship. On
the other hand, the daughter can be the confidante and empathize
with the mother, forming a coalition against the father. Mothers can
also serve as buffers, protecting the girls from the father. They can
provide encouragement and all forms of emotional and social support, even without conflict with other members of the family or
outsiders. Jarrett (1990b) found lower-income black daughters feeling strong solidarity with their mothers. Atypical relationships can
develop between the mother and the daughter, in which the expected rights and duties are not honored, as in the case of either a remote
or an overinvolved parent (Fisher 1986, 26–32). Variations in the
role of daughter in a father-absent versus a two-parent household
have not been fully explored, although there is some indication that
the daughter undertakes many more duties toward the mother and
the household in general if there is no other adult present (Lopata
1979). Daughters have been known to take on many of the responsibilities of the absent wife/mother/homemaker when the father is

left alone, which is one of the conditions in which father-daughter incest occurs (Russell 1984).

Children of the upper classes are often, in fact preferably, sent to "finishing" or other boarding schools (Ostrander 1985). Employed Issei (first-generation Japanese American) mothers sometimes sent their children back to Japan to be raised by their own mothers and other relatives, as a last resort (Glenn 1986, 210). Becoming a student or a worker away from home usually decreases the duties of the role of daughter, with an increase of commitment to outside relations. Employed daughters sometimes contribute to family income if they live at home, but they are no longer expected to send money and provisions back to the family if they live elsewhere. There does not appear to be a uniform financial agreement between a college student daughter and her parents concerning repayment of the cost of her education.

American and European daughters tend to increase identification with the mother when they themselves reach adulthood and become involved in similar roles (Entwisle and Doering 1981, 128). In fact, the image of her own mother improves significantly after the daughter starts raising her first child. Part of this is due to the amount of help she receives from the parent, especially in the lower class, where the kinfolk are less dispersed. Middle-class women more often hire help, at least for a short period of time after the birth of a child, and mothers come in after that.

The shift of roles by the daughter also provides her with a new perspective and better empathetic understanding of the complications of motherhood. In addition, "the hierarchical nature of the relationship becomes less problematic" (Fisher 1986, 126), so that duties of obedience, which become increasingly obnoxious as a woman matures, are relaxed. Not all mother-child relations become more symmetrical, as both persons can be locked into the duties or rights of their own cohorts. A lack of reciprocity can be resented, or actually enjoyed, by either (Fisher 1986, 53). Daughters with families of their own often receive many new rights from their parents, financial assistance, empathetic understanding of daily problems, baby-sitting or even more involved care of the children, and services such as help with shopping and household work (Goetting 1989). This was definitely the pattern established by "mum" and her daughters in boroughs of London studied by Bott (1957) and Wilmott and Young (1964). The mother insured that married daughters lived nearby by scouting apartments, and the women exchanged services, visited back and forth, shared work, and even ate meals together when the husbands were absent. Social scientists studying kinship relations have documented extensive interaction and exchanges of support systems between adult children, especially daughters, and their parents, especially mothers. In early years of the daughter's life within her own family of procreation, the flow of supports is mainly downward from the mother (Adams 1968; Shanas 1979b; Sussman 1965). Recent research confirms the continuation of this flow (Barnett 1988). Ethnic traditions reinforce the tendency of parents to help their adult children, and the closeness of the tie between mother and daughter results in a "fundamental asymmetry or 'tilt' in American kinship in favor of the wife's family" (Cohler 1988, 54). Modern daughters expect many such forms of support, which sometimes are not met by the busy mother.

Allegedly, there is much more tolerance by mothers of sexual activity of unmarried daughters, even of unmarried childbearing and rearing, in underclass black communities than among other groups (Jarrett 1990a; Staples and Mirande 1980). However, recent statistics of births identified only by the mother indicate that young white women are also bearing and keeping children (Cherlin 1981). A short news item in the *Chicago Sun Times Parade* ("Unmarried Mothers," 30 September 1990, 9) stated that "approximately 25% of all babies born in the United States in 1988 were born to unwed mothers." There is little research on the unmarried daughter's rights to continued help from the mother in these circumstances in white communities, probably because the trend toward keeping the baby is so new.

The Adult Daughter of Aging Parents. The role of daughter changes as parents become decreasingly capable of providing their own care, let alone providing support systems to others. Actually, this stage in the family life cycle may arrive gradually, unless a serious health problem develops. The decrease of the power of the male line, accompanying social development, has changed the relation of adults, both daughter and son, to their parents (Lopata 1991b). Transitional American society gradually removed the pressure on the son to take full responsibility for the welfare of his parents. In fact, even main economic supports are no longer expected of him. In the meantime, the daughter has been freed from arranged marriage and the need to leave her family of orientation for that of her husband. As the son's obligation to his childhood family decreases, so does that of his wife. She is now able to retain her relationships with her own family. The mother now does not need to depend wholly upon the son and is thus able to develop closer relationships with her daughter, no longer fearful of losing her early in life. A daughter also gains more positive attention from the mother as a child than was typical in the patrilocal family system, encouraging continued feelings of closeness.

It is during the mother's older years that the increased responsibility of daughters rather than of sons appears in modern families (see Lopata 1987c, especially chapters on Iran, Turkey, Korea, and India; also Lopata 1991b). Thus, the closer relationship between the parents and the daughter, rather than the son, throughout life leads to an increase in her flow of supports toward the older generation. Social scientists, whether or not influenced by Freudian ideas, have long concluded that her contributions are more natural than those of the son and daughter-in-law (Chodorow 1978). Some social scientists claim that this supportive relationship between an adult daughter and her aging parents is undertaken voluntarily, rather than as a consequence of familial obligations as in the past (Hess and Waring 1978a and 1978b). This supports my thesis concerning the shift from the patriarchally ascribed responsibility of the son and daughter-in-law to that of the daughter, who has more comfortable, and in adulthood, more egalitarian relationships with her parents, especially with her mother.

On the other hand, it may be that the daughter who is still in the transitional stage of family development when women took on most nurturant, supportive activity has simply been socialized to a sense of obligation to the parents, especially the mother (Hess and Waring 1978a and 1978b). In one study the daughters living within fifty miles of the aged parents who were not actively supportive of them felt very uncomfortable over the fact that a sister carried the main burden. The sons were obviously not socialized into giving much care, and thus felt no guilt over their failure to do so:

> The overall feeling conveyed by the data is the discomfort of the local sisters, but not the brothers, about being in the role of secondary caregiver, even though in reality they provided more help than the brothers. (Brody et al. 1989, 537)

"Being employed significantly decreased the hours of assistance provided by sons but did not have a significant impact on the hours of assistance provided by daughters" (Stoller 1983, 851). The importance of daughters rather than sons is evidenced by the likelihood that at least one daughter is living within easy support distance of a widowed mother, and the frequency with which they appear in her support systems (Lopata 1979). The Chicago-area mothers generally did not share housing with their children, although if the older woman lived with a child it was much more likely to be with the daughter's family than with an adult son, even if he were single.

Increasing frailty of parents, accompanied often by bouts of hospitalization and definite incapacitation, is not only physically, but also psychologically, difficult for daughters if they must "reverse roles," treating the mother or father as a dependent who lacks even decision-making skills. The older generation's social life space can wither, making the daughter the main supplier of a variety of supports (Fisher 1986).

The amount of time, energy, and sometimes money involved in caring for a parent may cause conflict with a daughter's other roles, in the family of procreation or even in an occupation. This is especially true if the woman is an only child. Daughters have been known to delay marriage or quit a job in order to provide supports for a mother or father, or both. Single adult children often bear the brunt of the care. A total of forty-two of the fifty never-married women studied by Simon (1987) were the primary caregivers for an ailing parent.

The families of procreation of a married daughter may express resentment over her new priorities, while she may resent their unwillingness to understand these (Kleban et al. 1989). Other researchers find daughter caregivers stressed by the addition of this set of obligations to the normal work load of other roles. Brody (1989) has drawn our attention to "daughters in the middle," caught in a complex set of high-priority obligations toward the parents, the husband, and the children.

The parents may also suffer in such situations, feeling the resentment from the caregiving daughter and being forced to acquiesce to demands from harried caregivers. The loss of power of decision making over their own lives can be an extremely frustrating experience. Mere contact and aid may not result in interpersonal intimacy between generations, especially if it is felt on both sides as being only obligatory. In fact, it may result in elder abuse by the stressed caregiver.

"Factors tending to attenuate intergenerational bonds" from the point of view of the daughter include diminishing opportunities, the demands of middle age, psychological barriers, and transitions. "Factors tending to preserve and prolong the intergenerational bond" include socialization and the sharing of values, role modeling, and special sentiments, as well as the presence of a healing-caring network (Hess and Waring 1978, 261).

A final duty of a daughter to her parents is to keep their memories alive, providing the grandchildren knowledge of their contributions to family lineage and heritage.

The Modern Form of the Role of Daughter

The evidence is overwhelming that the transitional stage in modernization has placed a major burden on women in the role of daughter, as it has in their other roles. Brody (1989), England and Farkas (1986), Horowitz, (1985), Lopata (1991b,) and all the other researchers studying the support systems of elderly parents report greater contribution and stressful concern on the part of the daughter than on the part of the son. Finley (1989) expects this system to continue until there is a societal reevaluation of the importance of the male source of support. At present, all agree that the institutionalization of women's housework, and the extension of this into care for others, is so strong as to resist any attempt to create a more egalitarian system of emotional and service support. Wilkinson (1988, 191) suggests the creation or expansion of extensive forms of support for dependent family members from voluntary social groups as a means of alleviating the burden placed on the female kin member, especially the daughter. If the predicted changes by which the responsibility for human welfare is better distributed among a variety of people and groups actually take place, as I believe they must for modern life to reach its potential, then the role of daughter, much like that of mother, will contain a more complex social circle. Its members can negotiate both the duties and the rights of what can now be a burden for the social person of daughter at the more dependent stage of the life course of the mother.

The Role of Daughter-in-Law

The relationship between daughter-in-law and mother-in-law appears more often in anthropological or sociological studies of more highly patriarchal family systems than of the modern American one. In the former, the younger woman is often seen as the victim (see Barnes

1987 on China; Ross 1962 on India). In a sort of hazing like in fraternities of the not-so-distant past, she often receives the same kind of treatment as did her mother-in-law when she was young. In addition, joint households often assign much of the homemaking work to the younger woman, the mother-in-law thus becoming the honored matriarch of the family.

The relation between the woman that grows out of the kinship system is expected to be difficult, since the two women are of different generations, have usually not been in contact prior to the younger woman's marriage to the son of the older woman, have had the relationship thrust on them by that event, and are in competition for the attention of the man who is the connecting link. The daughter-in-law may resent what she sees as interference in child rearing, which the older woman may perceive as simply providing help to the novice. However, the modern daughter-in-law has more power than in the past to negotiate with the husband for independence from his mother. In fact, contact can be relatively voluntary and limited. The daughter-in-law can treat the relation (with cooperation from the mother-in-law, of course) as one of friendship, minimal involvement, or "substitute mother" (Fisher 1986, 119). Although one of the duties of the daughter-in-law's role in traditional times was to respect and express positive feelings toward the husband's parents, many women are unable to feel those sentiments and are less likely in present times to control their expressions. The daughter-in-law's role may also be complicated by her husband's conflicts between his duties and rights in the role of husband and those in his role of son.

Most daughters-in-law are able to successfully separate relations with their own mothers from those with the husband's mother. Marotz and Cowan (1987) studied women who lived together on farms or ranches and who reported that they got along pretty well, using conflict-avoidance techniques. The sources of conflict were differences in values and goals, which often were not communicated adequately.

Sister

The role of sister is thrust upon a girl simply by birth or adoption and acknowledged family membership of herself and a sibling. Birth order is an important circumstance affecting the place of the newborn in the family, the social circle components, and treatment by others. The size, spacing, and gender distribution of the sibling group influence all members (Elder and Boverman 1963). It makes a great deal of difference whether the child is in the first, middle, or youngest position in the family, and whether the siblings are girls or boys. Duties and rights are assigned differently by parents and others according to such characteristics of the sibling structure. A brother will relate with a sister differently than will a same-sex sibling, and the number of years between children can generally decrease competitiveness and increase protectiveness.

An extremely important influence on the role of sister, as on all other sets of relationships, is the society within which it is carried out, with its culture and social structure. The location of the relation within that society, especially in its socioeconomic system, is also very important, as lower-class or lower-caste families usually relate differently than do upper-class ones. The role of sister can also vary among other societal subdivisions, such as religious, as in the case of the Quakers versus Catholics, or ethnic, as with Italian Americans versus Navaho Indians. It certainly makes a difference whether the sister can retain her role (i.e., relations with her circle) or loses it with marriage.

Cross-cultural analyses point to a greater interdependence among siblings in many parts of the traditional world than in middle-class America. Sibling groups share many functions, including work and responsibility, serving as substitutes for each other, being obedient to seniors, teaching and learning, playing and disciplining, and making sure that the family system operates smoothly (Weisner 1982, 308). In many such societies community and family are accentuated over individualism, and caregiving is a normal, ongoing aspect of life. The importance of the sibling group continues throughout life unless there is a geographic dispersal of members. In societies such as Egypt, for example, a sister is highly dependent on her brothers for mate selection, the provision of dowries, property inheritance, and so on. Such close interdependence fosters strong sentiments, not all of them positive.

The literature on siblings in transitional America is in interesting contrast to this cross-cultural description, in that it is scarce and often does not specify gender. Two revealing article titles are "Sibling Interaction: A Neglected Aspect in Family Life Research" (Irish 1964) and "The Sibling Relationships: A Forgotten Dimension" (Pfouts 1976). In fact, most recent studies of siblings have focused not on the role, but on the effects of such variables as birth order, gender, spacing, and "density" upon such characteristics as personality.

A few studies provide some insights. The small number and short age distance between siblings of recent decades allegedly promotes more competitiveness and cooperation in childhood and youth than was true in the past. In addition, mothers of transitional times devoted greater attention to children, again increasing the possibility of competition. Sisters reportedly feel moderately close to their siblings, more so than brothers, and more so toward their sisters than toward their brothers (Boverman and Dobash 1974). Adolescents feel closer to their older than to their younger siblings, implying an asymmetry of the relationships. Kammeyer (1967) found that the presence of younger brothers helped sisters learn feminine deference and demeanor, while the presence of older brothers made the younger sister more masculine or "modern."

Intense sibling loyalties can develop in cases of parental loss or child abuse (Bank and Kohn 1982). Such loyalty manifests itself by constant devotion, identification with the other, the ability to resolve interpersonal conflicts rapidly and openly, sacrifices for the other, the wish to be together to the point of strong negative reaction to separation, and defense of the other against outside threats. However, we need to know more about the factors that bind sisters and brothers to each other. As of now, only dire circumstances in the lives of the siblings appear to result in strong loyalty.

What happens as brothers and sisters become adults and old people? An extensive debate has been waged over the last forty years about the involvement of adult and aging siblings in each other's support systems. The discussion harks back to Parsons's (1943) statement that the modern American family is isolated from its kinship group, which includes siblings. Lee (1980) stated in his summary of the 1970s decade of research and theory on kinship that while the 1960s work was dominated by refutation of this thesis, the 1970s focused on studies of actual exchanges of supports. Most sociologists would agree that the middle-class American situation contrasts with that of working-class urban Britain, where the mother ("mum") guarantees contact among her daughters by her own activities. Even there, however, the sisters tend to disperse when the mother dies or if the sister's family of procreation moves elsewhere (Wilmott and Young 1960).

As in the ideal of friendship, which we will be examining later, other relationships and roles prevent many adult women from maintaining a strong focus on the role of sister. This is particularly true of women in the roles of wife and mother, especially if they move from the area occupied by their family of orientation, as so many Americans have done.

Most of the studies of the role of sister focus on older rather than middle-aged women and reach one of two mutually exclusive conclusions. On the one side are studies that argue that the role of sister is active among older Americans and pulls together not only the women but also male siblings. This reinforces the thesis that women take responsibility for keeping in contact with kin. Older women are more apt to communicate with their siblings than are older men. Closer sister relationships occur among older women who never married or had children than among those who had families of procreation (Shanas 1977). Thirty-one of the fifty never-married women studied by Simon (1987, 70) were sharing an apartment or house with a sister or brother in old age. Economic support, help in sickness, companionship, and emotional support were reasons for such arrangements. Several reported especially close relations with a sister. Sisters were very helpful as support providers and confidantes among black women facing serious personal problems (Chatters, Taylor, and Neighbors 1989, 764). In fact, researchers find that sisters, and sometimes brothers, are used as child and spouse substitutes (see also Shanas 1977). In addition, even for rural elderly not "enmeshed in an emotionally supportive network of kin relations," having a sister living in relatively close proximity may contribute to the life satisfaction of women (McGhee 1985, 90). It is possible that even "rivalrous feelings between sisters" may challenge them toward a livelier involvement in interaction or a fuller social life space.

In general, closeness and contact tend to remain constant over the years at whatever level is achieved in adulthood (Cicirelli 1982). Memories, however, may help increase feelings of acceptance and approval later in life. As Gold (1987) notes:

> The reduction in perceptions of resentment and envy indicate that older sisters and brothers may be able to "forgive and forget" in old age. . . . The findings here indicate that generational solidarity becomes more evident early in old age and grows throughout late life for many sibling dyads. (P. 30)

Gold adds that it is mainly the sister who contributes to such feelings of closeness, in both sisters-only and in sister-brother dyads. She focuses on the salience of the memories, rather than on more active support systems.

On the other hand, several researchers have questioned this "overheralded structure in past conceptualizations of family functioning" (Gibson 1972). A careful examination of the data used by sociologists such as Litwak (1965) and especially Sussman (1962) indicates that most of the supports flow up and down the parent-child line, rather than horizontally to siblings (Lopata 1978). "Siblings simply are not available for interaction in the metropolitan area for a large proportion of the sample. The sibling bond is not sustained at the same level throughout the life cycle, and becomes less prevalent among older people" (Rosenberg and Anspach 1973, 108). Not only is the role of sister relatively rarely activated among old women, but when it is, it can become a burden, creating strained relations with siblings. This is particularly true in cases in which one sister becomes the major caregiver while other sisters and brothers are locally available but much less active in the supports of older parents (Brody et al. 1989). In fact, there are numerous records of sibling abuse, including even homicide (Steinmetz 1987). As with other family abuse, it tends to go from brother to sister, although age is an important factor.

Siblings seldom appeared in support networks of widows in the Chicago metropolitan area, even when the respondents were given 195 chances to list a sister or brother (Lopata 1978 and 1979). We asked about four sets of supports, defined as the giving or receiving of objects or actions that the giver and the receiver perceive as supportive of a life-style (Lopata 1987b, 3). Support networks consist of people or organizations that provide supports. Support systems are sets of actions or objects and include the inflow and outflow of economic and service supports and social as well as emotional interaction. All but 19 percent of the widows have at least one living sibling, but "the average frequency of contact with such a collateral relative is just over 'several times a year'" (Lopata 1978, 357). Most of the widows do not report economic exchanges with anyone, let alone siblings. In addition, at most 10 percent of the women report a sibling within the service support system, and that is as a giver or receiver of help with decisions. Siblings appear as helpers with transportation, household repairs, shopping, yard work, child care, and so forth even less often than that. The same is true of social supports. Only 11 percent of the respondents report visiting or traveling out of town with siblings, and only 10 percent report sharing holidays with them. Fewer go to public places, share lunch, go to church, or engage in leisure games or sports with a brother or sister. Finally, and this is the most devastating finding to those who claim that close sibling relationships in adulthood and old age are common, very few siblings appear in the emotional support system. Fewer than 10 percent of the widows list a sibling as the person they most enjoy being with, to whom they tell problems, who comforts them when depressed, makes them feel important or useful, or who most often makes them angry. Only 10 percent feel closest to a sibling or would turn to one in times of crisis. All in all, siblings do not appear in 99 percent of the economic-inflow, 98 percent in the economic-outflow, 87 percent in the service-inflow, and 92 percent of the service-outflow systems. They are more frequently involved in the sentiment system, but even here, 74 percent of the women do not think of a sibling when answering those questions. On the other hand, if a woman lists a sibling, it is usually a sister and she is usually listed several, sometimes many, times (Lopata 1979 and 1987c).

Several articles in a special issue of the *American Behavioral Scientist* (Bedford and Gold 1989) devoted to the complexity of sibling relationships among older Americans, report a prevalence of conflict in many relations among sisters, the infrequency of sustained help, and the distress produced when such help is actually given. Support occurs mainly in brief crisis periods (Bedford 1989a and 1989b).

A number of factors can serve as mediators influencing the provision of supports by siblings, such as geographic proximity, social network structure, health and functional status, gender composition, and ethnicity (Avioli 1989, 57). Physical distance affects especially members of the lower social classes, who are not accustomed to using correspondence or even telephones for maintaining closeness, being mainly dependent upon face-to-face interaction, which can be hard to achieve with limited resources. Social distance, in terms of social class difference, is also important, although there is no consensus on its influence as a depressor of relationships. Bott (1957) found professional and generally more middle- and upper-class couples more involved in friendships with like-minded peers than with parents or siblings.

There are several explanations for the relative absence of siblings from the support systems of widows and of other adult or older sisters.

> The decline in the need for interdependence and shared functioning, and in the maintenance of a single family estate, is the primary underlying feature allowing for the remarkable mobility in the American sibling group. Bilateral inheritance has a great deal to do with the relatively equal investment in boys and girls in our society. The replacement of parents' material wealth with other forms of parental investment early in life, and lessened importance of having parents' skills transferred to sons, are both of enormous importance for the freedom and egalitarian treatment within the Western sibling group. (Weisner 1982, 325)

Siblings interact intensely in America, according to Weisner (1982), only when inheritance issues arise, because our "unusually egoistic family pressures" (325) increase chronic rivalry and personal possessiveness, especially among middle-class American siblings (see also Lamb and Sutton-Smith 1982).

All in all, the assumption that sibling relationships grow closer with aging has not been borne out in most research on transitional families. The growing literature on stepfamilies in modern times includes discussion of stepsisters, usually in early stages of entrance into that role. We do not know enough as yet to tell whether stepsisters retain active involvement in that role in later life.

Grandmother

One of the main advantages of old age, portrayed in highly romanticized terms, is that of being a grandparent. Images of a grandmother baking pies with her granddaughter or telling stories to the grandchildren abound in American folktales and literature. The wicked old stepmother is replaced by the kind old grandmother. The relationships are positively presented; negative aspects are not mentioned. The grandmother, deservedly in that role because she had children and raised them to value having families of their own in contact and cooperation with her, reaps all the benefits. She has companionship without constant care. The grandchildren and she are in contact for a limited number of hours, when both are on their good behavior, and then separate, leaving nothing but pleasant memories. She can read to them without worrying about their performance in schools. She can perform the traditional homemaking tasks such as cooking favorite foods without having to worry about diets or forcing the children to eat at the right time and in the right way. She can buy clothes or playthings, but need not worry about their maintenance. She can spend money on their entertainment rather than on their support. She can use money as gifts without undertaking major expenditures for teeth straightening or housing.

Although being active in the role of grandmother is voluntary, a woman has actually no choice as to when and under what circumstances it becomes available to her. Children produce their own children on their own timetables, not as a convenience to their own parents. "Normative time," so labeled by Neugarten (1973), occurs when the grandparent is ready and the community considers her to be at the appropriate stage of her life. If the event occurs too early or too late, or "off time," complications can occur, as indicated before in the case of unmarried black grandmothers (Burton and Bengtson 1985).

Traditional Times, Traditional Places

Grandmothers have traditionally had the right to help in, or even to dominate, the socialization process of the grandchildren. This was both a duty and a right in slowly changing societies in which they had accumulated knowledge and time freed from heavy subsistence work (Wong 1988). The middle generation was usually all too glad to turn over this function to the older one, being themselves too busy with social reproduction. A Puerto Rican grandmother living on the mainland reputedly has strong rights of control over her grandchildren, including that of removing them from the parents if she considers their behavior unsatisfactory (Ludwig 1977).

The right and duty to socialize the grandchildren is often accompanied by the total care of these beneficiaries in the grandmother's social circle. This is true of Thailand (Cowgill 1972), traditional China (Wong 1988; Barnes 1987), South Korea (Koo 1987), and many European countries (Mindel, Habenstein, and Wright 1988).

> Cooking, washing, cleaning, bathing are necessary repetitive chores at which grandmothers may substitute for younger mothers who may be involved in occupational roles away from home. At the same time, these grandmothers are serving as teachers and disciplinarians. In fact, it appears that it is often the grandmother who is the actual, if unrecognized, head of the household, the person who controls much of the daily routine of the members and supervises most of the activities of the children. (Cowgill 1972, 98–99)

The role can thus combine elements of the roles of homemaker and mother with those of grandmother. Role strain and role conflict often enter into this type of situation when two social persons in two different roles claim the same duties or rights. A mother and a grandmother may each feel that it is her main right to socialize a child her way, with the assistant conforming to her definitions of that situation. This occurs quite frequently between first- and second-generation immigrant families in America. On the other hand, there are situations in which the role of mother may be delegated by the biological mother willingly, or by community action, to the biological grandmother.

Conflict between the mother and the grandmother over the children is especially likely when more than one set of relationships operates concurrently in the same locale. This happens in three-generation households, when there is not a clear-cut division of authority and labor. As Ross (1962) found in urban India, and F. Adams (1972) in Mazaltepec, the grandmother can define her role more satisfactorily for herself when adult married children and their offspring reside in her home than when she lives in households dominated by the younger woman (see also Koo 1987). The higher the status of the elderly woman, the greater usually are her rights to determine her role of grandmother. In traditional and even modern China, a grandchild may be left behind by families moving away from the ancestral home or sent to the home of the grandmother to be raised by her or to care for the elderly (Barnes 1987, 213). Some American Indian communities allow children to leave their parental homes in cases of family conflict and to live with grandparents or aunts and uncles (Nelson 1988; Schlegel 1988).[4]

Transitional and Modern Forms of the Role of Grandmother

Many changes in the culture, composition, and social structure of societies have dramatically changed the real, rather than the ideological, role of grandmother. One basic conclusion by observers of these changes is that the role has decreased in importance for both the older woman and the grandchildren in transitional, urban America from times and places in which the kinship network was locally contained and mutually interdependent. Thus, the first reason given for this decrease is the weakening of the network that granted the grandmother rights and assisted her in her duties. The extended family has dispersed, and remaining members are limited in number, usually the parents of the children and possibly their aunts and uncles.

The weakening of the patriarchal structure of families means that the other grandparents, of which there can be several sets, must now be considered. Geographical separation of the grandmother and the major beneficiaries also makes their circle involvements more difficult.

Many demographic changes in the society can influence the attractiveness of grandparenting (Sprey and Matthews 1982). Modern grandmothers often are too busy to participate in that role on an extensive basis. Most have not modified their role cluster sufficiently to incorporate grandparenting, or at least to move it into prominence. Rather than making grandparenting a "career" of involvement, such women, too involved in other roles while the grandchildren are small, may find the youngest generation involved in its own life when they are ready to grandparent (Cherlin and Furstenberg 1986).

There are several recent trends that affect the age at which a woman acquires grandchildren. Among lower-class African American, Chicano, and Puerto Rican families, women can become grandmothers biologically while still in their twenties and thirties and feel very irritated over being pushed into a role that implies aging (Burton and Bengtson 1985; Jarett 1990b). They often have children and grandchildren of the same ages (Jarrett 1990a). Of course, if the present trend toward later marriage and motherhood continues, the role of grandmother may increase in importance in the future, as the new cohorts of women reach the age of retirement from public roles while grandchildren are still available.

Another reason why the role of grandmother may be decreasing in importance can be the gradual removal of major rewards. Being an active grandmother may be worth a great deal of effort not only in the absence of interesting competitive roles, but also when it is considered very important to society in general. This is likely to occur when there is power, or at least authority, connected with it, when the older woman is given the rights to determine the boundaries of the role, and when there is a complex social circle assisting and supporting her actions. Historical and anthropological research indicates that such circumstances were present in the past and in other societies, where the practical contributions of the role were valued. In such societies people envied families with grandmothers, assigned them sufficient rank that their demands on behalf of the children were honored and resources were provided for their performance of their duties. Of course, some of the descriptions of grandparents' power in other times and places may be exaggerated. Even great dowager grandmothers of future kings and queens may not have had the ultimate say in how the youngest generation was to be cared for and socialized. The social circle of grandmothers has often contained people who have equal, if not greater, say on these matters. The more important the youngster, the more complex his (and sometimes her) circle, of which the grandmother is only a small part, is likely to be. Thus, her role is influenced by the grandchild's current or future roles.

One of the characteristics of modern societies is the rapidity of social change, which makes much of the knowledge collected over years by the grandmother considered outmoded by the middle generation and its assisting personnel (Gutmann 1985; Lopata 1972, and 1976a). The children of immigrants, born and socialized in America, often resist the influence of their own parents over the children, wishing more "modern" contents and methods of socialization, as provided by Dr. Spock (1957) or other "scientific" sources (Lopata 1971b and 1976a). widows interviewed for the study *Women as Widows: Support Systems* (Lopata 1979) complained that their role of grandmother had withered into one of "baby-sitting," or simply watching that the child not be hurt or do anything destructive, rather than actively being involved in child rearing. In fact, many felt that their own children interfered with the building up of a relationship with the grandchildren.

In fact, one of the major reasons that American widows prefer to live alone, even to face loneliness, rather than share the households of their married children and their offspring, is the anticipation of intergenerational conflict. They imagine not only irritation with the grandchildren, but also, and often even more importantly, anger at their own offspring over their methods of rearing the youngsters (Lopata 1973c and 1979).

An earlier study of role modifications of older widows showed that, at the time of the interview, blacks in the Chicago metropolitan area had no advantage over their white counterparts when it came to sharing households, although many had experienced living with relatives in the past (Lopata 1971a and 1973c). The assumed centrality of matrifocal families among non-middle-class blacks led me to the assumption that many more black families would be headed by a maternal grandmother or have her living in a home headed by a daughter (Burton and Bengtson 1985). However, only a tiny number of Chicago-area widows ever had grandchildren living in the same residence. Interestingly enough the grandmother shared a home with granddaughters more often than with grandsons.

In spite of the infrequency among all the social races of three-generational households, I had expected grandchildren to be actively involved in the support systems of the widows. This hypothesis also proved incorrect. Grandchildren appeared in the economic support systems of widows, if they did at all, only as recipients of gifts of money. Only one-fifth of the references to people whom widows entertained at home, and one-fourth to those with whom holidays are spent, are to grandchildren. I also assumed a much greater contribution of such children in the emotional support systems—but was disappointed. Only 10 percent of the widows reported having a grandchild as one of the three persons with whom they most enjoy being, and about 6 percent as the person who most often makes them feel important or useful. Grandchildren are definitely not major contributors to the support systems of the vast majority of Chicago-area widows in two carefully selected samples. A few of the widows' comments about the third generation indicated irritation with the manner of deportment or lack of deference. On the other hand, some commented that they enjoyed the relationship and that it was part of their emotional support system. Cherlin and Furstenberg (1986) probed in greater depth and found that the generalized reference to "grandchildren" masked the fact that the older generation had favorites, who were emotionally very important. Even ethnically identified grandparents were not, for the most part, involved with grandchildren on a day-to-day basis. However, there was strong emotional investment in those children who were seen regularly.

The subject of grandparenting has recently drawn expanded attention from both popular and social science literature, undoubtedly accompanying increases in the numbers of the elderly and the growth of the field of social gerontology (see Bengtson and Robertson 1985).

The Social Psychology of Grandmothering

The deinstitutionalization of the role and its basic relationships has made available many alternate ways of grandparenting. The (1964) Neugarten and Weinstein study, a classic in the field, determined five different "styles" of such role involvement, all based more on companionate than on authoritarian relationships: formal, fun-seeking, surrogate parenting, as a reservoir of wisdom, and as a distant figure. This typology has been used in many studies, with additional embellishments of the basic five. The distant grandmothers can be detached or remote, passive or selectively investing themselves. A very important function of the more passive grandparents can be that of being the "family watchdog" who stands ready to help mainly in emergency situations but refrains from what might be taken as interference (Troll 1983). Many characteristics of the older woman, including her health, income, other family obligations, or personal stances to social roles, can also influence the social psychological aspects of role involvement. This role "can be either a gift or a curse, a reward or punishment for what one has done or been earlier" (Troll 1985, 135). Research on life-course changes in personality indicates a continuity of stances, a stability of styles in many roles that preceded that of grandmother.

Styles of grandparenting do not function in isolation from the social circumstances and background of interaction. We must remember that this role can be enacted with many different grandchildren. Unless all are within the same geographical area, social distance may be affected by resources available to undertake an alternative style. Add to this the changes and ambiguities of the role itself, even within each class, and other complications arise. Geographical proximity influences such relationships, as it does others. The match between expectations on the part of each generation is important: The closer these expectations are to each other and to an "ideological" view of the role, the easier it is to actually relate. The relative willingness and power of each generation to bargain and negotiate the relationship also contribute to interaction (Robertson 1977). The ages of all participants and the stages in their family cycle must be considered, according to Wood and Robertson (1973). There may be a generation gap in expectations, grandparents often expecting aspects of the role to be quite different from what the youngsters expect.

A combination of social class variables constructs the situation within which relationships flourish or remain formal or distant. Lower-class families of all social races allegedly give the role of grandmother much more centrality and vitality than do the middle classes (see Adams 1968; Staples 1988; Winch and Blumberg 1968). One change that could lead to an increase in the use of grandmothers as child rearers by middle-class mothers is the latter's movement into the labor force. However, such mothers tend to use day-care facilities, in spite of their inadequacies, rather than the grandmother, due to generational differences in ideas about human development. Other middle-class tendencies that seem to decrease the value of kin caretaking of children include an emphasis on leisure-time pursuits. Males' increasing longevity past retirement has turned the older generation toward fun rather than work. The grandparents brought up one family and resist being tied down by children. Being economically comfortable now with social security, they can pay for their own services, rather than depending on their children, which decreases their need for payback supports (Clavan 1978, 355; Lopata 1979).

Gutmann (1985) claims that Americans have repudiated gerontocracy, or the power of the elderly over the rest of the society. The middle-aged and older are refusing to face aging, wishing independence and autonomy from familism, hedonistically withdrawing from demands of closeness, narcissistically choosing only roles that provide pleasure rather than duties.

As the obligatory aspects of the role of grandparent decrease for the older generation, and as the middle generation finds alternative ways of caring for its children and focuses on nonfamilial activities, the factors facilitating voluntary relationships become more pronounced (Hess and Waring 1978a). The importance of the middle generation in either facilitating or interfering with grandparent-grandchild interaction cannot be neglected. Their feelings and viewpoints can push the others toward or away from each other. In fact, Robertson (1977) presents different dimensions of parental mediation influencing grandparent-grandchild relations. These include the parental perception of the significance of grandparenthood, of the appropriateness of the behavior of the grandparents, and of the rituals of contact. In addition, the means parents use to mediate between generations, the frequency of mediation, and the parents' attitudes about the equity of interaction are all important factors affecting the results.

A situation that recently received sociological and popular attention is the demand by grandparents for access to grandchildren in the case of divorce (Burton and Bengtson 1985, 65). The probability of continued contact is relatively high if they are the parents of the divorcée, less likely if it is the son who formed the connecting link. In modern society, the divorced wife has the right to remove the grandchildren from contact with the ex-husband's family if she wishes. This right is contrary to the traditional patriarchal system, in which the grandparents on the male line had stronger rights over the children than did the mothers. The creation of barriers to contact with grandchildren can be a serious shock to grandparents who have already developed loving relationships. The mother can even remarry and change the children's family name so that they are hard to trace. Such a cutoff is not likely to happen if the grandparents have property that can be inherited and subsequent legal battles are to be avoided. The sociopsychological aspects of involvement in grandmothering mean that some women suffer emotional withdrawal if grandchildren they had become attached to are no longer available for contact and mutual support.

Summary

Women's kinship roles, including kin keeper on either side, daughter, sister, or grandmother, have become sufficiently deinstitutionalized in the United States to allow voluntary engagement in adulthood. The forced interdependence that often created uncomfortable demands for work and subservience has decreased with independent sources of social integration. On the other hand, the prescribed, traditional support resources have simultaneously become optional, and people can, without recourse, be deprived of emotional or social comfort.

An interesting recent suggestion is to have the government allow large kinship networks to incorporate themselves as businesses, providing tax advantages in the form of write-offs for assistance with new business ventures, tuition funds, and wealth transfers (Wallis 1992, 44). Such a modern innovation could revitalize kinship in America.

Once having entered the role of daughter, even if without choice, a girl allegedly has the backing of society to insure that she receives adequate care, although many cases of neglect appear to slip by its notice. The role has a distinct life course, changing from high levels of dependence upon the mother in childhood, to comparatively egalitarian interaction in adulthood, and possibly a reversal in the parents' old age. There are also definite social class variations in how this role is carried forth and in the size and complexity of its social circle. In the extremes of social class position, greater importance is assigned to the role of daughter than in the middle classes.

An important aspect of this role in modern America is that it can be active even after marriage. In contrast to prior times and places, a woman does not have to neglect her family of orientation when becoming a daughter-in-law.

Sister relations were probably never significant in patriarchal families, since sisters dispersed upon marriage, joining the families of their husbands. Continued contact with the mother in modern times can insure sibling interaction in adulthood, but her death can weaken the link. Mobility, whether social or geographical, can decrease its salience, if positive feelings ever existed. Contact at funerals and weddings is not equivalent to continued interaction and supports. The role can be reactivated in old age, as other roles lose their significance and if circumstances permit.

There are many idealized images of the role of grandmother in all ethnic and racial subcultures in America's past. The role is now so highly deinstitutionalized that each grandmother develops, more or less voluntarily and in cooperation with circle members, her own relationships with her grandchildren. The more resources she has, the more she can demand or negotiate her terms for the role. The intermediary generation can function as her assistants, setting up the proper atmosphere and making interaction easy, or it can hinder it.

Grandmothers are known to vary considerably in their personal styles of involvement. However, it takes more than a style to carry forth a role, and many factors facilitate or impede this one. Many more women have now survived to grandmotherhood than in the past, and the deinstitutionalization of the role and the increasing individualization of American women mean that here too, as in other social roles, diversity abounds.

5

Occupation: Homemaker

One of the interesting characteristics of the role of homemaker in modern America is the high level of emotional and evaluative disagreement it draws. The woman in this role can be seen as a creative contributor not just to direct beneficiaries but to the society at large. On the other hand, the role can be seen as exploitive and demeaning to the titleholder, even if it is judged to be important to the beneficiaries.

The role of homemaker is undertaken by a woman who decides, more or less voluntarily, to manage a household and draws together a social circle involving everyone who benefits from her work and who contributes to her efforts—assistants, and suppliers of goods and services. The role can be performed by a man, who is interestingly still called a "househusband," while the older term *housewife* has been replaced by *homemaker* to include women other than wives. Very, very few men undertake the role of full-time househusband, carrying the main responsibility of managing the household and allocating tasks to circle members (J. Pleck 1983).

Housekeepers are usually defined as employees of homemakers or other managers of households.

The duties of this role, as of any other, depend upon the size and construction of the social circle and what must be done in interaction with each member. Its rights are also influenced by the relative status, or prestige location, of the homemaker and by her location in the organizational chart of the household's environment. The household is the basic unit of the role.

The social circle of the homemaker can be quite simple, consisting of a limited number of beneficiaries, residents, guests, other recipients of products and services she has created, and assistants. She could be the only beneficiary, if she were the only resident and never invited anyone into her home or offered services and products from the home without pay. Such a situation can be visualized in the case of a homemaker in a relatively isolated and self-sufficient American pioneer farm. Some circle members may be forced upon her by other decisions, as when in-laws or stepchildren move in with a husband, or residents invite guests. Most traditional homemakers have been embedded in a network of extended families and village neighbors with complicated work and product exchange systems. Modern homemakers have numerous assistants in the form of product and service suppliers. A social circle can be as complex as that of the White House, managed by the U.S. First Lady with the assistance of enormous staffs and with uncounted numbers of beneficiaries from all over the world.

Traditional Times, Traditional Places

Households have varied tremendously all over the world and throughout history. The young bride of the traditional rural Hindu family of India moved into limited quarters within the joint family household managed by her mother-in-law and had few rights until she herself became the eldest matriarch (Gujral 1987). Limited rights also went with homemaking in all ancestral homes in familistic cultures, in which each generation had the obligation to retain things for the future with little individualized change.

Aries (1965) describes the manor homes of Europe as very complicated centers of societal life, especially in countries without specialized political and economic meeting places. Within them lived a variety of people, while others visited for many reasons, often for extended periods of time. My own great-grandmother recorded in detail the work and the social activities connected with my grandfather's wedding in Poland in the 1870s (Znaniecka 1872). Literally hundreds of people, whom she had to organize, were involved as assistants, suppliers, and beneficiaries. Artificial orange trees to decorate the home were made by local women who were obviously given models, since such trees could not grow in the Polish climate. Visitors stayed for weeks, having traveled great distances in premodern conveyances.

Homemakers in charge of manor homes usually managed the whole estate when the husband was away for business or wars, even if his signature were required for legal transactions (Pinchbeck [1930] 1969). Servants and apprentices often lived within the employer's household. Many families either obtained young servants from villages or sent their own children as servants in the homes of others (B. Laslett 1973; P. Laslett 1971; Oakley 1974b). The homemaker trained and supervised these workers and provided the resources they needed to carry out their tasks. In all but recent times, this involved extensive production of goods, such as breads and clothing, from raw material (Andre 1982; Strasser 1978). Care of animals was often part of the role.

American history also provides many examples of complex social circles of homemakers. Demos (1973) details seventeenth-century family life in the Plymouth colony. Kessler-Harris (1981), Cowan (1983), Ehrenreich and English (1979), Hayden (1981), Rothman (1978), and numerous other social scientists have relatively recently reexamined American history in an effort to make more visible the work of women as homemakers and in informally paid activities and jobs. Studies of the contributions and problems of black and immigrant women trying to maintain households under extremely trying conditions emphasized the importance of the homemaker as the connecting link between the public and the private spheres of life. The creation of a home private sphere was especially difficult for women of color, due to the constant interference of public policies (Hurtado, 1989).

Many houses in American traditional times may have been relatively simple in terms of room specialization, as they were in Europe before privatization, but the large amount of work in and around them required the cooperation of numerous persons. Expansion in size changed human relationships, providing greater institutionalization of interaction and emotion. The household could contain the elderly, many children, unmarried relatives, servants indentured or in apprenticeships, boarders and lodgers, and the poor under guardianship (Hareven 1978b; Ryan 1979). All these people had to be provided space, fed, clothed, and cared for in illness; at the same time, they contributed their services in a complex of household work. Animals also had to be cared for. The establishment of homemaking was further complicated in America's early history by the absence of legal rights. European and American wives were legal minors, unable to own and control a dwelling until relatively recently. They remained in the home owned by the father until they married and entered the home owned by the husband, which then passed on to the son. Babcock and her associates (1975) document the consequences of such laws in *Sex Discrimination and the Law*:

> When a woman marries, she loses her domicile and acquires that of her husband, no matter where she resides or what she believes or intends. . . . As of 1974, only four states allowed married women to have separate domiciles from their husbands for all purposes; another 15 allowed women to have separate domiciles for voting, six for election to public office, five for jury service, seven for taxation and five for probate. (Pp. 575–76)

The extension of this norm, in the ritual of a new husband's carrying his bride across the threshold of "his" dwelling, has now been made obsolete by the simple fact that the couple usually shares a household even before marriage and that it is just as likely to have been hers to begin with as his.

Urbanization and industrialization, plus modern technology, contributed to changes in the roles of homemakers, the composition of their social circles, and the intertwinement of relationships of duties and rights. The expansion of the middle class and the increasing heterogeneity of the population added new dimensions to home management. The home changed its significance several times. By the turn into the twentieth century, "more than 70 percent of the population had lived in boarding houses at some time in their lives" (Lynes 1963, 51). Immigrants and young couples either could not afford, or did not want to maintain their own households. Apartment hotels proliferated. Charlotte Perkins Gilman ([1898] 1966) pushed for an American domestic revolution that would do away with private kitchens and introduce professional child care, but this never became popular. O'Neill (1969a) observes about Gilman:

What she could not have guessed in 1889 was the extraordinary affection Americans would demonstrate for the detached, self-contained, single family dwelling. (P. 45)

The Transitional Form of the Role of the Homemaker

The home that most American women have been managing throughout the transitional periods of social development is very different from that described by social historians of the traditional family era. It has been changing in terms of its place vis-à-vis the rest of the world, its composition, its relationships, and the values it represents. The role of homemaker in America has also been developing several unique characteristics, in contrast to other roles, and other times and places. Some of these are inherited from the past, others have evolved in recent times.

A transitional aspect of the role of homemaker is its indeterminate character, for there are great variations available to, and influencing, its titlebearer and the contributions made by others (Lopata 1966 and 1971b). Such a woman must, of course, command the necessary resources for even minimal involvement (such as money and other material goods, location, and the cooperation of others) and must operate within their limitations. A woman marrying a widower or divorced man who has custody of his children has less independence than one starting out with a new household. Even the former is likely to immediately introduce change or push for the establishment of a new home over which she has rights of selection and arrangement. Role making, as Turner (1978 and 1981) has termed the process of personal innovation in preexisting roles, is also more predetermined when the household has been established in the past than when a woman creates her own circle. In the latter case, the homemaker tends to be free of control by in-laws in location, although the husband's occupation usually imposes restrictions.

On the other hand, some of the influence by family members on the homemaker was replaced by that of "experts" by the end of the nineteenth century (Ehrenreich and English 1979; Rothman 1978). The "germ theory" of disease placed the responsibility for prevention upon the homemaker, requiring a completely different view of cleanliness than in the past. Doctors took over from household managers and midwives as the experts about what is good and healthy in daily life. The home became the haven for those who had to leave it to earn income or learn in school how to live within the modernizing world. The same trends that made the wife a personal dependent of the husband in transitional times also made the homemaker basically limited to meeting the needs of a husband and children. She is responsible in such times for making the home a virtuous, clean, healthy, safe, secure, and hospitable place for all beneficiaries.

An important characteristic of the homemaker role in transitional times has been the ideologically acclaimed, but usually unfulfilled, potential flexibility of the social circle. Beneficiaries can become assistants, under certain circumstances, by demand or negotiation. For example, all members of the household can join together, sharing in preparations for the entertainment of visitors. Or the homemaker may try to negotiate with circle members to have them give up some previously established rights of beneficiaries in order to help her manage the household on a permanent basis. The expansion of women's role clusters, and thus attempts to change the role of homemaker, is one of the major sources of conflict within families and other residential units. Homemakers experiencing role conflict are increasingly demanding that beneficiaries become at least partial assistants, although they do not go as far as Oakley (1974a) in her recommendation that the role be entirely obliterated through a division of responsibility, with the work added to other roles of residents. The dramatic popularity of Hochschild's *The Second Shift* (1989), which illustrates the failure of this attempt to turn husbands from beneficiaries into assistants or role sharers, indicates the reality of this problem. The same can be said about the conflict homemakers are having with children when they attempt to change these beneficiaries into assistants (Wittner 1980).

The modern household with shared homemaking is not here in great numbers (see also J. Pleck 1983)! Observers such as Bird (1979), Matthews (1987), and Hochschild (1989) stress the importance of early and explicit negotiation with future adult circle members, and socialization of children into their expected contributions. One of the problems is that arrangements for duties or rights made at any one stage of the role course may not be satisfactory later on and may have to be renegotiated again and again.

One unusual feature of the role of homemaker in this transitional society has been the ambivalence felt toward it by so many social persons, so that even women who claim to hate many aspects of it and who feel anger at the lack of cooperation from circle members often do not want to part with all the responsibility or identification with the role (Ferree 1987; Hertz 1986; Yogev 1981). The same can be said for circle members.

Stereotypes

One of the first things that impressed observers of the American scene for years is the stereotypical and negatively valued image of the housewife/homemaker (see, for example, de Tocqueville as quoted in Dulles 1965).[1] The devaluation of housewifery or home-making activity was actually the reason for my original study of American women that forms one of the bases for this volume. Several factors may have contributed to this situation. Within the last couple of centuries, social development dramatically expanded the public sphere of life located outside the home. The major part of productive work shifted from home-based territory to that public sphere, allegedly leaving only second-stage production to the home (Dulles 1965). The husband was removed as its co-manager, com-mitting most of his time and energy to outside activity. The develop-ment of complex structures to meet the expanding needs for formal education into cultures beyond that shared by the family, as well as the development of organized religion, mass communication, and recreation, led many observers to also devalue the home's contribu-tion to these institutions. The home was deprived of its location as a center of important societal events, serving instead as a place to which adults escaped from, or prepared for, the harsh, competitive outside world.

The household also shrank in complexity as unmarried older relatives, servants, and apprentices moved out (Coser 1973; Laslett 1978; Vanek 1978). For some reason, the size of the unit is associated with the importance assigned to it by many observers, who ignore the extensions of the role beyond its borders. Ignored also are the new values and technologies, such as environmentalism and con-sumerism, which have introduced new dimensions into the home-maker role but have not been given sufficient value to offset the loss of older tasks and relations. Observers repeatedly express surprise over the amount of time required to maintain a home, assuming that much of the activity is nothing but meaningless busywork.

The American view of the home as a simple and societally

unproductive unit has also contributed to the view of the homemaker either as a simple person engaged in repetitive and noncreative work or as completely alienated. The "domestication" of women, that is, their identification with, and limitation to, a circumscribed and privatized home, now being experienced in developing countries, has been influenced by Western ideologies (Glazer 1978; Matthews 1987; Rogers 1980).

The downgrading of the home and of the homemaker can be accounted for even more explicitly by changes in the American value system that accompanied the Protestant ethic (Weber [1904] 1958) and were reinforced by neo-Marxists' focus on the market value of work. The argument over whether domestic labor is productive or unproductive, only for private use or for exchange value, occupied major thinkers of the midtwentieth century to the extent that other systems of evaluating human activity were neglected. From the capitalist point of view, unpaid work is not of societal importance; from the point of view of the working class, unpaid work also provides no subsistence and is devalued. The early debates over use and exchange value have now been superseded by the growing recognition of the importance of unpaid work to societal welfare. The feeling that unpaid workers are inevitably being exploited remains and will undoubtedly continue until values other than market price gain importance.

The feminist movement of the 1960s and 1970s, influenced by Marxism, initially reinforced this negative stereotype of the role of homemaker, to the extent that Oakley 1974a) advocated its total elimination, as mentioned above. Ferree (1980, 110) calls the blame placed on feminism for contributing to the denigration of housewives "blaming the messenger for the message." It certainly constricted the value placed on all nonmarketable cultural products and social activity. Even Friedan (1963) bought into that value system when she recommended that women work only for money—for instance, painting not for pleasure but only to sell the product.[2] The attempt to find the "monetary value of housework" falls into that economic sphere (see Walker and Gauger 1973 and the extensive discussions in Glazer 1984). Fromm (1947) described Americans as obsessed by the "marketing mentality," which judges a person's worth by how much he or she is worth in the market. The application of criteria of the economic institution, such as task efficiency, to other institutional areas of life inevitably downgrades the relational aspects of social roles (see also Brown 1982). A perfect example of this is contained in the otherwise excellent analysis of household work by Carmi Schooler and his associates (Schooler et al., "Housework as Work," 1984 and Schooler et al., "Work for the Household," 1984). Both discussions of substantive complexity in the role of homemaker focus on things, ignoring the complexity of dealing with people. This they do systematically for low-status jobs, although they focus on complexity in dealing with people, rather than things, when describing higher status jobs.

Matthews (1987) explains the devaluation of the homemaker role by another set of factors associated with the home economics movement. America in the first half of the twentieth century underwent a broad social movement labeled "scientific management," fathered by industrial engineer Frederick Taylor (1911). Work patterns were examined in industry to determine more efficient uses of time and worker energy, and efficiency became the motto. Attention was then directed toward the home, with home economics as a new scientific field running parallel to, but gender-segregated from, the newly professionalizing occupations. According to Matthews (1987) and Strasser (1982), the home economics movement devalued the competence of women already performing the role of homemaker on the basis of their life experiences. It thus reinforced the placement of women in the home and the separation of men from it, then defined homemakers as inefficient in that role. In addition, it gradually redefined homemaking into a role whose main function is consumer activity (Matthews 1987, 171). Strasser (1982) judges the home economics movement even more strongly:

> With their advertising, the manufacturers joined the home economist—who welcomed them from the start—in their roles as household experts, perverting the role in the interest of selling goods. (P. 8)

Americans' negative image of the role of homemaker emerges not just from its gender identification, but also from a set of criteria that assigns high importance to activity involving those stages in the production of goods and services that are counted as part of the gross national product. Glazer (1980, 253) identifies state governments as contributing to the trivialization of housework, while Glazer and associates (1979, 162) argue that "businesses, schools, stores and others who provide services related to running a home and caring for children" assume that each home has a housewife with all the necessary time to adjust to their schedules.

The Life Course of the Role of Homemaker

Becoming a Homemaker

The social person of the homemaker needs only to manage a dwelling, to declare herself in the role, and to establish relations with at least two other persons. Unless she inherits the home, she sets one up by renting or buying space that meets the qualifications of such housing, which means in most of America that it has a roof, walls, doors, and windows, is heated and electrified, and has water and waste-disposal facilities. Such a dwelling in all but extreme poverty locations is usually divided into rooms, the basic ones being kitchen, bathroom, and bedroom. Multiple and special-function rooms of great variety can be included, each then furnished with objects judged necessary by the standards and resources of the homemaker to meet the assigned functions. Again, unless the woman inherits such objects, they must be purchased and adjusted for the use of the beneficiaries. Self-defined needs tend to change over the life cycle of the role, in response to changing needs of the beneficiaries or changing resources and wishes of the homemaker. One of the complications of the patriarchal heritage of modern America in all but the very recent past has been women's lack of sufficient economic independence to purchase or rent dwellings and fill them with the objects for modern living.

One of the trends frequently referred to by observers of population changes is the frequency with which both men and women now leave the homes of their parents (or parent) to set up independent housekeeping (Masnick and Bane 1980, 20; Sweet and Bumpass 1987, 82). In fact, demographers consider this as one of the dramatic shifts between 1960 and 1980. Cohabitation with others helps solve some of the problem of cost, as does improvement in jobs and wages. Pooling of resources occurs after the "yours or mine" dwelling decision is made. There are no strict norms as to duties and rights, beyond the minimum maintenance requirements for safety and local standards of cleanliness and appearance. The beneficiaries and assistants may refuse to allow the homemaker the rights of access and action or to accept the results of her work; they may remove themselves from the home; but there are few, if any, situations in which suppliers refuse to sell to or service a homemaker. Some unmarrieds share responsibilities and the work of management with cohabitors. However, studies of even countercultural communes and the kibbutzim movement indicate the difficulty of breaking down gender roles in household and even community life, regardless of the strength of egalitarian ideology (Gerson 1978; Zicklin 1983).

Entertaining guests and learning to shop for goods to be converted for home use and for services in and out of the housing unit are the frequent early steps of "becoming a homemaker." American women managing households without a husband or other permanent adult who can share the economic maintenance, responsibility, and work are increasing in number. There are several reasons a woman may have sole responsibility for a multiperson household: Other adult members can be incapacitated, as with elderly parents or a disabled husband or child; there may have never been a co-manager; a cohabitor may have left through desertion or entrance into a total institution (e.g. prison, armed forces, or hospital); or divorce may have split a marital pair that lived together in the past. The process of becoming a homemaker is thus also an indefinite one at present, with no precise turning point and frequent humorous commentary. Modern young women are not apt to think of themselves as homemakers unless and until marriage or motherhood. The role at first appears as a simple addition to other roles such as wife or friend, without major adjustments in the cluster. Social research indicates the inevitability of assignment of the role to women by husbands and everyone involved in helping to maintain the home or benefiting from its activities. In other words, people living in or entering the home tend to assume that the "main" adult woman is the homemaker.

There has been a very interesting change in the past thirty years in assumptions about the need for training for this role. After subject-specialized mass education became organized in America, the home economics movement insisted on teaching scientific management methods for homemaking. Courses on sewing, cooking, financial accounting, and so forth were added to schools at various levels. These were initially aimed at girls only. Students of both genders in our Wisconsin town now take courses in what is still called "home economics" and in what used to be called "shop." Home economics colleges still exist in many land-grant universities, though they are often renamed and inclusive of family study and even social work. The idea behind the nineteenth-century home economics movement, favored by Catharine Beecher and her sister, Harriet Beecher Stowe (1870), was to introduce scientific principles into home management. This aim is also evident in the numerous gender-specific mass-media publications.

The tie-in between this role and that of wife is suggested in the title of a chapter by Gates in Chapman and Gates (1977), "Homemakers into Widows and Divorcées: Can Law Provide Economic Protection?" In fact, the role used to be called "housewife," as indicated by the title of my 1971 book, *Occupation: Housewife,* and by that of Matthews's *Just a Housewife* (1987).

The 1950s and 1960s Chicago-area respondents were definitely split over whether modern homemakers were properly trained for that role, and over who was responsible for such training, the school or the home (Lopata 1971b). Over half did not consider housewives trained, and they blamed both the schools and girls' lack of interest. The higher the woman's education, the higher the family income, and the younger the children, the more the woman thought that training was necessary, and the more she used a variety of sources to obtain increased "on-the-job" learning (Lopata 1971b, 146). Employed urban women were the least likely to consider the role as something for which you need training and were the most apt to perform the role at minimal levels. Transitional dependence on official experts was apparent in their lists of useful past and current sources of knowledge. Primary relations, including with the mother and the home, were listed by mainly younger urban women as either past or current sources. The suburbanites, all of whom had children, used the older generation less frequently, turning more often to the mass media and peers for advice. These were the post–World War II mothers of the baby-boom generation who used the dramatic explosion of advice to homemakers in the media to revolutionize home life. They broke away from parental and urban patterns to create new variations on old roles in a new suburban environment (Gans 1967; Lopata 1971b).

Women who were asked similar questions in 1990 were much less concerned with the adequacy of their prior preparation or on-the-job training, which is not surprising in view of the cultural shift away from such total commitment (Lopata 1993c). They did not perceive as large a gap between pre- and post-homemaking involvement in that role as did the respondents of the feminine-mystique period.

The Expanding Circle

The next stage of the role of homemaker is that of the "expanding circle," when others, usually a husband and definitely children, are added. It usually takes full-time involvement with a small child before the woman sees herself, voluntarily or in consequence of the push by others and circumstances, as the "natural" center of the role and really incorporates it into the role cluster. Of course, some women, usually the younger ones of modern times, never really shift their identities in that direction, while others, usually the older, less educated ones, focus upon it. Some new homemakers find themselves overcome by the unaccustomed features and scope of the work at this stage, responding to constant demands in never-ending sequences (Lopata 1969b; Strasser 1982). The work is very different from any they experienced in the past. Traditional and even modern resources for easing the burden of tasks do not necessarily help to decrease worry and tension about doing things well. Social isolation can be bothersome when children are small, the climate harsh, and other adults absent most of the day (Andersen 1983).

Another problem of this stage of role involvement is the change demanded of everyone, of the social person and circle members, during the early stages of the creation and expansion of the circle. Skills and knowledge learned prior to entrance or early on the job can become useless, or even dysfunctional, as the circle of beneficiaries expands. Having learned to prepare an elaborate meal requiring hours of time does not help a homemaker with tiny babies to feed. Thus, competence gained at one stage does not automatically transfer to another stage.

The Peak Stage

The work and relationships of the peak stage are influenced by a combination of factors:

1. The number and ages of the beneficiaries: children, adult cohabitors, and anyone else (such as guests).
2. Their special needs.
3. The kinds of duties undertaken by the homemaker in relation to these beneficiaries because of societal, circle, or self-imposed demands.

4. The size and complexity of the home that must be maintained.

5. The number of items that must be maintained and the activities required to keep them in good condition.

6. The number of assistants and the type of help they provide, plus the duties directed toward them.

7. The number and variety of "labor-saving" devices or conveniences (e.g., prepared foods) designed to decrease the effort or time required to perform any of the tasks, in terms of not just time but also energy (Hartmann 1981; Schooler et al., "Housework as Work," 1984; Schooler et al., "Work for the Household," 1984).

8. The number and variety of new homemaking activities requiring organizational and activity time, especially in conjunction with the roles of wife and mother.

9. The location of the household and each task in relation to the assisting segment and to useful objects, plus the versatility of these services as sources of shifting duties and activities.

10. Competition from other roles in the homemaker's cluster and the social psychological aspects of her involvement (Lopata 1966, modified).

This stage is still very demanding and often harried, especially because it contains beneficiaries with highly divergent needs, and thus a multiplicity of assistants and suppliers. Women who lack financial resources, are unwilling to pull together such circle members, or have uncooperative beneficiaries (who are unwilling to also to be assistants) can find this stage especially stressful.

The Full-House Plateau

The full-house plateau occurs when the household is not apt to have new beneficiaries added to it. The social circle can expand, however, with the addition of new suppliers of goods and services to the home, or outside of it, and new associates of the main beneficiaries who enter the home. At the same time, the young members of the household gain in the ability to take care of many of their needs, decreasing the direct work, but not supervision, by the homemaker. At this stage the full-time homemaker is likely to find the job complex, but satisfying to the extent that she has mastered the tasks, negotiated satisfactory relationships, and added flexibility to the role (Schooler et al., "Housework as Work," 1984; Schooler et al., "Work for the Household," 1984). This is similar to being in the stage of a job when one's expertise is high.

The Shrinking Circle

The "shrinking circle" stage usually begins when the children start leaving and ends when the woman is left alone. Relationships are modified by the exit of circle members; assistants and suppliers are dropped or withdraw. For example, the decrease of a husband's involvement in his job may decrease the need for entertainment or special clothes preparation, while increasing work created by his constant presence (Szinovacz 1989). Children who were both beneficiaries and assistants withdraw from both segments of the social circle. On the other hand, changes in the role involvements of the homemaker may ease her role conflicts, as when she retires. The shrinking of the circle may result in the woman's neglecting her own self-care. For instance, cooking is something women feel they do for others, not for themselves, so many a widow creates health problems for herself by not getting good nutrition (Lopata 1973c, 1979). Her incentive to keep the house, and even herself, clean and with a pleasant appearance may disappear with the shrinking of the circle of beneficiaries.

Of course, any of these stages can be interrupted, or reversed, especially in our modern, mobile society and long-lasting life courses. Divorce can decrease the circle, remarriage can increase it. Widowhood can occur before the children leave home. Children who moved out in gestures of independence can return, often bringing with them spouses and children, turning the role back into that of the peak stage. Aging or widowed parents no longer can demand of adult offspring that they return to the ancestral home as in patriarchal times, but occasionally they have to move in with daughters, or sons, and their families. Realtors in several Chicago communities report that house owners are adding not only "granny" but also "children's families" units. The expense and shortage of adequate housing brings Americans back to household sharing, whether they prefer such arrangements or not, reactivating the role of homemaker.

The life course of the role of homemaker is affected by social class, the uses made of the house by all the beneficiaries, including the homemaker, and the life courses of the roles of circle members. One of the interesting consequences of the indeterminate nature of this particular role is that it expands in conjunction with some roles, such as that of mother, but contracts with others, such as that of employee. The stages of occupational involvement by the husband, of school involvement by the children, of dying by a circle member, and so forth, all impinge on the duties and rights of the homemaker. Her rights over the home and how it is used also vary by a number of other factors, such as her relationship to the official head of the household and inheritance rights following his or her death.

The Part-Time Homemaker

Much discussion in recent decades has focused on whether women have simply added a "second shift" (Hochschild 1989) to their lives, retaining a full-time involvement in homemaking while adding on a full-time job, or whether they have cut homemaking down to a part-time occupation with the help of cohabitors or with the decrease in household complexity. Numerous studies record a definite failure by women to cut down the role of homemaker to a part-time, shared commitment (see Aldous 1982; Berk 1985; Ferree 1980; Hochschild 1989; Model 1982). The person expected to share household responsibility and work is generally the husband, and husbands do not appear to change their ways even when the wife goes into full-time employment. Working-class men allegedly "help" more, while middle-class men give more lip service to sharing the work of home maintenance. Model (1982) and J. Pleck (1983), among others who have concentrated on the amount and type of household work undertaken by the husband, usually find a continued gender-segregation of tasks and a lack of feeling of responsibility for the solution of mutual problems by the husband. This means that the major responsibility for the household remains with the woman, who must assign, or negotiate for "help" with, the work much as in the past, although there appears to be more of that help in the present.

Homemaking and Household Composition

Another way of looking at the role of homemaker is in terms of household composition (see also Hartmann 1981, 383). The full-time homemakers of the study of middle-aged women (ages twenty-five to fifty-four) of the late 1970s were organized in the analysis into four major groups, with two subgroups, by complexity of the household (Lopata, Barnewolt, and Harrison 1985; Lopata, Barnewolt, and Miller 1987). The managers of households containing only adults (husband, adult children, or both) had the most ambivalent feelings about that role. They did not see homemaking as a complex job and perceived more advantages to full-time employment and less to full-time homemaking than did any other homemakers (Lopata, Barnewolt, and Harrison 1987, 227). Two-thirds would prefer full-time jobs, but various circumstances prevent them from having one, and they have not actively sought employment of recent years. Those who are the most committed to the role of homemaker, rather than having just drifted into it, are the women in this category who had children at an early age or those in the early stage of becoming a homemaker who plan on adding children to the household in the near future.

Closest to the adults-only households are the single-parent households, whose managers would really like to get a job, especially if they are on public aid, but who do not have the resources to do so. Some of these women are widows, but the majority either never were, or are no longer, married. They lack the education, skills, day care, health care, and sufficient money to create a positive presentation of self to prospective employers, or even to enter a job search (Hartmann 1981). We had originally thought that these women have the most complex job as homemakers, since they lack the assistance of a husband/father. However, analyses of various aspects of their role indicate that a husband added to, rather than ameliorated, the burden of household management (see also Stack 1975). Homemakers in single-parent households were able to set their own work schedules and duties, not needing to build these around a man's presence (Lopata, Barnewolt, and Harrison 1987, 231). Their overall self-esteem is low, with little in their past to provide positive feedback. Most come from disadvantaged families. They are not especially happy over full-time homemaking and in general lack strong commitments to any role except that of mother.

Managers of households with small nuclear families (husband, wife, and one or two pre-adult children) tend to be white, to be the most educated, and to have had in the past the highest occupation of all the homemakers in our sample. Their family income is relatively low, mainly because the breadwinner is still young (Lopata, Barnewolt, and Harrison 1987, 235). Unlike the blue-collar women studied by Rosen (1987), they chose to give up the earnings of a job, feeling they could manage financially and that it was more important to stay home with the small children. They see the role of home-maker as above average in complexity and see few advantages to full-time employment. They often explain that involvement in full-time homemaking is temporary, since they plan to return to the labor force in the future. Thus, their relatively high commitment to the role of homemaker is based on their commitment to the role of mother. They rate themselves higher on the items combined into the self-esteem scale than do the other homemakers.

Managers of large nuclear households with a husband and more than two children are not in numbers as overwhelmingly white as those with fewer children. They do not see the role as complex, although they rank it high in opportunity for creativity, the chance to see the product of the work, and time for self-development. Thus, they have reached the full-house plateau level and mastered the tasks of homemaking. The younger the woman, the more commit-ted she is to this role. There is a negative association between this commitment and self-esteem along the leadership dimension.

Sociopsychological Aspects of Role Involvement

The women at even the height of involvement in the role of home-maker do not necessarily assign it equal importance in the role cluster; many situations contribute to its placement. For one, the role has shifted in salience in American society over the centuries, with the movement into, and then away from, the ideology of "true womanhood" (Cott 1977). The importance women assigned this role, even during the 1950s at the height of the feminine mystique era, reflected strong variations. Only a third of the Chicago-area women who were both homemakers and employees in my initial studies even mentioned it when asked in open-ended questions which roles were important to them (Lopata 1971b, 48). On the other hand, almost two-thirds of suburbanites referred to it—but then they were at the peak stage of the life cycle of that role and of the suburban revolution of the American dream of home ownership. However, when forced to make a choice among twelve social roles most often involving women, the Chicago-area respondents were able to separate wife and mother from homemaker and differed by social class in the rank assigned the last-named role (Lopata 1971b, 57). Some were home-focused, and product- rather than person-oriented. They wanted the home to look perfect by their standards, and were irritated by constant disruptions by other residents and their guests (Lopata 1971b, 60).

By the late 1970s, the home-oriented woman had pretty much vanished. The study of metropolitan Chicago women aged twenty-five to fifty-four included again a list of twelve roles, of which only the four most important were elicited (Lopata and Barnewolt 1984). Employees who were not married or had no children ignored the role of homemaker almost entirely (1 percent of 1,833 respondents listed it). In addition, only a tenth of the wives and mothers who did not hold a job outside of the home placed homemaker in one of the top ranks, while 9 percent of husbandless mothers did so (see also Luxton's 1980 study of three generations of homemakers).

In general, women who ranked homemaker as third or fourth in importance tended to have rich family-dimension involvements, which is not surprising. Those with many salient roles outside of the home were less oriented toward its management.

There are, of course, important social class variations in a woman's sociopsychological involvements in the role of homemaker. Lower-class women are often overcome by the never-ending round of work involved in maintaining a home and a family, without adequate resources, and with additional complications such as the unemployment or absence of a husband (Luxton 1980; Milkman 1979; Rubin 1976). Both socialization and structural limitations of the environment tend to produce a passive stance (Kohn 1977; Schooler et al. "Housework as Work," 1984), or lead such women to seek out solutions that make them appear passive to associates (Wittner 1990; Milkman 1979).

The *Occupation: Housewife* (Lopata 1971b) working-class respondents tended to perform the role repetitiously and reactively. When asked to explain the rhythm of their work, the least educated and poorest Chicago-area respondents described a continuous round, reflecting the old adage that a woman's work is never done (Strasser 1982). Middle-class women asked for qualifiers of time of year, week, family schedule, and the like. The upper-class homemakers studied by Ostrander (1985) and Daniels (1988) used the home as the showplace for their class position, in terms of its appearance and the complexity of activities carried forth in it or from it. A perfect example of the class influence on homemaking is contained in etiquette books for wives of military or colonial officers and protocol rules for wives of political heads. The hostess obligations of the American ambassador's wife, including especially those for official dinners, can be extremely complex. She must not only arrange for the dinner and what is to be served, but also train the servants so as to avoid all awkward situations, select the seating arrangement according to norms of protocol, and insure that conversations flow to involve everyone (Hochschild 1969).

> Since the ambassador's wife is much of the time either a hostess or a guest, and since much of her important work is performed in those roles, she finds that often she is stationary, either on her "turf" or on someone else's. There is not much time for walking around in public. Rather, in private places she is in public. (Hochschild 1969, 84)

There are two other aspects of involvement in the role of home-maker that have drawn increasing attention from social scientists: the sentiments felt about various features of the role, and the self-images of women involved in it at different levels.

Sentiments and Self-Images

As Shehan, Burg, and Rexroat point out (1986; see also Shehan 1984), "studies comparing the mental health and well-being of employed wives and housewives proliferated during the 1970s" in response to the increased participation of American women in the labor force. Most of these studies concluded that "employed wives have better psychological health than housewives." The frequency of depression among housewives is associated with the stage of the family life cycle and the number and ages of children. The larger the number of beneficiaries, and the more needful they are of her care, the more depressed the homemaker is apt to be when she does not have the necessary resources (Pearlin 1975). This is not surprising, from the vantage point of role strain theory. The woman in the rapidly expanding and full-house stages of homemaking can feel overwhelmed, especially since the roles of wife and mother require more than just the work of those roles. The early stages of home-making include being tied down in the home, thus creating social isolation, which easily leads to depression (Shehan, Burg, and Rexroat 1986, 406).

An important aspect of a woman's satisfaction with this role, as with any other, is the fit between her expectations and reality (Ferree 1976 and 1980). Those women who purposely enter this role, vol-untarily expand the beneficiary segment of the social circle, and feel that the assisting segment is meeting its obligations, tend to be satisfied with it; those who are disillusioned with major features of it are likely to feel depressed or angry (Lopata, Barnewolt, and Miller 1985; Warren 1987). The assumption that modern American home- makers are not satisfied is often connected by the media with the assumption that those who are involved in it full-time envy employed women and see their lives as being more glamorous and less con- fining than their own. Thus, satisfaction can be expected of home- makers when the society reinforces their decision to enter and remain in this role full-time, and dissatisfaction when it publicly rewards employed women.

One frequently sees mass-media stories about the defensive stance of women who are not in the labor force, unlike the 1950s and 1960s, when full-time homemaking was the preferred form of involvement. I had found the *Occupation: Housewife* (Lopata 1971b) respondents generally satisfied with this role, their level of satisfac- tion increasing with an increase in personal resources, such as education, and with instrumental resources, such as money. Friedan argued, however, in *The Feminine Mystique* (1963) this satisfaction may have been only a polite veneer, underneath which lay serious concern over "the problem that has no name"—that is, the feeling of confinement and lack of personal identity and development. The late 1970s homemakers in the *City Women* study felt much less confined by that role, unless they lacked the self-confidence to function outside of it. At the two extremes for full-time homemakers, thus, are the younger, modern women who choose that full-time involvement and those who feel trapped in it, wishing for alterna- tives but unable to go through the barriers they feel are surrounding them. In between are the homemakers who do not feel strongly enough to make in-or-out decisions, or who do not define the situation in such terms, moving more or less freely between various levels of involvement.

Ann Oakley's (1947b, 192) study of London housewives in the peak stage of that role also found many women dissatisfied with the work involved. They complained of monotony, a long working week, and loneliness, though they were pleased with their auton- omy. Women with a history of high-status jobs were the most dissatis- fied, as the various tasks connected with the role did not produce the same level of satisfaction as their former jobs had. Cooking and shopping were among the most liked activities, a sentiment found also among American homemakers (Lopata, Barnewolt and Miller

1985). Schooler and associates (Schooler et al., "Housework as Work," 1984; Schooler et al., "Work for the Household," 1984) found one of the distressing aspects about the role of homemaker to be "responsibility over things outside one's control." The fact that the role itself is not necessarily depressing—definable as only repetitious, monotonous, and demeaning—is evidenced by their conclusion that women who are ideationally flexible may choose to do substantively complex household tasks.

The literature on depression among homemakers led to the inclusion of a series of fifty-one items of areas of competence and generalized characteristics in the *City Women* interviews (Lopata, Barnewolt, and Miller 1985). In brief, we found that full-time homemakers expressed less strong, less positive identification with areas of competence connected with leadership qualities than did the employed women. The exception was among the younger and more educated women who saw themselves as only temporarily in the role of full-time homemaker and identified themselves as competent and successful. One can but speculate as to the reason other full-time homemakers do not give themselves higher competence scores. Women with high scores may be more apt to stay in or return to the labor force, or the full-time homemakers may feel that their lack of leadership qualities precludes satisfactory employment. On the other hand, we can easily conclude that the role of homemaker does not provide feedback, in looking-glass form, or self-evaluations that can lead to high self-esteem (Schooler et al., "Housework as Work," 1984a; Schooler et al., "Work for the Household," 1984; see also Rosenberg 1979).

The Homemaker and Her Home

Of great interest to symbolic interactionists are the constructions of reality within which people live, and these include the home and things within it (see also Duncan 1982, Csikszentmihalyi and Rochberg-Halton 1981). One change in the relation between the home and the homemaker since traditional times is that most young women can start out on their own, instead of living for extended periods of time in households managed by other women, such as mothers, mothers-in-law, or boarding-house managers. A household—that is, the unit living in a home—has become simplified, while the house's physical structures are more complex, with diversification of room functions among families that can afford it. For example, each child is expected to have her or his own room. However, the design of these homes has remained mainly the job of male architects, while women have been mainly able only to modify its interior or add features. Hayden (1981) predicts in *The Grand Domestic Revolution: A History of Feminist Designs for American Homes, Neighborhoods, and Cities* that this will change in the future (see also Ardener 1981).

The symbolism of "the American Dream" has traditionally contained a picture of home ownership, made possible for many after World War II by federal low-interest mortgages. The suburban respondents of the *Occupation: Housewife* study (Lopata 1971b, 178–81) felt that life was better than they had visualized as teenagers, mainly because they had not anticipated living in such nice surroundings. The home was a source of pleasure, security, and status. The working-class Levittowners were very much involved in their homes and yards, which they individuated with decorative features from the mass-production base. It was not suburbia per se that had a strong impact upon former urbanites, but home ownership:

> The single most important source of impact is undoubtedly the house, even though most of the changes it encouraged in the lives of Levittowners were intended [by the developers]. The house is both a physical structure and an owned property. . . . Modernity encouraged improved housekeeping methods and allowed a bit more space time for wives. (Gans 1967, 277)

P. Rossi (1955) speaks of the "mystery" of home ownership that pushes people in that direction, and the Polish Americans whom I studied (Lopata 1976b) worked very hard to obtain this symbol of permanence and status.

Part of reality construction is the perceived fit between the person and her surroundings. A woman is apt to dislike her home if she considers it below her as a symbol of status. She may then just bide her time until she can move to a home that is better by her standards, or try to change the one she has if such upgrading improves its fit in the neighborhood. We asked women in the 1990 exploratory study if the house they were in was their "dream home." Only about a tenth of the respondents replied yes; the others complained about size, location, and appearance, but explained that their present homes were all they could afford at the time. Those who were pleased had lived in other places before, and had house-

hunted for a long time, or had had the house built to their specifi-
cations. Linking the home to one stage of life does not mean that
leaving it is psychologically impossible:

> Yes! In some way it is [my dream house], but I have dreams of a bigger
> home. This is my first house, it is like my baby. I have furnished it and
> have made it our home. Everything inside the house is us, we both
> have put a lot of work into the house. (Twenty-five-year-old home-
> maker anticipating needs for more space in next stage of the role)

Another woman, however, not satisfied with her house and unable
to leave for another due to financial constraints, kept adjusting it to
meet her self-defined needs.

> It is not what I perceived to be the home I would live in this long. It
> was to be my starter home, but with each project it became more of
> our own. We have totally redecorated the interior and exterior of the
> home. We added additional rooms and made a larger expanse of
> living areas. We upgraded baths and kitchen. . . . I would like to add
> a first floor family room but this is not financially feasible. (Forty-seven
> year-old with a husband and six children living in the household)

Almost all of the home owners had changed something about their
houses, starting with redecorating and including often considerable
remodeling. Renters seldom do more than paint, feeling it to be a
waste of time and money to individuate the place, even after years
of residence.

The Homemaker as a Link between Home and Society

Looking at the homemaker from the woman's point of view, as
Smith (1987), Glazer (1978), Bernard (1974 and 1981), and other
feminists recommend, we find that she is not limited to a relatively
isolated household, which other members are free to leave in order
to enter roles in other institutions, while she waits for them to return
to her hot soup and stroking support. Those homemakers who are
committed to this role, at least temporarily, by choice rather than
because of a lack of alternatives, tend to see themselves as centers
of a complex social circle that reaches far beyond the confines of the
home (Lopata, Barnewolt, and Harrison, 1987). Even in the midst of

the feminine mystique period, women extended into the wider community in several ways. They interacted with suppliers of objects and services, they provided such to others, and they saw characteristics of life outside of the home that had their imprint. For example, they liked to dress up their children for outside events. The recent demands that their contributions be recognized by others in the public sphere have definitely been helped by the feminist movement, but the activities were there before. The importance of this work has been mainly invisible to the male world and even undervalued by the women themselves (Daniels 1988; Finch and Groves 1983; Glazer 1984 and 1988). For example, the Chicago-area women of the 1950s and 1960s studies utilized twenty-six services brought to the home and thirty-three services outside of the home (Lopata 1971b, 168–71). Over half had daily newspaper delivery, and many received local papers. Very few had a live-in maid, that service having long been gone from most American homes, although about a fourth employed a cleaning woman who came in periodically. The use of external services was complicated by the fact that women who did not have cars were limited to weekend ventures. The more affluent and more educated used a variety of services; the less privileged were more geographically limited, but they tended to go out to get supplies more often. In addition, the full-time homemakers in suburbs exchanged services and goods with neighbors. Many of the ways they served as connecting links between the home and society actually fell into the supportive functions of the roles of wife and mother. The economic and political spheres of life did little to make it easier for homemakers to function—the allegedly work-saving technology and the transportation-consumer-professional-service complex were not actually designed with them in mind (Cowan 1983; Lopata 1971b and 1980a). Although some effort is now being made by the public sphere to ease the homemaker's life, the 1950s required entrance into a tremendous variety of specialty stores, children in tow.

Homemakers frequently mention their contributions of work and products to organizations in the religious, educational, occupational, political, and combined institutions of the community. Such contributions are made by women of all social strata. Black homemakers often spend days preparing food for Sunday church affairs. Rummage sales, picnics of a variety of groups, gala events of women's auxiliaries of men's clubs, fund-raising socials for women's or school groups—all these activities are expected of homemakers in most communities. The work can take considerable time, but it also provides opportunities for interactions that continue to link the home with the outside world.

The homemakers also speak with pride of seeing the products of their work in public: their children nicely dressed for school, neighbors commenting on the festive holiday look of the home, church members congratulating them for a potluck dish (Ferree 1976 and 1980). Recent studies have documented just how dependent public life is upon the unpaid work of women who bridge not only the spheres but also the specialized and often segregated areas of each institution. Glazer (1984 and 1988) has devoted a number of years to the study of women's benefits to the economic institution and, recently, to health services (see also Weintraum and Bridges 1979). Galbraith emphasizes:

> The conversion of women into a crypto-servant class was an economic accomplishment of first importance. . . . If it were not for this service all forms of household consumption would be limited by the time required to manage such consumption—to select, transport, prepare, repair, maintain, clean, service, store, protect, and otherwise perform the tasks that are associated with the consumption of goods. (Galbraith 1973, 79; Lopata 1984, 162).

Socialist feminists of the 1970s repeatedly listed the contributions to capitalist economy made by the consumer, who is very often the woman (see Gerstel and Gross 1987b; Hensen and Philipson 1990). Pictures and news stories have documented the fact that the former Communist/socialist countries depended on (mainly) women to stand for hours in line waiting for household goods, such as meats, breads, and even toilet paper. Even buying services can take time (Weintraum and Bridges 1979). Involvement in consumption, health care, education, and religion requires efforts by the homemaker, in addition to persons who directly work in these institutions. Certainly many organizations have recently cut back on personal services to members of the society. The buyer economy supplied milk, vegetables, bread, and knife sharpening directly to the consumer. The rising costs of labor shrank the personal delivery system.

It is interesting to note that some of these changes have followed a circular path. First, the consumer, student, or patient was in the power of experts whose esoteric knowledge was accompanied by a license and a mandate to determine their fate (Haug and Sussman 1968; Hughes 1971; Lopata 1976a). Next, rather than depending upon the vendor, such as a store owner or delivery employee, to provide the "best products for the lowest price," the consumer in the homemaking role, with sufficient education and coached by experts in the media, became an expert and a comparative purchaser herself. Much of what has been written about the woman as consumer in the "consumption society" and the role of homemaker ignores the complexity of this activity, which requires a great deal of time and knowledge to define the needs of families and other beneficiaries, to study alternative means of satisfying them, to locate products and services, to obtain these, to bring them home, to convert them for personal use, and to store them (Berk and Berk 1979; Glazer 1984).

In the field of health, women are expected to ensure the prevention of illness in family members and others whom they are helping to care for, as well as nurse them during illness and the dying process. This includes medicines and other items, actual physical care, presence at times of need, transportation to health facilities, and the following of experts' prescriptions (Glazer 1988). Attempts to cut back on expenses by medical personnel have resulted in recent increases in demands upon women. They must perform extended duties as caregivers, reversing the trend of the past century or so during which the medical profession and allied fields increased control over, and care of, the health of the nation. Of course, the private sector never really stopped caring for the sick, but it had decreasing control over decisions. The control has remained with the medical profession, having been taken out of the hands of pregnant women, mothers, wives, daughters, friends, and neighbors, but an increasing amount of the work has returned into the laps of homemakers.

Time shortages for women who handle demanding jobs and manage households are evident in some of the new services that have sprung up in urban centers. Homemakers expand their social circles to include providers of fully cooked meals and clothing, carpeting, furniture, and other objects delivered to their homes (Bergman 1986). They can shop for goods using the television. We can expect this trend to expand in the future as more and more women earn sufficient money to consider it worthwhile to pay others sometimes sizable amounts of money to undertake tasks.[3]

The Modern Form of the Role of Homemaker

Two recent changes may be contributing to an increase in the status of homemakers in modern times: One is the new recognition of the contributions they make to the functioning of society; the other is the realization of how complex and necessary their work is, even when it is compressed into "the second shift" (Hochschild 1989). Feminist social scientists have begun to reexamine the dependence of capitalist (and socialist) societies upon the activities and relationships of the homemaker (Daniels 1988; Glazer 1984; Glazer et al. 1979; Seccombe 1974). They join Galbraith (1973) in pointing to the importance of the work the homemakers do as "crypto-servants" or "servants" to capitalism— work that was previously or alternatively carried forth by paid workers (Eisenstein 1979; Glazer 1980). Various economists and related scholars have attempted to estimate the monetary value of the work involved in the role. Although such estimates diminish nonmonetary activity, they establish its importance in American eyes (Glazer 1978; Pyun 1972). The largely unsuccessful attempts, by the homemaker who also carries a paid job, to change the role and to increase the contributions of others to the maintenance of the home have also drawn attention to the role's complexity.

The difficulties experienced by social scientists trying to place the homemaker role in the occupational status structure have also drawn attention to the great heterogeneity of the ways it is carried forth (Bose 1980; Nilson 1978). The transitional evaluation of the status of the homemaker as dependent upon the status of the husband ignores her role involvements. Yet there has been a connection, at least in the transitional two-person-single-career past, between the complexity of the role of homemaker and the husband's occupation.

The modern homemaker has attempted to carry out this role with great flexibility, and her negotiations for cooperation from circle members have varied with her needs. These needs are adjusted to her other roles as well as those of circle members. Thus, she may become a full-time homemaker when involved full-time in the role of mother, shifting into part-time involvement as she returns to greater participation in outside roles, converting beneficiaries into joint managers and increasing contributions of suppliers.

Of course, the expanding cost of housing in modern America makes it more difficult for women to identify the role of homemaker with the ownership of a home that is her own and that she can modify to fit her needs. This may combine with other changes, such as an increased focus on external roles, to further decrease the importance of this role.

Summary

We have now examined the complexities inherent in the role of homemaker in transitional and modern American society. The role is entered into by the woman when she becomes a manager of a household and pulls together a social circle of beneficiaries, assistants, and suppliers. It is a very indeterminate role; it has no defined boundaries or standards of performance, although extremes are commented upon by participants and observers. Women do not generally prepare for this role. They pick up some knowledge from observation and by helping in the home of their families of orientation, and they count on their ability to learn on the job. Numerous experts are available, mainly in the mass media, to guide them in becoming homemakers and through the various stages. The household of modern times contains relatively few live-in beneficiaries. New products, services, and technologies may introduce greater variation in performance than was previously true of homemakers of different social classes.

Women also vary considerably as to the social psychological aspects of their involvement in the role of homemaker. Those with a rich family dimension in their social life space tend to regard it as more important than do those with a fuller involvement in other or multiple dimensions. Many aspects of the role are not sources of satisfaction, although seeing the product of the labor can be. The negotiation that is a constant part of this, as of any role, can be a source of pleasure or a constant irritant. A major problem on the current scene is the attempt by many women to change relationships with beneficiaries, getting them to move closer to the assistants' segment of the social circle. These beneficiaries tend to resist, expecting the wife/mother/homemaker to carry forth the duties of the role as performed during the feminine mystique days by their mothers and grandmothers.

The work of the homemaker extends beyond the home and the family, as people benefit from her services and the products she has created. It extends to life in other institutions. Although the role has faced many periods of being downgraded in importance, it seems to have survived and may be increasing in public opinion as the difficulties of managing a home and the invisible work of homemakers become more apparent.

The increasing refusal of women to carry all the burden of the duties of the homemaker role, with few rights, while also contributing to the breadwinning activity that makes possible the operation of the home, family, and community, will certainly introduce more modern variations of the role. The fact is that most women are not in highly demanding stages of the role course and that the number and needs of beneficiaries have decreased. For many women, this role can be a part-time involvement. The conflicts and concern expressed in the mass media really focus upon the woman who is combining full-time homemaking with the peak stages of the roles of wife, mother, and jobholder. This covers a relatively short period of time for most modern women. Those with limited resources are still having a hard time managing complex households. Those above the level of poverty or restricted assistance are finding greater expansion of the role into societal life, forming a link between the home and the beneficiaries, on the one side, and resources, on the other side.

6

The Job: Settings and Circles

Much work in modern societies has been organized into jobs, with specified qualifications, as well as duties and rights, for the social person and the members of the social circle. The universal characteristics of jobs include these: The worker is hired by an employing organization (or is self-employed) because she or he meets the desired criteria to perform specific tasks and relational duties in a usually predesignated social circle, and the worker is paid for job-related work and can be fired if she or he does not satisfy the requirements (or the worker can leave voluntarily). All jobs have specified locations or settings, whether within a limited space (e.g., behind a counter) or scattered (e.g., among offices of clients and any combination of locales in between). Whatever formal duties and rights tie the social person and circle members together in the role, no work organization can function without a complex informal system of interaction involving the cooperation of all.

We must also remember that not all work is organized into jobs, so that it is necessary to examine carefully not only what a person is doing at any time, but also her social relations, to determine if the interaction is part of a job or part of another type of social role. For example, much of the work done by wives or mothers, volunteers or homemakers, could be restructured into paying jobs, but the social relationships would be different. For instance, some of the actions of a wife are similar to those of a call girl. The logic of this separation is lost on people who speak of a mother's "going to work," when they mean that she has taken a job, as if the role of mother did not involve work.

Jobs contain not only tasks, which are evaluated by the U.S. Department of Labor by degree of complexity, but also sets of relations, since they are true social roles (see Kohn and Schooler 1983 and related papers).[1] The tendency to see only visible tasks, or technical job descriptions, especially in less prestigeful occupations, contributes to much of the simplistic evaluation of so many jobs. A perfect example of this is the role of cocktail waitress (Spradley and Mann 1975) in a male-dominated bar, who must negotiate and play games with customers and bartenders in order to accomplish the simple tasks of transmitting orders for drinks and delivering the drinks (see Harragan 1977, *Games Mother Never Taught You: Corporate Gamesmanship for Women,* for games at another occupational level). The Department of Labor's (1977) classification scheme determines whether the major focus of a job is work with data, people, or things and then evaluates the complexity with which these are manipulated. It has been the consistent thesis of this book that all jobs, like all social roles, involve at least some complexity of dealing with people, some negotiated interaction with circle members, which is often not recognized by the Department of Labor.

Since we cannot meaningfully examine many occupations in a book devoted to a variety of women's roles, we will concentrate on two main sets of characteristics of jobs that have a major influence upon women's relations. The first of these focuses on the role aspects (social person, circle, duties, and rights) of all employees. The second is the influence of the setting upon such relations (see also Pavalko 1988). Of course, locales also vary by many other factors, but what appears especially significant is the "ownership" of that locale, be it a bench, truck, office, or whole factory within which the role must be negotiated. Control over the space within which the job is carried forth provides at least some control over the rights and duties of the workers. Other characteristics of the setting, such as its "jointness" and boundaries, accessibility, and distribution of circle members, are important. All these factors influence the amount of control an employer, associate, or beneficiary has over the worker's independence and autonomy, the ease of working with others and of obtaining resources, access from outsiders, and rights. Let us first examine the role of employee in general, then focus on jobs in different settings.

The Entrepreneurial or Self-Employed Woman

One of the ideals of the American business community has been independent ownership. Whether offering a product or a service, the self-employed businesswoman organizes her own job with more or less freedom, pulling together a social circle, defining rights and duties. Constraints, of course, abound even for the self-employed, coming from the technical or relational aspects of the job (see the chapters in Lopata 1990). Governments at all levels promulgate laws and demand payment in the form of taxes. Beneficiaries, assistants, and suppliers must constantly be negotiated with, and the amount of control each segment has over the job varies considerably. The most autonomous is the individual professional, such as a psychiatrist, who operates from her own home or office.[2] Beneficiaries come to her because they need the service, acknowledge her superior control of esoteric knowledge, and grant her many rights, including a right to high payment. Other beneficiaries can have greater control, as do restaurants contracting for certain homemade meals, or women seeking the service of a beautician. Colleagues and coworkers make their own demands, such as conformity to a code of ethics, while employees must be supplied resources and paid.

Enterprising women (Bird 1976) have always managed to create their own businesses. Wives of whalers or traders who were gone for extended periods developed businesses of their own throughout American history. Widows often organized services or served as middle persons between producers and consumers (Christensen 1987b). There has been a recent regeneration of such activity, as more educated women, caught between their interest in economic independence and the rigidity of the occupational system, have organized their own businesses, with greater choice of activity, social circle, time, and space. A report that a high proportion of women with Harvard MBAs had dropped out of the corporate world within a few years led to studies of where they had gone—and the answer was not to full-time homemaking, but to companies they formed themselves (Kleiman 1986, 10). The Small Business Administration estimates that "the number of self-employed women in the United States grew 74 percent between 1974 and 1984" (Kleiman 1986, 10).

Many entrepreneurs start out working from the home or a small rented or privately owned shop or office. Beauticians and solo professionals like physicians, psychologists, lawyers, architects, artists, social workers, and music or other specialized teachers provide services. Others create objects to be sold within the home or to external businesses. Typical of modern times are catering, baking, or gourmet cooking establishments providing foodstuffs to private households or restaurants (see also Foerstner 1987). Shops specializing in antiques or other objects are often located in homes or communities of similar businesses. The beneficiaries might either come to the home for the service or goods or deal with an intermediary and never even interact with the producer. Suppliers also come to the businesswoman, or she goes out to fetch them herself (Christensen 1987c). Assistants can be hired from the outside, or household members can be used, with varying degrees of formality in the relationship.

As in the case of home-based employees, entrepreneurs working out of the home face problems if this is also the major setting for other roles. Boundaries between the job and those roles are not easily maintained (Christensen 1988a and 1988d). Frustration and anger are common among people who try working on nonhousehold (or even household) tasks in a home containing other people with whom other roles are shared, as any writer, artist, or academic will testify. Role conflict experienced by women in such circumstances is even greater than that of men, since the former are expected to take care of all home-related matters first, with no one to protect them from impingement by family roles (Beach 1989; Christensen 1988d). Women are expected to organize space, time, and their own behavior around a home-based husband, but the same rights do not seem to be guaranteed to the home-based woman worker who is also a wife, mother, daughter, neighbor, friend, community activist, and so forth.

Some businesses that start out on a home base grow sufficiently large or complex to require separate space, an office or a factory. A special variety are family-owned businesses headed by women. There are two ways in which a woman can own her business besides starting and building one herself: She can inherit it, usually after the death of her husband or father, or she can buy one started by others. Although Ward (1987) finds that 90 percent of American businesses are family owned, started after World War II, and with a still-living founder, almost inevitably a male, he makes no reference to women owners. A major problem of such businesses is family succession, because founders often do not train replacements and have trouble letting go of the firm, especially to a relative (Danco 1982). There are cases of widows running the business founded by their late husbands, although Danco (1982) does not consider this a good practice; he claims that few women are able to understand the complexities of a firm in its final form, even if they were originally involved in it, and even if it originated in the home. In this claim he reflects many of the attitudes of traditional businessmen. Daughters are only recently written up by the mass media as inheriting management of family businesses. Such a situation is still unusual, and there are reports of strain, even conflict, with circle members accustomed to working for the male founder. Traditional businesses do not approve of women in power (see Lopata, Miller and Barnewolt 1986 for some studies of such attitudes).

The most frequently given example of a very successful company founded and run by a woman who hired family members, including two sons, is Mary Kay Cosmetics. Acceptance by the business community is easier to get if the firm is stereotyped as appropriate for women. Some of the successful women business owners have formed a nationwide association.

Working for Someone Else: The Role of Employee

A person looking for a job and an established social circle wishing to fill a vacancy must find ways of coming together. Modern societies have developed complex methods for accomplishing this, including state and private employment agencies, interviewers who come to schools, and "headhunters" or executive search firms. These use allegedly rational methods to test and fit people to jobs and organizations. A frequent method, less costly to the employer, is that of placing advertisements in mass media with a readership likely to include potential candidates. Vacancies can also be filled by word of mouth—people already working in companies letting others know of openings. There are two problems with that method. In the first place, it limits the job seeker to people she knows, who are apt to be in traditional occupations. Since most women are still secretaries, lower-grade teachers, nurses or nurses aides, and so forth, friends and acquaintances are apt to provide information about positions of the same gender-segregated type. On the other hand, good jobs can also be learned about in this manner, as when a woman executive in a corporation brings in her friends, similar to the way the "old boy" network has always worked. Thus, the use of friends is an advantage for the job seeker at a high occupational level, while it can be a limiting factor for the job seeker at a more limited level. The other problem with using personal channels is the illegality of the word-of-mouth vacancy information system in modern times. All positions must now be advertised openly to prevent discrimination against minorities and women. Of course, the methods of matching jobs and persons are seldom as rational as alleged, and they vary considerably by occupation and employer.

Job-search procedures are influenced, of course, by a woman's knowledge of the labor market and by what kind of job she thinks she would be able to get, as well as by her wishes for certain characteristics of jobs, such as location. Socialization and education usually provide knowledge as to the kind of job she would like and the kind of organization she would like to be involved with and that is likely to accept her. Women who seek out jobs in male-dominated occupations usually have a prior connection, through relatives, friends, or co-workers (see Hareven and Langenbach 1978 and Cavendish 1982 on factory jobs; Lembright and Riemer 1982 on long-distance trucking; Walshok 1981 on women in crafts; and Epstein 1983 on lawyers). Schools often encourage preparation for traditional female jobs, perpetuating gender segregation in spite of mass publicity about recent changes.

Of course, many a woman job seeker never considers, or is considered for, most jobs. The doubly disadvantaged are women of color in the U.S. labor force (Smith and Tienda 1988). That category usually includes black, American Indian, Hispanic, and Asian women. Although women of employment age, regardless of race, are least apt to be in the labor force when they have small children, single mothers are often pushed into jobs for economic reasons, and more of these are of minority than dominant groups. Women of color, however, still have a long way to go to reach equality in the American labor force with white women, and certainly with white men, as far as occupation and earnings are concerned (Smith and Tienda

1988, 78). The failure of many women of color to break out of minority-female occupations, enabling first horizontal and then upward mobility, is also documented for California Chicano and Mexican immigrant women by Segura (1989) and regarding the professions, for black women by Sokoloff (1988). On the other hand, an "enormous decline in their overrepresentation in female-dominated professions" was experienced by white women in the years between 1960 and 1980 (Sokoloff 1988, 47).

The hiring procedures and the hierarchy of qualifications by which the person and the job are matched vary considerably by the main location of the work. A woman hired as a receptionist in an office of high-status architects may need mainly "good looks" (often including "acceptable" skin color) and good clothing, a "friendly," poised manner, a certain quality of voice, and the gatekeeping ability to distinguish acceptable from unacceptable visitors (Stone 1962 and 1981). On the other hand, a woman hired for a telecommuting job operating from her home needs only relevant skills and physical ability to perform the tasks well and on time; her appearance is irrelevant. Allegedly a physician's appearance within norms of propriety (usually defined in upper-middle-class manner, according to Bucher and Stelling 1977), is less important than her proven ability to take care of patients and cooperate with colleagues and service suppliers. As Hughes (1971) noted a long time ago, the fact that physicians have traditionally been men may interfere with a woman's attempt to pull together a social circle (see also Lorber 1984 and Walsh 1977). The gender, racial, age, and other characteristics that an employer finds acceptable in a candidate are affected by the distribution of such among circle members: administrators, colleagues, and clients (Epstein 1988).[3] The history of hiring for different jobs is replete with selection processes that focus on who can be "trusted—i.e., persons of the same gender, race, age, and so forth as those doing the hiring—and only lawsuits or governmental action have forced change in cases of gross discrimination (Kanter 1977). America has been halfhearted in administrating antidiscrimination laws.

Sex segregation of jobs in America, and elsewhere for that matter, is definitely a phenomenon that is resisting change (Hartmann 1990). For example, Cavendish (1982) observed when working in a factory in Britain that all the women were in stationary positions on the assembly line, while men had superior positions and rights of mobility. In fact,

a week before the Equal Pay Act became law, everyone was shunted
around so all the assembly line workers would be women, and all the
supervisors and higher grades would be men, and they wouldn't have
to pay higher rates to women. (P. 78)

Epstein (1988) and Reskin and Hartmann (1986) summarize
explanations of barriers to the entrance of women into some occupations that leave them mainly in jobs and positions with inferior
levels of pay, career line, autonomy, and other rights. These include
theories that "blame the victim," explanations that women are biologically, or through socialization, unwilling and unable to take
high-commitment and skill/knowledge jobs. Freudians, who influenced American culture to a large extent, claim that "biology is
destiny" and that women are created mainly for reproduction, so
that they should not be involved in competing roles (Epstein 1983,
198; see a strong statement of this position in Deutsch 1944). Others
see women as unwilling to invest in their "human capital" or in
extensive occupational preparation. Most researchers and theoreticians, however, look to structural and historical factors in order to
understand sex discrimination and segregation in the world of paid
work. Barriers they see include those to training and entrance opportunities, employer "taste" for workers who will fit into the ongoing system and who fight "reverse discrimination," the history of a
dual economy that has relegated women to the peripheral labor
market and sex-labeled jobs that make it difficult for all involved to
imagine women in other occupations, and many other formal and
informal institutional processes.

There are many cultural beliefs about gender and work that
make choice of nontraditional jobs, or even employment in general,
difficult for American women (Reskin and Hartmann 1986). These
are based on the strongly held assumption that there are innate
psychological differences between the genders, including that women
are "too good" for politics and the "dirty, competitive" world of
business and production, and that male-female relationships are
inevitably reduced to sexual encounters. Even legal barriers to full
employment still exist, founded on the protective laws of 1974,
which are often used to justify discrimination. Some of these have
just recently been rejected by the U.S. Supreme Court. People
advantaged by the existing system simply do not want to lose
benefits. Male workers in male-dominated and male-intensive occu-

pations, whose egos are founded on a chauvinistic view of their work, do not want "inferiors," be they women or members of racial and cultural minorities, entering, for fear of losing prestige and many other benefits. Clients of organizations of "experts," such as management consultants, lawyers, or doctors, do not want social inferiors to tell them what to do; at least managers of such groups claim this to be the situation when they refuse to hire a woman or black (Kanter 1977; Lopata, Miller, and Barnewolt, 1986).

Regardless of how well a person prepares for a prospective job through education, formal job training, and anticipatory socialization, on-the-job training is always necessary. This may be provided through secondary sources, but most jobs involve direct contact with circle members who precede the person at the location. It is here that many of the discriminatory practices are employed by superiors or co-workers. Social circle members, such as supervisors or co-workers, may refuse to provide the information necessary for adequate performance of duties and receipt of rights, as numerous studies have documented (e.g., Walshok 1981 and Schroedel 1985 for manual workers; Jurik 1985 for female correction officers; Epstein 1970 and 1983 for professionals; and Kanter 1977 or Harragan 1977 for management).

The size, complexity, and composition of social circles of jobholders vary considerably, the layers of closeness often being influenced not only by location and the size of the total organization, but also by the importance of the job to the organization and by the presence of intermediaries, such as the assisting staff surrounding the social person. Beneficiaries may be so removed from the person that no direct interaction takes place, or they can be so scattered that the person is the only representative of the company to have face-to-face contact with each. The latter is the case with traveling salespersons. Beneficiaries may enter a territory within which a whole assisting staff is present and forms an interacting network, as does a patient of a doctor in a hospital.

A good indicator of how a woman can define her relationship with circle members on the job is whom she considers to be the main beneficiaries of her service (Lopata, Barnewolt, and Miller 1985). An equal proportion of *City Women* respondents selected their employing company, or the bosses' customers, and their own "customers, clients, patients, or students." Identification with people who benefit from one's work is certainly different when the benefit is seen as direct ("my client . . .") rather than indirect (as the responsibility of the employer).

Although the beneficiary of a product or service can be quite depersonalized, the reference group, consisting of people whose judgment of performance is important, is usually much more specific. This was true of the *City Women* responses, the supervisor's judgment of performance being the most frequently listed by workers directly under the control of such a member of the organization (Lopata, Barnewolt, and Miller 1985). The judgment of co-workers and customers was important in this regard to only about a tenth of the respondents. Over a quarter of the women listed their own judgment of work performance as the judgment they respected the most. These differences are really significant, and one can imagine a woman's concern over the judgment of her work by these different people. Variations by occupations are interesting. For example, teachers consider their students as their main beneficiaries, but colleagues (other teachers) as their reference group. The claim that the beneficiary does not have the right to judge the performance has been a major point in the development of professionalization. Professionals reserve that right for themselves and their peers. This illustration also reemphasizes the importance of seeing the social role as involving a social circle with interacting segments rather than with isolated parts of a role set, à la Merton (1957a and 1957b).

Regardless of who is the beneficiary of an occupational role, the salaried or wage-earning worker has a definite package of duties and rights, often controlled by a complex administration, in relations with the employer. These include being in the assigned place during the designated or agreed-upon time period. The number and timing of hours of work have been the subject of strong dispute between employer and employee, assisted by unions and, finally, by governmental decrees (Steinberg 1982). The employee must fulfill her contract concerning her work, within the confines of the resources, including other people's performing their jobs and providing the social person her rights.

The employer must not only pay for the work, but must provide necessary resources, another subject of conflict between labor and management. If a worker who sews at the factory does not bring her own equipment and material, then these must be provided. The resources allegedly include environmental features and adequately trained, cooperative assistants and other circle members of adequate number. Either safety, comfortable working conditions, and so forth must be supplied, or the worker must agree to work under the conditions that exist. Unfortunately, as the history of work for women, and in many cases for working-class men, shows, businesses and even governmental agencies have failed to supply their workers with environments that are sufficiently safe and comfortable, resulting in serious accidents, illness, and even death. Many unions have been male-dominated and ignored problems raised by their women members, and many women work in settings with no union supervision (Kessler-Harris 1982; O'Farrell 1988; Schroedel 1985; see also Armstrong 1982).

Since employers have not voluntarily given up control over conditions and benefits, as Edwards documents in *Contested Terrain: The Transformation of the Workplace in the Twentieth Century* (1979), and unions have often been too weak or unwilling to confront the system, frequently the only resource for women fighting injustice is the government. However, a vast literature documents the failure of many states to prevent exploitation of workers. Some do not wish to interfere with the business sector or pass laws they do not have the strength or desire to enforce. The competitiveness of capitalism, or the benefits derived by the power elite in any other economic system, combine to create a history of exploitation of employees. Thus, the only alternative for a worker may be to quit a dangerous job and thus be deprived of its benefits, meager as they may be. Labor turnover is often simply a form of protest by workers fed up with inadequate resources and rewards.

The social circle of an employee may, and in fact often does, contain people who are not part of the employer's organization. They can be the beneficiaries, as is true of diners served by waitresses, clients by social workers, or patients by physicians. In other cases they can be colleagues, as among university scholars and scientists who consider others in similar jobs all over the world as people with whom to share ideas. Even assistants do not need to be in the same organization, and suppliers of goods and services usually come in from the outside. A worker who is attached to a particular setting must have some means of transportation of goods to and from her, while a mobile worker must have permission to enter the territory of others. Of course, the fact that segments of the social circle can be outside the authority of the employer or the jobholder makes more complex the negotiations, unless the common denominator of money balances duties and rights.

Sociopsychological Aspects of Role Involvement

One of the problems facing employers is employee "loyalty" or commitment to the job and all its components, and/or to the organization. The extensive literature on job training, motivation, satisfaction, and so forth comes from two directions: externally from economics and the social sciences, and internally from divisions of the organization whose function it is to hire the "right person," to provide prior or on-the-job training, and to keep workers. Our *City Women* study of the changing commitments of women to work and family roles utilized a career commitment scale, which proved discriminating among the employees along predictable dimensions (Lopata 1993c). Defining commitment in terms of the "side bets" a woman makes to insure continued involvement and a minimum of role conflict, à la Becker (1960), we find that the women most committed to their jobs undertook a long socialization and preparation period early in life or after involvement in an unsatisfactory job, rank the job as important in the role cluster, consider the job as complex and are pleased by this, see themselves as leaders and successful women, and tend to associate with others like themselves. In addition, often they are not married—ever or any more—and are without small children. They earn more than most of the Chicago sample, although we do not know if their commitment is a consequence of or a cause for that level of reward. They are in higher-status jobs, as sales agents, managers, and professionals.

In general, the greater the perceived complexity of the occupation, and the higher its objective status in the occupational structure, the higher the women's commitment (Lopata 1993c; see also all the relevant work of Kohn and Schooler 1983). Salesclerks, who often prepared for better jobs and held such in the past, are not highly committed. On the other hand, nurse aides who come from lower socioeconomic backgrounds and have little status or pay feel that they have been trained for the job and socialized into the ideology of the medical profession sufficiently, so that they consider themselves as performing very important work of high benefit to the patients. Their inability to retain a job for long periods of time is almost entirely due to external circumstances over which they feel they have no control. Clerical jobs vary in complexity and prestige within a company, from file clerks to executive secretaries, and the commitment scores reflect this. Another interesting finding is that professionals in "object-focused" jobs, such as statisticians, drafts-women, designers, and so forth, do not possess high commitment scores, while those who deal with people, such as personnel and labor relations workers, clergy, reporters, counselors, and so forth, are highly committed. Of course, commitment to an occupation or a career line may not be translated into commitment to an employer.

All employees find some aspects of their jobs more enjoyable than others, because of either the tasks or the relations with a segment of the circle. Irritating interaction with someone important to the job can ruin one's enjoyment of the job, as reported by most of the women in the trades interviewed by Schroedel (1985). Joanne Miller and associates (1980) explain some of the sociopsychological effects of occupational conditions, confirming the fact that women, as much as men, wish autonomy in their jobs, although they appear somewhat less concerned with mobility. McIlwee (1982. 315) found women in the first year of work in nontraditional jobs satisfied with mastering traditionally male-labeled skills, with intellectual and physical challenge, with help and support from some of their male co-workers, with the pay, with anticipated advancement, and with the prestige of holding such jobs. The intrinsic aspects of the work predominated as sources of satisfaction during the second year, and social relationships were reported as having improved. Of course, these are the women who survived all the hassles experienced early in their involvement in male-dominated settings. Women in female-intensive jobs report a lack of hassles, positive relations with others, security, and confidence in their ability to do the job, if detracting factors are not overwhelming (Lopata, Miller, and Barnewolt 1986).

The fact that outside observers may evaluate a job in terms of only its tasks, rather than its social role components, can lead to assumptions of inevitable alienation in many occupations. This leads to questions like Hobson's "Gender Differences in Job Satisfaction: Why Aren't Women More Dissatisfied?" (Hobson 1989). Hobson states that although most women's jobs are inferior in many respects to those of men, the holders express greater satisfaction. One of his tentative explanations is that women use different standards to compare their jobs to those of others. Another is that they focus on different aspects of work for satisfaction than do men (Hobson 1989, 385). However, he ignores the possibility that they see the job in role rather than task terms, while men concentrate on the tasks. Our study of city women in midlife indicates that his first assumption is realistic, since most women did not know enough about jobs from which they were excluded to use them in comparison to their own, judging mainly in terms of jobs similar enough to their own to be visible to their imagination in role-taking terms (Lopata, Barnewolt, and Miller 1985). Thus, our respondents saw their jobs as more complex than the "average job," often contradicting the complexity measures of the *Dictionary of Occupational Titles* (U.S. Department of Labor 1965 and 1977; see more-detailed analyses in Lopata et al., "Job Complexity," 1985). The main reason for this was their perception of the role in terms of the complexities of social relationships. Even the worker in the xeroxing center of a university may see herself as a center of a hub, negotiating priorities. Other studies of women's job satisfaction in different occupations show the importance of perceived complexity and selective job conditions (Miller 1980; Miller et al. 1980).

There are two ways of leaving a job: quitting, or being fired or released. The initiative comes from the worker or the employer. The second aspect of leaving is the direction of movement. One can search for, or be offered, another job, or withdraw from the labor force entirely. Many reasons force or encourage a person toward the latter action, the most typical for women being the desire to focus on other roles or retirement. Historically, women left paid employment to marry, or with the first pregnancy. Employer policies for occupations such as teacher or stewardess used to force women out at these events, and even now class-action suits appear in front of American courts claiming discrimination on such grounds. Women leave their jobs in ever-changing proportions and compositions of the female labor force, with or without pay or guarantee of return, as a result of pregnancy or to care full-time for small children. In the past such women did not return to regular employment except out of financial need, but the probability is now very high that they will.

Of recent interest to economists and sociologists has been the retirement of women with extensive labor force careers (see mainly Szinovacz 1982 and 1989). Previous comments on the effects of retirement on women focused on the husband's leaving his job.

Let us now look at the varieties of work settings by the type of ownership of the territory, ranging from home-based work for pay, to jobs taking the person into the territory of the beneficiary, or to bureaucratically controlled locales such as factories, offices, and multiple settings.

Settings: Home-Based Work

Throughout human history, work has been a bridge between the home and the external world. This holds true also for much of the work now organized into jobs in the formal economic market. By the seventeenth century, Europe had already witnessed the creation of many jobs away from the home, although domestic production has continued into modern times (Boserup 1970). Home production for exchange or for sale involves the whole family, and the role of the paid worker is hard to separate from the roles of homemaker, wife, and mother. The division of labor and assignment of raw material, tools, space, and contributions of others often remained the same for products used at home and those taken out for sale (Clark [1919] 1968). Women organized work groups in the home for the production of crafts or foodstuffs, or the provision of services, such as laundry, and the unit as a whole received the rewards, to be used for its welfare (Boserup 1970). Most job-related work connected with the formal system is different, in that each worker is treated as an individual unit, to be hired, located in the work group, and rewarded for her or his specific contribution.

Early industrialization in England involved the "cottage industry," or "putting out" system. One member of the family would usually go to a central locale to collect the material and bring it back, and then return the finished product (Lopata, Miller, and Barnewolt 1986). Pay was by product, not by worker or hours. Sometimes a middleman (usually a man) delivered to, and picked up from, the home. The introduction of factories did not stop the need for services and goods carried forth in the home. For example, wet-nursing of children of women employed in factories existed in France up until World War I. Customized sewing continues to take place at the home of the seamstress or the customer.

An interesting variation in the history of human production has been the somewhat isolated household operating with relative self-sufficiency, such as farms in the American westward-moving frontier (Pavalko 1988, 174–76). Such a farm required the cooperative work of the whole household, and contact with suppliers was minimal compared to urban households. Special projects required help from neighboring or transitory workers. Flying over the United States, one can still see otherwise isolated farms that are connected to the outside world by roads and to the mass media by television antennas.

Machinery driven by a single farmer has now replaced many farm workers, in contrast to most of the rest of the world where fields are still seasonally populated with laborers of all ages and both genders.

Although the increasing dependence in the world system upon jobs carried forth in places and organizations away from home underemphasizes and undervalues paid work carried forth in the household, that part of economic production contributes in varying proportion to the gross national product. In fact, it is receiving more attention at the present time, with the use of new technologies and entrepreneurial activity for the development of home-based objects and services. Toffler focused on "the electronic cottage" in *The Third Wave* (1981). Due to their own inflexibility, modern corporations have not moved as fast as Toffler predicted they would to develop telecommuting jobs, in which the employee uses electronic means to carry forth her work at a location external to the corporation (Costello 1988, 137). A 1989 *Newsweek* article, "Escape from the Office: High-Tech Tools Spur a Work-at-Home Revolt," also claims that this is the wave of the future, but adds that it is not a major trend at the present because many managers do not trust workers they cannot see (Schwartz and Tsiantar 1989, 59). Some businesses have experimented with supplementary telecommuting work of full-time employees, others with farming out work to self-employed contractors.

Millions of American women, unwilling to conform to the time and energy commitments of the male-based model of jobs at various stages of the life course, have begun to enter home-based paid work that reproduces the "putting out" system of cottage industries, and that of entrepreneurial activity of their own initiative (Christensen 1988c and 1988d). The article in *Newsweek* claimed that the office-at-home market is worth $5.7 billion (Schwartz and Tsiantar 1989, 58), and it has been estimated that 24.9 million people worked at home in 1988 (Holbert 1988). These figures, of course, included both men and women and both entrepreneurial and employee jobs. The latter kind of home-based worker is described by Hope, Kennedy, and de Winter (1976) as

> a person who is employed directly by a firm or by an intermediary or agent of a firm to carry out work in his or her own home, not directly under the control or management of that employer. (P. 88)

Home-based paid workers differ greatly, depending on the type of work and relations to the employer, but they function mainly as a "reserve army" to be used when the employer wishes to call for their work (Milkman 1979). The least advantageous or most exploitive is manual work, as in the garment industry; paid for by product, the employer not even covering such costs as electricity, heat, or damaged goods (Kessler-Harris 1982; Stansell 1986). The employees usually do not receive benefits such as health insurance, paid vacations, maternity leaves, or pensions. They are dependent upon the employer for work, which is often seasonal, always undependable, and invariably underpaid (Allen and Wolkowitz 1987; Brown 1982; Milkman 1979). They are isolated from other circle members of the employer's organization. The power of determining who works when is entirely in the hands of the employer.

Paid home-based work has elicited a great deal of criticism and many attempts to control it throughout American history. Interestingly enough, laws passed to prevent exploitation in the sweatshop types of home-based industries are now actually interfering with the independent entrepreneurial activity (Kleiman 1988). Not only the worker and her household, but also the neighbors, may be disturbed by home-based work. Many communities have passed zoning ordinances relating to people making a living by working at home (Butler 1988). Most of the ordinances are a result of complaints from neighbors about traffic, noise, odors, garbage, fire hazards, advertising signs or other visible demonstrations of the work. In order to satisfy communities, ordinances define home occupations in residential areas, restrict some and regulate conditions under which others may operate, as well as include enforcement procedures (Butler 1988, 192).

Although working conditions can be better for secretaries and others connected by home computer to the organization, the absence of external controls on the employee prevents many organizations from venturing in this direction. There are two types of home-based work in the white-collar domain. One is supplemental, or overflow, work that a regular jobholder occasionally takes home. The other is similar to manual work, in that independent, self-employed workers always work at home, never being located in the employer's office (Kraut 1988; Gerson and Kraut 1988). Such women can do all their work for one employer, in which case they tend to have higher benefits and work assurance, or have arrangements with more than one employer, which can result in a precarious ebb and flow of assignments.

Independent contracting, whether called "freelancing," "consulting," or "telecommuting," has its own variations. Christensen (1988b) found

> that nearly two-thirds of both manufacturing and nonmanufacturing firms reported relying on production or administrative support contracts in 1985. (P. 79)

Involuntary contractors are members of marginal economic groups that cannot obtain regular jobs in employing organizations because of a variety of personal limitations. They would prefer full-time, regular employment (Christensen 1988a, 83). Other independent contractors are in this position voluntarily, most being owners of small, unincorporated businesses, who want the autonomy of being their own bosses.

Whether home workers take such employment by choice or because they have no other alternative, their expanding use has many advantages to the employer. Christensen (1988b) points to structural changes in the U.S. economy as a major set of factors making it worthwhile not to have all workers in the same location. Foreign competition, utilizing cheap labor, provides a strong incentive to cut labor costs here. As the price of space increases in urban centers, having workers work from their own homes can cut all other expenses connected with maintaining a worker in an office or factory. Technological change makes possible the farming out of many white-collar or manual jobs. A third factor Christensen discusses is the shift from an industrial to a service economy, many of whose tasks can be carried out away from an office.

Although many women respond to advertisements and the hype of mass media to take on home-based jobs, feeling they could gain independence and flexibility, and although many are quite satisfied with such an arrangement, others have realized their many disadvantages. In addition to the role conflict similar to that faced by home-working entrepreneurs, employees so situated face isolation from the company's social circle, which means not only loneliness, but also the lack of important organizational information. The same is true for manual workers, whose interaction with the employing firm is formal and relationally minimal. Since so much of a job is contained in social relations, this narrows manual labor down to mainly tasks. Promotions within the system are impossible. And, of course, such workers are at a disadvantage compared to regular employees if they do not have a specified contract guaranteeing a certain amount of work, are paid lower wages or salaries, are not covered by company benefits such as health insurance, and have to use their own space, heat, and other resources.

The Beneficiary's Territory[4]

Another category of jobs requires the social person to enter the territory of the beneficiary—the customer, client, student, or patient— alone or as part of a team, to sell a product or provide a service. Such jobs range from that of a domestic who cleans the homes of her employers, to an interior decorator who transforms a store, a management consultant who develops a plan for the reorganization of a corporation, or a manufacturer's representative selling to a wholesaler or a physician's office. The main locus of power or authority may lie with the beneficiary, who can select the worker and decide what she should do and what her rights are, or she or he may forfeit many of these rights to the incoming "expert" whose knowledge or equipment can solve a major problem.

There are two basic types of beneficiary settings the worker may enter: the home or the organizational setting.

The Beneficiary's Home as the Setting

The jobholder who enters the beneficiary's home can be a performer of services, such as a servant, plumber, doctor, or beautician. Salespersons can provide objects (such as cosmetics) or services (such as insurance). The manager of a household serves as the connecting link between the home and the outside world, utilizing a great variety of services and objects. Those entering the home can do so for very limited amounts of time, once or repeatedly, with differing complexities of duties to the beneficiaries and rights of pay and other benefits.

The characteristics of the social person, the jobholder, are frequently established by agencies other than the customer, who either does not have the knowledge and authority to test ability, or who must accept the proof of tests performed by others. A master plumber who so advertises himself has been apprenticed and trained by the union and licensed by the state; a doctor has been educated by the medical profession and also licensed by the state; a cleaning woman has been trained and bonded by a service agency or accepted on the basis of a word-of-mouth recommendation. The choice of the home entrant by the customer often involves several steps: a local "expert" turned to for advice when several qualified persons are available (Katz and Lazersfeld 1955), a personal interview with a candidate, or a test performance.

The social person entering the home of the main beneficiary must, however, establish trust beyond the formal qualifications that got her there in the first place. The rights of access and movement within the home can be previously established or negotiated at entrance. The patient of a home-visiting doctor can restrict access to certain rooms, while allowing a freedom to manipulate the body that is not offered to people in other jobs, and guaranteeing cooperation of the patient's social circle. At the other extreme is the suspect who must give access to police officers with a search warrant. Other rights and duties of the jobholder must also be negotiated, at least at first contact, if there is to be continued interaction. The circle of the employee includes many more people than the customer.

The subject of private household servants received a great deal of attention from social scientists in the past decades, with the growing shortages of such workers and changes in their relations with employers (see Coser 1973, Katzman 1978, Rollins 1985). This occupation contains some interesting variations, as the power of the social person versus the employer increased with organization. The most powerless have been slaves, legally the property of the owners who could assign them tasks and determine whatever rights they wished (Rodgers-Rose 1980; Malson et al. 1988). In America, descendants of slaves were joined as servants by immigrant women (Katzman 1978).

Several changes on both the employer's and the worker's side have modified this relationship. On the employer's side, the amount of work carried out in the home decreased with urbanization, industrialization, and technology. Soap, bread, clothing, and other goods could be purchased with money, decreasing the need for extra workers in the home. Also, the cost of maintaining servants, in terms of space, clothing, and food, became prohibitive for most households in urban centers. Simultaneously, the dramatically expanding middle class increased the demand for at least partial household help.

On the other hand, fewer and fewer women were willing to work as live-in servants. The spread of democratic ideas and increasing opportunities for alternative occupations decreased the attractiveness of domestic service for all but such women who could not fit into new labor markets, such as older blacks, new immigrants, or imported domestics (Bernard 1981; Coser 1973). The great disadvantages of live-in employment, including the constancy of demands, the lack of privacy on the job, and limits on private life away from it, plus the demeaning nature of the relationship with the employer and related circle members, resulted in a shortage of workers and the modification of demands (Lopata, Miller, and Barnewolt 1986; Rollins 1985).

The changes on both demand and supply sides resulted in a decrease of live-in servants. The combined needs led to an increase in "day workers" who come into the employer's homes to perform more time-limited duties and receive rights more typical of jobs in modern societies (Katzman 1978). This meets the needs of most employers, who can no longer maintain multistaff households, and of the workers, who can live in their own homes. Other changes include the rise of new entrepreneurial businesses that formalize the relationship between the managers of a household and domestic servants, serving as intermediaries, providing workers with very specified duties and definite rights (Lopata, Miller, and Barnewolt 1986). Restaurants, catering businesses, and take-out places have generally replaced the home-based cook, and window-, furniture-, and clothing-cleaning establishments proliferate. Dealing with such organizations reduces the power of the beneficiary, converting an employer into a customer, and diminishes the intensity or primary quality of relations with employees.

The development of a relationship between an employer and a jobholder entering her home is particularly difficult in the direct sales field. The beneficiary knows very little about the seller, so that the first interaction must build trust very rapidly. There are four basic procedures used in direct sales, which mushroomed in the feminine-mystique years when homemakers spent a great deal of time in the home (Cox 1963, 43–45). Some of these have survived into recent times, with variations due to the daytime absence of so many potential customers. The first method follows the traditional door-to-door pattern of the peddler, although the title has been changed to "representative" due to the negative stereotype of high-pressure "foot-in-the-door" salespeople. While such items as vacuum cleaners and household cleaning products have been sold by men to homemakers and couples in the past, manufacturers of goods such as cosmetics, household objects, and jewelry have increasingly used saleswomen. The main reason that it took so long for direct-sales companies to utilize saleswomen, who allegedly would be less threatening at the doorstep than men, is the premodern company's fear of hiring women to travel and enter possibly dangerous places (Lopata, Miller and Barnewolt 1986).

A person in direct sales must rapidly develop a dyadic relation-ship with the customer and is highly dependent upon her or his cooperation, since she has no supports in the setting or even a team to assist in the presentation (Prus and Frisby 1990). This is undoubt-edly one of the most difficult jobs, dependent not so much on the product (although its name does carry weight in building trust) as upon the woman's ability to convert a suspicious stranger into a cooperating teammate.

A second method of direct sales is through referrals and prear-ranged appointments. Each time a sale is completed, the "demon-strator" asks the customer for names of friends, with a promise of gifts if the recommendation results in a sale. The third procedure is through the "party plan," in which elements of primary relationships are exploited for the secondary goal of making a sale. The whole program is based on home and neighborhood life, in that the dealer enlists hostesses to invite the guests (customers) and provide the homes (salesrooms) and refreshments in exchange for gifts. The dealer presides over the party, leading the games and making a sales presentation. She then takes orders for delivery later to the hostess, who in turn distributes the merchandise to the guests (Cox 1963, 46; see also Peven 1968).

Finally there is a "club plan," which works like a chain letter and is somewhat similar to the referral system, except that the buyer recommends a friend for "club membership." The members actually do not interact with each other, but continue buying items, such as silverware or china, through the seller until they have completed a set.

One of the interesting features of the direct-sales field is the training and selling method, purposely developed for the conver-sion of former full-time homemakers, with hardly any employment history, into the salesforce. Reinforcement contacts continue for years, in an effort to retain the saleswomen in a field noted for high turnover.[5] Peven (1968) compared the training meetings to religious revival sessions. Employers also provide the salesforce with props, in the form of samples or "gifts," even precanvassing catalogues (Cox 1963). Companies such as Avon have begun to experiment with different ways of merchandising their products, due to the frequent absence of a potential woman customer from the home during daytime hours so that calling "cold" (i.e., without an appointment) is not likely to produce a response (Deveny 1989).

A very difficult form of role strain, between the person and the demands of the job, is often experienced by insurance underwriters due to feelings of intrusion on the privacy of potential customers (Krugman 1969). Successful insurance agents select areas or methods of contacting clients that provide a set of prospects as similar to themselves as possible (Crane 1969).

The easiest aspect of direct selling is that of customer maintenance. For example, milkmen, when this was a frequent occupation, learned complicated methods to establish and retain customers, even to get rid of undesirable ones (Bigus 1972). Like the ballroom dance teacher who must keep the student happy, the milkman uses cultivating tactics of pseudofriendship. At least the teacher has the whole studio and colleagues to support her front- and backstage, a sort of support not available to sales workers (Lopata and Noel 1967).

The Beneficiary's Job Setting

Another type of job involves entering the work setting, rather than the home, of the customer. Some industries and organizations have started hiring women for the male-dominated occupation of sales representative. For example, pharmaceutical manufacturers now send "detail women" to offices of physicians and dentists, and book publishers assign women to universities in an extended territory. Such a person enters an establishment under the control of the potential or repeat customer and has to fit her demeanor to that of the surroundings, while showing genuineness, likeability, toughness, and so forth. She has no close colleagues; all those who do the same thing are competitors or in different locations. She is the only person from her own company, with not even a supervisor to lend support. Knowledge of the product and of the needs of the consumer can be quite complicated, and failure to have been sufficiently prepared is readily apparent.

Such assignments require not only entrance into "foreign territory" of the work space, but also travel, frequently for extended periods of time. Until very recently restaurants, hotels and motels did not know how to handle women business travelers, but now slick travel magazines are running articles showing adjustments being made for them. Prior "protectiveness" toward women, which was partly due to employers' fears that female employees might be sexually assaulted or embarrassed, as well as fears of lawsuits, have decreased (Berheide 1988; Coser 1975b). Women are now traveling independently (although I still get asked if I am going to visit a grandchild when I'm flying to a distant location).

The *City Women* study included two kinds of salesworkers: salesclerks and sales agents (Lopata, Barnewolt, and Miller 1985). The Chicago-area sales agents and representatives are very different from the salesclerks in background, occupational histories, construction of reality, and role clusters. They have more college education, initially and after returns, and more job training in the past and the planned-for future, which is specifically directed toward improving their success in the field. They initially trained to be clerical workers, but somewhere along the line they saw the benefits obtained by male agents in their firms and moved out of clerical work into more independent and profitable jobs. They are very satisfied with the occupation and consider it much more complex than an average job and as very important to the beneficiary. They are career oriented and expect to remain that way in the future. Women sales agents consider themselves to be competent, intelligent, creative, and healthy, and in general they have a higher self-esteem than either full-time homemakers or women in many other occupations, especially salesclerks. In addition, they earn more than two-and-a-half times what other salesworkers make. Thus, they have decrystallized their life patterns in midlife to free themselves from prior constraints and are reaping the benefits. Most do not have small children in the home and are freer than many women to travel and to work unusual and erratic hours. There is one complication in the picture: The husband does not appear to be as pleased by the wife's job as she is. This may be because the changes it has introduced into their married life have disrupted its prior rhythm and, possibly, the rights of the husband to the wife's work and attention. Secretaries may be easier to live with than are sales agents, even if their earnings are inferior. Salesclerks do not report similar problems.

Women now entering the great variety of sales jobs requiring new skills and presentations of self have formed mutual support, local, and national organizations with similarly involved persons. For example, the National Network of Women in Sales has branches in most American cities and suburbs, holding national conventions and publishing literature of interest to members. Much of the activity is very similar to what went on in now-defunct organizations of salesmen: sharing information on sales techniques, building self-esteem, and in general contributing to feelings of morale, esprit de corps, companionship, and similarity of experience. Colleagues in such organizations thus become part of the social circle, the employing organization and customers forming the other two major segments.

Jobholders may also enter as outsiders into organizational territory to perform services. This is true of, for example, accountants or management consultants, fields expanding to include women. A major American consulting firm with hundreds of experts had only one woman until relatively recently, claiming that this was not due to personal taste but to the fact that the clients did not want women telling them how to run their businesses. There were no blacks, male or female, in consulting positions, although such faces were visible in the back rooms of the central settings.

The outsider entering such a "foreign" establishment might have very tightly circumscribed rights of access to space and data, or might be allowed to wander about or to interview people if that is part of the contract. The employees must be told how to cooperate and when to protect the organization from unwelcome disclosure. Even the mass media show the complications of interaction in such situations—the outsider trying to get "guilty knowledge," the locals pretending there is none (Hughes 1971). Here, again, the consultant, accountant, or other specialist is frequently operating alone. However, the firm that tested her for the necessary qualifications, hired her, sent her on the assignment, and pays her is expected to back up her report and defend her actions, if it approves them—but usually not to the point of losing the account.

Outsiders also include office "temps," or temporary workers, sent by mushrooming firms specializing in filling special needs or finding replacements for absent workers, usually in clerical jobs (Gannon 1984). The workers obviously do not have the status of the consultant and face several other difficulties, including learning what needs to be done in the absence of the regular worker and being able to fit into the ongoing system. Social relations can be awkward, especially if the work team suspects that the "temp" may replace their colleague. The experience can be isolating, but women who sign up with the agencies like the flexibility of scheduling and often find the work interesting. Supposedly they are completely free to accept or reject assignments, but frequent rejection will lead to a decrease in calls from the agency.

Organizational Settings

One of the alienating aspects of jobs is the inability to call a setting one's own, with rights to protect it from invasion, particularly by higher-ups. Many jobs are carried forth in relatively large organizations, in space that the worker must personalize to build a setting for herself, such as a factory, prison, store, or office. Manual workers designate boundaries or become frustrated if they cannot do so. Howe (1977) dramatizes the irritation experienced by waitresses in the restaurant she studied over the lack of a safe and private space in which to change into their uniforms and store their street clothes. Attempts to build partial personalized space is evident when pool secretaries insert pictures or permanent flowers on the desk, while the "big shots" have walls to hang art indicating high culture, or at least million-mile awards from airlines (Kanter 1977). Much was made by industrial sociologists, and is now being made by bestseller books, about this allocation and use of space, physical and social, in large (and even small) business firms or factories (Margolis 1979; Pavalko 1988; Whyte 1956).

A very interesting relation between setting and occasional roles exists in "total institutions" (Goffman 1961) such as communities of nuns or armed forces bases. Cloistered nuns lived in their own settings, although owned by the Catholic Church (Ebaugh 1988). There is a great deal of debate concerning the integration of women into the American armed forces, since they are seen as impinging on men's occupations in men's territory (Rustad 1982). It is outside the purview of this volume to deal with such situations, since they encompass more than just the job.

Factories

Probably the most confining setting for a job is the factory floor where manual workers are located. Thanks to scientific management of the transitional times in modernization, assembly work has been divided into the most efficient system judged possible by the experts, with strict schedules. Such a factory setting is not similar to the rest of societal life; it is routinized, specialized, mechanically controlled, and depersonalized (in that each worker is replaceable), with a tight authority structure. Workers are not trusted to do their jobs right, often with cause due to the alienation produced by the setting, and thus supervised tightly without decision-making rights. For example, Cavendish (1982), studying women factory workers, noted that the engineers who came to solve machine problems did not even listen to the women, who knew what was going on. Supervisors have a great deal of control over the allocation of women to jobs and over their acceptance by co-workers (Reskin and Padavic 1988). This is particularly true when they can manipulate the labor force along gender, race, and class lines to prevent work manipulation by workers or organized protest (Hossfeld 1990). Zavella (1987), who studied their jobs and outside lives, reports that Chicano cannery workers in California adjust to going "through hell for three months" of intensive, seasonal employment simply because of the high pay and the unemployment insurance for the months when the canneries do not need them. They must work, and alternative jobs have their own disadvantages.

Work in the canning industries appears to have the same constraints, whether it be in the state of Washington or in Hawaii, or in Delaware in the 1920s and 1930s. The work is tedious, usually carried forth in an unhealthy environment and under constant time pressure. In addition, many of the jobs are dangerous, either in themselves or because of the employer's (and sometimes employees' failure to utilize protective devices (McCurry 1975). This holds true for women miners and those working with hot or heavy machinery (Kingsolver 1989; Walshok 1981; see also Stromberg, Larood, and Gutek's 1987 special volume of *Women and Work* devoted to occupational health issues). Interpersonal relations with co-workers are often limited to off-work hours, and the basic interaction is between the woman and her machine.

Women in factories often face additional problems, modified by their class and racial characteristics, the main one of which is sexual harassment. This is particularly true when they enter territory previously controlled by men. The macho image of so many jobs requires constant reference to subjects with which women are not comfortable, and the harassment can be very personal, even physical. Harassment in female-dominated occupations comes from male supervisors demanding sexual favors and punishing women who do not comply; in male dominated occupations, it takes the form of a constantly demeaning environment.

Attempts to modify the factory work system on the model of, for example, Scandinavian firms have not been very frequent or successful. Such experiments assign greater freedom to work teams to decide rights and duties and to benefit more directly from the economic success of their work. The redefinition, in the 1992 presidential campaign, of the American economic system as being in serious trouble, and the declared future policies of the Clinton administration, may force employers into a more modern organization of factory jobs.

In-depth studies indicate that women do not respond passively to the negative aspects of their jobs. They organize their work scheduling to fool machines and supervisors (see, for example, Cavendish 1982). They form networks and support groups and use the very logic with which the management tries to manipulate them to reconstruct their situation (Hossfeld 1990; Zavella 1987). They even cross racial and class lines to accomplish their purposes vis-à-vis the structure. Kessler-Harris (1982) summarizes women's part in the history of the labor movement in America (see also Kingsolver's 1989 *Holding the Line: Women in the Great Arizona Mine Strike of 1983*). The successful workers studied by Walshok (1981) were very task-oriented, interested in problem solving, skilled, and involved in a "network of competent, savvy peers" who supported them in their risk-taking work.

Men's Prisons

Two studies have recently given us a picture of how women correctional officers handle themselves and others in men's prisons (Jurik 1985; Jurik and Halemba 1984; Zimmer 1987). Women were introduced into the men's prison system in 1978 in an attempt at reform. Dramatic prison revolts and class-action suits led to a mandatory change in the philosophy guiding prisons, a change mainly from coercion to attempts at rehabilitation. Women were supposed to help introduce the reforms. However, extensive cultural and structural barriers—many of which occur in other male-dominated or changing settings—have prevented women from functioning effectively (Jurik 1985). These include the stereotypical image of women as physically and "mentally" weak and unsuited for the job of insuring safety for the staff and conformity by prisoners; polarization of tokenism; the informal "old guard" opportunities for advancement to which they were not admitted; inadequate prior experience (many of the men, but not the women, had been in the armed services or similar prior jobs), training, and on-the-job learning opportunities; ambiguity of the role itself; and inadequate implementation by the external authorities. The prisons were overcrowded, inadequately staffed, and thus dangerous, and the lack of trust from the male guards, who held such strong stereotypes of women, is partially understandable.

The women entering these settings were more educated than their co-workers, but in nonrelevant fields. Many were not married and were attracted to the job by the money and because they wanted to use the training. Thus they used different styles of relationships with the prisoners than were traditional or used by men. For example, they guarded by using communication and persuasion, in order to obtain voluntary cooperation (Zimmer 1987). They decreased the social distance from the prisoners, which the men tried to constantly maintain. Obviously, such differences in styles of interaction produced conflicts with the male guards.

Long Distance Trucks

Women truckers face sexual harassment and must develop their own style of relating with circle members, dock-loading and -unloading workers, truck stop personnel, and other truckers. Although the territory of the truck belongs to the drivers, at least while they are on the road, most women are in a subordinate position, 80 percent of the time driving double, with a boyfriend or husband in the main seat. The women consider themselves to be real truckers, able to solve any problem, but the men, who act as unintentional sponsors, are more interested in female companionship than in driving competency (Lembright and Riemer 1982, 472).

Stores, Restaurants, and Airplanes

Salesclerks are "stationary workers" in a depersonalized setting; their rights over a limited floor space are highly dependent upon characteristics of the establishment for making sales (Mills 1956). The physical arrangements of the store, the location of "stations" to which women are assigned, and the characteristics of the customers who are drawn to the store are not within their control. There is a great variation in settings, ranging from cost-cutting discount outlets that have proleterianized the job into one of merely writing up and packaging the order, to quality stores requiring the clerk to know the merchandise and help customers make selections they are satisfied with. Glazer (1984) points out that in many capitalist establishments, such as stores, the customer now performs some of the work of the employee. Some businesses even set up physical barriers preventing much clerk-customer interaction. On the other hand, many employers intensify the customer interaction of their salesforce, being convinced that service is their main contribution to the beneficiary (Benson 1984, 113). The selection of the social person for this job varies considerably, according to the image the store wants to project, which accounts in a major part for the lag in hiring blacks and other minority women (Benson 1984).

C. Wright Mills (1956, 172–74) classified women salesclerks by the personal styles with which they interact with customers while being careful not to antagonize colleagues. The competition is high when commissions are at stake, but the "saleslady" must constantly relate to the other women in the same job, while customers come and go. Mills also noted the difference between salesclerks in small towns, or shops that draw repeat customers, and those in large city department stores with mainly anonymous sales interaction. We found in the *City Women* study (Lopata, Barnewolt, and Miller 1985) that the job of salesclerk is a catchall, drawing women who consider it a temporary experience. They come from a variety of backgrounds and occupational histories. Most are not career committed and do not see the job as complex or as giving any chance for self-development, control over others, or independence. They are more oriented toward family roles than toward the job, although they do find companionship and their own earnings to be sources of satisfaction (see also Howe 1977). The merchandise is there, the customers come to the store and not to them, and they have few discriminatory decision-making rights. They do think that their performance of the job is more important than the job itself (Lopata, Barnewolt, and Miller 1985). However, there are women among them who have moved up from less prestigeful jobs, and the setting is often pleasant, requiring care of appearance and, if not customer deference, at least polite demeanor. Such salesclerks are much more satisfied with their jobs than are the ones who feel they have moved down in social status.

There is a great deal of gender segregation in the merchandise to be sold. Women are assumed to do better at selling cosmetics or clothes than at selling mechanical gadgets or major appliances

(Donovan [1929] 1974). The perfect example of gender specialization of objects is the car salesroom, which has traditionally been dominated by men, supported by the assumptions of management and clients that women cannot sell cars because they do not understand their mechanical functioning (the accompanying assumption is that all car salesmen do understand this). Lawson's (1990) study of women who are now entering the car salesforce found a high turnover due to the problems and hassles. The job is made especially difficult by the fact that the assisting segment of the circle, in the form of other salespersons, does not cooperate with them. Some women moved into the financial aspects of the business, while those in sales who survived on the floor developed personalized styles of interaction. These styles of relating to the male co-workers resemble stereotypical family roles, labeled as "mothering" and so forth, much as did the women in male-dominated armed-service units studied by Rustad (1982). One reason for the success of some women in this highly competitive field is the increase in female car buyers, who are likely to trust someone of their own gender more than a man. This factor is important, since the public's image of the car salesforce is quite negative.

Waitresses must meet several physical qualifications in order to take orders and bring food and drinks to the diners. The higher the prestige of the restaurant, the more appearances and style are important, although the highest-status establishments (or those trying for such a reputation) usually hire men, who carry, after all, more prestige than the most sophisticated waitress. The waitress deals directly with the beneficiaries, hostesses or maître d's, cooks, bartenders, other waitresses, and "busboys." Whyte's classic 1948 study concluded that the interactional problems of this job are enough to "make waitresses cry." Gender differences among members of the social circle are an important influence on this interaction, and also waitresses have a rather sexist "client classificatory system," according to Howe (1977, 102–3).

A variation on the role of waitress, but with many more complications, is that of flight attendant. Hochschild (1983) devotes a whole book, *The Managed Heart,* to a discussion of the selection, training, duties, and rights of this role. The title refers to the fact that stewardesses, as they used to be called before the title became gender-neutral, are extensively trained to manage their emotions in order to create a relaxed, "homelike" atmosphere in the airplane cabin, controlling difficult passengers without antagonizing them.

The role includes much more than serving food and drinks, although the beneficiaries are often unaware of these duties except in emergencies. The flight attendant can be in contact with the same passengers for extended periods of time, and can see some repeatedly if assigned the same route. Class-action suits have recently been filed against airlines for firing women who married while still on the job. Marital and parental status are no longer asked in hiring procedures, and the women's activities while not on the job are not a subject of concern, unless they embarrass the airline. There has been a shift in selection criteria, with males, older women, and minority women appearing more frequently.

Offices

In discussing the office as a setting of jobs, Pavalko (1988) interestingly limits it to the province of receptionists, secretaries, typists, bookkeepers, file clerks, bank clerks, and so forth. He then adds that this is a feminized work context. This limitation is not surprising, in view of prevalent stereotypes, but it ignores the fact that members of management, university scholars, and persons in many other male- or female-dominated or gender-neutral jobs are also in offices. It is impossible to look at the myriad jobs that are located in offices, so let us first examine those in which such a setting is the main center of activity, and then those for which an office serves only as a "home base" from which the jobholder moves to other locales to fulfill duties and receive rights.

Clerical Workers. Office workers in female-dominated jobs vary in the complexity of their work and social relationships, as well as their control over the setting (Feldberg and Glenn 1979; Lopata, Barnewolt, and Miller 1985; Lopata, Miller, and Barnewolt 1986; Malveaux 1980). There are great differences between the private secretary, who usually has her own office and moves up the organizational ladder with her boss, acquiring territory in fiefdom style as his assistant, and the more stationary pool typist, with limited rights or discretion in her work (Kanter 1977). On the other hand, the pool secretary may need very complex and negotiated interaction just because of her lack of power. File clerks can move around large territories, as illustrated by Howe in *Pink Collar Workers* (1977), having rights of access to other people's space but hardly any space of their own. Some become very possessive about their files, but most must allow others entry even to these (see also Benet 1972). Receptionists and phone operators can extend themselves great distances, as we see in one of the favorite skits by comedienne Lilly Tomlin. Computerization of the secretarial office has had mixed effects, most of which, however, are evaluated by observers as a process of deskilling and degrading, or proletarianization, of the work. One of the ways training schools are trying to upgrade the appearance of this category of jobs is by relabeling: They are now "office support workers." Regardless of the label or location, clerical workers interact with a wide variety of circle members. The organizational structure and size of the establishment obviously influence the relationships and the amount of negotiation necessary to fulfill obligations and receive rights.

Although many disadvantages appear at all levels of clerical jobs, most women are still located in them because it has been white-collar, "socially acceptable employment" (Lillydahl 1986) requiring relatively little education. As younger white women are broadening their horizons and gaining expanded job opportunities, they are decreasing their concentration here, as in other female-intensive occupations. This leaves space for minority women, who are moving into these white-collar positions in great numbers (Braverman 1974; Glenn and Feldberg 1977 and 1979; Sokoloff 1988).

The *City Women* clerical workers varied by the complexity of their jobs from file clerk to receptionist, secretary, and high-level office worker with more complex, executive, or specialized duties. Such employees also came from a variety of backgrounds and were distributed differently within the office setting. The women themselves are highly conscious of internal status differentiation and boundaries, and the ones with higher status are very conscious of the ceiling that prevents them from moving into managerial positions. One of the features that distinguishes their work from that of professional occupations is that few of them interact directly with people outside of the organizational setting except as representatives of management.

Managers and Professionals. The other people who work in offices, but not as part of that female-dominated domain of clericals, are in an even greater heterogeneity of jobs and social-person characteristics. Office-bound jobs tend to be of marginal professional more than managerial character, since management usually requires physical mobility into multiple settings. Office management jobs are actually similar to those of stationary factory employees, in that work must be brought in to the managers and the finished product removed. Many of the "object-focused" professionals in the *City Women* study spend most of their time in offices or their equivalents, such as laboratories—with small office spaces for writing up results—or studios. Here they manipulate data or create objects such as advertisements. The fact that they are focused in one location belonging to a larger organization does not mean that they conduct their roles entirely within its confines; they often go out to meet with colleagues, to conferences with others in the company, or to meetings with people in other organizations. One of the problems of scientists working in bureaucracies is that they have been socialized into cosmopolitan reference and membership groups with whom they continue interaction even when faced with ethical and loyalty conflicts (Gouldner 1957 and 1958; Merton 1968).

Doctors' and dentists' offices are the settings for most of the work of such professionals; the beneficiaries, assistants, and suppliers come to these offices from the outside, although doctors also function in hospital settings. Lawyers are usually required to use multiple locales to accomplish their purposes, but their basic setting is an office. Grade school teachers are often deprived of private offices and tend to convert the classroom into their own space (Lortie 1969 and 1975). The level at which the teacher is hired is dependent upon the match between her knowledge and the children's ages and assumed ability to learn. Teachers of very young children stay mainly in the same room and see the same beneficiaries the academic year 'round. As the age of the children increases, so does specialization by teacher, so that new groups are taught in the same place at different hours of the day. The race of the teacher is often associated with the race of the students, whites being greatly overrepresented in this occupation until recently. Token teachers of a different gender or racial identity than that of the dominant group can become quite isolated and alienated in urban public schools; their colleagues, and even the parents of the children in their classes, cooperate with them only minimally (Dworkin, Chafetz, and Dworkin 1986).

Universities and colleges, with the dual function of developing new knowledge and transmitting it to students and the world, require greater mobility of their professors. The professorial office is visited by students, colleagues, suppliers, building maintenance personnel, and so forth. The professor enters offices of others, classrooms, meeting locales, and food-serving establishments on campus. In fact, ideally, the professor can live a major part of the day and year within the confines of the organization. One way of understanding the real meaning of the resources available to academics in such a setting is to examine the problems facing people who have not acquired full membership (Smith and Hixson 1987).[6] Disadvantages of women adjunct professors not on the tenure track vis-à-vis those on the track, or already past the major career barriers, include inadequate office space and secretarial help, inconvenient course assignments, lack of necessary information for duty performance due to distance from the network, and lack of funds for attendance at professional meetings.

Hochschild (1992) recently studied people at various levels of jobs in a major corporation and noted the significance of placement of photographs upon the allotted spaces. Managers in private offices display formally framed family pictures on the desk or behind it on walls. Secretaries in pool locations stick their unframed pictures into slots of available objects with which they work. Factory workers draw out their photographs from wallets in their pockets.

Multiple Settings

No business, and no organization devoted mainly to other functions, such as a school or church, exists independently of its social milieu—which includes suppliers, external beneficiaries, competitors, and governmental agencies. Therefore, members of the organization who form the connecting link between it and the rest of the world are vital to its welfare. This includes the officers of the firm, the staff whose job is to collect data, and the salesforce, in the case of product or service manufacturers. It may include advertising specialists, lawyers, external accountants, and even managers' wives.

Those connecting-link jobholders may be seen as sufficiently important representatives of the company that the rest of the staff is treated as supportive and responsive to their needs. In other than home settings, the main obligation of the representatives is to make the organization look good or get accounts or new members. Religious personnel are generally expected to seek out and convert potential congregation members.

One of the problems of people in multiple settings that bridge cosmopolitan and local, or other mutually exclusive value systems and norms, is that of person-role strain or role-loyalty conflict (Gouldner 1957 and 1958). If the social circle contains groups that demand different behavior and interaction, the social person can be caught in a psychologically damaging double bind.

Many other jobs require movement from one setting to another, accompanied by changes in social circle and thus in relations and self-presentation. An interesting occupation that combines home, office, and other persons' locales is real estate sales. Traditionally a male-dominated occupation, based on the assumption that males know more about building construction and financial matters, its residential segment has become female-dominated within a relatively short period of time. The explanation for the shift is again in terms of gender qualifications: "Women understand homes better than men," and "women decide on homes and women sales agents are better at finding the right emphasis for persuasion." Realtors establish territories, or "farms," within which they keep track of householders, using word of mouth and other sources of knowledge to spot future vendors or sellers. The office provides the buyers, through advertisements, branches in other locales, or multiple listings. The agent must determine the best match between buyer and seller and negotiate between them, which is often a very delicate process, into which potential agents are carefully trained. Realtors have to be very careful to follow antidiscrimination regulations, while simultaneously not antagonizing colleagues and neighborhoods by selling to "undesirables" (Squires et al. 1987, 9; House 1977).

Kanter and Stein (1979) explain the complexities of multiple settings, made more difficult by male hostility, in a study of women in an industrial salesforce. There were few women in the organization they studied, and so they were highly visible, requiring modifications of behavior and the creation of new relationships by both the women and the various segments of their circles. For example, when out on the road with colleagues, women often felt very uncomfortable in dealing with the "male culture" of jokes, drinking, and general demeanor. Each woman had to develop her own way of dealing with such situations. Most did not find a similar problem with customers, in the latter's location, although awkwardness created by mistaken identity often followed a lack of clarification of the salesperson's gender by appointment arrangers. On the home base of the company, new situations arose with the introduction of women to the salesforce, as in relations with secretaries adjusted to men's style, or the need to develop comfortable relations with the wives of colleagues.

The same need for adjustment exists whenever the social person must change locales or a woman enters a relational context based on a male model of interaction. Relations with colleagues at the home base, with the protection of the organization, must be changed when in public or other settings in which a woman and a man are frequently treated as sexual or at least dating partners. The boundaries of norms of primary or leisure-time interaction and those of secondary relations are often hard to maintain or even understand.

Multiple settings have sometimes been forced upon women by the domination of certain territory by men. The biographies of women scientists, writers, and artists are full of refusals by established research centers or universities to allow them positions or the use of space. This situation was bad enough when the scholar or scientist was doing the same kind of work as her colleagues or husband who had official positions in these centers, but even more difficult when the woman was focused mainly on feminine subjects or viewpoints (Abir-Am and Outram 1987; Harding 1986, 242). As late as 1965, psychiatrist Erik Erikson explained the absence of women from positions in scientific centers and engineering as due to their "inner space," or womb, which makes "scientific training more or less peripheral to the intimate tasks of womanhood and motherhood" (see also Lopata, Miller, and Barnewolt 1984, 213–14). Rossi (1965), attending the same conference on women in the scientific professions, explained their scarcity in more sociological terms: socialization and organizational barriers to preparation and position. Many women who never reached prominence had actually undertaken the preparation for scientific careers, only to withdraw from active involvement later in life. Those who continued faced great problems, especially if their work required a special setting and resources available only at large and endowed centers such as universities.

The white "homosocial" male world of many occupations has made it difficult for persons with other characteristics—not just the female gender—to attain space within their settings at appropriate levels (Lipman-Blumen 1976a, 15). The cooperation of social circles is often absent or minimal, even when jobs are obtained. The difficulties facing people lacking the ideal social-person characteristics, or membership in the desired circle, are still apparent whenever we look at the distribution of workers in the American labor force, or within any large, complex organization such as a corporation, factory, or university.

Summary

Much human work has been organized in the modern world into individually held jobs. Employer and employee much reach an agreement as to the social person characteristics the employee must possess and duties and rights, including the necessary resources the employer must provide the employee. The employer usually has the greater power to define the situation. Beneficiaries of the work can be contacted directly, or so indirectly that the worker considers only the evaluation of a supervisor. Colleagues can be an invaluable asset, making even dreary routines companionate, or they can sabotage all efforts.

Not all women earning an income work outside the home. Some attempt to combine the job with family roles by locating the job in the home. There are two types of home-based paid work: that of entrepreneur and that of employee. The advantages for the woman employee are flexibility and autonomy; disadvantages are low pay, lack of many benefits, social isolation, and conflict with other home-based roles. Few households are organized to protect a woman from interference while she works at her job. The advantages for the employer are low expenses and not having to provide the work space and resources provided to in-company workers; disadvantages are mainly in the lack of control. The entrepreneur faces the same problems of business maintenance as are experienced in any independent economic venture. Independence is curtailed by the rights that must be granted all circle members plus any restrictions coming from governmental policies.

There are other settings within which jobs are carried forth. One is the home or job location of the beneficiaries, such as customers of saleswomen. The home provides more opportunities for the use of primary-relation interaction, while women who travel to the factories and offices of customers often face a heavily male-culture based world.

Organizational settings of jobs also vary, from factory stations to stores and restaurants or offices. Many of these settings are gender-specific, assigned so traditionally and because of stereotypical assumptions of management. Higher status settings tend to be male-intensive and male-dominated. Office-based jobs include those thought of as "feminine," such as clerical support staff, as well as those of most white-collar (dress and suit?) workers, such as professionals and corporate managers. The role, rather than the setting, determines relationships with circle members, but the location either facilitates or hinders these. Workers are highly aware of the importance of the setting as evidenced by the constant demands for "better," often defined in prestige terms, spatial resources on all levels of jobs.

Many jobs are actually carried forth in more than the base location, movement to beneficiaries, colleagues, administrators, or external persons or groups being required or advantageous. Women entering the public domain, in which so many relationships are organized around the male model of interaction, timing, and interest, find some locations easier to work in than others. The tendency to not try, or to withdraw from, jobs and careers that are reputedly hostile or that present too many barriers to success, combined with the very real presence of such barriers, continues the sex-segregated and sex-stratified system. Women who take other than the traditional roles must negotiate variations of style. One of the dramatic trends in recent years has been the willingness of so many of them to try to succeed in an ever-broader range of occupations.

7

Social Roles in the Rest of the World

We have finally reached the social roles of American women outside of the family and economic dimensions: in the rest of societal life and even in the world at large. This includes the roles of student, friend, neighbor, and member of a variety of community groups and social movements. These roles can be carried forth rather informally, or, within a highly structured social circle, they can aim at benefiting the social person, the group, or even larger segments of humanity.

Student

A member of modern societies is often involved with the formal school system at two periods in the life course: as a student in the early years after basic socialization by the family; and later as a parent of a student.

The history of women's involvement in the role of student in America is rather convoluted. Mass education was developed during transitional times with male beneficiaries in mind because the two-sphere ideology placed them in the public sphere of political and economic life for which extensive public knowledge was deemed necessary. It was assumed that women could learn all they needed to know from home, other women, and the church. (See Lopata 1981a, 14, for a summary of that argument). Extension of all but minimal formal schooling to women met with predictions of serious problems. Myerson (1927), for example, blamed higher education (high school and above) of women for the creation of "the nervous housewife": Schooling and employment had already led, and would increasingly lead, girls to refuse to be homemakers or to nervous breakdowns; women's minds were simply less able to absorb the kind of knowledge men's absorb, while educating them would produce individualization and decrease their willingness to contribute to family life. Musterberg (1905), a Harvard psychologist with a strong German background, saw dire consequences for the society at large from the education of women: It would weaken the system and lower the educational, and thus the scientific, achievement of American men, losing this society's ability to compete in the world.[1] Thus, the social-person characteristics in the role of student were deemed masculine, and absent in women or detrimental to their health if they were introduced to them. The social circles in higher education were all male-dominated. However, a new ideological movement of the nineteenth century provided a justification for increasing educational opportunity to women: It would make them better family members. Ehrenreich and English (1979) trace this shift to the idealization of the roles of mother and wife and to the influence of medical experts. Women were now seen as needing more complex knowledge in order to raise intelligent sons and help their husbands (Schwager 1987, 337). Their education was to be limited, however, to home economics and related subjects of use in family and homemaking roles. Thus, higher education was divided into two spheres.

The feminine mystique decades of the twentieth-century that limited women to family roles did little to encourage their involvement in the role of student beyond those legally and culturally prescribed norms, unless it prepared them to teach or nurse others before starting their own families. Women who entered higher education were allegedly looking for a husband who would be successful or, by contrast, they were interested in a career at the sacrifice of family roles. Furthermore, men did not want highly educated wives. For example, the marriage rates of Wellesley graduates between 1889 and 1908 were extremely low, although most of the women did not plan for a career (Frankfort 1977, 58–59). Rossi (1965) found few pioneers in her study of college students as late as in the 1960s. The psychiatrists of various forms influenced by Freud also found scientific and all other demanding careers inappropriate for women (Bettelheim 1965; Erikson 1965; Friedan 1963). In the meantime, Poland and the Soviet Union, needing women in science, engineering, medicine, and dentistry because of the loss of men during World War II, simply redefined women and these fields as appropriate to each other (Sokolowska 1965). These facts show the strength of the social-person stereotypes of areas of life. It is only recently that American universities have begun to reconceptualize science and other knowledge fields in an effort to make them more gender-neutral—mainly due to the direct push from feminists, or new governmental laws and policies. The Civil Rights Act of 1964, the 1972 Education Amendments Act and Title IX of the Equal Rights Amendment helped to force universities and related organizations that obtained federal money to cease discrimination (Mezey 1992; Sochen 1982). Such laws did not mean, however, that the social circle of the established university greeted women students gracefully or facilitated involvement in this role.

In spite of the debate about women and schooling and the hostility of male faculty and students, women were quietly expanding the number of years they spent in schools and the variety of establishments they attended (Solomon 1985). Many observers failed to understand the extent of this change in women's identities and their aspirations to educational achievement. Sewell and Hauser (1975) predicted only a slow change:

> In 1965, 12 percent of the adult male population and 7 percent of the adult women were college graduates. By 1985, these proportions are expected to rise to 18.6 and 12.5 percent, respectively. (P. 10)

Their predictions were pessimistic. By 1979–80 there was a 24 percent increase over 1975–76 in the number of women Ph.D.s (Lopata, Miller and Barnewolt 1986, 210–11). The *Chicago Sun Times* reported (Nelson 1989) that the Department of Education predicted that women would be receiving the majority of doctorates by the year 2000.

However, at all levels of higher education, prejudice and discrimination against women continue, especially in certain fields, due to the myths concerning women's abilities. The characteristics seen as necessary for work in mathematics and natural science are seen as lacking in women. One way of solving this problem is for women to fit the male model of student. Aisenberg and Harrington (1988) caution that a woman must transform herself into an active persona, prepared to be an autonomous expert, in order to succeed in academia. The fight includes changing not only the self, but, even more importantly, relations with all circle members in the role of student in preparation for changes in relations with circle members in succeeding roles. The other solution is the creation of a university, or part of one, that gives equal status to subjects and styles of learning and doing for which women have been already socialized (Howe 1977). This effort started as the very successful women's studies programs and is now pushing for a deconstruction of all traditional areas of knowledge.

An Example of the Effects of Schooling in Transitional Times

The effects of all these constructions of reality concerning education and women can be seen in the Chicago-area studies. The 1950s and 1960s women described in *Occupation: Housewife* (Lopata 1971b) had seldom reached more than a high school education, and few used that schooling to prepare for a multidimensional life space. Even then, however, variations in the consequences of the number of completed years of schooling were dramatic. It became apparent that formal schooling is an extremely important contributor to women's breadth of perspective, self-esteem, and ability to utilize the resources of the society in their involvement in social roles (see also Lopata 1981a, 19). The more education the woman had, the more complex and creative she was in her construction of reality and behavior. Her educational achievement also influenced whom she married and her life during and after marriage.

The same conclusion was reached independently in the widow-hood studies (Lopata 1973a, *Widowhood in an American City,* and 1979, *Women as Widows: Support Systems*). There was, however, one surprise in the findings: The more education a woman achieved, and the more middle-class life-style she and her husband developed while he was living, the more disorganized her life and self-concept became when he died. This is mainly due to such a woman's greater dependence on her husband, being a wife, and on being the wife of that particular husband. On the other hand, the more education she had, and the more middle-class her life-style, the more she was able to reorganize her life patterns and to develop a new social life space.

The reexamination of results from these two sets of studies leads to the conclusion that formal schooling has been of extreme importance to the social involvements of American women, even at a time when knowledge still tended to be organized into gender-specific areas (Lopata 1973a). The less formal schooling a woman achieved even then, the more apt she was to be socially isolated, to be unable to adjust to life changes, and to hold negative attitudes about social relationships. The increasingly voluntaristic nature of social involvement in more-developed and large-scale societies requires of members the kind of knowledge, thought processes, and competence that formal education provides.

The *City Women* study (Lopata, Barnewolt, and Miller 1985) reflected the continuation of a limited use of education for occupational futures by the older, transitional women, but a completely new view of it by the more modern respondents. The latter saw it as an ongoing activity, flexibly used to meet changing needs. Many of the younger women used school to prepare for specific occupations, anticipating life-course changes in other roles. However, a surprising 43 percent of the whole sample returned to school after assuming they had completed education earlier in life (Lopata, Barnewolt, and Miller, 1985).

The Role of Student at Reentry

The traditional educational system of American society was, and basically still is, designed for a young person who has gone through school with only scheduled interruptions since childhood. This applies also to higher education. Such young people are expected to live on campus or nearby and not to have competing marital and parental roles. The ideal of a university locates it in a small town in which it dominates the student's life. The student role is dominant; the circle contains faculty and administrators, service providers, and fellow students organized into classes, majors, and voluntary associations promoting sports, dating, and social life in general.

One of the really dramatic changes in the role of student has been reentry by American women (also men, but not as frequently during the regular schedule) of varied ages.[2] The presence of such students is not reflective of a stage in the "ordinary" life course, nor can it be accounted for in terms of the pleasure of being on campus. It is used as a means of changing role clusters. Reentry is a point of transition, often from full commitment to roles in the family institution and homemaking to expansion in the public sphere (Faver 1984). The midlife student movement is counted in the millions and includes various degrees of involvement and combination with other sets of relations (Schlossberg 1984).

The Chicago-area returnees helped to decrystallize the influence of family background, which had been evident in initial achievements: Women from advantaged households obtained more schooling the first time around than did their less fortunate counterparts. Race had virtually no additional impact on the women's education after parental socioeconomic status, mother's education, and the age of entry into motherhood were taken into account (see also Mott et al. 1977).

The returnees ended up with an average of two years' more schooling than did those with continuous involvement. They most often finished in the school system they started in, and the more education a woman obtained initially, the greater the probability of her return. Interestingly enough, there is a strong association between return to school and divorce. One suspects that either women contemplating divorce decide to prepare themselves occupationally, or return to school so changes the person as to make the marriage stressful or at least no longer satisfactory.

The youngest of our three cohorts of Chicago-area women were much more oriented toward an education that would prepare them for greater involvement in the world outside of the home than had been the older cohorts, but the age thirty-five to forty-five cohort was most apt to return to school and change its life-style, gaining higher incomes and job satisfaction. The same positive results came from specific job training in midlife.

Although both undergraduate and graduate higher educational institutions have become more flexible in the admission of nontraditional students by removing the upper age limits, age remains a pervasive identity affecting the social relationships of the student. An interesting study of the changes introduced in the construction of reality and social circles of older women returning to school is contained in Levy's (1990) analysis of "off-time" students in a prestigious university. Their social circle simply did not know how to handle such older persons in student-faculty or student-student relations. The problems were even more complicated if the older woman entered a male-dominated field, which she was more likely to do than her younger and more occupationally inexperienced counterparts. Friendships were difficult to make with co-students who were in other life-course stages. Problems in relations with younger faculty derived from differences in status, which are accentuated in university settings.

In the meantime, the reentry student goes through several life-course discontinuities in other roles, since formal schooling is usually not considered an appropriate involvement at her age by her other social circles. The problems are illustrated by developments and changes in friendships in settings with which the woman is still affiliated in her nonstudent life (Levy 1990). Involvement in the role of student can disorganize the woman's participation in roles that previously dominated in her life. A subject of interest to sociologists observing this trend toward reentry of adult women into higher levels of the educational institution has been the attitude of the husband. Suitor (1988) reports that, although the more educated husband expresses enthusiasm over his wife's effort, he does not translate this into instrumental support as a member of the student's social circle or in other roles. A less educated husband, who initially expresses worry and mainly negative attitudes, nevertheless extends more support, possibly in anticipation of an increase in family income. The more educated husband may find the changes in his wife's scheduling and commitment to be an inconvenience he does not need. He may also worry about the consequences of his wife's achievements upon their relationship.

Friend

The role of friend is surrounded by many interesting cognitive and emotional nuances in American society. This was apparent when a group of us, sociologists all, got together to talk about the possibility of putting together a book on friendship in the different contexts in which we were studying other roles and relationships (Lopata and Maines 1990). Most of us found a gap between the ideal picture of the perfect friend, totally committed to the relationship, willing to make any sacrifices, aware of all emotional and more practical needs, accepting of all behavior, and providing a very attractive "looking-glass" image of the self and reality in the settings we were studying (Cooley [1902] 1922). At least in American society, emphasis on the value of work for men in proper Protestant-ethic form and the value of "true womanhood" for women, devoted exclusively to the husband, children, and home, defines strong friendship as almost dangerous in that it could interfere with such commitments. In this highly competitive world men allegedly cannot trust each other with disclosures and intimacies, which could expose signs of weakness, while women allegedly are so competitive in their search for, and possessiveness about, men as to make each other unlikely friends. Raymond (1986), in fact, claims that it has been impossible for modern women to enter true friendships with each other in a man-made world, and found it only among lesbians, in convents, or among Chinese marriage resisters of a century ago.

In spite of all these alleged restrictions on friendship in this society, numerous studies point to its presence and variations among women. For example, Bernard documented extensive and multi-level friendships among women in *The Female World* (1981) and Smith-Rosenberg (1979) used letters and diaries of the mid-eighteenth and nineteenth centuries to bring to light networks of friends that provided emotional support, security, and self-esteem and that were central to the members' lives.

A variety of factors influence the social-person characteristics of people selected as friends, the composition of the social circle, and the packages of negotiated rights and duties. Americans vary greatly by stage of life cycle, generation, gender, ethnic and racial background, education, residence, and so forth in whom they identify as a friend. Sociologists have assumed that friendship is most apt to bloom among the elderly, since other roles are less demanding at that time of life. Yet, there is no consensus concerning such a frequency of friendship in old age. Pihlblad and Rosencranz (1968) found some older people in small towns of Missouri claiming all residents as friends, while others claimed to have no friends at all. Other elders spoke of the impossibility of developing relations now that could duplicate those with a lovingly described childhood chum. It appears that old age alone is not a sufficient factor in friendship formation. Physical proximity with people of the same age and marital and life circumstances are facilitating situations, as Hochschild found among women in *The Unexpected Community* (1973). Roberto and Scott (1984–85) tested equity theory on the friendship of elderly women using my support-systems framework and found that those who were "overbenefited," that is, who received more support than they gave, had the lowest morale. Those who were underbenefited, by their terminology, were pleased to be able to help a friend not as well off as themselves. Constraints, such as health or financial problems, can limit the formation of friendship in old age (Rook 1989).

Sources of contact with potential friends depend upon the social involvements of the person; the variety of these is influenced by the complexity of the social life space. During the transitional times of the feminine mystique, restrictions on direct involvement in the public sphere limited the sources to school in childhood, and to the neighborhood and voluntary associations in the roles of wife and mother. Women have expanded their involvements in more modern times, providing greater variations in sources of contact, with mixed results. On the one hand, a job can demand considerable time, especially when combined with the second shift at home, decreasing occasions for developing and maintaining friendships. On the other hand, the job provides opportunities for pleasant interaction, whether limited to such settings or carried into leisure-time activity. The mobility of many women, both social and geographic, almost necessitates a turnover of friends (see also Lopata 1975). It can also bring together people of strongly divergent social classes (Hess 1972; Matthews 1986). The opportunity of finding points of commonalty and divergence, facilitators and barriers, thus differs by setting.

The development of a friendship requires repeated social interaction, preferably, but not necessarily, face-to-face, that can increase perceptions of similarity (Adams and Blieszner 1989; Bell 1981). It is the perceived similarity of interests, reinforced by continued contact, rather than similarity of cultural background, that contributes to friendship formation (Gudykunst 1985, 281). The interaction must be egalitarian, although masters or husbands in asymmetrical relations can claim to be close friends with servants or wives. The person in the subservient position is less likely to so define the relationship.

Once established, friendship acquires a personalistic focus, each partner seeing the other as unique so that intercultural differences recede into the background. Jackson and Crane (1986) studied black-white friendships and concluded that contact is not enough to do away with prejudice and categorical discrimination. Even positive affective dispositions toward a person of another social race is not enough to support equality in the relationship. The best combination appears to include a black of a higher social status than the white, since equality of personal prestige does not offset categorical inferiority. White-black friendships appear more frequent in academia or the entertainment world than in the general population, where equality of interaction and commonalty of interests are less likely.

One of the findings of my various studies in the Chicago area is that some women, usually lower-class and less educated, do not define the role of friend as something that one can develop, assuming either that kin members are the only possible intimates or that such relations can be achieved only in childhood (see also Rubin 1976). The assumption that adults have trouble making friends appears to be prevalent, as evidenced by the existence of numerous for-profit organizations that educate people into the techniques of such development. Dale Carnegie's 1936 book and still popular courses teach people how to "win friends and influence people," etiquette publications abound, and the mass media are full of reports on ways people unaccustomed to developing close nonkin and nonjob relationships with others can learn how to do so. The military and multinational corporations, which force their members into frequent geographic movement, use shortcuts such as enforced socializing to create opportunities for social contact.

The role of friend necessitates not only purposeful development through efforts on both sides, but also maintenance activities (Blieszner 1989; Brown 1990). McCall and Simmons (1978) see friendships as incorporating increasing dimensions of self-identities. Although circumstances can create boundaries, especially when friends are not able to observe each other in other contexts, Little (1990) shows that the sharing of reminiscences, symbolic representations, and even letters can provide insights among buddies who have never seen each other's other selves. Of course, people may wish to segment their friendships, leaving parts of the self uninvolved.

Most observers point to the importance of a positive balance of benefits over costs for a friendship's maintenance. The costs frequently involve strain in relations with significant others who may be jealous of the time and closeness involved in the friend relationship. The benefits include empathetic understanding, even love, acceptance of even less than likable aspects of the self regardless of societal norms, the pleasure of association and sharing activities, protection from unpleasant self-images and sometimes even from unpleasant interaction, the provision of resources for reaching goals, and so forth. Many women stress the importance of friendships in the reconstruction of the self from traditional identities into feminist ones (Acker, Barry, and Esseveld 1990). Factors that underlie the selection of friends may differ from those that sustain or deepen the relationship (Brown 1990, 31–32). In order to exist as a role, of course, a relationship must include more than two people, in a set of friends or a setting of supporting circle members. In fact, a friendship is frequently embedded in a friendship network, with more or less freedom to form closer dyads (Baker and Hertz, 1990). The circle can provide resources, such as space and activity for contact among friends, and can protect them from interference by others. Thus, the relations does not exist in isolation.

Friendships are temporal, changing in characteristics and salience as other aspects of life over which choice is not always possible are modified. This happens, for example, when people move away, for a job or other reasons. Dubin (1956) found factory workers perfectly willing to change jobs even if it meant giving up friendships in the old locale. They knew they could replace them easily enough in the new setting. One of the problems of retirement is the impossibility of maintaining such relationships as the settings vanish.

Commitments to the role of friend, involving "side bets" to anchor this role, are often not sufficiently important to offset commitments to other roles. To paraphrase Janowitz (1968), modern friendships appear to involve limited liability and the willingness to give them up if their benefits fail to satisfy. At the same time, as diffused as friendships appear to be in our society, they also seem to contain rules that, when broken, create strains and often end the relationship (Duck 1986; Rook 1989; Matthews 1986). Violations of such norms include breach of confidence, invasion of privacy, or critical and unresponsive behavior. Sometimes friendships simply face not being revitalized over time. The failure of a dyadic relationship can create problems for the network in which it is embedded.

Whatever meaning the role of friend has for different people, its perceived absence tends to create feelings of social and emotional loneliness (Lopata 1969b; Weiss 1973). People need a variety of relationships (Weiss 1973). People are especially devastated when former friendships are broken off, especially when this does not happen through their own action and they think other people are involved in relations of satisfactory intimacy (see Lopata 1990).

Same-Gender and Cross-Gender Friendships

Two questions are usually raised in discussions of the role of friend: whether, and in what ways, friendships among women differ from those among men, and what are the characteristics of cross-gender relationships.

Although much attention has been given in the mass media and in social science literature to male "bonding" ever since Tiger's *Men in Groups* (1969) appeared, the general consensus appears to be that women form closer, more intimate friendships with each other than do men (Rubin 1985). Men more often lack a best friend or list a woman who does not identify the relationship as symmetrical. A New Zealand study found strong "gender differences in friendship patterns" (Aukett, Ritchie, and Mill 1988). Women's relationships were more intimate and emotional, involving talking, sharing, discussing personal problems, and self-disclosure. Men tended to share activities but to shy away from emotional involvement. Williams (1985) concluded that male colleagues were more instrumental in their support of each other, while women were more expressive.

Even women's same-gender and same-stage-of-life-course friendships can be constrained by involvement in competing roles. Fischer reported in 1982 that marriage restricted the possibilities of non-kin and non-neighbor friendships for women. In addition,

> Children clearly restricted the social involvements of their parents, especially of their mothers. Women with children at home had fewer friends and associates, engaged in fewer social activities, had less reliable social support, and had more localized networks than did otherwise similar women without children. (Fischer 1982, 253)

These conclusions were very similar to those I had reached almost thirty years before, accentuating the importance of looking at a person's role cluster in determining the social psychological aspects of involvement in any one role (Lopata 1971b).

The findings concerning same-gender friendships raise interesting questions concerning cross-gender relationships. Do women gain different benefits from men friends than from women friends? A difference can also be assumed for the men. Several studies address these subjects directly. Women college and graduate university students reportedly prefer same-gender relationships for intimacy and acceptance, but cross-gender friendships for companionship (Rose 1985). The latter is not surprising on a campus where dating is the prevalent companionship activity. Rose (1985) reports that men are more dependent upon significant women in their lives than women are on men. O'Meara (1989) cautions that cross-gender relationships must meet four major challenges:

> These include the private challenges of defining the nature of their emotional bond, regulating the role of sexuality, and dealing with the impact of gender inequality, and the public challenge of presenting the authenticity of the friendship to relevant audiences in the friends' social networks. (P. 539)

The problem of sexuality and the assumption by others in social circles that any relationship between a woman and a man must be based on this element is not surprising in a society that evaluates women mainly as sex objects. Adams (1985) entitled her article on the subject "People Would Talk: Normative Barriers to Cross-Sex Friendships for Elderly Women."

The differences in what women and men offer each other in friendship produce an asymmetrical relationship. Aukett, Ritchie, and Mill (1988) decided that men get more emotional support and therapeutic value from women friends than women get from men friends; women do not benefit equally in their cross-gender relations as they do from same-gender ones. Acker, Barry, and Esseveld (1981) explained that the new feminism in America at first strained cross-gender relationships, as women felt a strong need to develop greater independence from men and anger over their past subservient status, but the authors expect that in the long run it will help the formation of new, egalitarian friendships. Rubin (1985) found that gay men and straight women often were comfortable with each other and able to enter close friendship relations.

Couple-Companionate Friendship

One of the interesting aspects of friendship in this society is the increasing frequency of association between the role of wife and that of friend. Middle-class modern America insists that marital partners should also be "best friends" (Bell 1981; Rubin 1985). In addition, companionate marriage favors what I call "couple-companionate" relations. Women and men who marry are expected to convert their past friendships into relationships involving both mates and to develop new friendships with other couples. For example, change in friendship networks evolves even among college student couples as they deepen their involvement with each other (Milardo 1982). Joint networks help to preserve the couple relationship, while separate friendships "are more invested in one individual or the other than in the couple" (Milardo, 1982; 170).

The friendship conversion process by married couples can be difficult, unless there is sufficient communality among all the people involved in the couples. Block and Greenberg (1985) were wrong when they stated:

> A century ago, few married couples socialized . . . in more recent years, particularly in the last half century, the belief that women and men could be socially compatible emerged. (P. 138)

On the contrary, there is a long history of couple-companionate relations in European and American upper classes (see Veblen [1899] 1953; Znaniecki 1965). Compatible couples have long enjoyed many games and other pastimes together. Couples in modern times tend to do things together on Saturday nights or at other times if retired from paid employment, and share a variety of activities. The role of couple-companionate friend requires that each member treat the others symmetrically in what they do for each other's entertainment and expenses. For example, hospitality in the home should be reciprocated, unless there is an acceptable reason for alternative privileges. It is possible, of course, that the women can have separate personal friendships with each other, but couple-companionate occasions are to be symmetrical, within gender propriety norms.

One of the fascinating aspects of couple-companionate friendships is the source of the contact, the person who brings the other couple into the relationship. Babchuk and Bates (1963) claim that the husbands dominated as the originators of such relationships, at least among urbanites in Nebraska. I found that the wives gave themselves credit in most situations, even when the original contact was through the husband's job (Lopata 1975 and 1990). The wife, who is usually the "social secretary" for the middle-class couple, defines her contribution as the selection of couples from that milieu for close interaction. Claim of contribution gives the originator greater rights and obligations for continued maintenance.

Divorce and widowhood place great strains upon couple-companionate friendships, bringing forth the importance of symmetry and balance (Lopata 1973b, 1975, 1979, etc.). Widows are constantly faced with the fact that their married friends tend to withdraw, or to see them only when their husbands are absent (Adams 1983). Whether accurately or not, widows report that their married women friends are jealous of their possible relations with their husbands (Lopata 1973c). There is an awkwardness over transportation, payment of bills, and other interactional aspects, while past loyalties linger. "His friends" who allegedly became "our friends" revert to their original identity and fail to keep up the contact (Kitson et al. *Divorcees and Widows* 1980). Life circumstances become too different to maintain the feelings of "we-ness." Both widows and divorcees finally turn to other women in the same marital situation, although they feel deprived of male companionship (Adams 1983 and 1985; Adams and Blieszner 1989).

Neighbor

The role of neighbor is another component of a frequent nostalgia for the past. The village or small town is idealized as containing neighbors whom one has known throughout life, who are familiar with the family and all of its history, and who are always there to provide social and emotional support as well as help in emergencies (Fischer 1982). Anyone familiar with such communities, as contained, for example, in Reymont's description (in his Nobel Prize–winning *The Peasants* [1925]) of life in a Polish village, knows better than to accept such portrayals. However, this does not stop much of literature on urbanism from being extremely critical of an alleged lack of such ideally drawn neighboring. At the same time, early observers of suburbia were very negative about that style of life because of "too much" neighboring. Most were horrified by the alleged homogeneity, ease of interaction, and decrease of norms of privacy (Mumford 1961; Riesman, Glaser, and Denney 1950; Whyte 1956). What they neglected to note was that the women were turning to each other to create a new, revolutionary style of life, much as had the women studied by Willmot and Young (1960) who moved from a London borough to a suburb.

The concept of neighboring illustrates the difference between availability of a role and actual involvement. Our concern here is with neighbors as people who live within a self- and other-defined geographical "neighborhood," be it composed of apartments, homes within a dense but small territory, or farms scattered on individual acres away from others. It is, of course, possible to talk of people in a work setting or sharing a table at an official event as "neighbors," but I am limiting this discussion to residential proximity. Almost everyone has neighbors, but the role of neighbor involves active exchanges of rights and duties with people considered neighbors. The circle of neighbors may form an integrated network, all members being aware of belonging, communicating, and interacting with each other along established norms.[3] It is this form of neighboring upon which network analysts focus (Fischer et al. 1977; Fischer 1982). It is necessary to note here that our role theory does not negate the presence of such networks but also considers other persons with whom a neighbor may be involved who are not part of the network. For example, being a neighbor may require interaction with the neighbor's children, service and object providers, businesses, school personnel, and so forth.

Neighborhoods vary considerably in the relationships among their residents, as do individuals, communities, even societies. There can be pockets of intense neighboring even in a working-class community with minimal or restricted interaction among those living nearby. The forms and intensity of neighboring vary by the history of interaction, the abilities, desires, and resources of residents, and the competition this role has from other roles in each person's cluster. An important element in neighboring, as in friendship, is the match between the person and the neighbors in social class, race, ethnicity, age, and other common or division-creating characteristics (Lopata 1971b). People living in close proximity almost invariably come into some form of contact, but that can as easily lead to hostility or indifference as to friendly interaction.

The Transitional Form of the Role of Neighbor

Early studies of neighboring in American cities were usually incorporated into research on ethnic communities, prior studies having focused on rural or pioneer relationships. The Chicago school of sociology is famous for such interest in ethnic communities. Wirth's *Ghetto* (1928) is a classic of this type. Scholars studied the influence of increasing size, density, and heterogeneity upon social relations (Wirth 1938). Expansion of large, dense, and heterogeneous cities led scholars such as Stein (1960) to theories of community eclipse.

Social scientists reactivated their interest in neighboring after World War II, with the phenomenal growth of new, and the expansion of old, suburbs surrounding American cities. The G.I. Bill, which helped veterans obtain additional schooling, also assisted them with low-interest loans for the purchase of homes. The housing industry boomed, and mass media as well as sociologists followed people out of the city to see how they lived and related to each other. These various studies contribute to our understanding of factors that activate, or suppress, involvement in the role of neighbor.

For example, builder-designed communities, such as Park Forest, Illinois, were isolated from other settlements, and neighbors were highly dependent upon each other for all kinds of service and emotional supports (Whyte 1956). Upwardly and geographically mobile young residents often came from distances that prevented frequent contact with relatives and friends and made people willing to go through the stages of active neighboring. Most of the women in newly emerging communities developed a quite intensive involvement in the role of neighbor. The fact that urbanists such as Whyte (1956) and his associates and Lewis Mumford (1961) were quite disparaging concerning the women's "fishbowl" existence did not decrease the desire for such relationships, especially in Park Forest. Some of the Park Foresters complained of not having any privacy, but most were thrilled to have such social and support exchanges. Even women not socialized into middle-class forms of social interaction, such as the California residents described in *Working Class Suburb* (Berger 1960) or Levittowners in Pennsylvania, slowly replaced kinfolk with neighbors for support systems (Gans 1967). Active neighboring took place in the Canadian middle-class Crestwood Heights (Seeley, Sim, and Loosely 1956), but the higher status "exurbanites" around New York City engaged in selective interaction with those neighbors they deemed to be of equal status (Spectorsky 1955).

I first became interested in the neighboring relations of American suburban women in the 1950s when my husband and I moved with a small child to a suburb of Chicago (Skokie) while I was finished my dissertation at the University of Chicago. Having been brought up in a much more formal milieu in urban Poland, I was amazed as the informality of interaction in our neighborhood, which consisted of twenty new trilevel houses built by the same developer and containing mainly of young couples with children. This fascination turned into several research projects, summarized in *Occupation Housewife* (Lopata 1971b), to which numerous references have already been made.

The Chicago-area studies, many of which involved observation and open-ended interviews, produced a model of several forms and intensities of involvement in the role of neighbor, which are applicable to other settings. The forms were these: casual conversation when out of the dwelling for other purposes; borrowing and lending; exchange or one-directional services; invitational get-togethers by the women; men's socializing; and couple-companionate interaction in homes or even away from the neighborhood. All but one of these forms involved women, who, at that transitional period of American social development, stayed in the neighborhood during the day. These forms combined into several levels of involvement, as presented in table 1.

Table 1. Levels of Neighboring Interaction

None	Low	Medium	High
Anomic noninteraction	Casual	Institutionalized controls	Multiform
Institutionalized noninteraction	Seasonal	Self-imposed controls	Close
Justified noninteraction	Restricted to one form	Restricted to a few people selective	Causing uncomfortable strain in other social roles

Modified from Helena Znaniecka Lopata, *Occupation: Housewife* (New York: Oxford, 1971), p. 234

Noninteraction beyond the inevitable contact when occupying proximate territory, such as the mailroom or the garbage-disposal complex, involves anomic stances in dense, heterogeneous, and usually mobile areas in which people are simply not oriented toward personal exchanges. Institutionalized noninteraction is based on a local "consensus to so live," rather than on a lack of norms of neighboring (Lopata 1971b, 234). This is one way that people can prevent oppressive aspects of crowding, a construction of symbolic reality not available to animals. Justified noninteraction occurs when a person, or a set of neighbors, justifies a low level of interaction in situations of obvious expectations of greater sociability. Low levels can be casual, seasonal, or restricted to one form, while medium levels operate with controls, whether group- or self-imposed. Such levels abound among women who had been in intensive interaction in a past neighborhood and did not wish to duplicate it in the present one. Multiform, close involvement in the role of neighbor can create uncomfortable situations if the person does not know how to keep it in bounds.

Each community has its own norms for the duties and rights of the role of neighbor, varied by region due to climate and culture. The Midwest's norms fall somewhere between the conservative East Coast and the "instant friendship" of much of California. A specific neighborhood can change in its forms and content of neighboring over time, especially if it draws new populations with other tendencies. Social class and ethnic, as well as age and marital status, variations contribute their own styles of interaction, if perceived as homogeneous and matching. It is interesting to note that people in ethnic communities can completely ignore geographically close neighbors to enter the role with scattered others of the same identity (Lopata 1976b). Facilities for social contact such as parks, shopping malls, and taverns also contribute occasions for development of neighboring relationships. The distribution of housing units and of barriers can affect how people see each other and the amount of effort they make to enter neighboring roles. The location of the area vis-à-vis other institutional settings drawing people away from the immediate vicinity is also influential. This is one of the arguments made by conservatives against the busing of children out of neighborhoods. Many areas of central cities have so many resources for social involvement as to make benefits of neighboring negligible.

Finally, the personal characteristics of individuals and families contribute to the forms and intensity of involvement in the role of neighbor. Time spent in the area, competition from other roles, perceived similarity of interests with people living nearby, permanence of one's own settlement, and the rate of mobility of other residents all influence such relations. Transients, especially of backgrounds different from one's own, are usually looked upon with suspicion, and few efforts are made to invest in a relationship with them. The behavior of each person and even of other family members may attract or repulse potentially friendly neighbors. People differ not only in their ability to develop closer relationships with neighbors, but also in their interest in doing so.

There is a definite life cycle of the role of neighbor, its forms and intensity varying by the life cycle of the roles of the women and their families and by the cycle of neighboring in a particular area and of that role itself. The birth of a child, a child's entrance into the school system, and the role involvements of the husband/father or the wife/mother can move the role into a more focal place in the cluster or push it out to the outer layers. As children develop more independent sources of contact, the mothers can be deprived of the companionship of other neighborhood mothers. As a neighborhood ages, parks become deserted, and schools can close or consolidate with more distant ones; mothers are freed to enter new roles or reactivate old roles, as in taking a job or becoming a volunteer. A turnover of neighbors can break off a close relationship and result in less willingness to reinvest, or it can introduce people who are much more compatible. Increased income can provide the second car and mobility, decreasing dependence upon those living nearby. Established households require less emergency (and even daily) borrowing, lending, and exchanges of services.

A decrease in opportunities for, and interest in, the role of neighbor can be experienced differentially within a network, often causing strain. Women dependent upon the companionship and other benefits of such involvement can find that neighbors are too busy or wish to change the norms, forms, or intensity of the relationship. A change in leisure-time activities can separate a neighborhood network that played cards within the hearing of young children. Nonlocal friendships can replace the supports of nearby associates. Or someone made uncomfortable with an expansion of neighboring into higher levels may try to cool it, without having adequate techniques for doing so (Goffman 1967). Other problems can arise, as in friendships, making the costs of neighboring disproportionate to the benefits. I found frequent references to conflicts among children or over property rights as main reasons for withdrawal from active neighboring. In fact, such conflicts can split a whole neighborhood into warring camps (Lopata 1971b, 251).

Thus, the person most apt to be involved in the role of neighbor at a somewhat controlled high level in the 1950s and 1960s was a full-time homemaker with small children, a home owner living in a newly developed, middle-class suburb or urban fringe community of similar women. This is particularly true if she had been socialized into developing relationships with virtual strangers, aware of, and following, the norms of reciprocity and privacy. She was not apt to have highly supportive relatives within easy distance upon whom she could depend at all times. She was matched by many characteristics with her neighbors, having common interests and problems, and so developed an egalitarian exchange, not necessarily of the same supports.

The Modern Form of the Role of Neighbor

Suburban life and, to a lesser extent, urban life have been considerably modified since the feminine-mystique days, especially in areas that had previously almost exclusively drawn married full-time homemakers with children (see Stimpson et al. 1981; Lopata 1980a). The boundary between city and suburb has blurred, and living in an outside community is no longer a pioneering venture. Commercial and industrial activity has become more decentralized, providing jobs where only bedroom dwellings existed before.

Many of the women of metropolitan Chicago in 1990 display a different attitude toward the role of neighbor from that of the post–World War II homemakers. Fewer women have small children keeping them in the home and its immediate environment; more women do not marry, do not have children or have fewer than in prior cohorts, and do not stay home even when in the role of mother. The various questions as to forms and levels of neighboring often draw surprised comments—surprised that we expect such strong involvement. Neighboring has often narrowed to an exchange relationship, or close interaction with only one neighbor, and much less network involvement than in the past. Services that are now exchanged include the taking in of packages, mail, or other items in the daily or more lengthy absence of the other, a result of the frequency with which neighbor women are employed. Friendship is less often tied to the role of neighbor, as the women become less constricted to the local area. Education and income, indices of social class, still influence involvement in neighbor networks, especially in a network's size rather than intensity and emotional intimacy. Women of higher levels tend to know more neighbors and to visit more often, but the role is not as significant as among lower-class women, who develop longer lasting friendships with a few neighbors. The mixture of these two roles, friend and neighbor, is hard to separate.

The growing number of retirement communities and retired, leisure-oriented people may be increasing the importance of the neighbor role at that stage of life. More people are living longer and have the economic means to move to climates conducive to outdoor socializing. Retirement hotels or communities make special efforts to provide locales and events for neighboring and encourage the development of such roles as a means of keeping their residents happy (van den Hoonaard 1991). The expansion of such geographical areas in recent years certainly reinforces Rosow's (1967) and Hochschild's (1973) findings that age homogeneity provides an excellent resource for involvement in the role of neighbor.

Suburban and urban social relationships, including those of neighboring, have not been forgotten by social scientists, who still express negative evaluations of life in the outer areas. The strength of the rejection is still tied to an idealized image of the "dream house" in the "dream community." Baumgartner (1988) appears surprised that her affluent suburb of New York City contains people with hostile and indifferent attitudes, who nevertheless avoid open conflict with great restraint. Baldassare (1986) draws our attention to the trouble in paradise, exposing the assumption that paradise should be available in suburbia. Conflicts and anger at the way some communities have developed show involvement, even if negative, and accentuate the fact that the suburbs are not as homogeneous as originally portrayed. There is an increasing interest in the factors that create variations in the role of neighbor, in contrast to the original assumption of high levels of involvement. In spite of all the changes, unemployed women with small children are still most apt to depend on neighbors for social supports, while people involved in a multi-dimensional life space have broader and less intensive relations (Fischer et al. 1977; Fischer, 1982). Many people in many societies are still seeking the feeling and involvement of community life, judging by the frequency of active neighboring, especially in new towns (Thorns 1976). Women in Middletown were still engaged in neighboring exchanges in the 1980s (Caplow et al. 1982). Urban black communities can be seen as networks involving their residents (Oliver 1988), while neighboring contributes to residential satisfaction in Canadian cities (Michelson 1977). However, many of the recent studies of the role of neighbor in local areas exemplify Janowitz's (1968) thesis of the community of limited liability, in which members have multiple identifications and relationships, so that no single involvement can command strong commitment.

Roles in Communities

There are many social roles within the broader community, defined as a symbolic, territorial, or identity territory in which persons or groups are located (Hunter 1974; Lopata 1976b and 1994; Suttles 1972). This section of the chapter is focused on nonoccupational roles in voluntary associations in local, national and even international communities. Such groups can be identified by manifest (i.e., declared) functions or latent, more hidden functions, or by type of membership. People involved in such groups can be differentiated by level of commitment or position and type of activity. Complex social groups can work toward several purposes, and each member can be involved in one or a combination of them, at any level, at any stage of involvement. For example, a hospital auxiliary can benefit patients by providing objects (such as books) and services (such as companionship), while simultaneously benefiting members by offering social status in the community and activity outside of the home. It can train women in leadership roles or be part of a family's status-production work. Numerous characteristics or pervasive identities of social persons, such as gender, race, religion, ethnicity, and age, can serve as criteria for admission or rejection of potential members. So can interests, such as skiing or stamp collecting. Members may meet frequently or only through representatives. They can move up or down ladders of authority or status positions. In fact, it would be impossible to analyze all the combinations and permutations of characteristics of organizational roles, so I shall concentrate on a limited number of roles organized by breadth of beneficiary. It is important to specify these, because, unlike with the role of mother or wife, the beneficiaries are not always apparent even from the title of the group, and the roles of members are dependent upon these. The first type of group is organized to benefit only the members. The second consists of volunteers whose beneficiaries are external to the group but limited to the local community. The third includes activists or reformers on the national and/or global scale, whose beneficiaries are whole categories of beings, whether people or other species.

The social person characteristics and the activities of each association are more or less formally matched. The criteria of membership of social persons depend on manifest and latent purposes of the group, the duties required, and the rights and privileges offered. These obviously vary so much that generalizations are difficult to make. Some groups have gradations of membership, with scales of duties and rights (Clawson 1986). A woman can take an active part, with other activists, in the campaign to get Nestlé milk products withdrawn from markets in developing countries, without maintaining a lifelong membership in any reform group. Knowledge of the group and willingness to abide by its norms are universal requirements. So is the obligation to treat other members in the expected manner, to allow authoritative actions from those granted leadership privileges, to present the self in a manner not embarrassing to others, and to do the necessary work at the right time in the required setting.

Research on voluntary associations usually focuses on evidence of latent purposes, as in charitable groups that spend so much time selecting the right members and maintaining high-status activities as to indicate that their manifest purpose is really secondary in importance to social status. Only a careful examination of the actual criteria used to select members and the relative importance of activities can bring to light the conscious, or sometimes even unconscious, functions. Evaluative research can also focus on dysfunctional activities that interfere with main goals. Some researchers try to determine the reasons people join or avoid joining a particular group, or a category of such groups. This is especially true of associations designed to benefit people who often fail to take advantage of the benefits, as is true of those devoted to the elderly or the handicapped (Fisher et al. 1989).

The significance for women of participation in all kinds of voluntary associations has not been carefully researched. In studies devoted to the whole social life space, the role usually does not appear as the most important in women's role clusters, but this varies considerably by social class or special group affiliation. Some women and some groups have intensive interconnections, the networks functioning as a constant background to other roles, or even in a central location of the role cluster (see also the special issue of

Signs, Women in the American City [Stimpson et al. 1980]). What a person gains from membership and activity varies, of course, by the same sociopsychological aspects of involvement that apply to other roles.

Several researchers have recently studied the differences in the role of member in voluntary organizations as carried forth by women and by men. McPherson and Smith-Lovin (1982) drew on a large sample of noninstitutionalized adults in Nebraska and found differences having extensive consequences upon life and social influence. Women were members of smaller and different kinds of groups than were men. Small size in itself had negative consequences, in that it limited the number of potential contacts. Although they had the same mean number of memberships as did the men, the women limited themselves to "domestic, including youth, church-related, social charitable, neighborhood and community organizations," while men belonged to job-related organizations (union, professional, or business) or nondomestic organizations (fraternal, sports, veterans, political, hobby, and service and civic; McPherson and Smith-Lovin 1982, 901). The researchers accounted for the differences in terms of selective recruitment by high-powered, prestige organizations, which prefer high-status, high-income, high-mobility men, or selective joining by women in traditionally defined roles. They conclude that women join organizations that value their skills and interests, which tend to be local and small in size. These cannot "provide access to information about jobs, business opportunities or chances for professional advancement" and thus place women at a disadvantage vis-à-vis that world. This analysis fits beautifully into our role theory, in that it documents the importance of social person and social circle selection processes and the criteria.

We could say that such gender variation may be typical of Nebraskans but certainly not of such a cosmopolitan environment as New York City! It appears, however, that there are also status differences in the type and level of involvement by women in organizations in that city. Lawson and Barton (1980) studied the tenant movement in New York, which included organizations in buildings, neighborhoods, and larger federations. The movement was started by women on the local level and then spread geographically and horizontally. The authors found that the higher the level of the positions in the larger units that required negotiation with bureaucracies, and the higher the income of the tenants, the more the leaders were apt to be men (235).

The explanation for the divergence follows traditional gender roles. The fact that women started the tenant movement on the building level is due to their responsibility for the domestic sphere with its related problems. Such involvement brings them into contact with other women residents who share similar activities and content. Local participation is also more socially acceptable for them than is citywide activism. There is an additional gender difference in involvement in the movement. The men who enter, usually at a less local and higher level of leadership, are in the movement mainly for career reasons. Their expertise and knowledge of "bureaucratic manipulations" is transferable to other organizations, and they tend to move on. This rapid turnover at higher positions enables the women, who learn from them, to finally move into leadership positions. In making policy recommendations, the authors suggested that men should learn to utilize the local skills of women and combine these with formal, large-organization skills in developing and maintaining social movements. The opposite direction of organizational advantages was not recommended for the women.

A study of two organizations in the women's movement, however, provides guidelines stressing the advantages of a "formalized or bureaucratic structure." Staggenborg (1989) followed the history and format of the Chicago Women's Liberation Union, which did not survive, and the Chicago chapter of the National Organization for Women, which is still in existence. The former allowed more innovation, but was undermined by a lack of formalized structure and centralized division of labor. Although Chicago NOW is seen as disadvantaged by too much centralization and lack of contribution by subunits, its paid staff and organizational techniques are judged to assist continuity. These kinds of studies are sociologically interesting because of the underlying assumption that women are not able to organize effectively. Such a hypothesis is erroneous, in view of the history of women's groups the world over.

Member of Voluntary Associations

Women have been involved in community roles for centuries, although the definition of these varies by society and time. Religious communities abounded in Europe and have a complicated history in America. Women also participated in a variety of ways in courts of rulers. It is safe to say, however, that only a tiny proportion of past populations were involved in any but local groups. The vast majority participated in, without choosing, village life and informal group-ings, the church being the main formal organization. Thomas and Znaniecki (1918–20) described the Polish peasant of the early twen-tieth century as limited in the perspective to the *okolica*, the local area within which his or her reputation was contained. In spite of nationalistic movements by political rulers and the intelligentsia, most Europeans did not see, and were not interested in, the wider national cultural society, let alone the world.

The same can be said of the majority of less educated Americans. In addition, the emergence of the "Cult of True Womanhood" in the nineteenth century discouraged women from participation in public sphere activities that fell into the province of men. Foreign travelers like de Toqueville ([1835] 1936) and Harriet Martineau ([1837] 1966) were astounded by the lack of opportunity for women to be in-volved in the world outside of the home. In actuality, however, there were many local groups, formal and informal, of women who shared work or leisure time and church activities in colonial America. These groups blurred the boundaries between the role of neighbor and that of member of an association, with its formal characteristics of title, tests of membership, declared function, division of labor, and hierarchy of status. The increasing numbers of middle- and upper-class women in larger communities became involved in associations providing the role of volunteer in a wider arena:

> Volunteering broke it [the Cult of True Womanhood], for generations of leisured women who created new, unpaid jobs for themselves outside the home. It gave them public lives, ended their domestic isolation, and gave rise to organizations of women dedicated to insti-tutional reform in education, health care, and criminal justice, as well as the cultural and "moral" enrichment of society. (Kaminer 1984, 24)

Charity circles, anti-vice societies, and educational and politically oriented groups that were organized on a national scale helped the poor, insured the welfare of children, and worked to change the position and life of women. Antislavery and women's rights groups preceded and followed the Civil War. The Young Women's Chris-tian Association, the Women's Christian Temperance Union, and the National Consumers League are examples of early associations with a wide range of beneficiaries. It is interesting to note a basic difference between even these groups with broad goals: Some were oriented toward maintenance of the status quo, partly by solving some of its problems, while others were determined to reform the system itself. A few, but not many, were revolutionary, in that they aimed to overthrow the system and substitute a different one.

The role of status-maintaining volunteer remains even in modern times. Susan Ostrander (1985) comments on it in the world of upper-class women:

> The evidence presented in this chapter demonstrates that volunteer work provides certain personal advantages to upper-class women (such as the opportunity to advance to leadership positions without formal credentials, and to balance home and family responsibilities). But these personal advantages do not explain their overall commitment to this work . . . the women focus on class-specific reasons for doing volunteer work, such as noblesse oblige (which justifies privilege) and family tradition (which carries on the traditions of the class). These are the fundamental reasons for their commitment. (P. 138)

The level of commitment to this work is high, although the women downplay its importance to the community at large. Ostrander interestingly notes that

> upper-class women are not, for the most part, involved in direct service kinds of volunteer work. . . . Instead . . . [they] move quickly into leadership positions on the boards of their organizations. (P. 112)

However, volunteers managed by these upper-class women, who are themselves at least upper-middle-class in community status, contribute time and effort directly to the beneficiaries or at least raise funds used to do so. And the work civic leaders do definitely benefits the community, which could not exist in its modern form without it (Daniels 1988). Although their effort and careers within this world are mainly invisible, they can produce large sums of money, enabling the maintenance and growth of major community agencies. The patriarchal nature of the society is evident in the male dominance over the "important" positions in the same groups. The women's work and contributions are "backstage," while that of the males are front or center stage (Daniels 1988, 270). The backstage is in itself important, as it provides opportunities for others to accomplish the visible work, and it maintains the values of community, encouraging active participation of many other people. In general:

These women fund, organize and manage school, church, and neighborhood services. . . . All these efforts focus on two major lines of interest: voluntary activities in social reform and community welfare and cultural interests, community beautification, or "uplift." (Daniels 1988, xx)

Actually, their social reform efforts are limited to cleaning up any dysfunctional or inefficient aspects of the social system, rather than reforming the system itself.

Many of the traditional volunteer organizations also provide the female equivalent to the proverbial "old boy network" for the concentration of informal and even formal sources of power in the community. Domhoff concluded in *Who Rules America?* (1967) and *Who Rules America Now?* (1983) that persons listed in *Who's Who of American Women* were almost inevitably involved in a wide range of social groups with welfare, cultural, and civic activities. Membership roles carry appropriate obligations and rights of information and influence, as well as careful observance of norms of deference and demeanor (Ostrander 1985). Duties to fellow members include recognition and respect and strict adherence to the activities for which the group is known in the community. Unless the group is secret, which the vast majority are not, the need to maintain its reputation carries the obligation to meet its purposes, regardless of competition from other roles.

The presence of such status quo-maintaining organizations should not blind us to the recognition of many broader, reform-oriented women's associations. There is a whole history of more or less organized women's social movements pushing for dramatic change in American institutions, including those aimed at suffrage, protective legislation, mothers' rights over their children, the environment, and a variety of other economic and political rights for all Americans, as well as movements aimed against war and militarism. Those have not been the goals of groups maintaining the status quo.

Communities that depend upon volunteer workers and leaders are now facing major problems, as the same women who had the knowledge and ability to organize and carry out so many local activities are the very ones who can do similar work in a job. Wendy Kaminer concludes in *Women Volunteering: The Pleasure, Pain, and Politics of Unpaid Work from 1830 to the Present* (1984) that a community who "lived on its volunteers" is finding it hard to find substitutes (212). Certainly associations can hold meetings on eve-

nings and weekends, and some fathers are increasing their participation in "traditional women's things," but that still leaves much
daytime work undone. Who is to be a Brownie leader? The whole
ideology of volunteerism is questioned when people have to be
hired to do the work. It is the same problem that O'Donnell and
Stueve (1983) noted about the failure of employed middle-class
mothers to serve as the social agents connecting children to the
community. From the vantage point of the community itself, the
absence of these women has created a major void inadequately
filled by paid workers. Of course, not all women are employed;
many women of the upper and middle classes continue their activities with limited help. Attempts are made to socialize women of the
lower classes into less passive stances vis-à-vis their communities,
housing, and schools. An example of such efforts is the Organization
of the NorthEast in two of Chicago's most heterogeneous and prob-
lem-ridden neighborhoods. Women who traditionally did not venture out of home, church, and maybe a job have become active in
a variety of activities under the motto "Our Hope for the Future,"
meaning the children (Nyden et al. 1922). Men will undoubtedly be
forced to do more of the backstage work in the absence of women
who did it in the past.

One source of volunteers for traditional community work is
expanding in recent years. The developing concern over the graying
of America has resulted in a closer look at the voluntary association
membership of the elderly. The extensive survey *Older Minnesotans: What Do They Need? How Do They Contribute?* found many of
the elderly making volunteer contributions to others (Fisher et al.
1989). Their work was segregated to a certain degree by gender.
Women did welfare work of a personal nature, visiting people,
bringing food, helping the church function—all of which are extensions of family and homemaking activity. Men helped with male-
intensive work, such as house repairs, and were more active in
organizational management. Thus, gender assignment or selection
of activity, including leadership, does not end in old age.

Whatever the beneficiaries of the role of volunteer gain from this
activity, the social person also receives rewards. Involvement in the
role prevents, or at least delays, the "cycle of social breakdown,"
which Bengtson and Kuypers developed as a model of problems
associated with aging due to role loss and ambiguity of norms. Being
a volunteer with obvious duties and rights reconstructs feelings of

status and competence (Payne 1977). Activity in voluntary associations assists integration into the community, even at the lower-class levels, as Clemente, Rexroad, and Hirsch (1975) found among elderly black women. Ethnic and religious communities also provide resources for continued social involvement throughout the life course (Kitano 1988; Sklare 1971). The Polish Women's Alliance, founded in the 1880s and still active, has maintained a completely female staff of leaders, doctors, and lawyers (Lopata 1976b and 1993b). Problems occur if the community moves away to a secondary settlement, leaving behind the elderly, usually widowed women, who may be completely alienated from the new residents and their networks and thus become socially isolated (Lopata 1988a). In general, however, researchers find that voluntary associations are very important in the lives of the elderly, providing positive feedback to people who no longer have demanding roles upon which to focus (Cutler 1976).

In the meantime, women have been forming new types of associations based on new interests of their members. A major category of such groups has emerged from involvement in the more prestigeful and knowledge-demanding occupations. Occupational groups provide "networking" or contacts, information about jobs, and success stories as well as pointers. The newspapers and magazines of local communities, and occupational and professional journals, abound with announcements of meetings, training seminars, and opportunities for informal exchanges of problems and solutions (Kleiman 1980). I have recently been attending numerous meetings of Women in Sales, Women in Marketing, Women in Publishing, Women Business Owners, and so forth. Branches in different cities arrange for national meetings that much resemble those of the previously all-male National Sales Executives, except that the participants are much more open about barriers, lack of personal tools, and "helpful hints." These are examples of new forms of associations aimed at helping the members themselves. The main obligation of the member role is to transmit knowledge and skills useful in the occupation, as similar men's groups have done for years.

An example of an organization furthering the careers of members is the relatively new Sociologists for Women in Society. Consisting mainly of women (but with male members), it provides a journal aimed at making women and feminist theories more visible, conducts annual conferences with refereed scientific papers, has a mentoring program, and maintains a hotel suite at the American

Sociological Association's and related meetings for members to come together, talk, and arrange for social events. An important benefit to members is ease of involvement in a profession that traditionally was male-based and ignored women except as objects of sexual interest.

One of the new types of organizations in America (although similar, informal groups have usually existed in every community) is in the form of self-and-other help. These groups bring together people who have gone through a disorganizing experience, be it winning the lottery or the death of a significant other, or who are trying to solve personal problems. The most famous, and one of the oldest, is Alcoholics Anonymous (Denzin 1987a and 1987b). Silverman (1987) organized the initial Widow-to-Widow program at Harvard Medical School and studied similar groups as they sprang up all over the United States. Such organizations consist of widows who serve as mentors providing information about resources and confidante interaction at times of intense grief, as well as other widows to get together with to share experiences (Lopata 1973c and 1979). Self- or mutual-help groups are now being organized by women homemakers, according to Andre (1982). Their activities include food or babysitting cooperatives, cottage industries, and so forth.

Another part of the women's movement is aimed at opening up gender-restricted associations, much as the civil rights movement worked toward democratizing other restrictive groups. The pioneers have been tokens in groups composed mostly of the dominant gender or racial members. Clawson (1986) presents a historical picture of the Freemasons' and other quasi-Masonic groups' responses to women's demands for membership. The fraternals were purposely organized to exclude, and separate themselves, from, female influence. The formation of auxiliaries such as Eastern Star, as a compromise, allowed the membership in the main body to remain male-only. Wives of Rotarians can be "Rotary Anns"; American women could not join the Rotary itself until the U.S. Supreme Court declared such a membership policy unconstitutional. That decision created an uproar in some of the chapters. The June 1990 issue of *The Rotarian* contained a special section on women in Rotary. Although the cover story was titled "Women—Are They Changing Rotary?" the question was never really answered. Opposition is still strong among many male members, although one respondent said he had "mellowed a bit" (Nugent 1990, 27).

Member of Reform or Revolutionary Movements

Women's reform groups are often vaguely identified as part of the feminist movement, working for humanitarian and equal-rights causes (Mueller 1988). Although there have been some revolutionary groups at different times in American history since independence, they have not been as influential as groups that have limited themselves to reform.

Most historians trace the feminist movement to the Seneca Falls Declaration of 1848 (Sochen 1982). Women also organized farmers' alliances and employee groups, such as the International Ladies Garment Workers Union, and pushed for the vote for civil rights legislation (Hansen 1990). The activities of the Women's Christian Temperance Union certainly influenced political and private life (Gusfield 1963). Black women have been active in abolition, suffrage, and crusades against lynching, and for women's rights movements. Aptheker's *Tapestries of Life* (1989; see also Aptheker 1982) shows how resistance to patriarchal, racist, and class restrictions operates in the daily lives of women. Angela Davis (1988) reminds audiences all over the country of the importance of fighting racism and violence against women on the global scale.

Hartman, in *From Margin to Mainstream: American Women and Politics since 1960* (1989, vii), identifies three eras of the women's movement in America. The first lasted from "the birth of the nation to 1920," a period when women were not citizens and thus were unable to vote, hold office, or participate in party activities, so they had to exert influence indirectly, as did Abigail Adams. The second era lasted from 1920 till the 1960s—women had the vote but were not really integrated into the political system. Hartman dates the third era from the 1960s, when women began mobilizing actively to change major political policies toward their gender. Many scholars have analyzed these activities, successes, and failures (see, for example, Garland 1988, *Women Activists: Challenging the Abuse of Power*).

Examples of women's leadership in environmental protection abounded in the Public Broadcasting System's ten-hour program "Race to Save the Planet" in October 1990 (see *TV Guide*, 6–12 October 1990, 100). Women have organized to protest the militarization of this society, based on the mythology of maleness, which actually hurts the very people who play "war games" against real or hypothetical enemies (Allatt 1983; Enloe 1987). The Boston Women's Health Collective has three times published *Our Bodies, Ourselves* (1971, 1984, 1992), teaching women about the care of their bodies, and numerous protest groups have formed around the subject of human health.

An ongoing example of one form of women's pressure on the economic system is consumer activism (Bloom and Smith 1986). Some of the actions have been individual, such as complaints or personal boycotts against products, brands, or sellers, and legal action. Much, however, is organized through a variety of groups (see Warland, Herrmann, and Moore 1986 for a survey of such actions). The most dramatic has been the pressure to stop the distribution of Nestlé infant formula to less-developed countries because it resulted in a high mortality rate (Post 1986). Nestlé filed a defamation lawsuit in Switzerland to stop the boycott, but had to bow to pressure and settle out of court.

As Steinberg (1990) points out:

> Women have become an institutionalized force in American politics, with dramatic results: in the 1970s Congress passed 71 laws that were part of the feminist political agenda. Gains have been greatest in the extension of legal entitlement in employment and education, among them equal pay for work of comparable worth. (508)

Bernard (1979) summarized the extensive reform activity of various groups of women and their goals of the 1970s:

> They wanted protection for themselves against rape; they wanted an end to discrimination against them in education, vocational training, job opportunities. They wanted protection against "displacement" as housewives in middle life. They wanted recompense for their work in the home. They wanted credit on the same terms as men. They wanted into the social security system in their own names. They wanted a better public image in the media. An end to putdowns; changes in language, in forms of address. . . . They found issues that stunned the world, so long had they been swept under the carpet. (P. 285)

Participation in social movements can be undertaken at various levels and in various social roles. There is usually a core group of highly committed women who are involved in a variety of activities. It often includes both charismatic leaders, who draw new members or at least passive support for the cause, and bureaucratic leaders, who develop constitutions and organize activities. Around the cadre can be found specialists with unique talents who carry forth such work as publicity or special events and wider rings of participants, many of whom are involved only temporarily. The role of activist requires political savvy of a different type than is needed in the role of volunteer in local communities. Yet many of the social person skills are similar, in that a major function of such roles is to "educate" the powers that be, locally or in Washington, who are not interested in women's issues or who are bombarded by opposing groups. Newsletters, such as those produced by the National Organization of Women, have often been read by, and informed, male legislators (Hartman 1989).

Yet women have a long way to go (in spite of the Virginia Slims ads) to achieve equity, as is obvious from the gender distributions in all aspects of American life. Gelb and Palley (1982) claim that women still need to professionalize and even bureaucratize the members of their pressure groups if they are to be more effective in influencing national or state political leaders. The failure to pass the Equal Rights Amendment is an indication that women have not sufficiently coordinated their efforts. Of course, one problem is that women do not form a single block, having many, often contradictory, definitions of social problems and of their solutions, as is clearly evidenced in the abortion issue.

The absence of women in the seats of economic and political power in the United States reflects the strength of the dual-sphere world of the past and, obviously, in the present. Where are the women in high political offices? Other societies, such as Israel, Pakistan, India, and Britain, have elected women to their highest political positions—sometimes, but definitely not always, in consequence of class and political manipulation by stronger powers and the women's connections to powerful males. Even in those countries there is a large gap between the women in the top positions and those further down. Communist societies, which had an ideology of meritocracy, lacked a proportional representation of women in the ruling elite, or even in the next layers of officials. Although Papandreau (1988) states that "feminism is the most powerful revolutionary force in the world today," she adds: "Yet, significant numbers of women have not yet been able to break into that bastion of male power, the traditional political arena—electoral politics" (p. xiii). Those who comment on the failure of women the world over to acquire power point to the importance of both grass-roots and national organization and of funding for political office campaigns (Papandreau 1988). Flammang (1984), Mueller (1988), and various American mass-media publications keep counting the number of women holding various political offices in their own right (and not because of their connection as daughters, wives, or widows to strong males). Although contributors to Flammang 1984 and Mueller 1988 find a rather dramatic increase of women on the local and state levels, the few women reaching national attention have not been very successful in their bids for office. Women in their struggle to get access to power still face enormous barriers (Epstein and Coser 1981; see also Lipman-Blumen 1984). The painful experiences of watching Ferraro and Schroeder be defeated in their campaigns for the highest offices in the United States remind observers of the distance women have yet to come. So does even a glance at the corporate structure of the business world.

On the other hand, the mass media are full of the very recent movement of women into the political arena, which can be explained in part as a reaction to several national events that have dramatized inequality and the obvious degradation of women by American men. A front-page article in the 21 October 1992 issue of the *New York Times,* entitled "Women Advance in Politics by Evolution, Not Revolution," pointed out that even if all 108 women who were running for the 103d Congress had won, that would still have left Congress 80 percent male (Manegold 1992, 1A). The rather dramatic increase in the number of women who had at least won the primaries was accounted for by the financial help and training given to candidates by the National Women's Political Caucus, the National Organization for Women, the Women's Campaign Fund, Emily's List, and the Wish List, all of which have been formed in the last twenty-some years. These groups have also learned to distribute the millions of dollars they have raised to candidates who have a good possibility of winning, rather than to all women who are running for office.

Summary

The social roles discussed in this chapter are, or can be, interrelated. Social relationships do not exist alone, but are interwoven into larger fabrics. What is common to all these roles is the element of volunteerism, freedom from the kinds of pressures facing women in traditional society and even now in family roles. Friends are persons converted from strangers or acquaintances through a series of negotiations. Living next to someone does not necessitate entrance into the role of neighbor, nor does residence in a community or the world at large demand active membership in the activities of their groups. At the same time, all these roles require a social circle of same-minded persons who interweave their rights and duties through a division of labor in order to meet their mutual goals. Few friendships can exist without the support of others. The same is true of the circle of a neighbor or of an association member. No matter how one wants to revolutionize one's world, one needs the cooperation of many other persons, who can enter the social circles of each role with a whole range of their own sociopsychological forms of involvement.

When it comes to push and shove, American culture usually justifies neglect of any of these roles if they interfere with what are considered to be more important sets of relations, such as, for women, those of wife or mother. And yet, as the world widens and education and the mass media help broaden the *okolica*, or the arena within which women and men locate their social life spaces, involvement in all kinds of roles is unavoidable. Presumably the connection between the domestic arena and the larger community outside is constantly reinforced by children and friends' sharing activities, by neighborhood interaction, movement in and out of the role of student, and involvement in all sorts of groups at all stages of the life course. Thus, the boundaries between primary and secondary roles are also indeterminate and subject to negotiation with all involved.

The conclusions one can draw from women's involvements in roles outside of the family and occupations are similar to those developed in previous chapters. The overall pattern reflects the movement from traditional, ascribed involvements in the local scene, entered into with little choice and without awareness of the broader world by the majority of women. Transitional times, supported by increased education and individuation, freed women from being automatically embedded in these local relationships. This had a dual effect, expanding the number of women concerned with the larger community while simultaneously expanding the number and variety of social groups helping women achieve personal goals. However, structural and two-sphere restrictions still abounded. It appears that "modern" women are becoming more established in their broader and flexible identities and are turning their attention to concern with the world community through a variety of nonfamilial roles.

8

Life Spaces and Self-Concepts

American society has gone through tremendous changes, purposely introduced or felt repercussively since its traditional times. The processes of modernization and increased scale of organization or social development—whatever concept we use to summarize all the modifications—have been introducing a different way of life, experienced and contributed to by dissimilar people from the past (Coser 1991; Inkeles 1981; Inkeles and Smith 1974). We have been examining the roles of women, who have experienced and contributed to these changes differently than men have. Each gender has been affected in multiple ways, depending on social class with its racial and ethnic subgroups, the degree of urbanization, and, especially, education. Since men and women live together in that they share daily life in many settings, each is influenced by what happens to the other. In addition, since each social role contains circle members who, in turn, can now come from a variety of backgrounds and are involved in other social roles, what they do constantly affects their relationships. All these developments make it dysfunctional, even impossible, to adhere to social roles as fixed patterns of behavior.

The more rigid and inflexible the social person or circle members, the greater the probability of extreme role strain for both the changer and those living in the past. As we have noted throughout, role strain is anyway inevitably built into sets of relations, due to the complexity of demands and the needs for synchronization. It is impossible to be a traditional mother in transitional or modern times if the child is exposed to other types of interaction with other members of the mother's circle who do not cooperate with traditional rights and duties.

Not only role strain, but also role conflict, is inevitable in anyone's role complex, let alone when roles are changing in different ways or all the people involved are experiencing life at varied stages of modernization. Add to this people's need to be socialized and constantly resocialized to the world around them, and it is easy to see multiple sources of role conflict.

Interestingly enough, Americans individually and as a society either do not seem to realize all the consequences of changes they are experiencing, or are unwilling to introduce collective solutions to some of the problems, even when they publicly wring their hands about them. A perfect example of the inadequacy of the definition of current life is contained in the stereotypical view of role conflicts of modern [actually transitional] women.

Role Conflict

Much discussion of present-day American women focuses on the subject of role conflict (that is, conflict among the roles in which they are involved at any stage of life) as if it were a new situation and as if men did not face it. There are two basic sources for such a concern. One is nostalgia for the past that encompasses the strange idea that role conflict did not occur in the "good old days," because of institutional integration with clearly-set priorities (Coontz 1992). The second is a rather simplistic view of human beings. According to the first imagery, men and women had definitely defined, mutually congruent roles that connected activities in all institutions. Women, for example, were wives, mothers, homemakers, kin keepers, grandmothers, producers, members of religious congregations, neighbors, and so forth in a whole fabric moving along the life course, all circle members in each role supporting the rest. One need only read the ever-growing number of biographies and recently resurrected autobiographies of women in the U.S. past and in other societies to know how unrealistic that image was.[1] Role conflict abides in all known situations.

The fact that complex, "developed" societies contain relatively separated and segmented institutions and structures with highly divergent value and behavioral systems leads some observers to the assumption that uncontrolled role conflict is inevitable. Human beings, and especially women, are seen as incapable of dealing with complex social life spaces. Most of the current literature assumes, or even clearly states, that "modern" [actually transitional] societies force onto women much role conflict and that this is detrimental to their welfare.

On the other hand, some scholars, such as Simmel (1955), Sieber (1974), Long and Porter (1984), Marks (1977), and Rose Coser (1975a and 1991), find complex social systems to have positive consequences, allowing the development of complex human personality, and find traditional and more homogeneous cultures to be limiting. I agree with them in many ways and will return to this point.

One cannot deny the complexities of multiple role involvement in large societies. Most of their institutions have grown dissimilar in many values and role hierarchies, and most people's roles are not encompassed within a single institution. People are involved in more than one area of life and are thus faced with competing values and behavioral demands. For example, many scientists must give up some of their commitment to scientific openness and to control over their findings, which are required for membership in the scientific community, in return for a salary from a business company. Women lawyers trying to bring feminist norms into their practice face resistance even from women clients and secretaries who have been socialized into the male model of the lawyer role (Epstein 1983). In addition, circle members of one role often do not allow demands of another role to take precedence, insisting that duties to them take precedence over duties toward the other circle. Duties to clients on the job may be judged by employers as being more important than duties to children.

Awareness of at least partial segmentation of institutions in modern societies could lead to an understanding of the difficulties of involvement in roles that are located in different value systems that do not allow strong alternative commitments. Being a mother of small children and being a lawyer in a Wall Street firm are still almost mutually exclusive involvements (Epstein 1971 and 1983). It is hard to meet the standards of two greedy institutions at the same time (L. Coser 1974; Coser and Coser 1974; see also Pearson 1990).

There are two major settings of possible conflict inherent in the role clusters of American women, as seen from the perspective of "ideal typical" models only, that is, through the framing of selected characteristics. These are among roles within the family institution and between roles in it and in other institutions (Weber 1949).

Role Conflict within the Family Institution

Americans still require that women give highest priority to family roles, alternating between those of wife and mother. It is apparent from previous discussion that these two roles can easily conflict, as when the husband wants to make love but the wife/mother worries about waking the children (Rubin 1979). Much of the literature on the problems created by the birth and presence of children within a marriage focuses on the emotional, attentional, time, and energy demands on the husband and wife team versus the father and mother team. As Bettelheim (1962) noted when describing the advantages of the kibbutzim method of childrearing, the marital couple in the kibbutz system have time to themselves without interruptions from children, and the time devoted to the offspring is not interfered with by duties of housekeeping or husband-tending. He also pointed out that each child gets the attention needed for its stage of development without having to compete with other children of the same mother who have different needs. The role of mother is entered into by a woman each time separately for each child, unless she treats them as a single unit. Each child tends to place her at the center of her or his needs, treating her as a mother separate from the mother the other children have. Add to this the fact that the same man can be a multiple of fathers, as well as a husband to her, and the complexities increase.

In addition, a partial resolution of role conflicts at one stage of life may not work for long. The concept of "empty nest" somehow implied that role conflicts for mothers with several children and between that role and other roles subsided when offspring grew into adulthood. The life-course literature shows us how oversimplified that assumption was. The children may continue to need help in competition with each other, and the husband may resent the woman's continued focus upon motherhood. Although a husband does require "tending," and although his schedule and demands complicate life (see chapter 2), his removal from the household through divorce or death creates new sources of conflict for the woman. Vestiges of the role of wife that interfere with other relationships and her ambivalent emotions are apt to complicate adjustment to new life-styles and, for example, the role of mother. Of course, divorced and widowed women can experience feelings of freedom and competence and new ways of enjoying life.

Family roles can involve other forms of conflict. Add to the nuclear family the mother of the husband, and the complications can be unbearable, especially if she becomes one of the beneficiaries of the homemaker by moving in with them. Her idea of how her son should be treated or the children raised can conflict with all or some of the family members' ideas. The role of daughter may conflict with that of wife and mother. Differences in values, norms, and ideologies among people of different generations, cultural backgrounds, genders, and relationships, when brought into a close interactional setting, can result in emotional explosions, no matter how much people try to manage their feelings (Hochschild 1983).

There is likely to be another role conflict involved: that between the homemaker and the beneficiaries of her role who are also her husband, children, and so forth. Whatever she does to make the house socially presentable to evidence her expertise in that role is likely to interfere with their needs for play space or informality of clothes placement (otherwise known as "messing up" the bathroom and bedroom). Of course, the role of homemaker does not fit in the family institution in the first place, although it is usually so placed by all involved. That role really falls into the economic institution, being an occupational role, allegedly judged in this society by some of the same standards as other jobs. The homemaker is supposed to keep the home within certain appearance and comfort levels, clean and germ-free as much as possible, operating efficiently, rationally and according to all the norms of scientific management. At least, that is what the home economics movement and the mass media portray, pointing out that modern conveniences make this cognitively run system operative. Current observations by sociologists document the confusion between the contributions of technological change and the interpersonal dynamics of the role (see Cowan 1983, Hardyment 1988, and chapter 5 for examples). To state the main problem bluntly, the activities of homemaking have been organized into a role, taken out of the family and placed into the occupational system in its set of behavioral norms, while it remains in the family institution in the minds of the beneficiaries—if they are not paid lodgers and boarders in secondary relationship to the social person. The household beneficiaries often want the woman to run the home along economical and efficient norms, but giving priority to her obligations as wife and mother.

Although a number of observers have addressed themselves to role conflicts experienced by women within the family institution, it is the problem of carrying forth roles in different institutional settings that draws most attention. There are some comments about such role conflicts for American men with greedy jobs and family responsibilities (see J. Pleck 1983; also Pleck and Pleck 1980; Kimmel and Messner 1992), but it is the women who are pinpointed as suffering it to an almost debilitating extent.

Conflict between Family Roles and Those in Other Institutional Dimensions

The early literature on role conflicts of American women focused upon the roles of wife and jobholder, especially if the job made strong commitment demands or was of higher social status than that of her husband (see, e.g., Bird 1979; Ferber and Huber 1979).

Bird (1979) described "the personal, sometimes painful side" of the wife-jobholder conflicts in *The Two-Paycheck Marriage*. The titles of some of her chapters illustrate conflicts: "Coping with the Dream of a Perfect Home," "The Truth about the Money She Earns," "The Age Thirty Bind," and "The Two-Career Collision Course." The book was written from the woman's point of view and the problems are seen as hers, with relatively little attention to the man's reality. Whether the woman is a defiant working wife preferring to be employed although the husband wants her at home full-time, a reluctant jobholder although neither she nor her spouse wants her in that role, or a submissive employee pushed out of the home by the demands of the husband, she faces several role conflicts. Bird (1979) found that many couples are not comfortable with the money earned by the wife because they do not openly acknowledge the need, especially if it is large enough to threaten the man.[2] Regardless of size, it is often treated as not sufficiently significant to warrant the husband's cooperation in the wife's "second shift" of homemaking and parental roles. Bird's chapter on the two-career collision course focuses on the conflicting demands of the marital partners' greedy occupations in terms of time, energy, and attention commitment, solution of emergencies, transfers, and so forth. Whose crisis is the most important? When does love conquer all, including ambition? Bird notes:

> Most of the married women in *Who's Who in America* have husbands who are not listed in their own right, including anti-feminists Phyllis Schlafly and Marabel Morgan, author of *Total Woman*. . . . A man who gives up his own career for his wife's can expect raised eyebrows— and so can his wife. (P. 208)

One of the concerns of this gender-stratified society is that the wife's higher education and occupational activity can decrease the husband's productivity, an additional commentary on how much the men are dependent upon backup wives and may suffer when such demands are made upon them. Ferber and Huber (1979) actually found support for this anxiety among academic men. Those with wives of higher role status outside of the marriage produced less than those with wives without demanding occupations. Ostrander (1985) and Daniels (1988) also explain that upper-class women cannot even allow their volunteer roles to interfere with their more direct obligations to the husband, although he is a beneficiary of even that work. A wife's friendships can be seen as competing with the husband's demands for attention, especially if he feels left out and considers the wife as his "best friend," which many men seem to do in the absence of male confidants.

The lack of equality between husband and wife in carrying forth life-sustaining and life-style work, which produces role conflict for women, is documented by many other social scientists, such as Hertz (1986; see also the contributions to Gerstel and Gross 1987a and 1987b). Hochchild's analysis in *The Second Shift* (1989) focuses on the problems of work and personal interaction facing a couple when both the husband and the wife are employed. Interviewing both partners, and even observing them at great length in the home, Hochschild analyzed not only the sources of conflict but also the methods by which different couples managed to survive without breaking up. The problems include the fact that few marriages actually involve the sharing of the home shift, although the woman is definitely overextended in her duties and obligations. Hochschild found some very interesting ways in which both husbands and wives justify the husband's not sharing in responsibilities, which she labels "gender ideologies." Each human being exists within a constructed reality, that is, within a process of constructing meaning in all of life's situations. Each couple then must create a mutual constructed reality at least to an extent that makes coexistence possible. According to Hochschild, such a construction is often forged at great cost to the wife. It is basically the wife who needs greater help from the husband, while both of them either do not see or else explain away the asymmetry.

Thus, personal conflict often occurs between the employed husband and the employed wife concerning his resistance to her strong outside commitments and efforts to change home maintenance into a shared activity, that is, to make the role of homemaker one of joint responsibility and work. Men resist simply because they do not want to give up all the benefits of a superior position, especially if these have been previously established (Goode 1982). Although many men (though not all) admit that they need, or else that they use, the "extra" income brought in by an employed wife, the fact that this income is usually smaller than the husband's provides the justification for not sharing the work. The realization by middle-class men that the wife's lower pay is not her fault, and that the couple has frequently favored his search for occupational advantages at the cost of her job, does not diminish his use of greater earnings as a reason for dispensation from work and responsibility (Gerson 1985). It does make a difference, however, whether the job held by the wife preceded marriage or was undertaken after the family patterns became established with a full-time homemaker as the backup to a greedy family (Coser and Coser 1974). It is difficult for the woman to unhinge the prior dependence upon her, just as it is hard for the middle-aged wife and mother to separate her identity from dependence upon the husband and children (Rubin 1979).

Most literature on the role conflicts of American women focuses not on those between an occupation and the role of wife, but on the conflicts between an occupation and the role of mother, or even potential mother. The mass media, at least, worry that some women may not want to be mothers at all. The panic created by the "biological clock," which eventually cuts off the possibility of becoming a mother (whether in fact or psychologically) was already a major subject of the 1970s. It has become increasingly so in recent years as women postpone role conflict with careers by postponing pregnancy. The panic over role conflict is mainly due to the definition of the role of mother. The demands of motherhood in American society are such that they are expected to interfere with any activity away from the home base, be it of a volunteer, an organizational, or an occupational nature. Children get sick, and it is the mother who must transport them from wherever this occurs and stay home with them. School, doctor, service, and activity appointments for the offspring are usually available only during working hours, on the assumption that a mother is always available. School closings for whatever reason neglect the problems of empty houses, and indignation over "latchkey kids" neglects the fact that some mothers cannot leave work when children return from school. Middle-class mothers are also expected to have time to serve as the social agents linking children to the community (O'Donnell and Stueve 1983).

Going as far back as Komarovsky's *Women in the Modern World* (1953) we find that about a third of highly educated post–World War II women avoided possible role conflict by becoming unmarried career women and another third became full-time homemakers. The women who combined career and motherhood felt guilt but had good help with the care of children by live-in, trained servants. Any other method of dealing with problems of child care in the absence of a full-time mother or full-time cooperation from other family members was reportedly extremely difficult. The occasional "career woman" of the past familistic era had not only servants but also support from many sources because she was so unusual (Hunt and Hunt 1982). It was also helpful to have an unusually cooperative husband (Holmstrom 1973). Having a complex support network is also typical of successful women in the public sphere in other societies, most of whom come from upper-class families.

Of course, problems can occur when people are involved in more than one role in institutions other than the family. Some of these appear endemic to American women; others are faced by both genders. Friendship can be seen as interfering with occupational roles, especially in bureaucracies. As mentioned in connection with institutional separation, people working for a bridging organization may experience conflicting demands from groups in the two neighboring institutions. In addition, they may face role conflict within their life course, as when the job requires behavior contrary to what they learned in the role of student or what they expect to follow in future roles.

Societal Solutions to Role Conflicts of Women

American society of the transitional times has not admitted, or even understood, how it has created and contributed to the role conflicts of its women, nor has it taken on as much responsibility as other countries for creating solutions. It fails to recognize that women's "personal troubles" arise out of societal changes and that these have serious social problems as consequences (Mills 1956). Although it acknowledges that modernization, especially industrialization and urbanization, has made inevitable many of these social problems, its value system and power structure do not allow adequate assistance to people who are going through them. In fact, the main solution to the dramatic changes of the last two centuries, the division of the world into the private and the public, is itself a major cause of role conflict for its members. Society has allowed its men to solve role conflicts by neglecting the private aspects of self and life—roles of husband, father, friend, and neighbor. It has pushed and socialized women to solve them by neglecting involvement in roles defined as public. It also ignores the fact that this is an artificial division and that women are constantly in the public sphere in what are called "private" roles or in almost invisible public roles. This the society does by defining women's public involvements as secondary both for them and for the whole, while preventing their access to powerful roles.

The artificial boundaries between public and private lead to the pretense that private and public are separate and ought to be occupied by separate types of persons. In fact, the ideology contains major contradictions. On the one hand, the private is defined as sacredly immune from interference, especially in the form of public responsibility for its welfare. On the other hand, American society impinges upon the alleged private sphere with its laws and policies any time it wishes to do so. In the case of policies concerning women, it tries to keep women out of important roles in the public sphere, ignores their actual presence in that sphere, and interferes with their roles of wife, mother, and homemaker.

Kamerman and Kahn (1978; see also Kamerman 1977; Kahn and Kamerman 1975) studied family policies of the major industrializing societies and found the United States to be the least cooperative. It is most unwilling to introduce policies that could alleviate or at least decrease social problems, blaming these instead on the relatively powerless mother/wife/homemaker/employee. Solutions are left to individual action, although the problems are often, if not usually, beyond personal control.

In fact, the late 1980s and the 1990s have been witnessing an allegedly strong backlash against women's efforts at breaking down the barriers between private and public domains (Faludi 1991). Deep in its heart, this society wants women back in the home, in nineteenth-century fashion, even when they cannot maintain themselves economically from that setting and although modern life and education have considerably changed pervasive and role identities. The theme Rose Coser pointed to in "Stay Home Little Sheba" (1975b) has not been revised much since then. Americans worry about the effects on the children of having an employed mother, in spite of the conclusion by many researchers that there are no serious negative effects (see the summary of this research in Hoffman 1987). They do not worry about the effects of a father so engaged, nor does the worry result in the provision of alternative community or governmental solutions. The mass media favorably publicize stories of women who decide to give up their careers to stay home (Trost 1990a, B1). These traditional attitudes were brought into the open by the conservative, religious right during the 1992 presidential campaign. It is now trying to organize a grass-roots movement to offset any governmental policies aimed at decreasing conflicts for family members that might be introduced by the Democratic administration.

It is interesting, if worrisome to symbolic interactionists, to note that all the concern over stressful role conflict of women focuses on a limited range of time and thus neglects sixty or so years in their lives (see also Long and Porter 1984). This backlash ignores women who do not have any children and most of the life course of those who do. It generalizes to all women and is strongest in rejecting those who are entering occupations or the political, religious, or other spheres of life in influential roles. The underlying assumption is that all of a woman's life must be organized around these few years when the demands for exclusive commitment to each major role are highest. This happens when she is building a career, entering a love relationship that is still expected to last many decades (with all the negotiations with the social circle that that entails), and being a mother to one or more young children. The failure of American society to recognize and adjust to this life squeeze makes the years between entering the major roles and reaching a stabilized stage difficult. It is possible that, at some time in the future, the scheduling of the life cycles of major roles will be sufficiently sequenced to interfere less with each other. It is also possible that role commitment will not be so "greedy" as to exclude strong (but not twenty-four-hours-a-day) involvement in more than one role.

Of course, one way women's temporary role conflicts during greedy stages of role involvements could be eased is through actions of the employing organizations, rather than governmental agencies, but the economic institution has been organized around a model of male workers who can commit themselves to the job without regard for other commitments (see also Coser 1991). The male worker is seen as either not responsible for any dependents, be they disabled relatives or children, or as having a backup person to solve all the troubles arising from such involvements. Women who are also committed to other roles besides the job and thus refuse to meet the male model of behavior, or who are expected by employers to do so, are kept in inferior positions at inferior pay or in unstable jobs. It is going to take some time, and the revolt of many employees, for employers to reorganize work to meet employee needs because they realize such action will also benefit the company (Schwartz 1992). Arrangements that would make life easier for employees include: flextime, flexplace, part-time employment with benefits, job sharing, temporary assignments, and leaves for medical, parental, and other reasons. Most of these variations on the traditional work schedule actually benefit the organization, according to a survey by the American Marketing Association; they produce higher morale, reduced tardiness, reduced turnover, and easier recruitment of new employees (Rothman and Marks 1987, 196). An extensive article in the *Wall Street Journal* indicates that some bosses are adjusting (Hymowitz 1990). Some employing organizations even set up child-care centers nearby (Trost 1990a). And yet Rothman and Marks (1987) reported several years ago that only 12 percent of employing organizations have developed some form of flexible work schedule to accommodate the needs of employees arising from role conflicts. This figure had risen to just about 15 percent by the middle of 1990 (Trost 1990b).

The reexamination of work and career scheduling has not been helped by existing powerful pressure groups and other organizations whose leaders could introduce changes but do not, or by male members of other circles of women. Economic and political institutions have a long way to go to make life more humane for the society's members, including men.

Role-Conflict Solutions by Women

There are two major ways in which women can ease some of the life squeeze of role conflicts: through collective action and through individual action. Transitional women organized the fight for freedom from traditional restrictions, for abolition of slavery, and for suffrage and equality of opportunity, but they sought individual solutions to their personal role conflicts and felt inadequate or guilty if the problems remained. Part of their problem has been an ambivalence concerning basic values, and possibly a belief in the reality of a two-sphere world. In view of their inner conflicts , how did, and how do, these women, who are still far from being able to negotiate a modern life, deal with experienced role conflicts? The vast number of studies that document problems faced by women in "modern" times who are wives, mothers, homemakers, and jobholders come to the same conclusion: Women are the only ones who are assigned, and take on, the responsibility of solving role conflict. Many women are aware of this and make hard choices (Gerson 1985) along the way, trying to decide which roles to enter, and balancing costs and rewards, including not just the quality and benefits of the job, but also the types of sharing they can expect from "understanding bosses" or cooperative husbands/fathers/home-co-maintainers. Many career-oriented women simply postpone or decide not to enter competing roles, especially that of mother, but even that of wife. However, the pressure toward motherhood is high in this society, and usually comes also from the husband, although the pressure toward fatherhood does not appear to translate into shared parenting. Women have usually succumbed to this pressure and taken the path of least resistance by becoming mothers and giving up careers, even jobs, in spite of the low status of full-time homemakers (Bird 1979; Gerson 1985). Some, as we saw earlier, consciously sequence their role involvements, but often at a cost to success, given the rigid career lines of many occupations.

Many mothers settle for inferior jobs, as numerous studies have documented (see Lopata, Miller, and Barnewolt 1984; Lopata,

Barnewolt, and Miller 1985). The same is true in Britain, where the price of convenient hours or location is a woman's inability to get a job that is either as rewarding as the job she gave up to become a mother or equal to her prior training (Sharpe 1984). Certain occupations in both countries, mainly in service industries, have benefited considerably from this cheap and expendable labor, and an ideology about women's unreliability has grown to justify discrimination in hiring, firing, and job assignment.

Women who insist on following demanding careers in combination with family roles also find individual solutions.[3] Extended families, especially their female members who have traditionally been the main supports of mothers with competing roles, are decreasingly available with increasing geographical mobility and labor force participation. Given sufficient income, many women hire "nannies" or other servants, although the problems associated with this action are legion, according to all mass-media and social science reports. The pool of women willing to take on those roles in preference to other jobs is shrinking; often the remaining candidates have only passing interest in the job or have inferior social person characteristics.

Women decrease conflict between homemaking and other roles by simply decreasing the amount of work they do in the home, adding more assistants to provide such services as cleaning, food preparation, and purchasing and delivering goods. Entertaining company at home is one of the first activities to be given up by multirole women, decreasing or simplifying the numbers of beneficiaries of the role (Bird 1979). The delegation of work to others, avoidance of duties and rights deemed unnecessary, and compartmentalization of time and mind are effective strategies for many women. In the meantime, the woman whose roles are all in the expanding stage who does feel stressed can only do the best she can and hope for the plateau stage, when skills have been learned, negotiations bring satisfactory sequences of relationships, and changes flow into each other.

Some couples have worked out alternate scheduling to insure that the children have a parent present whenever they need one. However, most husbands and wives work matching schedules (Pleck and Staines 1982). Some couples have returned to the world of Mom-and-Pop businesses, working together out of the home or in a manner enabling family care (see chapter 6). Hunt and Hunt (1982) call these "integrators," couples who are able to bring together businesses and family roles.

Whatever the individual solutions, the net result is overall inefficiency for the society as a whole and for each woman who must reinvent the wheel of solutions common to so many others at the same stage of the life course. (Spalter-Roth and Hartmann 1990; documented *in Unnecessary Losses: Costs to Americans by the Lack of Family and Medical Leave* ; see also Hyde and Essex 1990 for multiple analyses). And this in a society that prides itself on rationality and efficiency in solving problems!

The Complexity of Social Life Spaces

There are two aspects of this situation that need closer examination. One is the questionable assumption that complex life spaces inevitably produce problems; the second is the general image of American women that permeates American culture.

Although the mass media and much of social science literature portray Americans as living in too complex a world, facing serious role conflicts, constantly stressed, harried, nervous, and in a difficult relationship with each other, there are some voices of dissent. These speak of the advantages of complex roles and multidimensional life spaces. Rose Coser takes this idea even further in "The Complexity of Roles as a Seedbed of Individual Autonomy" (1975a) and her book *In Defense of Modernity: Role Complexity and Individual Autonomy* (1991). Segmented social roles provide a variety of role partners differently positioned and not equally involved, which necessitates constant negotiation. People in such life spaces need to constantly articulate their stances, to think out the consequences of their actions in view of their empathetic understanding of others' constructions of reality. Coser refers to Kohn and Schooler's (1983) work showing that complexity of the work environment is associated with complexity of personality and with intellectual flexibility. Referring back to George Herbert Mead (1934), Coser illustrates the effects of social complexity with his game stage of social development. The more complex the game, the more positions a person must understand in order to plan her present and future behavior. Even conflict creates the need for distancing and thinking out one's rights and duties, which can result in greater flexibility and individual enrichment.

The same can be said of complexity of the role cluster—its spread into multiple institutional dimensions, visualized as a social life space. One role may actually support another, as when membership in a professional organization and friendship among scientists assist scientific production. Crane (1968), Merton (1968), and Lewis Coser (1984) found the most productive scientists to be ones with complex sociometric connectedness networks, who are involved in many interactions and roles that communicate and disseminate knowledge. People with complex kinship roles may obtain emergency and regular help with any role, including work brought home from a job.

The growing number of social scientists who have undertaken a life-course perspective also point to the importance of complex role involvements (Moen, McClain and Williams 1989). Contributors to Baruch and Brooks-Gunn's *Women in Midlife* (1984), especially Baruch (1984) herself, stress the psychological well-being that accompanies multiple roles in those years, as Payne (1977) had observed regarding the elderly. Baruch, Barnett, and Rivers (1983) found women pleased to have multiple roles, mastery over their lives, and independence. Such women had a strong sense of selfhood and self-worth that came from successful role performance and the ability to coordinate involvements. They were freed from dependence upon the husband's approval for their feelings of mastery, a dependence which was more typical of married full-time homemaker (Baruch, Barnett, and Rivers 1983, 40). In fact, the authors state:

> But one of the most positive findings of our study is that involvement in multiple roles has a strengthening effect on well-being—for both Mastery and Pleasure— for women. This contradicts the conventional wisdom so directly that it made us ask why. Where did those old notions come from? (P. 140)

They answer this question with references to the mental health field, which assumed there would be serious problems when women left the home to enter the labor force (see also Friedan 1963 and Harris 1979). According to Baruch and her associates, the expectation of great stress came from what they called a "limited model" of resources available to human beings. This model refers to energy as being drained by each effort leaving less energy for other activities. Neglected are the stimulating and energizing aspects of many activities. Interestingly enough, they also found that the limited-resources model is applied more frequently to women than to men, possibly flowing from nineteenth-century medical imagery of the "frail lady" (140–41). Mental health experts gave greater weight to stress emanating from role conflicts of women with external commitments than to stress based on domestic involvements.

Marks (1977) calls this a "scarcity" approach to energy, time, and commitment, tracing it back to Freud and numerous other theoreticians who use the metaphors of spending, draining, leaking out, or dribbling away of energy. The result of both the theoretical and the empirical work is the conviction that people in modern society are overwhelmed by demands from multiple roles (Marks 1977, 973).

Marks (1977, 926) favors the expansion approach to human energy, following Durkheim, who saw complex social involvement as enriching and revitalizing. Marks applies the same argument to time and commitment, pointing out that many activities are stimulating and can be carried out simultaneously. He argues that concerns about role strain and role conflict limit the view of human potential for complex behavior. The conclusion that people can wither when faced with a simplistic life after more complex social involvement is recognized by everyone who finds inadequate the Cumming and Henry (1961) thesis that people "disengage" voluntarily from social roles as they grow older.

Returning now to Simmel (1955) , Sieber (1974), Coser (1975a and 1991), and Long and Porter (1984), and developing their ideas further, we find a very optimistic view of modern life. Simmel (1955) pointed out that conflict is not inevitably debilitating. In fact, the segmentation of institutions and social structures has enabled modern individualism. It gives people much more freedom to choose and negotiate, to have a unique life-style, than is possible in more homogeneous societies with a greater interdependence of institutions. One can carry the feeling of being a unique individual wherever one goes, in contact with a variety of others who are also unique and thus able to create or modify social roles to fit themselves and circle members, rather than conforming to culturally established norms of behavior (see also Turner 1962, 1968, 1978, and 1981).

Gains of role accumulation can include the acquisition of new rights, status security and enhancement, ego gratification, and feeling of competence. The rights may include greater authority and resources (Sieber 1974). However, there is a serious question as to whether women are as yet gaining all these benefits from increased role accumulation, since so may find that adding a job and contributing to the family economic welfare do not guarantee rights and privileges, certainly not within the family (Long and Porter 1984). One can but optimistically predict that the cumulative effects will come as all the roles of women's social life spaces increase in importance and as America enters the modern world at least in this aspect of its life and social structure.

Sociopsychological Aspects of Social Life Spaces

The questions remain, how do social roles influence the self-concepts women carry around with them through the life course, and how have these changed with shifts from traditional to transitional and modern societal times? These questions cannot be adequately answered at the present time, because there is not enough data from carefully worked research, but some insights can be gained from my ongoing studies of Chicago-area women, begun in 1956. As mentioned before, the reexamination of results from all this work points strongly to the significant effects of formal schooling on the social involvement of American women. Schooling definitely affects the complexity with which women perceive and act in the roles of wife, mother, kin member, friend, and participant in voluntary associations. In addition, the less formal schooling a woman achieves, the more apt she is to be socially isolated, to hold negative attitudes about social relationships, and to be unable to adjust to life changes. The increasingly voluntaristic nature of social involvement in more socially developed and large-scale societies requires of members the kind of knowledge, thought processes, and competence that formal education provides. This conclusion is reinforced by comparative studies of support systems of widows in different societies (Lopata 1987c and 1987d).

Modernization or social development of complexity brought expanded education, in terms of the percentage of the population being educated and the amount of knowledge transmitted to it. We can posit that women (and men, too, of course) in a modern society, having received a formal education that involves the manipulation of abstract ideas, have learned to think out and plan their lives and to participate in the larger world. Abstract thinking enables the person to anticipate the consequences of alternative decisions, without having to experience them in concrete form. Women can make their decisions autonomously (Coser 1975a; Inkeles 1981; Inkeles and Smith 1974; Simmel 1971), but in cooperation with circle members of the roles they choose to enter. They are not isolated human beings and are not dependent upon a single, or limited, source of social involvement and thus identities (Troits 1986). Social roles contain social relationships, and modernization does not necessarily lead to isolated independence, as some thinkers have claimed; it can lead to negotiated and voluntary interdependence based on self-development (Cancian 1978). Of course, this idealized image of development of human potential assumes a society that has removed tradition-based barriers to individual achievement and has stopped forcing dysfunctional stereotypes upon the young.

The ideal typical woman in such a modern, developed society is able to build a congruent construction of reality that brings into the framework her generalized and specialized conceptions of herself, her commitments, her actual role involvements, the positively evaluated benefits of such, the pleasure of such role complexity, and the support she perceives herself to receive from circle members in each of the roles within her role cluster (Lopata 1980b; 1993a).

However, not all members of an allegedly modern society, even in its urban centers, have been sufficiently socialized and educated to take advantage of available resources to build individualistically congruent constructions of their own reality. This is particularly true of women in patriarchal, rapidly changing settings. We can hypothesize that two types of women will have the most internally congruent constructions of reality at the present time. One type would be located in less changing and more homogeneous pockets of such a society, the second near the forefront of social change. What factors influence such settings, and what happens to women in the transitional middle, caught by both traditional and modern views of women and opportunities for role involvements?

The traditional women whom I interviewed in the 1950s and 1960s were married home owners in new, or new areas of older, suburbs with at least one pre–high school child and no outside employment. They represented the vast majority of women in such settings, being there with the help of the GI Bill and often socially mobile husbands. Of roles such as careerwoman, artist (or other self-expressive role), concerned citizen, or neighbor, or even member of a religious group, none was considered anywhere near as important as roles in the home. Their constructions of reality, including commitments, perceptions, and self-concepts, within the family and homemaking roles, varied considerably by social class and especially by education, but were highly traditional when it came to outside involvements (Lopata 1971b). The more educated respondents perceived their world and themselves and their homemaking and family roles in much more complex and creative ways than did their less educated counterparts. Those married to more educated husbands in more-prestigious jobs tended to place the role of wife above that of mother, while the working-class women definitely stressed the role of mother, often forgetting to mention that of wife. However, Spock (1957) was very much evident among the middle-class women who worried about their ability to meet all the requirements of good motherhood. The husbands of the less-educated respondents were seen mainly as breadwinners, while they themselves ranked high the role of homemaker (Lopata 1966). The questioning of this whole value system and the restriction of women to the home—a questioning brought forth by Friedan in *The Feminine Mystique* (1963)—had not yet surfaced, and the women's main concerns were financial or maternal.

The transitional women whom I have studied since the 1970s have been much more heterogeneous along several dimensions in addition to social class. They vary considerably in how they sequenced the entrances and exits of their roles and in how well they had anticipated the consequences of their choices upon the goals they visualized with more or less clarity. Many were socialized into a circumscribed world by parents with little education or other resources, many of whom were themselves socialized in foreign countries or American rural areas, and simply followed the traditional patterns of life, completing limited schooling, working for pay and having some "cheap amusements" along the way, marrying and/or having children, and deviating little from the standard (Peiss 1986). They resemble the 1950s women in their home orientation more than any other group, except that they feel much more restricted, being aware of the alternative life-styles publicized by the mass media. Others of a similar background have been able to decrystallize the effects of such a background, mainly by entering occupations that offered a new look at what women can do, achieving new educational levels or job training, and becoming resocialized into new life-styles and self-concepts (see Epstein 1992 for changes in the self-concept). A third category had all the advantages of higher social class, which built positive self-images, and either went the traditional route or committed themselves early to educational and occupational involvement that enabled them to enter multidimensional life spaces. Some of the advantaged women also went back to school. In fact, the higher her original educational achievement, the more likely is the woman to return to school or obtain new or further job training in later years. Divorce has often been associated with occupational or educational change, in chicken-or-egg sequence. Many women now combine roles in their cluster in a variety of ways and with degrees of flexibility, changing their life spaces in response to life-course shifts.

Since so much of the concern over American women is focused on the alleged conflict between full-time homemakers and full-time employees, I will limit my discussion here to the construction of reality centered around these two mutually exclusive forms of commitment (see also Lopata and Barnewolt 1984).

There appears to be an increasing number of "modern" women who have created relatively internally congruent realities, in that they are involved in the roles they rank as very important and that they prefer. They can be either full-time homemakers or full-time employees. They see many advantages to their involvements, they have a comparatively high self-esteem, and they perceive their environments (particularly the husband, if there is one) as supportive. They fit other roles around their basic commitment.

The most highly congruent homemakers are relatively young and educated, with a background of comparatively high-status jobs. They are married and mothers of small children, which is why they choose to be at home. They are able to do so, but not necessarily because of a high family income. In fact, need, as established by family income without the wife's earnings in comparison to other respondents, is not a significant factor. This finding surprised us, in view of the frequent assertion that all employed mothers must work for financial reasons. Such mothers scaled down their expenses from preparenthood times and learned how to live on more limited incomes. Of course, each had an employed husband. What is important is the conscious decision these mothers of younger children have made to leave the labor force, at least temporarily, because they consider such action necessary for the welfare of their families. They find their husbands supportive of this decision. The generalized characteristics and areas of competence in their self-concept reflect a much higher self-esteem than that of older and less educated full-time homemakers, who usually scored lower than did the employees (see Lopata 1980b; Lopata, Barnewolt, and Miller 1985). A surprising conclusion, in view of the 1956 study, is that these voluntary homemakers do not find their role highly complex, in spite of their having higher levels of education than the less congruent homemakers. It is possible that they do not define homemaking as equivalent in complexity to that of prior or future jobs.

I had expected to find other types of homemaker with congruent constructions of reality, and I found one: mothers of large families, with a husband and three or more children, in the full-house plateau stage of that role. They have been socialized to be homemakers and have mastered the role sufficiently to look upon themselves as successful and to experience relatively little role conflict. They are pleased with their situations, although they often live on relatively restricted incomes and in rather flat social life space. They tend not to be geographically or socially mobile, but they are not sufficiently bothered by the mass media's image of the "modern woman" as having an outside career to question themselves. They are quite different from the first category of congruent homemakers and are critical of what they consider the others' "uptight" life-style, especially what they see as the others' pushing their children in developmentally detrimental ways. They express traditional values and are also critical of the actions of the congruent employed women.

The least congruent transitional full-time homemakers are not involved in that role at its expanding circle or full-house plateau stages, in that the home does not contain small children but may have a husband. They appear to lack justification for being out of the labor force, and often express the wish to get a job. However, the older ones do not have the skills and knowledge to get employment, having been disadvantaged early in life in terms of family and educational background. They never did hold a good job and do not visualize themselves as able to function successfully in the world of work outside of the home. On the other hand, they do not find homemaking complex. They do not hold images of themselves as leaders or as successful or competent women, and so they have a very different content to their self-concepts than do the congruent employees or the more congruent homemakers.

The most congruent employees can be either unmarried or married, but most do not have small children in the household (although there are some with that combination in the role cluster who have worked it all out). Most are apt to have been employed a longer proportion of time since finishing school in more prestigious and better paying jobs than the less congruent jobholders or homemakers at any but the highest level of congruence. In fact, they appear either to have avoided roles that compete with their career commitment or to have reached a stage in life course, external supports, or self-confidence where they do not feel major conflicts. They like their jobs, find them complex, and find many advantages to employment. If married, they are very apt to report that the husband is supportive, although he seldom shares equally in home-making or child rearing, a not surprising find in view of all the reports of other researchers. Those with the cluster of wife-mother-career explain with great satisfaction how they maintain this.

The least congruent employees are working for pay because they feel they have to, although they would rather stay home; or they try to stick to a career although they are unable to resolve guilt or role conflict with motherhood. Some report supportive attitudes on the part of the husband for such employment; others do not. Some simply do not like their jobs and see many advantages to full-time homemaking. Others worry about the children and about not having enough time and energy to carry forth the home-based roles the way they would like to. These represent the typification of the "modern, conflict ridden" women of the mass media and public outcry. However, they are only one of many different categories of women along this congruence dimension. It must be remembered that they are being studied at one point in their life course and in their role's life cycle. Some may change considerably due to person-ally or externally induced events.

In spite of all the negative evaluations of this society and of women's role modifications in all spheres of life, positive changes are evident throughout the life spaces of Americans. Both women and men are entering new roles or developing negotiated flexibility in old ones. There is excitement surrounding those people and groups that experience voluntarily introduced and even repercus-sive reconstructions of reality in their own world and those of circle members in a variety of roles.

In the long run, a major influence of "the female world" (Ber-nard 1981) upon transitional American society may be the conse-quence of the different activities of many different women and their associations. This influence can remove the artificial division be-tween the public and the domestic spheres simply by the way women's pervasive identities express themselves in all interaction—as the ranges of relationships expand, so do the various forms of these identities. Douglas in *The Feminization of American Culture* (1977) and Lenz and Myerhoff in *The Feminization of America: How*

Women's Values Are Changing Our Public and Private Lives (1985) document changes in this society and its way of life. Lenz and Myerhoff trace women's influence on language, friendship, politics, the workplace, religion, the arts, the family, health care, and the protection of life through pressure for peace and against war. The emerging men's movement may work toward the same goals from the other direction, making roles and relationships more flexible and negotiable, less norm-restricted (see Turner 1978 and 1981).

Conclusions

We have examined the major roles of American women, in historical perspective and with the help of a symbolic interactionist social role framework. The ways the roles of wife, mother, kin member, daughter, sister, and grandmother in the family dimension and the roles of women in other institutional dimensions have evolved are ingrained in the evolution of American society and are now influencing where it goes. This interdependence of social changes has been deeply affected in recent decades (a very short period of time in human history) by the feminist movement and the actual behavior of women vis-à-vis social roles outside of the family institution. Women previously marginal to the occupational world have entered the labor force, almost before the development of an ideology questioning past barriers to the public domain. They have also pushed for greater involvement in the local, national, and international political, religious, scientific, military, health, and nonoccupational economic spheres of life. In fact, most of the changes have been forced on society by women, with little help from their male companions, public agencies, or economic establishments.

The interdependence of women's involvement in all roles of their social life spaces have decrystallized the effects of their backgrounds, early socialization, and prior choices, making more flexible the life cycle of each role and the women's whole life course. The processes and rapidity of personal changes and of changes in the public sphere have produced many role strains and conflicts, which have been loudly commented upon by the mass media and objected to by those who benefited from the status quo. Educational institutions have been more responsive to demands for modification than have other areas of life, with pockets of slow adjustment in academic roles. Occupational structure appears to have been very slow to change, taking advantage of power to perpetuate convenient stereotypes and practices. Religious groups are accepting token women and token reformulations, but have a long way to go.

And so it is—a great deal of change and a great deal of resistance. Women have taken advantage of openings, modified prior involvements, and fought vestiges of the transitional past by individual actions and in cooperation with others. Some have been pushed in directions they did not choose or with which they are still uncomfortable. Some have taken advantage of former and new resources to build complex, flexible social life spaces with involvements in many roles in several institutions. Some experience a great deal of stress, especially in view of the minimal encouragement and assistance they receive from their circles and the society at large. Many men in their social circles have resisted new demands that threaten their advantages. They are often fearful of responding to the demands of their female partners in many roles, braced by the inflexibility of images of masculinity and of the structures of greedy institutions to which they feel committed by necessity.

The idea that these are times of transition assumes that we know what the next model of role involvement will be. Futurists attempt to paint the picture of various types of utopias. In the meantime, the growing pressure of social groups and of individual choices appears to be gradually moving mainstream American social structure and culture into a more open system of role involvement for both women and men. All the intelligentsia's talk of a postmodern society neglects the fact that most Americans have yet to create and take advantage of a fully modern one.

A major conclusion of this book is that the potential for role conflict exists whenever human beings are involved in more than one role. The degree and frequency of conflict depend on many factors, including the coexistence of high-intensity stages in multiple role involvements. The frequently heard statement among Americans that role complexity is necessarily debilitating, producing major problems for people in multidimensional social life spaces, is based on a limited or scarcity model of human resources: of time, energy, love, commitment, and so forth. The view of American women as overwhelmed by multiple role involvements is based upon this model and upon the nineteenth-century picture of women as frail and unable to meet the challenges of public life. It is thus tied to the image of a two-sphere world. Downplaying role conflicts within the family institution, the current concern over the activities of modern women focuses upon their entrance into the public sphere. It generalizes to women of all ages, although it is explained in terms of the coexistence of high-intensity stages in the roles women undertake in only a small time period of their life course. In other words, women are still discouraged from strong commitments in the occupational and related worlds, from investing in side bets of education and training, and from sequencing roles, on the assumption that, sooner or later, they will face tremendous role conflicts. All of the life course is thus ideally constricted by the fact that certain years of certain women's lives might require strong commitments in more than one role. Simultaneously, little effort is made by the occupational world, or the society at large, to modify the timing of career stages to enable sequencing of high-intensity stages in more than one role.

An almost inevitable conclusion of the mass media and many social scientific studies of the disastrous consequences of role conflicts for American women is that women should avoid such conflicts by not entering, or by withdrawing from, situations that might bring them about. Since total responsibility motherhood is so highly valued, the withdrawal they appear to be demanding is from the public world of occupations, politics, and other community involvement. Other solutions, ones that might actually benefit men and establishments in the public sphere, are not seriously considered. The Protestant ethic is doing well in the corporate, managerial, and professional worlds—employing high-status and high-pay people. These greedy organizations demand that the lives of their workers be organized around one model of work scheduling. Yet it is possible that flexibility will be introduced in the future, and make the worst forms of role conflict obsolete. Until then, women in increasing numbers are showing that they are able to manage in complex social life spaces, and that their response to challenge is to become invigorated rather than pathetically wilted or withdrawn.

Notes

Chapter 1. Social Roles of American Women

1. This book is not the place to argue the pros and cons of modernization or social development theory, or whether American society at large is now in the postmodern stage. I am simply using the concepts of traditional, transitional, and modern to cover sweeping changes in the roles of women.

2. Turner (1962, 24) refers to roles as "meaningful groupings of behavior," but my emphasis on sets of relations is more appropriate to interactionist perspectives.

3. Znaniecki (1965), whose definition of social role is, with modifications, the basis of this study, used the concept of social circle rather than social group, since people associated in a social role may not form an organized whole, as exemplified by the patients of a doctor. Social circle is a more useful concept than that of role set, which is used by Merton (1957 and 1968) and his followers because it shows the interrelationships among its members, as well as the person's relationships with its segments.

4. The symbolic interactionist perspective on social roles, as here developed, is very different from the analysis that deals "only with institutionalized roles, linked to recognized social status" (and is thus limited to a social structural

framework), as presented by Mirra Komarovsky (1973, 649). Although our definition pulls together the micro and macro levels of sociological analysis, it approaches the subject as a set of negotiated relations within established patterns. The culture of a particular group provides the model for the relationships. The traditional view of social role, based on Linton's (1936) anthropological analysis of status as position and role as the more or less conformist *behavior* of one person in that position, is used by Komarovsky (1973), Parsons (1937, 1951), and others, as brought together by Biddle and Thomas (1966).

Also frequent, but impossible to use in studies of human interaction, is the view of social role as a set of expectations of behavior by the position holder. That use requires additional concepts to explain what actually occurs in life—the interaction rather than the expectation. The symbolic interactionist perspective makes irrelevant the artificial polarization of sociology and psychology into which Komarovsky (1973) pushes herself. The differences between the analysis used here and other perspectives on social roles will be increasingly apparent as we examine the shift from the traditionally conformist to the negotiated roles of American women.

5. Of course, the mother must wait for many of the rights from the children to be activated until the children are socialized into their roles. In the meantime, others ideally contribute to the rights later carried forth by the children, such as dressing and feeding them.

6. My original formulation of the concepts of role cluster, institutional richness, and social life space first appeared in the original manuscript of *Occupation: Housewife*, which was written in the late 1960s but was not used in the final product by Oxford University Press. I used abbreviated versions in Lopata 1969b and 1987e.

7. Many languages introduce great variations in noun, pronoun, verb, and adverb by gender, making gender-neutral communication impossible. For example, my mother, an American with English as her first language, frequently evoked smiles among Poles when she spoke their language, since she imitated my father's vocabulary. The need for specifying gender is important when variations in imagery must be acknowledged. Even English, which is quite simple as far as gender allocations are concerned, requires caution in the use of singular pronouns. I will use the female pronoun throughout, unless there is a reason to bring forth a male image, since this book is devoted to the social roles of women.

8. I am drawing on a number of my own studies as material for this theoretical reformulation of existing knowledge of the history and contemporary roles of women. All the studies took place in the metropolitan Chicago area. The first of these was conducted in the 1950s and 1960s and involved in-depth interviews with suburban and urban homemakers and urban employees. *Occupation: Housewife*, published by Oxford University Press in 1971, contains the insights derived from these studies. I then entered two major research projects focused on widows as women who had reached a stage of life that required modifications of their social roles. *Widowhood in an American City* (Lopata

1973c) involved women aged fifty to sixty-four and sixty-five plus. *Women as Widows: Support Systems* (Lopata 1979) developed a support-systems framework that was replicated in studies in many countries of the world (see Lopata 1987c, 1987d). The next project that makes theoretical and data contributions to this volume focused on the changing commitments of American women to paid work and family roles. Emphasis on background, occupational reality, and role clusters was developed in a two-volume work entitled *City Women: Work, Jobs, Occupations and Careers*. The first volume, subtitled *America* (Lopata, Miller, and Barnewolt 1985), analyzed various sources of knowledge about the occupational history and present involvements of women in America; the second, subtitled *Chicago* (Lopata, Barnewolt, and Miller 1985), drew upon an extensive sample of 1,877 Chicago-area women aged twenty-five to fifty-four. Cheryl Allyn Miller looked at the background, school, and work histories of the women, organized into twenty-six occupational categories. I analyzed their occupational construction of reality, and Debra Barnewolt examined their role cluster. A study now in process concerns itself with the social integration of modern suburban women in the suburb, their homes, and the role of homemaker. I shall be referring to these studies from time to time in this book.

Chapter 2. The Role of Wife

1. Bernard Farber (1966) claims that the complexities of modern times require serial marriages through the life course, each stage experienced with a partner of different characteristics. Of course, the same individual may change to meet the needs of each stage.

2. Komarovsly documented in *Blue-Collar Marriage* (1964) that "blue-collar or manual workers (skilled, semi-skilled and unskilled) constituted, in 1963, 48.9 percent of employed white persons and 79.7 percent of employed Negroes" (4). The families were involved mainly in traditional lifestyles, or the slow process of transitional change.

Chapter 3. The Role of Mother

1. Feldmen (1981) found that intentionally childless couples have more highly interactive marriages than intentional parents, but that these groups were "similar in their levels of marital happiness and in the extent to which they have egalitarian marriages" (593, 598).

2. Berrueta-Clement (1984) followed three- to four-year-old children receiving early childhood education into age nineteen to determine the consequences of a special Perry Preschool program. One conclusion is the importance of the quality of the program, which includes parent (mainly mother) involvement. The second conclusion is the undeniable benefit of early educational

preparation, especially of children living in poverty. They note that it is unfortunate that the vast majority of children in poor families, who are most at risk for later educational failure, are not served by similar programs.

3. Barbara Ehrenreich and Deirdre English document the extensive growth of "experts," especially since "the century of the child" in *For Her Own Good: 150 Years of Experts' Advice to Women* (1979). The end result has been the treatment of "motherhood as pathology." I found the women reported on in *Occupation: Housewife* (Lopata 1971b) to be very concerned over the role of mother, seeking experts whenever they could find them, although they often received contradictory advice. It is not that the newly expanding knowledge on child development was scientifically wrong, but that it was presented in such piecemeal fashion, and in such a style, as to create anxiety on the part of conscientious mothers unable to develop their own style of relationship with their children. Ehrenreich and English predict greater self-assertiveness on the part of women who insist on their right to define their duties.

Chapter 4. Social Roles in Kinship Networks

1. I have decided not to enter here into discussion of the complex topic of network analysis. Interest in the establishment of network methodologies and characteristics, started by anthropologists, appears to have peaked in the 1970s. Schneider (1980) uses the concepts of kin groups and networks interchangeably, although the degree of organization varies considerably in these social units.

2. Students in several family classes whom I asked to trace family histories often reported that their informants simply lacked information about whole branches of the mother's or father's kinfolk. This is particularly true in cases of divorce, which often cut off the relatives of the noncustodial parent.

3. As I will document in chapter 8, there is an increasing tendency for young women to decrystallize the effects of family background, mainly through the use of education, which supplies knowledge, skills, and self-confidence to operate in a larger world with more choices than predicted on the basis of the background limitations.

4. Of course, the easy movement of children to grandmothers for varying amounts of time among Native American families in the Southwest (Nelson 1988; Schlegel 1988) was facilitated by the matrilineal nature of some of these societies. The women trusted each other with their children since they belonged to the same lifelong kinship unit.

Chapter 5. Occupation: Homemaker

1. Matthews (1987). "If one could accurately pinpoint the exact time when the phrase 'Just a housewife,' made its first appearance, it seems likely that the

period under discussion [1920s] might have been that time. Certainly the likelihood that domesticity could be a fully adequate prop for female self-esteem had greatly diminished by 1930. The consumer culture along with the hedonism it spawned sounded the death knell both for housewifery as a skilled craft and for mother as the moral arbitrator. And yet the overwhelming majority of American women were still housewives for the better part of their lives" (pp. 193–94).

My original title for the *Occupation: Housewife* book was *I'm Just a Housewife*, because that was the phrase most often used by women asked to identify themselves during the 1950s and 1960s (Lopata 1971b; see also Friedan 1963). The publisher, Oxford University Press, considered that title insufficiently dignified at that time, although it recently came out with a book titled *Just a Housewife* (Matthews 1987). It appears that the negative identification and its connotations have not died out even in the 1990s.

2. It is surprising that the feminist efforts to redefine the role of homemaker have been so dependent upon this economic framework. Trying to determine how much a family would have to pay for the various activities performed by the homemaker reduces her role to that of hired helper, ignoring commitment and interactive components.

3. *Glamour* magazine (1989, 110) recently listed information on timesaving services under the title "Ease Holiday Pressures: Let Someone Else Do It":

> In a season filled with pressures and obligations, fitting yet another last-minute errand into your overloaded schedule can be the last straw. More and more businesses provide time-saving services—particularly pickup and delivery—to ease your load. And the price you pay is often as low as a $2 tip. As you write out your "do it" list, think again: What could someone else do for me? Many dry cleaners and laundries now offer pickup and delivery. There are video stores that pick up, pet food stores that deliver and diaper services that provide disposable as well as cloth diapers. Grocery stores and many restaurants (not just pizza and Chinese) deliver, of course, as do some drugstores. You can order stamps and tickets and check your bank balance by phone. Some hairdressers and manicurists will come to you to save waiting at a salon. If your SOS requires more than convenience, a personal service firm may be the way to go. These jacks-of-all-trades will do almost anything—from Christmas shopping to party planning to waiting in line to renew a driver's license. Just having someone come in to clean—especially before or after a party—could salvage your holiday spirit. Some companies charge by the task; others by the hour ($10–25 is average) — not cheap, but sometimes, your time—and sanity—are worth it.

Chapter 6. The Job: Settings and Circles

1. The occupations in *City Women: Work, Jobs, Occupations, Careers,* volume 1, *America,* and volume 2 *Chicago,* were organized by level of complex-

ity. For example, the professionals were aggregated into those in "object-focused (statisticians, sculptors)" teaching, health/welfare, and in "people-focused (counselors, ministers)" jobs.

2. Susan Berkun, a young lawyer with two small children, explained some of the problems of running her practice from the home, problems that have driven her back into a law firm. She had originally developed a successful career line in a prestigeful, large, Chicago-area firm. After the birth of the children she tried to negotiate a more flexible schedule with this definitely greedy institution. This proved impossible, so she quit to start her own legal practice, specializing in tax law, which is her forte. The presence of children in the home made it impossible to do professional counseling on the telephone—she couldn't persuade clients or other lawyers to her argument with screaming children in the background. Her work was constantly interrupted, and the problems of maintaining professional behavior with the constant impingement of the mother role was impossible. She recommends that any professional or business entrepreneur arrange for members of the family to be absent during hours of occupational work. A further difficulty was the tendency of clients and others in the social circle of the lawyer to call at all hours, which they could not do in an office with established hours.

3. I will never forget how fast my husband, a management consultant, was pulled off of a job when I unwillingly told his age to an older representative of a major manufacturing company whom he was advising. The man was furious that such a "youngster" was telling him how to run his department.

4. It is difficult to find a term other than *beneficiary* that covers the segment of the social circle toward which the activity is directed and that is assumed to be most benefited. I also use the terms *customer* and *client* in this chapter, when appropriate. Sometimes the people assumed by the social person and/or the organization to be the beneficiary do not construct reality the same way, as in the case of men prisoners in the circle of prison officers. The social person can be the beneficiary of her own work, as is true of students and patients.

5. Any organization experiencing rapid employee turnover is concerned with this problem, trying to solve it at various points in employee search or career. Direct-sales companies such as Tupperware invest heavily in training and constant reinforcement. See Peven's (1968) comparison of its training procedures to religious revival events.

6. My mother, who obtained her law degree from the University of Chicago in 1915, had to sit outside the classroom in several courses because the professors were worried that her presence might distract the male students.

Chapter 7. Social Roles in the Rest of the World

1. De Tocqueville stated in his *Democracy in America* ([1835] 1936) that if egalitarian education were spread "over whole earth, the human mind would

gradually find its beacon lights grow dim and men would fall back into darkness" (p. 421).

> [De Tocqueville] favored the aristocratic system by which upper-class families provided extensive education to their youth, at home with tutors and govern-esses or in special schools. Peasants and other class members were assumed by him to obtain all the learning they needed from role models at home or in the apprenticeship system. (Lopata 1981a, 12)

2. My husband was initially rejected by Northwestern University when he applied for the Ph.D. program in economics at an over-thirty-five age, although he had completed an M.S. in that field at the age of twenty-two. His was not a unique situation, as most universities until rather recently were operating on a short-life-span model and did not want to "waste" resources on people who could not devote their entire adulthood to a career. There were also questions as to the desirability of students who changed their minds in midlife, rather than an appreciation of personal flexibility of career involvement. Although increasing numbers of midlife women started returning to school during the 1970s, it was not until such prestigious colleges as Radcliffe or Mundelein, specifically addressed themselves to such a potential student body that this became a publicly acknowledge group of persons in higher education. Loyola University of Chicago has a whole program of counseling and socialization for returning students, regardless of age. Davis and Bumpass (1976) questioned the traditional sequencing of school, marriage, and employment.

3. Although network analysis has been extensively used in research on neighborhoods, the concept of social circle enables us to see how non-neighbors, such as service providers, are brought in to facilitate or hinder neighboring. For example, we can see how neighbors can decrease interdependence with the expansion of shopping facilities or the introduction of voluntary associations which draw upon a selected number of co-residents.

Chapter 8. Life Spaces and Self-Concepts

1. *The Peasants: Fall, Winter, Spring, Summer* by Ladislaw Reymont (1925), a Nobel Prize–winning novel of life in a small Polish village, provides a perfect description of families involved in highly emotional role conflicts.

2. The fact that husbands may not be supportive of high earnings of wives comes from the *City Women: Chicago* (Lopata, Barnewolt, and Miller 1985) study. Our sample contained two sets of salesworkers: clerks and agents. The agents entered that occupation later in life, having left mainly secretarial jobs and obtained specialized training. They are now earning much more than before, and two-and-a-half times what the salesclerks make. However, few report that their husbands think work is "good for the wife" or that it is an "advantage to

have a working wife." Salesclerks regard their husbands as appreciative of the money they bring home. The lack of support by the husbands of sales agents may be due to the inconvenience placed on the family by the irregular hours and work patterns of sales agents, but we wonder how much the increase in earnings by the women contributes to it.

3. Carolyn Heilbrun (Amanda Cross), a professor of literature at Columbia University and also an author of murder mysteries, responded, when asked during a speech at Wellesley College how she finds time to do everything: "There are only two of us at home, and we meet our children in restaurants."

References

Abbott, Grace. 1938. *The Dependent and the Delinquent Child.* Vol. 2 of *The Child and the State.* Chicago: University of Chicago Press.

Abir-Am, Pnina G. and Dorinda Outram, eds. 1987. *Uneasy Careers and Intimate Lives: Women in Science, 1989–1979.* New Brunswick, N.J.: Rutgers University Press.

Acker, Joan, Kate Barry, and Joke Esseveld. 1990. "Feminism, Female Friends, and the Reconstruction of Intimacy." In *Friendship in Context,* 75–108. *See* Lopata and Maines 1990.

Adams, Bert. 1968. *Kinship in an Urban Setting.* Chicago: Markham.

———. 1988. "Fifty Years of Family Research. What Does It Mean?" *Journal of Marriage and the Family* 50:5–17.

Adams, Frances McLeavey. 1972. "The Role of Old People in Santo Thomas, Mazaltepec." In *Aging and Modernization. See* Cowgill 1972.

Adams, Rebecca. 1983. "Friendship and Its Role in the Lives of Elderly Women." Ph.D. diss., University of Chicago.

———. 1985. "People Would Talk: Normative Barriers to Cross-Sex Friendships for Elderly Women." *The Gerontologist* 25:605–11.

Adams, Rebecca, and Rosemary Blieszner, eds. 1989. *Older Adult Friendship: Structure and Process.* Beverly Hills, Calif.: Sage.

Aisenberg, Nadya, and Mona Harrington. 1988. *Women of Academe: Outsiders in the Sacred Grove.* Amherst: University of Massachusetts Press.

Aldous, Joan, ed. 1982. *Two Paychecks: Life in Dual-Earner Families.* Beverly Hills, Calif.: Sage.

Allatt, Patricia. 1983. "Men and War: Status, Class, and the Social Reproduction of Masculinity." In *The Public and the Private,* edited by Eva Gamarnikow, David H. J. Morgan, June Purvis, and Daphne Taylorson, 47–61. London: Heinemann.

Allen, Sheila, and Carol Wolkowitz. 1987. *Homeworking: Myths and Realities.* New York: Macmillan Education.

Anda, Diane de, and Rosina M. Becerra. 1984. "Support Networks for Adolescent Mothers." *Social Casework* 65:172–81.

Andersen, Margaret L. 1983. *Thinking about Women: Sociological and Feminist Perspectives.* New York: Macmillan.

Andre, Rae. 1982. *Homemakers: The Forgotten Workers.* Chicago: University of Chicago Press.

Anspach, Donald F. 1976. "Kinship and Divorce." *Journal of Marriage and the Family* 38:323–30.

Aptheker, Bettina. 1982. *Woman's Legacy: Essays on Race, Sex, and Class in American History.* Amherst: University of Massachusetts Press.

———. 1989. *Tapestries of Life: Women's Work, Women's Consciousness, and the Meaning of Daily Experience.* Amherst: University of Massachusetts Press.

Ardener, Shirley, ed. 1981. *Women and Space: Ground Rules and Social Maps.* New York: St. Martin's.

Aries, Philippe. 1965. *Centuries of Childhood.* New York: Random House.

Armstrong, Peter. 1982. "If It's Only Women It Doesn't Matter So Much." In *Women, Work, and the Labor Market,* edited by Jackie West, 27–43. London: Routledge & Kegan Paul.

Aukett, Richard, Jane Ritchie, and Kathryn Mill. 1988. "Gender Differences in Friendship Patterns." *Sex Roles* 19:57–66.

Avioli, Paula Smith. 1989. "The Social Support Functions of Siblings in Later Life." *American Behavioral Scientist* 33:45–57.

Babchuk, Nicholas, and Alan P. Bates. 1963. "Primary Relations of Middle-Class Couples: A Study of Male Dominance." *American Sociological Review* 28:374–84.

Babcock, Barbara Allen, Ann Freedman, Eleanor Holmes Norton, and Susan C. Ross. 1975. *Sex Discrimination and the Law: Causes and Remedies.* Boston: Little, Brown.

Backett, Katheryn C. 1982. *Mothers and Fathers*. New York: St. Martin's.

Bahr, Harvey M. 1976. "The Kinship Role." In *Role Structure and Analysis of the Family,* edited by F. I. Nye, 61–79. Beverly Hills, Calif.: Sage.

Baker, Wayne, and Rosanna Hertz. 1990. "Communal Diffusion of Friendship: The Structure of Intimate Relations in an Israeli Kibbutz." In *Friendship in Context. See* Lopata and Maines 1990.

Baldassare, Mark. 1986. *Trouble in Paradise: The Suburban Transformation in America.* New York: Columbia University Press.

Bank, Stephen, and Michael D. Kohn. 1982. "Intense Sibling Loyalties." In *Sibling Relationships. See* Lamb and Sutton-Smith 1982.

Barnes, Denise R. 1987. "Wives and Widows in China." In *Widows: The Middle East, Asia, and the Pacific. See* Lopata 1987c.

Barnett, Rosalind C. 1988. "On the Relationship of Adult Daughters to Their Mothers." *Journal of Geriatric Psychiatry* 21:37–50.

Barnewolt, Debra. 1986. "Social Role Importance: An Interplay of Experience and Expectation in the Lives of Chicago Area Women." Ph.D. diss., Department of Sociology, Loyola University of Chicago.

Bart, Pauline. 1971. "Depression in Middle-aged Women." In *Woman in Sexist Society,* edited by Vivian Gornick and Barbara K. Moran, 163–86. New York: Basic Books.

Baruch, Grace. 1984. "The Psychological Well-Being of Women in the Middle Years." In *Women in Midlife. See* Baruch and Brooks-Gunn 1984.

Baruch, Grace, and Jeanne Brooks-Gunn, eds. 1984. *Women in Midlife.* New York: Plenum.

Baruch, Grace, Rosalind Barnett, and Caryl Rivers. 1983. *Lifeprints: New Patterns of Love and Work for Today's Women.* New York: McGraw-Hill.

Baumgartner, M. P. 1988. *The Moral Order of a Suburb.* New York: Oxford University Press.

Beach, Betty. 1989. *Integrating Work and Family Life: The Home-Working Family.* Albany: State University of New York Press.

Becerra, Rosina M. 1988. "The Mexican American Family." In *Ethnic Families in America. See* Mindel, Habenstein, and Wright 1988.

Becker, Howard S. 1951. "The Professional Dance Musician and His Audience." *American Journal of Sociology* 57:136–44.

———. 1953. "Becoming a Marijuana User." *American Journal of Sociology* 59:235–42.

———. 1960. "Notes on the Concept of Commitment." *American Journal of Sociology* 66:32–42.

Bedford, Victoria. 1989a. "Understanding the Value of Siblings in Old Age." *American Behavioral Scientist* 33, 33–44.

————. 1989a. "Sibling Research in Historical Perspective: The Discovery of a Forgotten Relationship." *American Behavioral Scientist* 33:6–18.

Bedford, Victoria H. and Debra T. Gold, eds. 1989. *Siblings in Later Life: A Neglected Family Relationship.* [Special issue]. *American Behavioral Scientist* 33 (September/October).

Beecher, Catherine E., and Harriet Beecher Stowe. 1870. *The American Woman's Home.* New York: J. B. Ford.

Bell, Robert R. 1981. *Worlds of Friendship.* Beverly Hills, Calif.: Sage.

Benet, Mary Kathleen. 1972. *The Secretarial Ghetto.* New York: McGraw-Hill.

Bengtson, Vern L., and E. deTerre. 1980. "Aging and Family Relations: A Decade Review." *Marriage and Family Review* 3:51–76.

Bengtson, Vern L., and Joan Robertson, eds. 1985. *Grandparenthood.* Beverly Hills, Calif.: Sage.

Bennett, Amanda. 1983. "Population Lid: China Cajoles Families and Offers Incentives to Reduce Birth Rate." *Wall Street Journal,* 6 July, 1 and 16.

Benson, Susan Porter. 1984. "Women in Retail Sales Work: The Continuing Dilemma of Service." In *My Troubles Are Going to Have Trouble with Me,* edited by Karen Brodkin Sacks and Dorothy Remy, 113–24. New Brunswick, N.J.: Rutgers University Press.

Berger, Bennett. 1960. *Working Class Suburb.* Berkeley: University of California Press.

Berger, Peter, and Hansfried Kellner. 1970. "Marriage and Construction of Reality." In *Patterns of Communicative Behavior,* edited by Hans Dreitzel, 50–73. London: Collier-Macmillan.

Bergmann, Barbara R. 1986. *The Economic Emergence of Women.* New York: Basic Books.

Berheide, Catherine-White. 1988. "Women in Sales and Service Occupations." In *Women Working: Theories and Facts in Perspective,* edited by Ann Helton Stromberg and Shirley Harkess, 2d ed., 241–57. Mountain View, Calif.: Mayfield.

Berk, Richard A., and Sarah Fenstermaker Berk. 1979. *Labor and Leisure at Home: Content and Organization of the Household Day.* Beverly Hills, Calif.: Sage.

————. 1985. *The Gender Factory: The Apportionment of Work in American Households.* New York: Plenum.

Bernard, Jessie. 1973. *The Future of Marriage.* New York: Bantam.

————. 1974. "The Housewife: Between Two Worlds." In *Varieties of Work Experience,* edited by Phyllis L. Steward and Muriel G. Cantor, 49–66. New York: Wiley.

————. 1979. "Women as Voters: From Redemptive to Futurist Role." In *Social Roles and Social Policy: A Complex Social Science Equation,* edited by Jean Lipman-Blumen and Jessie Bernard, 279–86. Beverly Hills: Sage.

———. 1981. *The Female World*. New York: Free Press.

———. 1983. "The Good Provider Role: Its Rise and Fall." In *Family in Transition,* edited by Arlene S. Skolnick and Jerome H. Skolnick, 155–75. Boston: Little, Brown.

Berrueta-Clement, John R. 1984. *Changed Lives*. Ypsilanti, Mich.: High/Scope Press.

Bettelheim, Bruno. 1962. "Does Communal Education Work? The Case of the Kibbutz." *Commentary* 33:117–25.

———. 1965. "The Commitment Required of a Woman Entering a Scientific Profession in Present-Day American Society." In *Women and the Scientific Professions,* 4–17. *See* Rossi 1965.

Biddle, Bruce J., and Edwin J. Thomas. 1966. *Role Theory*. New York: Wiley.

Bieder, Robert E. 1973. "Kinship as a Factor in Migration." *Journal of Marriage and the Family* 35:429–39.

Bigus, Odis. 1972. "The Milkman and His Customers." *Urban Life and Culture* 1:131–65.

Bird, Caroline. 1976. *Enterprising Women*. New York: New American Library/Mentor.

———. 1979. *The Two-Paycheck Marriage*. New York: Rawson Wade.

Blake, Judith. 1974. "Coercive Pronatalism and American Population Policy." In *The Family: Its Structure and Functions,* 2d ed., edited by Rose Coser, 276–317. New York: St. Martin's.

Blieszner, Rosemary. 1989. "Developmental Processes of Friendship." In *Older Adult Friendship,* 108–26. *See* Adams and Blieszner 1989.

Block, Joel, and Diane Greenberg. 1985. *Women and Friendship*. New York: Franklin Watts.

Bloom, Paul N., and Ruth Belk Smith, eds. 1986. *The Future of Consumerism*. Lexington, Mass.: Lexington Books.

Bluestone, Barry, and Bennett Harrison. 1982. *The Deindustrialization of America*. New York: Basic Books.

Blumer, Herbert. 1969. *Symbolic Interactionism: Perspective and Method*. Englewood Cliffs, N.J.: Prentice-Hall.

Blumstein, Philip, and Pepper Schwartz. 1983. *American Couples: Work, Money, Sex*. New York: Morrow.

Bohannan, Paul J. 1963. *Social Anthropology*. New York: Holt, Rinehart & Winston.

Borg, Susan, and Judith Lasker. 1988. *When Pregnancy Fails: Families Coping with Miscarriage, Stillbirth, and Infant Death*. Rev. ed. Boston: Beacon.

Bose, Christine. 1980. "Social Status of the Homemaker." In *Women and Household Labor,* 69–87. *See* Berk 1980.

Boserup, Ester. 1970. *Woman's Role in Economic Development.* New York: St. Martin's.

Boston Women's Health Collective. [1971] [1984] 1992. *The New Our Bodies, Ourselves.* New York: Simon & Schuster.

Bott, Elizabeth. 1957. *Family and Social Network.* London: Tavistock.

Boverman, C. E., and R. M. Dobash. 1974. "Structural Variations in Inter-Sibling Affect." *Journal of Marriage and the Family* 36:48–54.

Braverman, Harry. 1974. *Labor and Monopoly Capital.* New York: Monthly Review Press.

Brody, Elaine M. 1989. *Women in the Middle: Their Parent Care Years.* New York: Springer.

Brody, Elaine M., Christine Hoffman, Morton Kleban, and Claire Schoonover. 1989. "Caregiving Daughters and Their Local Siblings: Perceptions, Strains, and Interactions." *The Gerontologist* 29:529–38.

Brown, Bradford B. 1990. "A Life-Span Approach to Friendship." In *Friendship in Context,* 23–50. *See* Lopata and Maines 1990.

Brown, Clair (Vickery). 1982. "Home Production for Use in a Market Economy." In *Rethinking the Family: Some Feminist Questions,* 151–67. *See* Thorne 1982.

Bucher, Rue, and Joan G. Stelling. 1977. *Becoming Professional.* Beverly Hills, Calif.: Sage.

Burton, Linda M., and Vern L. Bengtson. 1985. "Black Grandmothers: Issues of Timing and Continuity of Roles." In *Grandparenthood,* 61–77. *See* Bengtson and Robertson 1985.

Butler, JoAnn C. 1988. "Local Zoning Ordinances Governing Home Occupations." In *The New Era of Home-Based Work,* 189–200. *See* Christensen 1988c.

Cain, Virginia, and Sandra L. Hofferth. 1989. "Parental Choice of Self-Care for School-Age Children." *Journal of Marriage and the Family* 51:65–77.

Callan, Hilary, and Shirley Ardener. 1984. *The Incorporated Wife.* London: Croom Helm.

Cancian, Francesca. 1987. *Love in America: Gender and Self-Development.* New York: Cambridge University Press.

Caplow, Theodore, Howard M. Bahr, Bruce A. Chadwick, Reuben Hill, and Margaret Holmes Williamson. 1982. *Middletown Families: Fifty Years of Change and Continuity.* New York: Bantam.

Carlson, Margaret. 1992. "All Eyes on Hillary." *Time,* 14 September, 28–33.

Carlson, Patricia, Marian Simacek, William F. Henry, and Ida M. Martinson. 1984. "Helping Parents Cope: A Model Home Care Program for the

Dying Child." In *Childhood and Death,* edited by Hannelore Wass and Charles A. Corr, 113–27. New York: Hemisphere.

Carnegie, Dale. 1936. *How to Win Friends and Influence People.* New York: Simon & Schuster.

Cavendish, Ruth. 1982. *Women on the Line.* London: Routledge & Kegan Paul.

Chafe, William Henry. 1972. *The American Woman: Her Changing Social, Economic and Political Roles, 1920–1970.* New York: Oxford University Press.

Chapman, Jane Roberts, and Margaret Gates. 1977. *Women into Wives: The Legal and Economic Impact of Marriage.* Beverly Hills, Calif.: Sage.

Chatters, Linda M., Robert Joseph Taylor, and Harold W. Neighbors. 1989. "Size of Informal Helper Network Mobilized During a Serious Personal Problem among Black Americans." *Journal of Marriage and the Family* 51:667–76.

Cherlin, Andrew J. 1981. *Marriage, Divorce, Remarriage.* Cambridge: Harvard University Press.

Cherlin, Andrew J. and Frank F. Furstenberg. 1986. *The New American Grandparent: A Place in the Family, A Life Apart.* New York: Basic Books.

Chodorow, Nancy. 1978. *The Reproduction of Mothering: Psychoanalysis and the Sociology of Gender.* Berkeley: University of California Press.

Chodorow, Nancy, and Susan Contratto. 1982. "The Fantasy of the Perfect Mother." In *Rethinking the Family,* 54–75. *See* Thorne 1982.

Christensen, Kathleen. 1988a. "Independent Contracting." In *The New Era of Home-Based Work. See* Christensen 1988c.

————. 1988b. "Introduction: White-Collar Home-Based Work—The Changing U.S. Economy and Family." In *The New Era of Home-Based Work. See* Christensen 1988c.

————, ed. 1988c. *The New Era of Home-Based Work: Directions and Policies.* Boulder, Colo.: Westview.

————. 1988d. *Women and Home-Based Work.* New York: Henry Holt.

Cicirelli, V. G. 1982. "Sibling Influence throughout the Life Span." In *Sibling Relationships,* 455–62. *See* Lamb and Sutton-Smith 1982.

Clark, Alice. [1919] 1968. *Working Life of Women in the Seventeenth Century.* New York: Kelley Reprints.

Clavan, Sylvia. 1978. "The Impact of Social Class and Social Trends on the Role of Grandparent." *The Family Coordinator* 27:351–57.

Clawson, Mary Ann. 1986. "Nineteenth-Century Women's Auxiliaries and Fraternal Orders." *Signs* 12, 40–61.

Clemente, Frank, Patricia A. Rexroad, and Carl Hirsch. 1975. "The Participation of Black Aged in Voluntary Associations." *Journal of Gerontology* 30:469–72.

Cohler, Bertram J. 1988. "The Adult Daughter-Mother Relationship: Perspectives from Life-Course Family Study and Psychoanalysis." *Journal of Geriatric Psychiatry* 21:51–72.

Cooley, Charles Horton. [1902] 1922. *Human Nature and the Social Order.* New York: Scribner's.

Coontz, Stephanie. 1992. *The Way We Never Were: American Families and the Nostalgia Trip.* New York: Basic Books.

Corcoran, Mary, Greg J. Duncan, and Martha S. Hill. 1988. "The Economic Fortunes of Women and Children: Lessons from the Panel Study of Income Dynamics." In *Black Women in America,* 97–113. *See* Malson et al. 1988.

Coser, Lewis. 1973. "Servants: The Obsolescence of an Occupational Role." *Social Forces* 52:31–40.

———. 1984. *Refugee Scholars in America: Their Impact and Their Experiences.* New Haven: Yale University.

———. 1974. *Greedy Institutions.* New York: Free Press.

Coser, Lewis, and Rose Laub Coser. 1974. "The Housewife and Her 'Greedy Family.'" In *Greedy Institutions. See* Coser 1974.

Coser, Rose Laub. 1975a. "The Complexity of Roles as a Seedbed of Individual Autonomy." In *The Idea of Social Structure: Papers in Honor of Robert K. Merton,* edited by Lewis A. Coser, 237–630. New York: Harcourt Brace Jovanovich.

———. 1975b. "Stay Home Little Sheba: On Placement, Displacement, and Social Change." *Social Problems* 22, 470–80.

———. 1991. *In Defense of Modernity: Role Complexity and Individual Autonomy.* Stanford, Calif.: Stanford University Press.

———. 1992. Personal Correspondence.

Costello, Cynthia B. 1988. "Clerical Home-Based Work: A Case Study of Work and Family." In *The New Era of Home-Based Work,* 135–45. *See* Christensen 1988c.

Cott, Nancy F. 1977. *The Bonds of Womanhood: Women's Sphere in New England, 1780–1885.* New Haven: Yale University Press.

Cowan, Ruth Schwartz. 1983. *More Work for Mother: The Ironies of Household Technology from Open Hearth to the Microwave.* New York: Basic Books.

Cowgill, Donald O. 1972. "The Role and Status of the Aged in Thailand." In *Aging and Modernization,* edited by Donald O. Cowgill and Lowell D. Holmes, 91–101. New York: Appleton-Century-Crofts.

Cox, Claire. 1963. *How Women Can Make Up to $1000 a Week in Direct Selling*. New York: Van Nostrand.

Crane, Diana. 1968. "Social Structure in a Group of Scientists: A Test of the 'Invisible College' Hypothesis." *American Sociological Review* 34:335–352.

Crane, Lauren Edgar. 1969. "The Salesman's Role in Household Decision-Making." In *Salesmanship: Selected Readings,* edited by John M. Rathwell, 98–110. Homewood, Ill.: Irwin.

Csikszentimihalyi, Mihaly, and Eugene Rochberg-Halton. 1981. *The Meaning of Things: Domestic Symbols and the Self.* New York: Cambridge University Press.

Cumming, Elaine, and William E. Henry. 1961. *Growing Old: The Process of Disengagement.* New York: Basic Books.

Cutler, Stephen. 1976. "Membership in Different Types of Voluntary Associations and Psychological Well-Being." *The Gerontologist* 16:335–39.

Danco, Leon A. 1982. *Inside the Family Business.* Englewood Cliffs, N.J.: Prentice-Hall.

Daniels, Arlene Kaplan. 1988. *Invisible Careers: Women Community Leaders in the Volunteer World.* Chicago: University of Chicago Press.

Davis, Angela Y. 1988. *Women, Culture, and Politics.* New York: Random House.

Davis, Kinsley. 1940. "The Sociology of Parent-Youth Conflict." *American Sociological Review* 5:523–35.

———. [1949] 1966. "Status and Related Concepts." In *Role Theory. See* Biddle and Thomas, 1966.

Davis, Nancy J., and Larry Bumpass. 1976. "The Continuation of Education after Marriage among Women in the United States." *Demography* 3:161–74.

Demos, John. 1973. *A Little Commonwealth: Family Life in Plymouth Colony.* New York: Oxford University Press.

Denzin, Norman K. 1987a. *The Alcoholic Self.* Newbury Park, Calif.: Sage.

———. 1987b. *The Recovering Alcoholic.* Newbury Park, Calif.: Sage.

Deutsch, Helene. 1977. *The Psychology of Women.* New York: Grune & Stratton.

Deutsch, Morton. 1954. "Field Theory in Social Psychology." In *Handbook of Social Psychology,* edited by Gardner Lindsey, 412–487. Cambridge, Mass.: Addison-Wesley.

Deutscher, Irwin. 1964. "The Quality of Postparental Life." *Journal of Marriage and the Family* 26:52–59.

Deveny, Kathleen. 1989. "Can Avon Get Wall Street to Answer the Door?" *Business Week,* 20 March, 123–24.

Dobrofsky, Lynne R., and Constance T. Patterson. 1977. "The Military Wife and Feminism." *Signs* 2:675–84.

Domhoff, G. William. 1967. *Who Rules America?* Englewood Cliffs, N.J.: Prentice-Hall.

———. 1983. *Who Rules America Now: A View for the '80s.* Englewood Cliffs, N.J.: Prentice-Hall.

Donovan, Frances R. [1929] 1974. *The Saleslady.* New York: Arno.

Douglas, Ann. 1977. *The Feminization of American Culture.* New York: Avon Books.

Dubin, Robert. 1956. "Industrial Workers' World: A Study of the Central Life Interests of Industrial Workers." *Social Problems* 3:131–42.

Dulles, Foster Rhea. 1965. *A History of Recreation: America Learns to Play.* New York: Appleton-Century-Crofts.

Duncan, James. 1982. *Housing and Identity: Cross-Cultural Perspectives.* New York: Holmes & Meier.

Duvall, Evelyn. 1954. *In-Laws: Pro and Con.* New York: Association Press.

Dworkin, Anthony Gary, Janet Saltzman Chafetz, and Rosalind J. Dworkin. 1986. "The Effects of Tokenism on Work Alienation among Urban Public School Teachers." *Work and Occupations* 13:399–420.

Ebaugh, Helen Rose Fuchs. 1988. *Becoming an Ex: The Process of Role Exit.* Chicago: University of Chicago Press.

Edwards, Richard. 1979. *Contested Terrain: The Transformation of the Workplace in the Twentieth Century.* New York: Basic Books.

Ehrenreich, Barbara. 1983. *The Hearts of Men: American Dreams and Flight from Commitment.* Garden City, N.Y.: Anchor.

Ehrenreich, Barbara, and Deirdre English. 1979. *For Her Own Good.* Garden City, N.Y.: Anchor.

Eichler, Margrit. 1973. "Women as Personal Dependents." In *Women in Canada,* edited by Marylee Stephenson, 36–55. Toronto: New Press.

Eisenstein, Zillah. 1979. *Capitalist Patriarchy and the Case for Socialist Feminism.* New York: Monthly Review Press.

Elder, Glen H., Jr., and Charles E. Bowerman. 1963. "Family Structure and Child-Rearing Patterns: The Effect of Family Size and Sex Composition." *American Sociological Review* 28:891–906.

Emmerman, Lynn. 1990. "Mixed Blessings: Five Couples Talk about Their Interracial Marriages." *Chicago Tribune Magazine,* 9 September, 13–18.

England, Paula, and George Farkas. 1986. *Household, Employment, and Gender: A Social, Economic, and Demographic View.* New York: Aldine.

Enloe, Cynthia. 1987. "Feminists Thinking about War, Militarism, and Peace." In *Analyzing Gender: A Handbook of Social Science Research,* edited by Beth B. Hess and Myra Marx Ferree, 526–47. Beverly Hills, Calif.: Sage.

Entwisle, Doris, and Susan G. Doering. 1981. *The First Birth: A Family Turning Point.* Baltimore: Johns Hopkins University Press.

Epstein, Cynthia. 1970. *Women's Place: Options and Limits in Professional Careers.* Berkeley: University of California Press.

————. 1971. "Encountering the Male Establishment: Sex-Status Limits on Women's Careers in the Professions." In *The Professional Woman,* edited by Athena Theodore, 42–73. Cambridge, Mass.: Schenkman.

————. 1983. *Women in Law.* Garden City, N.Y.: Anchor.

————. 1988. *Deceptive Distinctions: Sex, Gender, and the Social Order.* New Haven: Yale University Press.

————. 1992. "Changes in Structure: Changes in the Self." Paper presented at the annual meeting of the American Sociological Association, Pittsburgh, 22 August.

Epstein, Cynthia, and Rose Coser, eds. 1981. *Access to Power: Cross-National Studies of Women and Elites.* London: Allen & Unwin.

Erikson, Erik H. 1965. "Concluding Remarks." In *Women and the Scientific Professions,* 232–45. *See* Rossi 1965.

Eskilson, Arlene, and Mary Glenn Wiley. 1987. "Parents, Peers, Perceived Pressure, and Adolescent Self-Concept: Is a Daughter a Daughter All of Her Life?" *Sociological Quarterly* 28:135–45.

Faludi, Susan. 1991. *Backlash: The Undeclared War against Women.* New York: Crown.

Farber, Bernard. 1966. "Kinship Laterality and the Emotionally Disturbed Child." In *Kinship and Family Organization,* edited by Bernard Farber, 69–78. New York: Wiley.

Farber, Bernard, Charles H. Mindel, and Bernard Lazerwitz. 1988. "The Jewish American Family." In *Ethnic Families in America,* 400–437. *See* Mindel, Habenstein, and Wright 1988.

Faver, Catherine A. 1984. *Women in Transition: Career, Family, and Life Satisfaction in Three Cohorts.* New York: Praeger.

Feldberg, Roslyn, and Evelyn Nakano Glenn. 1979. "Male and Female: Job versus Gender Models in the Sociology of Work." *Social Problems* 26:524–38.

Feldman, Harold. 1981. "A Comparison of Intentional Parents and Intentionally Childless Couples." *Journal of Marriage and the Family* 43:593–600.

Ferber, Marianne, and Joan Huber. 1979. "Husbands, Wives, and Careers." *Journal of Marriage and the Family* 41:315–25.

Ferree, Myra Marx. 1976. "Working-Class Jobs: Housework and Paid Work as Sources of Satisfaction." *Social Problems* 23:431–41.

————. 1980. "Satisfaction with Housework: The Social Contract." In *Women and Household Labor,* 89–112. *See* Berk 1980.

————. 1987. "Family and Job for Working-Class Women: Gender and Class Systems Seen from Below." In *Families and Work*, 289–301. *See* Gerstel and Gross 1987a.

Finch, Janet. 1983. *Married to the Job: Wives' Incorporation in Men's Work.* Boston: Allen & Unwin.

Finch, Janet, and D. Groves. 1983. *A Labour of Love.* Boston: Routledge & Kegan Paul.

Finley, Nancy J. 1989. "Theories of Family Labor as Applied to Gender Differences in Caregiving for Elderly Parents." *Journal of Marriage and the Family* 51:79–86.

Fischer, Claude. 1982. *To Dwell among Friends: Personal Networks in Town and City.* Chicago: University of Chicago Press.

Fischer, Claude, Robert Max Jackson, C. Ann Steve, Kathleen Gerson, Lynne McCallister Jones, and Mark Baldassare. 1977. *Networks and Places: Social Relations in the Urban Setting.* New York: Free Press.

Fisher, Lucy Rose. 1983. "Mothers and Mothers-in-Law." *Journal of Marriage and the Family* 45:187–92.

————. 1986. *Linked Lives: Adult Daughters and Their Mothers.* New York: Harper & Row.

Fisher, Lucy Rose, Daniel P. Mueller, Philip W. Cooper, and Richard A. Chase. 1989. *Older Minnesotans: What Do They Need? How Do They Contribute?* St. Paul, Minn.: Amherst H. Wilder Foundation.

Flammang, Jane A., ed. 1984. *Political Women: Current Roles in State and Local Government.* Beverly Hills, Calif.: Sage.

Foerstner, Abigail. 1987. "Home Again: Increasingly Businesswomen Are Finding There's No Place Like It." *Chicago Tribune*, 12 April, 6–15.

Forcey, Linda Rennie. 1987. *Mothers of Sons: Toward an Understanding of Responsibility.* New York: Praeger.

Fowlkes, Martha R. 1980. *Behind Every Successful Man.* New York: Columbia University Press.

Frankfort, Roberta. 1977. *Collegiate Women.* New York: New York University Press.

Friedan, Betty. 1963. *The Feminine Mystique.* New York: Norton.

Frohock, Fred M. 1986. *Special Care: Medical Decisions at the Beginning of Life.* Chicago: University of Chicago Press.

Fromm, Eric. 1947. *Man for Himself.* New York: Rinehart.

Furstenberg, Frank, Jr. 1990. "As the Pendulum Shifts: The National History of Teenage Childbearing as a Social Problem." The Duvall Distinguished Lecture, National Council on Family Relations, 11 November, Seattle.

Furstenberg, Frank Jr., Leon Gordis, and Milton Markowitz. 1969. "Birth Control Knowledge and Attitudes among Unmarried Pregnant Adolescents: A Preliminary Report." *Journal of Marriage and the Family* 31:34–42.

Furstenberg, Frank, Jr. and Graham Spanier. 1984. *Recycling the Family: Remarriage after Divorce.* Beverly Hills, Calif.: Sage.

Galbraith, John Kenneth. 1973. "The Economics of the American Housewife." *Atlantic Monthly,* August, 78–83.

Gallup, George H., Jr. and Frank Newport. 1990. "Who Wants Kids? Nearly Everybody." *Chicago Sun Times,* 3 June, 3.

Gannon, Martin J. 1984. "Preferences for Temporary Workers: Time, Variety, and Flexibility." *Monthly Labor Review,* August, 26–28.

Gans, Herbert. 1962. *The Urban Villagers: Group and Class in the Life of Italian-Americans.* New York: Free Press.

———. 1967. *Leavittowners.* New York: Pantheon.

Garland, Anne Witte. 1988. *Women Activists: Challenging the Abuse of Power.* New York: Feminist Press, City University of New York.

Gates, Margaret. 1977. "Homemakers into Widows and Divorcees: Can the Law Provide Economic Protection? In *Women into Wives,* 215–32. *See* Chapman and Gates 1977.

Gelb, Joyce, and Marian Lief Palley. 1982. *Women and Public Policies.* Princeton: Princeton University Press.

Genevie, Louis, and Eva Margolies. 1987. *The Motherhood Report: How Women Feel about Being Mothers.* New York: Macmillan.

Gerhardt, Uta. 1980. "Toward a Critical Analysis of Role." *Social Problems* 27:556–69.

Gerson, Judith M., and Robert E. Kraut. 1988. "Clerical Work at Home or in the Office: The Difference It Makes." In *The New Era of Home-Based Work,* 49–64. *See* Christensen 1988c.

Gerson, Kathleen. 1985. *Hard Choices: How Women Decide about Work, Career, and Motherhood.* Berkeley: University of California Press.

Gerson, Menachem. 1978. *Family, Women, and Socialization in the Kibbutz.* Boston: Lexington Books.

Gerstel, Naomi, and Harriet Engel Gross, eds. 1987a. *Families and Work.* Philadelphia: Temple University Press.

———. 1987b. "Introduction to Work in and from the Contemporary Home." In *Families and Work,* 153–61. *See* Gerstel and Gross 1987a.

Gibson, Geoffrey. 1972. "Kin Family Networks: Overheralded Structure in Past Conceptualizations of Family Functioning." *Journal of Marriage and the Family* 34:13–24.

Giles-Sims, Jean, and Margaret Crosbie-Burnett. 1989. "Stepfamilies." *Family Relations* 38:19–23.

Gilligan, Carol. 1982. *In a Different Voice: Psychological Theory and Women's Development.* Cambridge: Harvard University Press.

Gilman, Charlotte Perkins. [1898] 1966. *Women and Economics.* New York: Harper Torchbook.

Glamour. 1989. "Private Time: Ease Holiday Pressures: Let Someone Else Do It." December, 110.

Glazer, Nona. 1978. "Housework: A Review Essay." In *Family Factbook,* edited by Helena Z. Lopata, 87–93. New York: Marquis Academic Media.

———. 1980. "Everyone Needs Three Hands: Doing Unpaid and Paid Work." In *Women and Household Labor,* 249–73. See Berk 1980.

———. 1984. "Servants to Capital: Unpaid Domestic Labor and Paid Work." *Review of Radical Political Economics* 16:61–87.

———. 1988. "Overlooked, Overworked: Women's Unpaid and Paid Work in the Health Services "Cost Crisis."" *International Journal of Health Services* 18:119–37.

Glazer, Nona, Linda Majka, Joan Acker, and Christine Bose. 1979. "The Homemaker, the Family, and Employment: Some Inter-relationships." In *Women in the Labor Force,* edited by Ann Foote Cahn, 155–169. New York: Praeger.

Glenn, Evelyn Nakano. 1986. *Issei, Nisei, War Bride: Three Generations of Japanese American Women in Domestic Service.* Philadelphia: Temple University Press.

Glenn, Evelyn Nakano, and Roslyn L. Feldberg. 1977. "Degraded and Deskilled: The Proletarianization of Clerical Work." *Social Problems* 25:52–64.

———. 1979. "Clerical Work: The Female Occupation." In *Women: A Feminist Perspective,* edited by Jo Freeman, 2d ed., 313–38. Palo Alto, Calif.: Mayfield.

Glenn, Norval D., and Charles N. Wever. 1988. "The Changing Relationship of Marital Status to Reported Happiness." *Journal of Marriage and the Family* 50:317–24.

Glick, Paul C. 1989. "Remarried Families, Stepfamilies, and Stepchildren: A Brief Demographic Profile." *Family Relations* 38:24–47.

Goetting, Ann. 1989. "Patterns of Support among In-Laws in the United States." Paper presented at the Eighty-Fifth Annual Meeting of the American Sociological Association, San Francisco, August.

Goffman, Erving. 1961. *Asylums: Essays on the Social Situation of Mental Patients and Other Inmates.* New York: Anchor.

———. 1967. *Interaction Ritual: Essays on Face-to-Face Behavior.* Garden City, N.Y.: Doubleday.

Gold, Deborah. 1987. *Siblings in Old Age: Their Roles and Relationships.* Chicago: Center for Applied Gerontology.

Goode, William. 1960. "A Theory of Role Strain." *American Sociological Review* 25:483–96.

———. 1963. *World Revolution and Family Patterns.* New York: Free Press.

————. 1982. "Why Men Resist." In *Rethinking the Family,* 131–50. *See* Thorne 1982.

Goody, Jack. 1983. *The Development of the Family and Marriage in Europe.* Cambridge: Cambridge University Press.

Gouldner, Alvin W. 1957. "Cosmopolitans and Locals." *Administrative Science Quarterly* 2 (December): 281–306; 2 (March 1958): 444–80.

Grubb, Norton W. and Marvin Lazerson. 1982. *Broken Promises: How Americans Fail Their Children.* New York: Basic Books.

Gudykunst, William B. 1985. "An Exploratory Comparison of Close Intracultural and Intercultural Friendships." *Communications Quarterly* 33:270–83.

Guillemin, Jeanne Harley, and Lyda Lytle Holmstrom. 1986. *Mixed Blessings: Intensive Care for Newborns.* New York: Oxford University Press.

Gujral, Jaya Sarma. 1987. "Widowhood in India." In *Widows: The Middle East, Asia, and the Pacific,* 43–55. *See* Lopata 1987c.

Gusfield, Joseph. 1963. *Symbolic Crusade: Status Politics and the American Temperance Movement.* Urbana: University of Illinois Press.

Gutmann, David L. 1985. "Deculturation and the American Grandparent." In *Grandparenthood,* 173–81. *See* Bengtson and Robertson 1985.

Halem, Lynne Carol. 1982. *Separated and Divorced Women.* Westport, Conn.: Greenwood.

Halpern, Sydney A. 1989. *American Pediatrics: The Social Dynamics of Professionalism, 1880–1980.* Berkeley: University of California Press.

Hansen, Karen V. 1990. "Women's Unions and the Search for Political Identity." In *Women, Class, and the Feminist Imagination,* 213–38. *See* Hansen and Philipson 1990.

Harding, Sandra. 1986. *The Science Question in Feminism.* Ithaca, N.Y.: Cornell University Press.

Hareven, Tamara K. 1987a. "The Dynamics of Kin in an Industrial Community." In *Turning Points,* edited by J. Demos and S. Boocock, 151–81. Chicago: University of Chicago Press.

————. 1978b. *Transitions: The Family and the Life Course in Historical Perspective.* New York: Academic Press.

Hareven, Tamara K., and Randolph Langenbach. 1978. *Amoskeag: Life and Work in an American Factory-City.* New York: Pantheon.

Harragan, Betty Lehan. 1977. *Games Mother Never Taught You: Corporate Gamesmanship for Women.* New York: Warner.

Harris, Barbara. 1979. "Careers, Conflict, and Children: The Legacy of the Cult of Domesticity." In *Career and Motherhood: Struggles for a New Identity,* edited by Alan Roland and Barbara Harris, 55–86. New York: Human Sciences Press.

Hartman, Susan M. 1989. *From Margin to Mainstream: American Women and Politics since 1960*. New York: Knopf.

Hartmann, Betsy. 1987. *Reproductive Rights and Wrongs: The Global Politics of Population Control and Contraceptive Choice*. New York: Harper & Row.

Hartmann, Heidi. 1981. "The Family as the Locus of Gender, Class, and Political Struggle: The Example of Housework." *Signs* 6:366–94.

———. 1990. "Capitalism, Patriarchy, and Job Segregation by Sex." In *Women, Class, and the Feminist Imagination*, 146–81. *See* Hansen and Philipson 1990.

Haug, Marie R., and Marvin B. Sussman. 1968. "Professional Autonomy and the Revolt of the Client." *Social Problems* 17:153–61.

Hayden, Delores. 1981. *The Grand Domestic Revolution: A History of Feminist Designs for American Homes, Neighborhoods, and Cities*. Cambridge: MIT Press.

Heisel, Marsel A. 1987. "Women and Widows in Turkey: Support Systems." In *Widows: The Middle East, Asia, and the Pacific*, 79–105. *See* Lopata 1987c.

Henze, Lura, and John Hudson. 1974. "Personal and Family Characteristics of Cohabiting and Noncohabiting College Students." *Journal of Marriage and the Family*. 36:722–26.

Hertz, Rosanna. 1986. *More Equal than Others: Women and Men in Dual-Career Marriages*. Berkeley: University of California Press.

Hess, Beth. 1972. "Friendship." In *Aging and Society*, vol. 3: *A Sociology of Age Stratification*, edited by Matilada Riley, M. Johnson, and Anne Foner, 357–93. New York: Sage.

Hess, Beth, and Joan M. Waring. 1978a. "Changing Patterns of Aging and Family Bonds in Later Life." *Family Coordinator* 27: 303–14.

———. 1978b. "Parent and Child in Later Life." In *Child Influences on Marital and Family Interaction*, 241–74. *See* R. Lerner and Spanier 1978.

Hobson, Randy. 1989. "Gender Differences in Job Satisfaction: Why Aren't Women More Dissatisfied?" *Sociological Quarterly* 30:385–99.

Hochschild, Arlie. 1969. "The Role of the Ambassador's Wife: An Exploratory Study." *Journal of Marriage and the Family* 31:73–87.

———. 1973. *The Unexpected Community*. Englewood Cliffs, N.J.: Prentice-Hall.

———. 1983. *The Managed Heart*. Berkeley: University of California Press.

———. 1989. *The Second Shift: Working Parents and the Revolution at Home*. New York: Viking Penguin.

———. 1992. "Beyond the Second Shift: Denying Needs at Home or Contesting Rules at Work." Paper presented at the annual meetings of the National Council on Family Relations. 8 November, Orlando.

Hoffman, Lois. 1987. "The Effects on Children of Maternal and Paternal Employment." In *Families and Work,* 362–95. *See* Gerstel and Gross 1987a.

Holbert, Ginny. 1988. "If You Must Work, There's No Place Like a Home Office." *Chicago Sun Times,* 16 October, B.M. 3.

Holmstrom, Linda L. 1973. *The Two-Career Family.* Cambridge, Mass.: Schenkman.

Hoonaard, Deborah van den. 1991. "The Aging of a Retirement Community." Ph.D. diss., Department of Sociology, Loyola University of Chicago.

Hope, Emily, Mary Kennedy, and Anne De Winter. 1976. "Homeworkers in North London." In *Dependence and Exploitation in Work and Marriage,* edited by Diana Leonard Barker and Sheila Allen, 88–108. London: Longman.

Horgan, Ellen Somers. 1988. "The American Catholic Irish Family." In *Ethnic Families in America,* 45–75. *See* Mindel, Habenstein, and Wright 1988.

Horner, Matina S. 1972. "Towards an Understanding of Achievement-related Conflicts in Women." *Journal of Social Issues* 28 (February):157–76.

Horowitz, Amy. 1985. "Sons and Daughters as Caregivers to Older Parents: Differences in Role Performance and Consequences." *The Gerontologist* 25:612–17.

Hossfeld, Karen J. 1990. "Their Logic against Them: Contradictions in Sex, Race, and Class in Silicon Valley." In *Women Workers and Global Restructuring,* edited by Kathryn Ward, 149–78. Ithaca, N.Y.: Cornell University Press.

House, J. D. 1977. *Contemporary Entrepreneurs: The Sociology of Residential Real Estate Agents.* Westport, Conn.: Greenwood.

Houseknecht, Sharon K. 1987. "Voluntary Childlessness." In *Handbook of Marriage and the Family,* 369–95. *See* Steinmetz 1987.

Howe, Louise Kapp. 1977. *Pink Collar Workers: Inside the World of Women's Work.* New York: G. P. Putnam's Sons.

Huber, Joan. 1980. "Will U.S. Fertility Decline toward Zero?" *Sociological Quarterly* 21:481–92.

Hughes, Everett C. 1971. *The Sociological Eye.* Chicago: Aldine Atherton.

Hughes, Helen MacGill. 1977. "Wasp/Woman/Sociologist." *Society/Transaction.* August, 69–80.

Hunt, Janet G., and Larry L. Hunt. 1982. "Dual-Career Families: Vanguard of the Future or Residue of the Past?" In *Dual Paychecks* 41–62. *See* Aldous 1982.

Hunter, Albert. 1974. *Symbolic Communities: The Persistence and Change of Chicago's Local Communities.* Chicago: University of Chicago Press.

Hurtado, Aida. 1989. "Relating to Privilege: Seduction and Rejection in the Subordination of White Women and Women of Color." *Signs* 14:833–55.

Hyde, Janet Shibley, and Marilyn J. Essex. 1990. *Parental Leave and Child Care: Setting a Research and Policy Agenda.* Philadelphia: Temple University Press.

Inkeles, Alex. 1981. *Exploring Individual Modernity.* New York: Columbia University Press.

Inkeles, Alex, and David H. Smith. 1974. *Becoming Modern: Individual Change in Six Developing Countries.* Cambridge: Harvard University Press.

Irish, Donald P. 1964. "Sibling Interaction: A Neglected Aspect in Family Life Research." *Social Forces* 42:279–88.

Jackson, Mary R., and Marie Crane. 1986. "'Some of My Best Friends Are Black . . .': Interracial Friendships and Whites' Racial Attitudes." *Public Opinion Quarterly* 50:459–86.

Janowitz, Morris. 1968. "The Community of Limited Liability." In *The American City,* edited by Anselm Strauss, 368–72. Chicago: Aldine.

Jarrett, Robin. 1990a. "A Comparative Examination of Socialization Patterns among Low-Income African-Americans, Chicanos, Puerto Ricans, and Whites: A Review of the Ethnographic Literature." New York: Social Science Research Council.

———. 1990b. "Gender Roles among Low-Income Black Women." Manuscript, Chicago: Loyola University of Chicago.

———. 1992. "A Family Case Study: An Examination of the Underclass Debate." In *Qualitative Methods in Family Research,* edited by Jane Gilgun, Kerry Daly and Gerald Handel. 172–97. Newbury Park, Calif.: Sage.

Joffe, Carole E. 1977. *Friendly Intruders: Childcare Professionals and Family Life.* Berkeley: University of California.

John, Robert. 1988. "The Native American Family." In *Ethnic Families in America,* 325–63. *See* Mindel, Habenstein, and Wright 1988.

Johnson, Colleen Leahy. 1985. *Growing Up and Growing Old in Italian-American Families.* New Brunswick, N.J.: Rutgers University Press.

———. 1988. *Ex Families: Grandparents, Parents, and Children Adjust to Divorce.* New Brunswick, N.J.: Rutgers University Press.

Johnson, Elizabeth S. 1981. "Older Mothers' Perceptions of Their Child's Divorce." *The Gerontologist* 21:395–401.

Johnson, Miriam M. 1988. *Strong Mothers, Weak Wives: The Search for Gender Equality.* Berkeley: University of California Press.

Jurik, Nancy C. 1985. "An Officer and a Lady: Organizational Barriers to Women Working as Correctional Officers in Men's Prisons." *Social Problems* 32:375–88.

Jurik, Nancy C., and Gregory J. Halemba. 1984. "Gender, Working Conditions, and Job Satisfaction of Women in a Non-traditional Occupation:

Female Correction Officers in Men's Prisons." *Sociological Quarterly* 25:551–66.

Kahn, Alfred J., and Sheila B. Kamerman. 1975. *Not for the Poor Alone: European Social Services*. New York: Harper Colophon.

Kamerman, Sheila B. 1977. "Public Policy and the Family: A New Strategy for Women as Wives and Mothers." In *Women into Wives*, 195–214. *See* Chapman and Gates 1977.

———. 1980. *Parenting in an Unresponsive Society*. New York: Free Press.

Kamerman, Sheila B., and Alfred J. Kahn. 1978. *Family Policy: Government and Families in Fourteen Countries*. New York: Columbia University Press.

———. 1989. *Privatization and the Welfare State*. Princeton: Princeton University Press.

Kaminer, Wendy. 1984. *Women Volunteering: The Pleasure, Pain, and Politics of Unpaid Work from 1830 to the Present*. Garden City, N.Y.: Doubleday.

Kammeyer, Kenneth. 1967. "Sibling Position and the Feminine Role." *Journal of Marriage and the Family* 29:494–99.

Kanter, Rosabeth Moss. 1977. *Men and Women of the Corporation*. New York: Basic Books.

Kanter, Rosabeth Moss, and Barry A. Stein. 1979. "The Gender Pioneers: Women in an Industrial Sales Force." In *Life in Organizations*, edited by Rosabeth Moss Kanter and Barry A. Stein, 134–60. New York: Basic Books.

Kantrowitz, Barbara, and Pat Wingert. 1980. "Step by Step." Special Issue on *The 21st Century Family: Who We Will Be, How We Will Live. Newsweek*, Winter/Spring, 14–17.

Katz, Elihu, and Paul E. Lazarsfeld. 1955. *Personal Influence*. New York: Free Press.

Katzman, David M. 1978. *Seven Days a Week: Women and Domestic Service in Industrializing America*. New York: Oxford University Press.

Kessler-Harris, Alice. 1981. *Women Have Always Worked: A Historical Overview*. New York: Feminist Press.

———. 1982. *Out to Work: A History of Wage-Earning Women in the United States*. New York: Oxford University Press.

Kidwell, Jeannie S. 1981. "Number of Siblings, Sibling Spacing, Sex, and Birth Order: Their Effects on Perceived Parent-Adolescent Relationships." *Journal of Marriage and the Family* 43:315–32.

Kimmel, Michael S., and Michael A. Messner. 1992. *Men's Lives*, 2d ed. New York: Macmillan.

Kingsolver, Barbara. 1989. *Holding the Line: Women in the Great Arizona Mine Strike of 1983*. New York: ILR (International Labour Review).

Kitano, Harry H. L., 1988. "The Japanese American Family." In *Ethnic Families in America, 258–75. See* Mindel, Habenstein, and Wright, 1988.

Kitano, Harry H. L., Wai-Tsang Yeung, Lynn Chai, and Herbert Tatanaka. 1984. "Asian-American Interracial Marriage." *Journal of Marriage and the Family* 46:179–90.

Kitson, Gay, Helena Z. Lopata, William Holmes, and Suzanne Meyering. 1980. "Divorcees and Widows: Similarities and Differences." *American Journal of Orthopsychiatry* 50:291–301.

Kleban, M. H., Elaine Brody, Claire Schoonover, and Christine Hoffman. 1989. "Family Help to the Elderly: Sons-in-Law Perceptions of Parent Care." *Journal of Marriage and the Family* 51:303–12.

Kleiman, Carol. 1980. *Women's Networks.* New York: Lippincott & Crowell.

———. 1986. "Women Climb Off the Corporate Ladder to Build Their Own." *Chicago Tribune,* 30 June, 5–10.

———. 1988. "Cottage Industries Battle to Stay In-Home." *Chicago Tribune,* 29 August, section 4, 6.

Knapp, R. J. 1986. *Beyond Endurance: When a Child Dies.* New York: Schocken.

Kohn, Melvin L. 1977. *Class and Conformity: A Study of Values.* 2d ed. Chicago: University of Chicago Press.

Kohn, Melvin L., and Carmi Schooler. 1983. *Work and Personality: An Inquiry into the Impact of Social Stratification.* Norwood, N.J.: Ablex.

Komarovsky, Mirra. 1953. *Women in the Modern World: Their Education and their Dilemmas.* Boston: Little, Brown.

———. 1962. *Blue Collar Marriage.* New York: Vintage Books.

———. 1973. "Presidential Address: Some Problems in Role Analysis." *American Sociological Review* 38:649–62.

Koo, Jasoon. 1987. "Widows in Seoul, Korea." In *Widows: The Middle East, Asia, and the Pacific,* 56–78. *See* Lopata 1987c.

Kourvetaris, George. 1988. "The Greek American Family." In *Ethnic Families in America.,* 76–108. *See* Habenstein, and Wright 1988.

Krauskopf, Joan M. 1977. "Partnership Marriage: Legal Reform Needed." In *Women into Wives,* 93–121. *See* Gates, 1977.

Kraut, Robert E. 1988. "Homework: What Is It and Who Does It?" In *The New Era of Home-Based Work,* 30–48. *See* Christensen 1988c.

Kriesberg, Louis. 1970. *Mothers in Poverty: A Study of Fatherless Families.* Chicago: Aldine.

Krugman, Herbert E. 1969. "Salesman in Conflict: A Challenge to Marketing." In *Salesmanship,* 25–28. *See* Crane 1969.

Lamb, Michael E. 1978. "Influence of the Child on Marital Quality and Family Interaction during the Prenatal, Perinatal, and Infancy Periods." In *Child*

Influences on Marital and Family Interaction, 137–63. *See* R. Lerner and Spanier 1978.

Lamb, Michael E., and Brian Sutton-Smith. 1982. *Sibling Relationships: Their Nature and Significance across the Lifespan.*Hillsdale, N.J.: Erlbaum.

Landers, Ann. 1976. "If You Had It to Do Over Again—Would You Have Children?" *Good Housekeeping,* June, 100–101, 215–16, 223–24.

Langman, Lauren. 1987. "Social Stratification." In *Handbook of Marriage and the Family,* 211–49. *See* Steinmetz 1987.

Larwood, Laurie, Ann H. Stromberg, and Barbara A. Gutek, eds. 1985. *Women and Work.* Vol. 1. Beverly Hills, Calif.: Sage.

Laslett, Barbara. 1973. "The Family as a Public and Private Institution: An Historical Perspective." *Journal of Marriage and the Family* 35:480–92.

———. 1978. "Family Membership, Past and Present." *Social Problems* 25:476–91.

Laslett, Peter. 1971. *The World We Have Lost: England before the Industrial Age.* New York: Scribner's.

Lauritzen, Paul. 1990. "What Price Parenthood?" *Hastings Center Report,* March/April, 39–46.

Lawson, Helene. 1990. "Service Values-Profit Goals: The Divided Selves of Car Sales Women." Ph.D. diss., Loyola University of Chicago.

Lawson, Ronald, and Stephen E. Barton. 1980. "Sex Roles in Social Movements: A Case Study of the Tenant Movement in New York City." *Signs* 6:230–47.

Lee, Gary R. 1980. "Kinship in the Seventies: A Decade Review of Research and Theory." *Journal of Marriage and the Family* 42:923–34.

Lembright, Muriel Faltz, and Jeffrey W. Riemer. 1982. "Women Truckers' Problems and the Impact of Sponsorship." *Work and Occupations* 9:457–74.

Lenz, Elinor, and Barbara Myerhoff. 1985. *The Feminization of America: How Women's Values Are Changing Our Public and Private Lives.* New York: St. Martins.

diLeonardo, Micaela. 1987. "The Female World of Cards and Holidays: Women, Families, and the Work of Kinship." *Signs* 12:440–53.

Lerner, Daniel. 1958. *The Passing of Traditional Society.* New York: Free Press of Glencoe.

Lerner, Richard M., and Graham B. Spanier. 1978. *Child Influences on Marital and Family Interaction: A Life-Span Perspective.* New York: Academic Press.

Levinson, Daniel J. 1978. *The Seasons of a Man's Life.* New York: Ballantine.

Levy, Judith. 1990. "Friendship Dilemmas and the Interaction of Social Worlds: Re-Entry Women on the College Campus." In *Friendship in Context,* 143–70. *See* Lopata and Maines 1990.

Liebow, Elliot. 1967. *Tally's Corner*. Boston: Little, Brown.

Lillydahl, Jane H. 1986. "Women and Traditionally Male Blue-collar Jobs." *Work and Occupations* 13:307–23.

Lindgren, Ralph J., and Nadine Taub. 1988. *The Law of Sex Discrimination*. New York: West.

Linton, Ralph. 1936. *The Science of Man*. New York: Appleton-Century.

Lipman-Blumen, Jean. 1976. "Toward a Homosocial Theory of Sex Roles: An Explanation of the Sex-Segregation of Social Institutions." In *Women and the Workplace: The Implications of Occupational Segregation*, edited by Martha Blaxall and Barbara Reagan, 15–31. Chicago: University of Chicago Press.

Little, Roger. 1984. *Gender Roles and Power*. Englewood Cliffs, N.J.: Prentice-Hall.

———. 1990. "Friendship in the Military Community." In *Friendship in Context*, 221–35. *See* Lopata and Maines 1990.

Litwak, Eugene. 1965. "Extended Kin Relations in an Industrial Democratic Society." In *Social Structure and the Family: Generational Relations*, edited by Ethel Shanas and Gordon Streib, 290–23. Englewood Cliffs, N.J.: Prentice Hall.

Long, Judy, and Karen L. Porter. 1984. "Multiple Roles of Midlife Women: A Case for New Directions in Theory, Research, and Policy." In *Women in Midlife*, 15–31. *See* Baruch and Brooks-Gunn 1984.

Lopata, Helena Znaniecka. 1966. "The Life Cycle of the Social Role of Housewife." *Sociology and Social Research* 51:5–22.

———. 1969a. "Loneliness: Forms and Components." *Social Problems* 17:248–62.

———. 1969b. "Social Psychological Aspects of Role Involvement." *Sociology and Social Research* 53:285–98.

———. 1971a. "Living Arrangements of Urban Widows and their Married Children." *Sociological Focus* 5:41–61.

———. 1971b. *Occupation: Housewife*. New York: Oxford University Press.

———. 1972. "Role Changes in Widowhood: A World Perspective." In *Aging and Modernization*. edited by Donald Cowgill and Lowell Holmes, 275–303. New York: Appleton-Century-Crofts.

———. 1973a. "The Effect of Schooling on Social Contacts of Urban Women." *American Journal of Sociology* 79:604–19.

———. 1973b. "Self-Identity in Marriage and Widowhood." *Sociological Quarterly* 14:407–18.

———. 1973c. *Widowhood in an American City*. Cambridge, Mass.: Schenkman.

———. 1975. "Couple Companionate Relationships in Marriage and Widowhood." In *Old Families/New Families,* edited by Nona Glazer-Malbin, 119–49. New York: Van Nostrand.

———. 1976a. "The Expertization of Everyone and the Revolt of the Client." *Sociological Quarterly* 17:435–47.

———. 1976b. *Polish Americans: Status Competition in an Ethnic Community.* Englewood Cliffs, N.J.: Prentice-Hall.

———. 1978. "Contributions of Extended Families to the Support Systems of Metropolitan Area Widows: Limitations of the Modified Kin Network." *Journal of Marriage and the Family* 40:355–64.

———. 1979. *Women as Widows: Support Systems.* New York: Elsevier/North-Holland.

———. 1980a. "The Chicago Woman: A Study of Patterns of Mobility and Transportation." *Signs* 5 (Spring): S161–S169. Special issue entitled "Women and the American City."

———. 1980b. "The Self-Concept: Characteristics and Areas of Competence." Paper presented at the annual meeting of the American Sociological Association, New York.

———. 1981a. "American Women: Education and the Construction of Reality." *Quarterly Journal of Ideology* 3:11–24. Special issue entitled "Gender and Ideology".

———. 1981b. "Widowhood and Husband Sanctification." *Journal of Marriage and the Family* 43:439–50.

———. 1984. "Social Construction of Social Problems over Time." *Social Problems* 31:249–72.

———. 1987a. "Widowhood and Social Change." In *Widows: The Middle East, Asia, and the Pacific,* 217–29. *See* Lopata 1987c.

———. 1987b. "Widowhood: World Perspectives on Support Systems." In *Widows: The Middle East, Asia, and the Pacific,* 1–23. *See* Lopata 1987c.

———, ed. 1987c. *Widows: The Middle East, Asia, and the Pacific.* Durham: Duke University Press.

———. 1987d. *Widows: North America.* Durham: Duke University Press.

———. 1987e. "Women's Family Roles in Life Course Perspective." In *Analyzing Gender: A Handbook of Social Science Research,* edited by Beth B. Hess and Myra Marx Teree, 381–407. Newbury Park, Calif.: Sage.

———. 1988a. "Polish American Families." In *Ethnic Families in America,* 17–42. *See* Mindel, Habenstein, and Wright, 1988.

———. 1988b. "Support Systems of Widowhood." *Journal of Social Issues* 44:220–28.

————. 1990a. "Friendship: Historical and Theoretical Perspectives." In *Friendship in Context,* 1–19. *See* Lopata and Maines 1990.

————. 1990b. *Current Research on Occupations and Professions: Societal Influences.* Greenwich, Conn.: JAI Press.

————. 1991a. "Role Theory." In *Social Roles and Social Institutions: Essays in Honor of Rose Laub Coser,* edited by Judith R. Blau and Norman Goodman, 1–11. Boulder, Colo.: Westview.

————. 1991b. "Which Child? The Consequences of Social Development on the Support Systems of Widows." In *Growing Old In America,* 4th ed., edited by Beth B. Hess and Elizabeth W. Markson, 39–49. New Brunswick, N.J.: Transaction.

————. 1993a. "The Interweave of Public and Private: Women's Challenge to American Society." *Journal of Marriage and the Family* 55:176–90.

————. 1993b. "Career Commitments of American Women: The Issue of Side Bets." *Sociological Quarterly* 34:257–77.

————. 1994. *Polish Americans,* 2d rev. ed., New Brunswick, N.J.: Transaction.

Lopata, Helena Znaniecka, and Debra Barnewolt. 1984. "The Middle Years: Changes and Variations in Social-Role Commitments." In *Women in Midlife,* 83–108. *See* Baruch and Brooks-Gunn 1984.

Lopata, Helena Znaniecka, Debra Barnewolt, and Kathryn Harrison. 1987. "Homemakers and Household Composition." In *Current Research on Occupations and Professions,* edited by Helena Z. Lopata, 219–45. Greenwich, Conn.: JAI Press.

Lopata, Helena Znaniecka, Debra Barnewolt, and Cheryl Allyn Miller. 1985. *City Women: Work, Jobs, Occupations, Careers.* Vol. 2: *Chicago.* New York: Praeger.

Lopata, Helena Znaniecka, and Henry Brehm. 1986. *Widows and Dependent Wives: From Social Problem to Federal Policy.* New York: Praeger.

Lopata, Helena Znaniecka, and David Maines, eds. 1990. *Friendship in Context.* Greenwich, Conn.: JAI Press.

Lopata, Helena Znaniecka, Cheryl Miller, and Debra Barnewolt. 1984. *City Women: Work, Jobs, Occupations, Careers.* Vol. 1: *America.* New York: Praeger. Published in paperback in 1986 as *City Women in America.*

Lopata, Helena Znaniecka, and Joseph R. Noel. 1967. "The Dance Studio: Style without Sex." *Transaction/Society,* 4 (January/February): 10–17.

Lopata, Helena Znaniecka, Kathleen F. Norr, Debra Barnewolt, and Cheryl Allyn Miller. 1985. "Job Complexity as Perceived by Workers and Experts." *Sociology of Work and Occupations* 12:295–415.

Lopata, Helena Znaniecka, and Barrie Thorne. 1978. "On the Term 'Sex Roles'." *Signs* 3:718–21.

Lorber, Judith. 1984. *Women Physicians: Careers, Status, and Power.* New York: Methuen.

Lortie, Dan C. 1969. "The Balance of Control and Autonomy in Elementary School Teaching." In *The Semi-Professions and their Organization,* edited by Amitai Etzioni, 1–53. New York: Free Press.

Lortie, Dan C. 1975. *Schoolteacher.* Chicago: University of Chicago Press.

Losh-Hesselbart, Susan. 1987. "Development of Gender Roles." In *Handbook of Marriage and the Family,* 535–63. *See* Steinmetz 1987.

Ludwig, Constance. 1977. "The Social Role of the Grandmother among Puerto Ricans on the Mainland." M.A. thesis, Department of Sociology, Loyola University of Chicago.

Luxton, Meg. 1980. *More than a Labour of Love: Three Generations of Women's Work in the Home.* Toronto: Women's Educational Press.

Lynes, Russell. 1963. *The Domesticated Americans.* New York: Harper & Row.

Malson, Micheline R., Elisabeth Mudimbe-Boyi, Nean F. O'Barr, and Mary Wyer, eds. 1988. *Black Women in America: Social Science Perspectives.* Chicago: University of Chicago Press.

Malveaux, Julianne M. 1980. "Moving Forward, Standing Still: Women in White Collar Jobs." In *Women in the Workplace,* edited by Phillis Wallace, 101–29, Boston: Auburn.

Manegold, Catherine S. 1992. "Women Advance in Politics by Evolution, not Revolution." *New York Times,* 21 October, 1A, 15.

Margolis, Diane Rothbard. 1979. *The Managers: Corporate Life in America.* New York: Morrow.

Marks, Stephen R. 1977. "Multiple Roles and Role Strain: Some Notes on Human Energy, Time, and Commitment." *American Sociological Review* 42:921–36.

Marotz-Baden, Ramona, and Deane Cowan. 1987. "Mothers-in-Law and Daughters-in-Law: The Effects of Proximity on Conflict and Stress." *Family Relations* 36:385–90.

Martin, Elmer P., and Joanne Mitchell Martin. 1978. *The Black Extended Family.* Chicago: University of Chicago Press.

Martineau, Harriet. [1837] 1966. *Society in America,* edited by Seymour Martin Lipset. Garden City, N.Y.: Doubleday.

Masnick, George, and Mary Jo Bane. 1980. *The Nation's Families 1970–1990.* Boston: Auburn.

Matthews, Glenna. 1987. *Just a Housewife: The Rise and Fall of Domesticity in America.* New York: Oxford University Press.

Matthews, Sarah. 1986. *Friendship through the Life Course.* Beverly Hills, Calif.: Sage.

deMause, Lloyd. 1974. "The Evolution of Childhood." In *The History of Childhood,* edited by Lloyd deMause, 1–73. New York: Psychohistory Press.

McAdoo, Harriet Pipes. 1980. "Black Mothers and the Extended Family Support Network." In *The Black Woman,* 125–44. *See* Rodgers-Rose 1980.

McCall, George J., and J. L. Simmons. 1978. *Identities and Interactions.* New York: Free Press.

McCurry, Dan. 1975. *Cannery Captives: Women Workers in the Produce Processing Industry.* New York: Arno.

McGhee, Jerrie L. 1985. "The Effects of Siblings on Life Satisfaction of the Rural Elderly." *Journal of Marriage and the Family* 47:85–91.

McIlwee, Judith S. 1982. "Work Satisfaction among Women in Nontraditional Occupations." *Work and Occupations* 9:299–355.

McKain, Walter. 1969. *Retirement Marriage.* Storrs, Conn.: University of Connecticut.

McPherson, J. Miller, and Lynn Smith-Lovin. 1982. "Women and Weak Ties: Differences by Sex in the Size of Voluntary Organizations." *American Journal of Sociology* 87:883–904.

Mead, George Herbert. 1934. *Mind, Self, and Society, from the Standpoint of a Social Behaviorist,* edited by Charles Morris. Chicago: University of Chicago Press.

Merton, Robert. 1957. "The Role Set." *British Journal of Sociology* 8:106–20.

———. 1968. *Social Theory and Social Structure,* enlarged ed. New York: Free Press.

Mezey, Susan. 1992. *In Pursuit of Equality: Women, Public Policy and the Federal Courts.* New York: St. Martin's.

Michaels, Gerald and Wendy Goldberg, eds. 1988. *The Transition to Parenthood.* New York: Cambridge University Press.

Michelson, Williams. 1977. *Environmental Choice, Human Behavior, and Residential Satisfaction.* New York: Oxford University Press.

Milardo, Robert M. 1982. "Friendship Networks in Developing Relationships: Converging and Diverging Social Environments." *Social Psychology Quarterly* 45:162–72.

Milkman, Ruth. 1979. "Women's Work and the Economic Crisis: Some Lessons from the Great Depression." In *A Heritage of Her Own,* edited by Nancy F. Cott and Elizabeth H. Pleck, 507–41. New York: Simon & Schuster.

Miller, Barbara. 1981. *The Endangered Sex: Neglect of Female Children in Rural North India.* Ithaca, N.Y.: Cornell University Press.

Miller, Brent C. 1987. "Marriage, Family, and Fertility." In *Handbook of Marriage and the Family,* 565–95. *See* Steinmetz, 1987.

Miller, Cheryl Allen. 1981. "The Life Course Patterns of Chicago Area Women." Ph.D. diss., Department of Sociology, Loyola University of Chicago.

Miller, Joanne. 1980. "Individual and Occupational Determinants of Job Satisfaction." *Sociology of Work and Occupations* 7:337–66.

Miller, Joanne, Carmin Schooler, Melvin Kohn, and Karen Miller. 1980. "Women and Work: The Psychological Effects of Occupational Conditions." *American Journal of Sociology* 85:66–94.

Mills, C. Wright. 1956. *White Collar.* New York: Oxford University.

Min, Pyong Gap. 1988. "The Korean American Family." In *Ethnic Families in America,* 199–229. *See* Mindel, Habenstein, and Wright 1988.

Mindel, Charles H., Robert W. Habenstein, and Roosevelt Wright, Jr., eds. 1988. *Ethnic Families in America.* 3d ed. New York: Elsevier.

Model, Suzanne. 1982. "Housework by Husbands: Determinants and Implications." In *Two Paychecks,* 193–205. *See* Aldous 1982.

Moen, Phyllis, Donna Dempster McClain, and Robin Williams, Jr. 1989. "Social Integration and Longevity: An Event History Analysis of Women's Roles and Resilience." *American Sociological Review* 54:635–47.

Monagle, Katie. 1989. "Court Backs Two-Mom Family." *MS,* October, 69.

Mosher, Steven W. 1983. "Why Are Baby Girls Being Killed in China?" *The Wall Street Journal,* 25 July, 9.

Mott, Frank, Steven Sansell, David Shapiro, Patricia Brito, Timothy Carr, Rex Johnson, Carol Jusenius, Peter Koenig and Sylvia Moore. 1977. *Years for Decision: A Longitudinal Study of the Educational, Labor Market, and Family Experiences of Young Women, 1968 to 1973.* Columbus: Ohio Center for Human Resource Research, College of Administrative Science, Ohio State University.

Mueller, Carol M. 1988. "Continuity and Change in Women's Political Agenda." In *The Politics of the Gender Gap: The Social Construction of Political Influence,* edited by Carol M. Mueller, 284–99. Newbury Park, Calif.: Sage.

Mumford, Lewis. 1961. *The City in History.* New York: Harcourt Brace & World.

Musterberg, Hugo. 1905. "The American Woman." In *The Making of America,* vol. 1, edited by John D. Morris and Robert M. Lafollette, 402–96. Chicago: John D. Morris.

Myerson, Abraham. 1927. *The Nervous Housewife.* Boston: Little, Brown.

Nelson, Dale. 1989. "Women to Get Most Doctorates, Study Shows." *Chicago Sun Times,* 28 December, 8.

Nelson, Sarah M. 1988. "Widowhood and Autonomy in the Native American Southwest." In *On Their Own: Widows and Widowhood in the American*

Southwest 1848–1939, edited by Arlene Scadron, 22–41. Urbana: University of Illinois Press.

Neugarten, Bernice. 1973. *Middle Age and Aging.* Chicago: University of Chicago Press.

Neugarten, Bernice, and Karen K. Weinstein. 1964. "The Changing American Grandparent." *Journal of Marriage and the Family* 26:199–204.

Newman, Katherine S. 1988. *Falling from Grace: Experiences of Downward Mobility in the American Middle Class.* New York: Free Press.

Nilson, Linda Burzotta. 1978. "The Social Standing of a Housewife." *Journal of Marriage and the Family* 40, no. 3:541–48.

Nugent, Jo. 1990. "We're All Rotarians." *Rotarian,* June, 26–27.

Nyden, Philip, Joanne Adams, and Maryann Mason. 1992. *Our Hope for the Future: Youth, Family, and Diversity in the Edgewater and Uptown Communities.* Chicago: Loyola University of Chicago.

Oakley, Ann. 1974a. *The Sociology of Housework.* Bath, England: Pitman.

———. 1974b. *Women's Work: A History of the Housewife.* New York: Pantheon.

———. 1981. *Subject Women.* New York: Pantheon.

O'Bryant, Shirley L. 1987. "Attachment to Home and Support Systems of Older Widows in Columbus, Ohio." In *Widows: North America,* 48–70. *See* Lopata 1987d.

O'Donnell, Lydia, and Ann Stuave. 1983. "Mothers as Social Agents: Structuring the Community Activities of School-Aged Children." In *Research on the Interweave of Social Roles: Families and Jobs,* 112–29. *See* E. Pleck 1983.

O'Farrell, Brigid. 1988. "Women in Blue-Collar Occupations: Traditional and Nontraditional." In *Women Working,* 258–72. *See* Berheide 1988.

Oliver, Melvin L. 1988. "The Urban Black Community as Network: Toward a Social Network Perspective." *Sociological Quarterly* 29:623–745.

O'Meara, J. Donald. 1989. "Cross-Sex Friendship: Four Basic Challenges of an Ignored Relationship." *Sex Roles* 21:525–43.

Omolade, Barbara. 1986. *It's a Family Affair: The Real Lives of Black Single Mothers.* Latham, N.Y.: Kitchen Table: Women of Color Press.

O'Neill, William. 1969. *Everyone Was Brave.* Chicago: Quadrangle.

Osborn, D. Keith, and Janie D. Osborn. 1978. "Childhood at the Turn of the Century." *Family Coordinator* 27:27–32.

Ostrander, Susan A. 1984. *Women of the Upper Class.* Philadelphia: Temple University Press.

Overvold, Amy Zucherman. 1988. *Surrogate Parenting.* New York: Pharos Books.

Papandreau, Margarita. 1988. "Foreword. Feminism and Political Power:

Some Thoughts on a Strategy for the Future." In *Women, Power, and Policy: Toward the Year 2000,* edited by Ellen Boneparth and Emily Stoper, xi–xix. New York: Pergamon.

Papanek, Hanna. 1973. "Men, Women, and Work: Reflections on the Two-Person Career." *American Journal of Sociology* 78:852–72.

———. 1979. "Family Status Production: The 'Work' and 'Nonwork' of Women." *Signs* 4:775–81.

Papanek, Hanna, and Gail Minault. 1982. *Separate Worlds: Studies of Purdah in South Asia.* Delhi: Chanakya.

Parsons, Talcott. 1951. *The Social System.* Glencoe, Ill.: Free Press.

———. 1943. "The Kinship System in the Contemporary United States." *American Anthropologist* 31:22–38.

Parsons, Talcott, and Robert Bales. 1955. *Family: Socialization and Interaction Process.* Glencoe, Ill.: Free Press.

Paskowicz, Patricia. 1982. *Absentee Mothers.* New York: Universe Books.

Pavalko, Ronald M. 1988. *Sociology of Occupations and Professions.* Itasca, Ill.: Peacock.

Payne, Barbara P. 1977. "The Older Volunteer: Social Role Continuity and Development." *The Gerontologist* 17:355–61.

Pearlin, Leonard. 1975. "Sex Roles and Depression." In *Proceedings of the Fourth Life-Span Developmental Psychology Conference: Normative Life Crisis,* edited by Nancy Datan and Leon Ginsberg, 191–208. New York: Academic.

Pearson, Kandace. 1990. "Illusion and Reality: An Examination of the Position of Women in Small Law Firms." M.A. thesis, Department of Sociology, University of Wisconsin, Milwaukee.

Peiss, Kathy Lee. 1986. *Cheap Amusements: Working Women and Leisure in Turn-of-Century New York.* Philadelphia: Temple University Press.

Peterson, Gary W., and Boyd C. Rollins. 1987. "Parent-Child Socialization." In *Handbook of Marriage and the Family,* 471–507. *See* Steinmetz 1987.

Peven, Dorothy. 1968. "The Use of Religious Revival Techniques to Indoctrinate Personnel: The Home-Party Sales Organization." *Sociological Quarterly* 9:97–106.

Pfohl, Stephen J. 1978. "The 'Discovery' of Child Abuse." *Social Problems* 3:310–23.

Pfouts, Jane H. 1976. "The Sibling Relationships: A Forgotten Dimension." *Social Work* 21:200–204

Pihlblad, T., and Howard Rosencranz. 1968. *Old People in the Small Town.* Columbia: University of Missouri.

Pinchbeck, Ivy. [1930] 1969. *Women Workers and the Industrial Revolution, 1750–1850.* London: Bass.

Pineo, Peter. 1966. "Disenchantment in Later Years of Marriage." In *Kinship and Family Organization,* 229–39. *See* Farber 1966.

Piven, Frances Fox, and Richard A. Cloward. 1977. *Poor People's Movements: Why They Succeed, How The Fail.* New York: Pantheon.

Pleck, Elizabeth H. 1983. "The Old World, New Rights, and the Limited Rebellion: Challenges to Traditional Authority of Immigrant Families." In *Research on the Interweave of Social Roles: Families and Jobs,* 91–112. See Lopata and Pleck 1983.

Pleck, Elizabeth H., and Joseph H. Pleck. 1980. *The American Man.* Englewood Cliffs, N.J.: Prentice-Hall.

Pleck, Joseph. 1983. "Husband's Paid Work and Family Roles: Current Issues." In *Research on the Interweave of Social Roles: Families and Jobs,* 251–333. *See* Lopata and Pleck, 1983.

Pleck, Joseph, and Graham L. Staines. 1982. "Work Schedules and Work-Family Conflict in Two-Earner Families." In *Two Paychecks,* 63–88. *See* Aldous 1982.

Polit, Denise F., and Toni Falbo. 1987. "Only Children and Personality Development: A Quantitative Review." *Journal of Marriage and the Family* 49:309–25.

Post, James E. 1986. "International Consumerism in the Aftermath of the Infant Formula Controversy." In *The Future of Consumerism,* 165–78. *See* Bloom and Smith 1986.

Prus, Robert, and Wendy Frisby. 1990. "Persuasion as Practical Accomplishment: Tactical Maneuverings at Home (Party Plan) Shows." In *Current Research on Occupations and Professions,* vol. 4, edited by Helena Z. Lopata, 133–652. Greenwich, Conn.: JAI Press.

Pyun, Chong Soo. 1972. "The Monetary Value of a Housewife." In *Women in a Man-Made World,* edited by Nona Glazer-Malbin and Helen Youngelson Waehrer, 187–93. Chicago: Rand McNally.

Rainwater, Lee, Richard P. Coleman, and Gerald Handel. 1959. *Workingman's Wife: Her Personality, World, and Life Style.* New York: Oceana.

Rapp, Rayna. 1982. "Family and Class in Contemporary America: Notes toward an Understanding of Ideology." In *Rethinking the Family,* 168–87. *See* Thorne 1982.

Rapping, Elayne. 1990. "The Future of Motherhood: Some Unfashionably Visionary thoughts." In *Women, Class, and the Feminist Imagination,* 537–48. *See* Hansen and Philipson 1990.

Raymond, Janice G. 1986. *A Passion for Friends: Toward a Philosophy of Female Affection.* Boston: Beacon Press.

Reiss, Ira, and Gary R. Lee. 1988. *Family Systems in America.* New York: Holt, Rinehart & Winston.

Reskin, Barbara F., and Heidi I. Hartmann, eds. 1986. *Women's Work, Men's Work: Sex Segregation on the Job.* Washington, D.C.: National Academy Press.

Reskin, Barbara F., and Irene Padavic. 1988. "Supervisors as Gatekeepers: Male Supervisors' Response to Women's Integration in Plant Jobs." *Social Problems* 35:536–50.

Reymont, Ladislas. 1925. *The Peasants: Fall, Winter, Spring, Summer.* 4 vols. New York: Knopf.

Riesman, David, Nathan Glaser, and Reuel Denney. 1950. *The Lonely Crowd.* New Haven: Yale University Press.

Roberto, Karen A., and Jean Pearson Scott. 1984–85. "Friendship Patterns among Older Women." *International Journal of Aging and Human Development* 19:1–10.

Robertson, Joan. 1977. "Grandparenthood: A Study of Role Conceptions." *Journal of Marriage and the Family* 39:165–74.

Rodgers-Rose, La Frances, ed. 1980. *The Black Woman.* Beverly Hills, Calif.: Sage.

Rodman, Hyman. 1990. "The Social Construction of the Latchkey Children Problem." *Sociological Studies of Child Development* 3:163–74.

Rodman, Hyman, and David J. Pratto. 1987. "Child's Age and Mother's Employment in Relation to Greater Use of Self-Care Arrangements for Children." *Journal of Marriage and the Family* 49:573–78.

Rogers, Barbara. 1980. *The Domestication of Women: Discrimination in Developing Countries.* London: Tavistock.

Rollins, Judith. 1985. *Between Women: Domestics and Their Employers.* Philadelphia: Temple University Press.

Rook, Karen S. 1989. "Strains in Older Adults' Friendship." In *Older Adult Friendship,* 166–94. *See* Adams and Blieszner 1989.

Rosaldo, Michelle Zimbalist. 1974. "Women, Culture, and Society: A Theoretical Overview." In *Women, Culture, and Society,* edited by Michelle Zimbalist Rosaldo and Louise Lamphere, 17–42. Stanford, Calif.: Stanford University Press.

Rose, Suzanna M. 1985. "Same- and Cross-Sex Friendships and the Psychology of Homosociality." *Sex Roles* 12:63–74.

Rosen, Ellen Israel. 1987. *Bitter Choices: Blue-Collar Women In and Out of Work.* Chicago: University of Chicago Press.

Rosen, Lawrence, and Robert R. Bell. 1966. "Mate Selection in the Upper Class." *Sociological Quarterly* (Spring): 157–66.

Rosenberg, George S., and Donald F. Anspach. 1973. *Working-Class Kinship.* Lexington, Mass.: Lexington Books.

Rosenberg, Morris. 1979. *Conceiving the Self.* New York: Basic Books.

Rosenthal, Carolyn J. 1985. "Kinkeeping in the Family Division of Labor." *Journal of Marriage and the Family* 47:965–74.

Rosow, Irving. 1967. *The Social Integration of the Aged.* New York: Free Press.

Ross, Arlene. 1961. *The Hindu Family in Its Urban Setting.* Toronto: University of Toronto Press.

Rossi, Alice. 1965. "Barriers to the Career Choice of Engineering, Medicine, or Science among American Women." In *Women and the Scientific Professions,* edited by Jacquelyn A. Mattfelt and Carol G. Van Aken, 51–127. Cambridge: MIT Press.

———. 1968. "Transition to Parenthood." *Journal of Marriage and the Family* 30:26–39.

———. 1985. "Gender and Parenthood." In *Gender and the Life Course,* edited by Alice Rossi, 161–91. New York: Aldine.

Rossi, Peter. 1955. *Why Families Move.* Glencoe, Ill.: Free Press.

Rothman, Barbara Katz. 1986. *The Tentative Pregnancy: Prenatal Diagnosis and the Future of Motherhood.* New York: Penguin.

Rothman, Sheila M. 1978. *Woman's Proper Place: A History of Changing Ideals and Practices, 1879 to the Present.* New York: Basic Books.

Rothman, Sheila M., and Emily Menlo Marks. 1987. "Adjusting Work and Family Life: Flexible Work Schedules and Family Policy." In *Families and Work,* 469–77. *See* Gerstel and Gross 1987a.

Rubin, Lillian. 1976. *Worlds of Pain: Life in the Working-Class Family.* New York: Basic Books.

———. 1979. *Women of a Certain Age.* New York: Harper & Row.

———. 1983. *Intimate Strangers: Men and Women Together.* New York: Harper & Row.

———. 1985. *Just Friends: The Role of Friendship in Our Lives.* New York: Harper & Row.

Russell, Diana E. H. 1984. *Sexual Exploitation: Rape, Child Sexual Abuse, and Workplace Harassment.* Sage Library of Social Research, no. 155. Beverly Hills, Calif.: Sage.

———. 1986. *The Secret Trauma: Incest in the Lives of Girls and Women.* New York: Basic Books.

Rustad, Michael L. 1982. *Women in Khaki: The American Enlisted Woman.* New York: Praeger.

Ryan, Mary P. 1979. *Womanhood in America: From Colonial Times to the Present.* 2d ed. New York: New Viewpoints.

Sanchez-Ayendez, Melba. 1988. "The Puerto Rican American Family." In *Ethnic Families in America,* 173–95. *See* Habenstein and Wright 1988.

Scanzoni, John H., and Leta Scanzoni. 1981. *Men, Women, and Change.* 2d ed. New York: McGraw-Hill.

Schlegel, Alice. 1988. "Hopi Family Structure and the Experience of Widow-hood." In *On Their Own: Widows and Widowhood in the American Southwest 1848–1939,* edited by Arlene Scadron, 42–64. Urbana: University of Illinois Press.

Schlossberg, Nancy. 1984. "The Midlife Woman as Student." In *Women in Midlife,* 315–39. *See* Baruch and Brooks-Gunn 1984.

Schnaiberg, Allan, and Sheldon Goldenberg. 1989. "From Empty Nest to Crowded Nest: The Dynamics of Incompletely-Launched Young Adults." *Social Problems* 36:251–69.

Schneider, David. 1980. *American Kinship: A Cultural Account.* 2d ed. Chicago: University of Chicago Press.

Schooler, Carmi. 1984. "Serfdom's Legacy: An Ethnic Continuum." In *Work and Personality,* 261–77. *See* Kohn and Schooler 1984.

Schooler, Carmi, Melvin L. Kohn, Karen A. Miller, and Joanne Miller. 1984. "Housework as Work." In *Work and Personality,* 242–60. *See* Kohn and Schooler 1984.

Schooler, Carmi, Joanne Miller, Karen A. Miller, and Carol N. Richtand. 1984. "Work for the Household: Its Nature and Consequences for Husbands and Wives." *American Journal of Sociology* 90:97–124.

Schroedel, Jean Reich. 1985. *Alone in a Crowd: Women in the Trades Tell Their Stories.* Philadelphia: Temple University Press.

Schwager, Sally. 1987. "Educating Women in America." *Signs* 12:333–72.

Schwartz, Felice. 1992. *Breaking with Tradition.* New York: Warner Books.

Schwartz, John, and Dody Tsiantar. 1989. "Escape from the Office: High-Tech Tools Spur a Work-at-Home Revolt." *Newsweek,* 24 April, 58–60.

Scott, Marvin, and Stanford Lyman. 1968. "Accounts." *American Sociological Review* 33:46–62.

Secombe, Wally. 1974. "The Housewife and Her Labour under Capitalism." *New Left Review* 83 (January–February): 3–24.

Seeley, John R., Alexander Sim, and Elizabeth W. Loosely. 1956. *Crestwood Heights.* New York: Basic Books.

Segura, Denise A. 1989. "Chicano and Mexican Immigrant Women at Work: The Impact of Class, Race, and Gender on Occupational Mobility." *Gender and Society* 3:37–52.

Selingmann, Jean. 1990. "Variations on a Theme." *Newsweek,* Winter/Spring. Special Issue entitled 'The 21st Century Family: Who We Will Be, How We Will Live.'

Settles, Barbara H. 1987. "A Perspective on Tomorrow's Families." In *Handbook of Marriage and the Family,* 157–80. *See* Steinmetz 1987.

Sewell, William H., and Robert M. Hauser. 1975. *Education, Occupation, and Earnings.* New York: Academic Press.

Shae, Nancy. 1941. *The Army Wife*. Rev. ed. New York: Harper's Brothers.

Shanas, Ethel. 1977. "Family-Kin Networks and Aging in Cross-Cultural Perspective." In *The Family,* edited by Peter Stein, Judith Richman, and Natalie Hannon, 300–307. Reading, Mass.: Addison-Wesley.

———. 1979a. "The Family as a Social Support System in Old Age." *The Gerontologist* 19:169–74.

———. 1979b. "Social Myth as Hypothesis: The Case of the Family Relations of Old People." *The Gerontologist* 19:3–9.

———. 1980. "Older People and Their Families: The New Pioneers." *Journal of Marriage and the Family.* 42:9–15.

Sharpe, Sue. 1984. *Double Identity: The Lives of Working Mothers.* New York: Penguin.

Shehan, Constance. 1984. "Wives' Work and Psychological Well-Being: An Extension of Gove's Social Role Theory of Depression." *Sex Roles* 11:881–99.

Shehan, Constance, Mary Ann Burg, and Cynthia A. Rexroat. 1986. "Depression and the Social Dimensions of Full-Time Housewife Role." *Sociological Quarterly* 27:403–21.

Sicherman, Barbara. 1975. "Review Essay: American History." *Signs* 1:461–85.

Sieber, Sam D. 1974. "Toward a Theory of Role Accumulation." *American Sociological Review* 39:567–78.

Silverman, Phyllis. 1987. "Widowhood as the Next Stage in the Life Course." In *Widows: North America,* 171–90. *See* Lopata 1987d.

Simmel, George. 1955. *Conflict and the Web of Group Affiliations,* edited by D. Levine. Chicago: University of Chicago Press.

Simon, Barbara Levy. 1987. *Never Married Women.* Philadelphia: Temple University Press.

Sklare, Marshall. 1971. *American Jews.* New York: Random House.

Skolnick, Arlene S. 1983. *The Intimate Environment: Exploring Marriage and the Family.* Boston: Little, Brown.

Smith, Catherine Begnoche, and Vivian Scott Hixson. 1987. "The Work of University Professor: Evidence of Segmented Labor Markets inside the Academy." In *Current Research on Occupations and Professions,* vol. 4, edited by Helena Z. Lopata, 159–80. Greenwich, Conn.: JAI Press.

Smith, Dorothy. 1987. *The Everyday World as Problematic: A Feminist Sociology.* Boston: Northeastern University Press.

Smith, Shelley A., and Marta Tienda. 1988. "The Doubly Disadvantaged: Women of Color in the U.S. Labor Force." In *Women Working,* 61–80. *See* Berheide 1988.

Smith-Rosenberg, Carroll. 1979. "The Female World of Love and Ritual." In *A Heritage of Her Own,* edited by Nancy F. Cott and Elizabeth H. Pleck, 311–42. New York: Simon & Schuster.

Sochen, June. 1982. *HerStory: A Record of the American Woman's Past.* 2d ed. Palo Alto, Calif.: Mayfield.

Sokoloff, Natalie J. 1988. "Evaluating Gains and Losses by Black and White Women and Men in the Professions, 1960–1980." *Social Problems* 35:36–53.

Sokolowska, Magdalena. 1965. "Some Reflections on the Different Attitudes of Men and Women toward Work." *International Labor Review* 92:35–50.

Solnit, Albert J. 1984. "Parenthood and Child Advocacy." In *Parenthood: A Psychodynamic Perspective,* edited by Rebecca S. Cohen, Bertram J. Cohler, and Sidney H. Weismann, 227–38. New York: Guilford.

Solomon, Barbara Miller. 1985. *In the Company of Educated Women.* New Haven: Yale University Press.

Sommerville, John. 1982. *The Rise and Fall of Childhood.* Beverly Hills, Calif.: Sage.

Spalter-Roth, Roberta, and Heidi J. Hartmann. 1990. *Unnecessary Losses: Costs to Americans of the Lack of Family and Medical Leave.* Washington D.C.: Institute for Women's Policy Research.

Spectorsky, A. C. 1955. *The Exurbanites.* Philadelphia: Lippincott.

Spender, Dale. 1980. *Man Made Language.* London: Routledge & Kegan Paul.

Spicer, Jerry W., and Gary D. Hampe. 1975. "Kinship Interaction after Divorce." *Journal of Marriage and the Family* 17:113-119.

Spock, Benjamin. 1957. *Baby and Child Care.* New York: Cardinal/Pocket.

Spradley, James, and Brenda Mann. 1975. *The Cocktail Waitress: Women's Work in a Man's World.* New York: Wiley.

Sprey, Jetse, and Sarah H. Matthews. 1982. "Contemporary Grandparenthood: A Systematic Transition." *Annals, AAPSS* 464 (November): 91–103.

Squier, Ann D., and Jill S. Quadagno. 1988. "The Italian American Family." In *Ethnic Families in America,* 109–37. *See* Mindel, Habenstein, and Wright 1988.

Squires, Gregory D., Larry Bennett, Kathleen McCourt, and Philip Nyden. 1987. *Chicago: Race, Class, and the Response to Urban Decline.* Philadelphia: Temple University Press.

Stack, Carol B. 1975. *All Our Kin.* New York: Harper & Row.

Staggenberg, Suzanne. 1989. "Stability and Innovation in the Women's Movement: A Comparison of Two Movement Organizations." *Social Problems* 36:75–92.

Stansell, Christine. 1986. *City of Women: Sex and Class in New York 1780–1860.* New York: Knopf.

Staples, Robert. 1988. "The Black American Family." In *Ethnic Families in America,* 303–324. *See* Mindel, Habenstein, and Wright 1988.

Staples, Robert, and Alfredo Mirande. 1980. "Racial and Cultural Variations among American Families: A Decennial Review of the Literature on Minority Families." *Journal of Marriage and the Family* 42:887–903.

Stein, Maurice. 1960. *The Eclipse of Community*. Princeton: Princeton University Press.

Steinberg, Ronnie. 1982. *Wages and Hours: Labor and Reform in Twentieth-Century America*. New Brunswick, N.J.: Rutgers University Press.

———. 1990. "Radical Challenges in a Liberal World: The Mixed Success of Comparable Worth." In *Women, Class, and the Feminist Imagination,* 508–34. *See* Hansen and Philipson, 1990.

Steinmetz, Suzanne. 1987. "Family Violence: Past, Present, and Future." In *Handbook of Marriage and the Family,* edited by Marvin Sussman and Suzanne Steinmetz, 725–65. New York: Plenum.

Stephan, Cookie White, and Walter G. Stephan. 1989. "After Intermarriage: Ethnic Identity among Mixed-Heritage Japanese-Americans and Hispanics." *Journal of Marriage and the Family* 51:507–19.

Stimpson, Catharine R., Elsa Dixler, Martha J. Nelson, and Kathryn B. Yatrakis, eds. 1981. *Women and the American City*. Chicago: University of Chicago Press.

Stoller, Eleanor Palo. 1983. "Parental Caregiving by Adult Children." *Journal of Marriage and the Family* 45:851–58.

Stone, Gregory. 1962. "Appearance and the Self." In *Human Behavior and Social Process,* edited by Arnold Rose, 86–117. Boston: Houghton Mifflin.

———. 1981. "Appearance and the Self: A Slightly Revised Version." In *Social Psychology through Symbolic Interaction,* edited by Gregory P. Stone and Harvey A. Farberman, 187–202. New York: Wiley.

Strasser, Susan. 1978. "The Business of Housekeeping: The Ideology of the Household at the Turn of the Twentieth Century." *Insurgent Sociologist* 7:147–63.

———. 1982. *Never Done: A History of American Housework*. New York: Pantheon.

Stromberg, Ann H., Laurie Larood, and Barbara A. Gutek. 1987. *Women and Work*. Newbury Park, Calif.: Sage.

Stryker, Sheldon. 1980. *Symbolic Interactionism: A Social Structural Version*. Palo Alto, Calif.: Benjamin/Cummings.

Sue, Stanley, and James K. Morishima. 1982. *The Mental Health of Asian Americans*. San Francisco: Jossey-Bass.

Suitor, J. Jill. 1988. "Husbands' Educational Attainment and Support for Wives' Return to School." *Gender and Society* 2:482–95.

Sussman, Marvin B. 1962. "The Isolated Nuclear Family: Fact or Fiction." In

Selected Studies in Marriage and the Family, edited by Robert Winch, 49–57. New York: Holt, Rinehart & Winston.

———. 1965. "Relationships of Adult Children with Their Parents in the United States." In *Social Structure and the Family: Generational Relations,* edited by Ethel Shanas and Gordon Streib, 62–72. Englewood Cliffs, N.J.: Prentice-Hall.

Suttles, Gerald. 1972. *The Social Construction of Communities.* Chicago: University of Chicago Press.

Sutton, John R. 1983. "Social Structure, Institutions, and the Legal Status of Children in the United States." *American Journal of Sociology* 88:915–47.

Sweet, James A., and Larry L. Bumpass. 1987. *American Families and Households.* New York: Russell Sage Foundation. Boston: Auburn House.

Szinovacz, Masimiliane, ed. 1982. *Women's Retirement: Policy Implications of Recent Research.* Beverly Hills, Calif.: Sage.

———. 1989. "Retirement, Couples, and Household Work." In *Aging and the Family,* edited by S. J. Bahr and E. T. Peterson, 33–58. Lexington, Mass.: Lexington Books.

Taylor, F. W. 1911. *Scientific Management.* New York: Harper and Row.

Teachman, Jay D., Karen A. Polonko, and John Scanzoni. 1987. "Demography of the Family." In *Handbook of Marriage and the Family,* 3–36. *See* Steinmetz 1987.

Thomas, W. I., and Florian Znaniecki. 1918–20. *The Polish Peasant in Europe and America.* Boston: Richard G. Badger.

Thorne, Barrie. 1982. "Feminist Rethinking of the Family: An Overview." In *Rethinking the Family: Some Feminist Questions,* edited by Barrie Thorne with Marilyn Yalom, 1–25. New York: Longman.

Thorne, Barrie, Cheris Kramarae, and Nancy Henley, eds. 1983. *Language, Gender, and Society.* Rowley, Mass.: Newbury House.

Thorns, David C. 1976. *The Quest for Community: Social Aspects of Residential Growth.* London: Allen & Unwin.

Tiger, Lionel. 1969. *Men in Groups.* New York: Random House.

Tilly, Louise A., and Joan W. Scott. 1978a. *Women, Work, and Family.* New York: Holt, Rinehart & Winston.

———. 1978b. *Working Life of Women in the Seventeenth Century.* New York: Holt, Rinehart & Winston.

Toffler, Alvin. 1981. *The Third Wave.* New York: Bantam.

Tocqueville, Alexis de. [1835] 1936. *Democracy in America,* edited by J. P. Mayer. Garden City, N.Y.: Doubleday.

Touba, Jacqueline Rudolph. 1987. "The Widowed in Iran." In *Widows: The Middle East, Asia, and the Pacific,* 106–32. *See* Lopata 1987c.

Treas, Judith, and Vern L. Bengtson. 1987. "The Family in Later Years." In *Handbook of Marriage and the Family,* 625–48. *See* Steinmetz 1987.

Troits, Peggy A. 1986. "Multiple Identities and Psychological Well-Being: A Formulation and Test of the Social Isolation Hypothesis." *American Sociological Review* 48:174–87.

Troll, Lillian E. 1983. "Grandparents: The Family Watchdogs." In *Family Relationships in Later Life,* edited by Timothy Brubaker, 63–74. Beverly Hills, Calif.: Sage.

———. 1985. "The Contingencies of Grandparenting." In *Grandparenting,* 135–49. *See* Bengtson and Robertson 1985.

Trost, Cathy. 1990a. "Careers Start Giving in to Family Needs." *Wall Street Journal Marketplace,* 18 June, B1.

———. 1990b. "Marketing-minded Child-Care Centers Become More than 9–5 Baby Sitters." *Wall Street Journal Marketplace,* 18 June, B1.

Trost, Jan. E. 1979. *Unmarried Cohabitation.* Vasteras, Sweden: International Library.

Turner, Ralph. 1962. "Role Taking: Process versus Conformity." In *Human Behavior and Social Processes,* edited by Arnold Rose, 20–40. Boston: Houghton Mifflin.

———. 1968."The Self Conception in Social Interaction." In *The Self in Social Interaction,* edited by Chad Gordon and Kenneth Gergen, 93–106. New York: Wiley.

———. 1978. "The Role and the Person." *American Journal of Sociology* 84:1–23.

———. 1981. "The Real Self: From Institution to Impulse." In *Social Psychology through Symbolic Interaction,* 203–20. *See* Stone 1981.

U. S. Department of Labor. 1965. *Dictionary of Occupation Titles.* Vol. 1, *Definitions of Titles.* 3d ed. Washington, D.C.: U.S. Government Printing Office.

Vandepol, Ann. 1982. "Dependent Children, Child Custody, and the Mother's Pensions: The Transformation of State-Family Relations in the Early 20th Century." *Social Problems* 29:220–35.

Vandervelde, Maryanne. 1979. *The Changing Life of the Corporate Wife.* New York: Mecox.

Vanek, Joann. 1978. "Housewives as Workers." In *Women Working,* 392–414. *See* Berheide 1988.

Veblen, Thorstein. [1899] 1953. *The Theory of the Leisure Class.* New York: Mentor.

Veevers, Jeanne E. 1980. *Childless by Choice.* Toronto: Butterworth.

Visher, Emily B., and John S. Visher. 1979. *Stepfamilies: A Guide to Working with Stepparents and Stepchildren.* New York: Brunner/Mazel.

Walker, Kathryn, and William H. Gauger. 1973. *The Dollar Value of Household Work*. Ithaca, N.Y.: Cornell University.

Wallis, Claudia. 1985. "Children Having Children." *Time*, 9 December, 78–90.

———. 1992. "The Nuclear Family Goes Boom." *Time*, Fall, 42–44. Special issue.

Walsh, Mary Roth. 1977. *Doctors Wanted—No Women Need Apply: Sexual Barriers in the Medical Profession*. New Haven: Yale University Press.

Walshok, Mary Lindenstein. 1981. *Blue-Collar Women: Pioneers on the Male Frontier*. Garden City, N.Y.: Doubleday Anchor.

Ward, Barbara. 1963. *Women in New Asia*. Paris: UNESCO.

Ward, John. 1987. *Keeping the Family Business Healthy*. San Francisco: Jossey-Bass.

Warland, Rex H., Robert O. Herrmann, and Dan E. Moore. 1986. "Consumer Activism, Community Activism, and the Consumer Movement." In *The Future of Consumerism*, 85–95. *See* Bloom and Smith 1986.

Warren, Carol. 1987. *Madwives: Schizophrenic Women of the 1950s*. New Brunswick, N.J.: Rutgers University Press.

Wearing, Betsy. 1990. "Leisure and Crisis of Motherhood: A Study of Leisure and Health amongst Mothers of First Babies in Sydney, Australia." In *The Family as an Asset,* edited by Stella Quah, 122–55. Singapore: Times Academic Press.

Weber, Max. 1949. *The Methodology of the Social Sciences,* edited by E. Shils and H. Finch. Glencoe, Ill.: Free Press.

———. [1904] 1958. *The Protestant Ethic and the Spirit of Capitalism*. New York: Scribner's.

Weinbaum, Batya, and Amy Bridges. 1979. "The Other Side of the Paycheck: Monopoly Capital and the Structure of Consumption." In *Capitalist Patriarchy and the Case for Socialist Feminism*, 190–205. *See* Eisenstein 1979.

Weisner, Thomas S. 1982. "Sibling Interdependence and Child Caretaking: A Cross-Cultural View." In *Sibling Relationships,* 305–27. *See* Lamb and Sutton-Smith 1982.

Weiss, Robert S. 1973. *Loneliness: The Experience of Emotional and Social Isolation*. Cambridge: MIT Press.

Weitzman, Lenore. 1981. *The Marriage Contract: Spouses, Lovers, and the Law*. New York: Free Press.

———. 1985. *The Divorce Revolution: The Unexpected Social and Economic Consequences for Women and Children in America*. New York: Free Press.

Whyte, William F. 1948. *Human Relations in the Restaurant Industry*. New York: McGraw-Hill.

————. 1955. *Street Corner Society: The Social Structure of an Italian Slum.* Chicago: University of Chicago Press.

Whyte, William H., Jr. 1956. *The Organization Man.* New York: Simon & Schuster.

Wilkinson, Doris Y. 1988. "Mother-Daughter Bonds in Later Years: Transformation of the 'Help Pattern'." In *Family and Support Systems Across the Life Span,* edited by Suzanne K. Steinmetz, 183–95. New York: Plenum.

Williams, Dorie Giles. 1985. "Gender, Masculinity-Femininity, and Emotional Intimacy in Same-Sex Friendship." *Sex Roles* 12:586–600.

Williams, Norma. 1990. *The Mexican American Family: Tradition and Change.* Dix Hills, N.Y.: General Hall.

Willie, Charles, and Susan L. Greenblatt. 1978. "Four 'Classic' Studies of Power Relationships in Black Families: A Review and Look to the Future." *Journal of Marriage and the Family* 40:691–94.

Wilmott, Peter, and Michael Young. 1964. *Family and Class in a London Suburb.* London: Routledge & Kegan Paul.

Wilson, William Julius. 1987. *The Truly Disadvantaged.* Chicago: University of Chicago Press.

Winch, Robert, Scott Greer, and Rae Lesser Blumberg. 1967. "Ethnicity and Extended Familism in an Upper Middle Class Suburb." *American Sociological Review* 32:265–76.

Winch, Robert, and Rae Lesser Blumberg. 1968. "Societal Complexity and Familial Organization." In *Selected Studies in Marriage and the Family,* edited by Robert F. Winch and Louis Wolf Goodman, 70–92. New York: Holt, Rinehart & Winston.

Wirth, Louis. 1928. *The Ghetto.* Chicago: University of Chicago Press.

————. 1938. "Urbanism as a Way of Life." *American Journal of Sociology* 44:1–24.

Wittner, Judith. 1977. "Households of Strangers: Career Patterns of Foster Children and Other Wards of the State." Ph.D. diss., Department of Sociology. Northwestern University.

————. 1980. "Domestic Labor as Work Discipline: The Struggle over Housework in Foster Homes." In *Women and Household Labor,* 229–47. *See* Berk 1980.

————. 1990. "A Resource for Women? Domestic Violence Court and Feminist Research." Manuscript, Loyola University of Chicago.

Wong, Morrison G. 1988. "The Chinese American Family." In *Ethnic Families in America,* 230–57. *See* Mindel, Habenstein, and Wright 1988.

Wood, Vivian, and Joan Robertson. 1973. "The Significance of Grandparenthood." In *Time, Roles, and Self in Old Age,* edited by Jay Gubrium, 278–304. New York: Behavioral Publications.

Wrobel, Paul. 1979. *Our Way: Family, Parish, and Neighborhood in a Polish-American Community*. Notre Dame. University of Notre Dame Press.

Wylie, Philip. 1955. *Generation of Vipers*. New York: Holt, Rinehart & Winston.

Yogev, Sara. 1981. "Do Professional Women Have Egalitarian Marital Relationships?" *Journal of Marriage and the Family* 43: 865–71.

Young, Malcolm. 1984. "Police Wives: A Reflection of Police Concepts of Order and Control." In *The Incorporated Wife*, edited by Hilary Callan and Shirley Ardener, 67–88. London: Croom Helm.

Zavella, Patricia. 1987. *Women's Work and Chicano Families: Cannery Workers of the Santa Clara Valley*. Ithaca, N.Y.: Cornell University Press.

Zelizer, Viviana. 1981. "The Price and Value of Children: The Case of Children's Insurance." *American Journal of Sociology* 86:1036–56.

———. 1985. *Pricing the Priceless Child: The Changing Social Value of Children*. New York: Basic books.

Zicklin, Gilbert. 1983. *Counterculture Communes: A Sociological Perspective*. New York: Greenwood.

Zimmer, Lynn. 1987. "How Women Reshape the Prison Guard Role." *Gender and Society* 1:415–31.

Znaniecka, Zofia Pin de Saint Pau. 1872. Unpublished diary.

Znaniecki, Florian W. 1965. *Social Relations and Social Roles*. San Francisco: Chandler.

Index

The Politics and Economics of Appeasement
British Foreign Policy in the 1930s

The German original of this book has received the highest praise from international scholars and reviewers. Not only is it an attempt to evaluate a large number of primary sources from many archives, it also provides a comprehensive synthesis of Britain's policy of appeasement *vis-à-vis* Nazi Germany. The author argues that the problem of rearmament offers the key to an understanding of British domestic and foreign policy in the 1930s. Having chosen rapid rearmament as the issue area of his challenge to the British Empire, Hitler forced Britain to embark upon a counter-strategy of economic appeasement because a counter-strategy of military build-up was unacceptable for social and economic reasons. The author has also made a major contribution to the more general debate on how foreign policy-making and domestic policies are inter-related and may be linked analytically via the 'hinge' of military power and the financial burdens it imposes upon nations.

Gustav Schmidt has written widely on German and British history in the nineteenth and twentieth centuries. He is a founding member of the Workshop for German Scholars of British History and has been Visiting Professor at Emory University, Atlanta (1984) and at the University of Toronto (1985). He now teaches as Professor of International Politics at the University of Bochum in West Germany.

Gustav Schmidt

The Politics and Economics of Appeasement
British Foreign Policy in the 1930s

Translated from the German by
Jackie Bennett-Ruete

ST. MARTIN'S PRESS
New York

First published in the United States of America in 1986

Printed in Great Britain

ISBN 0–312–62617–7

Library of Congress Cataloging-in-Publication Data

Schmidt, Gustav, 1938–
    The politics and economics of appeasement.

    Translation of: England in der Krise.
    Bibliography: p.
    Includes index.
        1. Great Britain—Foreign relations—1910–1936.
2. Great Britain—Foreign relations—1936–1945.   3. Great
Britain—Foreign relations—Europe.   4. Europe—Foreign
relations—Great Britain.   5. Great Britain—Foreign
economic relations.   6. World War, 1939–1945—Causes.
I. Title.
DA578.S35613   1986   327.4104   85–32109
ISBN 0–312–62617–7

Contents

Preface

There has been a lively and unceasing interest, both among the public and among scholars, in British foreign policy before the Second World War, between Hitler's rise to power and the outbreak of war. It is thanks to the research which has resulted from that interest that we have access to large amounts of information on the events and decisions of the 1930s.[1] A number of the available documents have raised important questions; this appears to be the appropriate moment, therefore, to attempt an assessment which draws out the fundamental principles and basic outlines of British foreign policy.

Starting from the assumption 'that the problems which the majority of the political actors regarded as determinants of their political actions provide at the same time clues about the conditions of political events',[2] research into appeasement has tended to explain the developments of the 1930s in terms of a 'subjective' appreciation of the situation of Britain; in terms of what were seen or postulated to be the country's interests. In this context a multitude of interacting motives and processes have been identified.[3] Most of the literature to date has tended to reconstruct how

1. Gustav Schmidt, Introduction, and 'Das Zusammenspiel sicherheitspolitischer, wirtschaftlicher und ideologischer Faktoren in der englischen Weltpolitik und die Restrukturierung der internationalen Politik', in: Karl Rohe, ed., *Die Westmächte und das Dritte Reich 1933–1939. Klassische Großmachtpolitik oder Kampf zwischen Demokratie und Diktatur?*, Paderborn 1982, pp. 9–27, 29–56.

2. Klaus Hildebrand, 'Geschichte oder "Gesellschaftsgeschichte"?', in: *HZ*, 223 (1976), p. 349.

3. Of the many review articles, I would refer here to Bernd-Jürgen Wendt's and J.A.S. Grenville's reports to the Braunschweiger Schulbuch–Konferenz, in: *Internationales Jahrbuch für Geschichts- und Geographieunterricht*, XVII (1976), pp. 248–275 and 236–247; D.C. Watt, 'The Historiography of Appeasement', in: A. Sked/Ch. Cook, eds., *Crisis and Controversy*, London 1976, pp. 110–29; Anthony Adamthwaite, 'War Origins Again', in: *JMH*, LV(1984), pp. 100–15.

1

the actors viewed the situation and how they viewed their own role within it. In public statements, at conferences, in diplomatic exchanges as well as in internal memoranda and minutes, so the argument goes, British politicians had always emphasised a fundamental British interest in bringing about a 'general European settlement'. British foreign policy, it is said, did not merely aim to maintain 'normal' bilateral relations but also to secure conditions of regularity within the framework of a multilateral international system. Consequently, it has been deemed possible to gauge the basic outlines of Britain's behaviour in international affairs by studying the changes in her relations with other powers and variations in her position within the hierarchy of international politics. The assumption is that in the aftermath of the First World War and the Great Slump, two options were open to British foreign policy, namely:

(1) to acquiesce to changes not only in the economic but also in the power-political status quo on the Continent as well as in the Far East, insofar as (or rather in order to ensure that) they occurred by peaceful means;

(2) to accommodate itself to the security concerns of those countries and regions to which Britain considered herself tied by a 'strategic community of fate' (*strategische Schicksalsgemeinschaft*).

Although official British policy was designed to combine both options, a reconciliation of the two divergent positions proved possible only in the shape of compromise formulas put forward by Britain. What emerged, in other words, were compromises on paper only.

Two major orientations can be identified among the scholarly controversies on British foreign policy. Although both advance sophisticated arguments, they do no more in essence than to trace, more or less consciously, those lines of conflict and those debates on 'facts' or hypotheses which were introduced into the discussion by the respective protagonists and participants in the events of the epoch under investigation. Both research orientations view it as their task to identify the circle of decision-makers who, during the crisis situations of the 1930s, made attempts to implement their favoured solutions of negotiation and 'peaceful change', thereby engaging in 'appeasement', in the sense that they were prepared to make advance concessions to potential disturbers of the peace. This approach uses such terms as 'pro-German', 'pro-French' and 'anti-communist' or combinations of these as a way of identifying underlying motives.[4] Its arguments are complemented by a tendency to explain the successes or failures of British attempts at mediation in terms of the openness or inflexibility with which other powers interpreted their own interests. As regards the sins of omission or commission of British policy-makers, the critics of appeasement on the Right tend to measure this policy by the traditional yardstick of balance-of-power politics.[5] Critics on the Left, on the other hand, tend to apply the criteria of the system of collective security. Both camps deem appeasement to have been found wanting. The 'appeasers' and their defenders have attempted, on the other hand, to counter such criticisms, by arguing that they were neither blind to the dangers of Nazism nor that they had any sympathy with the aims of the Hitler regime, certainly not as far as its ambitions *vis-à-vis* the Soviet Union and Eastern Europe were concerned. Ultimately, they attempt to turn the tables on the critics by charging them with having adhered to illusions, be it in respect of France, Russia or of any other purported threat.

As attempts to come to terms with the British past, interpretations which follow the above pattern – whether they cast Neville Chamberlain as the 'villain of the piece' or whether they attempt to justify his policies – have a part to play in our understanding of the epoch under discussion. In the final analysis, however, interpretations which place personalities at the centre are just as unsatisfactory as hypotheses which are informed by theories of society.[6] By the latter we mean those hypotheses which maintain that the possession of economic power carries with it power positions in politics, and which even go so far as to present certain socio-economic interests as having a monopoly in the shaping of political events *without examining* whether the transmutation of economic benefits and opportunities into 'political assets' is actually successful. Instead, it is simply taken for granted that power is just as easily realisable in the business of politics as 'financial power' (*Geldmacht*) is assumed to be by businessmen accustomed to deploying it successfully in their economic operations. Yet the

---

4. The prototype is Martin Gilbert, Richard Gott, *The Appeasers*, London 1963, 1967[2]; Adamthwaite, *France and the Coming of the Second World War, 1936–1939*, London 1977; Nicholas Rostow, *Anglo-French Relations 1934–1936*, London 1984.

5. Winston Churchill, *The Second World War*, London 1948–1954; Robert Vansittart, *Mist Procession*, London 1958; A.J.P. Taylor, *The Origins of the Second World War*, New York 1968[2], picks up arguments advanced in Vansittart's 'Lessons of my Life', but in *The Trouble Makers: Dissent over Foreign Policy, 1792–1939*, London 1957, sympathises with the 'radical' view on foreign policy.

6. W. Röhrich, *Gesellschaftssysteme und internationale Politik. Sozialökonomische Grundrisse*, Stuttgart 1976.

problem is precisely that of determining whether 'different uses of power require different sources of power'. Is it correct that success in politics is tantamount to political power? Who disposes of political power? Are there identifiable political power élites which decisively participate in the transformation, for example, of *Geldmacht* into crucial decisions relating to situations which are of significance to a society and its politics as a whole? And do such political élites carry any weight, even if some of their members have no links with those economic forces and cannot rely on them? Do these political élites succeed in preserving the relative autonomy of their operational sphere against attempts by economic forces to turn politicians into agents and subordinates of their command centres? In short, the issue at stake is that of whether British history[7] provides any significant examples of political configurations in which political coalitions have 'unhinged' alignments of socio-economic interests, thus making it possible to talk in terms of the 'policy of the political system'.[8]

This book aims to elucidate both the domestic determinants of British diplomacy and policy towards Germany and to analyse how the repercussions of international crises and pressures from abroad affected the balance of forces and decision-making processes at home. Armaments policy functions in the context as a focus for both aspects of our investigation. We are concerned, on the one hand, 'with the internal preconditions of a material and institutional kind which guided the conception and execution of British foreign policy'.[9] In this context foreign policy is defined as the 'broad spectrum of political–diplomatic as well as economic–financial activities involving different protagonists and groups of protagonists of an official, semi-official and private kind'.[10] On the other hand, the task we have set ourselves is that of investigating changes

---

7. The fundamental criticism of Tom Nairn and others on the 'English disease' is based on the assumption that 'political elites' in Britain manage to run the country on their terms. This view is also implied in D.A. Kavanagh, 'Crisis Management and Incremental Adaptation in British Politics: The 1931 Crisis of the British Party System', in: G. Almond, S.C. Flanagan, R. Mundt, eds., *Crisis, Choice, and Change*, Boston 1973, pp. 152–223.

8. Karl Rohe, 'Ursachen und Bedingungen des britischen Imperialismus vor 1914', in: Wolfgang J. Mommsen, ed., *Moderner Imperialismus*, Stuttgart 1971, pp. 63–5; G. Schmidt, 'Wozu noch "politische Geschichte"?', in: *Aus Politik und Zeitgeschichte*, B 17/75.

9. E. Forndran, 'Zur Theorie der internationalen Beziehungen', in: E. Forndran, F. Golczewski, D. Riesenberger, eds., *Innen- und Außenpolitik unter nationalsozialistischer Bedrohung*, Opladen 1977.

10. B. J. Wendt, 'Strukturbedingungen der britischen Südosteuropapolitik am Vorabend des Zweiten Weltkriegs', in: F. Forstmeier, H.-E. Volkmann, eds., *Wirtschaft und Rüstung am Vorabend des Zweiten Weltkriegs*, Düsseldorf 1975, p. 301.

in the constellations of international politics, and of examining which of the changes in the international sphere decisively influenced British interests. A further question we shall be raising here is that of whether the external pressures on British policy threw up problems which were different from those which would have emerged from the interplay of domestic forces inside the country. All these are problems which this study will deal with in some detail.

Finally, special attention will be paid to the following two aspects of British policy:

(1) We will be attempting to explain the fact that, from about 1938 onwards, both Government and Opposition put foreign policy at the centre of their respective overall policy, whereas in the years covered by this book, 1930 to 1937, the trend was rather in the opposite direction. Throughout this earlier period, the aim was to prevent British politics from becoming completely swept up in the dynamics of foreign affairs.

(2) We will be investigating the failure of British groups and individuals responsible for security policy and for industry and commerce to coordinate their potential leverage at the negotiating table in order, firstly, to stabilise Britain's position in foreign relations and, secondly, to offer an appropriate response to the 'nationalist–political' challenges of Germany (and Japan).

There is of course a rule that changes in economic power and in military power are likely to be in the same direction. We also know that economic power and political–strategic power can be utilised for divergent and even opposing purposes or, at any rate, that they may have divergent impacts. A capacity to use power in a calculated manner therefore depends on whether it is the public authority ('the state') or market forces which successfully claim to have control over the two above-mentioned sources of power and mobilise them towards the same objective. In Britain, however, politicians and industrialists were preoccupied with developing intermediate solutions. Moreover relations between the two were influenced by mixed bodies such as the Department of Overseas Trade and the Bank of England, with its informal direction of the banking system.[11] At the same time, there were interdepartmental conflicts in London at the political level, and conflicts over objec-

---

11. D.C.M. Platt, *Finance, Trade and Politics in British Foreign Policy, 1815–1914*, Oxford 1968; C.A. Wurm, *Internationale Kartelle in der britischen Außen- und Wirtschaftspolitik 1919–1939*, Habilitationsschrift Bochum 1983.

tives which took place at the economic level, between pressure
groups or between the manufacturers and the trading houses and
trusts with global connections.[12] These must of course be seen
against the background of global rivalries, between the economic
interests of the financial, commercial and industrial enterprises, on
the one hand, and tensions between the diplomatic and consular
services and 'economic' interests, on the other.

The English translation is taken from the two main analytical
sections of the German original of this book; Chapters I and II
have been deleted. The analytical and descriptive foundations of
this book were laid in discussions of the determinants of appeasement policy in the first two chapters of the original, where
appeasement was seen to have arisen, firstly, out of developments
in the field of foreign policy and, secondly, out of concomitant
processes of opinion-formation inside Britain. I have not included
the original Chapter I, which deals with the diplomatic history of
the period and makes extensive reference to sources and secondary literature, because I have assumed that readers will be familiar
with these developments in international relations and British
foreign policy from the numerous English-language studies on the
subject. There are many studies in existence of the Manchurian
crisis of 1931, the Abyssinian War, the remilitarisation of the
Rhineland, the Spanish Civil War, the *Anschluss* of Austria in 1938
and the crises of Munich and Czechoslovakia up to the outbreak of
war in 1939. Cuts have been made in the original Chapter II with
regard to details on the personality profiles of the main actors.
Those sketches that have been retained are designed to clarify the
methodological purpose of such profiles, which is to extend the
horizons of analysis of British foreign policy in this period by
studying the ways in which those charged with administering
British foreign relations perceived developments abroad and how
they distilled strategies from them by framing them within their
own judgemental matrices.

The Introduction, which follows this Preface, aims to bring the
following points into focus:

(1) To formulate and recapitulate the central hypotheses of this
study.

(2) To present those analytical concepts – 'economic appeasement' and 'armaments policy' – which guide the general direction

---

12. C.A. Wurm, 'Der Exporthandel und die britische Wirtschaft 1919–1939', in: *VSWG*,
LXVIII (1981), pp. 191–224; G. Schmidt, *Der europäische Imperialismus*, München 1985.

of our arguments.

(3) To reflect upon the frame of reference and upon the notion of 'economic appeasement' as well as the 'hinge function of armaments policy' in their relationship to each other. The object of these sections is in particular to examine the following questions relating to appeasement. Firstly, what degree of significance should be accorded to those economic factors in British foreign policy which in a particular way (and in a way to be more closely analysed) constitute 'economic appeasement'? Taken as analytical categories these economic factors comprise (i) the subjective involvement of individuals, groups, branches of industry and commerce and of other organised collectives; (ii) points of reference which can be objectivised; and (iii) objective conditions constituting the broad framework of action. Secondly, can 'armaments policy' (as defined and elaborated in this book) be seen as the key structural element of the British political system and its external relations during the 1930s?

Ultimately, this book aims to demonstrate that an interpretation which focuses centrally on armaments policy (and on its hinge function in linking domestic and foreign affairs)[13] provides a more plausible explanation of the period than one that makes the model of 'economic appeasement' the starting-point of its enquiries.

Chapters III and IV of the German original have been translated in full and form Chapters I and II of the present volume. However, footnotes have been restricted to the citation of primary sources and indispensable supplementary references. The reader who is interested in the full range of sources on which this study is based is asked to look at the German original in which cross-references, references to, and assessments of, the historical background may also be found. The same applies to the Bibliography, which has also been shortened. It has however been updated to include titles which have appeared since the publication of the German original.

The publication of the English translation owes much to the energy of Dr Marion Berghahn. My thanks are due to her and to her editor, Mr Chris Turner, for taking such care over the manuscript. I am also grateful to those colleagues who supported the idea of a translation and to Inter Nationes for financing it. The difficult task of translation was mastered with much sensitivity and

---

13. G. Schmidt, 'Politisches System und Appeasement-Politik, 1930–1937. Zur Scharnierfunktion der Rüstungspolitik für die britische Innen- und Außenpolitik', *MGM*, 1979/2, pp. 37–53.

intellectual effort by Jackie Bennett-Ruete, Karl Kimmig and Volker Berghahn. Finally, I would like to thank my assistant, Heinz-Werner Würzler, for helping with the revision of the footnotes and with the correction of the proofs.

Introduction

Students of appeasement have been fascinated and mesmerised by the 'Munich syndrome'. 'Munich 1938' stands for a 'diplomacy of illusion' which led its protagonists into 'wishful thinking' and blinded them to 'strategic reality'.[1] It is seen as a 'readiness to make large concessions for the sake of Anglo-German amity [which vitiated] one of the basic tenets of traditional policy, [i.e. the] maintenance of the balance of power in Europe'.[2] It is also said to have been a 'policy of weak nerves' which short-sightedly abandoned the interests of third powers for the sake of preserving Britain's own interests. Finally, it is assumed to reflect Britain's inability to cut a good figure from a position of weakness.

This study has a different starting-point. By focusing deliberately and – as will be shown – with good reason on the period 1930–37, it tries to get at the foundations and basic outlines of British foreign policy between the Great Slump and the outbreak of war. The profound impact which critical analyses of the concept of appeasement have hitherto made, results, on the one hand, from the assumption that there was an alternative to appeasement in the 1930s. This alternative is seen to have been that of 'resistance to Germany's *Drang nach Osten*' on the basis of a 'more energetic diplomacy'. However, opportunities for resistance are said to have been eradicated or undermined by the appeasers' success in out-manoeuvering the advocates of the alternative strategy and in circumventing the 'accumulated wisdom' (*Amtsweisheit*) of the Foreign Office. The evidence shows, however, that neither Churchill nor Eden nor the Labour Opposition offered a genuine

1. Brian Bond, *British Military Policy Between the Two World Wars*, Oxford 1980, p. 338.
2. Anthony Adamthwaite, 'War Origins Again', *JMH*, LVI (1984), pp. 100–115.

alternative.[3] They, too, spoke in favour of appeasement on a number of issues; for example, in respect of Italy and Japan. This would seem to indicate that any simple juxtaposition of appeasers versus anti-appeasers does not conform to reality. The most that existing critical studies have achieved has been to identify the advocates of appeasement *vis-à-vis* Germany and to show who was prepared to tolerate Japanese or Italian expansion; they also show who recommended satisfying colonial, economic and/or power-political claims in the process.

If we accept the notion that all of these were in some sense 'appeasers', we are forced to look for a methodology which focuses more centrally on structural factors and, above all, on the question of determinants on British policy; to ask what were the rules of participating in the political game and what were the orientation-points and restrictions influencing British policy. From the debates outlined above, it emerges also that there were limits to the extent to which the so-called appeasers were prepared to make concessions. The extent of their determination to preserve 'essential national interests' depended on how they viewed the interconnections between points of crisis outside Europe (e.g. in the eastern Mediterranean or in the Far East) and British policy towards continental Europe; it also depended on where they thought pressure might best be applied to prevent 'fascist' challenges[4] from arising simultaneously. According to existing research, three interconnected aspects of British foreign policy have to be considered if it is to be understood in its entirety:

(1) The global dimension of British foreign and security policy, an examination of which is said to demonstrate the reasons why Britain was unable simply to concentrate on supporting the concerns of France and other partners in the European security system.

(2) Political and socio-economic factors. In whatever combination they influenced behaviour and actions (and differences must be emphasised), these factors are said to have determined the British interest in preserving the peace at almost any price.

(3) The extent of British willingness to safeguard the national interest against aggressors. A focus on this aspect of policy is

3. Neville Thompson, *The Anti-Appeasers. Conservative Opposition to Appeasement in the 1930s*, Oxford 1971; David Carlton, *Anthony Eden: A Biography*, London 1981.

4. Wolfgang J. Mommsen, L. Kettenacker, eds., *The Fascist Challenge and the Policy of Appeasement*, London 1983; D. Dilks, ed., *Retreat from Empire: Studies in Britain's Foreign Policy of the 20th Century*, London 1981.

deemed capable of demonstrating the determination with which the appeasers of Germany resisted concessions to Japan and/or Italy, or conversely, with which the appeasers of the latter resisted concessions to Hitler.

However, scholarly debates become somewhat sterile if they merely repeat the charges and counter-charges of contemporary commentators and confine themselves to asking which of the two sides was correct. Was it, it is asked, more useful to appease Mussolini's Italy or Japan than the Third Reich? What might have been the benefits of such a policy for Britain? The debating of such questions is bound to lapse into polemics if no attempt is made to explain the room for manoeuvre of British policy against the background of the policies and politics of the times. To gauge the extent of this manoeuvering space, we have to consider, on the one hand, the changes of position undergone by other decisive actors and factors in the world economy, in the European state system and in the Middle and Far East. We have therefore to assess the significance of the relative retreat of France from Eastern Europe and of the changing role of the United States and France in the world economy. On the other hand, we must also examine the objective preconditions for action, as well as the assumptions of actors – insofar as these are objectifiable – on the framework within which their activities were combined. We have, for example, to consider how far public opinion was prepared to tolerate certain policy changes or to take cognisance of financial constraints. In an early phase at least (1927–32), the domestic and foreign policy considerations which motivated the setting of 'financial limits' were not yet made subject to the restrictions which were to be seen, with hindsight, to have required the setting of different priorities than those encapsulated in measures derived from the Ten Years' Rule (or from budgetary and monetary policies). A further 'objective' constraint on shifts towards a high-level armaments economy was of course the impossibility of making any such changes overnight.

The fundamental presupposition on which this book is based is therefore that politics is always confronted with the necessity of dealing with the consequences of previous policies.[5] It follows

5. G. Schmidt, 'Das Einmaleins politischer Konflikte: Zum Verhältnis von Regime-Unterschieden und Großmachtambitionen in den deutsch-englischen Beziehungen im Zeitalter des Imperialismus', in: *GG* 1985, and in: *War and Society*, 1986. For a methodological explification of this tenet cf. Karl Rohe, *Politik. Begriffe und Wirklichkeiten*, Stuttgart 1978.

from this that appeasement must be explained first and foremost within the context of political prognoses and uses of British room for manoeuvre, at a time when British policy faced a 'new set of conditions': the Great Slump, the domestic financial crisis of 1931, the 'German Peril', and so on. It was in this context, through both action and inaction, that the range of options open to future British policy was outlined:

> For a fully adequate analysis it is necessary to amend a state-power argument to take account of the impact of past state decisions on domestic social structures as well as on international economic ones . . . Great Britain and the United States have both been prevented from making policy amendments in line with state interests by particular societal groups whose power had been enhanced by earlier state policies . . . Once entrenched, Britain's export industries and, more importantly, the City of London, resisted policies of closure . . . The British state was unable to free itself from the domestic structures that its earlier policy decisions had created, and continued to follow policies appropriate for a rising hegemony long after Britain's star had begun to fall.[6]

However convincing Krasner's analysis may be, it has not prevented him from committing the grave error of applying it to long-term trends between 1846 and 1945. He has overlooked the fact that Britain between 1931 and 1933 made a break with precisely the traditions with which he is concerned. The policies between 1931 and 1933 shattered the 'domestic structure' of the free-trade era. Moreover, by turning towards empire isolationism and protectionism ('Ottawa' and the 'sterling bloc'), Britain in turn made a major contribution to the transformation and disruption of the world economy and of world politics. If the task of analysis is to clarify the connections between the societal conditions determining political action and the impact of political decisions on 'domestic structures', then we must not ignore the political changes which took place across this hundred-year period. On the one hand, there were realignments within coalitions of domestic political interests (leading to the development of a new 'governing synthesis');[7] on the other, there was an adaptation to the actions of

6. St.D. Krasner, 'State Power and the Structure of International Trade', in: *World Politics*, XXVIII (1976), p. 318, cf. pp. 341ff.

7. Gilbert Ziebura, Franz Ansprenger, Gerhard Kiersch, eds., *Bestimmungsfaktoren der Außenpolitik in der zweiten Hälfte des 20. Jahrhunderts*, Berlin 1974, p. 39; St. Hoffmann, *In Search of France*, New York 1965[2].

other countries in the field of foreign and trade policy. In the context of developments such as these, 'politics' is able to nullify the restrictive effects of certain traditions or even replace them with alternative structures.

And yet appeasement persistently continues to be interpreted by observers clinging obstinately to notions of the 'Munich syndrome' as a period of failure in which Britain deviated temporarily from the glorious successes by which her position in world politics was traditionally characterised. The more or less conscious implication of this interpretation accords with our definition of appeasement *politics* – in the sense that it is seen to have created structures. But they were structures which led to Britain's derailment from the tracks of a traditional world power. The moral reproach against the appeasers which united both Churchill and the Labour Party has its deeper roots in this interpretation. As the successors and 'heirs' to Chamberlain's policy, they believed they had been robbed of Britain's future. After the end of the Allied coalition war, this attitude on the part of the anti-appeasers – Churchill and Eden, but the Atlee government no less so – did not, however, undermine their belief that British policy could steer and maintain an intermediate course between the superpowers. In an attempt to bring the issue here more sharply into focus, it is perhaps permissible to resort to a kind of contrafactual history and deduce from this illusion that the alternative strategies fought for by the anti-appeasers before 1939–40 represented an overestimation of the room for manoeuvre for the establishment of a British 'order', whether of the balance-of-power or collective-security/Concert of Europe variety. The crucial point is that research on appeasement must confront the question of how long the 'objective' conditions under which Britain might have retained a world-power role persisted. Was it up to the outbreak of the Second World War, as the anti-appeasers have argued; or had this role already come to an end in the 1930s? And how far did the policy of the 1930s, by withdrawing from a world-power role, reinforce and accelerate the demise of a 'positive' tradition?

Put differently, the issue at stake is that of whether and in what respects the appeasement period represents a departure from tradition, and to what extent that tradition was in any case positive. Existing research (and above all the West German contributions to this debate) has traced a line of continuity precisely in the fundamental interest of a declining imperial power in maintaining peace – peace, it should be added, among the great powers. One such contribution to the debate from K. Hildebrand attempts to encapsulate the political–diplomatic and socio-economic determinants of this search for peace in the concept of 'British interests'. His interpretation takes up Herz's point that it is necessary to stress Britain's interest in the peaceful co-existence of divergent regimes and systems; but it extends this argument by including determinants considered to be continually at work within the political culture of Britain.[8] 'British interests' are thus seen to comprise the domestic and foreign political elements of a peace strategy which contrasts with the continuing sense of hubris believed to have been the hallmark of German national history from William II to Hitler.[9]

It is certainly necessary to raise the question of continuity – however differently it may be posed – if we are to attempt an interpretation of British appeasement. However, in order to be able to provide a coherent answer, we must firstly define our questions, more clearly and, secondly, make clearer distinctions between divergent levels of analysis. As to the first point, we must ask what is the time-span within which the question of continuity is to be considered. Is it the period after 1935–36, after 1933 or after 1930–32 which constitutes the beginning of our time-unit; and is 1938–40 to be the terminating point of this period? Which elements of the preceding epoch are still essential in considering the phase of appeasement itself? Internal continuities (i.e. the persistence of the 'Treasury view' or of 'Baldwin–MacDonaldism'), on the one hand, and the Great Slump, the financial crisis of 1931, and so on, on the other, may be taken as indications that the beginning of our time-unit should be 1930–32.[10] By implication, then, the 'search for a general European settlement' (1933–38) is to be seen here as a continuation of the attempt to achieve a 'political truce', which was the hallmark of British foreign policy in

8. K. Rohe, 'Großbritannien: Krise einer Zivilkultur?', in: Peter Reichel, ed., *Politische Kultur in Westeuropa*, Bonn 1984, pp. 167–193; K. Hildebrand, 'Zwischen Allianz und Antagonismus. Das Problem bilateraler Normalität in den britisch-deutschen Beziehungen des 19. Jahrhunderts (1870–1914)', in: H. Dollinger et al., eds., *Weltpolitik–Europagedanke–Regionalismus*, Münster 1982, p. 326.

9. G. Schmidt, *Politische Tradition und wirtschaftliche Faktoren in der britischen Friedensstrategie 1917–1919*, Habilitationsschrift Münster 1971; K. Hildebrand, *Preußen als Faktor der britischen Weltpolitik 1866–1870. Studien zur Außenpolitik Großbritanniens im 19. Jahrhundert*, Habilitationsschrift Mannheim 1972.

10. G. Schmidt, 'Das Zusammenspiel sicherheitspolitischer, wirtschaftlicher und ideologischer Faktoren in der englischen Weltpolitik und die Restrukturierung der internationalen Politik', in: Karl Rohe, ed., *Die Westmächte und das Dritte Reich 1933–1939*, Paderborn 1982, pp. 29–56.

the period from 1930 to 1932. The collapse in the international system after 1933–34 – that is, the disintegration of the systems of Versailles and Washington – are ample reason for the historian to analyse events in terms of an antagonism of systems, with Britain and Nazi Germany appearing on the stage as protagonists. However, account will also have to be taken of the fact that the actors on both the British and also the German side did not at first respond to the emergence of this particular structure of conflicts by reorientating their policies accordingly. It is in view of the gradual nature of their accommodation to contemporary realities that it becomes necessary, as we shall see below, to pose the question of continuity in a very specific way. Taking the period from 1930–32 to 1938–40 as the time-span of our analysis also involves the assumption that periods of continuity are in no sense identical with 'balance of power' phases, but instead that they span such periods as the 'Locarno period' in British policy.

What therefore constitutes this continuity? In the first instance, our premise must be that British foreign policy, ever since the country's appearance as a world power, had always involved a balancing act between the resources of the British Isles and the world-wide dispersal of the aims and interests of its politicians and citizens. Did the 1930s therefore represent the first point at which Britain had to acknowledge that her policies were unlikely to end as happily as in preceding decades and centuries? Up to the First World War, the country had always been able to make economic, territorial and other gains at the end of the great wars of the modern period. But after 1930–32 there was a growing feeling among those administering British foreign relations that in all these respects Britain could only expect losses in future. This meant that the nightmare of a 'world power in decline' which had frequently been conjured up was likely to become real should Britain make another effort at power-politics.

This in turn raises the question of different levels of analysis; for it appears to be important for an assessment of the scope for manoeuvre of British foreign policy to ask whether or not the economic and military structures of world politics underwent a profound change around 1930.[11] If indeed they did, then we must ask further in what respects this worked to the detriment of

11. Gilbert Ziebura, *Weltwirtschaft und Weltpolitik 1922/24–1931*, Frankfurt am Main 1984; G. Schmidt, ed., *Konstellationen internationaler Politik 1924–1932. Politische und wirtschaftliche Faktoren in den Beziehungen zwischen Westeuropa und den Vereinigten Staaten*, Bochum 1983 (cf. the author's 'Dissolving International Politics'?, ib. pp. 348–428).

Britain's position. More particularly, was it on the economic level or on the level of security politics that decisive policy impulses originated? As far as the *international economy* is concerned, the determining developments took place both in the arena of world trade and of international financial relations. The 'regionalisation' of the world economy, the creation of currency blocs (the franc bloc and sterling bloc) and customs unions or other forms of trade agreements were indicative of an increasing introduction and expansion of protectionist policies in response to escalating competition. The American Smoot–Hawley Tariff gave a decisive boost to this trend, as did rapid currency devaluations and restrictions on currency and capital movements. Britain, having lost its position as the leading industrial nation, had no choice but to note the irrevocable loss of its position as the 'world's banker'. The reverse side of this coin was Britain's rediscovery of the 'national economy' as a feasible political alternative.[12] It was to be combined with what was identifiable as an additional – if minimal – opportunity to attain a useful level of autarchy, by means of a 'new imperial economic policy'. This shift towards a 'national economy' appeared to many contemporaries, particularly among the Tories and in the Labour Party, as a belated reorientation and adaptation, triggered by the 1931 crisis, to the realities of the British competitive position within the international economy of the twentieth century. To these circles this reorientation opened up political vistas behind which the European continent declined in importance.

Changes on the level of security interests were, however, no less far-reaching. Although Britain was reluctant to return to a 'policy of strength' *vis-à-vis* its main opponent, Germany (which would have involved engaging in an arms race, aggressive economic diplomacy and the propagation of an alternative model of politics), London nevertheless wanted to retain the option of

---

12. Criticism of what is seen as the unjustified influence of the City — the 'finance' factor — on British policy and (foreign) economic relations, which underlies for example the analyses of S. Pollard, R. Skidelsky, T. Nairn, Rubinstein and others, assesses the increased attention paid to the domestic economy in the 1930s as a theoretically positive development. At the same time it laments the illogicality of the measures through which the National Government and the Conservatives attempted to eradicate the causes of the 'English disease'. See G. Schmidt, Karl Rohe, eds., *Krise in Grossbritannien? Historische Grundlagen und aktuelle Dimensionen*, Bochum 1982 (Arbeitskreis Deutsche England–Forschung, I); I. Kramnick, ed., *Is Britain Dying?*, Ithaca 1979; S. Blank, 'Britain: The Politics of Foreign Economic Policy, the Domestic Economy, and the Problem of Pluralistic Stagnation', in: Peter Katzenstein, ed., *Between Power and Plenty*, Madison 1977.

mobilising its political strength. In so doing, it hoped to be in a position to wait out direct conflict with an aggressive Germany. In the course of our analysis, we will then hope to demonstrate the advisability of making a conceptual distinction between a 'policy of strength' and 'political strength'.

Structural changes in the world economy and in world politics amounted to an accumulation of factors all of which negatively affected the role Britain had become accustomed to playing. We propose to define this accumulation as representing a *crisis*, the features of which will be described in greater detail below. This crisis demanded of the actors, on the one hand, that they make the 'proper' sacrifices and, on the other, that they create, through determination and political mobilisation at home, the preconditions under which survival could be secured, despite changes in the framework of international relations.

What sacrifices, or what reductions in 'overcommitments' might then be seen in this context to have been potentially correct? Were they in the first instance to involve the abandonment of the gold standard and of the City's role as world banker? Taking this step would have meant Britain drawing the final conclusion from her failed attempts in the 1920s to act as the 'lender of last resort' and as a clearing-house in the circulation of international finance. Was it also necessary for Britain, as Bonar Law had first suggested in 1922 during his brief period as prime minister, to give up her role as 'guardian of the peace'? Or should it be considered more useful for her to have concentrated on finding a substitute solution, to function as an unarmed international police force for the world, comparable to the law-and-order forces at home? Taking such steps would have implied a continuation of the course embarked upon by Britain in 1919–22 and modified in 1927, whereby she limited her guarantees in respect of the 'European balance'. Thirdly, there is the question of whether abandoning the role of 'guardian of peace' might have opened up an opportunity for a shift to a more vigorous policy of stimulating the domestic economy. Such a policy, which was initiated in principle, might then have provided a basis from which increased efforts could be made in the service of a national security policy. And would not an augmentation of Britain's defence potential have offered a secure fall-back position for British diplomacy?

The question of continuity must also be posed on the basis of evidence derived from the appeasement period itself. In our investigation here, we shall therefore be concerned with the following questions: Is British foreign policy marked throughout by support for 'peaceful change'? Is this 'peaceful change', as Britain's preferred mode of behaviour towards the outside world, the mirror image of intentions which informed the code of conduct of the British power élites in domestic affairs? Do such domestic determinants have a bearing on British policy *vis-à-vis* Germany, and if so, what is the extent of their impact in the 1930s in comparison with other epochs, and in what forms do they find expression?

From the opposite standpoint, we shall also be asking why British policy prior to the Second World War was so distinctly different from the balance-of-power doctrine adhered to before 1914, and why it so consciously rejected that latter policy? After all, objectively speaking 'Anglo-German antagonism' was much more marked in the 1930s than before the First World War. And yet the differences between the two political systems as perceived by British actors, led them to adopt a strategy which aimed primarily to avoid external conflict. The decisive factors in this respect were the experiences which Baldwin, Neville Chamberlain, Simon and Runciman had had as 'seconds-in-command' during the Great War. When, by the 1930s, they had advanced to key positions within the power élite, they sought to take advantage of the lessons they had learned in this earlier period.[13] The acceleration of changes in the world economy and in world politics during the First World War and the Great Slump induced the decision-makers to assess other lessons from past experience. In relation to foreign trade, they aimed to follow France's lead in activating the benefits of the imperial past. In foreign policy they were inclined to sit out any inconveniences arising from the Central European situation. The former strategy required capital commitments; according to the decision-makers, if these were to be made, they should be for the development of a 'sterling zone'. The latter strategy was reflected in their hope that the 'security–political life-line of the 1920s' – that is, the Ten-Year Rule strategy of preparing for a European war on a long-term basis – could be perpetuated, if not by the letter, then at least in spirit.

Britain's aversion to alliance commitments, and her discrediting of them as power diplomacy in both senses of the word, are distinctive features of appeasement. In the following, we shall be asking whether, over and above this, they are also a characteristic

---

13. J. Barnes, K. Middlemas, *Baldwin. A Biography*, London 1969; Martin Gilbert, *The Roots of Appeasement*, London 1967; Corelli Barnett, *The Collapse of British Power*, London 1972; W.R. Rock, *British Appeasement in the 1930s*, London 1977.

of Britain's world-power consciousness; that is, of a calculation that she could and should regulate goal conflicts autonomously and coordinate resources with objectives single-handedly and under her own authority. Certainly Britain's basic attitude betrays her propensity to retreat into isolationism and go it alone. It is also an indication of her reservations against according primacy to foreign policy. Or to put it another way, Britain's attitude betrays a preference for the idea that it is the task of diplomacy to guarantee 'freedom to develop society without outside interference'.[14] Ultimately, our investigation here will lead us back to our original question of why the decision-makers 'internalised' their role of being the opponents of German militarism before 1914, yet, at least in public, flatly rejected the organisation of an international resistance movement to National Socialism in the 1930s.

The attitude of the appeasers is certainly connected to the fact that they carried within them the shock of 1917–18, the crisis year of the First World War. It was during that year that Britain's allies effectively dropped out of the war: Russia did so permanently; France temporarily. As a result, Britain had to bear the brunt of the war, losing, on the one hand, practically the whole of the generation which would have moved into leadership positions in the 1930s and, on the other, falling behind the United States in the world economy.[15] For its protagonists, appeasement represented an attempt to implement the 'doctrines' formulated by Milner, Amery and others in the situation of 1916–18 as a counterargument to the Western Front strategy of the military (Haig/Robertson) and the Middle East/Balkan strategy of Churchill and Lloyd George.[16] This counter-position had been explicitly developed in anticipation of a renewed rise of German power which it was thought would occur from about the middle of the 1930s, independently of any potential decisive defeat of Ludendorff and German militarism in the First World War.

Given the ambiguities of the Locarno strategy, it is not easy to

14. Richard Löwenthal, 'Freiheit der Eigenentwicklung', in: U. Scheuner, ed., *Außenpolitische Perspektiven des westdeutschen Staates*, vol. I: *Das Ende des Provisoriums*, München 1971, pp. 11–15.

15. G. Schmidt, 'Politische Tradition und wirtschaftliche Faktoren in der britischen Friedensstrategie 1918/19', in: *VZG*, XXIX/2 (1981), pp. 131–188; Carl P. Parrini, *Heir to Empire. United States Economic Diplomacy, 1916–1923*, Pittsburgh 1969, points to the fact that Washington and American industry nevertheless were concerned about British rivalry and competition.

16. G. Schmidt, *Politische Tradition*, (note 9).

provide a clear-cut answer to the question of whether appeasement can be linked to 'Locarno diplomacy'.[17] Official British policy
was certainly committed to continuing its multifarious endeavours
to orientate Germany towards the West, to avoiding any commitment of the Western powers to an Eastern Locarno, and to supporting moral and economic recovery. Other commentators on
Locarno, principally its critics, also regard it as characteristic of
the favouring in Locarno policy of a diplomatic Four-Power constellation which would bypass the Soviet Union, on the one hand,
and the smaller European powers, on the other. However, by the
1930s some of the important policy prerequisites and special
conditions of the Locarno era had disappeared. While Austen
Chamberlain had always insisted on Anglo-French partnership,
London claimed a leadership role *vis-à-vis* France in the 1930s.
Moreover, not only was the US no longer prepared to function as
midwife and samaritan for the restoration of Europe, but Great
Britain also appears to have regarded the retreat and reserve of the
US in a positive light and thus not to have pressed wholeheartedly
for a renewal of commitments on the part of Washington and Wall
Street.

The distribution of domestic power which had obtained in the
1920s and during the Locarno period, remained unchanged in the
1930s. It was indeed consolidated and strengthened when existing
close correspondences in the policies adopted by the higher
echelons of leadership in the two parties officially coalesced in the
National government of Baldwin and MacDonald after 1931. If we
assume that Hitler's seizure of power represented a discontinuity
with the Weimar tradition – certainly in terms of domestic policy
and, as far as foreign policy was concerned, at least in its methods
of interest articulation – then we must also ask whether Britain,
because of the continuity of her political system at home, ought to
have changed her foreign and security policy to deal with structural changes on the German side, instead of extending the policy
of 'political truce' she had adopted towards Brüning to a policy of
'political truce' towards Hitler. The answer we will give to this
question below will show that it was not just a matter of Britain
failing to undertake analyses of the German threat after 1933 and to
react to the deterioration of the situation by appropriate means.
Rather we shall also have to examine in Chapters I and II what the
continuity of domestic politics consisted of in Britain and why that

---

17. Jon Jacobson, *Locarno Diplomacy. Germany and the West 1925–1929*, Princeton 1972.

continuity furthered the continuation of the foreign policy of 1930–32 rather than an adaptation to, or imitation of, the diplomatic postures adopted by Germany.

Finally, we should stress here that appeasement cannot merely be seen as one stage in a long-drawn-out process beginning at the end of the nineteenth century, in which Britain gradually sacrificed power.[18] It is also, and above all, one variant of a dilemma which the policies of 'liberal Britain' had faced repeatedly in the age of nationalist and social revolutions. Hence appeasement must be located within the frame of reference of a history of peaceful co-existence[19] between regimes with divergent ideological and power-political orientations.

Starting from these points and preliminary considerations, we can now formulate what will be the *guiding idea* of this study. Appeasement as British foreign policy in the 1930s was propelled by a paradoxical attempt to solve, or at least to regulate, conflicts by means of diplomacy and political strength at a time which was marked rather by the end of diplomacy. British policy was faced with a *crisis*, with the negative effects of an accumulation of changes, none of which seemed to bear promise of relief either at home or abroad. The crisis arose out of the failure of diplomacy to paper over the long-term cracks which split the global reach of Britain's objectives, her commitments and the resources at her disposal, from traditional means and methods of resolution. It arose out of the distrust of Britain's allies, as well as her opponents, in British diplomacy; no longer were they receptive to the traditional approaches of that diplomacy. Since diplomacy could no longer cushion the external pressures upon Britain, there was bound to be

18. Paul M. Kennedy, 'The Tradition of Appeasement in British Foreign Policy 1865–1939', in: *British Journal of International Studies*, II (1976), pp. 195–215, introduces this favourite German view of British foreign policy during the 20th century into English writing on Apeasement. Presseisen's attempts to clarify the contours of the appeasement problem by drawing a comparison between Munich and the Amiens peace agreement is in many ways successful. Criticism becomes necessary however precisely at the point at which he fails to take into consideration the objective differences between Great Britain's situation vis-à-vis Napoleon and Hitler, or the differences in the international situation around 1803 and in 1937/40. In my view, a comparison of this kind can only be meaningful if it begins in the period of 'relative decline'; in any other context, what is achieved is at best only a collection of interesting policy elements, which present themselves only on the basis of the comparability of action in different periods to counter the advance of a hegemonic power with whom confrontation has become unavoidable. Ernst L. Presseisen, *Amiens and Munich: Comparisons in Appeasement*, Den Haag 1978.

19. H. Herzfeld, 'Zur Problematik der Appeasement-Politik', in: *Aus Politik und Zeitgeschichte*, B16/63; John H. Herz, 'Sinn und Sinnlosigkeit der Beschwichtigungspolitik', in: *PVS*, V (1964), p. 389.

increased pressure on British policy to safeguard the viability and efficiency of its socio-political system, and thus to generate political strength. This pressure became all the stronger in the 1930s when France resigned her responsibilities within the European security system, and the US relinquished her jurisdiction over the regulation of the international economy, both countries thereby losing the authority they had held in the decade after the First World War. A final source of pressure was the challenge posed by Germany to all her opponents, most notably Britain, when she had been subjected, as had Britain in the 1920s, to the imposition of restrictive ceilings on her economic power position and her security policy. Now, in the 1930s, she made rapid moves to catch up with the opposition. This about-turn in German policy confronted Britain with new problems both in the economic and the security sphere which British political society would not have generated within its own realm. These problems became condensed in the *armaments question*, which was to become the hinge linking domestic and foreign policy, and was hence to emerge as the centrepiece of British politics. 'Britain in Crisis' – this was the title of the German original of this study, and it also encapsulates the constellation in which the country was forced to orientate its policy towards armaments. The particular turn taken by Britain's armaments policy arose as a result of Hitler's posing of a threat at a time when Britain was confronted with general problems of political reorientation, and when France and the United States had more or less reneged on their commitments to international security. It is for all the above reasons that armaments policy and its relationship with the British political system occupy the centre of this book.

Another central theme we will be pursuing in the following relates to a further aspect of the continuity question. The domestic about-turn of 1931–32 and the resultant policies of consolidation ('national economy'; sterling stabilisation; regeneration of the domestic market; 'inter-imperial trade') tended to neglect considerations of the European connection in relation to economic interests – despite the fact that Britain was faced with the danger of a re-emergence of the old Anglo-German antagonism through Britain's attempts to protect her security interests, which were liable to overshadow an economic development orientated towards the domestic market and the Empire.[20] The problems which arose

20. G. Schmidt, 'The Domestic Background to British Appeasement Policy', in: W.J. Mommsen, L. Kettenacker, eds. (note 4), pp. 101–124.

in this context are the subject of debates below on the character, aims and methods of '*economic appeasement*'. The events and problems which present themselves for analysis under the dual headings of 'The Armaments Question' and 'Economic Appeasement' have many points of empirical convergence. Yet the differences between the two areas are equally marked. There are continuous determinants on foreign economic policy which all interpretations of economic appeasement can take as their reference point in order to establish how official decision-makers and unofficial political actors attempted to create an autonomous sphere of action, for economic appeasement as a political strategy, related to existing interest structures. However, the main point is that when analysing the external economic relations and activities to be found under 'economic appeasement', we are dealing with interest- and power-constellations which are different from those of the security–political sphere.

The *hinge function of armaments* for Britain's policies at home and abroad[21] is marked by a distinctive form of interaction between the political system and foreign relations. In the wake of fundamental postwar reorientations and of the peace settlement in 1918–20, armaments policy came to be based on the assumption that Britain would be able to cope with difficulties in the field of foreign policy more easily than with the problems of 'labour' at home.[22] For what

21. G. Krell, 'Zur Theorie der Rüstungsdynamik im Ost-West-Konflikt. Ein kritischer Überblick über die verschiedenen Ansätze', in: *PVS*, XVII (1976), pp. 446ff., offers a survey on the range of subjects and topics combined in the notion 'Rüstungsfrage'. The studies of Volker R. Berghahn, *Der Tirpitz–Plan*, and M. Geyer, *Aufrüstung oder Sicherheit? Die Reichswehr und die Krise der Machtpolitik, 1924–1936*, Wiesbaden 1980, are very good examples for doing such a study.

22. 'Labour' as a concept does not simply refer to the labour movement, by which is meant primarily the Trades Unions, but to the 'vicious circle' syndrome which is seen to arise out of the severe stresses of the mobilisation situation. On the basis of the fact that 'labour' becomes more crucial than any other factor in an armaments economy - not to mention its centrality within a war economy - it is assumed that labour will demand an appropriate price for its services. Since industry also demands higher profits than is 'normally' the case, or rather profits guaranteed by the State, the total price required by labour was seen by numbers of contemporary figures to be likely to rise sharply. Men such as Simon, Runciman, Hoare, Inskip and Neville Chamberlain foresaw a complete remoulding of England's social profile. This particular 'spiral' of events was forecast on numerous occasions by key Cabinet ministers and their advisers. For one of many examples, I would refer the reader here to Neville Chamberlain, 25.4.1937, cit. in Feiling, *The Life of Neville Chamberlain*, p. 292. On the factual relationship between armament and inflation — its first appearance in 1937 and its practical effects by 1939 — see H.W. Richardson, *Economic Recovery in England, 1932–1939*, London 1967, esp. pp. 284f., p. 233. Assumptions made at the time on the part of the government may be broadly summarised in the notion that the war would render social reforms unavoidable. For discussions of this in the fifties and sixties, see P. Abrams' survey, 'The Failure of Social Reform: 1918–1920', in: *Past and Present*, 24 (1963), pp. 43–64. The first formulation of these ideas had come from Hankey in his

was at stake in those latter conflicts was not just a change in the domestic balance of power in favour of the Labour Party, who represented the 'natural' governing party in a country where blue-collar and white-collar workers constituted the largest section of the working population; rather it was more far-reaching changes in the socio-economic sphere, in the structure of the existing system and in British political culture. The way problems relating to the notion of 'labour' were handled in Britain was to be markedly different from practices developed on the European continent.

However, it is certainly misleading to conclude from the goals outlined at the time for appeasement, or from the fact that appeasement cast itself in the role of diametric opposition to the militant strategy of the totalitarian Nazi regime[23] that British foreign policy did in fact mould both aspects of appeasement into a single policy. Certainly some of the appeasers, as well as a number of their apologists, argued for the introduction of measures for a peaceful revision of the international status quo as well as for a stabilisation of the domestic system by means of reform. But a coordinated approach never really emerged. Neither the MacDonald cabinet, nor Baldwin and Chamberlain initiated domestic reforms as a preliminary to or at the time of the appeasement initiatives which they announced annually between the winters of 1933/34 and 1937/38.[24] The deficiencies in British social and economic policy in the 1930s are so glaring that it becomes impossible to see Britain as the opposite of the German case. Nazi Germany was without doubt the country in which the link between a policy of threat and expansionism abroad and an open repression strategy at home can be most cogently demonstrated. Yet it cannot be counterposed to the image of a 'model' Britain in

---

response to the protest movements of 1919 and to the disarmament and demobilisation restrictions imposed on Germany in March 1919. On the genesis of these ideas, see Howard, *Continental Commitment*, esp. pp. 77f.; Gibbs, *Rearmament*, pp. 3f. In the following, the notion of 'labour' will be deployed, and is to be understood, in a dual sense: firstly, 'labour' in the sense of trades unionism, and secondly, 'labour' as a progression from armaments inflation to social unrest to pressures for concession and for realignments in the distribution of social forces.

23. K. Hildebrand, 'Hitlers Ort in der Geschichte des Preußisch-Deutschen Nationalstaats', in: *HZ*, 217 (1973), pp. 584–632; id., 'Innenpolitische Antriebskräfte der nationalsozialistischen Außenpolitik', in: H.U. Wehler, ed., *Sozialgeschichte heute*, Göttingen 1974, pp. 635–651.

24. The appeasement initiatives are analysed by James T. Emmerson, *The Rhineland Crisis, 7 March 1936. A Study in Multilateral Diplomacy*, London 1977; K. Middlemas, *Diplomacy of Illusion. The British Government and Germany 1937–1939*, London 1972; Bernd-Jürgen Wendt, *Economic Appeasement. Handel und Finanz in der britischen Deutschlandpolitik 1933–1939*, Düsseldorf 1971.

which a peaceful foreign policy was accompanied by reforms at home.

It is, however, legitimate to argue that there existed a different kind of connection between social appeasement at home[25] and peaceful change abroad.[26] Unlike the government of the Third Reich, the British government did intend to deal with difficulties at home by making domestic gestures and taking account of other political and social groups. They did not try to deflect attention from domestic difficulties by embarking upon an aggressive foreign policy. Since the turn of the century, both Liberal and Conservative governments had been trying to gain room for manoeuvre in domestic politics by gradually dismantling British commitments within the international system.[27] They then used that room to initiate tax reductions, expansions of the social insurance system, and so on (i.e. relief policies which had a socially pacifying effect), or to promote the extension of house-ownership (i.e. strategies of conserving existing social structures). The government did not wish to see these policies obliterated by Hitler's foreign coups except in an emergency. Thus 'the Treasury feared that Germany's action would result in the product of their effort to regain control over expenditure being snatched from their grasp at the last moment'.[28]

The hope, then, was that freedom of action in fiscal policy would help immunise Britain against phenomena which had manifested themselves on the Continent in various forms of open or latent civil war.[29] If it is possible to define German foreign policy as 'an unsuccessful attempt to preserve the domestic status quo (and to destroy the international status quo) by means of rearmament, following only too soon by the realisation that [rearmament] jeopardised the domestic status quo',[30] then British policy in the

---

25. M. Cowling, *The Impact of Labour 1920–1924. The Beginnings of Modern British Politics*, Cambridge 1971; id., *The Impact of Hitler. British Politics and Policies 1933–1940*, Cambridge 1975; B.-J. Wendt, 'Großbritannien — Demokratie auf dem Prüfstand: Appeasement als Strategie des Status quo', in: E. Forndran et al., eds. (Preface, note 9), pp. 11–31.

26. M.N. Medlicott, *Britain and Germany: The Search for Agreement 1930–1937*, London 1969; id., *From Metternich to Hitler. Aspects of British and Foreign History, 1814–1939*, London 1963; W.N. Medlicott, *British Foreign Policy since Versailles 1919–1963*, London 1968[2].

27. This is the contention of Medlicott's studies (s. note 26). G. Monger, *The End of Isolation: British Foreign Policy 1900–1907*, London 1963, was the first to demonstrate the inter-action between social reform and 'Entente' politics of the Liberal Governments.

28. R.P. Shay, *British Rearmament in the Thirties: Politics and Profits*, Princeton 1977, p. 197.

29. The arguments advanced by N. Chamberlain, Lord Weir, Leith-Ross, Runciman are analysed below.

30. Volker R. Berghahn, *Rüstung und Machtpolitik*, Düsseldorf 1973, p. 69.

fields of security, armaments and foreign affairs in the 1930s may be seen by contrast as motivated by a fear of destabilisation of the domestic status quo, which led – at least temporarily and within certain limits – to a greater willingness to accept changes in the international status quo. The limits to which appeasement could go before a turning-point was reached were clearly outlined by the appeasers themselves. As Lord Lothian put it, 'Germany, by a policy of oppression and destruction of the Czech nation, was destroying the only basis on which a powerful development of German life would have been reconcilable in the long run with the continued existence of Europe'.[31]

It is frequently suggested that appeasement may be seen as a strategy for avoiding external conflict which served the class politics of the Conservatives, by cementing the existing soció-economic order.[32] There are two objections to a short-circuiting of historical developments which blurs the distinction between conservative policies and the policies of the Conservatives. These are (1) the documentary evidence to the contrary and (2) the basic character of British politics. Both issues will be discussed in turn below.

In the 1930s certain Conservatives operating in opposition to the Right pressed the government to step up rearmament. They objected to 'colonial' as well as to 'economic' appeasement and accused the cabinet of violating the British national interest. At the same time, the willingness at least to tolerate appeasement and to approve the guiding philosophy of official diplomacy (i.e. its commitment to peaceful change'; 'limited liability', etc.) was not confined before 1938–39 to those who had voted for the National government. Support came also from 'class interest' groups which figured otherwise as rivals in questions of social and economic policy.[33] Relatively independently of party-political stances, the

---

31. Lothian, quoted in: J.R.M. Butler, *Lord Lothian (Philip Kerr), 1882–1940*, London 1960, p. 229.

32. B.-J. Wendt, in: Forndran, ed. (note 25), pp. 18, 22; id., *Aspekte* (cf. note 3 Preface), pp. 266ff.; M. George, *The Warped Vision. British Foreign Policy 1933–1939*, London 1963, combines the 'class-based' foreign policy–thesis with an assertion of anti-bolshevism, i.e. Britain actively encouraging 'Germany's, 'Drang nach Osten': G. Niedhart, *Großbritannien und die Sowjetunion 1934–1939*, München 1972, demolishes this argument.

33. The general explanation is provided by Samuel Beer's 'group politics'–interpretation of British politics; cf. Samuel H. Beer, *Modern British Politics*, London 1969; D.A. Kavanagh, 'An American Science of British Politics', in: *Political Studies*, XXII (1974), p. 264. — To give an example: 'Economic appeasers' were inclined to 'free trade', 'restoring international economy' etc., and opposed to the favourite topics of Government propaganda ('Ottawa', 'Sterling bloc', 'domestic economy' etc.); the 'imperialists' within the Conservative Party formed a caucus to

experience of the First World War in particular allowed an appreciation of the restrictive conditions of political action.[34] This experience had shown that a shifting of resources towards armaments, even in an *ad hoc* fashion, was likely to lead to struggles over the distribution of these resources not only between classes but also between different branches of industry. Moreover, the country's competitive position with regard to the postwar world market was likely to be adversely affected. Only a small number of opponents of appeasement, Churchill among them, wished to go through the same experience again by embarking upon a policy of rapid rearmament in the 1930s.

The Labour Party and the trade unions tried to circumvent the question of rearmament as a response to the German challenge. They did so by asserting that the peaceful states held a sufficient military superiority and by demanding that this superiority be used for an appropriate policy of collective security, designed to contain and deter the aggressor politically and diplomatically. The government parties denied the fact that the situation constituted a state of emergency which necessitated alliance commitments. They espoused the notion of 'limited liability' as a corollary of flexibility in foreign affairs. And flexibility, in contrast to Churchill's bloc policy or the notion of collective security on the Left, was seen to allow Britain the option of committing no resources to an armaments economy either at home or abroad. It was with this goal in mind that the appeasers invoked the argument that the international situation did not yet rule out the possibility of achieving a 'general settlement' with the Third Reich (and/or Japan, Italy). After the crises of 1938 (the *Anschluss* and 'Munich'), foreign policy became the arena in which divergent political forces tried to enhance their public image. The strategy of 'limited liability', which had hitherto provided a common basis for international politics by shielding British domestic politics against developments on the Continent, was at this point put in jeopardy. It was at this point that the British partners in the West European collective security system were asked to pay their risk-premiums in full. While British society and politics displayed an ever more visible polarisation, foreign policy became the issue which was to lead to

---

prevent the Government's testing of 'colonial appeasement'.

34. G. Hollenberg, *Englisches Interesse am Kaiserreich*, Wiesbaden 1974, pp. 45f., 85, advances an interpretation which suits the conditions before World War I, but — in its methodological implications — could also be applied to an analysis of the inter-war period; See Chapter II, 'Political System', below.

the regrouping of political forces. In other words, it was Britain's perception of global shifts occasioned by the aggressive policies of conflict-prone countries such as Japan, Italy and Germany, which caused her to redefine her diplomacy, and which solicited reactions from various groups within the country.

This new situation was a consequence of the fact that the options which British decision-makers began now to perceive lay almost exclusively outside the parameters which interest groups and opinion leaders had begun to formulate on their own initiative. In 1938 the decisive groups within the government (which in their internal debates were, of course, also concerned to preserve their own influence) initially favoured courses of action which departed from the 'limited liability' strategy as little as possible. The opposition inside the government, by contrast, considered a change of direction and a rapprochement with the USSR overdue. This was also the view of the right-wing and the left-wing Opposition. During a second phase in 1939, the government, pursuing its aim to retain power, changed to a policy of rapid rearmament and arms mobilisation. It was a policy which the right-wing Opposition had long advocated, but which the left-wing Opposition had rejected as a manifestation of class politics. In putting the British economy on a war-footing, the government was, of course, aware that the left-wing Opposition would at least have to tolerate rapid rearmament, including the introduction of military service as a means of countering the perceived foreign threat.

The parameters within which armaments policy evolved as symptom and symbol of a British diplomatic and military response to the German challenge were drawn by economic difficulties of a structural and financial character, on the one hand, and by certain political markers, on the other. Any study of British foreign policy has to take account of the fact that security policy aimed to preserve the freedom of Britain to develop as she saw fit. In other words, it was linked to the expectation that the relative autonomy of decision-making in all questions relevant to the development of British society and politics had to be upheld.[35] It was for this reason too that shades of isolationism became visible in the fabric of British foreign policy.[36] To this isolationist pattern must be added

---

35. K. Hildebrand, this author and Karl Rohe have developed these ideas in a number of studies; cf. notes 5, 9, and Preface, notes 2, 8.

36. K. Hildebrand, '"British Interests" und "Pax Britannica"', *HZ*, 221 (1975), pp. 623–639; cf. G. Hollenberg, pp. 45f.

the German challenges[37] which cut across the thrust of British policy and reflected the shifts in the international balance of power of the 1930s. The political constellation which resulted from this and which is encapsulated in the armaments question makes it impossible to interpret the foreign policy of this period exclusively from the perspective of the domestic conditions of diplomacy. The 'hinge function' of armaments policy, which links domestic and foreign policy, has two corollaries: firstly, the constellation of forces inside Britain, the country's resources (in the widest sense of the word) and prevailing perspectives focusing on the question of armaments; and secondly the debates inside the government on whether or not to launch foreign policy initiatives along the lines of preventive diplomacy, as well as British reactions to acute conflict situations within the international system, revolving on a concern to limit damage both at home and abroad. Britain's freedom to develop autonomously was to be protected against unilateral pressure to adapt to power-shifts in the international economy as well as in world politics. Moreover, the government endeavoured to limit the repercussions and side-effects of German aggressiveness upon the British position within the international system and upon Britain's security partners.

Appeasement is hence not merely to be seen as a result of the effects which the 'hinge function of armaments policy' produced. It represents also a relentless attempt to make that hinge work in directions desirable for Britain and actively to promote the mutual interaction of domestic and foreign policy. Once again, then, the approach and the central perspective of this book may be summarised as follows. Once the militancy of the Nazi regime had caused German foreign policy to take an aggressive turn, forcing armaments to the top of the agenda in debates on the German challenge, other nations, and Britain in particular, were pressed into a conflict which successive British Governments had been hoping to avoid for reasons of domestic politics. The public manifestation of this policy of evasion had been the 'voluntary' arms limitation of the 1920s and the reluctance shown by Britain to rearm in 1931/33 and after 1935/36. As our analysis of 'economic appeasement' will show, London found it impossible to reproduce Nazi Germany's success in constituting the options and preferences determined by the state of British society and politics into topics for debate within German politics.[38]

37. G. Schmidt, 'Das Zusammenspiel . . .', in: K. Rohe, ed., (note 10).
38. Hoare (in 1934) and Neville Chamberlain (1938–1940) claimed there was a chance of

It is the purpose of this study to unravel the whole complex of problems at stake in appeasement and to provide a profile of the years 1930 to 1937. In this context we shall first have to investigate how and why Britain formed a space for manoeuvre in the actual 'crisis management' of 1938/40 which had been created by the policy of appeasement during 1930–37.

---

playing on the 'will to peace' of the 'common people' in Germany; others reminded decision-makers of Hitler's awareness of the incidences that combined to the 'Dolchstoß-Legende', and reports on reactions of the German people on troops marching in front of Hitler seemed to confirm the meaning of their 'peace strategy'. There is no doubt that such arguments served as alibis, but this must not blind us to the fact that policy was founded on these assumptions. The calculus of economic appeasers will be dealt with in the chapter 'Economic appeasement'.

I

Economic Appeasement

As has been mentioned in the Introduction, our interpretation of the policy of appeasement approaches the subject from the perspective of a political system which was shaped by the hinge function of armaments linking domestic and foreign policy. This interpretation constitutes a competing explanatory model to those analyses which focus on trade and finance. Like this book, such analyses also start from the structural conditions on which Britain's interest in the preservation of peace was founded. Britain's need for peace, so the argument continues, was linked with Britain's position as a trading nation and as the hub of a world-wide commercial network which would have been threatened by military conflict. Such a conflict would in turn have led in the long run to the British Empire losing its status as a great power.[1]

Since these explanatory models are supported by innumerable documents containing official and private statements, it has been easy to quote evidence from every period in British foreign policy to underline the economic aspect of Britain's peace efforts. Such interpretations can further assume that economic factors and aspects, on the one hand, and restrictive socio-economic conditions, on the other, played a central role in British politics and therefore also in her foreign relations. If the general view is added that British foreign policy in the 1930s was one of appeasement, it

---

1. G. Niedhart, 'Appeasement: Die britische Antwort auf die Krise des Weltreichs und des Internationalen Systems vor dem Zweiten Weltkrieg', *HZ*, 226 (1978), pp. 67–88; B.-J. Wendt, *Economic Appeasement*,; id, 'Großbritannien — Demokratie auf dem Prüfstand: Appeasement als Strategie des Status quo', in: E. Forndran et al., eds., *Innen- und Außenpolitik unter nationalsozialistischer Bedrohung. Determinanten internationaler Beziehungen in historischen Fallstudien*, Opladen 1977, pp. 11–31. — Eden, HofC., Parl. Deb., 14 March 1934, vol. 287, col. 390; Statement Relating to Defence, Cmd. 4827(1935), p. 2.

31

is easy to conclude that British foreign policy was guided by 'economic appeasement'. As C. MacDonald put it: 'Economic appeasement was not merely a diplomatic gambit on the part of Britain. Chamberlain always believed that a settlement with Germany was essential to British economic interests'.[2] MacDonald and others not only try to identify the elements 'essential to British economic interests' but also rely on statements relating to British foreign policy. Both combined, in their view, add up to 'economic appeasement'. To be sure, there is some validity in this view: trade with Germany would have guaranteed employment in a number of 'depressed areas' in Britain's export-orientated economy; British foreign policy[3] was searching for ways to reintegrate Germany into the 'Western' economy and did not wish to see it merged with the state-managed, 'Bolshevik' trade systems. But the crucial point is whether these tendencies worked in the same direction and whether they really shaped British policy towards Germany and Europe or whether they were checked and constrained by the opposition of the ministries in charge of the economy (Treasury, Board of Trade, Agriculture, etc.).

Furthermore, any interpretation favouring the notion of 'economic appeasement' must look into the following questions: (1) whether Neville Chamberlain in fact held the view that (political) conflicts could be solved by economic approaches and means; (2) whether Chamberlain (or equally British governments responsible for the turn towards 'economic nationalism' in Britain) was prepared and willing to negotiate economic settlements with Germany if that meant granting German products access to British (and overseas) markets, i.e. retreating from '1932' (import duties, 'Ottawa', etc.); (3) whether Chamberlain and his associates believed that the Third Reich would alter its 'national economy' with a view to help Britain's export industries out of economic distress by increasing their share of German markets and thus to improve Britain's balance of trade.

It is essential therefore to consider German and British politics at the time of the World Depression. In both cases, comparative military 'weakness' was counterbalanced by an interest in economic success. Germany felt that her 'weakness' prohibited the conclusion of treaties since these would acknowledge her dependence on the 'stronger' country. Conversely, until Germany had

2. C.A. MacDonald, 'Economic Appeasement and the German "Moderates" 1937–1939', *Past and Present*, 56 (1972), p. 105.

3. Eden's initiative in March–May 1937 is a case in point; see below.

regained her position as a 'strong' nation, the use of political and military power was likewise thought to be inadvisable:

> We shall first have to concentrate our political activity on economic questions, in order to avoid in all circumstances warlike complications which we cannot cope with at the present time . . . By means of a statement that the objectives of our policy are exclusively economic and financial we can succeed in breaking up the front that has now been formed against us out of concern about surprise actions by Germany.[4]

A second school of thought arrived at a negative view of economic appeasement because it took account of this situation as well as of Britain's renunciation of any counter-strategy to the development of Germany's economic power on the Continent.

In view of the general validity of these approaches, which constitute the frame of reference of interpretations of economic appeasement, it is not surprising that the concept has been so enlarged as to include literally everything that happened after 1933, or was rumoured to have occurred in Anglo-German economic relations. Despite the broad array of theses and building-bricks which make up the explanatory model, they give no answer to the question of what is economic appeasement in the strict sense of the word. Only the most popular versions and variants on offer are sketched below. Accordingly, economic appeasement has been interpreted as:

(1) The recognition of *Mitteleuropa* as a zone of German influence corresponding to Germany's dominance in the foreign and economic affairs of her neighbours;[5] it remains to be shown that this element was of varying importance to, and exercised different functions for, the economic appeasement strategies of individual interest groups and lobbies.

(2) The settlement of credit and payment transactions between the City and German importers of raw materials,[6] the inference in certain cases being that this occurred with the knowledge and consent of the British government: 'It is highly improbable that

4. Neurath, Meeting of German Ministers, 7 April 1933, DGFP, ser. C, vol. 1, p. 260.

5. MacDonald, *Moderates*, p. 111; Wendt, *Economic Appeasement*, pp. 418ff.; M. Gilbert, R. Gott, *The Appeasers*, London 1967[2], pp. 189ff., 220; H.I. Nelson, *Land and Power. British and Allied Policy on Germany's Frontiers 1916*–1919, London 1963, pp. 325ff.

6. P. Einzig, *In the Centre of Things*, London 1960; Einzig pressed his views in his articles in *Financial News* and by supplying information to Labour MPs, Boothby and supporters of Churchill. On the Compensation Brokers Ltd. (1936) see Wendt, *Economic Appeasement*, pp. 405ff.; correspondence between Tiarks/Piggott and Norman, Leith-Ross, November 1936, T 177–30.

any open credits have been granted even by the most pro-German of London firms . . . so long as loans, as opposed to those short-term commercial credits, are prohibited, it cannot be said that the City is providing money with which Germany can finance her rearmament programme. On the other hand, it is not true to say that no credits have been granted'.[7] Plans for such cooperation through the financing of raw material imports were submitted to the Board of Trade, the Treasury and the Foreign Office but were in fact usually put aside by the government agencies as 'impractical', as were proposals which can be seen as modified versions of proposals to solve the reparations problem in the 1920s put forward by cabinet ministers such as Amery and Churchill. They wanted Germany to share in the industrial development of parts of the Empire (Africa), in addition to the supply of valuable industrial goods which were to be set off as reparation payments along the lines of the Wiesbaden Agreement between France and Germany.

In the 1930s similar views were expressed: Germany was to be given access to sources of raw materials in return for such 'development aid'.[8] One can indeed take any sign of readiness to negotiate on raw materials, rather than using them as a political lever, as an indicator of economic appeasement policies. This seems all the more plausible in view of Germany's low stockpiles (in many cases only sufficient for two months), the vulnerability of her economy to export embargoes (e.g. by Russia and by Rumania in March 1936) and in view of the fact that in 1936–37 shortages of raw materials prevented industry from working at full capacity.

(3) A readiness to revise or correct the financial and economic strategies adopted between 1931 and 1932 which were known to have been disadvantageous to Germany:[9] this version was expressed in the formula aimed at reviving the triangular trade system. The interest of some Dominions (Canada and Australia) in such a solution ensured that this version had a lasting effect on the political processes determining British foreign policy.[10]

(4) Appeasing dictators with economic concessions at the ex-

---

7. Nigel Law to Sargent, 6 May 1936, C 3524/99/18, FO 371–19 932, p. 139f.: for details see T 160–573, F 13 460/011–012; FO 371–17 687, pp. 131ff.; FO 371–17 688, pp. 367ff.; FO 371–16 693, pp. 99ff.; FO 371–19 933, pp. 227f.

8. Piggott-Tennant/Lehnkering-Ribbentrop project, March 1935, C 1980/25/18, FO 371–18 822, pp. 117ff.; Leith-Ross rejected the ideas, id., p. 124; cf. Interdepartmental Committee, Report, 13 Oct. 1922, C 14394/201/18, FO 371–7506.

9. Vansittart, 'The World Situation and British Rearmament', 31 Dec. 1936, C 8898/4/18,§ 26; Pinsent to Foreign Office, FO 371–19 888, pp. 75ff.; cf. Wendt, *Economic Appeasement*, p. 60f.; see below, notes 85f.

pense of others[11] and a readiness to cede certain areas of trade to Germany: this readiness was connected with efforts to divert the pressure of German competition into specific areas, thus excluding German trade from those areas, the loss of which could be more harmful to British interests.[12] Such calculations also extended to armaments exports: 'If we bottle in even legitimate German activities, we may raise internal pressure [in Germany] to bursting point. The line of explosion would moreover be in our direction if we seem in German eyes to be responsible'.[13]

(5) A way of shielding economic recovery from the consequences of the World Depression[14] by emphasising London's willingness to negotiate with the Hitler regime, particularly in moments of crisis.

(6) An attempt to bring Germany back into a system of multilateral trade and bilateral exchange or to persuade her to liberalise her foreign economic policy with various offers or concessions because of her multiplying function within and for the world economy. Success would ease Britain's economic difficulties, in particular her balance of payments deficit.[15]

The gist of this proposition is that agreement with Germany was to create conditions to redress the balance of payments deficit and to protect British interests (the Treasury) by not expanding armament production at the expense of export production. Britain's readiness to avoid her economy being determined by an expanding armaments production for as long and as far as possible and, in view of this even to tolerate the import of armaments, led to precarious episodes in Anglo-German relations. Corresponding exploratory talks accompanied the government's toleration of raw materials imports essential to Germany's arms production by subsidiaries of British international companies operating in Germany (Dunlop, Mond-Nickel, Shell Oil Company, etc.): such operations were permitted with the proviso that they were conducted on the principle of short-term commercial credits or cash payments. The

---

10. Hall-Scheme: C 4758/99/18, FO 371–19 933, and in Jones-Mss., Class E, vol. 1, No. 10; see below § 8.-H. Butler to Foreign office. 17 July 1936, C 5197/99/18, FO 371–19 934, pp. 1ff., 5ff.. On inter-imperial trade relations see H.J. Richardson, *British Economic Foreign Policy*, London 1936, p. 124; Wendt, *Economic Appeasement*, pp. 32ff., 402ff.

11. Gilbert, Gott, *Appeasers*, ch. 13 'Czech Gold', pp. 209ff.; Einzig, *Centre*, pp. 186ff.

12. G.W. Rindell to Newton, 27 Nov. 1936, C 6731/99/18, FO 371–19 949.

13. Newton to Rindell, 24 Sept. 1936, C 6731/99/18, FO 371–19 949.

14. MacDonald, *Moderates*, pp. 106ff.; Wendt, *Economic Appeasement*, pp. 87ff., 449ff., 21, 27.

15. Wendt, *Economic Appeasement*, pp. 15, 377ff., 435; MacDonald, *Moderates*, pp. 105ff.

economic appeasers' opinion that their concrete proposals offered only slender prospects for effecting a change in the German political system will be studied in greater detail below; nevertheless, the links between economic appeasement and the armaments question were central to their activities.

(7) As an expedient course which the Western powers would have to take because of their economic need for peace, should the explanation given by Hitler, Schacht and the Foreign Ministry to Lloyd George, Lothian and Ward Price prove to be correct that Germany's 'weekend coups' were an escape from bottle-necks and social tensions.[16] The Western powers would at the very least have to indicate that other escape routes existed than risky but prestigious actions to the 'reasonable' forces within Germany.

(8) As a tactical preventative measure taken against the threat of an economic 'Rapallo':[17] 'what is a serious danger is the extent to which [Germany] is moving away from the economic system of Western Europe into an idiosyncrasy of attitude not unlike that of Russia ... Russia can supply so many of German needs ... a division might establish itself between two economic systems in Western and Eastern Europe. It is therefore of urgent importance to restore Germany to her normal place in the Western European system'.[18] In view of the fact that both the German and Russian economies complemented each other, which was stressed by both countries, the 'economic appeasers' estimated the danger of a formation of such an economic bloc as being particularly high should Britain and the British Empire revoke or drastically reduce the terms of the agreement on fixed exchange ratios with Germany. This variation was supplemented by the idea that Britain could participate in the Russian state trade market through cooperation with German business. In this way Britain would possibly find replacements for those markets which she had lost because of

16. The locus classicus is N. Chamberlain's statement in the Cabinet on 19 Febr. 1938; R.A.C. Parker, 'Ökonomie, Aufrüstung und Außenpolitik Großbritanniens vor 1939', in: H.A. Volkmann, F. Forstmeier, eds., *Wirtschaft und Rüstung am Vorabend des Zweiten Weltkriegs*, Düsseldorf 1975, pp. 266ff.; MacDonald, *Economic Appeasement*, p. 105; R.M. Meyers, *Britische Sicherheitspolitik 1934–1938*, Düsseldorf 1976, pp. 419ff.; cf. Eden—Memorandum, C.P. 42(36), debated in Committee on Germany, 17 Febr. 1936, Cab. 27–599.

17. Wigram-Sargent-Ashton-Gwatkin Memorandum, 'Britain, France and Germany', 21 Nov. 1935, see ch. I of German original; (Jebb-) Eden-Memorandum, The Economic Aspect of Foreign Policy, 28 May 1937, W 11034/5/50, FO 371–20 659; cf. Wendt, *Economic Appeasement*, pp. 437ff.; M. Gilbert, *The Roots of Appeasement*, London 1967, pp. 153ff.

18. (Jebb) Eden Memorandum, The Economic Aspects of Foreign Policy, 28 May 1937, W 11034/5/50, FO 371–20 659. On the connection between this perception of threat and the 'escalation theory' see below, notes 87ff.

trade barriers raised under the banner of economic nationalism.

(9) The readiness of captains of industry (a) to try bilateral direct methods, (b) to do this by referring to the payments and naval agreements and contrasting the usefulness of the high-level Schacht–Norman talks as the correct road with the futility of the diplomatic methods recommended by France, and (c) to voice sympathy for the attack by the National Socialist regime on the postwar structure, the 'Versailles System'. The conduct of these captains of industry is said to have demonstrated a pattern of behaviour which it was worth imitating and which the politicians understood and adopted. The successful method of economic diplomacy of 'direct contact with the right people on the German side at the right time' is said to be discernible in the view that supported taking up Hitler's offers as long as they were 'fresh'; that is to say, precisely in moments of crisis.[19] A decisive factor for the captains of industry was that the most important questions could never be negotiated in Geneva or in other international forums: on the contrary, Great Britain had to enter into direct talks with Germany over questions of mutual concern and, if necessary, to conclude bilateral agreements. This position is said to have impressed influential cabinet advisers (Jones, Hankey and Leith-Ross), but also to have been behind the secret contacts or behind the readiness of the 'Service Departments' to feel their way towards an armaments convention via an exchange of information.[20]

These various definitions of economic appeasement, whose plausibility in detail is incontestable, have been made part of an argument to the effect that certain commercial and financial circles which had many links with the German economy could have urged the British government to represent their interests *vis-à-vis* Germany. Moreover, particularly Wendt, Gilbert and Mac-Donald, apart from analysing the network of influence between the government and economic interests, have shown that government circles were taken by a view which makes it possible to subsume under 'economic appeasement' declarations of interest and private trade and financial relations encouraged or tolerated by the government. In this context, 'economic appeasement' amounts to the calculation that reaching economic compromises with Germany might be initiated with a hope to reduce domestic tensions inside the Third Reich and hence of an international

19. Lord Riverdale to Hankey, 9 March 1936, FO 371–19 891, pp. 238f.
20. See ch. I of German original, especially notes 182 and 338.

détente. They also took the view that the government (i.e. Neville Chamberlain) hoped that a welcome by-product of successful economic appeasement would be a revival of the British economy and a consolidation of its (party-) political position.[21]

What this interpretation fails to emphasize with equal clarity is that the maxim of exploiting the existing differences between the 'moderates' and the 'extremists' in Germany had been recognised and acted upon in different ways at different times. In all probability a stronger inclination existed at cabinet level by the late 1930s (i.e. under Chamberlain's government), 'to do all we could to encourage the "moderates"'[22] than prevailed at the beginning or around the middle of that decade. Britain's readiness to 'appease' with economic means was less pronounced at the time when big business still possessed a relative autonomy (at least according to the results of research into the power structure of the Third Reich) than after October 1936, when Schacht began to lose power.[23] This relative autonomy manifested itself in the then strong position of Schacht and his influence on foreign policy and rearmament via his foreign-trade policies and in particular his currency and raw materials policies.

However, the fact that the readiness for economic appeasement came at a time when it was less likely to find a response within the German power structure, is not the only objection to the predominant view in the literature on economic appeasement. The critique of interpretations of British foreign policy to be found in this literature has to be conducted at different levels and from several perspectives.

The definitions, motives and calculations of the economic appeasers cover a wide range of political events! Consequently, one could be forgiven for thinking that British foreign policy can only be described in terms of economic appeasement.[24] Several questions have to be asked, however:

21. Wendt, *Economic Appeasement*, pp. 420, 423, 526; MacDonald, *Moderates*, pp. 108, 112, 124.

22. Cabinet meeting 30 Nov. 1938, Cab. 57(38), Cab. 23–96; cf. D.N. Lammers, 'From Whitehall after Munich: The Foreign Office and the Future Course of British Policy', *HJ*, 16 (1973), pp. 831–856; C 15084/42/18, FO 371–21 659.

23. M. Cowling, *The Impact of Hitler*, Cambridge 1975, pp. 299f., 145ff.; Wendt, *Economic Appeasement*, pp. 548ff., 73ff.; on Schacht's position and the political power structure in the Third Reich: P. Hüttenberger, 'Nationalsozialistische Polykratie', *GG*, 2 (1976), pp. 432ff.; D. Petzina, 'Vierjahresplan und Rüstungspolitik', in: Forstmeier, Volkmann, eds., *Rüstung und Wirtschaft*, pp. 66ff., 72f.; H.E. Volkmann, id., pp. 104ff.

24. The following argument stresses the necessity to distinguish between economic appeasement as a label (in the sense of Max Webers 'ideal type') and the many events, actions and

(1) Was the British government prepared to pay the economic price which it would have had to pay as its contribution to a 'general settlement'; that is, could or would it make sacrifices in the area of economic policies which were a matter of internal dispute?

(2) The general trend of British policy after '1931' was to avoid anything which endangered the priorities of domestic (economic and social) policies or which engaged Great Britain in political conflict on the Continent. Did this not mean that 'official' British policy had to restrain itself in matters of foreign economic policy (outside the sterling bloc)?

(3) Has each element to which the concept of 'economic appeasement' refers the same common denominator so that we are presented with a consistent and plausible explanation when all the elements are put together?

(4) Should not the individual pieces of evidence be seen in the context in which they interact with one another? If seen in this context, it may emerge that they had other functions or meanings than if they were combined with explanatory reasons which themselves relate to a specific context.[25] A further question is whether support for a single specific objective (economic appeasement) can be seen as working towards the same end, although measures, ways and means of achieving this aim differ, or whether the disagreement over the choice of a suitable starting-point meant that a broad support for economic appeasement could only partially be mobilised. For example, did the pressure groups and lobbies which advocated moves towards détente because of the balance-of-payments situation also take the view promoted by others that Britain had to do 'something' to influence the struggle for power in Germany in favour of the moderates? One line of argument combines the first and second aspect and suggests that the power and success of economic appeasement can thereby be demonstrated.[26] Yet on closer inspection this was not really the case, because the first group merely envisaged advantages for

---

intentions, which occurred in Anglo-German economic relations before, during and after Hitler's seizure of power in 1933.

25. On the variety of meanings see M. Wight, 'The Balance of Power', in: H. Butterfield, M. Wight, eds., *Diplomatic Investigations*, Cambridge 1969, pp. 149ff.; E.B. Haas, 'The Balance of Power: Prescription, Concept or Propaganda', in: J.N. Rosenau, ed., *International Politics and Foreign Policy*, New York/London 1961, p. 318ff.

26. MacDonald, *Moderates*, correlates statements by 'economic appeasers' (Jebb, Ashton-Gwatkin) to views expressed by Leith-Ross and N. Chamberlain, but ignores the different

Britain and regarded foreign trade with Germany only as a side-show; that is, not centred on the question of how 'economic' links could restore 'normal' working agreements in politics. All this leads to the question as to how seriously this line of argument should be taken. Can aspects which are characteristic of one group of economic appeasers be added to those points of view important for another group or are these groups not opponents to all intents and purposes? Before the British government could begin an economic appeasement offensive, they had to decide what to offer; their choice was determined by the fact that concessions should not provoke any protest from those British pressure groups affected by those concessions. Nevertheless, they were supposed to offer Germany enough advantages to induce her to give serious consideration to the desired changes for her economic structure or of her basic political line concerning questions of war and peace. If the government chose to negotiate one of several proposals, it then had to ask itself whether the interests and intentions which influenced its decision were identical to, or at least compatible with, the motives and calculations of those who first put the proposal forward. The government also had to ask whether the choice of a specific option for diplomatic action also took the interests and calculations of those who had opted for a different negotiating agenda into account. Was it therefore certain that the supporters of economic appeasement approved all advances towards achieving a common goal, or did they make their support dependent on their own preferred strategy being adopted?

(5) Were initiatives in favour of economic appeasement which emanated either from economic interest groups or from trade-cycle forecasts and assessments of the economic situation coordinated with the advances made by representatives of specific economic appeasement strategies, entrenched within the political centre of things? Since different uses of power require different

---

conclusions drawn by the one and the other. In a similar manner, Wendt, *Economic Appeasement*, p. 431, quotes the Liberal opposition spokesman on foreign affairs, White, as pressing the Government to embrace 'economic appeasement' after the failure of political appeasement; but Wendt pays no regard to the massive criticism in White's speech of the economic foreign policy of the National governments. The criticism of the government's record and the policy of the government cannot be referred to as economic appeasement. In another instance, Wendt, *Appeasement 1938*, Frankfurt 1966, p. 139, defines economic appeasement as a response to a set of domestic problems and to structural changes in the 20th century, but then follows the line of thought which P. Einzig and Gilbert, Gott have introduced into the debate on economic appeasement.

sources of power, the transformation of 'economic' influence into 'political' assets and political opportunities is exactly the point that begs the question.

(6) Can the influence of economic appeasement strategies be traced back to links with specific economic interest groups or did 'political strategies' merely make use of economic factors on the assumption that economic questions alone were capable of providing starting-points for appeasement?[27] Are we perhaps looking at political groups which propagate economic policies but which cannot be characterised as being tied to vested economic interests? Did the economic concept of 'economic appeasement' prove to be an instrument with which political support groups could be organised into a rallying movement? Or was the course of events rather that different interest groups took and promoted economic appeasement as a frame of reference for their activities, but could not be convinced to pursue a goal-orientated policy in the sense of economic appeasement strategies?

The list of questions could be extended; it is, however, more important that we give the concept of 'economic appeasement' sharper contours. Its limitless use is something of a hindrance for analytical purposes. The following section will firstly attempt a preliminary definition of the concept and then proceed to look at three areas, at three levels: (a) The interrelation between selective economic data and political calculations in the context of a specific economic appeasement strategy; in this context the concrete proposals – the 'grand' and 'small' solutions – will be considered; (b) the direct connections between the economic situation, economic interests and the effects of economic appeasement; and (c) the third level will present evidence that the initiatives of the economic appeasers had to give way to those who preferred a 'political approach'. This means that the circumstances under which economic appeasement and the political approach were seen as alternatives[28] in the decision-making process will have to

27. The controversy between the champions of a political approach and the 'economic appeasers' forms section 9 of this chapter. For the British, political motives were dominant both in Germany's colonial claims and in Britain's stance in the question of raw materials.

28. See below, pp. 180ff. To give an example: Runciman, President of the Board of Trade, who had opposed Lloyd Georges 'knock out'-strategy 1916/18 and criticised the Treaty of Versailles, supported appeasement as a preventive diplomacy ('early move'-strategy) and acknowledged German claims to 'equal rights'; with a view to Britain's economic recovery and to Britain's place in world economics, he supported Chamberlain's, Weir's and Simon's 'limited liability'-views. For these and other reasons, 'appeasement' found favour with him. But he was

be given particular attention.

1. Preliminary Conceptual Remarks

The analysis of economic appeasement has to distinguish between the following areas:

(1) The intentions, and chances for the realisation, of the ideologies of different groups of influence ('action-related programs').

(2) The objective criteria which strategies of economic appeasement rely on or refer to.

(3) The key arguments indicating the direction of specific economic appeasement strategies.

The precondition for, and yard-stick of, economic appeasement is the intensity of economic interaction at an official level (government, central banks) and between leading organisations (Federation of British Industry, Reichsverband der Deutschen Industrie, Chambers of Commerce) and economic policy organisations, individual regions and industries. The extent of mutual dependence, of cooperation and competition, between economic groups in Britain and Germany may indeed be decisive when considering whether these groups were trying to create as organised groups a favourable climate in Anglo-German relations. However, this does not as yet say anything about whether their interventions pursued the same goals as those of, for example, Ashton-Gwatkin, Leith-Ross and other appeasers in the Foreign Office and the Treasury. It remains to be analysed whether or not the programmes developed by top officials contained similar economic and political expectations of a future compromise between Germany and Britain as

---

critical of and very concerned about the economic projects put forward by the Economic Section of the Foreign Office, by Piggott/Tennant (Lehnkering), Tiarks/Piggott, private bankers, etc. Runciman can be viewed as an economic appeaser only if economic appeasement is defined as an effort to sponsor or prolong Britain's economic recovery; in this case, it would be hard to identify anyone in the 1930s who did not qualify as an economic appeaser. Runciman's case demonstrates his ambivalance towards economic deals (does an arrangement favour Britain without harming or even facilitating Germany's position) and his proclivity to appeasement for political reasons ('guilt complex'; German legitimate grievances, etc.). We should remember that Britain in her crisis adopted economic measures which seriously affected the Brüning Government's room for maneouvre; the measures taken considered Britain's 'needs' and neglected Germany's and France's growing financial, economic and strategic apprehensions; Ch.W. Chappius, 'Anglo-German Relations 1929–1933: A Study of the Role of Great Britain in the Achievement of the Aims of German Foreign Policy', University of Notre Dame, Ph.D. 1966, pp. 238f.

the trade-offs promoted by those economic interest groups which were directly affected.[29]

Pressure applied by economic interest groups was, furthermore ambivalent; they could only be relied upon in a very limited way to act as a load-bearing pillar of economic appeasement policy. On the one hand, the Federation of British Industry, the Association of the Chambers of Commerce and export circles, amongst others, tried to obtain 'state help' to ward off German competition, particularly in phases when the balance of trade and/or payments pointed to a rapprochement with Germany (at least according to MacDonald and Wendt).[30] On the other hand, their recommendation to imitate German methods so as to achieve a symmetrical agreement between competing German and British industries belonged to the standard formulas used by the economic advisers to the government (Leith-Ross, Ashton-Gwatkin), who rejected threats or sanctions against Germany as unsuitable, even detrimental, and thus remained open for economic appeasement. In inter-ministerial discussions since the First World War it had been a matter of dispute as to whether an economically 'weak' but rearming Germany or an economically strong Germany presented the greater threat. Ashton-Gwatkin recommended constructive British measures to eliminate the economic causes of German aggressiveness; he saw these causes in Germany's 'have-not' status and thought to have identified an escape route in the opening-up of export outlets which could relieve the excess pressure: 'full economic recovering is therefore impossible with Germany in her

29. According to Wendt, *Economic Appeasement*, pp. 286f., 273ff., 190ff., 627, the British government had their views included in the Payments and Trade Agreements. The economic departments – Treasury, Board of Trade, Department of Overseas Trade – did not support the projects of Tennant, Piggott, Tiarks; cf. Nixon, 16 Jan. 1935, C 794/635/18, FO 371 – 18 869, pp. 102ff. On the other hand, the regions and branches which profited from the Trade and Payments Agreements founded 'pro-German' pressure groups; the Anglo-German Fellowship was a kind of 'thank you' act; E.W.D. Tennant, *True Account*, London 1957, pp. 178ff., 193ff.; Wendt, *Appeasement 1938*; H. Pickles, President of the British Wool Federation, *The Times*, 8 Jan. 1936; The German Trade Development Board (*The Times*, 1 April 1936, p. 11) and the Anglo-German Fellowship found favour with the coal export, cotton and wool trades, chemical industries and City banks.

30. The Federation of British Industries pressed for a cancellation of the Payments Agreement in late 1935, whilst the Foreign Office prepared the working agreement–initiative (Nov. 1935–March 1936); Ramsden (FBI) to Runciman (Board of Trade), 16 Dec. 1935 to 5 Febr. 1936, FO 371-19 917, pp. 117–119. In 1934, the FBI had criticized the government for the failure to apply the terms of the Act that established clearing offices towards Germany; FBI to Runciman, 21 Sept. 1934. The Board of Trade pointed to the benefits for British trade and claimed that the agreements guaranteed British interests. The Empire Industries Association, but the FBI, too, pressed the case of protectionism, and had no liking at all for the criticism of the economic appeasers (see below).

present state'; 'for a lean Germany we have ourselves to pay by loss of trade'.[31] Leith-Ross understood the formula in a similar way in as much as he thought that an economically weak Germany was more threatening to peace than a strong one.[32] His fears were based on the assumption that in an economically weak Germany the 'radicals' would be encouraged. However, another set of reasons was really decisive for him. He argued, both before the Nazi seizure of power[33] and in 1935–38, that a restrengthened Germany would be faced with demands from domestic forces, in particular from the trade unions, who would press for higher wages and improved social benefits; in this way they would move towards a British 'situation', and this in turn would lead to an increase in imports. The economic appeasement effects of Leith-Ross' recommendations, if that is what they might be called, arose from his view that the socio-economic factors at work in Germany were similar to those of the British socio-political system. This appraisal was based on the assumption that, because of its specific historically developed structures, German, just as British industry, would not flourish in times of high protective tariffs and that both systems could make full use of their capacities and achieve other economic aims only under 'free-trade conditions'. From Leith-Ross's point of view, the German problem had thus shifted to a political level: for him the solution to Germany's and hence to Europe's, problems lay in endeavours to achieve a 'political truce'; therefore this political approach had to precede offers of economic settlement.

It cannot be denied that those socio-economic groups with interests in Germany supported economic appeasement to a certain extent and also contributed to providing it with political substance. Commercial and financial relations, as it were, provided the British and German sides with indicators as to where bridge-building could begin.

The question was, however, whether bridge-building could succeed at all and whether diplomatic and/or economic negotiations could – metaphorically speaking – agree on the material and the load-bearing capacity of this bridge and the apportionment of the building costs. It was, furthermore, a question of whether the diplomats would thereby function as agents of interested parties or

---

31. Ashton-Gwatkin, 20 Febr. 1935, minute to C 1266/635/18, FO 371 – 18 869, p. 150.
32. On Leith-Ross see below, §8
33. Leith-Ross note on conversations with Flandin, Rueff, Dec. 1931/Jan. 1932, 10 Jan. 1932, C 273/29/62; see notes 437ff. of German original, ch. III, Economic Appeasement.

whether, because of the 'anormal' political frame of reference, they would be building the bridge – called 'economic appeasement' – using calculations other than those employed by 'businessmen'. British politicians and captains of industry knew that the German economy had lost its autonomy, at least in foreign affairs, to 'politics'. Did British business interests, albeit for different reasons, also become an 'object' in the politician's calculations when they devised economic appeasement strategies? In the changing climate of opinion concerning the causes and future effects of certain transformations within the world economy or world politics, officials and politicians disposed of the supposed interests of economic groups in such a way that the respective programme for economic appeasement was capable of making coalitions or accommodating other officials, who favoured different approaches and instruments, in order to remain on the 'winning side'. But this part of politics neither controlled nor shaped the 'autonomous' wielding of economic power by economic interests.

In moving towards a definition, my proposition is to reserve the term 'appeasement' to evaluations which comply with the following set of criteria: (1) specific actions resulting from the process of competing for overall political responsibility; and (2) attempts to influence and shape the government's stance on overall relations with Germany. Thus 'economic appeasement' does not exhaust itself in the articulation of the interests of different groups who possessed or recommended economic links with Germany. Whilst the attempts by individual City bankers, by Bradford mill owners, and so on, to lobby the government in London as well as German partners help to illustrate Anglo-German economic relations, even the sum total of such networks of interest cannot be described as economic appeasement policy. It is also insufficiently defined simply by adding the measures and considerations of (foreign) policy decision-makers to the effects of direct business transactions, important as they are for the total picture.[34]

The politicians' measures or considerations, originating from prognostications about the economy, e.g. an observation of fluctuations in the British balance of payments, aimed at achieving

---

34. MacDonald, *Economic Appeasement*, pp. 106, 108; Wendt, *Economic Appeasement*, pp. 305ff., 561ff.; id., *Appeasement 1938*, pp. 14, 90f. The Board of Trade, the Treasury, the Department of Overseas Trade, the Ministry of Agriculture regarded 'protectionist' interests as their constituency. Wendt (*Economic Appeasement*, pp. 250ff., 270ff.; *Appeasement 1938*, pp. 57ff.) refers to these policy constraints, but does not reflect on the consequences for *economic* appeasement.

'peace' on the economic and currency front and were, therefore, at pains to remove political obstacles by means of negotiations. In these instances, an interest in stabilising Britain's balance of payments was paramount, whereas questions of which measures would lead to an easing of the economic and political situation in Germany were pushed into the background. In interdepartmental committees, which met to examine the set of proposals for economic appeasement drawn up mainly within the Foreign Office, the emphasis shifted from concessions which might possibly help the (internationally orientated) 'moderates' in the Third Reich in their positional warfare against the 'autarkists'; it focused instead on demands which the German side was to meet to improve the economic–financial situation of Britain. If we relate economic appeasement to both groups everything happening in the field of Anglo-German economic relations may be classified as economic appeasement (with the exception of those areas in which the relationship was predominantly competitive and supported by state interventionism). Arguing on these lines has, of course, some merit insofar as economic factors were the linch-pin of the argument for both groups and insofar as both aimed at calming the political atmosphere. However, such an interpretation of economic appeasement fails to distinguish between events which were, as indicated above, intended directly to favour the British economy and those which were to influence the politico-economic power structure in Germany in favour of the 'peace party'.

Since analytical definitions should not be contradictory and a frame of reference should comply with the principle of clarity, it is expedient to limit the concept of 'economic appeasement' to certain more specific types of 'political' interest calculations which operated with economic variables. Whereas all forms of appeasement necessarily involve intentions or attempts to influence the political conduct of the other side, and all such approaches rested in turn on the assumption that a positive response from Germany was still in the offing, economic appeasement relies on economic measures for producing the desired political change, because it starts from the assumption that a 'behavioural disorder' can be explained by economic causes. But these effects on the power structure cannot, in general, be expected from 'normal' trade relations, even if the latter continued after '1933' in spite of the deterioration of political conditions. Economic appeasement must, therefore, link 'economic' interests with politically designed transactions and thus go beyond specific economic relations.

The economic appeasers did not expect improvements in the balance of trade alone to be sufficient to deal with political danger-spots. Rather they reasoned that an extension of economic relations between both countries would lay the foundation for a gradual intensification of interactions. Thus they hoped to create a counterbalance to the dangers posed by ideological conflict and rearmament; they feared that if Britain did not implement 'economic appeasement', confrontational patterns and values would dominate relations and drive both sides into conflict; that is, war. The economic appeasement strategy indeed contained the pedagogic appeal to create or to maintain a constellation of interests and support groups which would retain a structure of influence powerful enough to guarantee a minimum standard of social and political behaviour in Germany. This appeal was aimed first and foremost at those groups currently or formerly interested in Anglo-German business. The strategies of the economic appeasers attempted, on the one hand, to profit from the fact that economic interest groups, keen to trade with Germany, claimed that a renunciation of exchange relations would not only damage Germany but Britain as well. On the other hand, this strategy demanded that these 'interests' should conduct themselves in a political way; that is, that they must organise and establish themselves as a counterbalance to other influences – for example to the protectionists – if they wanted to maintain trading opportunities with German partners, who were seen as the 'enemy' by others within the British economic system. If these trading and financial interests played a 'political role' in accordance with economic appeasement strategy, then economic interaction between Germany and Britain would be promoted in such a way that relations would develop their own dynamic; it would thus stabilise peace by providing a counterbalance to the confrontational patterns which would arise from the escalation of ideological conflicts in the wake of the arms race.

The priorities and orientations of economic appeasement strategies varied according to circumstances; it also depended on the reading of the writing on the wall. As far as the interest groups were concerned, the proposals arose from their awareness of acute balance of payments problems or of the problems of individual industries and regions interested in trade with Germany.[35]

35. Tennant and other founders of the Anglo-German Fellowship calculated that economic links would 'moderate' German foreign policy; they were more lenient towards Germany's political claims than any of the 'economic appeasers' (incl. Lothian and Jones). Members of the

Although the economic appeasement strategies of the politicians tried to capitalise on this, their proposals resulted from their analysis[36] of the causes of these 'problems' and, above all, from their predictions of the consequences both for the German and British body politic if the prescriptions of economic appeasement were not applied. The principal difference between these two positions is that the first concept concentrates on the (desired) German contribution to the solution of British problems, whereas the second hoped that British protection would enable moderate circles in Germany to improve economic conditions and thus undermine the justifications for control of the German economy by the state.

It would be an a-historic approach simply to relate the concept of economic appeasement, on the one hand, to concrete economic relations and their economic consequences and, on the other hand, to the political hopes attached to them. The explanatory model sketched so far could just as easily be used to explain Anglo-German relations before 1914 as those of the 1920s and 1930s. To be sure, there are continuities and they can be, and are being, used to challenge simplifying polemical labels.[37] Any interpretation of economic appeasement must, however, consider the change of the terms of debate within Britain resulting from the transition to 'protectionism' in 1931–33; that is, it must explain the configuration of traditional and newly developing vested interests in the disputes over ways to solve Britain's economic problems and how to react to the different turn of events resulting from the Great Depression in Britain and Germany. In Britain recovery measures and the finance of armaments had first charge on policy

---

Anglo—German Fellowship, e.g. Beharrell (FBI), Leverhulme, D'Arcy Cooper, Courtauld, were called upon to form an advisory committee to N. Chamberlain on supply and production under the rearmament programme in the aftermath of 'Munich'.

36. The economic appeasers, as well as Leith-Ross and the FBI, regarded talks between industrialists as a chance to improve Anglo-German relations. There were a number of suggestions from both sides to start discussions and negotiations on market sharing agreements; eg. Waley (Treasury) to Wigram/FO, 26 April 1935, C 3485/25/18; 4 May 1935, C 3722/25/18, FO 371–18 822. A memorandum from the British banks (July 1936) argued for 'conciliation' instead of conflict, advocated 'piecemeal'–procedures, and the maintenance of strength and efficiency; the authors assumed that the 'Nazi moderates' did share their preferences, i.e. free trade and arms limitation; German Foreign Ministry Archives, 5481 H.

37. Wendt, 'Der blockierte Dialog', *MGM*, 17 (1975), pp. 201ff., and G. Niedhart, *Großbritannien und die Sowjetunion 1934–1939. Studien zur britischen Politik der Friedenssicherung zwischen den beiden Weltkriegen*, München 1972, pp. 15ff., demolish the interpretations of M. George, *The Warped Vision. British Foreign Policy 1933–39*, Pittsburgh 1965; A. Rothstein, *The Munich Conspiracy*, London 1958, and similar studies which reduce 'appeasement' to sheer anti-bolshevism.

commitments; in Germany the priority given to rearmament, combined with employment programmes and the acceptance of deficits, presented a formidable threat to world peace. An interpretation of economic appeasement has, therefore, to broaden its scope and analyse the socio-political motives behind British efforts to obtain a general settlement with the Third Reich.[38] In this respect one has to differentiate between groups of appeasers within government circles: Neville Chamberlain, Simon, Weir, Leith-Ross, Inskip, Kingsley Wood, Brown and Runciman wanted to implement Britain's rearmament without a 'dislocation of industries, inflation and social unrest', which they saw 'as a threat to the whole social order';[39] with this aim in mind they were prepared to offer colonial, political or economic concessions in exchange for an agreement on arms limitations. The second group wanted their socio-political motives behind economic appeasement to be complemented and insisted that it should also cover domestic appeasement. This group, with its leanings towards 'centre-left movements', argued and postulated that a 'social policy' which corrected the hardships of a liberal-capitalist economic and political system was a prerequisite to any strategy aiming at peace-keeping and maintaining or restoring the international economy. Their foreign policy was motivated by a desire to free world trade as much as possible from restrictions experienced since the First World War and particularly since the Great Depression: 'The real programme of recovery must cover international peace and the restoration of international trade as well as industrial reconstruction at home.'[40] For them, liberal societies had to salvage useful aspects of state interventionist activities designed to alleviate *domestic* social distress. But the accommodation with the spirit favouring the growth of national welfare policies at home was at the same time regarded as an obligation to infuse '*international*' norms into international affairs; that is, spawn international cooperation and reinforce international regimes as barriers to the states' take over of the whole range of international relations. In other words, the acknowledgement of state interventionism in domestic 'welfare' affairs was intertwined with an appeal (and a warning) to push for the (re)cre-

38. Wendt, *Economic Appeasement*,; R.P. Shay, *British Rearmament in the Thirties. Politics and Profits*, Princeton 1977; K. Robbins, *Munich 1938*, London 1968, have regard to the 'societal' factors in British foreign policy.

39. See ch. II: 'Political system', §§1 and 6.

40. Lothian to Lloyd George, 20 Dec. 1934 (referring to Lloyd George's Conquering Prosperity programme), GD 40–17, vol. 283, p. 360.

ation of liberal-international elements in world politics and in the international economy.

We may generalise that representatives of economic interests seldom agree with the socio-political and socio-cultural motives imputed to them by politicians, journalists and social scientists. It therefore follows that an analysis of economic appeasement policies has the task of examining firstly whether attempts at economic appeasement were of relevance to an economic issue area and whether economic interests were behind those initiatives which emerged in the context of economic appeasement strategies. Secondly, the analysis has to establish how, if it existed at all, the link between the two aspects came into being. The 'theoretical', structural framework of economic appeasement strategies must consider economic forecasts and the experience of economic relations between associations, specific industries, companies, and so on; however, the linch-pin of the interpretation would seem to lie in the socio-political area.[41] The most consistent economic appeasement strategy took into account explanations of structural changes of the state as well as changes in the relationship between state and economy, overshadowed by a crisis in which economic nationalism had asserted itself. The advocates of this specific strategy watched and judged developments after the First World War, especially after the World Depression – which were experienced as a self-fulfilling prophecy – from the vantage-point of a liberalism 'willing to learn'. Their economic appeasement strategy would be misunderstood if one overemphasised either the 'appeasing-of-the-dictators' component or if one relied too strongly on the influence and continuity of specific economic interests and of contacts that were conducted after '1933' at various levels.[42] The economic appeasers adhered to a concept of a 'free(er)' world economy and in this sense pursued economic interests. They assumed that Britain and the US, as leading industrial nations, depended firstly on the export of their products and on the import of raw materials. Secondly – and this is in some ways linked with the first point – since both states were capitalist economies, investment and reproduction opportunities had to be

41. The initiatives in 1936/37 were based on the improved conditions in world trade and on the importance of the standard of living debate; with Britain turning to 'real' rearmament and facing the problems of a defense loan, the economic appeasers attempted to turn this situation to their advantage. See below on the Bruce-Butler-McDougall project and the economic appeasers' interest in the Leith-Ross–Schacht talks.

42. See below, pp. 165ff. (on Leith-Ross).

found. This was why they advocated a world (economic) order where other states refrained from 'artificially' ('politically') restricting trade and capital transactions and where states hoped to maintain certain living standards. The concept bears similitudes to the 'open door' policy of C. Hull, and this explains why Lothian for one – recognising the common interests and ideologies – wanted to promote Anglo-American cooperation.[43]

A look at the chronology of economic appeasement initiatives helps to clarify the analytical framework further. The fundamental fact remains that the peak of economic appeasement initiatives did not occur in the recession (from the autumn of 1937) but at the beginning of the renewed expansion of world trade (1936–37). Indeed, Leith-Ross and the economic appeasers at the Foreign Office saw the upturn in the economy in the summer of 1936 as a starting point; their jointly elaborated views which were steered through an interdepartmental committee on trade policy, were considered by the Cabinet Committee in June 1937. However, the 'Roosevelt depression' blocked the implementation of this 'programme' from the autumn of 1937.[44] Alongside the upturn in world trade, the social policy theme of 'living standards' was, the main focus of deliberations at that time.[45]

The chronology of economic appeasement also shows that efforts to relax economic tensions intensified in the aftermath of the crisis of March 1936. They were made with a view to preventing Germany from using the tactical success of a political breakthrough exclusively for building up *Mitteleuropa* as a spring-board for ambitions of world domination, whilst pursuing at the same time the consolidation of her military sovereignty and sealing off her western front. For the economic appeasers it was a matter of Britain offering German leaders alternatives to the concept of a 'closed economy' based on rearmament, and of a 'Fortress Europe'; that is, a repetition of the violent solution implemented in 1918 at Brest Litowsk. Only economic appeasement, they believed, could prevent a Second World War. The steps which they wanted to be taken along this path were, in some respects, also indicative of

43. Lothian to Jones, 15 Febr. 1928, GD 40–17, vol. 228. p. 288; Hull–Lindsay conversation, 21 July 1936, BT 11–589. For details, see ch. I, notes 401ff. of German original. The ambivalences of Anglo-American relations are clearly demonstrated in D. Reynolds' study, *The Creation of the Anglo-American Alliance 1937–1941*, London 1981.

44. See below, pp. 159ff.

45. On the activities of the Economic and Financial Organization of the League of Nations see M.D. Dubin, 'Transgovernmental processes in the League of Nations', IO, vol. 37 (1983), pp. 469–493.

what they wanted to be done in Britain. Ultimately, everything pointed in the same direction: reintegration into a 'free' world, based on a division of labour. For them economic appeasement consisted of assistance to Germany at each stage of their plan. This plan asked for the dismantling of trade barriers, for changes to their respective currency rates, for the abolition of foreign-exchange controls, and so on. The analysis of these stages will, however, show that economic interests in Britain, to whom a definite role had been ascribed in this scenario, did not want to play their role. It is also doubtful whether the economic appeasers, who introduced particular concepts into the governmental decision-making process, in any way sought to test or improve the chances of carrying their proposals through by resorting to prior consultation with economic interest groups concerned.[46] The fate of their initiatives in governmental departments dealing with economic matters will be dealt with below.

Apart from basing a definition of economic appeasement on chronological indicators, it has to establish the general context in which the strategy and its advocates were placed. In the continuing debate on British foreign policy in the 1930s, economic appeasement saw itself as an alternative programme to the Anglo-French defence alliance, which demanded that rearmament should be guided by the requirements of a defensive community. Economic appeasement by contrast, aimed to maintain, at least temporarily, a peacetime economy. The offer of economic cooperation was taken to be the only remaining choice to sound out Germany's attitude, once she had succeeded in disregarding the economic and military restrictions of the Treaty of Versailles. Since politicians in Britain accepted as a matter of fact that the country was unable to prevent a revision of the territorial status quo by Germany, but did not necessarily want to encourage territorial revision, 'economic appeasement' was the only option available. In a situation where an economic switch in the direction of a war economy was taking place in Germany (Four-Year Plan), the offer of world-wide economic cooperation was regarded as the one chance to keep the door open for negotiating an arms limita-

---

46. F. Ashton-Gwatkin, a member of the British negotiating 'team' on the Payments and Trade Agreements, was of course familiar with commercial and financial interests; he established contacts with A.G. Glenday, Chief Economic Adviser to the FBI. Nonetheless, in an interview (Nov. 1965) Ashton-Gwatkin stressed that he based his memoranda on his study and reading on British economic history, reports and the press, and that he went to the Board of Trade for information rather than getting in touch with the interests concerned.

tion agreement. This would have created a situation in which the other powers, particularly Britain, could have footed their rearmament bill in a more flexible way rather than using up financial reserves by entering an arms race with Germany. Exactly how this measure of flexibility could be attained was the central theme of economic appeasement strategies.

If we try to summarise the line of argument so far, these are the corner-stones of economic appeasement as an analytical framework:

(1) On the strength of Britain's economic interdependence with Germany – in terms of re-exports, of the role of Germany in British business on the Continent and in Russia, of the tripartite trading system Germany/United Kingdom/British empire, of the integrated structure of international companies, and of exchange relations between specific German and British industries, and regions, and so on – she was interested in reviving an international economic system in which London functioned as the banker and broker of the world and in which Anglo-German economic relations played a central role. Economic appeasement strategies thus referred to conditions which had been changed considerably by the First World War and the Great Depression,[47] and it is quite clear that they reflect a desire to restore pre-1929 conditions in the sense of a return to the linkage between the Dawes Plan and the Locarno System.[48]

(2) In order to identify the groups which advocated economic appeasement within the circle of power élites in the decision-making process, the following arguments characteristic of the strategy should be used as orientation points. Firstly, European economic recovery is said to be a prerequisite of, or at the very least an adjunct to, rebuilding the competitiveness of Britain's industry and finance: the aim is to re-establish the City as the financial centre of world trade, to return to normal and traditional channels of trade and to renew conditions within the world econ-

47. Lothian, 'The Roots of our present discontent', *The Round Table*, March 1936, pp. 229–238.

48. N. Chamberlain's statement in the House of Commons, 14 March 1933, which marked the Dawes–Locarno epoch as a point of reference for British foreign policy, was quoted by economic appeasers in order to remind the Government to pursue a sound foreign economic policy; see below note 221. Hoare's speech in Geneva in Sept. 1936 offered the economic appeasers another platform and they charged the Government to pick up the threads; the Morton plan (TH. Jones, *Diary with Letters, 1931–1950*, London 1954, pp. 220f.), the Bruce/McDougall and the Hall schemes and Lothian's 'diplomacy' were attempts to exploit Hoare's Geneva speech; see below notes 282, 286.

omy where Britain's service industries (banks, shipping) could once again be earners of income. In terms of politics, this liberal restoration is seen to compete with the imperial economic policy of Conservatives as well as with aims championed by Labour and the Keynesians, with the last two seeking to attain steady growth by stimulating the domestic economy and by increasing mass purchasing power or with the help of a public works programme.[49] Although they were willing to agree to modify the free-trade system in the direction of the creation of a low-tariff area,[50] the economic appeasers drew a clear line at the notion of imperial tariff unions. For example, Lothian and Ashton-Gwatkin both adhered to a '4-to-5-worlds' doctrine,[51] but at the same time demanded a proper free-trade area and not – as 'Ottawa' had stipulated – agreements between protectionist governments which not only excluded third parties but also inhibited the trade between participants.[52] 'Imperial preference' to their minds had not meant tariff reductions, but tariff increases for third states and very minor preferences for the partners of the Ottawa Agreements. This system therefore preserved old structures and gave 'politics' precedence over 'economics'.

Secondly, because of Germany's central position in economic relations of many countries in general and the repercussions of Germany's withdrawal as a customer for reasons of insolvency in particular, European recovery would only be achieved if Britain supported attempts to facilitate Germany's access to raw materials through credits, through political assistance, and so on. The intention behind this was that German politics should no longer be in a position to advance a 'legitimate' grievance, and then to claim that

49. Lothian to Lord Meston, 11 March 1936, GD 40–17, vol. 310; Lothian to Lloyd George, 11 Jan. 1935, GD 40–17, vol. 293; Lothian, Socialism and Peace, Speech at National Liberal Federation Convention 1934, GD 40–17, vol. 439; Lothian, Liberal Policy, 7 Sept. 1933, published in March 1934, Liberal Party programme, GD 40–17, vol. 147; Lothian to Hirst, July 1937, GD 40–17, vol. 347.

50. Lothian, 19 Febr. 1933, Observer (this article summarises the views which he presented in a memorandum to Baldwin, Chamberlain, Simon, Hankey, W. Fisher, Vansittart, on return from a visit to the U.S.A.); Lothian, The American Debt Negotiation, 16/17 Febr. 1933, GD 40–17, vol. 200, combines criticism of 'Ottawa' with an attack on protectionism.

51. Lothian to Buell (Foreign Policy Association), 28 May 1930, 'The Empire and Free Trade', GD 40–17, vol. 431, pp. 147–150; Lothian to Hirst, July 1937, GD 40–17, vol. 347.

52. In fairness to the MacDonald–Baldwin cabinets it must be stressed that London aimed at a 'lower tariff' union; the British delegation and the Cabinet accepted the terms of debate which emerged in the Ottawa negotiations. R.N. Kottmann, *Reciprocity and the North Atlantic Triangle, 1932–1938*, Ithaca 1968; R.C. Snyder, 'Commercial Policy as Reflected in Treaties from 1931 to 1939', *AER*, 30 (1940), pp. 787–802; A.A. Stein, 'The hegemon's dilemma: Great Britain, the United States, and the international economic order', *IO*, 38 (1984), pp. 355–386.

Germany had no alternative but to use force in order to get her share of the world's resources. The fact that, despite the intervention of the US, Germany remained undefeated on the Eastern Front in the First World War and that she had sought to secure an autarkic raw-materials empire in the Treaties of Brest Litowsk and Bucarest, was seen as a warning by the economic appeasers[53] from which they concluded that Britain (as the centre of the Empire–Commonwealth) and the US must allow Germany – at least in principle – to share in their advantages in raw materials in order to remove, or at least to weaken, the economic causes of war; that is, the German *Drang nach Osten*.[54]

Thirdly, Britain had to regain the initiative in international politics to create conditions in which a second phase of recovery could succeed; the forecasts of economic development emphasised the need to expand exports within the context of an expanding world trade.

Fourthly, British politics should act in accordance with its own decisions to the effect that Britain could not affect developments in the arena of European (power) politics since she did not want to take on any new commitments;[55] hence the only means of satisfying her peace needs lay in the economic field.

Finally, the development of the German economy in the direction of autarky was the most dangerous threat to world peace; economic appeasement was to break this vicious circle.

Within the circle of decision-makers, elements of this line of argument were chiefly employed by the staff of the Economic Section at the Foreign Office.[56] They arranged their decisive points of view under the following headings:
– Conditions of peace in international affairs.
– Conditions of peaceful change in domestic politics.
– Conditions for 'working agreements' in accordance with interna-

53. J.L. Garvin, *The Economic Foundations of Peace*, London 1919, had a renaissance in the 1930s; in his editorials, Garvin returned to his arguments (*The Observer*).
54. See below, §§7 and 8 of this ch. For Lothian, 'political truce' and 'economic disarmament' formed a unit; however, in his talks in Berlin he emphasised the political-psychological aspects, whilst in his meetings with Canadian and U.S. members of the administration and their advisors he pointed to the economic aspects of international relations. As a representative of 'liberal England' and in this manner a partner to C. Hull and Mackenzie King, Lothian regarded his diplomatic missions as a contribution to the restoration of the North Atlantic Triangle, which — from his point of view — was a prerequisite of a defense community of the western (Anglo-Saxon) democracies.
55. Leeper, 26 June 1936, minute to Hall-Scheme, FO 371–19 931; Eden added 'I agree' to the note of the head of the information department of the FO.
56. D.G. Boadle, 'The Formation of the Foreign Office Economic Relations Section, 1930–1937', *HJ*, 20 (1977), pp. 919–936.

tional interdependencies.

The strategy of economic appeasement is a mixture of different policies arising from distinct but compatible proposals derived from the analyses of these different topics.

The main features of their strategy were already fixed before the National Socialists seized power in Gemany. The proposals were first and foremost aimed at increasing the efficiency of British foreign policy by improving the coordination of economic and political interests and views in the British decision-making process. The setting up of a 'general staff' – of a 'politico-economic intelligence' centre at the Foreign Office – was to provide the institutional framework for such coordination.[57] The Economic Section was eventually set up, after several attempts, in 1930–31, when the dominance of economic questions in international politics brought home the necessity for international coordination and was stimulated by virtue of the fact that German foreign policy adopted similar procedures.[58] The Economic (Intelligence) Section was not given the chance, however, to advise the foreign secretary on important questions during the World Depression[59] of 1930–33 and later. In any case, the strategies which the Economic Section of the Foreign Office wished to contribute to foreign policy decision-making were outlined prior to the setting-up of the department and remained the point of reference for opinions provided by the Economic Section in the day-to-day business of the 1930s.[60]

The first significant application of their strategies was proposed by the economic appeasers in 1931 and 1932 when nationalist tendencies were permeating British economic politics. The memorandum 'Changing Conditions of British Foreign Policy', pre-

57. V. Wellesley, A Proposal for the Establishment of a Politico-Economic Intelligence Department in the Foreign Office, 1 Dec. 1930, W 2306/441/50, FO 371–15 671, esp. pp. 29ff. During the First World War, Wellesley had pressed similar views; the Department of Overseas Trade did not realise his proposals.

58. Wellesley, minute, 8 May 1931, FO 800–283, p. 329; Wellesley regarded Ritter's section in the German Foreign Office as an efficient instrument for the merging of economics and foreign policy; Britain's unawareness of the Zollunionprojekt in 1931 caused Wellesley to urge a decision on his proposal.

59. The Bank of England and the Treasury disputed the right of 'laymen' in the Foreign Office to any say in the formulation of British foreign economic policy, and in fact the FO was denied an influence in the decision in September 1931 and in 'Ottawa'. Dalton (in the Foreign Office) and the Board of Trade wanted to limit the responsibilities of that section if it had to be established; A. Henderson to MacDonald, 13 and 20 March 1931, FO 371–15 671.

60. Ashton-Gwatkin to Leith-Ross, 10 March 1938, FO 371–21 701; Ashton-Gwatkin, Economic Survey, W 6928/1195/20, FO 371–18 497, pp. 306–376 A, is based on the ideas presented in the Wellesley–Memorandum, 1 Dec. 1930 (see note 57).

pared by Sargent and Ashton-Gwatkin[61] on the instruction of the foreign secretary, Reading, and presented on the agenda of the cabinet on 2 December 1931, warned that a policy which concentrated on Britain, the Empire and Commonwealth would weaken Britain's negotiating power, separate Britain from Europe and reduce opportunities for exerting economic leverage. As an alternative they advocated that the tariff be applied as a diplomatic weapon in a different – more 'appropriate' – manner. Since this economic issue was thought to be of decisive importance for British foreign policy as a whole, the government should not simply evaluate the tariff question from the domestic and inter-imperial standpoint, but rather should instrumentalise the tariff question with a view to forcing the hand of adversaries and reluctant powers to consent to a policy of international cooperation rather than one of 'beggar-my-neighbour'. The stabilisation of sterling as the key currency and the threat of adopting protective tariffs was to effect an 'all-in settlement'; that is, an appropriate solution to the complex politico-economic questions of reparations, disarmament, security and the Great Depression:

> A high protective tariff, combined with Empire preference, implies a measure of dissociation from Europe, a corresponding diminution of our influence over European affairs and possibly a growth of economic antagonism . . . In negotiation an element of the unknown is of great value, and the knowledge that we have the tariff power . . . will . . . incline the recalcitrant nations of the continent, and even perhaps, the United States, to listen to our views on world recovery. To our foreign policy, therefore, this tariff question is all important.[62]

This 'Sargent Chain' has already been referred to and interpreted as a key to an understanding of economic appeasement.[63] It is, however, necessary to add two points if the significance of economic appeasement within the context of British foreign policy is to be assessed:

(1) There was always – within the Foreign Office and in any case at cabinet level – an influential official and/or minister who put

---

61. Sargent–Memorandum, 26 Nov. 1931, W 12 949/12 949/198; 2 Dec. 1931, Cab. 23–69
62. Ibid. Ashton-Gwatkin's review, presented to Leith-Ross, 10 March 1938, FO 371–21 701, stresses the defeat in 1931/32 and its consequences.
63. M. Gilbert, *Roots*, pp. 130ff. coined the phrase 'Sargent chain'. The 1931 memorandum and (Jebb) Eden's 'Economics and Foreign Policy', 17 March 1937, sent to N. Chamberlain, W 6363/5/50, FO 371–21 215, are the main products of the 'general staff' – work of the Economic Section and/or its members.

forward the opposite of this 'economic' perception of British foreign policy.[64] In 1931 this official was Vansittart. In his memorandum 'The United Kingdom and Europe', he called attention to the question of disarmament and with his model of a political solution stole the march on the economic strategies.[65] Wellesley vainly lamented the folly of British politicians who favoured negotiations on disarmament just when the financial, monetary, commercial international systems on which so much of Britain's way of life depended were in disarray. The juxtaposition of the economic appeasement approach against the political approach remained essentially intact throughout the 1930s.[66]

(2) The insistence of the economic appeasers that the causes of economic nationalism had to be overcome to prevent the 'crisis' from spreading to the entire political sphere also implied that they would have liked to have seen the recommended practice of international cooperation in the economic arena to be applied to international relations in general. This programme of an 'all-in settlement' included the following prescriptions on economic management which were derived from their view of international planning:[67]

- Agreements on currency stabilisation;
- Arrangements for an international system of granting stand-by credits in the event of balance of payments deficits;
- An international quota system for the production and distribution of finished goods.[68]

64. Vansittart, 15 Dec. 1931, revised C.P. 4(32), 1 Jan. 1932.

65. Vansittart and Selby had discovered the 'Old Adam' in German foreign policy, i.e. the appropriateness of Eyre Crowe's magisterial memorandum of 1 Jan. 1907; they judged developments in Europe from the perspective of nationalist revival and derived their strategy of 'political approach' from this assessment.

66. On the 'economic disarmament' and 'tariff truce' – schemes of 1927 and 1929–32 see notes 50 and 65 of German original.

67. Lothian, Jones and L. Curtis urged the formation of an economic study group, within the Royal Institute of Internatinal Affairs, with a view to the integration of international economics into the research agenda of the RIIA; the experience of 'Dawes' and Locarno helped to shape the idea; Garfield's Institute of International Politics in Williamstown, which launched the study of international planning, served as a model. Lothian–Jones correspondence, June 1925, Jones-Mss, Class E, vol. 7, no. 48, and Class W, vol. 13, nos. 66/67; Curtis to Jones, 20 August 1922, Jones-Mss, Class W, vol. 1, no. 118.

68. Amongst others, Chancellor Brüning, in the winter of 1930 proposed a world economic conference; topics included restrictions on production and international quota agreements. The Anglo-American dispute on the Stevenson Rubber scheme induced Lothian to raise the question of international planning with US ambassador Houghton. On international cartels see C.A. Wurm, *Internationale Kartelle in der britischen Außen- und Wirtschaftspolitik 1919–1939*, Habilitationsschrift Bochum 1983, and H.W. Würzler, 'Bericht', in: G. Schmidt, ed., *Konstellationen internationaler Politik 1924–1932*, Bochum 1983, pp. 237–277.

These suggestions to improve the working of the world economic order were to be gradually realised. In a process of give and take, the European nations were to offer and obtain some political and economic concessions which the economic appeasers hoped would result in a revision of the status quo; the method of an 'all-in settlement' was to insure that no power would ever be isolated (i.e. France) or allow another power (i.e. Germany) to reap the benefits and to seize the initiative. The Treasury, however, objected to the economic prescriptions which the economic appeasers wished to include in the negotiating package. To give one example: in the cabinet, the Treasury used criticisms of its economic policy contained in the Sargent–Ashton-Gwatkin document as an excuse to demand its withdrawal.[69] The intervention of the Treasury meant that one could concentrate on disarmament, without taking economic aspects, emphasised by the Foreign Office Economic Section, into account; as a result, the economic appeasement package was filed away.

Members of the Economic Section, in particular Ashton-Gwatkin and Jebb (from 1 January 1936), however, continued to use every opportunity in day-to-day business to air arguments based on their alternative strategy. Occasionally they were able to modify the wording of memoranda circulating in the cabinet or speeches given at the League of Nations. They also expressed their principal ideas during official and private visits to Germany.[70] Thomas Jones,[71] Lothian,[72] Barrington Ward (Hall Study Group),[73] E. H. Carr,[74] Harold Butler (ILO)[75] and G. Cassell[76] developed

69. Sargent – note, 10 Dec. 1931, C 92/172/62.

70. Ashton-Gwatkin, 24 July 1936, C 5685/99/18, FO 371 – 19 934, note on conversations with directors of the Reichsbank (on occasion of the standstill negotiations). Lothian timed his visits to Berlin, to Canada and the U.S.A. – in the autumn 1934, in the winter 1935/36, before the Imperial Conference 1937 – with a view to returning with 'fresh' information on the views of Roosevelt, Hitler, Mackenzie King, et al., before 'decision-making' in Britain moved into the final stage of Anglo-French and/or Anglo-French-German or inter-imperial meetings. See note 401ff. in ch. I of German original and below, pp. 122ff. (note 246ff.)

71. Jones, *Diary with Letters*, pp. 175ff., 220ff., 240ff. As former (deputy) secretary to the Cabinet, he remained at the centre of things; he had contacts especially to study groups and to pro-German economic interests (Tennant). Jones wanted to proceed on the basis of Hoare's Geneva speech (i.e. the raw materials question).

72. On Lothian see M. Cowling, *The Impact of Hitler*, pp. 133ff., 231ff.; J.R.M. Butler, *Lord Lothian (Ph.Kerr) 1882–1940*, London 1960, pp. 215f. See below notes 78, 231ff., resp. notes 55 and 209ff. of German original.

73. Barrington-Ward, leader writer of *The Times*, was co-author of the Hall-Scheme, 'An International Policy for the British Empire', Jones-Mss., Class E, vol. 1, No. 10; cf. Basil Liddell-Hart, *Memoirs*, 2 vols., London 1965–7; D. Maclachlan, *In the Chair. Barrington-Ward of The Times 1927–1948*, London 1971; M,D. Dubin, 'Transgovernmental process'.

74. E.H. Carr (Wilson Chair, University of Wales), 14 Oct. 1936, 'Public Opinion as a

similar ideas and thus constituted the nucleus of the support group which will be referred to below.[77]

The main features of the economic appeasement strategy will be dealt with in two stages. Firstly, the *escalation theory*,[78] which existed in outline before 1933, will be discussed, followed by an analysis of comments made by the economic appeasers within the Foreign Office in debates which occurred as part of the political process, particularly after mid-1934. Although there is an inner connection between the two stages, it is necessary to treat them separately since the economic appeasers only developed the escalation theory in rough outline and never formulated it into a complete theory. Consequently, it has to be 'reconstructed' by us. After the escalation theory, a second strategy will be considered which was supported by influential members of the government, military leaders and captains of industry. This will help to define

---

safeguard to peace', IA, vol. 15, pp. 846–862; id., 'League of Peace and Freedom', IA, vol. 14(1935); id., *Conditions of Peace*, London 1942. Carr had been deputy head of the Southern Section of the Foreign Office; M. Newman, 'The Origins of Munich. British Policy in Danubian Europe, 1933–37', *HJ*, 21(1978), pp. 378ff. regards Carr as a counter–force to Vansittart in the Office.

75. Harold Butler, director of the International Labour Office, considered the 'standard of living'-problem as an issue that could be launched with a view to bringing democracies and dictatorships to the negotiation table; thus he sponsored the McDougall scheme, approached Eden and arranged international pressure to get the topic on the agenda; Butler to Eden, 14 March 1936, C 2213/99/18, FO 371–19 932, pp. 197ff., 294ff; C 2140/99/18; Eden supported his ideas and passed his proposals to the Board of Trade and the Treasury, 17 July 1936, FO 371–19 934. See below, §8; Wendt, *Economic Appeasement*, pp. 324ff.

76. G. Cassell, 'From Protection through planned economy to Dictatorship (Cobden Lecture)', 10 May 1934, Lothian-Mss., GD 40–17, vol. 278, pp. 770f: the title fascinated Lothian, who forwarded the lecture to Sinclair, 18 May 1934.

77. The elements of the 'escalation theory' were part of the general debate on the compatibility of international co-operation and 'nationalisation'; the economic appeasers turned this set of arguments into a system of warning signals. Leading politicians argued on the same lines, e.g. Th. Inskip, 9 Dec. 1935 and 29 May 1936, HofC, Parl. Deb., vol. 307, col. 589f. On the relationships between Inskip and Lothian or Th. Jones see Jones, *Diary with Letters*; Gilbert, Roots; Gilbert, Gott, *The Appeasers*.

78. Lothian, 'The economic role of Liberalism', *Spectator*, Oct. 1934; id., 'Where are we going?', *Round Table*, March 1930, pp. 217–241, and GD 40–17, vol. 429, pp. 627–687; id., *Liberalism in the Modern World*, 1933; review of Dalton's 'Practical Socialism', *Politica*, June 1935; id., *The Industrial Dilemma*, 1926; id., 'Liberalism and Labour', *New Statesman*, 1935; id., 'The Eclipse of Democratic Civilisation', *Contemporary Review*, no. 814 (Oct. 1933); id., series of articles on the United States, 4 to 25 March 1928, *Observer*. Lothian introduced his basic principles into political debates on various occasions, e.g. Letter to the Editor of *The Times*, 11 Febr. 1936; Parl. Deb., HofL, 6 and 19 Febr. 1936; article, *News Chronicle*, 16 June 1936; his criticism on Ottawa – HofL., Parl. Deb., 9 Nov. 1932, vol. 85, col. 1163–1172 and on the World Economic Conference in London, 24 May 1933, HofL., Parl. Deb., vol. 87, col. 1019–1025, form the platform of his interventions later on. His views were the basis of manifestoes of the Council of Action for Peace and Reconstruction (Sept. 1935) and March 1936 (9–11 March 1936).

more clearly the peculiarities of the economic appeasement strategy of Ashton-Gwatkin, Lothian, Barrington Ward and others. Both strategies – and this is what makes the comparison meaningful – were prepared to deliver *Mitteleuropa* to Germany as a zone of economic influence and thus were resigned to appeasement *à la* Munich. However, this renunciation of Central Europe has a different significance in the context of the escalation theory than it has for the strategy of the second group of appeasers.

2. Economic Appeasement: the Escalation Theory

The economic appeasers were confronted with two challenges: the problems of collaboration between the two sides of industry and the dangers of 'state' (war) socialism or 'state' capitalism, on the one hand, and the arguments of an undiluted industrial-capitalist *laissez-faire* liberalism on the other.[79] By correlating 'social appeasement' in the domestic sphere with Britain's role in world politics and in the international economy, they wanted to give leadership to other states. Their operative ideal might be interpreted as a modified version of Britain's role as 'workshop of the world' and peace-keeper which she had performed as the first liberal great power during the First Industrial Revolution:

> It has taken a long time and bitter experience to convince [people] that international cooperation to prevent war is better than competitive armaments and national sovereignty. It may take as long and bitter economic suffering to convince them that complete freedom of trade with its correlative international cooperation for dealing with problems of currency and exchange is better for everybody. . .than tariffs and national self-interest.[80]

Their economic appeasement strategy refers back to two tendencies. On the one hand, there was the notion that liberalism had

79. Lothian, 'The Roots of Our Present Discontent', *Round Table*, March 1936, pp. 229–238; id., 'Nationalism, Socialism, and the Liberal Mind', Dec. 1934, Speech to the Eighty Club, GD 40–17, vol. 440; Lothian to Lloyd George, 11 Jan. 1935, GD 40–17, vol. 293; id. to Rathbone, 4 Sept. 1935, GD 40–17, vol. 113; id. to Duncan, 9 March 1933, vol. 263; id. to Flexner, 13 Febr. 1933, vol. 263; see references in note 78. H.V. Hodson (economic expert) *Round Table* IA, vol. 15, pp. 873f.; F. Ashton-Gwatkin, 21 Dec. 1936, quoted as annex 3 in M. Gilbert, *Roots*, pp. 212–214.

80. Lothian, Jan. 1930, *Manchester Guardian*, GD 40–17, vol. 412, p. 606; cf. Lothian to Grigg, 26 April 1933, GD 40–17, vol. 269; Lothian to Mackenzie King, 9 March 1939, GD 40–17, vol. 374.

to take self-correcting measures.[81] This implied a readiness both to acknowledge the specific regulatory functions of the state in the economy and to allow international planning[82] to lead capitalism in the international arena out of the anarchy of economic nationalism and its acceptance of the uncontrolled play of free-market forces. As Roosevelt put it in May 1933, 'The [World Economic] Conference must establish order in place of the present chaos by a stabilisation of currencies, by freeing the flow of world trade, and by international action to raise price levels. It must, in short, supplant individual domestic programs for economic recovery by wise and considered international action'.[83] On the other hand, the economic appeasement strategy took up proposals[84] to coordinate the role played by the US and the Empire–Commonwealth as the capital base and raw-material base of the world economy within the framework of an Anglo-American partnership. The economic potential of these two leading world economic powers was not only to be used to gear and steer international economic relations, but also to adjust the domestic political conditions in the rest of the world to the 'operative ideals' of the two Anglo-Saxon democracies; the idea was to create penetrated systems similar to those which came into existence at the time of the Dawes Plan.[85] The main intentions behind this particular economic appeasement

81. Lothian, Jones, Ashton-Gwatkin knew M.J. Bonn, F. Hayek, L. von Mises, W. Lippmann('The Great Society') and valued their writings; they had contacts with J.W. Dafoe and the Foreign Policy Association, i.e. advisors to King (Canada) resp. Hull (U.S.A.); J.W. Dafoe, Public Opinion and World Politics, 1933; id., 'Ottawa and World Trade', 15 May 1932, Baldwin-Mss., vol. 98, pp. 93–104. The writings of J.A. Salter influenced Lothian's ideas; J.A. Salter, *The Framework of an Ordered Society*, 1933; id., *Political Aspects of the World Depression*, 1932; id., ed., *The World's Economic Crisis and the Way of Escape*, 1932; id., ed., *The Causes of War*, 1932.

82. Williamstown, Institute of Politics, Lectures Programme 'World Economic Planning', 1931–1933, Lothian-Mss., GD 40–17, vol. 254, pp. 868ff.; Lothian, 'Europe at the Cross-Roads', *Round Table*, June 1926, vol. 16, pp. 492ff. On the circumstances favouring international cartels and/or negotiations on the forming of international cartels see League of Nations, 1944 Report, pp. 51ff., 61ff.; see notes 103f. of German original. Cf. J. Radkau, 'Renovation des Imperialismus im Zeichen der "Rationalisierung" ', in: I. Geiss, J. Radkau, eds., *Imperialismus im 20. Jahrhundert*, München 1976, pp. 242f.

83. Roosevelt–Message to the World Economic Conference, 16 May 1933, FRUS 1933 vol. 1, p. 144; E.B. Nixon, ed., *F.D. Roosevelt and Foreign Affairs*, Cambridge, Mass. 1969, vol. 1, p. 126.

84. Eden's memorandum 'The Economic Aspects of Foreign Policy', May 1937, referred to proposals and ideas aired with a view to the London Conference in 1933; the memorandum was drafted by Ashton-Gwatkin and Jebb; on the recommendations of the experts, the instructions to the British and American delegations etc. see Wendt, *Economic Appeasement*, pp. 120ff.; Ch. Kindleberger, *The World in Depression, 1929–39*, London 1973, pp. 204ff., 211ff. For details see note 65 of German original.

85. W. Link, *Die amerikanische Stabilisierungspolitik*, Düsseldorf 1970, p. 505.

strategy were therefore, firstly, to move the *laissez-faire* liberals towards 'organised capitalism' and, secondly, to endeavour to organise an efficient Anglo-American partnership as the spearhead of international planning, thereby constructively contributing to the securing of peace.[86] The strategy can in effect be described as a trade-off: in return for access to raw materials and the provision of commercial credits, the 'haves' demanded that the 'have-nots' respect the values of the Anglo-Saxon economic system and comply with the international practice of fulfilling contractual obligations. The analogy with the pattern of social-liberal reform policies with the aim of stabilising the political system and domestic economy, is obvious.

On the other hand, the economic appeasers reproached British, French and American policy for gambling away the opportunity, or worse, for not even starting upon the task of reorganising international relations after the First World War. The product of this failure was in their view the Third Reich.[87] They pinpointed the Treaty of Versailles and economic nationalism as the 'roots of the present discontent'. They accused the British government of pandering to these tendencies in 1931–32 by adopting such fiscal measures as a 10 per cent import duty and 'imperial preference'. Furthermore, they interpreted Hitler's use of violence in politics as an escape from economic difficulties.[88] In this way they minimised the strategic intentions behind Germany's diplomatic coups as exceptions in a chain of accidental errors which did not even seem inexcusable. It was believed that in order to prevent similar disturbances, the Western powers would have to muster enough courage to correct the mistakes they had made in the postwar

86. Lothian, 'Nationalism, Social Liberalism, and the Liberal Mind', Dec. 1934, Lothian Mss., GD 40–17, vol. 440, pp. 987ff.; Lothian to Crowthers (*News Chronicle*), 22 Febr. 1934, GD 40–17, vol. 272, pp. 171f.; Lothian, 'Europe's Parting of the Ways', 25 Dec. 1929, article for the *Frankfurter Zeitung*, GD 40–17, vol. 428, pp. 578ff.; Lothian, Speech to US Chamber of Commerce in London, vol. 412, pp. 129–135. Similar ideas were aired by W. Layton's Peace and Liberty discussion group, which became the Next Five Years Group. On the 'middle way'–'philosophy' and the centre-left movements see A. Marwick, 'Middle Opinion in the Thirties: Planning, Progress, and Political "Agreement"', *EHR*, 79(1964), pp. 285–298; H. Macmillan, *The Middle Way*, 1937; id., *Winds of Change*, London 1966, pp. 327f., 335ff.; M. Gilbert, ed., *Plough My Own Furrow. The Story of Lord Allen of Hurtwood*, London 1965.

87. Ashton-Gwatkin held the U.S.A. responsible — politically and economically — for the 'miseries' and defaults of the international system; — comment on Allen-memorandum, 'The United States and British Interests', A 2847/228/45, FO 371–20 659, pp. 266ff.; cf. Wendt, *Economic Appeasement*, pp. 60f., 336f. Lothian, *The Roots of our Present Discontent*; id. to Lloyd George, 13 Jan. 1932, GD 40–17, vol. 265; Lothian, 10 Dec. 1932, Queen's Hall Speech, vol. 435, pp. 554ff.; Hodson, in: IA, vol. 15, p. 873.

88. Lothian to E. Rathbone, 4 Sept. 1935, GD 40–17, vol. 113.

period. The susceptibility of the appeasers to Hitler's claim[89] that 'economic encirclement' – through import restrictions, through the stifling of German exports by People's Front governments, and so on – would favour 'Bolshevism' in Germany discloses at the same time their socio-political motives in their attempts to stabilise a 'free' economic system.

They maintained that a Second World War could only be prevented if British (or, better still, Anglo-American) efforts sought to break the unfortunate causal chain which was assumed to lead to the aggressiveness of Germany and other 'have-not' powers. They demanded resolute and speedy action as well as the use of effective measures. Since they attributed the misery of the German economy and the threat of an explosion to the bungled policies of the Allies in the aftermath of First World War and the Great Depression, they made believe that the Western powers could effect a regime change in Germany by correcting their foreign and world policies; that is, by switching to an economic 'peace strategy'. The momentum of their economic appeasement strategy lay in a specific construction of the causal chain; the ideas of this 'escalation theory' remained tied to a 'liberal' world-view.

The above-mentioned notion of a causal chain presupposes that economic depressions cause political conflict and even war; the political advice which the economic appeasers offered culminated in 'economic appeasement' becoming a strategy of graduated measures designed to combat this threat in the endangered nations. The economic appeasers contrast the inevitability of specific developmental stages in a country marked by economic nationalism with correspondingly graduated economic help from abroad. In their opinion, only such intervention, rather than an 'arms race and alliance policies', could save the peace.

In a broader perspective the economic appeasement strategy was seen as the answer to two dangers threatening the vital principles of Great Britain and the Commonwealth:

(1) In their opinion the First World War had introduced the principle of class struggle in a new way all over the world. The use of all available means and powers of nations in 'total' war, they believed, had drawn the state unalterably into economic life. In these circumstances the state was faced with the dilemma of

---

89. Hitler–Lloyd George meeting, 6 Sept. 1936, in: Jones, *Diary with Letters*, pp. 241ff., 197ff., 214ff., 224; cf. Phipps to Vansittart, 14 Nov. 1936; Phipps' report was referred to in the Cabinet's and the committees' debate on 'The Role of the British Army' and the basic orientation of British foreign policy in 1936/7.

whether to intervene in favour of the working class or of 'capital' in order to improve prospects in a world market afflicted by the chronic economic crisis which resulted from the misguided provisions of the Treaty of Versailles. Since the state had to take sides, it could no longer act as the mediator in compromises between divergent social forces. What complicated matters further was that, as neither 'Labour' nor 'Capital' could settle their disputes on their own, nor could they be resolved by 'parties' which were vying to form a government, the intervention of the state in domestic and international economies became the important factor influencing the attitudes and behaviour of actors within the socio-political systems; consequently, the pattern of social conflict was transformed into the struggle between 'state socialism versus state capitalism'. The laws and customs of the constitution, the basic rules of representative democracies, which stand and fall with the type of tolerant pluralist society, were thought to be (permanently?) suspended once the process which took place on the European continent spilled over to Great Britain and the Empire–Commonwealth. As soon as the state intervened in favour of one side, the other would adopt counter-revolutionary tactics in order to win over the state to its aims. In the end, the antithesis of socialism and capitalism was assumed to produce the deadly rivalry between revolutionary communism and counter-revolutionary fascism.

(2) The chances for Britain and the Commonwealth to develop their way of life depended not only on peaceful (constitutional) change within their own territories, but also on the survival of 'constitutional systems' in the rest of the world. If the chain of events described in (1) above repeated itself in all nations, with the (initial) exception of Britain and the Dominions, then the tide would not, in the long term, stop at the Commonwealth, scattered as it was over five continents. On the contrary, one member after another would be drawn into the global conflict between 'state socialism' and 'state capitalism'; between movements on the Left and those on the Right. The Commonwealth was therefore believed to have a vital interest in preventing the formation of such blocs. It must try to keep alive or re-establish a basis in other nations so that the increasingly grave situation developing between the *opposing* forces of socialism and capitalism would not lead to the antagonism of communism and fascism. The forms which state intervention would take in several countries, especially in Germany and Russia, were seen as a consequence of the fact that

the imbalance of productive forces and realisable surplus value forced the state to put pressure on society with a view to organising the country in such a way that it would fare relatively well in an international comparison. Because of economic and technological developments, only very few countries could regulate their problems internally, but since the dependence of almost all countries on imports and exports brought them into a relationship with others, the forces of 'organised capitalism' or 'advanced socialism' would also become commodities capable of import or export. The Empire–Commonwealth, seen purely from an economic point of view, was thought to be able to cope with a quest for self-sufficiency; and yet this was precisely what it must not do. It was in a position to isolate itself from the conflict between fascism and communism, but would in that case be unable to affect events in the international environment. Should conflict arise between the two forces, the Empire–Commonwealth would not be the *tertius gaudens*, since, if only for geographical reasons, individual members would become involved in the conflict and its 'isolated' unity would be undermined. Above all, however, the Empire–Commonwealth would be forced into the role of adversary because communism and fascism would be struggling to gain ground at the expense of constitutional democracy. The Commonwealth had to prevent a course of events resulting in a situation in which the democratic camp would be forced to take sides in the battle between the two systems, both of which were its deadly enemy. The camp of representative constitutional democracies had only one option left; that is, to bring the principles of their own eco-political system to bear on international politics – it had to introduce to the national economies the principle of tolerance through the internationalisation of commercial and financial-monetary links. This was believed to be the only way to limit further advances of the interventionist state.[90]

The analysis of the economic appeasers identified the following

---

90. Lothian, 1 Oct. 1935, statement for Columbia Broadcasting Services, Lothian Mss., GD 40–17, vol. 300; similar 'messages' were sent to Flexner, 13 Febr. 1935 (vol. 263) and P. Duncan, 9 March 1933 (vol. 263); see notes 78f. above. Cf. Jones, *Diary with Letters*, pp. 408f.; Baldwin, 18 Nov. 1936, Glasgow Herald; Baldwin, 20 Oct. 1936, HofC.; Central Office, Hints for Speakers, no. 3600 (Nov. 1936); Eden/Lord Avon, Facing the Dictators, London 1962, pp. 82f.; on Inskip see note 77. The 'fear' that Germany would follow the 'bolshevic' example (i.e. state socialism resp. state capitalism) was a background factor to the attempts of economic appeasers to re-integrate Germany into the international economy; see notes 17, 13, 64 and 178 of German original.

dangers to world peace:[91]

(1) That the continuation of the World Depression would be used to increase state influence on the economy and to legitimise the regulatory functions of state power.

(2) That the state would see itself forced to intervene in the economic process and to instrumentalise capitalism for its national economic policy of job creation at any price, particularly in those countries which were disadvantaged in various ways.

(3) Should these governments channel this more or less forced identity of state and economy into the sector of arms production – that is, couple job creation schemes with rearmament – it could be anticipated that in due course 'state capitalism' or 'state socialism' would be transformed into a war economy.[92]

(4) That this transformation was imminent or had already begun in Germany by 1935–36;[93] it was, therefore, necessary for Britain to initiate 'international' economic activities.

From about the end of 1935 the economic appeasers identified the start of a development in Germany in which the links of the causal chain could be described in the following way:[94] 'nationalism' developing into economic nationalism of various sorts (as reflected in currency manipulations, foreign-exchange controls, protective tariffs, etc.); 'economic nationalism', stimulated by security-policy arguments, would expand national boundaries and penetrate into neighbouring countries; this transformed/expanding

91. See notes 71 to 75; H.D. Henderson, *The Inter-War Years and Other Papers*, Oxford 1943/1955, pp. 236–295, heavily critisised the assumptions and correctness of the economic thought of the economic appeasers; Henderson chaired the Economic Advisory Council of the Government.

92. Pinsent's reports from Berlin induced Ashton-Gwatkin and Jebb to urge 'economic' appeasement to their superiors in order to 'liberate' Germany from the devious circle of rearmament, 'Wehrwirtschaft'/autarky, and drive to war: minutes on C 4487/99/18, 15 June 1936; on C 4501/99/18, 25 June 1936, FO 371–19 933, pp. 263, 273ff.; Ashton-Gwatkin-Jebb statement, 31 Jan. 1936, FO 371–19 884, pp. 44ff., and FO 371–19 888, pp. 75ff. Cf. Wendt, *Economic Appeasement*, pp. 324ff., 437ff., 450ff.

93. Ashton-Gwatkin/Jebb, 31 Jan. 1936, FO 371–19 884, pp. 44ff. On the situation in Germany in 1936 see D. Petzina, 'Rüstungspolitik', in: Forstmeier, Volkmann, eds., *Wirtschaft und Rüstung*, p. 71. Following Ritter's remarks, Ashton-Gwatkin and Jebb regarded Göring's appointment as a support to Schacht resp. the stance of the 'Moderates'; C 3309 (30 April 1936), C 3357 (2 May 1936), C 3431/99/18 (5 May 1936), FO 371–19 932; cf. *The Times*, 28 April 1936; Pinsent registered a decline of Schacht's influence, 30 March 1936, C 2706/99/18, FO 371–19 932, p. 21f.

94. The economic appeasers defended their strategy against Vansittart, e.g. 30 June 1936, C 4758/99/18, FO 371–19 933, p. 332; Ashton-Gwatkin argued that the payments agreements had encouraged the 'sounder elements' in the Third Reich: 20 Nov. 1934, C 7540/1/18, FO 371–17 689, p. 225. The basic arguments are in Lothian, 10 Dec. 1932, address to Liberal Meeting, GD 40–17, vol. 435, pp. 554–556. See notes 81 and 82 of German original, and below note 479.

'national economy', coupled with national prestige and ambitions, would come under the direction of an aggressive party leadership aiming at a total identification of politics and economics. Since the economic appeasers regarded the danger of such a transformation as imminent, but did not yet consider it to have been completed, they could still present their strategy as viable. But if the escalating process occurred, as was the argument of their opponents, economic appeasement would be an illusion; it misunderstood the true state of affairs; namely, that the policies of the National Socialist regime were the cause of economic difficulties and not *vice versa*. The economic appeasers were opposed to a development which deprived the economy of its own momentum and subjected economic forces to the rule of political will and transformed it into an instrument of militant nationalism. As soon as this stage had been reached, that nation-state organised as a 'combat unit' would turn away from the 'comity of nations' and only listen to its own uncompromising laws based on the satisfaction of its prestige and would withdraw from the world economic system. It would occupy a front-line position against interdependence, which would be vilified as dependency, and eventually it would seek to take the offensive to destroy the mechanisms of, and conditions for, the functioning of the world economic system. The economic appeasers held that business interests are contradictory, not susceptible to unmediated transformation into coherent state policy. The economic factors which, in the opinion of the economic appeasers, would by nature promote a world division of labour, would progressively lose their influence and role as regulatory norms once the described escalation occurred; they would weaken in line with the aggressiveness with which these nations propagated their level of achievement and their growth in power as being superior to that of the older liberal systems, which they depicted as decadent. They would also weaken to the extent to which these nations would dominate initiatives in inter-state relations and international politics. At this stage of the development they would no longer articulate 'legitimate grievances', but misuse their economic potential as they turned on weaker individual trade partners (isolated by the general wave of economic egoism) and back up economic penetration with threats of military action. The principle of self-help would thereby be pushed to extremes, and measures of economic aggression would be tantamount to a declaration of war on the world division of labour. Economic nationalism in this phase was seen to turn into 'war socialism' and to become a manifestation of militarism. Adherents to the 'liberal' principle had to succeed in maintaining the weight of economic factors in those nations which were susceptible to economic nationalism in order to prevent a confrontation between militant systems (i.e. the final stage of the escalation process), on the one hand, and those countries which had achieved economic recovery and consolidation, on the other. The regeneration and intensification of economic interdependence was seen by the economic appeasers as the only means by which the autonomy of economic factors in those countries could be renewed and protected in the long term. However, this could only be attained if interdependence was firmly established in key sectors of capability; namely, access to raw materials and capital markets and the creation of export outlets. The economic appeasers speculated that participation in intensified economic transactions would create sufficient dependencies for every state to find it difficult to extricate itself from this network. This appeared effectively to offer a guarantee that methods of peaceful change would become the dominant form of conflict resolution. Participation in international trade would compel each partner to comply with the regulating norms and, to a certain extent, to respect political rules and conventions. Economic interdependence was thought to have a restricting, if not allaying effect on unrestrained power-political ambition and egocentric-militant nationalism.

The expectation that a change of course induced from 'outside' could work in countries which were susceptible to economic nationalism arose from the presumption that even systems where the merger of economics and politics had advanced considerably retained a fundamental interest in 'good' foreign relations. Reports from the Third Reich gave the economic appeasers welcome proof of the accuracy of their estimates. They took these reports as signals that Germany's interest in the question of raw materials was not merely guided by a concern with arms production, but might serve different purposes. The reports related to views expressed by Schacht, the staff of the Foreign Ministry and reputable German journalists who argued that offers of 'equality of access to raw materials' from the West – in particular from Great Britain – could have a positive influence on Hitler's foreign policy. German statements (e.g. by Ribbentrop and Kordt) that in March 1936 Hitler had suggested economic–political agreements to Baldwin, and only after they had been rejected resorted to the Four-Year Plan, reflected, however, more the wishful thinking of the economic appeasers than they did Hitler's intentions.[95]

Hopes for the success of an economic appeasement strategy *vis-à-vis* Germany were founded on the following observations and basic views about the course of contemporary German history:

(1) The defensive attitude of German economic circles in 1918–19 towards attempts at nationalisation, the pleas of large industrial associations to adopt the Dawes Plan and Schacht's rejection of National Socialist economic policies in the 1930s, led them to hope that resistance inside Germany against a uniform society regulated or totally organised by the state[96] continued to exist and that it would be worth while supporting these forces by considerate actions on the part of the West.

(2) In general they regarded transnational cooperation – for example, international cartels as a form of 'private international planning' – as a means of rolling back economic and political nationalism.[97] Even within the Empire–Commonwealth in the 1920s, and the more so after 'Ottawa', they realised that industrialisation was primarily guided by economic nationalism, with no regard for an international division of labour. To them, the crucial defect of that wrongly conceived 'industrialisation' was that it turned against the principle of international welfare; that is, if one wished to increase one's own exports, one had to care for 'liberalising' imports. They expected politicians to pay heed to this idea and tackle the serious problems of adjusting industries and agricul-

95. E. Kordt, *Nicht aus den Akten*, Stuttgart 1950, p. 165; J. von Ribbentrop, *The Ribbentrop Memoirs*, London 1954, pp. 98ff.; Conwell-Evans to Th. Jones, 16 June 1937, Jones-Mss., Class E, vol. 1, no. 32; Lothian, 5 May 1937, report on talk with Schacht, GD 40–17, vol. 204; Phipps to Foreign Office, 1 Sept. 1936, C 5156/99/18, FO 371–19 933. Guinness-Report, C 5928/99/18, 14 August 1936, FO 371–19 934: The Germans wait on Britain 'giving a lead'; the internal feud between moderates and extremists was said to be not yet decided.

96. The economic appeasers referred to and relied on reports on Schacht (via Jäckh), on meetings with Schacht or directors of the Reichsbank and on Schacht's appeals to the British government to lend support to his efforts with regard to international economic policies; e.g. Phipps to Foreign Office, 7 June 1935, C 1284/635/18, FO 371–18 871. Lothian expected the German 'revolution' to pass into 'evolution' like any other revolution: Lothian to Coupland, 11 July 1935, GD 40–17, vol. 300.

97. Lothian, The Unemployment Problem, 10 June 1930, GD 40–17, vol. 134; id., Industrial Dilemma, 1926; Wellesley-Memorandum, 1 Dec. 1930, p. 19 (note 57); Ashton-Gwatkin, Economic Survey, FO 371–18 497, pp. 311ff.; Allen–Report, 10 June 1931, on meeting and resolutions on international meeting of Members of Parliament, Prague, 25 to 29 May 1931, T 172–1766; All Souls Meeting, 11/12 July 1931, Jones-Mss, Class C, vol. 4, No.73; Leith-Ross, 'The Position of Germany', 2 March 1938, note to Van Zeeland Committee. On problems of the economies and the international economy in the interwar period see I. Svennilson, *Growth and Stagnation in the European Economy*, Geneva 1954; D. Aldcroft, *The Inter-War Economy*, pp. 155ff.; Kindleberger, *World in Depression*, pp. 105ff. On amalgamations, mergers etc. in Britain see note 86 of German original.

ture – both in relation to changing patterns of world trade and to their balance in the national economies – with that principle in mind.

The line of argument which culminated in a firm belief in the value of *international cartels* provides the second focal point of their strategy alongside the psychological–political approach of the escalation theory. This second argument was rooted in their 'reading' of economic history and economic theory; it starts from the proposition that the World Depression was caused by a global tendency to overproduce, which again had to be seen in the context of nationalism.[98]

The economic appeasers incorporated into their theory which had grown out of their perception of a political threat the widely held belief of the twenties that structural distortions were the cause of chronic underemployment of labour and capital. Thus the 'lessons' drawn from these economic developments constituted a cornerstone of their peace strategy. They welcomed the rationalisation movement, advocated industrial efficiency and concentration in the banking and industrial sectors and sought to make use of the 'positive' aspects of these developments for their political strategy.[99]

In their view, the economy was developing along the following lines:[100] By too vigorously promoting, from a position of a misguided economic nationalism, their generally legitimate industrial development, the less-developed countries not only endangered the international economic order but also undermined the prospects for the success of their justifiable desire to achieve economic independence. The excessive measures taken were bound to produce unbalanced conditions in the home market by increasing the costs of agricultural production and thus weakening the base for industrial take-off. With regard to the pattern of growth in the world market, such overrapid industrialisation meant an increase in the overcapacity already existing in the world economy.

98. Ashton-Gwatkin/Jebb., *German Expansionism*, C 807/4/18, FO 371–19 884, pp. 46ff.; see below on their proposal to pursue the raw materials question and Hoare's Geneva speech. Cf. Arndt, *Economic Lessons*, p. 232.

99. Ashton-Gwatkin, Economic Survey, II: The Post-War Period, W 6928/1195/20, FO 371–18 497, pp. 306–376 A; the criticism is directed to economic nationalism as the driving force behind 'industrialisation', not against industrialisation in 'developing' countries as such; this criticism relates to the Dominions (Australia, Canada) as well as the states of 'New Europe'.

100. Lothian, 'The Roots', *Round Table*, March 1936, pp. 229–238; id., 'Where are we going?', *Round Table*, March 1930, GD 40–17, vol. 429, pp. 672–687; Lothian, 'Europe at the Cross-Roads', June 1926, *Round Table*, vol. 16, pp. 489ff.; Lothian, 12 Oct. 1932, Liberal Meeting, GD 40–17, vol. 435, pp. 534ff.

Their interaction would be bound to reinforce the trend towards protectionism; every government would shield itself against exports resulting from the overcapacity of others by erecting trade barriers such as quotas and exchange restrictions.

The evils of economic nationalism, which had already led to increased conflict before the First World War when the industrial nations resolved to subsidies and tariff policies, spread to the new nation-states after the war. They copied the 'bad' examples and therefore aggravated the problem by aiming at a disproportionate economic independence. This would inevitably affect international relations, since governments were constantly confronted with demands to protect national labour from imported unemployment. Governments dropped the guiding principle of economic liberalism; that is, that an increase in the productive capacity of individual countries could benefit all participants in the world economy only if a network of agreements existed which allowed for a division of labour and free access to markets.[101] Economic nationalism implied, however, that nations would exploit their jurisdiction in fiscal, financial and monetary affairs in order to create 'artificial' – and this included legalised (statutory) – advantages for their own citizens at the expense of foreign competition; the requirements of world trade were thus being ignored.

Britain, according to the economic appeasers, was and remained the one country which could not overcome her structural economic problems single-handedly, but was dependent on world trade. Great Britain was to use her dependence on world trade to demonstrate that foreign trade was not a zero-sum game in which 'one man's loss is another man's profit'. Advanced diversified economies should rather regard other economies orientated towards a division of labour as each other's best customers who could increase their production by exchanging goods and services. Anglo-German commercial and financial relations were thought to have been a case in point. The economic appeasers knew, however, that the structure of the British economy had to be adapted to changes in the world market. In their view this adaptation demanded a relocation of capital and labour from 'old declining export industries' towards 'modern' ones, capable of competing in the

101. Jones to Kerr (Lothian), 24 June 1925, Jones-Mss., Class W, vol. 3, no. 66; Wellesley-Memo. (note 57), p. 18f.; Lothian to Skelton, 6 Jan. 1926, Some Notes on an Economic Policy for Great Britain, GD 40–17, vol. 412, pp. 100ff.; (Skelton was a member of Macmillan's Industry and Democracy Group and was regarded as one of the big hopes of the Conservative Party); Lothian, 28 May 1930, The Empire and Free Trade, GD 40–17, vol. 431, pp. 131, 160ff.

world market. This programme, which had been presented by the economic appeasers on various occasions before 1931,[102] became even more attractive to them at the time of the World Depression and above all after 1934–35. They saw their fears about the consequences of an imbalance between the domestic and the world economy confirmed. But at the same time they urged that every country, including Britain, should deal with the 'weak spots' in the competitive position of its economy. The first task was therefore to improve industrial relations; secondly, dislocations brought about by the burden of high taxation had to be rectified through a revision of taxation policy, and finally those new industries had to be encouraged which, thanks to quality production and cost advantages, satisfied domestic demand. It was from this secure base that these industries would have a fair chance of competing successfully for a share in the world market. Britain's dependence on imports in other areas appeared to be so large that other countries would be unable to claim to be affected by selective British protective measures (such as tariffs protecting infant industries) as these were the exception rather than the rule.

Another of their arguments related to the failure of numerous attempts to conclude a 'tariff truce';[103] that is, efforts to remove trade barriers (duties, quotas and currency restrictions) through agreements between governments as discussed at the League of Nations' conferences and at international conferences from Brussels in 1920 to Stresa in 1932. To them the only chance for re-establishing multilateral trade was to effect the gradual roll-back of economic nationalism. They saw the reduction of overcapacities in the international sphere as a complementary strategy to the growing rationalisation movement in the domestic arena; meanwhile, cartels were to extend their domestic functions to the international level. The economic appeasers were aware that national economies, including Great Britain's, would have to insist on retaining protection of one sort or another against a flood of

102. Ph. Kerr (Lothian), 'Britain's Place in the World. A Competitive Age', 22 Sept. 1929, *Observer*; Lothian, 'The Macmillan Report', *Round Table*, Sept. 1931, vol. 21, p. 807ff.; Lothian, 'British Industry and the Future', *Round Table*, autumn 1925, vol. 15, pp. 692–716; id., 'The World Economic Conference', *Round Table*, spring 1927, vol. 17, pp. 267–286; id., 'Reflections on the Industrial Situation', *Round Table*, vol. 17, pp. 748ff.; id. 'The Economic Future of Great Britain', ibid, pp. 534ff.; id., 'Towards Industrial Renaissance', *Round Table*, vol. 19 (1929), pp. 255ff. and 'Unemployment', ibid, pp. 465ff. On Wellesley and Ashton-Gwatkin see notes 57ff.

103. Arndt, *Economic Lessons*, p. 230, 235; Kindleberger, *World in Depression*, pp. 77f., 131ff., 135; Kottmann, *Reciprocity*, pp. 39ff., 54ff., 65ff., 75ff., on 'economic disarmament' and tariff truce proposals and negotiations.

products from abroad; however, this need would not block the return to a world division of labour. The best way to maintain and develop multilateral relations, and at the same time to practice unavoidable quota restrictions, was to establish specific forms of organisations. These were to be constituted in the national arena by producers with the aim of countering the effects of ups and downs in the economy by regulating production and by maintaining costs and prices. Moreover these organisational structures were to be organised in a way facilitating their transfer to the international arena. This might involve tough negotiations between the cartelised industries of various countries. Those interested in a more conscious and stronger orientation of British foreign policy towards economic needs had advocated 'self-organisation' of British industry with a view to strengthening its international bargaining power even before and during the First World War.[104] A more efficient economic structure was seen by them as a necessary precondition and supporting factor of such an orientation. The 'positive' sides of rationalisation in Germany and France in the 1920s provided a further stimulus for inviting the example of their competitors.[105] They expected international forms of cooperation – between Germany and France, possibly between Germany and Russia – to occur; if British capitalism failed to organise, this would happen without British participation, and international cartels would ignore British interests if the country's industry failed to keep up with her competitors.[106]

104. Wellesley, *On Commercial Policy*, 1917; on this, see G. Schmidt, *Politische Tradition* (Habilitationsschrift Münster 1971); Wellesley, 1 Dec. 1930 (see note 57), pp. 19ff., 21f.; Ashton-Gwatkin, Economic Survey, pp. 311ff., 335ff; Ashton–Gwatkin/Jebb., 31 Jan. 1936, C 807/4/18, FO 371–19 884, pp. 46f. The Balfour of Burleigh Committee (1915/16) and the Balfour Committee on Industry and Trade had studied the problems; Wellesley and Ashton-Gwatkin.referred to these reports in order to stress Britain's deficits with regard to an effective reorganisation of production and marketing structures. International cooperation and rationalisation as instruments of international economics and politics were favourably discussed around 1930; Wigram, 8 Jan. 1932, 'Review of Franco–British Differences', FO 800–292, p. 6.; Sandeman Allen to Treasury, May 1931, T 172–1766; Ashton-Gwatkin, 15 Febr. 1935, C. 794/635/18, FO 371–18 869, pp. 102f.; W. Link, in: M. Knapp, ed., *Die USA und Deutschland 1918–1975*, Düsseldorf 1978, pp. 87ff., 91; P. Berkenkopf, 'Internationale Industriekartelle und ihre Bedeutung für die Gestaltung der weltwirtschaftlichen Beziehungen', *Weltwirtschaftliches Archiv*, vol. 28(1928), pp. 300–317; R. Boyce, 'America, Europe, and the Triumph of Imperial Protectionism in Britain, 1929–1930', *Millenium*, vol. 4(1975), pp. 63ff.
105. The Economic Section gathered reports from France, Germany, etc. during 1930/31 (i.e. the initiative to establish a 'general staff' within the Office) and again in 1933/34 when the Economic Section prepared guidelines for the diplomatic service on reporting on the economic aspects of foreign policy.
106. Wellesley, 1 Dec. 1930, p. 13. On international cartels see C.A. Wurm, *Internationale*

Another component of the rationalisation process was even more important for the strategy of the economic appeasers:

> [This is a process which] by the elimination of waste ... tends to produce such a close interlocking of all the main factors of production as to amount to trading on a national cooperative and collectivist rather than upon a competitive and individualistic basis ... the more perfect the process of integration becomes, the more it lends itself as an instrument of policy in the furtherance of political ends; and this is particularly the case when it comes under the controlling influence and direction of the state. Under the pressure of world competition this tendency is likely to increase.[107]

The economic appeasers appreciated the ambiguities of the tendency towards cartelisation. In their opinion the process of concentration and cartelisation had, in conjunction with militarism, led to the dangerous constellation of the prewar period. But this constellation was also the result of external influences. As Wellesley reminded his superiors, it was the impending threat of a success of the tariff reform movement in Britain after 1903 that 'threw the commercial and industrial class into the arms of the military party' in Germany (see below).

Since they expected the process of industrial concentration to advance in the wake of intensified competition – as reflected in industrial combinations, mergers and syndicates – they recognised the danger that these organisations might become tools of state policy. Demands for state protection from foreign competition which were advanced by business could quickly lead to a situation where the economy had to accept state control, even if it was opposed to such forms of intervention.[108] Rationalisation could, in this case, be turned into a highly effective political weapon. It might even be stronger than that of rearmament. Before 1933 the economic appeasers warned that a disarmed Germany would exploit her structural advantages in the economic sphere.[109] Rationalisation could serve as a basis for the systematic economic penetration of other countries in the form of (1) commercial

---

Kartelle (note 68); Würzler (see note 68), and A. Teichova, 'Concentration, Combination, and Cartelization in Central and South-East Europe since 1920' (Papers in East European Economics, 19); id., *An Economic Background to Munich: International Business and Czechoslovakia, 1918–1938*, Cambridge 1974.

107. Wellesley-Memo., pp. 4f., 19ff.
108. Ibid., pp. 4 and 22.
109. Ibid., pp. 7ff.

penetration, by which overproduction would be shifted onto a partner through exports; (2) industrial penetration, by which the establishment of subsidiaries, branches, and so on, would overcome tariff barriers; and (3) financial penetration, by which finance capital would gain control of companies operating in foreign countries. Since these 'partners' would resist Germany's attempts at penetration, it was to be expected that modern industrial developments, and the forms of 'organised capitalism' accompanying the process, would determine the structure and future course of international politics.[110]

However, the economic appeasers hoped to be able to defuse the elements of conflict which were contained in this trend. Since the rationalisation or, alternatively, the politicisation of the process of economic concentration was almost inevitable, it was thought necessary to remove the political (nationalistic) pretext. This was to be achieved by neutralising the national political effects of cartels through genuine international cartels:

> insofar as they [international cartels] serve purely economic ends . . . they may be said to be truly international. In that case they constitute in a sense counterbalancing influences which transcend political boundaries and make for stability and peace. Such influences deserve encouragement. But if . . . they form part of a policy aiming at political domination through economic control, then they become a most dangerous instrument of nationalism.[111]

Here lies the root of the economic appeasers' aim to keep politics and economics separate; that is, to safeguard their respective autonomy. Although they recognised that such a separation was anachronistic under postwar conditions, the political considerations outweighed the consequences to be drawn from their knowledge of economics and history. Nevertheless, their peace strategy aimed at re-establishing the autonomy of the economy against its distortion by politics in order to use it as a base for the reconstruction of international economic interdependencies which, in turn,

110. Ibid., p. 5. A.Teichova's studies demonstrate that no country combined the 3 methods of penetrating foreign economies, but rather concentrated on either financial, commercial or industrial penetration; Teichova, *Munich*, pp. 380–382; id., 'Die deutsch-britischen Wirtschafts-interessen in Mittel-Ost und Südosteuropa am Vorabend des Zweiten Weltkriegs', in: Forstmeier, Volkmann, eds., *Wirtschaft und Rüstung*, pp. 275ff.

111. Wellesley-Memo., p. 19; cf. Sargent/FO-Memo., 22 July 1931, C 5610/172/62, FO 371–15 189, p. 175f. (see pp. 53ff. of German original); FO-Memo., 'German Economic Penetration in Central Europe, the Balkans, and Turkey', 17 August 1936, R 4969/1167/67, FO 433–3, no. 13; cf. Wendt, *Economic Appeasement*, pp. 402ff., 413ff.

would render the relaxation of political conflicts possible.

The appeasers started from the assumption that the World Depression would reinforce the efforts of individual nations to improve the efficiency of their economies and to minimise their susceptability to external disturbances. The only chance of preventing the inherent danger of a collision of such perfected national economic units lay in the attempt to further the growth of the 'positive' (i.e. internationalist) aspects of the rationalisation process: if the trend towards larger units could be steered in the direction of international cartels and could perhaps even be guided through them, international cooperation and economic interdependence would constrain nationalism. Seen in this light, the economic appeasers based their strategy on the idea that by establishing workable international agreements and international cartels, they could create a counterbalance to the exploitation of the concentration movement in support of nationalist economic policies.[112]

The economic appeasers argued, as D. Mitrany was to do later, that the abandonment by Western states of *laissez-faire* principles in response to the World Depression and their introduction of national economic and social plans, would heighten nationalist sentiment and increase the potential of international conflict. They favoured international planning to reduce friction and to help develop an international consciousness.[113] In their view the problem to be solved was how the inevitability of rationalisation and concentration could be turned into an advantage. They were disturbed by the fact that cartel policies in the field of raw materials (e.g. rubber), which were dominated by only one partner, produced tensions even between countries which had normal political relations (i.e. Great Britain and the US).[114] Recognising the ambivalence of modern economic movements, they recommended that the instruments of integration and penetration should be employed to serve economic ends; efforts in this direction would have to

112. Wellesley-Memo., p. 20.

113. M.D. Dubin, *Transgovernmental Process*, pp. 492/493.

114. Wellesley-Memo., p. 22. On the Stevenson Rubber Restriction scheme and cartel negotiations (raw materials) during the 1920s, see I.M. Drummond, *Economic Policy*, pp. 116f., 49f. The United States picked the rubber issue as evidence of Britain's lack of interest in international settlements; Bingham to Eden, 17 July 1937, W 13 991/97/50, FO 433–3, no. 39, p. 113; H. Feis, 1 April 1937, quoted in A.A. Offner, *American Appeasement: United States Foreign Policy and Germany 1933–1938*, Cambridge/Mass., 1969, p. 179f. On Lothian's activities and Hoover's distrust of Britain see FO 371–11 168 (A 3163/10/45; A 4969/10/45, June 1926–August 1926) (see notes 101, 102 of German original).

override all attempts to use economic advantages for national power politics (imperialism).[115]

That this proposal was assumed to work in the best interests of the parties concerned, can be demonstrated by an example which preoccupied the minds of economic appeasers.[116] With a view to breaking the deadlock of Anglo-American economic relations, Lothian reminded both sides of the advantages of a Rubber Agreement. As Britain recognised that her capital was limited, she should invite the US to invest in the exploration and development of raw materials in the British Empire; this would offer the USA not only an opportunity to stockpile resources but also a fair chance of influencing price structures; the US had always complained about the British practice of restricting output by raising prices. The advantage to Britain of such an international agreement made the concession worthwhile: American capital invested in the British Empire would stimulate economic development and increase the demand for British manufactured goods. Indeed, the 'orderly marketing' arrangements might not simply offer economic gains; they might well further common interests in a variety of areas and even spill over into international politics; that is, the Anglo-American 'security community'. It would take a long time for this to become effective, but the economic appeasers nevertheless held that Anglo-American cooperation had to be pursued.

The experience of the 1920s showed them that things could go wrong in Anglo-American relations; they therefore emphasised that more attention needed to be paid to the impact of the raw-materials question on world politics. In the area of industrial raw materials only international cooperation, and possibly international regulations and controls, could limit the danger of a violent reaction to the bottle-necks created by monopolistic controls:[117]

---

115. Ashton-Gwatkin, Economic Survey, p. 373f.
116. Lothian, 18 Febr. 1926, Speech to American Chamber of Commerce in London, on economic co-operation, GD 40–17, vol. 412, pp. 129, 131, 133f. The instructions to the American delegation to the London (World) Economic Conference referred to agreements on production and distribution of 'international' raw materials; cf. Kindleberger, *World in Depression*, p. 215; League of Nations, Economic, Financial and Transit Department, Raw Material Problems and Policies, 2 parts, London 1946, pp. 50ff.: RIIA, Information Paper No. 18: Raw Materials and Colonies, 1936; RIIA, Information Paper, No. 18/1941, World Production of Raw Materials. A conference organised by the American Academy of Political Science, 10 to 14 May 1926 raised the topics for the first time, i.e. it did not just deal with the problems of raw materials in time of war; Proceedings, Part II: Raw Materials in Relation to International Peace and Economic Prosperity, vol. 12 (1926), pp. 113–224.
117. Wellesley-Memo., p. 22. Cf. Report of Interdepartmental Committee on Freedom of Access to Colonial Raw Materials, W 195/195/18, §§19 to 22, FO 433–3, no. 63, p. 622.

Everything points to some form of international rationalization policy that will rob the various systems of their nationalist and competitive character and unite mankind in an universal system of economic cooperation. International rationalization on a complementary basis is the only safeguard against overproduction and its attendant evils.[118]

In the 1930s the best way to divert these organised business interests from notions of self-sufficiency, which relied on protectionism, towards methods which offered protection without totally blocking multinational trade, appeared to lie in utilising such interests in the service of economic peace strategies. The whole set of their recommendations aimed at re-establishing the Triangular Trade System could only be realised if the industries concerned were organised in such a way that they could themselves participate in international negotiations. The economic appeasers ruled out the alternative of quotas being negotiated by governments since this involved the danger of a further politicisation of economic questions. However, they could not help but register another fact of life and try to make the best of the tendency it revealed. Just as associations of British industry,[119] the economic appeasers demanded that Her Majesty's government not only support British industry in international cartel negotiations as a counterbalance to German but also to French and Czechoslovakian industries, which were all more strongly subjected to their respective national economic policies. The economic appeasers preferred governments to ratify their trade agreements, but did so not in order to work out the structure or the details of the schemes. Certain excesses which they related to 'overcommitments' of governments and ensuing signs of 'economic reasonableness' as-

---

Ashton-Gwatkin recommended 'coordination of marketing . . . international agreements for the control of production and orderly marketing of certain commodities . . . to raise prices to a moderate degree and eliminate wild speculative movements'; he presented his views on a request from Foreign Secretary Hoare to outline concrete proposals as a contribution to his speech at the League's meeting in Sept. 1935; Ashton-Gwatkin took the chance to apply his basic ideas to an international statement of the British government; Ashton-Gwatkin referred to the Coljin Committee as still existing machinery and to Germany's membership in the Consumer's Committee of the International Rubber Regulation Committee; Ashton-Gwatkin, 7 Sept. 1935, FO 800–295, pp. 209ff., Hoare's Geneva Speech contained the 'catchwords' of the economic appeasers, FO 800–295, pp. 192–195; see below notes 282, 286.

118. Wellesley-Memo., p. 25; Ashton-Gwatkin, Economic Survey, pp. 311ff.

119. Wellesley-Memo., p. 18; Hall-Scheme (see notes 207–209), p. 22; on the talks between the FBI and the Reichsverband der deutschen Industrie see Wendt, *Economic Appeasement*, pp. 492ff., 522ff., 540f., 553f., 561ff.

serting a correction of the terms of such agreements, in their view proved the soundness of their own approach. The willingness of some branches in British industry to modify protectionist agreements in order to obtain their 'raw materials' (i.e. semi-manufactured goods) more cheaply on the Continent was seen by the economic appeasers as a sign not only that they were pursuing the right policies but also that they could expect their plan to be realised.[120] They observed that certain sectors and groups within British industry experienced challenges even in areas where the British supposedly held monopoly positions; British industry should, therefore, be content if it secured market opportunities through quota agreements.[121] These observations strengthened the view of the economic appeasers that those interests that were directly affected moved, for reasons of their own, in the same direction as their own proposals and schemes for 'economic reconstruction'. They took this kind of changing perspective as an example that economic factors were beginning to operate in favour of modifying or even revising the protectionist stance which asserted itself in 1931–32.[122]

Starting from a critique of the Ottawa system, the economic appeasers developed a comprehensive solution, which will be looked at in detail below. They joined the political debate by addressing themselves to the armaments question, just as their opponents regarded this as the central problem of the policy-making process. By demanding 'economic disarmament', they showed their commitment to the ideas of liberalism. Since protectionism, in its 'modern' form of state intervention in the economy, in particular in foreign trade, went against the needs of a specialised world economy, they forecast that the abandonment of liberalism would lead to conflict. If Britain insisted on protectionism – that is, obstructed access to the home market and misused the Empire's monopoly on important raw-material markets – she would not only provoke retaliation but would also write off her political influence which was based on her role in world trade and on her financial links. It was thought to be even more unfortunate if

120. The authors of the Hall-Scheme refer to the International Raw Steel Cartel (1935); on this see Wurm (note 68) and H.W. Würzler, *Großbritanniens Interesse an der westeuropäischen Stahlverständigung und die Gründung der Internationalen Rohstahlgemeinschaft (1924–1926/27)*, Ph.D. Bochum 1985; F. Benham, *Great Britain under Protection*, London 1940, pp. 182f., 188ff.
121. Hall-Memo., p. 16.
122. The Economist and the British Export Gazette, as well as 'Lancashire' industries criticised the protectionists' claim for import restrictions; Ottawa and the Trade Treaties on a compensatory basis had reduced British export opportunities.

Britain's economy set in motion and accelerated the trend to equip national economies with economic and eventually military means in the 'struggle for existence'. If the British government subordinated economic interests to political objectives or considerations beyond the transition period of short-term crisis management or simply prolonged the transitional measures, they would turn the last bastion of peaceful internationalism into a citadel of economic nationalism.[123] If, on the other hand, Britain intended to maintain the conditions in which her preferred option of 'peaceful change' and 'general settlements' could thrive, she had to encourage the functioning of the appropriate standards and preconditions, above all in the sphere of economics.[124] The economic appeasers conceded that *laissez-faire* liberalism had become an anachronism and that measures taken by the British government to attain economic recovery and restore 'normality' in Britain, namely the concentration on support for the domestic economy and imperial links, were unavoidable in the situation of 1931–32.[125] According to their judgement, however, the emergency measures should be temporary. They challenged the line of argument favouring 'imperial preference' and 'protectionism'.[126] They disputed the reasonableness of Britain's adopting the motto of 'everyone is master of one's own fate' and of practising the credo of 'British [Empire] interests always first'. If the protectionists claimed that Great Britain and the British Empire were still leading the world in terms of shares of the world's imports, Britain had to have a foreign policy appropriate to these realities. But if Britain, as protectionists advocated, restricted her capital exports and 'foreign' investments to within her empire and justified this change by pointing to security policy implications of (colonial) imperial preference, they had to be reminded of the consequences of their policy. If Britain locked her capital up in the Dominions and colonies, history might repeat itself; had not Australia, for example, experienced difficulties in servicing her debts and asked for larger exports in order to pay for the debts? If

123. Wellesley-Memo., p. 22; see ch. II 'Political system' re Inskip, Runciman, and below on Leith-Ross.

124. Wellesley-Memo., p. 23.

125. Wellesley-Memo., p. 23, 26; Ashton-Gwatkin, W 6928/1195/20, FO 371–18 497, pp. 371, 373ff.; Lothian, August 1935, 'The Peace Aspect of Reconstruction'; Lothian, 16 June 1936, *News Chronicle*. The background is the fact that the devaluation of the £ Sterling was a functional equivalent to a general tariff; the import restrictions, introduced in addition to devaluation, enforced the effect on foreign competitors; Memoranda of the Economic Advisory Council to Board of Trade, 24 and 25 Sept. 1931, FO 371–15 671, pp. 199, 215ff.

126. Amery, *Political Life*, vol. 3, pp. 203–207.

this happened again, Britain would have to reduce imports from 'the rest of the world' in order to cope with the requests of her 'imperial' debtors. How could this chain of events contribute to world recovery? Instead intra-imperial trade would cut into world trade. Furthermore, did the protectionists really want to live with the prospect of increasing imports from the Dominions? There was one way to avoid a fateful outcome: provision of capital exports and Empire-wide investments; for this strategy to work, however, there had to be more planning than the protectionists (i.e. Conservatives) were prepared to support.

Without wishing to repeal the Ottawa Treaty[127] and the sterling bloc[128] completely – which they regarded not only as unfeasible but also as inappropriate – the economic appeasers thought that this integrated market had to be fitted as a 'new unit' into a world economic order that was to evolve from the World Depression. However, this was only feasible, if the British 'bloc' was stripped of practices directed against other regional systems or economies. On a concrete level, one possible solution in their view lay in linking Germany and France to a customs union with the British Empire and the United Kingdom.[129] They held that it was import-ant that measures of crisis management were not perpetuated in a system of economic nationalism, since conflicts between large-scale economies would in that case be unavoidable. Rather, the British government should direct its efforts to linking general trends of world-wide economic development – concentration,

127. Ashton-Gwatkin and Chalkley represented the Foreign Office at the Ottawa negotia-tions; partly supported by the Board of Trade/Runciman, they advocated the principles of international trade, but to no avail; Ashton-Gwatkin, 5 Jan. 1933, W 238/238/50, FO 371–17 318, pp. 98ff. The Liberals (Sinclair, Samuel, Lothian) left the National Government because 'Ottawa' in their view spoiled the chances of the World Economic Conference; Lothian to Samuel, 25 Sept. 1932, and Samuel to MacDonald, 16 Sept. 1932, Lothian-Mss., GD 40–17, vols. 145 resp. 269; Lothian, Liberal Meeting, 12 Oct. 1932, GD 40–17, vol. 435.

128. Ashton-Gwatkin/Selby-Memorandum, Jan. 1933, W 890/278/50, FO 371–17 318, pp. 116ff., rejected the (Wardlaw-Milne) proposal to insulate the £-bloc. The breakdown of the London Conference favoured the formation of the £-bloc: S. Strange, *Sterling and British Policy. A Political Study of an International Currency in Decline*, London 1971, pp. 44ff., 55ff.; Drum-mond, *Economic Policy*, pp. 119ff.; Clay, *Lord Norman*, pp. 409ff.

129. Ashton-Gwatkin, 23 Dec. 1935, comment on C 8070/635/18, FO 371–18 873, p. 129. The idea of a lower tariff union implied criticism of 'Ottawa'; Dafoe ('Winnipeg Free Press') and Mackenzie King favoured a lower tariff union; Hull supported the idea: Dafoe to Halifax, 16 May 1932, Baldwin-Mss., vol. 98, pp. 93ff.; the British government intended to proceed on similar lines: Middlemas, Barnes, *Baldwin*, pp. 675ff.; Kottmann, *Reciprocity*, pp. 16ff. Later, London saw no chance of returning to the proposals: Baldwin's reply to a Deputation of the Peace and Economic Co-operation Movement, 21 March 1937, PREM. 1–212, p. 2. The Hall scheme favoured the lower tariff union concept.

industrial combines, rationalisation – to the positive elements of 'liberalism'; that is, freedom of movement, a world division of labour and cooperation between the (larger) new units.[130] This analysis of economic developments led them to a number of proposals which, in writings on appeasement, are generally regarded as indicators of economic appeasement. The list of proposals included a recognition of Germany's leading role in *Mitteleuropa* – perceived as 'a sort of Ottawa economic Mitteleuropa'.[131] There were also to be market-sharing agreements between branches which were organised in cartels and so on.

They merely had to develop a continuity thesis in order to be able to adhere to the consequences of their policy even *vis-à-vis* the Nazi regime. The aforementioned escalation theory comprised such an argument: economic nationalism leading to a domestic economy organised, regulated and misused by the state (state economy), and thence leading to autarchy and finally to militarist expansionism.[132] Their commentaries on the crises of the 1930s had all the symptoms of self-fulfilling prophesies. This was, however, linked with an interest in, and a hope of, blocking the escalation process, provided that Britain took initiatives of the right kind. Thus it was necessary that Great Britain, whose economic prospects depended in the long run on a return to a free world-market economy,[133] did not turn emergency measures implemented during the crisis into a dogma.

An historical analogy also served to underpin their rejection of protectionism: According to the economic appeasers, J. Chamberlain's tariff reform campaign had driven the industrial and com-

130. Ashton-Gwatkin, Economic Survey, pp. 311ff., 373ff.; Lothian to Buell, 30 April 1935, GD 40–17, vol. 289; Lothian, 'Europe at the Cross-Roads', *Round Table*, June 1926, vol. 16, pp. 494ff.; Lothian, The Empire and Free Trade, 28 March 1930, GD 40–17, vol. 431, pp. 147ff.

131. Lothian to Smuts, 16 March 1937, GD 40–17, vol. 333, pp. 880–886; Lothian, Speech at Chatham House, 29 June 1937, IA, vol. 16(1937), pp. 870ff.; Lothian to N. Henderson (Berlin), 13 Sept. 1937, vol. 347. Halifax hold similar views: Halifax to Phipps, 1 Nov. 1938, BD, 3ser., vol. 3, no. 285. According to an interview with Lord Harvey, Eden's PPS in 1936/38, on 18 Nov. 1964, Eden compared Germany's influence in its 'backyard' to American impact on Middle and Southern America; Eden would have recognised *Mitteleuropa* as an economic unit, if it came about peacefully; these arguments resemble closely the thoughts of Ashton-Gwatkin and Jebb. ·

132. On rationalisation see above, notes 103, 112f. Ashton-Gwatkin/Jebb, 31 Jan. 1936, C 807/4/18, FO 371–19 884, pp. 46ff. is a direct application of the 'escalation theory' to day-to-day 'office' politics; cf. Butler to Eden, 14 March 1936, C 2104/99/18, FO 371–19 932; Jebb minute, 25 March 1936, ibid., p. 294; Sinclair to Lothian, 18 May 1934, Lothian-Mss., GD 40–17, vol. 278, pp. 770f.; Memorandum of the Peace and Economic Cooperation Delegation to the Prime Minister, Prem. I–212 (8 Febr. 1937).

133. Ashton-Gwatkin, 15 Oct. 1934, comment on C 6844/1/18, FO 371–17 688, p. 79.

mercial classes in Germany – who were looking forward to Germany's future in the markets of the world and advocated *Weltmacht ohne Krieg* – into the arms of the militarist party and had thereby provoked that unholy alliance between militarism and a rationalisation movement in Germany, which was seen as one of the most important structural causes of war before 1914.[134] Drawing on this historical parallel was designed to support their current warning that Britain should not in principle depart from her liberal stance, but should present to the world a credible alternative to state socialism or state capitalism. The economic appeasers thus criticised the German élites less than those power élites in Britain who wanted to extend and complete protectionism initiated in 1931–32. Consequently, they called upon the government to modify the emergency measures, since they had to a certain extent exported the crisis from Britain to other areas, in particular to Central Europe. The revision of foreign economic policy should signal Britain's willingness to enter into negotiations for a reordering of the world economy; that is, to regulate the second phase of the recovery process not in a national but in an international context. As long as Germany still purported to respect British interests, Britain should seize the initiative: the progress made in her economic recovery and the resources of the British Empire–Commonwealth appeared to justify taking the risks which such a course involved.[135]

3. Economic Appeasement and *Mitteleuropa*

Economic appeasement would not be of paramount importance to students of British foreign policy if all we had to determine was the influence of the proponents of the escalation theory; that is, the Economic Section, the group around Lothian, centre-left movements and some others, as well as the connections between them.

---

134. Wellesley-Memo., pp. 6 and 4.

135. Ashton-Gwatkin, C 400/99/18. FO 371–19 931, p. 37; see below, note 380. Ashton-Gwatkin's suggestions approached the views put forward by Schacht, in Nov. 1935: C 7493/635/18, FO 371–18 873, pp. 25 ff. On German (and French) criticism of 'Ottawa' and British protectionism see Leith-Ross, 'The Financial and Economic Situation in Germany', 14 March 1932, C 2234/77/18, and Waley to Sargent, 18 March 1932, FO 371–15 936; Berlin Embassy to Foreign Office, 30 August 1932, C 7486/7486/18, FO 371–15 954; *The Times*, 14 Nov. 1932; Berlin Embassy to Simon, 28 Nov. 1932, FO 371–15 954, pp. 12f.; RdI, *Geschäftliche Mitteilungen*, vol. 14 (1932), no. 24. On trade diversions due to 'Ottawa', the Import Duties Acts. etc. see D. Kaiser, *Economic Diplomacy and the Origins of the Second World War. Germany, Britain, France, and Eastern Europe 1930–1939*, Princeton 1980.

Theirs is the most consistent 'strategic concept', but this, of course, is not the case if one measures its impact on politics.

Their concept was based on an economic analysis and aimed at applying economic factors (methods, ideas, factual relations, patterns of behaviour) to political problems. Their line of reasoning also provided impulses for political action and indicated the main thrust of their political initiatives. It is an economic appeasement strategy in its most undiluted form. Their chances of success were, however, limited partly because of the dynamics of the German development and partly because they represented the strategies of an opposition within the government. The strategies designed by Ashton-Gwatkin, Jebb and their followers among the 'attentive public' not only had political opponents, who maintained that Germany's economic difficulties were a consequence of the ruling regime's policies and that, therefore, only a political approach to the German problem should be considered; they also had to compete with appeasement strategies based on very different evaluations of the world situation and pursuing very different political ends.

Of these competing strategies of appeasement, which relied on, and deployed, economic means, the conception of one group has been chosen for closer analysis as it was well established in important departments and propounded by men like Eyres-Monsell, Swinton, Hankey, Cranborne, Sargent, Chatfield and Inskip in cabinet committees and in the cabinet itself. This second grouping responded to a certain extent to the escalation theory but actually put other 'political' aspects at the centre of its peace strategy. The approach of this second group was moreover informed by an aspect which also figured in the strategy of the first group, albeit less prominently.

The spokesmen of the second group took the view[136] that economic bottle-necks were the cause of aggressive military

136. This strategy is one of 'economic appeasement' insofar it expects appeasement effects to result/derive from conceding an economic *Mitteleuropa* to Germany/Third Reich. This solution was proposed and supported by Amery (Empire Industries Association), Swinton, Hankey, Simon, Dawson (The Times), Eyres-Monsell, O'Malley (Southern Section of the FO), Chatfield. Even circles who regarded themselves as anti-appeasers (after Munich!) argued in 1937/38 in favour of granting *Mitteleuropa* to Germany; since Britain was not capable of defending the status quo it had to aim at improving relations with all the 'great' powers: All Souls Meeting, 18 and 19 Dec. 1937, Nicolson-Mss.; Nicolson-Diary, 22 Dec. 1937 and 22 March 1938. As soon as the 'economic appeasers' (esp. Lothian) discovered that 1) Hitler (and not the 'Moderates') determined German foreign economic policy and 2) German *Ostpolitik* aimed at dominance and forceful change of the territorial 'order' in 'New Europe', they advocated (balance of) power politics; to Lothian this meant alignment with the U.S.A. and Canada.

regimes in Italy, Japan and Germany. However, they attributed these bottlenecks more to a lack of *Lebensraum* and not, as the first group, to dysfunctions of the world economic system, which they felt could be accounted for by wrong decisions taken by the established industrial nations. In connection with the view that large-scale economies such as that of the US, the Empire–Commonwealth or even the USSR would by themselves make a contribution to a lasting peace, the second group maintained that regulatory functions, which the saturated Western powers were claiming or had claimed for themselves, also had to be conceded to the leading rising powers such as Germany, Japan and Italy. This meant that they applied the categories which dominated their imperial thinking to German, Japanese and Italian demands for 'parity'.[137] Since, with few exceptions (such as Amery, who took a different position on Austria), they regarded British economic and even strategic interests in the 'hinterland' claimed by Germany or Japan as *quantités négligeables*,[138] they could afford to denigrate the 'victims' of the expansionist policy of Germany in the Balkans and of Japan in China. At all events, they regarded it as more important to arrange for an 'order' which would accommodate Germany (and Japan) without involving lasting disadvantages to Britain, than to declare the status quo or the interests of small, and above all quarrelsome, nation-states (or in the case of China, the War Lords) as sacrosanct. In their opinion 'small' nations had to accommodate the leading economic power in their region. Such a 'surrender' did not necessarily mean political-military risks for the established world powers. On the contrary, they maintained that the 'nationalism' of the small powers would provide an effective barrier against all attempts by the 'leading' economy in a particular region to achieve political dominance in the wake of an expansion of its economic sphere of influence. They were more disposed to the view that Germany would be absorbed by so many problems in *Mitteleuropa* (as Japan would be in China), and especially in 'political' conflicts, that they would be unable to expand beyond the sphere of interest which had been conceded to them.

As Cadogan and Simon put it on two different occasions:

137. F. Whyte, lecture at Royal United Services Institute, 8 Jan. 1936 (on Japan); Lothian, 29 June 1937, 'Germany and the Peace of Europe', IA, vol. 16, pp. 870–893. On Milner & Amery (during the First World War) see my 'Politische Tradition' and ch. I/4 of German original.

138. C.F. Remer, *Foreign Investments in China*, New York 1933, pp. 99, 138; W.R. Louis, *British Strategy in the Far East 1919–1939*, Oxford 1971, pp. 6ff.; S.L. Endicott, *Diplomacy and Enterprise: British China Policy 1933–1937*, Manchester 1975, pp. 19ff., 22f.

No ring is going to keep Germany in, as she is going now [e.g. rearmament]. If she acts, it is surely better that she should act to the East . . . that will at worst occupy her energies for a long time and may well prove a lesson and not a stimulus.[139]

It cannot surely be suggested that Germany could conquer and rule so many diverse elements. And if she could, I should have thought her hands would be full enough without any adventures against us.[140]

The time which Germany would need to settle her 'Balkan troubles' could be used by Great Britain to overcome her deficiencies in armaments and economic policies, caused by decisions of 1919 and 1932–34, to consolidate her own economic sphere of influence and generally to mobilise her strength.[141] Conceding the 'hinterland' (i.e. *Mitteleuropa*) to Germany did not necessarily mean that the Third Reich would gain a comparative advantage to the detriment of Britain.

Characteristic of this group is the idea (which to a certain extent even became an unshakeable belief) that Britain's ability to mobilise her moral, industrial, economic and military strength in an emergency was unmatched. Her financial power, defined as the fourth arm of her defence forces, would allow her eventually to extend her superiority *vis-à-vis* Germany and thus to create an element of security for herself and her partners in Western Europe. As this group put great emphasis on financial strength as a security factor and thought that time was on Britain's side in this field, they rejected proposals and suggestions of other groups which recommended providing financial support for Germany in the hope of achieving a change in German policies once Berlin had been helped to overcome its financial difficulties. Hankey, Swinton, Eyres-Monsell, Chatfield, Cranborne and others preferred to have Central/South-Eastern Europe 'released' into Germany's sphere of economic influence, as a concession of this kind

---

139. Simon, 17 April 1935, notes on Stresa conference; cf. Simon-Diary, 11 August 1936; and see Ch. I, notes 208ff., 233ff. of German original.

140. Cadogan-minute, 28 May 1937, on C. 3621/270/18 (Lothian report on talk with Hitler), FO 371-20 735, pp. 239.

141. Sargent and Vansittart challenged Lothian's views and charged him of defeatism: FO 371-20 735, pp. 235ff.; I. Colvin, *Vansittart in Office*, London 1965, pp. 144ff. Lothian's speech to the German-British Society was an attempt to correct this impression; he warned German leaders not to underestimate Britain's strength: 3 June 1936, C 4184, FO 371-19 906. Lothian tried to improve Britain's position in American opinion with a view to buying arms and tools in spite of the Johnson Act and Neutrality Laws.

would help Britain to gain much needed time for her industrial–military and moral rearmament whilst, at the same time, they expected and hoped that such a concession would dissipate and deflect German energy. However, they resisted proposals put forward by Lothian, Ashton-Gwatkin, Jebb and, for a while, Eden,[142] who not only recommended conceding economic superiority in Central and South-Eastern Europe to Germany but also alleviating her shortage of foreign currency and raw materials. They did not rule out credit facilities or joint ventures in markets not falling within the sphere of influence of either power. For them 'finance' was to be used for political ends; that is the stabilisation of particular political systems. In their opinion, Bolshevism had been a serious alternative in German domestic politics in 1930–32; the appropriate provision of credit facilities was to counteract the recurrence of such a situation. However, the main emphasis of the groups around Ashton-Gwatkin and Lothian/Jones was on recreating international interdependence and the idea of a penetrated system among 'Western' industrial societies. This was to be achieved, as we have argued, in the course of re-establishing financial, capital and commercial links which would spare Britain having to chose between the extreme perversions of state interventionism which had emerged in National Socialist Germany, on the one hand, and Bolshevik Russia, on the other.

The approach of Hankey/Chatfield/Cranborne and the economic appeasement strategy of Ashton-Gwatkin differed in important details, particularly with regard to the sacrifice expected from third parties in Central and East-Central Europe. They disagreed over the relevance of nationalism and its function for the re-establishment of a world economy and for securing peace and differed in their evaluation of the 'time factor'. They also disagreed in their assessment of the relationship between politics and economics. The second group maintained that the nationalism of small nations would give them strength to resist any misuse of Germany's economic superiority for politico-military ambitions of hegemony. They further presupposed that economic interest groups on the German side would recognise that capacity for resistance and, in their own interest, would object to the use of military methods for the subjugation of *Mitteleuropa* just as strongly as they would

---

142. Lothian, 11 May 1937, GD 40–17, vol. 203, pp. 264ff.; cf. Wendt, *Economic Appeasement*, pp. 348ff.; H. Nicolson-Diary, 16 June 1937, pp. 295f., refers to plans on forming a China consortium with a view to distracting Germany from her 'Drang nach Osten' (South Europe and Russia).

oppose their own subjugation to the aims of the 'one-party state'. In Germany's economic 'hinterland' the economic dominance of the Reich could be expected to quell the excesses of the economic nationalism of the small nations. It was not thought possible that Germany could break the political will of these 'units' to remain independent. For Ashton-Gwatkin and Jebb, for Lothian and other supporters of the escalation theory, on the other hand, the nationalism of the 'successor states', of *Zwischeneuropa*, was incapable of resistance and thus did not present a countervailing power. The problem of nationalism which concerned them was of a different order. They focused on the divergence of the leading world economic powers from, and their non-compliance with, the standards of a functionally divided economic system in general and the change of direction in British foreign economic policy of 1931–32 in particular. Whilst Ashton-Gwatkin and Lothian urged that Britain was short of time and, therefore, called for prompt action so as to mitigate social and political tensions arising from Germany's accelerated economic development, Hankey, Cranborne, Swinton and their followers took a long-term perspective which was based on a faith in the strength of British finance and the potential of British 'will power'. This contrast bears on another difference. Hankey and Swinton urged the government to invest more heavily in the economy, particularly in order to highlight the nation's interest in defence and to stress the needs of the armaments industry as against those of the exporters and consumers. Ashton-Gwatkin and Lothian, on the other hand, did not wish, as a matter of principle, to open up the economy to political inroads, even if in practice they did not want to exclude 'state measures' to deal with an emergency.

Whether the different emphases in the two strategies weakened the impact of economic appeasement is hard to establish. Against the background of the domestic economic and political power constellations in Britain the differences became blurred with other controversies. For the Board of Trade, the industrial federations and, above all, the National Union of Farmers, the guiding principle was that especially in economic questions Britain must safeguard her own interests above all else.[143] Since those groups which had stakes in their business connections with Germany did not have much to set against the political weight of economic

---

143. W. Elliot, Minister of Agriculture, was regarded as the champion of economic nationalism in Cabinet; cf. Drummond, *Economic policy*, pp. 232ff., 108ff. See below pp. 146ff. and Ch. II, §6.

nationalism at home, chances that the proposals of the economic appeasers would be realised were slim. The policies which the first group of economic appeasers wished Britain to adopt – revision of Ottawa, modification of tariff policies, credit facilities – became bogged down by the resistance of 'vested interests' inside the country.

Furthermore, the compromise formulas, developed by the two groups, which ultimately reached the cabinet (through interdepartmental committees), rarely contained economic concessions which might have induced totalitarian regimes to 'liberalise' their domestic or foreign policies. This applies equally to the most salient point on which both strategies were in agreement, namely Britain's disinterest in *Mitteleuropa*. The Germans were already successfully implementing their strategies and tactics of penetration, so that they saw no reason even to consider British economic or, to an even lesser degree, political counter-demands; the Germans did not even indicate an interest in negotiated settlements. Although various influences, above all the views of the military and of large parts of the Conservative Party, pushed in the same direction as the two strategies described above, British governments – at least before the end of 1937 – did not declare themselves in favour of a deal which implied the recognition of a 'Monroe-like *Mitteleuropa*'.

Elements of the economic appeasement strategies, as we have portrayed them, can be discovered at a later stage in British foreign policy. The ideas of the second group (Hankey, Chatfield and others) concerning *Mitteleuropa*, became part of official British soundings; for example, Halifax's visit of November 1937, when the trust invested in the strength of small-power nationalism and its resistance to Germany had at least become doubtful.[144] Basic elements and assumptions of the economic appeasement strategy, as we have defined it by reference to ideas proposed by Ashton-Gwatkin and Lothian long before 1937, advanced to 'official' positions when the tide had already turned.

(1) When in 1938 – after the Halifax visit of November 1937 – the 'political approach' had petered out, the British government launched proposals which had been recommended by the economic appeasement strategies and which had merely been the subject of internal foreign policy debates until then. In Munich,

144. L.G. Schwoerer, 'Lord Halifax's visit to Germany, November 1937, *The Historian*, 32(1970), pp. 353ff.; K. Middlemas, *Diplomacy of Illusion*, pp. 133ff.; Harvey-Diaries, pp. 59ff.; Eden, *Facing the Dictators*, pp. 508ff.; All Souls Meeting, 18/19 Dec. 1937.

Chamberlain raised the issue of economic relations with Central/ South-East Europe and, within the framework of Anglo-German economic cooperation, conceded German predominance in this area to Hitler.[145] The precondition for such an arrangement was to be a demarkation of interests between both powers; this was thought to include German concessions, possibly to the effect that the Third Reich promised 'good conduct', whilst the British withdrew economic aid to promote the latent resistance of the affected nations to Germany's policy of economic–political–military penetration.[146]

(2) The plainer it became that Hitler – as opposed to Schacht or Göring, who were seen as exponents of the 'moderates' – had no interest in colonial deals or in economic appeasement and absolutely none in changes in domestic policy as hoped for by the appeasers, the more pronounced became the attempts to supplant diplomatic efforts and approaches at the foreign-policy level with negotiations between leading industrialists.[147] Captains of industry had long recommended that 'meetings of businessmen . . . might perhaps be a suitable means of bringing about a return to common sense'.[148] However, contacts and soundings at this level had been watched sceptically by the Foreign Office and proposals to build on Schacht–Norman talks or on visits paid by top people in the military hierarchy were more likely than not to provoke debates in the cabinet. Although it is difficult to date shifts of emphasis and 'atmosphere' precisely, it can be said with certainty that 'semi-official' contacts were welcomed in 1938. As a last resort to defuse international tensions, politicians were more eager than hitherto to promote the necessary conditions for successful direct negotiations between different branches of industry. Considering that the economy and the political system had become increasingly interlocked as rearmament intensified, this recourse to a key element of

145. K. Feiling, *N. Chamberlain*, p. 376; DBFP, 3rd ser., vol. 2, no. 1228, pp. 639ff. Cf. Teichova, *Munich*, pp. 380ff.; the same applies to Chamberlain's policy towards Japan (in 1934): Chamberlain-Diary, 9 Oct. 1934, N/C 2/23A.

146. Hawtrey (Treasury)-Wills (Board of Trade) correspondence, 27–31 May 1938, 'Financial Pressure on Germany', BT 11–1006; 'Means of financial pressure in the event of war, with special reference to Germany and Japan', 12 March–27 May 1938, T. 160–769, F 15456; F.P. 54 and F.P. 74(36), Cab. 27–627.

147. FBI-Memo., 'Origin of Anglo-German Industrial Conversation', FBI/S/Walker/110; cf. Wendt, *Economic Appeasement*, pp. 413ff.; on Japan see Drummond, *Economic Policy*, pp. 134ff.

148. Berlin Embassy to FO, 7 June 1935, C 4653/653/18, FO 371–18 871, pp. 41ff. The 'political' heads of the Foreign Office opposed such bilateral methods since they did not want any repetition of the Payments and Naval Agreements. The Board of Trade and the Treasury did not favour the projects of Piggott, Tennant, et al. (March–April 1935, C 1980, C 3485, and C 3722/25/18, FO 371–18 822, pp. 117ff., 125f., 169ff., 182f.).

economic appeasement strategies came very late in the day.[149]
The top managers in industry and the representatives in meetings
of industrialists, who were aware of the profound changes in
international and domestic politics, urged more emphatically than
hitherto that a political rapprochement between the leading
figures of the Third Reich and Japan, on the one hand, and London,
on the other, was indispensable. They also asked the British
government to provide them with guarantees; British industrialists
were prepared to enter into agreements with their opposite
numbers from 'politicised national economies' only if such
guarantees were given prior to the summit conferences of private
industry.[150] This demand was reasonable, since the instrumentalisa-
tion of foreign trade for political ends and the mobilisation of
'economics' for purposes of arms production had underlined the
revival of *Drohpolitik*. The proponents of economic appeasement
strategies had offered their advice with a view to achieving, on the
one hand, a convergence of the socio-political systems through
negotiations between competing interests over market-sharing
and 'orderly' market agreements and zones of influence and, on the
other hand, through the gradual renunciation of political weapons
in economic competition (currency restrictions and manipulations, politically motivated tariff preferences, etc.); they had advocated their ideas but had also added a warning: their proposals
would work on condition that 'actions' were taken in good time.
When British 'official' policy in 1938–39 welcomed meetings
between industrialists, and industrialists in their turn demanded
support from the government against the failure of their summit
diplomacy, the actual situation differed markedly from the scenario
envisaged by the economic appeasement strategies.

This is not to say that – before 1938–39 – nothing happened
which fits into an interpretation of 'economic appeasement', or
that the recipes contained in economic appeasement strategies

149. L. Kettenacker, W. Lenz, 'Lord Kemsleys Gespräch mit Hitler', *VfZ*, 19 (1971), pp.
305 ff.; H. Metzmacher, 'Deutsch-englische Ausgleichsbemühungen im Sommer 1939', *VfZ*,
14(1966), pp. 369ff.; B. Martin, *Friedensinitiativen und Machtpolitik im Zweiten Weltkrieg
1939–1942*, Düsseldorf 1974. M. Cowling, *Impact of Hitler*, pp. 154, 205, warns against making
too much of the talks. In 1936, the Cabinet followed recommendations of Interdepartmental
Committees to support industrial conversations between individual branches — BT 11 — vols.
433, 442, 735, and 1045.; Jebb-Eden-Memo., to N. Chamberlain, 17 March 1937, W
6363/5/50, FO 371-21 215, pp. 183 (Germany) and 189 (Japan). On American negotiations
with Japan concerning voluntary export restriction schemes see D. Junker, *Der unteilbare
Weltmarkt. Das ökonomische Interesse in der Außenpolitik der U.S.A. 1933–1941*, Stuttgart 1975, pp.
153ff.
150. Glenday, 23 March 1937, Tariff and Trade Treaties Committee, FBI/C/2/1937.

worth their name were adopted by the government only when 'reality' was likely to disappoint the expectations. But what has been said so far amounts to the conclusion that the strategies of economic appeasement, outlined here on the basis of records covering the 1930–37 period and by reference to the genesis of the underlying ideas as they emerged in the 1920s, were not determining Britain's official foreign policy as a whole or in essential parts. Although these strategies were making advances, different approaches won the day. These approaches saw to it that initiatives conforming to the 'ideas' of economic appeasement were kept within the confines of *intra*governmental debate. They were *not* fed into *inter*governmental or diplomatic negotiations. To be made part of 'official' policy after the policy of appeasement had come to be regarded as synonymous with one-sided 'surrender' to aggressors, contradicted the main assumptions under which the champions of the two types of economic appeasement had thought their sets of recommendations to be operative. Their strategy implied that Britain, in one way or another, was still in a 'position of strength', albeit relatively so. That time was running out, was an argument in order to encourage decision-makers to lead the way and influence the course of events; it was not meant in the sense of 'appeasement' as a justification for 'buying time' and with a view to making sure that if Hitler began to attack, he would not hit the British first.

4. 'Grand' and 'Small' Solutions: the Array of Economic Appeasement Proposals

If one studies the details of the proposals submitted by the economic appeasers in the more limited period of 1934–37, it is important to realise the gap between the narrowness of their concrete offers and their view that there was a serious danger of an explosion in Germany. This gap also accounts for the note of scepticism which characterises their proposals for action.[151] They knew that these proposals represented anything but an ingenious way out. They acknowledged that their detailed proposals had to operate within the constraints of British domestic politics and at the same time were not to go too far in meeting the German side

---

151. Ashton-Gwatkin, 11 March 1936, C 1651/4/18, FO 371–19 889, pp. 18f.; Ashton-Gwatkin/Jebb, 31 Jan. 1936, C 807/4/18, FO 371–19 884, pp. 46ff.

in case concessions were then misused to advance German power. If, on the other hand and notwithstanding the watering-down of, and straight opposition to, their suggestions within the 'government by committee' system, they stuck to their strategy, this was essentially because of two circumstances. To begin with, they shared the view that Britain and France could endure the loss of prestige resulting from the successful German coups to no more than a limited extent and, therefore, had to ensure that the next *'fait accompli'* be prevented; but 'preventative diplomacy' could launch initiatives only in the economic field. This was the field in which the 'West' possessed some advantages at least.[152] Secondly, their escalation theory endowed the individual initiatives of their action-related programme with an inner 'consistency', whatever the criticisms that might be made on points of detail. Before turning our attention to the question of how to place economic appeasement strategies[153] within the framework of British foreign policy, it seems appropriate to examine the detailed proposals of the economic appeasers in terms of how they fared when they were confronted in interdepartmental and intradepartmental meetings with alternative scenarios for a 'preventative diplomacy', and how they then responded to criticisms disputing the usefulness of the 'economic approach'. We shall have to distinguish between the 'comprehensive' and 'small solutions'. Whilst the small solutions remained in the context of economic relations, in the 'grand solutions' economic components were imbedded in, or determined by, expectations of comprehensive conflict resolutions. The economic 'substance' and consequences of these proposals were not always assumed to be attainable by their proponents.

The economic appeasers classified 'colonial appeasement' (i.e. the return of colonies)[154] as a possible political deal; they did not, however, see it as contributing to the solution of the problems

---

152. Ashton-Gwatkin/Jebb, C 807, pp. 2 and 6. Similar views were forwarded by Dawson (*The Times*) and Liberals (Opposition), cf. Cowling, *Hitler*, pp. 132f.

153. For the following economic appeasement refers to the Economic Section of the FO, to Lothian and Th. Jones.

154. Ashton-Gwatkin, 'Germany's Economic Position', Annex to Wigram-Sargent-Memo. 21 Nov. 1935, Phipps-Mss., 5/5, pp. 120–123; cf. Wendt, *Economic Appeasement*, pp. 321ff. Sargent, 30 Nov. 1935, FO 371-18 851, p. 175; Wigram-Sargent-Memo., §31, labelled 'colonial appeasement' as 'Danegeld'. The issues at stake were Tanganyika, Togo and Cameroon, i.e. subject matters which, because of agreements during the First World War, involved France; on these soundings in 1936/7 see R. Tamchina, 'Commonwealth und Appeasement', *NPL*, 21, pp. 471–489; id., 'In Search of Common Causes: The Imperial Conference of 1937', *JICH*, 1(1972), pp. 88ff.; R. Ovendale, 'Appeasement', pp. 34f., 47ff. See note 141 of German original and pp. 404ff. of German original.

they had identified.[155] Since they realised that their main aim of normalising world trade could not be tackled straightforwardly, they concentrated on identifying the proper intermediate steps;[156] the colonial solution did not belong here:

> We shall be able to escape the redevelopment of the 1914 alliance system . . . only if we can prove that through the League there is a reasonable chance of finding a reasonable place in the sun for all nations. And that place in the sun includes territorial and economic aspects. The pressure for that most difficult thing – the transfer of territory – will lessen in proportion as security for raw material and markets can be obtained for all nations in other ways.[157]

'Colonies', as they preferred to view the problem, should be part of a comprehensive *economic* scheme; that is, lending itself to the economic ends of their own peace strategy. Their first option as a starting-point for negotiations with Germany, which could and should comply with the raw materials question, [158] was the formation of a comprehensive preferential trade and/or a tariff system which included Poland and the countries of South-Eastern Europe. Additionally, or alternatively, they envisaged a division of markets

155. Ashton-Gwatkin and Jebb recognised that the colonial question was a problem of power and prestige and that it would be impossible in view of the Abyssinian crisis and German rearmament to get 'public opinion' to agree to colonial deals; C 400/99/18, 1 Jan. 1936, FO 371–19 931, pp. 35ff.; Jebb, 24 June 1936, FO 371–19 933, pp. 319ff.; Hall-Scheme, pp. 2f., Jones-Mss., Class E, vol. 1, no. 10.

156. Ashton-Gwatkin/Jebb-Memo, 31 Jan. 1936, C 807/4/18, FO 371–19 884, pp. 44ff.; Ashton-Gwatkin, 4 March 1936, FO 371–19 889, pp. 18f.; cf. FO 371–19 888, pp. 75ff., and FO 371–19 933, pp. 322ff.

157. Lothian, The Peace Aspect of Reconstruction, August 1935, GD 40–17, vol. 113, pp.131ff.; cf. Cowling, *Hitler*, pp. 89f., 110 ff. Schacht, the key figure of German 'moderates' (from the point of view of economic appeasers), urged 'colonial appeasement', whereas the economic appeasers preferred the pursuit of the raw materials question started with Hoare's Geneva speech (FO 800–295, pp. 191–195). The Treasury rejected concessions on raw materials: C 2847/99/18, FO 371–19 932 (April 1936); on Chamberlain see Cowling, *Hitler*, p. 154.

158. Ashton-Gwatkin, 21 Nov. 1935, C 400/99/18, FO 371–19 931, pp. 35ff.; 23 Dec. 1935, FO 371–18873, p. 129. In his view, the Clearing- and Trade Agreements had already established 'preferential areas': C 397/8/18, FO 371–19 917, pp. 147f. In the internal discussions of the FO on whether to start the working agreement initiative with an Air Pact (New Locarno) proposal or with raising the raw materials question, the meeting on 14 Febr. 1936, chaired by Eden, resolved on the Air Pact; C 998/4/18, FO 371–19 885, p. 275. It was decided to separate the raw materials question from the 'working agreement' procedure and transfer this problem to the League of Nations; the sense of the meeting was that it was up to Germany to raise the raw materials issue; the FO expected that Germany had to offer something if Germany wanted progress with regard to raw materials. Cf. C 796/4/18, 3 Febr. 1936, FO 371–19 884, p. 21.

between Germany and Central/South-Eastern Europe, on the one hand, and Britain, North-Eastern Europe and Scandinavia, on the other hand.[159] In their view the Compensatory Trade and Clearing Agreements had paved the way for establishing a 'preferential area'. They rejected the view that their scheme was dangerous; they believed Germany to have reached the limits of her commercial penetration of her neighbours and that the prospects of her being able to establish *Mitteleuropa* as a *Zollverein* were dim indeed. Seen in realistic terms, Britain's economic ties with Northern Europe were stronger than Germany's, and this *de facto* position could serve to counterbalance German preponderance in South-Eastern Europe. A 'preferential bloc' of this kind would therefore provide Germany with a chance for economic recovery. Anyway, Britain's interests related much more to stimulating the German economy because of the multiplication effect of Germany's reintegration into world trade and less in direct exchange relations with Germany's 'hinterland'. Moreover, the actual development of the past (few) years was pointing in the direction of preferential areas. The economic appeasers therefore recommended acknowledging the truth of Friedrich List's telling argument that the Danube countries had the same significance as a market for Germany's industrial surplus as the mid-West for industrial America.[160] The argument of the economic appeasers suggested that, even when one dealt with Nazi Germany, traditional British interest in a prosperous Germany should take precedence over other points of view:[161] An economically 'satiated' Germany would moderate her political aims sooner than a military rearmed but economically weak Germany.[162]

The proposal constituted a variant of another working hypoth-

159. FO-Memo., 17 August 1936, 'German Economic Penetration in Central Europe, the Balkans and Turkey', §11, R 4969/1167/67, FO 433–3, pp. 82, 85ff. On the structure of the central and south-east European economies and their relationships with Germany see notes 145 and 151 of German original.

160. Ashton-Gwatkin, 24 July 1936, C 5685/99/18, FO 371–19 934, p. 88; Ashton-Gwatkin, 21 Nov. 1935, C 400/99/18, FO 371–19 931, p. 36.

161. Collier, 22 Nov. 1935, FO 371–18 856, pp. 147f., and Vansittart, 1 Dec. 1935, VNST 2/24, were critical on the political consequences of Ashton-Gwatkin's suggestions; the Board of Trade (G (36) 7, 26 Febr. 1936, Cab. 27–599) refuted the economic appeasers' suggestion for economic reasons. On the debate after 'Munich' see Lammers, *From Whitehall*, p. 840; MacDonald, *Moderates*, pp. 121, 126. Similar arguments dominated the internal American debate on policy towards German penetration in Latin America, cf. Junker, *Weltmarkt*, pp. 208, 260ff.; P.A. Varg, 'The Economic Side of Good Neighbourhood Policy', *Pacific Historical Review*, 45(1976), pp. 47–71.

162. Ashton-Gwatkin, C 400/99/18, FO 371–19 931, pp. 36ff.; cf. Wendt, *Economic Appeasement*, ch. 2.; Gilbert, *Roots*.

esis of appeasement policy, which holds that Britain, in taking Germany's demand for equal status seriously, could exercise a moderating influence on Germany. Following the Payments Agreement of 1934 and the Naval Agreement of 1935, the recognition of 'equality' in the area of foreign-trade policy was to be the next move among the various attempts to accommodate Germany.[163] The idea was that by granting Germany an 'economic Monroe Doctrine', she would respond accordingly; that is, arrange her predominance in *Mitteleuropa* in such a way as to make it acceptable to the countries concerned and to the Western powers so that they found it possible to live with such a German predominance. The political initiative of the winter of 1934–35 and the 'working agreement' approach of 1935–36 reflect their schedule for negotiating a general settlement with these ideas in mind.[164] From the point of view of the economic appeasers, a compromise did not contain merely risks. They expected Germany to be unable to purchase all the products of the economically dependent neighbouring states; consequently there was no hope of her achieving a monopolistic position. As the largest import market in the world, Britain remained, in their opinion, an attractive supplementary market for that region.[165] It was important to improve international trade, as this and only this provided a platform for the operation of economic appeasement strategies: 'I myself believe, however, that this nearly mortal complaint [on the cancerous nature of Nazism] will yield to the radio-active treatment of increased world trade' instead of 'cutting out Hitlerism with a knife'.[166] An additional attraction of this model was that as soon as the economic situation and trade in the German 'economic empire' experienced an upswing, Britain could also derive benefits from the restoration of economic relations in Central Europe.[167]

This line of thought was open to different sorts of criticisms.

163. Ashton-Gwatkin, C 400, pp. 36f; Wendt, *Economic Appeasement*, pp. 290ff. The willingness to 'resign' to the 'facts' is influenced by the view that the states of 'New Europe' had crossed British proposals and sided with France at crucial stages of British 'German policy'.

164. Cranborne, 17 March 1936, FO 800–296, pp. 139–142, FO 371-19 894, pp. 234f.; Stanhope, 26 Nov. 1935, FO 371-18 860, p. 137. On Lothian and Ashton-Gwatkin see notes 130ff.

165. Ashton-Gwatkin/Jebb, 31 Jan. 1936, C 807/4/18, p. 3 and 6, FO 371-19 884, pp. 46f. Ashton-Gwatkin, 27 Oct. 1938, C 14 471/42/18, Annex E, FO 371-21 659; cf. Lammers, *Whitehall*, pp. 837f., 840.

166. Jebb, 16 March 1936, on C 1558/4/18, FO 371-19 888, p. 76. Cf. Lord Gladwyn, *The Memoirs of Lord Gladwyn*, London 1972, p. 55; see note 193.

167. Ashton-Gwatkin, 16 March 1936, and 25 March 1936, FO 371-19 932, p. 294, and FO 371-19 892, pp. 202f.; see note 165.

Some expressed their criticism indirectly by attacking the free trade illusions of the American secretary of state, Cordell Hull; all of the critics disputed the adequacy of such a model for solving European conflicts. Only Germany would profit from improved economic terms of trade between herself and central South-Eastern Europe and the general improvement in trade relations. The Third Reich would not respect a 'liberal' international regime in any arena of trade, finance or security. Therefore improved market conditions in *Mitteleuropa* could not be expected which would induce the powers-that-be in Berlin to share the general interest in the maintenance of peace between Germany and the Western powers.[168] The economic appeasers not only considered helping to find outlets for Germany's exports, but also assisting this development by facilitating her access to raw materials and credits. They maintained that Germany depended on capital from the West (i.e. finance and raw materials) to develop her 'Monroe' zone. Because of this the Western powers were believed to have an effective lever at their disposal to prevent Germany from resorting to protectionism, and they even saw a process to this effect being under way in Germany.[169] Disputing such arguments, the critics of economic appeasement emphasised that, quite to the contrary, Britain would have to employ 'pre-emptive purchase' methods in order to bail out Germany's neighbours from their economic dependence on Berlin.[170] The economic appeasers countered this point by asserting that resort to such combative methods would signal the end to all hopes to release German foreign trade from its subordination to the political ends of Nazism.

The economic appeasers opted for the expedient of allowing German economic expansion in central South-Eastern Europe; they did so mainly because alternatives which they judged to be more effective appeared to be blocked by the power constellations in the British economic and socio-political system.[171] One of these alternatives concerned the opening-up of the British market to

168. Lammers, *Whitehall*, p. 837; MacDonald, *Moderates*, pp. 121, 126; Wendt, *Economic Appeasement 1938*, pp. 124ff.; Gilbert, Gott, *The Appeasers*, p. 196.

169. Ashton-Gwatkin, 'German Economic Penetration in the Danube Valley', 27 Oct. 1938, pp. 11–18, FO 371-21 659; Lord Gladwyn, *Memoirs*, pp. 53ff.

170. Swinton, *Memoirs*, pp. 164ff.; Einzig, *In the Centre*, pp. 91ff.; BT 11–1077 (re Jugoslavia) and BT 11–903 (re Romania). Similar French pre-emptive purchase initiatives did not fare better; agricultural interests resisted purchase of Romanian wheat and French investors were not keen to drop 'capital' into Southeast European ventures.

171. The 'Food & Defence' lobby, Empire Industries Association and other vested interests/ protectionists rejected the basic ideas of economic appeasement, i.e. 'liberalising' commercial policy and solving the raw materials problem.

German exports; this 'grand solution' will be considered below. The economic appeasers let it be understood, however, that the *Mitteleuropa* solution alone would not be sufficient to entice Germany into a compromise. Peaceful German penetration of *Mitteleuropa* would contribute to their main aim of a general European settlement only if British policy was coupled with other proposals, relating to the raw materials question or to the opening-up of British export markets to German products. They maintained that it was only possible to restrain violent German expansion to the east, if Germany had to fear serious consequences, such as the loss of markets which were controlled by Britain.[172] Referring to this proviso, they objected to the charge that in their view Britain could successfully combat the National Socialist movement[173] by giving way to German expansionism and freeing Germany from economic bottle-necks.[174] In their response to such allegations, the economic appeasers made clear that they merely intended to propose effective methods for influencing the course of developments in Germany, *if this was thought desirable for* political reasons. Their message was to direct policy-making to the key issue; namely, that the German problem had, above all, an economic context without being primarily an economic problem.[175]

However, their plea that they could keep the 'German peril' in check with their suggested revival of world trade, and especially of German trade with the rest of Central Europe and with the United Kingdom, could not conceal the fact that the proposal promoted a strengthening of Germany without offering a guarantee that the instruments for controlling the growth of German power would apply and work. The weakness of the proposal was precisely that

172. Ashton-Gwatkin/Jebb, C 807; Ashton-Gwatkin, 4 March 1936, FO 371-19 889, p. 18ff.,; FO 371-19 888, pp. 75ff.; Barringdon-Ward to Jones, 16 July 1936 Jones-Mss., Class E vol. 1, no. 10 = FO 371-19 933, pp. 322ff. (Hall-Scheme). The Board of Trade and Treasury representatives, Q. Hill and Waley, had raised the objections to the economic appeasers' proposals in interdepartmental talks preceding the 'working agreement' initiative of the FO; 17 Jan 1936, C 397/8/18, FO 371-19 917, pp. 147ff.; FO 371-19 932, pp. 202ff.; Lord Gladwyn, *Memoirs*, pp. 54f.; Board of Trade Memo., G (36)7, 26 Febr. 1936, Cab. 27-599.

173. Pinsent comment on Ashton-Gwatkin/Jebb-Memo., 7 March 1936, in: Phipps to FO, FO 371-19 888, p. 77.

174. Butler urged the British government to 'test' German offers and diverge from France's policy of signing on the dotted line; Ashton-Gwatkin and Jebb supported Butler's position; minutes, 16 March 1936, FO 371-19 892, pp. 202f. and FO 371-19 932, pp. 294f. (25 March 1936).

175. Jebb, 16 March 1936, on C 1558/4/18, FO 371-19 888, p. 76; Lothian to C. Hull, 12 Oct. 1937, GD 40-17, vol. 347; Lothian, Dec. 1935, Round Table, pp. 103-105. On the rather similar currents of debate in the State Department see R.N. Gardner, *Sterling-Dollar-Diplomacy*, p. 10; Junker, *Weltmarkt*, p. 197.

the economic appeasers knew, just as their adversaries, that it contained nothing to attract the Germans. Germany's economic influence in Central Europe had effectively gone as far as the proposals went; consequently nothing was to be expected in exchange from Hitler that might really relieve Britain of any of her own problems and bottle-necks.[176] Nevertheless, British foreign policy kept the question of concessions in *Mitteleuropa* on the table (Halifax visit November 1937). It wanted neither to increase the gravitational pull exerted by Germany at the centre by declaring London's renunciation or disinterest nor did it wish to add to British commitments.

The economic appeasers would have preferred the idea of a German 'preference area' in central South-Eastern Europe to be combined with commercial and political offers (reduction of import restrictions and trade barriers). This, however, was wrecked by the resistance of the Board of Trade, the Import Duties Advisory Committee and the majority of the cabinet, all of which did not agree either to a revision of protectionism or to a renunciation of the British rights contained in a number of most-favoured-nation agreements. Because of Germany's political success in the March crisis of 1936, the proposal was in any case no longer of any practical value.[177]

In these circumstances the 'credit question' became more important. Press reports and parliamentary questions kept the debate alive. German complaints about her lack of raw materials and German pressure on subsidiaries of international concerns (Dunlop, ICI, Mond-Nickel, Shell) to import and stockpile raw materials led observers to focus attention on the City, which had remained the centre for reimbursement credits and other ways of financing raw material transactions.[178]

176. Wigram, 20 May 1936, C 3746/4/18, FO 371–19 906; Pinsent to Waley, 15 June 1936, C 4487/99/18, FO 371–19 933, p. 266 (concerning devaluation of the Reichsmark and British supportive action).

177. Jebb, 16 June 1936, on C 4074/99/18, FO 371–19 933, pp. 197ff.

178. Meetings between Schacht and Norman were always accompanied by reports and rumours that the 'City' was keen to grant credits in order to facilitate German imports of raw materials; N. Law to Sargent, 4 Sept. 1934, C 6019/1/18, FO 371–17 687; Leith-Ross to Waley, 14 Sept. 1934, C 6370/1/18, FO 371–17 688; Phipps to FO, 7 Nov. 1935, C 7493/635/18, FO 371–18 873; Phipps to FO, 26 Sept. 1935, FO 800–295, p. 251; Waley to FO, 18 Nov. 1935, C 7748/635/18, FO 371–18 873; Law to Sargent, 10 Dec. 1935, C 8213/635/18, FO 371–18 873. The Treasury (Morrison, N. Chamberlain) asserted in the House of Commons that the Bank of England had only in Dec. 1934 granted a £750,000 credit to facilitate the repayment of commercial credits to British subjects (23 March 1936, HofC). Cf. Wendt, *Economic Appeasement*, pp. 344ff.

The economic appeasers were aware that German exports had risen and that the imports of raw materials had increased; the export quota, however, was not sufficient to satisfy the requirement for raw materials.[179] The economic appeasers did not want to promote German government loans in London to be guaranteed by Britain and France.[180] They knew that the Hitler regime would not allow itself to be 'bought' and that it did not look for credits and loans which would only multiply Germany's problems in the long term.[181] In the eyes of both the Germans and the economic appeasers, the question of credit facilities remained bound up with the question of exports. The German side was concerned with maintaining 'such economical credits as would naturally arise from a reviving trade'. From their perspective the credit question represented an appropriate option insofar as it amounted to nothing more than ordinary forms of short-term commercial or bank credits; these could, moreover, be regarded as the grease to the mechanism which was to set world trade in motion. Since world trade itself had not provided sufficient commercial credit facilities until now, Britain, as the financial, trading and commodity-market centre of the world, had to weigh up the pros and cons of financially assisting Germany's imports of raw materials in the hope of accelerating world trade.[182] When German agitation over the colonies reached its peak at the Nazi Party Rally in 1936, the economic appeasers also interpreted the campaign as an attempt to mobilise public opinion in favour of granting credits to Germany.[183] In talks with Schacht, Ashton-Gwatkin learnt that the German 'moderates' looked upon the credit question in much the

179. FO-minutes, 16 June 1936, FO 371–19 932, p. 196; on German foreign trade see H.E. Volkmann, 'Außenhandel und Aufrüstung', in: Forstmeier, Volkmann, eds., *Rüstung und Wirtschaft*, pp. 85ff., 101ff.

180. Eden and the 'political' heads of the FO rejected Government guaranteed loans, 23–30 Dec. 1935, C 8205/635/18, FO 371–18 873, p. 191; Phipps to Eden, 21 Oct. 1936, Simon-Mss. Ashton-Gwatkin and Jebb did not rule out government guaranteed loans; they considered financial assistance an essential element of any 'deal' which involved the 'conversion' of German armaments production capacity into 'civil/export' production: Ashton-Gwatkin, 16 March 1936, FO 371–19 892, p. 203; Ashton-Gwatkin/Jebb, 31 Jan. 1936, C 807/4/18, p. 4, FO 371–19 884.

181. Ashton-Gwatkin, note on his talks in Berlin, 21–23 July 1936, C 5685/99/18, FO 371–19 934, pp. 88f.; Phipps' comment on Ashton-Gwatkin's views were rather critical: C 5928/99/18, FO 371–19 934.

182. Jebb minute, 28 April 1936, on C 3110/99/18, FO 371–19 932, p. 80; Ashton-Gwatkin to Kirkpatrick (Berlin), 23 March 1936, C 1558/4/18.

183. FO minutes on Einzig's articles in *Financial News*, Nov. 1936, C 7986/98/18, FO 371–18 930. In Sept. 1936 Phipps had prophesied that Ribbentrop would like to start his ambassadorship with a big bang, similar to the Naval Agreement; Phipps added, however, that the City would react in a negative way to such agitation.

same way as the economic appeasers.[184] Schacht did not want 'large new credits' for the introduction of stabilising measures; but he did ask for 'some additional reimbursement credits . . . to come from the market'. Schacht promised not to cancel long-term debts on condition that a lowering of interest was made possible during the conversion operations. He declared his readiness to adjust Germany's currency – which would allow a reduction in export subsidies – on condition that the other countries took no measures to counteract a German 'devaluation'. Quotas and trade barriers were gradually to be reduced at the same time.

The fact that the detailed proposals submitted by the economic appeasers were similar to points which the diplomatic reports represented as Schacht's opinion and that their procedural proposals concentrated on establishing consultations at the level of the Schacht–Norman or Leith-Ross–Schacht talks induced the opponents of economic appeasement, in particular Vansittart, to force a decision against moves in the economic sphere.[185] Since Norman shared the economic appeaser's assumption that an 'explosion' was imminent in Germany and that a British wait-and-see policy was therefore dangerous, Vansittart thought it necessary to obtain a pledge from Norman that he would consult with the Foreign Office before he entered on his 'international diplomacy' again. This was even more necessary as rumour had it that Norman was strongly influenced by Schacht at meetings of the governors of Central Banks. Vansittart also encouraged Einzig's campaign against Norman, the City and the Treasury. Furthermore, the Foreign Office asked the Bank of England for a statement on the raw materials and credit question. The Treasury and the Bank of England reported back that neither they nor the City were considering expanding the credit limit to Germany and emphasised that such steps would only be considered when the German government had changed its political stance. They also pointed out that the German government did not want to increase its debts, but was looking for outlets for her exports.[186] The Bank of England and the Treasury evaded the question of commercial and bank credits since

---

184. Leith-Ross report of talks with Schacht in Badenweiler, 4 Febr. 1937, Phipps-Mss. 3/4, pp. 45–68; cf. Eden-Memo., May 1937, 'The Colonial Question; 70371-20735, pp. 194ff.

185. Vansittart to Eden, 5 Nov. 1936, FO 371–19 930; cf. Vansittart minute on Leith-Ross to Waley (re talk with M. Norman), 19 Sept. 1934, C 6370/1/18, FO 371–17 688.

186. Leith-Ross to FO, 3 Nov. 1936, C 7986/97/18, FO 371–19 930. The Treasury directive in spring 1937 asked the banks to grant no more credits to Germany: Einzig, *In the Centre*, pp. 72ff.; on the embargo on foreign loans in general see Howson, *Domestic Monetary Management*, p. 143; Howson/Winch, *Economic Advisory Council*, pp. 109, 111ff.

these were not controlled by them; however, they did try to shrug off as foolish the allegation that Germany would gain from the 'free pound' account of the Payment Agreement; that is, that Germany would be able to finance imports[187] of raw materials needed for arms production from this account. Industrialists engaged in Britain's rearmament, such as Lord Riverdale, one of the architects of the 'shadow industry', warned against the tendency 'to take any more of one's money into Germany than one can possibly help'.[188]

A third option which could serve as an intermediate step towards the normalisation of world trade concerned currency stabilisation; the economic appeasers, however, did not expect much to come of this. Although Britain could lend supporting cover to a reordering of currency relations, involving the devaluation of the German mark and its ensuing stabilisation[189] – as in the case of the devaluation of the franc – it would have been difficult to push such an operation at home; to provide 'covering fire' for a devaluation of the mark would have meant renouncing all measures against increased German competition engendered by devaluation.[190] From the point of view of foreign policy, this solution offered little prospect of politically desirable 'side-effects'; insofar as they were desired by the economic appeasers, these related to their main aim of removing 'artificial' (politically motivated) barriers to an exchange of goods and services. Their terminology registered

187. Jebb, 3 Nov. 1936, FO 371-19 930; cf. T 177-30. On German raw materials imports and exchange problems see Volkmann, *Außenhandel*, pp. 96ff., 133ff., and Wendt, *Economic Appeasement*, pp. 405ff.; Einzig, *Economic Appeasement*, pp. 96ff.

188. Lord Riverdale to Hankey, 9 March 1936, FO 371-19 891, p. 237; cf. Kirkpatrick (Berlin) to Wigram, 2 March 1936, C 1590/99/18, FO 371-19 931, p. 218.

189. Ashton-Gwatkin report on informal discussions with Waley (Treasury), Q. Hill (Board of Trade), Wigram and Jebb upon 'positive' elements of an economic policy toward Germany: 17 Jan. 1936, C 397/8/18, FO 371-19 917, pp. 147ff. In Nov. 1935 Schacht had given the impression, in talks with Norman, that Germany might devalue the Reichsmark; the Treasury was interested in discussing the 'technical' implications; these soundings should be bilateral, i.e. exclude France, Phipps to FO, 6 Nov. 1935, C 7493/635/18, FO 371-18 873, and C 8205/635/18 (10 Dec. 1935); Eden-Norman, 10 Jan. 1936, C 208/99/18, FO 371-19 931. For more details, see note 176 of German original.

190. In winter 1936/37 Leith-Ross favoured depreciation of the £ Sterling, but found no favour with the Bank of England (Clay) and the Treasury and Chamberlain — see Sayers, *Bank of England*, vol. 2, pp. 474f.; Leith-Ross recommended a devaluation to Germany (see below); Waley proposed the devaluation of the Reichsmark in the interdepartmental discussions (see note 189). The motive behind Leith-Ross' proposal can be surmised from this statement to Vocke (Reichsbank) in Jan. 1933: exchange controls - as an alternative to devaluation - would lead Germany onto the 'Russian' track; this fear is an important constituent of 'economic appeasement' strategies; J. Schiemann, *Die deutsche Währung in der Weltwirtschaftskrise 1929–1933*, Bern/Stuttgart 1980, pp. 185ff., informs on Leith-Ross' contacts with the Reichsbank in 1933.

practices such as exchange restrictions as characteristic of the 'Russian–Bolshevik system'; in order to reinstate capitalism (albeit tempered by 'orderly marketing agreements', etc.) and to reintegrate Germany into the 'Western economy', they wanted efforts to be made that would prevent Germany from following the 'Russian example' and thereby turning the 'state socialist' or 'state capitalist' alternative – in the sense of their 'escalation theory' – into a serious and immediate challenge to the Western economy. To lure Germany away from perfecting her 'controlled economy' and thus from lining up with the 'Russian-type' economy, more was needed than a promise to 'stand still' whilst Germany devalued the mark. Not only could devaluation do no more than remove the symptoms; the provision of British aid would have to be limited and thus would not be sufficient to compensate Germany if she acceded to British demands and demonstrated 'good behaviour'; for example, a gradual withdrawal of currency restrictions, of a 'managed currency', and so on, which was upsetting to trade.[191] Britain's limited flanking support which a currency stabilisation would provide could not invalidate Germany's arguments in favour of a 'controlled and managed currency'. These arguments held that Germany could not afford the repayment of debts abroad and could not increase imports as long as she was not allowed to expand her exports.[192] Besides, Hitler left no doubt that his government opposed devaluation because it would increase the costs of imports to a level higher than that to be achieved by increased export earnings.

5. The 'Grand Solution': Anglo-American Partnership and the 'New Imperial Economic Policy'

When ruminating upon the 'small solutions', the economic appeasers were confronted time and again by the question of how to find outlets for German exports.[193] They remained guided by the slogan

---

191. Pinsent to Waley, 15 June 1936, C 4487/99/18, FO 371–19 933, p. 266. Pinsent had warned that Germany's economy was 'warped' to such a degree – because of the impact (repercussions) of managed currency – that return to normalcy would require much time; C 2872/99/18/, FO 371–19 932.

192. Schacht linked his proposal to consider devaluation of the Reichsmark to various conditions, e.g. reduction of Germany's debt services, improved situation for German exports, readjustment of the main currencies; Febr./March 1935, C 1824/635/18, FO 371–18 870, pp. 235 ff.; FO 371–18 873, pp. 291ff.; Waley to FO, 27 June 1936, C 4679/99/18, FO 371–19 933.

193. Jebb, 16 March 1936, on C 1558/4/18, FO 371–19 888, p. 76; Gladwyn, *Memoirs*, p. 55.; Jebb, 16 June 1936, C 4074/99/18, FO 371–19 933, pp. 197f.

that 'if goods cannot cross international frontiers, armies will'.[194]

In their opinion, Britain, by changing her tariff policy – that is, by adopting a 'grand solution' – could contribute to the establishment of larger markets for Germany's export surplus and open up cheaper markets for Germany's agricultural and raw material needs in the Dominions, South America and in the sterling-bloc countries than those offered by the countries of Central and South-East Europe. They felt, therefore, that Britain had to add something of her own resources to a *Mitteleuropa* offer, particularly if she wanted to prevent the economic dependence of the countries concerned from turning into economic subjugation.[195] Here are two statements to this effect:

The only hope of moderating the German drive to the East (which is going on now and which she holds to be inevitable) and reducing it to something which would not take the form of actual military aggression, lies in the British Empire taking more German goods.[196]

There is little doubt, indeed, that Germany will soon be so strong, that she will prefer war even against an Anglo-French-Russian coalition to general internal bankruptcy – for that is what the alternative will be – unless . . . some kind of 'outlet', 'expansion' . . . is found before bankruptcy becomes inevitable.[197]

Pronouncing that, 'if we do nothing, we are in for a war',[198] the economic appeasers felt obliged to spell out the terms of a grand solution; that is, a scheme capable of influencing the politics and the economy of the Third Reich. In this context the following questions had to be dealt with: (1) Would Germany respond to the proposals? (2) Did the material and political conditions prevailing

194. Lindsay to Eden (on talk with Hull), 23 Jan. 1936, BT 11–589, pp. 282–288; cf. Ashton-Gwatkin/Jebb, 31 Jan. 1936, C 807/4/18, FO 371-19 884.

195. Ashton-Gwatkin/FO-Memo., 'German Economic Penetration in Central Europe, the Balkans, and Turkey', 17 August 1936, R 4969/1167/67, FO 433-3, pp. 83f.

196. Bruce to Stanhope, reported in Jebb minute, 10 June 1936, on C 5197/99/18, Eden/FO to Runciman/Board of Trade, FO 371-19 933, p. 325. In his conversations in Berlin, Ashton-Gwatkin gained the impression that Germany's financial problems were still manageable; everything depended on an up-turn in world trade, i.e. British stimulating measures: 24 July 1936, C 5685/99/18, FO 371-19 934, pp. 89f.

197. Ashton-Gwatkin/Jebb, 31 Jan 1936, C 807/4/18, pp. 2, 6.

198. Jebb, 2 July 1936, FO 371-19 933, p. 334; cf. Ashton-Gwatkin/Jebb, C 807, p. 2; Bruce proposed to the British Government that it should provide Germany with an alternative to increasing arms production; Bruce referred to the McDougall Scheme (see below), M. MacDonald to Eden, 10 Oct. 1936, FO 411-19, p. 108. Jebb had worked with the authors of the McDougall scheme; see below note 498.

in Britain allow for redeeming the offers made? (3) Could Britain control the side-effects of economic actions on the 'security arena'? If not, could Britain nevertheless take the risk that economic appeasement might equip the German war-economy instead of reintegrating Germany into an international peacetime-economy?

(1) As long as important sections of the German 'political economy' voiced an interest in a gradual return to world trade, the economic appeasers felt there was a chance of interesting Germany in a restoration or normalisation of world trade which was so important for Britain; even after 'Munich' many actions continued to be interpreted as showing a readiness to bring about détente. A further indication was Germany's own attempts to overcome her economic difficulties by increasing exports. It was for precisely this reason that they believed it essential to provide markets for her goods. They reckoned that the pressure of events that had induced the US and Britain to return to 'liberal' practices and principles in their relations with the rest of the world and in their bilateral relations would also lead Germany back into the international economy.[199] Of some importance to their judgement were a number of signs that the Barter Trade Agreements which Germany had concluded were not enough and that she might therefore wish, by learning from her own experiences, to return to multi-lateralism.[200]

In actual fact, however, the New Plan of September 1934 had already pointed Germany in another direction. In order to direct the German economy away from world trade even in those sectors where autarky was out of the question, a complex system of import and export controls was to ensure that capital-goods industries had first charge on man-power and raw materials. Dependence on the import of industrial raw materials required for arms production was regarded as disadvantageous and was, therefore, to be regulated by the state in such a way as to insure that nothing upset the development of the armaments sector.[201] Attempts to

199. Phipps to FO, 30 Sept. 1936, C 6852/99/18; cf. Economic Relations Office, 'Review of Events', C 7953/7746/62, 6 Nov. 1936, FO 433–3, No. 22, pp. 148f.

200. Correspondence Pinsent (Berlin)/Hill (Board of Trade), Oct. 1935, C 7093/25/18, FO 371–18 822; Ashton-Gwatkin and Jebb gathered information from meetings with their German opposite numbers in the committee work on behalf of the Standstill and payments agreements and from the reports of the Committee of Economic Information (see below).

201. On the development of German foreign trade and the concentration on a group of countries see Volkmann, *Außenhandel*, pp. 89ff., 103f.; W. Carr, *Arms, Autarky, and Aggression. A Study in German Foreign policy 1933–1939*, London 1972, pp. 52ff.; Petzina, *Autarkiepolitik*, pp. 46ff.; cf. FO-memo., 11 March 1938, C 1822/541/18, FO 371–21 701, pp. 455ff.

force Hitler to face 'economic facts' failed largely because of external conditions, such as the worsening of the terms of trade since 1935–36; but Schacht also suffered a series of setbacks in his battles with the Armed Forces High Command, the Air Force and the Ministry of Agriculture; these developments and the orientation of those industries, which were geared to the home market, towards Göring as the 'economic dictator', reduced Schacht's influence. The ruling party[202] could afford to ignore Schacht's plea of April 1937 to cut arms production and take advantage instead of expanding world trade to enhance German exports.

(2) The German argument, that they could resolve their shortage of foreign exchange and import difficulties only by increasing exports, met with a positive response in Britain and the British Empire.[203] Thanks to her connections with the Empire and the sterling-bloc countries, Britain had recovered a 'position of strength' in matters of raw materials and foreign exchange; this meant that she could operate as a partner who had something to offer, but at the same time maintain her controlling position.[204] Furthermore, Britain's recovery had advanced to a level which enabled her to look beyond her immediate needs and to take account of the international economy.[205] Equally, by the summer of 1936,[206] the

202. See note 191; Torr (FO) stressed that 'planned foreign trade' suited German purposes and that any hope of Germany's reintegration into international trade was therefore rather speculative; Torr, C 4679/99/18, FO 371–19 933, pp. 302; id., 23 June 1936, on C 4501/99/18, FO 371–19 933, p. 270.

203. Germany's terms of trade took a turn for the worse after 1934; see Petzina, *Autarkiepolitik*, pp. 31ff., and Volkmann, *Außenhandel*, pp. 84ff., 97. *The Economist* and *Financial News* (Einzig) hoped that the improved price structure for 'primary products'/commodities would allow the countries in central and south-east Europe to return to the markets of the world and liberate their economies from dependency on Germany (and the barter trade agreements).

204. Hall scheme: 'An International Policy for the British Empire', Barrington Ward to Jones, 16 July 1936, Jones-Mss., Class E, vol. 1, no. 10 = C 4759/99/18; Hall-memo., pp. 1, 10, 15. On the genesis of the Hall scheme see Lord Gladwyn, *Memoirs*, pp. 63f.; FO 371–19 933, pp. 322ff.; Jebb, 16 June 1936, and Ashton-Gwatkin, 25 June 1936, FO 371–19 933, pp. 197ff., 273f. Bruce, Australia's High Commissioner and delegate to the League of Nations, presented the gist of the Hall scheme in his speech to the League of Nations, Oct. 1936: FO 411–19, p. 108; MacKenzie King, Canada's Prime Minister, presented similar proposals at the Imperial Conference 1937, cf. Ovendale, *Appeasement*, pp. 27, 40ff.

205. Eden asked the Board of Trade and the Treasury to investigate the practicability of the Hall scheme; Eden to Runciman, 17 July 1936, C 5197/99/18, FO 371–19 933, pp. 329ff., and FO 371–19 934, pp. 1ff.; Bruce talked to Eden on the issue in Geneva – 3 July 1936, FO 371–19 934, pp. 1ff., and FO 371–19 933, pp. 318, 322ff. The Treasury rejected the main thrust of the Hall scheme and of the suggestions of an interdepartmental working group: Wigram report, 22 June 1936, FO 371–19 933, p. 198; Jebb, 25 June 1936; ibid., p. 322. In spite of the opposition made known in preliminary discussions, Eden requested an investigation.

206. Hall scheme, pp. 1, 10, 15. With regard to Japan, the authors of the Hall scheme hoped

wholesale price of primary products had made a recovery. This meant that it was in everybody's interest to consolidate the pattern of world trade and to restore the traditional channels of trade. This was therefore thought to be the moment to break the vicious circle that had led to protectionism all over the world in 1931–32:

> The contraction in the British adverse balance with industrial Europe has been accompanied by a proportionate contraction in Europe's adverse balance with the rest of the world . . . Primary producers need sterling if they are to meet their obligations, and unless their trade with industrial Europe provides them with sterling, which is only possible if the European countries have acquired sterling balance by trade with the United Kingdom, they cannot sell to Europe and Europe cannot buy from them.[207]

The prerequisites for tackling the German complaint about restrictions on her exports had been given (particularly in 1936–37) and the countries depending on a flourishing international economy were encouraged to take up the German problem while the favourable conditions lasted.

(3) The economic appeasers had inherited a ready-made solution[208] from debates during the First World War to cope with the issue of 'security', which came to the fore in connection with the debate on whether or not the provision of financial and economic aid might solve the economic dilemma. If the 'comity of nations' succeeded in reintegrating 'national economies' into an interdependent international economic system, the relationships would become so interlocked that any country would find it difficult to uncouple itself, should it so desire for political ends. Efforts to sponsor interdependency were, in the opinion of the 'economic appeasers', the best guarantee that countries felt themselves obliged to take political factors into consideration, to refrain from resorting to power-politics and to work for peaceful resolutions of conflicts:

---

that — thanks to their improved terms of trade — the 'developing' countries would import Japan's 'cheap' products; thus, Japanese competition would be 'distracted' to different markets, whereas the 'old' industrialised countries would exchange their products; Hall scheme, p. 8; Jebb, 24 June 1936, FO 371-19 933, pp. 319ff. Similar ideas shaped Cordell Hull's reciprocal trade policy concept.

207. Hall scheme, p. 10.

208. J.L. Garvin, *The Economic Foundations of Peace*, London 1919.

[It is] important to start talking the economics of peace as soon as we can. There is still a chance of giving the Germans some sort of vested interests in a settlement, and no settlement can last which is purely political . . . The ideal thing would be that it should be pressed upon the home government by the overseas Empire. This would provide the right kind of driving force and influence public opinion here . . . in the right direction.[209]

The implementation of this concept depended in part on the quality and substance of Britain's contributions; that is, whether the offers tempted Germany sufficiently to bring about her reintegration into the world economy. Another prerequisite was that Britain's 'position of strength' in the issue area was maintained. Both prerequisites were seen to be fulfilled in two respects: firstly, if there was the cooperation between Britain/the British Empire and the United States as the leaders in the raw material and capital markets of the world; secondly, if there was an 'imperial economic policy'. In both instances the conclusions of the economic appeasers were derived from the following argument: No one disputed that the 'nationalistic' measures which Britain had taken during the emergency of the World Depression had left their imprint on the political situation in the world and particularly in Germany. So, why not assume conversely that a revision of 'Ottawa', in conjunction with a more international orientation of American economic foreign policy and, above all, the coordination of both strategies, would relieve tensions in the world and in Germany?[210] If imperial preference and the devaluation of the pound in 1931–32 had accelerated 'nationalist' tendencies, turning competition into 'economic warfare' and thus contributing to the disruption of the European trading and financial system, agreements on currency stabilisation or a truce on tariffs and/or market sharing arrangements between industrial federations, and so on, ought to restore 'normal' conditions of multilateral economic exchanges.

209. Hall-scheme, pp. 1, 10; see note 204.
210. Hall-Memo., p. 4; Lord Gladwyn, Memoirs, p. 63; the lower customs union proposal relates to this aim, see below note 214. Jebb, 17 March 1937, FO 371-21 215, p. 179; Eden-Memo., ibid, pp. 182, 192; Atherton (US Embassy, talk with Eden, 24 Febr. 1936, A 1784/890/45, FO 371-19 834, pp. 132ff.; Jebb, 24 June 1936, FO 371-19 933, p. 320; FO 371-19 888, p. 76 (minute on C 1558/4/18). The economic appeasers urged the pursuit of the Hall scheme since they took Pinsent's report to mean that action had to be now if they wanted to break the vicious circle; Pinsent to FO, 15 June 1936, C 4487/99/18, FO 371-19 933, pp. 263ff.

However consistent this comprehensive appeasement strategy may have been, it had its weak points. To begin with, it linked British initiatives and room for manoeuvre to the state of Anglo-American relations, even to the point that the historian begins to ask himself if economic appeasement was a means of improving Anglo-American relations or if the Anglo-American 'partnership' was a prerequisite of Britain's search for a general European settlement. Seen from another point of view, the realities of the 'politics' of the international economy pointed towards an economic appeasement strategy which was based on a revision of Ottawa, on a 'new imperial economic policy', as presented by the study group working with Professor Hall.[211] The common denominator of both concepts of economic appeasement is the plea for an 'economic policy of collective security' that was to operate on the basis of an understanding with both France and the US;[212] it was thought of as an alternative to peace strategies which relied upon military alliances. The strategy of the economic appeasers was to be a substitute for such 'obsolete' defence measures and eventually to replace them; by identifying the proper way of removing the causes of war (i.e. by redressing political grievances and political tensions caused by the crises in the world economy), 'economic' appeasement was tackling the 'German problem' in the context of a comprehensive 'peace effort'.

These claims could be honoured only if the action-related programme aimed not merely at promoting economic growth but also provided guarantees of 'good conduct' to any country belonging to the economic community:

> Economic readjustments aimed at an increasing volume of trade must be to some extent revocable in character so that they will provide their own sanctions ... if there is not in the political sphere a substantial betterment of relations as a result of economic easement.[213]

---

211. The main ideas of the Hall scheme were urged by Bruce, by Mackenzie King, on Eden; see notes 204/205.

212. Ashton-Gwatkin/Selby, Jan. 1933, W 890/278/50, FO 371–17 318, p. 120; Lothian to Grigg, 26 April 1933, GD 40–17, vol. 269; Lothian, Chatham-House lecture, 26 July 1937. The debate on a reform of the League of Nations, i.e. infusing a new spirit into Article 19 and vivifying the Economic, Financial and Social Sections of the League, incl. the ILO, on the one hand, and getting the raw materials and standard of living issues on the agenda of international politics, on the other – was championed by the economic appeasers; they thought that the reform of the League would attract the United States and induce them to join or at least cooperate with the League; cf. Cowling, *Hitler*, pp. 231ff. on Sinclair, White and other Liberals who put forward these ideas in Parliament; see below notes 277, 282, 286.

213. Garvin, *Economic Foundations*; Hall-Memo., p. 4. The customs union idea was thought to

Mindful of Garvin's *Economic Foundations of Peace* (1919), the economic appeasers of the 1930s made it part of their credo that 'encouragement of a fat Germany' was meaningful only if it was 'part and parcel of some much wider scheme'.[214] The idea of a customs union appeared to them to be capable of dealing with both the growth aspect and the security aspect of their peace strategy. Britain and the British Empire were thus to transfer the idea of increased consumption, which had been successfully applied to their domestic economies,[215] to their foreign economic policies instead of continuing the policy of bilateral (reciprocal) concessions along the lines of 'Ottawa' and of the commercial treaty system. If Germany became a partner in a larger economic unit and feared the loss of her largest market (i.e. the British one),[216] she would think twice before overstepping her economic predominance in Central and South-Eastern Europe and misusing her Monroe-type zone for politico-military purposes.[217] If Germany were incorporated into the 'economic foundations of peace'[218] in a way which corresponded to her 'legitimate' aspirations and capabilities and shared both in the economic advantages and in the political obligation to behave well, one could expect the motivation for an aggressive foreign policy to disappear; to the economic appeasers 'aggressiveness' was a response to encirclement and *vice versa*. Should Germany, however, fail to honour the status of equality which would be accorded to her on joining the economic peace system, she would provoke a 'collective defence' response; that is, economic sanctions and, if the worst came to the worst, even military counter-measures.

This strategy referred back the proposals developed in the First

---

suit these purposes. Ashton-Gwatkin suggested considering Germany's entry into a customs union (lower tariff union) of the British Empire/United Kingdom; 23 Dec. 1935, FO 371–18 873, p. 130; Lord Gladwyn, Memoirs, p. 63. The reasoning behind this proposal is an awareness that offering equal access to colonial raw materials would not impress the powers-that-be in Germany; if Britain wanted to interrupt the escalation she had to face up to Germany's exchange problems; Ashton-Gwatkin, 7 Sept. 1935, FO 800–295, p. 213.

214. Lord Gladwyn, Memoirs, p. 63; cf. Hall scheme, p. 4.

215. Hall-Memo., p. 3; Ashton-Gwatkin to Vansittart, July 1936, C 4758/99/18, FO 371–19 933, p. 331 (talk on consultations between FO, Board of Trade and Treasury on the Hall scheme); Eden to Runciman, 17 July 1936.

216. Ashton-Gwatkin, 23 Dec. 1935, FO 371–18 873, p. 130; see notes 164 and 174 of this chapter.

217. Ashton-Gwatkin/Jebb, 31 Jan. 1936, C 807/4/18, p. 6, FO 371–19 884.

218. References and/or similiarities to Garvin's 'Economic Foundations of Peace' are in Lothian article, 16 June 1936, *News Chronicle*; Ashton-Gwatkin, note for Leith-Ross, 10 March 1938, FO 371–21 701, p. 4. The basic idea is to be found in article 4 of the Atlantic Charter.

World War and at the time of the Paris Peace Conference in 1919. Thinking on the 'economic foundations of peace', then, had the dilemma of the mid-1930s very much in mind, which was how to make Germany's recovery as a major economic power in Central Europe (which was in Britain's interest) compatible with the aims of security policy; that is, of preventing the rise of Germany as a military and militant power. Military alliances and legal agreements, as envisaged by the League of Nations, were regarded as inadequate by the proponents of this strategy as early as 1919 (and later in the 1930s). Such solutions were not deemed capable of tackling the twin problems of redressing legitimate grievances whilst at the same time restraining the 'devious' ambitions of one of the great powers. The real answer to the dilemma was to establish a collective system of economic security which would protect individual countries and international politics from the social consequences and symptoms of an economic depression[219] and thus prevent the rise of 'assertive' powers.

The identification of economic difficulties as lying at the root of international conflicts implied that the economic appeasers staked everything on the dual effect of economic influence: the US, the United Kingdom and the British Empire could, if expedient, employ their raw-material and capital resources to stimulate multilateral exchange relations by practising an open-door policy in their territories, or they could put increasing pressure on members of the international community to behave peacefully:[220]

> If we were prepared, particularly in cooperation with the United States, to offer financial support to countries which need it, progress with the restoration of normal international trade would be more rapid and we might in return be in a stronger position to press for modifications in the political sphere.[221]

The prospects of success were implied by the logic of the position. Since the Dominions and the US could largely satisfy Germany's requirement of raw materials and since Germany would also remain dependent to a considerable extent on these sources of supply,[222] the terms of striking a bargain seemed obvious. The

---

219. See note 218 above.

220. Hall memo., pp. 4f. The authors made 'open door'/equal access to colonial raw materials conditional on other colonial powers' (= France) reciprocal action and on acceding (disarmament conventions) arms agreements.

221. F. Phillips (Treasury) note, 7 June 1937, T 188–175; see above note 48.

222. The Hall memo. dwells on the Dominions' economic interests in trade with Germany

only thing to do was to trigger the mechanism. This could be done with the help of standby credits, adjustments to the exchange rate, and so on.[223] As matters stood in the autumn of 1936, circumstances invited action; the Tripartite Agreement of September 1936 between the 'liberal' democracies – which was accompanied by the devaluation of the French franc – had been successfully concluded and world trade was steadily improving. The British and French governments considered bargaining with Germany along the line that the 'have' powers would approach the financial and raw material issues with a view to persuading the Third Reich to restrain its political interventionism in Central and South-Eastern Europe (and in Spain). Within French government circles,[224] as the economic appeasers learnt, the opinion was gaining ground that in order to win American moral and material support it was necessary to show a willingness to negotiate both on the question of debts and with Germany. Reports from the Third Reich indicated that the Germans (Schacht) were willing to talk and even likely to agree to discussing political and economic issues. Amongst the various projected ideas the favourite was the setting-up of a 'private' trading and finance company. Provided with British, French and American capital, it was to regulate the raw materials markets and prices and to facilitate imports into 'have-not' countries through the granting of long-term credits. Since this company would be financially dependent on the Western powers, international control would be retained over developments in this sphere.[225]

The economic appeasers considered the superiority of the economic resources of the United Kingdom/British Empire, or of an Anglo-American partnership, to be a lasting condition which would yield a position of strength; in this regard the risks accompanying any appeasement strategy appeared to be supportable. They could equally well have presented this pattern as a powerhouse which would supply Germany, Japan and other 'have-

---

and other European countries. Wendt, *Economic Appeasement*, pp. 191, 337–402, has a comprehensive analysis of these relationships.

223. On Schacht's hints at devaluating the Reichsmark, on market sharing agreement see notes 3, 168, 176 of German original; on pressures to lift the embargo on foreign loans, see Wendt, *Economic Appeasement*, pp. 348ff., 435, and Howson, *Domestic Monetary Management*.

224. R. Girault, 'Léon Blum: La dévaluation de 1936 et la conduite de la politique extérieure de la France', *RI*, 13(1978), p. 106.

225. Lothian to Cordell Hull, 12 Oct. 1937, GD 40–17, vol. 347, p. 353f. See notes 205ff., 211.

nots', if they were prepared to comply with an established set of rules, norms and conventions: 'No nation today will "fatten the Tiger" with colonial or territorial revisions or with trade or financial agreement unless they feel that there is also some security that such action will not be used for their own violent undoing'.[226] The inherent advantages of these 'grand solutions', so the economic appeasers reminded decision-makers, was that Britain/British Empire (and the US) had a natural superiority in the economic sphere, in marked contrast to their situation as a military power; thus instead of preparing for the game of power-politics, the Anglo-Saxon 'civic cultures' were to concentrate on employing their resources to persuade the nations of the world to participate in 'competitive cooperation'. Even if they let others avail themselves of the resources of their 'imperial' economies, the British and the Americans would still maintain their leadership.

The economic appeasers were aware that the application of their recommendations required some kind of 'international planning' and hence control of national resources. They saw the necessity of improving the performance and efficiency of British foreign economic policy; to this end, they favoured cartels and in general they aimed at a higher 'organisation of capitalism' and pushed for co-operation between politicians and industrialists. These were some of the unspoken assumptions behind their foreign (economic) policy proposals and plans.[227] In contrast, the 'executive' departments – the Board of Trade and the Treasury – continued to emphasise that they intended to keep state intervention in trade and industry to a minimum; this offered the best protection from the temptation to 'politicise' trade relations between primary producers (British Empire) and importers of raw materials (Germany as well as Britain) with a controlling involvement in overseas trade. The economic departments in particular resisted the idea of exercising any influence in favour of facilitating raw material imports into Germany, as this would provoke protests from those British industries already demanding protection from foreign, and in particular German, competition.[228]

The intragovernmental decision-making process and the foreign-

---

226. Lothian to Hull, see note 225. Roosevelt's policy towards Japan is rather similar to the 'German' policy of Lothian and the economic appeasers.

227. See above on 'escalation theory' and the concept of rationalisation/international planning.

228. Pinsent–Ribbentrop talk, 29 March 1935, Pinsent to FO, 2 April 1935, C 2824/25/18, FO 371–18 822, pp. 160f.

policy network did not create the constellation which the economic appeasers had hoped for. The appeasers and like-minded forces in the US did not find a way forward to arrange for constructive cooperation and thus failed to direct policy towards the desired Anglo-American partnership; instead, we have an 'indirect' alliance of forces who succeeded in asserting themselves. Leith-Ross and Vansittart, on the one hand, and Feis and Moffat, on the other, got their way in that they convinced their superiors to judge economic relations with, and economic stakes in, German (and Japanese) affairs in the context of the general political goals of the German (and Japanese) regime.[229] The State Department and Roosevelt held that the superior economic power of the US (and of the United Kingdom/British Empire) were fitted to exert a countervailing pressure on aggressive regimes. Contrary to the main theme of economic appeasement strategies, the 'haves' should not make tempting offers but rather keep their advantages in reserve in order to force Germany and Japan to respect the rules and norms of the comity of nations. Offers of cooperation were, in their opinion, only to be made when the democracies had demonstrated their willingness to defend their way of life and had employed their instruments of pressure – such as the threat of a long-distance blockade, methods of pre-emptive purchase, credit facilities for those countries threatened by Germany and Japan etc., with a view to teaching Germany's rulers a lesson and possibly effecting political changes in Germany as well as in Japan. These, of course, were policies which were considered by the economic appeasers to be undesirable. They refused to admit that the actual situation before 1938–39 required a one-sided 'political' approach; they continued to argue that the indicators within their collective economic security system still allowed for a dual-track policy of offering cooperation while keeping (the threat of) sanctions in reserve.

If the strategy was not merely to remain a paper document but was to be put to the test, the economic appeasers had to fight to improve the set of conditions favourable to Anglo-American cooperation and/or draw attention to their concept of an imperial economic policy aimed at replacing that conglomerate of bilateral trade agreements, the Ottawa Settlement. They were less troubled by another crucial aspect. This was the question of whether a

---

229. Junker, *Unteilbarer Weltmarkt*, pp. 197ff.; H.J. Schröder, in Knapp, ed., *Die USA und Deutschland*, pp. 126ff.; see below part III on the political approach (Vansittart, Leith-Ross, N. Chamberlain, Runciman).

strategy that had been conceived before 1933 as a device for preventing the rise of nationalism–militarism in Germany and the breakaway of that country from the comity of nations, was still applicable to conditions after the National Socialists had come to power. They were satisfied to learn from reports and from their own visits and meetings that inside Germany influential forces kept on struggling for a return to 'normality', though not for the overthrow of Hitler and the National Socialist regime. The disposition of economic appeasers led them to believe that their strategy was built on firm ground; the Anglo-American partnership or the coordination of an imperial economic policy could make the world safe for peace; the 'German problem' was just one, although the most telling, of the various troublespots that had to be dealt with by an economic peace strategy. But economic appeasers had to fight to have British foreign policy adhere to this 'grand strategy'; they had to promote the coordination of British and American peace efforts if they wanted to demonstrate that theirs was not a 'diplomacy of illusions'.

Thus the 'grand solutions' of economic appeasement became entangled in intragovernmental in-fighting. But the economic appeasers entered 'bureaucratic politics' with the handicap of outsiders. Worse, when they perceived conditions to be favourable and pressed for testing their proposals, another development intervened which greatly occupied the British government. Since early 1936 the US stubbornly pursued negotiations on an Anglo-American Commercial Treaty.[230] The coincidence of the British 'working agreement' initiative in late-1935/early-1936 with Hull's pressure for a trade agreement with Great Britain pushed economic appeasement into the arena of commercial talks. This refers, of course, to the proposals of the economic appeasers and not – to the same degree – to official British foreign policy, which pursued different goals and did not intend to become tied up with American politics:

> I feel . . . that this point [inter-imperial consultations with regard to a revision of Ottawa in favour of a reorientation of Anglo-American

---

230. An American initiative in spring 1935 started the talks; Runciman's visit to Washington in January 1937 marked the official stage of the negotiations. FO-Memo., 13 March 1937, A 1968/228/45, FO 371–20 659, pp. 105ff., reviews the development; Allen-Memo., 'United States and British Imperial Interests', 15 March 1937, A 2847/228/45, FO 371–20 659, pp. 264ff., analyses the issues at stake. For more details on Anglo-American Trade negotiations see notes 206f. of German original.

policy] is closely bound up with our German policy. If . . . we succeed
in negotiating some settlement or even a truce with Germany . . . there
would be no compelling reason for getting out of our way to please
Cordell Hull . . . If . . . the prospect of any settlement with Germany
receded into the background, it may well be a matter of the highest
importance to explain the dangers of the situation to the Dominions and
ask them to make some sacrifices in the Common cause.[231]

For reasons of their own, the economic appeasers began to link
their 'German policy' to their endeavours to promote Anglo-
American cooperation. To begin with, the economic appeasers,
and Lothian in particular, welcomed the fact that like-minded
American and Dominion representatives[232] were joining the debate in Britain insofar as such interference reinforced their pressure on Whitehall to take the lead in open-door diplomacy; they
regarded Britain as belonging to a 'penetrated' (Anglo-Saxon)
system and therefore thought such intervention legitimate.[233]
Being aware of the limits of their influence, they expected their
ideas to have a greater impact on Whitehall, if the US and the
Dominions brought their message home to the British government. Secondly, the stakes to be deployed in the 'grand solution'
were not at the disposal of the British government alone, but had to
be used under some sort of joint control with the Dominions:

At the most, in this field [the revision of Ottawa] the immediate
question seems to be whether we can persuade the Dominions to allow

231. Jebb/Eden-Memo., 'Economics and Foreign Policy', 17 March 1937, FO 371–21 215,
p. 194a, ibid., pp. 185ff., 194f. Chamberlain's statement to the Imperial Conference and his plea
to agree on an Anglo-American Trade Agreement is to be viewed in this perspective; cf. R.
Tamchina, *In Search of Common Cause*, p. 90f.; Kottmann, *Reciprocity*, pp. 173f., 205ff., 214; cf.
Jebb, 11 June 1937, W 11 812/393/18, FO 371–21 247, pp. 66ff.

232. Jebb urged turning favourable statements by Canadian politicians, by Bruce and
McDougall to advantage. At the Imperial Conference, the Dominions agreed in principle to
revise partially imperial preferences in order to facilitate the conclusion of trade negotiations
between Britain and the USA; Toynbee, *Survey of International Affairs*, 1937, vol. 1, pp. 63; N.
Mansergh, *Commonwealth Affairs*, 1, pp. 88ff.

233. Lothian asked Jones for information on Lloyd George's/Jones' interview with Hitler
before he departed for Washington (autumn 1936); in order to 'warn' Hitler and Japan, Lothian
appealed to Mackenzie King to make another effort at linking trade liberalisation (i.e. Canadian–American Treaty as a model for an Anglo-American Agreement) with uniting western
democracies; Lothian to Jones, 14 Sept. 1936, Jones-Mss., Class W, vol. 13, no. 83. Lothian
regarded an international coalition of 'liberal' governments as an alternative to protectionist/
conservative influences; see notes 40 and 55 of German original. On Lothian's activities and
meetings with King and Roosevelt in 1936 and 1937 see notes 209 and 250 of German original.
Tweedsmuir to Baldwin, 8 April 1937, Baldwin-Mss., vol. 97, pp. 184–187, urges Baldwin to
accomodate the U.S.A. with a view to facilitating Anglo-American cooperation, rather along
the lines of Lothian's pleas.

some relaxation of Ottawa in favour of the USA and whether we ourselves would modify our silk duties in favour of France.[234]

In actual fact, any progress in negotiations with the US as well as with Germany required the consent of Canada, South Africa and others, to change the terms of the Ottawa Agreements, especially if the individual cases of revision fitted the aims of the 'grand solutions' as conceived by the economic appeasers.[235] Their hope was that a debate which started off with 'Ottawa is not enough' might actually produce a turn to the restoration of multilateral trade relations. Furthermore, some of the key issues of economic appeasement – such as the opening-up of British markets to German goods – were prominent in Anglo-American Trade Talks, since the US requested access to the British markets for a similar range of products as Germany did; therefore both the prospects of an American Trade Agreement with Britain and the imprint of the economic appeasers on Britain's 'working agreement' offer to Germany were intrinsically interlocked with essential economic interests of the Dominions and the sterling-bloc countries.[236] Domestic and foreign criticism of 'Ottawa' certainly provided the economic appeasers with a political starting-point to ask for a reorientation of British foreign (economic) policy; they triggered off a debate on the link between British imperial trade policy with Anglo-German and Anglo-American policy.[237] They had been aware for some time of Canada's growing interdependence with the US economy, of Australia's interest in trade with Germany and Japan, and of South Africa's increased foreign trade with Germany.

234. Leith-Ross, 25 Febr. 1937, T 188–175.; see note 239 below.
235. See above note 228; In February 1936, Lothian asked Mackenzie King to approach his opposite numbers in the other Dominions in order to defuse international tensions by helping to improve the situation of countries such as the Third Reich; a reform of the League and an offer of economic cooperation, starting in the field of raw materials, were the suggested terms of debate; Lothian to King, 18 Febr. 1936, and Lothian to Hull, 16 Febr. 1936.
236. FO officials suggested combining the deliberations on the working agreement initiative towards Germany with the reply to Atherton's proposals for improving Anglo-American economic relations: minutes, 19 to 27 Febr. 1936, on Eden- Davis interview, 7/8 Febr. 1936, C 888/4/18, FO 371–19 884. Jebb advocated the linkage; he regarded the Dominions' willingness to a modification or even revision of the Ottawa agreements (due in 1937) as a prerequisite for progress in negotiations with the U.S.A. as well as with Germany; an international framework was thought to facilitate the position of the Dominions' governments within their domestic constituencies.
237. N. Davis-Eden conversation, 7 Febr. 1936, C 889/4/18, FO 371–19 933; FO to Board of Trade, 2 March 1936. Hull's conversations with Lindsay induced Eden — in June/July 1936 and in late 1936 — to press the Board of Trade and the Treasury to interdepartmental committee work.

The important thing from the point of view of economic appeasers was how to prevent certain developments drifting apart and endangering the British Commonwealth economy. If Britain wished to avoid being bypassed by these movements, she had to initiate a new, coherent 'imperial economic policy':[238]

> I agree that [the Ottawa question] ought to be taken up at the Imperial Economic Conference and that the best line of approach is . . . bringing in the USA. But I fear that the Dominions will be much more ready to reduce British preferences in their markets than to accept reductions of their preferences in our market . . . and I expect that, notwithstanding the importance they attach to good relations with the USA, ministers will be extremely reluctant to make any substantial modification in the Ottawa policy.[239]

Before our analysis of economic appeasement strategy can be carried a step further, a few remarks on the general situation are necessary. The intragovernmental debate on the pros and cons of the contributions to the 'peace offensive' that aimed at preventing the Rhineland crisis and – in the aftermath of that crisis – at limiting the consequences of Hitler's triumph, ran parallel to the British reaction to the American drive to start negotiations on a trade agreement.[240] The procedure was, however, different in both cases: *vis-à-vis* Britain, the US was the moving spirit and quite prepared to force London's hand; in the area of economic appeasement, the British adversaries conducted the discussion internally among themselves rather than with their opposite numbers in Germany. In both cases, however, an examination of the details of the proposed bargains proved that both the economic appeasers and the US were asking too much of the British government. With regard to (1) the preferences granted to the Dominions, (2) the subsidies protecting British agriculture and (3) the impending claims on public expenditure, it was, in the opinion of interdepartmental committees, not possible even to come any-

---

238. The catchword 'Ottawa is not enough' implied, with regard to Jebb, Ashton-Gwatkin, Lothian, a British effort to remain in touch with tendencies in the Dominions to align with the USA or with Japan and Germany (in economic affairs) Britain had to 'invent' a new imperial economic policy in order to maintain London's position in the centre of the Commonwealth; the catchword implied a preventive economic diplomacy within the Empire. Jebb, 6 July 1936, C 4760/99/18, FO 371–19 933, pp. 355f. For details see note 210 of German original.

239. Leith-Ross to Ashton-Gwatkin, 25 Febr. 1937, T 188–175.

240. See note 272. The Board of Trade rejected the proposal to combine the German and the American question.

where near to fulfilling the wishes on the American list; nor was it realistic to hold out a prospect of cancelling the policy commitments made in 1931–32 to such an extent that one could count on the willingness of Germany to respond by turning towards 'peacetime economics' instead of proceeding on her path from economic nationalism to war-prone autarky. Departmental representatives stressed that there was no politically feasible way of altering the British quota system for agricultural products; any change in the system would occasion a storm of protest from the National Farmers Union, without facilitating a rapprochement with the US. They did not even think it advisable to force the process of consultation with the Dominions over a revision of 'Ottawa'. On the contrary, they, and subsequently their ministers, thought it dangerous to start the ball rolling. They believed it would be an invitation to the Dominions to confront Britain with a collective *démarche* at the 1937 Imperial Conference. The economic appeasers – as well as the Liberal and Labour Opposition in Parliament – envisaged their demands as aiming at the restoration of the Triangular Trade System with a view to inducing the heads of the Dominions and the British government to prepare a joint action. The departments, and above all the Board of Trade, warned that the Dominions would only too readily seize upon this item on the agenda in order to exert 'joint pressure' on Britain; that is, to press Britain into making all those sacrifices which both the US and Germany (and Japan) demanded from the British Empire;[241] the Dominions would want compensation from Britain before agreeing to anything in the way of an Anglo-American or Anglo-German 'rapprochement'.

However, Britain was disadvantaged by the structure of her trade relations with the US,[242] particularly in the agricultural sector, which was important to the Roosevelt administration for domestic reasons. The American government's effort obviously

---

241. Zetland recommended to Chamberlain British concessions in order to improve Anglo-American relations, Zetland to Chamberlain, 6 May 1937, T 188–175 (Committee on Trade Policy). Troutbeck-Memo., 5 March 1937, A 1704/228/45, FO 371–20 659, p. 28; FO-Memo., 'Anglo-American Trade Discussions', 13 March 1937, A 1968/228/45, FO 371–20 659, pp. 105ff.; Committee on Trade Policy Report, C.T.P. (37)11, 11 July 1937, §§12ff., FO 371–21 247. The important Anglo-Canadian Trade Agreement was concluded in February 1937, before the Imperial Economic Conference was officially announced. There were slight chances that the U.S.A. might accomodate the Dominions; see Tamchina, *In Search of Common Cause*, p. 91; Drummond, *Economic Policy*, pp. 89ff.; Mansergh, *Survey*; Ovendale, *Appeasement*, pp. 15ff., 38ff. On the Imperial Economic Conference see T 160–681 682, F 14 601/1–5; T 160–750, 755/756, F 14 239/01–03, F 14 239/1–19.

aimed at providing an outlet for American agricultural exports in the British market; the repercussions of an Anglo-American agreement on the Dominion supplies and sterling-bloc partners (Argentina) which accepted the American line could be disastrous; 'imperial trade' was a stabilising factor in Britain's economy. In addition, Britain's industrial exports to the United States were unlikely to compensate for 'sacrifices' on account of agriculture; the trade deficit in Anglo-American commercial relations was so large and the economic situation in America at the time of the trade negotiations, the so-called Roosevelt Depression, so unfavourable that a formidable opposition (FBI, NUM, Imperial Economic Union) protested against starting negotiations.[243] As regards the American demands, the British market also had no more than limited scope for expanding its capacity to absorb their industrial goods. Nevertheless, the economic appeasers expected Whitehall to coordinate economic and political interests and perspectives by linking the American and German aspects of its peace strategy. Organised business interests feared that the National government would be willing to sacrifice industrial interests for the sake of political advantages that might result from a Trade Agreement with the US.[244] They did not see how the British government could induce the Americans to do something about the depreciation of the dollar; no commercial settlement would be sound without the American authorities acting at the monetary end of the relationship. Moreover, British industrial and agricultural interests demanded that the National government insist in its negotiations for a renewal of the Ottawa Agreements (due to expire in 1937) that the Dominions pay their due by applying 'reciprocity'; that is, by granting 'real' preferences to British products. Finally,

---

242. In 1937 the USA exported £ 114 mill. to Britain and imported £ 31 mill. from Britain; the surplus of £ 83 mill. was nearly three times as large as the total British exports to the U.S.A. The main concern was that the USA, due to domestic pressure from the farmers' unions, would dump their agrarian over-production on the British market, thus competing with the Dominions and threatening the mechanisms of the £-bloc. The British Government changed, in spite of the protest of the NFU, the levy subsidy system and introduced in November 1937 the deficiency payments system; on this and the complicated negotiations with the Dominions and British agrarian interests see Drummond, pp. 109ff.

243. FBI to Prime Minister/Board of Trade, 'Proposed Anglo-American Trade Agreement', 11 Dec. 1937, FBI/C/2/1937B; *The Times*, 22 Nov. 1937; P. Hannon, 18 Jan. 1938, *Manchester Guardian*; *The Times*, 9 June 1937 (on a protest by 150 MP's/Empire Industries Association); cf. Wendt, *Appeasement 1938*, p. 58. Allen-Memo., 'The US and British Imperial Interests', 15 March 1937, A 284/228/45, FO 371–20 659, pp. 264–309.

244. Empire Committee, Minutes, 3 March 1938, FBI/C/2/1938.

the Federation of British Industries (FBI) discovered an interest in market-sharing agreements and/or international cartels with the proviso that the British Empire remained reserved for British exports; the idea was that by such methods the 'old industrialised' nations (Britain, Germany) could hold their own against 'cheap producer' countries (i.e. Japan, but also the Dominions and some colonies), and raise the level of export prices.

If Britain was to proceed with, and conclude, a trade agreement with the US,[245] she either had to offer the Dominions compensation for the transfer of a part of their share of the British market to the US (or to Germany) or had to convince the Dominions that even marginal concessions made to the US or Germany would stimulate world trade from which they too would profit. Otherwise Britain had to take the opposite road and at least convince the US that she should make some concessions to the Dominions in order to reduce pressure from the Dominions on the United Kingdom. In spite of these difficulties, the economic appeasers urged the government to take the lead; as long as economic forecasts looked promising – that is, as long as Britain's recovery, the rise in the price of raw materials and the increase in world trade were being recorded – the economic appeasers did not feel compelled to abandon their proposals.

Indeed, the economic appeasers, and Lothian in particular, succeeded in forming influential circles which included the American Special Envoy in London, Norman Davies, representatives of the Dominions and Members of Parliament belonging to the Centre-Left. Because of the social position of these networks and self-styled diplomatic missions,[246] the economic appeasers met with a certain success in arousing the interest of influential cabinet ministers (Baldwin, Simon, Eden, Inskip) and advisers of leading

245. In the end, Britain reduced or cancelled duties on wheat, cotton, rice, vehicles/tractors, tools; the US reduced tariffs on British textiles and metal products — cf. Kottmann, *Reciprocity*, p. 266.

246. Lothian wanted to meet Eden before he departed to Canada and the US; on return, he informed Eden on his talks with King and Hull (13 Febr. 1936); and invited Eden to Blickling; Eden could not make it before 6/7 March 1936. Lothian wrote in February to King and Hull, to the editor of *The Times* and spoke in the House of Lords, appealing to them to pursue Hoare's Geneva speech (raw materials question); see Lothian-Mss., GD 40–17, vol. 310; for details see notes 217f. of German original. Davis was familiar with Lothian and the 'Cliveden set'; as a banker, he knew Europe; he claimed to be Roosevelt's right hand man; Baldwin regarded Davis a busy-body; Davis 'personal' diplomacy was called off when the suggested Chamberlain-Roosevelt meeting turned awkward; see Ovendale, *Appeasement*, pp. 17ff.; Eden, *Facing the Dictators*, pp. 530, 535ff.; Offner, *Appeasement*, pp. 181f.

politicians (Jones) for their general ideas and concrete individual proposals, such as a reform of the League of Nations in order to attract the cooperation of the US and Germany:

> We are so tied up with Geneva and with personal contacts with European statesmen that, without Dominion pressure, it will be extraordinarily difficult to limit our commitments. And if anybody can awaken the US to the fact that liberty – including its own – may be at stake, it will be the Dominions and not Great Britain. It is therefore the Dominions who hold the key of the position. Once they face the fact that the League is dead, they alone can call a new League into being which, because it will have a core of invincible strength and practise in freedom, may accomplish incomparably more than the old.[247]

They wanted to infuse a new spirit into the League and to salvage the useful elements of the League's machinery, such as the International Labor Office (ILO) and the Economic and Financial Organisation. Promoting this idea in the mid-1930s was to them an effort to revive the vision of the reconstruction period of 1917–20, which had predicted the collapse of a purely 'political' League of Nations. In accordance with their 'social-liberal' commitment, they advocated an international rescue operation; just as 'new state interventionism' after the 1929–32 depression had stimulated national welfare policies designed to alleviate domestic social distress, 'liberal democratic societies' were now urged to put socio-economic models on the agenda of international politics. The profound interests of the rulers of the Third Reich in raising living standards in Germany, on the one hand, and the response to their ideas when they tested them on the American and the Dominion governments, on the other, persuaded the economic appeasers to push for an international conference to establish standards for adoption on a national basis.[248]

---

247. Lothian to Smuts, 8 July 1936.

248. Jebb hoped that Roosevelt would be informed on the McDougall Memo., i.e. the standard of living issue, and that Roosevelt would raise the matter with Runciman in January 1937; Jebb, 9 Jan. 1937, W 373/5/50, FO 371–21 215, p. 6. Roosevelt and Mackenzie King discussed the standard of living issue; King raised the proposal at the Imperial Economic Conference and in his meeting with Hitler; King styled himself a representative of North American interests at the Imperial Conference. Bruce had provided the American Ambassador in London with a copy of the McDougall memorandum; this induced the American Section of the FO to accuse the Dominions of trying to divert American pressure on the Empire to Britain: Allen memo., A 2847/228/45, §38, p. 21, FO 371–20 659, p. 296; Jebb minute on W 373/5/50, 9 Jan. 1937, FO 371–21 215, pp. 5f.

However, by referring to, and calling for, the intervention of the US, Dominions, and German 'moderates', and by advising the government to respect the current thoughts of the Opposition in Britain, the economic appeasers did not make headway with regard to their real concerns. The effect was to widen the common denominator of influences affecting the government's policy, which was definitely to commit Britain to Western Europe.[249] The economic appeasers aimed at demonstrating how much their escalation theory fitted the actual problem; this was the problem that Britain's reaction to the imminent changes in the economic policies of Germany in 1936–37 had to correspond with the task; Britain's peace strategy had to reflect policies designed to salvage useful aspects of economic interdependence. The inherent weakness of the appeasers was the reverse side of their (supposed) source of strength: it was claimed that an identity of interest existed with partners with which any British government had to associate – the US and the Dominions. The 'defect' of this line of argument was that it reminded the government of the proposals which they had been hearing from the Opposition for years.[250] The repetition of the criticisms simply produced a defiant reaction from ministers and civil servants in charge of official policies since 1931–32; they remained convinced that their decisions were appropriate to the circumstances then and now.[251] They, and above all Neville Chamberlain,[252] underlined their belief in 'Ottawa' and in a fiscal policy in the face of international criticism.

However, the economic appeasers were no less obstinate; they

---

249. The Foreign Policy Committee of the Cabinet debated in summer 1936 on proposals for reforming the League of Nations; the Cabinet made no changes with regard to its stance on strategic-political aspects (see Ch. I of German original); concerning economic foreign policy, Eden was instructed to state Britain's interest in participating in the League of Nations procedure on the Van Zeeland proposals (4 July 1936); see below on Van Zeeland Committee.

250. The economic appeasers as well as Hull regarded 'Ottawa' as a barrier to a revival of world trade; Hull had taken issue with 'Ottawa' on the occassion of discussing 'tariff truce' at the London Conference 1933; he launched a campaign in early 1936; FRUS, 1933, vol. 1, pp. 743f.; on 1936 cf. Wendt, *Economic Appeasement*, pp. 331ff. Hull further was critical of Britain's bilateral commercial treaties and clearing agreements (see below).

251. Board of Trade Minutes, 21 Jan. 1937, BT 11–755; the Board of Trade asked for plain speaking toward Washington; the FO's instructions to Lindsay — 22 Jan. 1937, BT 11–755 — passed the Board's arguments and provisoes to the American Government. The Board of Trade argued that Britain had to combine clearing and trade agreements since British recovery, foreign trade and debt services were bound up together. Hull regarded the British position to be determined by 'pressure groups'/vested interests; FRUS, 1936, vol. 1, pp. 656–666. 11 April to 26 May 1936.

252. N. Chamberlain, *The Times*, 10 Dec. 1937, p. 18; Chamberlain's speech was a reply to Hull's statement on American economic foreign policy and its criticism of imperial preference, etc. (20 Sept. 1937).

became even more assertive as international politics confirmed their warnings: in the (no longer distant) future, Britain and the US were said to become the targets of those 'national-political economies' which were susceptible to the 'ideology' of the 'one-party state' and the commands of 'vested interests'. If Britain and the US did not wish to wait and see for this drama to unfold, they should attempt to take advantage of their existing economic superiority and try to stop the plunge into 'catastrophe'. The economic appeasers joined the contest of interests, strategies and personnel for determining governmental actions. They operated through complex intradepartmental and interministerial committees with pretentious operative ideas but weak supporting power. Persons high-up in the American or Canadian hierarchy shared their ideas, but they could hardly ever point to instances of actual cooperation. Thus their blunt proposals amounted to no more than the suggestion that there was an identity of views between themselves, on the one hand, and the declaration of intentions and estimates of interest of specific American or Dominion politicians, on the other. Since their conception comprised the same arguments and guiding principles to be found in reports prepared by groups of experts for the World Economic Conferences of 1927 and 1933, they were heartened by signs that the US was also moving towards rediscovering the same 'international common sense' which pervaded their 'blue-prints'.[253] Conversely, they advanced compelling reasons that Britain should meet the US halfway; the offers which they felt would interest the Americans in cooperation over a strategy to reduce friction and to help develop international 'planning' and international consciousness resulted partly from their common criticism of 'Ottawa', partly from their concept of 'rationalisation'; they suggested, for example, that the US, in as much as they were a consumer, should have a seat and vote on the steering committee on raw material cartels for tin and rubber.[254]

However, from the American point of view concessions in both areas meant no more than a gesture which could assist in remedying legitimate grievances. Furthermore, 'trade outlets', 'lower-tariff union', 'open door', 'raising of living standards', and so on,[255]

253. Roosevelt, 16 May 1933, cf. Nixon, *F.D. Roosevelt and Foreign Policy*, vol. 1, p. 126. N. Davis transmitted Lothian's views to Washington and Hull's remarks to Lothian and Jones; Jones, *Diary with Letters*, pp. 337ff., (7 May 1937). Cf. H.J. Schröder, *Deutschland*, pp. 177ff.

254. Hall-Memo., p. 5. Leith-Ross, 9 July 1937, Report on meeting of the Economic Committee of the League of Nations and the meeting of the International Chamber of Commerce at Berlin, C 5139/71/62, FO 433–4, no. 38.

255. The formulas are defined in the Hall memorandum, and in McDougall memo., 'Eco-

did not guarantee that the economic appeasers and their American and Dominion companions agreed with their practical, concrete ideas and tactical preferences. The prime ministers and high commissioners of some Dominions (MacKenzie King, Hertzog, Massey, Smuts and Bruce) inundated the British government with schemes and procedural proposals which reflected the spirit that came to be incorporated into several joint memoranda (the Hall Scheme, McDougall Memorandum which led to the Van Zeeland and Bruce Committees of 1937–38 and 1939, respectively). However, the Dominion leaders had just as little leeway as the government in London to remove, for example, protective import duties, quotas and various kinds of restrictions which discriminated against foreign, especially German, products. It was even more unthinkable to go further and, instead of equating development with the import of capital funds from Britain, to be more reserved in their borrowing; as a gesture this might encourage the City and New York to think big; that is, to contemplate a large-scale conversion operation that would have to accompany any grand scheme of offering Germany an alternative to her 'war-prone economy'; if economic appeasement was to stop Germany's economy being wholly dominated by arms production, it had to offer capital for the conversion of her production structure into a peacetime economy: Apart from the highmindedness of these schemes, Dominion leaders could not help but consider the profitable aspects of any 'appeasement bargain'. The detailed advances were based more strongly on the economic interests of their own countries[256] and less considerate of whether they were likely to appease the National Socialist regime. Whitehall therefore suspected, when they learnt of the Dominions' proposals, that Australia, Canada and South Africa had their own commercial interests in mind and wanted to pass to Britain the 'economic appeasement' buck of making concessions to Germany and the US.

As to Washington's part in an economic appeasement venture, London was preoccupied with American neutrality legislation, which was accompanied by the slogan 'no entanglement in Euro-

nomic Appeasement', W 373/5/50, Bruce to Eden, 21 Dec. 1936, FO 371–21 215. The McDougall memo. was published by the League of Nations, Economic Committee, 46th session, Report to the Council, 'Remarks on the Present Phase of International Economic Relations', Sept. 1937, C.358.M242, 1937.

256. Troutbeck minute, 14 Jan. 1937, on W 373/5/50, FO 371–21 215, pp. 9f.; Jebb, 10 June 1936, FO 371–19 933, pp. 324ff., commented on Bruce's talk with Stanhope that Australia demonstrated its interest in opening the European-German markets for her products; cf. FO 371–19 949, p. 187.

pean affairs', as well as by accusations against Britain and pro-British influences in the US. London did not discover any sign of cooperation or reciprocity in American policy that corresponded to the 'partnership' envisaged by the economic appeasers. No wonder that the Foreign Office and the cabinet perceived Cordell Hull's foreign (economic) policy as bearing the marks of selfishness. Opponents of the economic appeasers could, therefore, reject not only their demands with a good conscience, but could also refute proposals put forward officially by the US and the Dominions. The plea of the economic appeasers that if Britain removed the sting from international criticism with gestures of conciliation and tangible concessions, America and the Dominions would cooperate in her peace strategy, was not born out by the facts. Their opponents were annoyed about this kind of interference in their affairs. Consequently, there was also no prospect of Britain obtaining support and help from her critics in the topical question of defence policy, especially from the US and the Dominions, which were sympathetic to a course of appeasement.[257]

The economic appeasers did not accept that their trust in the policies of Roosevelt, Hull, Mackenzie King, Smuts and others was of no importance when it came to shaping Britain's foreign policy. On the contrary, they asked people in charge to test, and cooperate in, calls for action aiming at a liberalisation and stabilisation of the world economy.[258] They referred to Cordell Hull's declarations: 'In the years that lie ahead, an adequate revival of international trade will be the most powerful single force for easing political tension and averting the danger of war'.[259] In addition, the economic appeasers maintained that a positive response to American and Dominion economic 'designs' would improve relationships

257. In his talks with N. Davis and Morgenthau N. Chamberlain left no doubt that he expected American initiatives in the security arena (either with regard to the situation in the Far East or by relaxing the neutrality laws): Offner, *Appeasement*, pp. 181f.; Kottmann, *Reciprocity*, pp. 144f., 204ff. Middlemas, *Diplomacy of Illusion*, pp. 144ff.; A.J.P. Taylor, ed., *Off the Record*, London 1973, pp. 67ff. (Crozier interview with Chamberlain, 17 Dec. 1937). On arms deliveries and production see D. Hall, *North American Supply*; Tamchina, pp. 93f.; Earl of Avon, *Facing the Dictators*, pp. 480ff.

258. The economic appeasers did not approve of Hull's policy on all accounts. Ashton-Gwatkin was more sceptical on American support than Lothian. Mackenzie King, whose government had agreed on a 'liberal' trade agreement with the USA and thus dealt a blow to 'Ottawa', pressed London to follow the same example; confronted with opposition in his party and within the cabinet and anxious about electorial perspective, King later on became more sympathetic to Britain's reluctance to comply with American requests.

259. Hull, 10 Febr. 1937, quoted in A.G.B. Fisher, 'Economic Appeasement as a Means to Political Understanding and Peace', *Survey of International Affairs*, 1937, vol. 1, p. 56; Hull to Eden, 6 April 1936; Hull to Lindsay, 28 March 1936; Lindsay to Eden, 21 July 1936, in: BT

generally and prepare the ground for collaboration in the security arena.[260] But if one evaluates Hull's intentions, it has to be conceded that their adversaries got the better of the economic appeasers. Hull and his close colleagues did not understand the formula to mean outlets for German exports in the same sense as the appeasers.[261] The successful conclusion of a trade agreement with Great Britain was designed above all to win the decisive battle in Congress and to prove the advantages of his policy of concluding Reciprocal Trade Agreements. If the Roosevelt administration succeeded in gaining access to the agricultural markets of industrial Britain, Washington would secure the required leverage to bring the lingering negotiations with Argentina and Uruguay to a conclusion favourable to American export interests. In other words, although Hull cast the Reciprocal Trade Agreement in the role of a constructive policy to secure peace, he in effect treated it as an instrument to force American interests on those trading partners which had traditionally been important to her. The administration needed 'success' – particularly in the shape of an agreement with Britain – to break the resistance of influential interest groups back home, such as the agricultural block in Congress, and to arrive at further agreements with Latin American partners.[262] Washington played the game of foreign economic policy with a view to its domestic audience and cared less about how the world, and especially the economic appeasers, judged the performance and what they expected of the spectacle.

It was of little help to the economic appeasers in Britain that

---

11–589. Lothian put Hull's ideas to the British public: 16 June 1936, *News Chronicle*; Lothian, *The Times*, 11 Febr. 1936. Lindsay warned his Government to cold-shower C. Hull, although Lindsay had his doubts on Hull's ability to get on with Congress: Lindsay to FO, 5 Febr. 1936, A 1302/1293/45, FO 371–19 834, pp. 9ff. Lothian attempted to coordinate Canadian and American influences and bring that pressure to bear on Whitehall.

260. Hall-Memo., p. 8; cf. All Souls Meeting, 18/19 Dec. 1937; see above, notes 78, 79, 95.

261. Hull regarded German hegemonic policy in central and south-east Europe as a danger; Schröder, in: Knapp, ed., *Deutschland*, pp. 126ff. But in the State Department and in the American attentive public, views similar to the economic appeasement strategy were held; Darlington memo., 31 Dec. 1937, in: Gardner, *Sterling-Dollar Diplomacy*, pp. 10f.; State Department (West European Section) to Davis, 16 Febr. 1937, 'Contribution to a Peace Settlement', cf. Schröder, *Deutschland*, p. 177. Hull's Reciprocal Trade Agreement policy was to counteract/contain European, especially German competition on the markets of Latin America: P.A. Varg, *Good Neighborhood Policy*, pp. 50ff.

262. Since the first round of reciprocal trade agreement negotiations had favoured American industrial exports, the treaty with Britain was destined to bring advantages home to the agricultural interests; the British Government was aware that Roosevelt had to care for the farmers as an essential element of his electorial constituency; Tweedsmuir to Baldwin, 8 April 1937, Baldwin-Mss., vol. 97, pp. 184ff.; cf. Kottmann, *Reciprocity*, pp. 118f., 196, 218.

Roosevelt and Hull held the Republicans responsible for the Great Depression in the same way that the economic appeasers had blamed the conservative forces in the National government for 1931–32. As for Hull and Roosevelt, criticism of Britain ('Ottawa') appeared to be simply the reverse (external) side of their rejection of the tariff, monetary and financial policies of their Republican predecessors. What mattered for Hull was that the protectionists remained masters of the situation in London and the Empire–Commonwealth.[263] For the economic appeasers and to an even greater extent for their opponents in Britain, on the other hand, it was important that Hull and Roosevelt remained powerless *vis-à-vis* protectionist interests in their efforts to reverse the policies of the Republican administration.[264] In other words, the economic appeasers in Britain were decisively less important for Hull than his policies were in the tactics and strategies of the economic appeasers.

However, in British politics it was of some benefit to the economic appeasers that on taking up his post the foreign secretary, Anthony Eden, proposed improving relations with the US and the Soviet Union, thus hoping to enlarge the scope of British foreign policy. As one of Eden's supporters in the House of Commons put it, the general idea was: 'In the immediate future, we should aim at reducing our own vulnerability, military and moral: military by strengthening our air defences, moral by at least offering a colonial settlement. We should bear in mind, whatever line of policy was contemplated, its effect on American opinion'.[265] This meant that Eden's operative ideals came close to the strategies pursued by the economic appeasers at the Foreign Office. Since American foreign policy and, more importantly, the British Embassy in Washington emphasised[266] that any initiative to improve the state of Anglo-American relations had to proceed via the economic arena, Eden looked into the economic aspects of Brit-

263. Hull termed Britain's bilateral trade agreements – especially the Spanish, Danish and Argentine treaties – 'economic nationalism'; London had to concede that the disavowal of the most favoured nation clause was due to the pressure of 'vested interests'. To Hull, Britain's 'entry' into his reciprocal trade agreement system was crucial; his criticism of imperial preference and 'Ottawa' sometimes amounted to a crusade. On the other hand, Hull tried to lure Britain into his 'system'; he stressed the common interest of the U.S.A. and the United Kingdom in preventing the industrialisation of developing nations proceeding at the expense of the U.S.A. and Britain; Lindsay to FO, 28 March 1936, transmitting a note from Hull, and Lindsay to FO, 31 July 1936, BT 11–589; C. Hull, *Memoirs*, vol. 1, p. 525.

264. Junker, *Unteilbarer Weltmarkt*, pp. 12f. Hull and Roosevelt accused Hoover and the Republicans of giving rise to protectionism all over the globe.

265. Nicolson-Diary, 22 Dec. 1937.

266. Lindsay to FO, 18 Jan. 1937, tel. no. 10, BT 11–755.

ain's 'American policy'. The economic appeasers took the dictum
that in the US one could commit every misdeed as long as it was
labelled economic appeasement,[267] as an invitation to push the
British foreign secretary into coordinating the 'working agreement' methods he envisaged for Germany with the general policies
proclaimed by Cordell Hull.[268] To this end Eden put the case for an
improvement in Anglo-American relations at the Imperial Conference of 1937; according to him, these could only be expected
to make progress in the economic arena. The political importance
of a trade agreement should not be underestimated, because – so
Eden argued – the success of Britain's military forces in the event
of war might depend to a large extent on a modification of America's neutrality legislation: 'If this [conclusion of the trade agree-
ment] involves sacrifices, it is a sacrifice for peace and a sacrifice
for our security'.[269] No doubt from the British point of view, trade
negotiations made sense only if they related to (prospective)
assistance in matters of security; Hull expressly refuted this linkage, arguing 'that an agreement with Britain on trade comported
no agreement whatever in the nature of a mutual political or
defense policy'.[270] Nevertheless, the perspective of improved
Anglo-American relations was just as important in the arguments
of the economic appeasers as the reference to elements of moderation in German and French politics.[271] Signs such as these
nourished their hopes and were thought to contribute to making
their appeasement initiatives plausible.

Meanwhile the Board of Trade, which was assigned the task of
examining the practicability of American requests for economic
cooperation, delayed comment on this matter just as they had on
the question of approaching Germany on terms suggested by the

267. Davis–Eden conversation, 20 April 1937, C 3148/71/62, BT 11–755. With this remark
Davis opened his statement on Washington's interest in Anglo-American trade negotiations.
This is to be viewed in the context of Mackenzie King's and Roosevelt's accord to press for an
international economic Conference and present this idea to the Imperial Economic Conference.; cf. Kottman, *Reciprocity*, pp. 162ff.; Ovendale, *Appeasement*, pp. 16ff., 38ff.

268. Atherton-Eden conversation, 24 Febr. 1936, A 1784/890/45, FO 371–19 834, pp.
132ff.; see note 233, and ch. I: 'Dominions' in German original.

269. Eden statement at Imperial Conference, A 4808/228/45, FO 371–20 661.

270. Hull, Memoirs, vol. 1, p. 529.

271. In his conversation with Eden and Cranborne; 20 April 1937, C 3148/71/62, BT
11–755. Davis viewed the Lansbury-Hitler interview as an indication of German moderation
and interest in a general settlement; in the same manner he regarded French willingness
(expressed by Spinasse) to consider the grant of credits to Germany as an encouraging signal.
Eden, however, insisted that a political agreement had to precede financial transactions and that
it was up to Germany to take the first step.

economic appeasers.[272] The Board of Trade's assessment of the proposals was that they barely scratched the surface of the problems which interested the economic appeasers, but were essentially aimed at Britain's general foreign economic policy.[273] At the same time, the Board persuaded the Foreign Office to drop any plans of starting talks with Germany about a preferential area in Central and South-Eastern Europe. Supported by the Treasury, the Board raised its voice for keeping the problem of Anglo-American economic relations separate from the question of an 'economic' approach to Germany. Whereas in the view of the economic appeasers and of Eden both questions were interlocked because they belonged to the problem of overcoming economic nationalism, the Board of Trade took Cordell Hull's appeal, that Britain should return to Cobden's principle of international peace and understanding, simply as an American device to harness Britain to a system of trade agreements suited to the expansion of America's exports. Whilst American foreign economic policy aimed at a British *volte-face* concerning 'Ottawa', they would themselves hold on to the symbols of their own economic nationalism; high tariffs and indirect trade barriers, albeit hidden in the rhetoric of multilateral trade, reciprocity, non-discrimination, and so forth.

In the early stages of their initiative Washington only desired a declaration from the Chancellor of the Exchequer or the Board of Trade to clarify two points: (1) that Britain and the British government were still committed to their earlier efforts to dismantle trade barriers and were willing to help with the recovery of world trade, and (2) that Britain shared the 'operative ideals' of Cordell Hull's foreign economic policy. When Britain adopted delaying tactics, the Americans reacted with massive pressure mounted from April 1936 onwards. These policies confirmed the Board of Trade and the Treasury in their suspicions that the US was mainly interested in subjecting Britain to her own political and economic interests. The economic appeasers were unsuccessful when, at their instigation, Eden put their proposals together and instructed them to

272. Troutbeck, 16 March 1936, A 1302/1293/45, FO 371–19 834, p. 8; Troutbeck, 27 April 1936, A 3607/890/45, FO 371–19 834, pp. 195ff.; cf. BT 11–589 and BT 11–755. The British government, due to pressure from the Board of Trade, informed Washington in April 1937 that the American demands and proposals were neither economically nor politically feasible; *FRUS*, 1937, vol. 2. pp. 23ff.; Hull, *Memoirs*, vol. 1, pp. 526ff.; Kottmann, *Reciprocity*, pp. 160ff.; Jones, *Diary with Letters*, pp. 337ff. (7 May 1937).

273. Runciman realised this during his conversations in Washington; he defended the British position by repeating the gist of his and Chamberlain's public statement; BT 11–755, FRUS, 1937, vol. 1, pp. 1ff., 8ff.; Hull, *Memoirs*, vol. 1, pp. 520ff.; Kottmann, *Reciprocity*, pp. 159ff.

compile a comprehensive memorandum; Eden approached the Board of Trade and the Treasury with the suggestion that they should no longer oppose exploratory talks because of overriding political concerns. The Board's answer to the official request from the Foreign Office was a rebuff.

British policy appeared to comply with American demands in that it took up the phraseology of Hull's campaign;[274] for instance, in memoranda (25 May 1936), in statements in the House of Commons (Runciman, 15 July 1936) and later in the Economic Committee of the League of Nations (4–5 October 1936). However, this did not prevent the US from attacking and repeating her criticisms of the practice of British trade and payments agreements (with Spain and Argentina).[275] The Board of Trade, the Treasury and the American 'section' of the Foreign Office found the accusations, which the Americans believed to be justified, to be school-masterly.[276] Indignation in British government circles at the continuing pressure from the US rose even more since the departments responsible felt that Britain had already given, or at least begun to give material substance to the restructuring of the international economy by joining the Tripartite Agreement concerning the devaluation of the franc and by her initiatives for the creation of the Committee on Raw Materials at the League of

274. The formulae were 'lowering of trade barriers', 'equality of trading opportunities', etc. Hull's 'diplomatic' demands on Britain were of a different nature: 1) Britain should acknowledge the RTA-policy as 'heir' to Britain's liberal tradition; 2) Britain should turn her back on 'economic nationalism' (i.e. revise the bilateral trade and clearing agreements), 3) Britain should aim at multilateral tariff reduction/'economic disarmament', 4) Britain should support an American initiative to convene an international trade conference, 5) Britain should urge Dominion governments, esp. Australia, to reduce protectionism; Hull note, 28 March 1936; Lindsay to Eden, 21 July 1936; Mallet to Eden (report on conversation between Hull and the Prime Minister of New South Wales), 29 August 1936, in: BT 11–589; Lindsay to FO, 18 Jan. 1937; Board of Trade/FO to Stirling, 30 August 1937, BT 11–755; FO minutes on Eden-Davis conversation, 20 April 1937.

275. Hull was dissatisfied with London's replies; Hull referred to American press comments, Lindsay to Eden, 21 July 1936. Hull transmitted his criticism in two notes, see summary in FO-memo., 19 Sept. 1936, A 7548/890/45, FO 371–19 834. Jebb agreed — with regard to the Runciman-Roca-Agreement (Argentine) — that Hull's charges were true and he recommended meeting the Americans, since Britain would profit from lowering trade barriers; Vansittart rejected well-meaning gestures.

276. Troutbeck, 29 Sept. 1936, A 7857/293/45, 'Mr. Hull's Economic Policy', FO 371–19 835, pp. 83ff., Troutbeck analysed American foreign economic policy since 1934 (RTA-Act). The Government countered American charges by pointing to the fact that Britain still offered the largest import market in the world and that American tariffs surmounted Britain's duties; Washington was accused of criticising treaties they obviously had never read and studied; correspondence between FO and Washington Embassy, Jan. to April 1937, BT 11–755; Cabinet meeting 20 Jan. 1937, top 7, Cab. 23–87, pp. 70f.

Nations and the Van Zeeland Committee.[277]

Britain's record could easily stand up to any comparison, in particular with that of the US. In view of this, how is the pressure emanating from Washington to be explained? The push and drive was seen as another attempt to gain Britain's central place in the world economy; it was a design to bind Britain to American reciprocal trade agreement policy and thereby to substitute American leadership for Britain's.[278] London interpreted Cordell Hull's reproaches that Britain was contravening the principles of her own foreign economic policy with her bilateral trade agreements, in as much as these agreements restricted equality of access to British markets, as the reverse side of his attempt to offer America's multilateral trade system as the hard-core of a sound international economic order.[279] Whitehall's anger over Hull's unswerving praise of his economic recipe for securing world peace was matched by a feeling of weakness with regard to trade agreement negotiations:[280] the fact that Britain already imported four times as much from the USA than she exported was seen as a poor negotiating position.[281] The basic assumption was that Britain just could not afford to restrict American imports; but how could Britain increase her share in the American market? The biased nature of trade relations made it difficult for Britain to envisage

277. Britain supported in April 1937 the establishment of the Van Zeeland Committee; this is to be viewed in the context of Anglo-French talks on Schacht's meeting with Delbos in August 1936 and as an attempt to calm down the opposition's request on acceding to King's and Roosevelt's initiative to convene a World Economic Conference; The U.S. Government regarded Hoare's Geneva speech as indicating Britain's willingness to participate in attempts to 'liberate' foreign and international trade and judged Britain's performance according to Britain's complying to this standard: Troutbeck, 27 April 1936, A 3607/890/45, FO 371–19 834, pp. 195ff. The Van Zeeland Committee reported in January 1938; the Roosevelt recession of 1937/38 sapped response to its recommendations: T 160–761, F 14 735/1–5, 'Proposed International Action for Reduction of Trade Barriers' (22 May 1936–2 Dec. 1938); T 160–762, F 14 735/03/1–4; T 160–770, F 15 853; Eden, 20 Sept. 1937, LofN, *Official Journal*, Special Supplement, no. 169 (1937), p. 65.

278. C. MacDonald, *The United States, Britain and Appeasement 1936–1939*, London 1980.

279. Troutbeck-Memo., 29 Sept. 1936, A 7857/293/45, FO 371–19 835, pp. 83ff. Whereas the U.S.A. increased their imports from $ 976 mill. in 1934 to $ 1,210 mill. in 1935, Britain's imports were stagnant, although the total was higher than the US figure ($ 2,044 mill.).

280. Eden-Bingham conversation, 19 Sept. 1936, A 7548/890/45, FO 371–19 834, pp. 258ff.; the preceding analysis is based on this document; cf. A 4455, 25 May 1936, see note 275.

281. RIIA, Information Department Papers, no. 22 'Anglo-American Trade Relations', March 1938; see note 206 of German original. From the British point of view Anglo-American Trade Negotiations served political purposes; Chamberlain had no easy task in convincing the Cabinet that Britain had to 'take' the Agreement; but Chamberlain was aware that Roosevelt, Hull, Morgenthau were not prepared to compensate Britain in the security arena for adhering to the commercial contract.

fresh concessions to the USA, especially since she had little room for manoeuvre in those markets which interested the US (agricultural products) because of her traditional links with countries which, in 1933, were united within the sterling bloc.

Whilst the economic appeasers could not play the American card profitably in intragovernment debates, they did succeed in mobilising public opinion and forwarding motions to Parliament. *Ad hoc* alliances (such as the Council for Action for Peace and Reconstruction, the Next Five Years Group, members of the Labour Party[282] and left-wing Conservatives) criticised the government's policies on lines similar to the interventions by the Americans, the Dominions and the economic appeasers; in some instances they referred *expressis verbis* to American and Dominion policy statements. Efforts in both Houses of Parliament and in a press campaign were combined in order to convince the government of the need to follow up with deeds the open-door initiatives announced in Hoare's speech at Geneva.[283] Alluding to these tendencies the former cabinet secretary Thomas Jones wrote to the prime minister, Stanley Baldwin, in the middle of February 1936, at the peak of the debates in the House of Commons and of American diplomatic pressure, that not only Britain's most important 'allies' (i.e. the US and the Dominions) but also the Labour movement made their support and cooperation in the event of a crisis conditional on the government tackling both rearmament and 'economic cooperation, recovery and peace'. 'The moral of that is to put as much energy into a new economic policy for Europe as we are now putting into rearmament'.[284] The government reacted to this pressure in a number of ways. It skilfully lent its public support to the ideas which were put to it; by so doing, it

282. Lansbury (5 Febr. 1936), Lloyd George (5 Febr. 1936), Sinclair (13 Febr. 1936) and Lothian (19 Febr. 1936) asked the Government to pursue Hoare's Geneva speech; Lothian to Murray (League of Nations Union), 13 Febr. 1936; Lothian, Letter to the Editor of *The Times*, 11 Febr. 1936; H. Butler memo., C 2213/99/18, and C 2140/99/18, with Jebb and Ashton-Gwatkin minutes (25/26 March 1936), FO 371–19 932, pp. 294f., 297ff.; Blessing of the German Reichsbank expressed the wish that Britain would follow up Hoare's ideas, Blessing to Pinsent, 2 March 1936, Phipps to FO, 5 March 1936, C 1556/99/18, FO 371–19 931, pp. 210f. Later in the year they asked the Government to proceed on the basis of the Tripartite Agreement (Sept. 1936). Davis' conversation with Eden on 7 Febr. 1936 covered much the same ground. Amery and D. Sandys founded the Imperial Group, since they feared the Baldwin government might subdue to the pressure from the centre left movements.

283. Jones, *Diary with Letters*, p. 175 (21 Febr. 1936); cf. League of Nations Union Resolution, 23 April 1937; the Canadian representative in London, V. Massey supported Lothian and Jones; Pearson was a member of the Hall group; see notes 217/18 of German original. Lothian, Letter to the Editor of *The Times*, 11 Febr. 1936.

284. Jones, *Diary with Letters*, pp. 175f.

was able to ward off diplomatic pressure from the US and the Dominions. Whilst leading members of the cabinet toured the country spreading the message of economic appeasement in their constituencies, particularly during the winter of 1936/37,[285] and delivered similar speeches at the annual meetings of the League of Nations, hardly anything came of these rhetorical efforts in inter-departmental and committee proceedings. The art of dealing with policy directives in a dilatory fashion made certain that the suggestions would end in the cul-de-sac of interdepartmental conflict – in this instance between the Foreign Office and the Board of Trade – or in intradepartmental disagreements.[286]

By stipulating that proposals for comprehensive settlements must first be examined by the appropriate ministries, the government could in fact delay the advance of those schemes which thwarted its own politically motivated initiatives; it was, however, faced time and again with the task of considering the ideas suggested, not least because the government had in the past paid tribute to some of the proposals. For example, the memorandum of the Locarno powers of 19 March 1936 took up the suggestion of the economic appeasers to arrange a world economic conference; the government limited this however with the proviso that such a conference would make sense only if Germany furnished evidence of her good 'conduct' in political crises.[287]

The foreign secretary, Anthony Eden, integrated important components of the concept of the economic appeasers into the

285. Hitler's speech on 30 Jan. 1937 and Blum's speech on 24 Jan. on the one hand and the forthcoming decision on a defence loan on the other shaped the context; Eden started the campaign when he called on Germany to adhere to the Tripartite Agreement (5 Nov. 1936, (HofC); he pursued the same track with speeches to his constituency (Leamington, 20 Nov. 1936), to the Foreign Press Association (12 Jan. 1937) and in the House of Commons (19 Jan. 1937). Baldwin's Guildhall speech (9 Nov. 1936) and a speech at Glasgow (Glasgow Herald, 28 Nov. 1936) carried the same arguments, as did speeches by Halifax (19 Nov. 1936, HofL) and Chamberlain (29 Jan. 1937, Birmingham). The structure of these speeches was rather similar: They stressed progress in British rearmament and warned Germany against challenging Britain; on the other hand they offered economic assistance once Germany had acceded to serious talks on arms limitation. The background factors are stated in Leith-Ross, *Money Talks*, pp. 236ff., and T 172–180]

286. The economic appeasers wanted to link the raw materials question and the discussion on reforming the League of Nations, i.e. to lay the 'economic foundations of peace' (Garvin); see above. In September 1936 Eden began to adopt the ideas presented to him by Bruce, Ashton-Gwatkin/Jebb. In 1937 the economic appeasers reminded the Cabinet of the need to meet criticism at home and abroad by coming forward with concrete suggestions to give substance to Hoare's initiative; Jebb, 'The Raw Materials Enquiry and Open Door', 15 April 1937, FO 433–4, p. 121, = W 7253/393/98; Ashton-Gwatkin/Jebb, 12 June 1937, W 11 815/393/18; Jebb, 11 June 1937, W 11 812; FO 371–21 247, pp. 66ff. and 78ff.; Leith-Ross, 20 July 1937, W 14 052/393/98, FO 433–4, no. 40.

287. Eden, 26 March 1936, HofC.

official position of British foreign policy; he did so on the assumption that Germany's obvious economic difficulties might lend themselves to attaining an agreement on arms limitation within the framework of an economic settlement.[288] Against the background of a press campaign initiated by Germany (which was countered by Eden listing how and when Britain had administered economic aid and political relief to Germany after 1919), Eden formulated a programme for a British peace initiative after the Rhineland crisis in almost the same words as those used by Jones, Lothian, Butler, Jebb and Ashton-Gwatkin, the latter two being actively involved in shaping the policy statement:

> We are prepared to do our best . . . by working for European appeasement to secure that others have butter in a world that has no need for guns . . . If we withdraw within ourselves, increase our individual isolation, if we continue to pile up armaments to the utmost of our economic strength and beyond it, we shall perpetuate the evils from which we suffer today and bring the world nearer to an even greater disaster than that from which it is only just beginning to recover. That way lies madness.[289]

Feeling compelled 'to correlate the rising burden of defence liabilities to the whole of our available resources' – that is, productive capacity, maintenance of confidence in Britain's financial stability and to the accepted policy in regard to social expenditure – Neville Chamberlain and Baldwin introduced appropriate provisions in the Defence White Paper of 1936.[290] Unofficial and official advisers to the prime minister were even more outspoken: 'I could only urge a dual policy for the government, rearmament and an equally vigorous attack on economic nationalism, because it is the economic misery of Germany which is held to be likely to bring about the explosion'.[291]

288. In his statements at the League of Nations on 25 Sept. 1936 and 20 Sept. 1937, Eden put forward the economic appeasers' set of ideas; in his letters to the Board of Trade and the Treasury (2 March 1936, 17 July 1936, 17 March 1937) he requested of interdepartmental committees that they 'test' the proposals.

289. Eden, 12 Jan. 1937 to Foreign Press Association; Eden, 19 Jan. 1937, HofC. The speeches (see also note 285) are counter-offensives to German (Goebbels) 'cannons instead of butter'-slogans. The strategy was to raise the 'standard of living' issue and bring the factor 'German people/will to peace' to bear on German politics; see ch. I of German original. Cf. G. Schmidt, 'The domestic background to British appeasement policy', in: W.J. Mommsen/L. Kettenacker, eds., The Fascist Challenge and the Policy of Appeasement, pp. 101–124.

290. Cabinet meetings of 25 Febr. and 2 March 1936, see below ch. II.

291. Jones, 25 Febr. 1936, Diary with Letters, pp. 177f.; cf. Earl of Avon, Facing the Dictators, pp. 323ff.

The verbal similarities between official statements and the standard thesis of economic appeasement strategy demonstrate above all the government's willingness to take up the formulas which were currently being expressed in 'public opinion'. This process of adaptation at the same time denied a firm foothold to the critics of government policy. Taking up the opposition's formula, however, meant neither that the government wanted to adopt a League of Nations course as advocated by the Labour Party nor did it represent a move away from protectionism and imperial preference as a first step in applying the recipes of the economic appeasers.

6. The 'Grand Solution': 'New Imperial Economic Policy'

In contrast to the package of proposals which were contingent upon Anglo-American cooperation, the 'grand solution', relying on a 'new imperial economic policy', could count on more favourable political conditions.[292] Almost all British opinion and interest groups held the view that the mechanism of the Triangular Trade system should be revitalised, thereby reviving world trade and helping to ease the world political situation. It was, of course, a matter of debate as to what Britain could and should do to stimulate this development. The recommendation of the economic appeasers that Britain merely had to relax import restrictions and imperial preferences to start serious talks was, however, by no means everybody's first choice.

The economic appeasers could rightly claim that their schemes took account of a number of important economic developments. These referred primarily to the fact that the British Empire had the largest share of world imports in the 1930s. The structure of the economies and of economic relations among the members of the Empire–Commonwealth were very varied and correspondingly opened up a multiplicity of opportunities and exchange possibilities. Accordingly, a peace strategy coordinating these potentials and facilities could expect to be met with interest in Europe – with Germany as a key factor. Basically their programme – and the Hall

---

292. On the Hall scheme see notes 203, 207f.; members of the study group were: Professor Noel Hall; Sir George Schuster; R. Barrington Ward; Pearson (Canada House), F. McDougall (Australia House), Enfield (Ministry of Agriculture), Jeff and Leeper (FO); C 4759/99/18, FO 371–19 933, pp. 322 ff.; Jones Mss, Class E, vol I, no. 10; Lord Gladwyn, *Memoirs*, pp. 63ff. The proposals are summarised in Eden's letter to Runciman, 17 July 1936, C 5197/99/18, FO 371–19 934, pp. 1ff., 5ff.; cf. FO 371–19 933, pp. 318, 322ff. See below note 302.

Scheme in particular – envisaged a pattern of multilateral trade; it would come into being if Britain restored 'world trade channels' and revoked the 'fiscal revolution' of 1931–32:

> Tariff adjustments by ourselves designed to admit more semi-finished goods from industrial Europe into this country in exchange for the admission of increased quantities of Dominion primary products into European industrial countries and increased purchases of finished products by the Dominions from us.[293]

A new cycle would 'take off' once Britain expanded her imports; this would stimulate the economies of partner countries, and Britain could reckon with increased income from foreign investments. World trade could only be restored if a financially stable power took the initiative, which, after 1935–36, meant primarily Britain. In view of the state of her economic recovery Britain could afford a temporary worsening of her balances, allowing her partners to avoid a crisis. The proposal took account of the fact that the Dominions had found other markets than Britain in Europe for their products and that conversely not only Britain but also European countries began to penetrate the Empire's market. All that would be required was to link higher British exports to primary producers with higher British imports from Europe[294] as the first stage; the reason why this was expected to work was that some of Britain's exports to the Empire would in any case consist of exports, such as automobiles, based on semi-finished goods (rolled metals, sheet metals, etc.) imported from Europe.[295]

From the point of view of the economic appeasers, both Britain and the Dominions could afford this change in policy since by 1935–36 they had, or were beginning effectively to, overcome the 1931 crisis.[296] In view of the upswing in individual countries and in world trade since the second half of 1936, which was reflected in rising prices and buying power (particularly in primary producing countries),[297] it 'only' depended on stabilising the trend with pro-

---

293. Hall-Memo., p. 9; cf. (Jebb) Eden-Memo., 'Economics and Foreign Policy', 17 March 1937, W 6363/5/50, FO 371–21 215, pp. 182,192; Jebb, 24 June 1936, FO 371–19 933, pp. 319ff.

294. Hall-Memo., p. 19. On the Treasury's criticism see notes 204, 212 of German original.

295. Hall-Memo., pp. 12f.

296. Hall-Memo., pp. 1, 10, and 15; EAC (S.C.) No. 25 = C.P. 341(36) = W 2380/5/50, 18 Dec. 1936, 'Survey of the Economic Situation', §53; EAC (S.C.) no. 26 = C.P. 77(37), 1 March 1937 = W 5821/5/50, 19 Febr. 1937, 'Economic Policy and the Maintenance of Trade Activity', § 17; cf. T 160–771, F 19 429.

297. Kindleberger, *World in Depression*, pp. 245f., 263f.

cyclical measures; that is, Britain tolerating an increase in imports. Alleging that 'Ottawa' did not allow for this expansion, the economic appeasers urged the extension of the imperial and trade-agreement system centred on Britain into a multilateral trading system by including Germany, France and other European industrial nations.[298] At all events 'Ottawa' had to be revised, as it was vital for Britain to find new outlets for her exports alongside those markets which she had secured on the basis that her traditional customers promised to take her exports in exchange for assurances that Britain would purchase their products.[299] Since the buying power of these partner countries was limited and would remain so, the success of the first phase of the recovery process would not be sufficient in the long term. The economic appeasers proposed reducing tariff rates where the import of semi-finished and other products was essential if production was to be more economical. In this way they hoped to promote the expansion of British exports.[300] Furthermore, the British government was urged to declare that it welcomed and would support international industrial agreements concluded by British industrial organisations with reference to market-sharing arrangements, prevention of cut-throat competition and so on.[301]

These proposals of the economic appeasers were applauded in government circles, albeit belatedly. The scheme worked out by a study group (led by Professor Hall) with the active participation of economic appeasers, was originally timed for presentation at the annual conference of the League of Nations in 1936.[302] Sup-

298. P.E.P, no. 36 'Ottawa is not enough'; Committee on Trade Policy, CTP(37)11, §§34–35; Hall-Memo., pp. 3 and 5; Ashton-Gwatkin discussed his suggestion to talk with Germany on customs union with Vansittart, 2 July 1936, C 4758/99/18, FO 371–19 933; Ashton-Gwatkin, 23 Dec. 1935, FO 371–18 873, pp. 129f. Jebb/Ashton-Gwatkin, 16 June 1936, FO 371–19 933, pp. 197ff. The 'new imperial economic foreign policy' was an attempt to maintain the Empire-Commonwealth: Ashton-Gwatkin, 30 June 1936, FO 371–19 933, pp. 355ff. The economic appeasers and Leith-Ross suggested that German competition in third markets would diminish if German products found their way to the British market; Germany would earn currency that might be spent on the purchase of British Empire products; CTP(37) 11, §§34–35, 7 June 1937, FO 371–21 247; (Jebb) Eden-Memo., W 6363/5/50, FO 371–21 215, pp. 182f., 192f.

299. Hall-Memo., pp. 13, 17; it was thought that 'Ottawa' did not allow for further increases. Leith-Ross, Balance of Payments, 7 Dec. 1936 (see below).

300. Hall-Memo., p. 17.

301. The FBI, Leith-Ross, the Economic Section of the FO, and industrialists put this demand to the Government.

302. Jebb, 'Scheme for Economic Solution of the German Problem', and his notes on the genesis of the Hall scheme; the Hall-Memo. and Ashton-Gwatkin's talk with Vansittart, 2 July 1936, are the main documents for this analysis; C 4757/4759/99/18, FO 371–19 933; Jebb., 9 Jan. 1937, W 373/5/50, FO 371–21 215, p. 5 on the connection between the McDougall

plementary to the Tripartite Agreement on Currency Stabilisation, the proposal, aiming at restoring 'old trade-channels', hoped to create a snowball effect in favour of a freer world economy. Since Runciman and Neville Chamberlain did not yet see an occasion for such a reorientation of Britain's foreign economic policy, the group had to wait for 'better times'. When the economic forecasts submitted by respected experts and by the government's advisory committees confirmed their assumptions, the economic appeasers immediately came up with a variation upon their scheme.[303] They demanded that the Tripartite Agreement be supplemented by a foreign (economic) trade arrangement re-establishing the Triangular Trade System. However, they ignored the fact that it had already been difficult to achieve a currency agreement and that this agreement had remained more or less ineffective. Furthermore, they took insufficient account that governments can influence economic developments much less than they can decisions affecting central banks and foreign exchanges.[304]

Moved by the 'lobbying' activities of the Australian High Commissioner, Bruce, on the other hand (who also played an important role in the League of Nations) and, on the other hand, by reports on the economy from the Committee on Economic Information and various experts, the foreign secretary, Eden, took up the ideas of the economic appeasers again towards the end of 1936 and officially requested that the Chancellor of the Exchequer set up interdepartmental committees; the 'terms of reference' reflected 'economic policy in the light of changes in the economic situation and the international political position since 1932'[305] and invited investigations into the propriety of criticisms of the measures

scheme and the pursuit of the Tripartite Agreement (Eden, 5 Nov. 1936, HofC); Economic Relations Section (FO), 6 Nov. 1936, 'Recent Moves in the Direction of International Economic Relations', C 7953/7746/62, FO 433–3.

303. (Jebb)Eden-Memo., 'Economics and Foreign Policy', 17 March 1937, W 6363/5/50, FO 371–21 215, pp. 182ff.; Eden, May 1937, 'The Economic Aspects of Foreign Policy'; cf. Wendt, *Economic Appeasement*, pp.437ff.

304. Strang, 13 Jan. 1937, FO 371–21 215, pp. 70f. (in his criticism of the McDougall scheme).

305. Chamberlain convened the Interdepartmental Committee on 4 May 1937; it reported on 7 June 1937; the Foreign Policy Committee of the Cabinet debated on the report in mid-June 1937 and suggested the directives to the British delegation to the Geneva 'raw materials' conference; T 160–770, F 15 583, 'Economic policy in the light of changes in the economic situation and the international political position since 1932'; cf. T 160–762, F 14 735/03/1–4; on the genesis and the terms of reference of the Committee see Leith-Ross papers, T 188–175; the report followed the thinking of Leith-Ross, Jebb, Schuster, Hodson, Salter, i.e. it advocated revision of 'Ottawa' and reductions of trade restrictions; CTP (37), §35, FO 371–21 247.

taken in 1931–32. The report of the Interdepartmental Committee on Trade Policy, which resulted from this request, recommended that, at the very least, imports of semi-finished and finished products should not be rendered more difficult and that consideration should be given to removing restrictions. The argument behind this was that if Britain took more products from continental Europe, her competitors might retreat from these markets (i.e. in the Far East, in South America and in the British Empire) or at least abandon their cut-throat methods. Beyond this the industrial nations of Europe would be able to use their exchange earnings from exports to Britain to buy raw materials from the British Empire, thus boosting trade within the sterling bloc.[306]

In order to defend their case against objections from the economic departments which concentrated on economic factors, the economic appeasers increasingly emphasised the 'political' aspects. They were tired of hearing the standard criticism which emphasised the primacy of a political approach with reference to the 'German problem'; they also noticed the increasing pressure exerted by German politics on British politicians. They selected their arguments according to their estimation as to whether they corresponded with, or at least went some way towards, the predispositions of the decision-makers.

In order to pass on their message to the 'inner circle' of decision-makers, they had to meet the 'atmosphere' halfway. They realised that they had made no headway as long as they had based their agitation solely on the argument that 'Ottawa' is not enough'.[307] It was not enough to contrast the prevailing view, which saw the extension of inter-imperial trade as automatically resulting in the revival of world trade,[308] with the notion, substantiated by expert opinions,[309] that a world-wide upswing in trade

306. CTP(37), §35, FO 371-21 247.

307. See note 298; P.E.P. no. 36, 30 June 1936 'Ottawa is not enough'. McDougall/Bruce-Memo., 'Economic Appeasement', W 373/5/50, FO 371-21 215, pp. 14–39; Ashton-Gwatkin, 6 July 1936, C 4760/99/18, FO 371-19 933, pp. 355/6. The McDougall scheme was produced by the study group which presented the Hall scheme; Jebb, 9 Jan. 1937, FO 371-21 215, pp. 5ff. Bruce outlined the proposals to the Birmingham Chamber of Commerce, *The Times*, 25 Febr. 1937; a leader 'The End and the Means', applauded the scheme, *The Times*, 25 Febr. 1937. Its author, Barrington Ward, was a member of the group. The practical proposition, i.e. to call an international economic conference on social and economic subjects, was forwarded by King and Roosevelt; on the Bruce Committee and the economic activities of the League of Nations see Dubin, *Transgovernmental Process*.

308. N. Chamberlain, 4 Febr. 1934, HofC; cf. Chamberlain, in *The Times*, 10 Dec. 1937, p. 18.

309. On the EAC reports of 25 Dec. 1936 and Febr. 1937 see note 296.

would occur only if at least some of the 'emergency' measures of crisis management were removed. They therefore emphasised the advantages of a strategy which highlighted the aspect of raising the standard of living: 'Healthy growth of international trade, accompanied by an improvement in the general standard of living, is an essential step to political appeasement'.[310] Before Neville Chamberlain, Simon, Halifax and others were willing to adjust British foreign and domestic policy to the requirements of 'defence' and of an arms race,[311] they were keen to test the seriousness of Hitler's professed interest in raising the standard of living; the economic appeasers also expected Germany to be interested in this perspective.[312] They therefore suggested that Leith-Ross use his pre-arranged talks with Schacht[313] to sound out this idea with a view to finding out whether the dictatorships and the Western democracies could reach agreement on the basis of joint undertakings to improve the standard of living.[314] By promoting the improvement of welfare services, the cheapening of retail prices, the extension of laws regulating terms of employment within the framework of the ILO and related 'social' plans, the Western democracies should at the same time demonstrate their ability to attain a higher standard of living ('prosperity for all').[315]

The proposal aimed at upgrading those sections of the League of

310. The final report on the Imperial Economic Conference, Cmd. 5482, §22, contains the formula: 'healthy growth of international trade, accompanied by an improvement in the general standard of living, is an essential step to political appeasement.' Mackenzie King reported to Chamberlain that Hitler and Göring stated in his conversations with them that Germany aimed at improved living conditions; King to Chamberlain, 6 July 1937, C 5187/5187/18, FO 371-20 750, pp. 325ff.

311. The FO and the Treasury were kept informed, thanks to comprehensive analyses of the Berlin Embassy, on the repercussions of German arms economy on the standard of living; Simon to Tweedsmuir, 24 Nov. 1936; Simon: minutes on Henderson's report of a conversation with von Neurath, 22 May 1937, Berlin tel. no. 320, Simon-Mss.

312. See above notes 248 and 307. Lothian, Letter to the Editor of *The Times*, 11 Febr. 1936; Lothian, *News Chronicle*, 16 June 1936; Mackenzie King discussed the subject with Roosevelt and with Hitler on his visit to Berlin.

313. Ashton-Gwatkin and Jebb suggested that Leith-Ross should discuss the McDougall scheme in his talks with Schacht; they expected the standard of living question to come to the fore, i.e. to lay aside the colonial question (at least during the period of dealing with the McDougall scheme); Jebb, 9 Jan. 1937, minutes on W 373/5/50, FO 371-21 215, p. 6a. Schacht and Delbos/Blum had agreed on 28 August 1936 to postpone the colonial issue whilst talks on international economics proceeded. Leith-Ross to Chamberlain, 4 Febr. 1937, Phipps-Mss., 3/4, pp. 56–68 (= C 958/78/18, FO 371-20 725); Leith-Ross report, 6 July 1936, C 4897/78/18, FO 371-20 728, pp. 299ff.; Leith-Ross, 9 July 1937, C 5139/71/62, FO 433-4, pp. 109–112; Leith-Ross, *Money Talks*, p. 253; cf. Wendt, *Economic Appeasement*, pp. 449ff; Middlemas, *Illusions*, pp. 111ff.

314. Jebb minute, 9 Jan. 1937, FO 371-21 215, p. 6.

315. Nicolson-Diary, 10 June 1937; Schuster was a member of the Hall group.

Nations machinery which were not yet compromised by the political collapse of 'Geneva'. The economic appeasers wanted to employ these institutions, and especially the ILO, in the context of their strategy, and this seemed to suggest itself because the head of the ILO, Harold Butler, had established contacts with them. If this plan succeeded, the proponents of economic appeasement could hope to mobilise 'mass' support, if the organisations behind the ILO lent their influence to a campaign for raising the standard of living as an essential step to political appeasement.[316]

This shift in emphasis did not simply reflect an intention to bypass domestic and inter-imperial vested interests in official foreign economic policy; its primary design was to focus on issues which were equally attractive to Labour and Liberals and thus suitable for an all-party intellectual effort. All of this points to the common roots of economic appeasement and 'social appeasement'.

The guiding principles and phrasing of the proposals gave rise to the suspicion that they were aimed more at accommodating Washington than Whitehall.[317] The authors of the economic project and their associates left no doubt that they regarded their political strategy as superior in the sense that their decision for talks would please Roosevelt and Hull as well as Hitler.[318] Their starting point, that British policy had to react to the criticisms of 'Ottawa', involved an obligation to design a platform for talks not only with the US but also with Germany, both of which were critics of 'Ottawa' abroad. We have already dealt with their view that British policy could not offer anything of material substance in talks with Germany without securing American approval. Conversely, Britain's policy had to dispel America's objections to imperial preference and trade agreement policies, if it wanted to size up its opportunities *vis-à-vis* Germany.

British policy has killed the system of international trade, which made

---

316. On the McDougall scheme see notes 248, 255, and 307. H. Butler, the director of the ILO, had provided a number of suggestions to the schemes of 'Economic Appeasement' (Hall-and McDougall memoranda). The investigations of the ILO and the Economic Section of the League are mentioned by Arndt, *Economic Lessons*, p. 247, and Dubin, *Transgovernmental Process*.

317. Troutbeck minute, 14 Jan. 1937, on W 373/5/50. The propositions of Lothian, Jones, Jebb, Schuster, the All Souls meeting (18/19 Dec. 1937) were phrased with a view to their effect on Washington. Jebb report, 15 April 1937, W 7253/393/98, §§36 and 43; Jebb memorandum, 11 June 1937, W 11812/393/98, FO 371–21 247, pp. 66ff.

318. Jebb minute, 9 Jan. 1937, FO 371–21 215, p. 7. The opponents of the economic appeasers asserted that Goebbels' 'Kanonen statt Butter'–campaign indicated what the German rulers were up to; Waley to Pinsent, 19 June 1936, C 4501/99/18, FO 371–19 933; see below §III.

the greatness of England during the nineteenth century. It is no contribution to economic appeasement to say that we might have had much more protection, and to advise others to give up exchange controls and quotas. The fact is that our policy (tariffs, agriculture, Dominions) leaves us with no contribution that we can make to economic appeasement, and we can only make a contribution by reversing the policy. This would be impossible now. We can never return to the opportunity of 1931. It is remarkable that we are able to open our doors as wide as we are doing to the United States of America. That is the most practical and probably the only effective step towards economic appeasement that we are able to take in present circumstances. This step does not lead in the direction of Germany, France, Italy or Japan . . . The future seems to be developing along the lines of large preferential groups – *Großraumwirtschaft* . . . If this is so, our consolation must be that our own particular group is the richest and the most powerful. If we add the United States of America as our associate, then its future economic and even political influence will be the decisive factor in the twentieth century.[319]

Against the background of these difficult politico-economic relations between Britain, the Dominions and the US and of social problems at home that could be expected to accompany the transition to a fully-fledged defence economy, Ashton-Gwatkin, Jebb, Hall and other appeasers emphasised the socio-political aspects more strongly and favoured world-wide action in the shape of a conference to raise living standards. Seen in this light, the question arises as to whether their proposals for economic appeasement initiatives were no less concerned with social tensions in Britain than they were with the German question.

We certainly cannot ignore this question for the purposes of our interpretation of events. As we have shown, their detailed proposals were open to massive criticism. How then could the economic appeasers proceed with their plans in the face of this? Was it that they bore these criticisms because they were so sure of their 'social' motives? The criticisms of their opponents were based on three standard hypotheses:[320]

(1) Economic means would work much too slowly; in present

319. Ashton-Gwatkin to Leith-Ross, 10 March 1938, FO 371–21 701. The economic appeasers pointed to the fact that Japan rather than Germany would benefit from a revision of preferential treatment in the colonies; Jebb, 17 March 1937, FO 371–21 215, p. 179; Eden-Memo., 'Economics and Foreign Policy,' 17 March 1937, FO 371–21 215, pp. 182f., 192f.; the details were provided in an India Office memorandum to the Cabinet Committee on Germany in Febr. 1936, G (36), Cab. 27–599.

320. Strang minute, 13 Jan. 1937, on McDougall-Memo., FO 371–21 215, pp. 7f.

circumstances, direct and more speedy instruments were needed to come to grips with the problems of influencing the disagreement between 'moderates' and 'extremists' in Germany from the outside.

(2) Economic actions would never be sufficient to banish the National Socialist 'devil', since Hitler's seizure of power could not simply be explained by economic factors.

(3) The National Socialist regime had consciously chosen to reduce the standard of living to further different priorities (national strengthening of state power); it would continue to endure these conditions should the alternative be to renounce their power ambitions.

The economic appeasers objected to these points on the grounds that the very same reservations applied to alternative measures – sanctions (see above, points 1 and 2) – and that their concern was to find a way out of the cul-de-sac in which negotiations over political issues had invariably ended. They maintained that economic offers – be they the opening-up of export outlets or the joint effort to raise living standards – were more fitting to the real problem because the National Socialists also had to cope with the problem of legitimising the regime by introducing welfare policies designed to alleviate domestic social distress.

Against a background both of contemporary and subsequent criticisms, the question must be asked, whether the economic appeasers envisaged 'appeasing' the National Socialist regime or rather aimed at addressing the German problem within the framework of a comprehensive strategy, which originated from the idea of conserving the British way of life, Britain's 'socio-political culture'. and the Empire. The *quid pro quo* which the economic appeasers expected from Germany in effect amounted to more than the concessions offered by Britain. This is also true if one looks at specific details; for example, the renunciation of export subsidies should Britain promise to rule out retaliatory measures against Germany as was the case at the time of the devaluation of the franc after the Stabilisation Agreement of September 1936.[321]

Primarily, however, this *quid pro quo* would have provided additional cover in their dispute with the advocates of protectionism[322]

---

321. (Jebb) Eden-Memo., 17 March 1937, W 6363/5/50, FO 371–21 215, p. 192a. The economic appeasers hoped that France would revise (liberate) its quota system at least with regard to industrial imports; see notes 346f. of German original.

322. The economic appeasers urged the British government to press for a reduction of quota systems; the Van Zeeland Committee was to tackle this issue: W 6363/5/50, FO 371–21

who, as continental experiences demonstrated, could expect to strengthen their position as British rearmament gradually got under way. The call of the economic appeasers for negotiations and agreements with Germany can be seen in this context as a strategy motivated by socio-political considerations. Their intention to encourage a change in direction in Germany also meant that Britain was no longer forced to follow Germany's example. The full significance of their approach, namely to fight economic national-ism wherever and however it manifested itself, is, therefore, that they wished to induce a change in Germany through concessions which at the same time would help to maintain or reactivate the principles of an enlightened liberalism in Britain: 'The economic crisis in this country which will in the long run be provoked by our own armaments expenditure will be largely relieved by the in-crease in international trade induced by a settlement.'[323]

Economic Development, Economic Forecasts and Economic Appeasement

The characterisation of economic appeasement referred to at the beginning of this study relies on impressive and comprehensive evidence. This does not, however, establish that economic ap-peasement determined British foreign policy in the 1930s. Even if one accepts that the World Depression (1929–32) and the de-pression of 1937–38 were likely to bring economic considerations and interests to bear on foreign policy, thus requiring any consist-ent interpretation to consider economic elements in Britain's external relations, two lines of argument speak against an overesti-mation of economic appeasement. Firstly, it cannot be taken for granted 'that the structures of political society are a direct reflec-tion of socio-economic structures'.[324] By concentrating on hypoth-eses and points of view generally associated with a socio-economic approach, all non-economic interests and factors can all too easily be minimised which could be and were relevant to a

---

215, p. 193. On the economic appeasers' campaign against protectionism and their fears of an unholy alliance between militarism and protectionism see below, and notes 79f.

323. Economic Section, 8 Febr. 1937, comments on Leith-Ross–Schacht meeting of 2 Febr. 1937 (at Badenweiler), C 958/78/18, FO 371–20 725, pp. 224ff., 226.

324. Karl Rohe, *Politik. Begriffe und Wirklichkeit*, Stuttgart 1978; J. Kocka, in H. A. Winkler, ed., *Organisierter Kapitalismus*, pp. 26f.; E.O. Czempiel, in: E. Krippendorff, ed., *Internationale Beziehungen*, p. 27.

strategy of appeasement. These non-economic interests were paradoxically often mobilised through economic measures and for economic reasons. The plethora of interests, influences, actors in influential positions, of issues and perceptions of problems which dominated British policies and politics in the 1930s and shaped appeasement, cannot, of course, be isolated from and played off against economic constellations and cycles. They are, however, not structured in a way which permits the direct transformation of economic interests into the arena of foreign relations. The British political system, shaped and formed as it is by traditions and conventions in general and by the special circumstances surrounding the issue of defence in interwar Britain in particular, resists interpretations which trace British appeasement policy back to a multifaceted economic interest determined by trade and finance.

Defence and arms production are interlocked with economics and economic interests of a wide variety, and both defence and economics were very important for Britain's foreign policy between the wars; but it would be totally misleading to neglect or ignore the non-economic factors impinging on the issue of defence and the story resulting therefrom – a story which had momentum of its own.

Secondly, the findings of our investigation of the intragovernmental decision-making process also contradict the proposition to see the roots of British appeasement policy in the economic sphere. In the continuing contest of policy recommendations on how to settle the 'German problem' both with respect to British interests and to a workable European peace system, a coalition of officials, advisers and cabinet ministers prevailed time and again, which maintained that economic and financial measures were admissable as supplementary measures but could never properly prepare the ground for a lasting arrangement between political powers. The perspectives of Britain's 'peace strategy', so they proclaimed, had to be derived from their 'political approach'; this argument will be analysed in more detail below.

The relationships between economic development, economic policy and appeasement/foreign policy interest us here in the context of two questions:

(1) Was there a time in the process of economic recovery or a focus in an economic policy which was dedicated to relieving Britain of 'crises' when foreign economic policy initiatives, focusing on the cooperation of Germany, required an 'accommodation' of German political ambitions?

(2) Did those interest groups which regarded foreign economic policy activities as an essential condition of economic growth, propose economic appeasement; that is, the cure of German (and possibly at the same time British) economic and/or political problems by offering 'material' economic benefits to Germany's rulers? Were they, in as far as they had any established influence on British economic policies, reliable allies of the economic appeasers in policy-making contests when facing such opponents as the Treasury, the Board of Trade, the Ministry of Agriculture, the Department of Overseas Trade and other institutions?

Both aspects will now be considered. The keynote of this analysis comes from official statements according to which British economic policy strove to achieve economic recovery in two stages.[325] Although Britain, as the leading import and export nation, stood at the centre of the storm, the world economic crisis effected Britain less directly than the rest of the world.[326] In the first phase it was therefore important to shield Britain from the spillover effects of any disruptive factors; emergency measures were introduced with a view to keeping the national economy free from the effects of alterations in exchange rates or in world trade. The crisis hit Britain primarily as one of finance and confidence;[327] accordingly, crisis management concentrated on attaining a balanced budget and improving the balance of payments by a 'revolution' in fiscal policy,[328] by devaluation[329] and by an embargo on foreign loans.[330] Many of the nations that had been hit harder by

325. N. Chamberlain, 4 Febr. 1936, HofC., Parl. Deb., vol. 261, cols. 279ff.; E.A.C. (S.C.) 21, 18th report, 29 July 1935, pp. 4f., Cab. 24–256. The economic appeasers referred to public statements of the government, i.e. tried to suggest that their action programmes (Hall- and McDougall scheme) were the better part of British policy.

326. W. Koren, 'Britain's economic recovery. Policies of the National Government', *Foreign Policy Report*, 31 July 1935, vol. 11, pp. 130ff.; W.A.P. Manser, *Britain in Balance*, London 1971; Phillips, Maddock, *Growth of the British Economy*, pp. 114f.; see note 296/7 of German original.

327. Howson, *Monetary Management*, pp. 75ff.; Sayers, *Bank of England*, vol. 1, ch. 17; Skidelsky, *Politicians and the Slump*, ch. 12; J.L. de Wilde, 'Currency Stabilization and World Recovery', *Foreign Policy Report*, 28 August 1935, vol. 11, p. 156; L.J. Williams, *Britain and the World Economy 1919–1970*, London 1974; Pollard, *Development*, pp. 212ff., 224ff.

328. Howson, Winch, *Economic Advisory Council*, pp. 122ff.; Howson, *Monetary Management*, pp. 70, 92ff.; on the 'Treasury view' and the capital fund theory see Youngson, *Economy*, pp. 254ff.

329. On the £ : $ relation during the crisis and in the 1930s and the effect of the devaluation of Sterling (by about 30%) see Sayers, *Bank of England*, vol. 2, pp. 419–430; Howson, *Monetary Management*, pp. 84ff.

330. The embargo on foreign loans (June 1932) was destined to shelter the debt conversion operations; in July 1934 the Government abolished the embargo on loans to Dominions, but insisted on 'tied loans'; Chamberlain, 11 July 1934, HofC., vol. 292, cols. 1260f.; see note 302 of German original.

the crisis devised and adopted protective measures of a different type, such as exchange controls, import quotas and the freezing of foreign debts. Partly in response to these restrictions, British policy followed the trend and completed her set of emergency measures. It generally favoured the substitution of imported industrial goods by domestic products[331] and introduced import surcharges to shelter 'trade-impacted' branches. But the main impulse to the domestic economy was the policy of cheap money.[332]

In order to maintain export outlets for the products of traditional export industries, the government rather skilfully employed the advantages of Britain's pattern of trade – in her trade agreement negotiations[333] Britain used her capacity to import specific, mainly agricultural, products as a bargaining counter; threatening retaliation, Britain got Denmark, the Netherlands and many other 'complementary' economies to import a given volume of staple goods from Britain in exchange for British assurances to purchase an agreed amount or percentage of agricultural produce. In its relationship with the Dominions, Britain at first aimed at some sort of a 'lower customs union' and later adopted the device of imperial preference;[334] the advantage was that Britain accommodated the Dominions' demand to increase tariffs on retained industrial imports of all competitors, including Britain, but granted British exporters a preferential rate. This package of measures – going off the gold standard, devaluation of the pound (by some 30 per cent), conversion of debts[335] and a cheap money policy, the establish-

331. Howson, *Monetary Management*, p. 111; Aldcroft, 'Impact of British Monetary Policy,' and other authors maintain that devaluation was at first more effective than tariffs; 'the big post-tariff increases came in 1934 when the tariff was made permanent' (Howson, p. 111).

332. The Bank rate was reduced to 5% in February 1932, and to 2% since 30 June 1932; on 'cheap money policy' see Sayers, vol. 2, pp. 430ff.; Nevin, in: Pollard, ed., *The Gold Standard and Employment Policies between the Wars*, London 1970; Alford, *Depression and Recovery?*, pp. 17ff., 38.

333. Board of Trade, C.P. 187(33), 26 July 1933, Cab. 23–75, pp. 359ff.; cf. J.H. Richardson, *Economic Foreign Policy*, pp. 101ff.; H.W. Richardson, *Economic Recovery*, pp. 260f.; Britain increased her exports to the group of trade treaty countries 1932 to 1934 by 33%, to Empire countries by 12% and to 'third' countries by 5%; G.P. (35)10, p. 8, March 1935, Cab. 27–584; E.A.C.(S.C.) 21, 18th report, §§25ff., Cab. 24–256.

334. Politically, the advantage of imperial preference was that this system allowed for protection of industries in the Dominions and at the same time for granting preferential treatment to the 'Ottawa' partners; in economic terms, 'Ottawa' did not contribute to an increase of British exports; G.P. (35)58, §97, p. 22, Cab. 27–584; Hancock, *Problems of Economic Policy 1918–1939*, pp. 198–230; Arndt, *Lessons*, pp. 132ff.; Drummond, *Economic Policy*, pp. 91ff.

335. The big conversion, announced on 30 June 1932, was followed by a number of smaller operations; Sayers, *Bank of England*, vol. 2, pp. 430ff.; Hicks, *Finance of British Government*, pp. 380f.; Howson, *Monetary Management*, pp. 69ff.; 87ff.

ment of an Exchange Equalisation Fund, the creation of the sterling bloc, Import Duties Act, Imperial Preferences – did not simply signal a turning away from the policy goals of the postwar period to re-establish London as the clearing house of a multilateral liberal economy and to conserve the international utility of the London money market. It also marked the attempt to create an alternative, relatively autonomous economic and currency system that was to provide shelter for its central member; that is, Britain.[336] An aversion to making British taxpayers provide a safety-net for world-wide loans to countries claiming to deserve capital aid for rehabilitating their economic fabric, was not in fact new to British foreign (financial) policy,[337] but the concentration on the sterling bloc meant a change towards financial and political isolationism unusual for Britain; since roughly 60 per cent of Britain's net liabilities were held by members of the sterling bloc, its formation took a lot of the pressure, on the monetary front, off British foreign policies. In comparison with 'emergency' and temporary measures by the governments to stimulate the home market and the exchange of goods, services and payments within the Trade Treaty and sterling-bloc systems, London's declarations on its continued 'international' stance were not very convincing. These statements argued that Britain must first put her own house in order so as to provide a basis for international action aiming at a realignment of currencies (exchanges), price increases as an adjunct of the restoration of prosperity and for the delivery of world trade from restrictive protectionist measures.

The first aim – to assist industrial recovery 'at home' – had been achieved by late 1933 and continued, albeit more slowly, throughout 1934 and 1935. In the last quarter of 1934 Britain's industrial production once more reached its 1929 level. World trade, however, had only recovered very little from the depression during this period, and the start of the second phase was, therefore, problematic because it aimed at supplementing the domestic growth through an expansion of exports.[338] The ratio of exports to the

336. S. Strange, *Sterling and British Policy*, pp. 55ff; Francis, *Britain's Economic Strategy*, pp. 151 ff.; Ellsworth, *International Economy*, pp. 383ff. About 60% of Britain's net liabilities were placed with countries belonging to the sterling bloc, thus alleviating the pressure on the £ and providing shelter against international irritations and intimidations.

337. Leith-Ross, 6 May 1932, FO 800–286, p. 601 (quoted in note 262, ch. I of German original); T 177–10; BT 11–223; cf. G. Schmidt, *Politische Tradition*, on the 1917–1921 period.

338. GP(35)58, §95, p. 23; cf. Aldcroft, *The Inter-War Economy*, pp. 245f.; Howson, *Monetary Management*, p. 118; H.W. Richardson, *Economic Recovery*, p. 49; Kindleberger, *World in Depression*, p. 244.

GNP had declined from 17 per cent in 1929 to 10 per cent in 1938; however, the share of investment goods exports rose.[339] The question was now whether Britain, during the second stage, had more to gain in the field of foreign trade or from promoting continuing internal recovery by keeping up the impetus of those expanding sectors which could help to accelerate the recovery of the economy as a whole – iron and steel, car manufacturing, electrical, chemical and building industries and manufacturing engineering. Unlike the economic advisers, the Committee on Economic Information, as well as some top Treasury officials, the chancellor of the exchequer and the government rejected deficit spending (public borrowing for public works) as an instrument of economic policy.[340] They believed that the export industries would not be helped sufficiently by such measures, whereas domestic industries (both house-building and iron and steel) were effectively assisted by the main instrument of British economic policy; that is, 'cheap money'.

The government had committed itself to an overseas trade policy in order to sustain recovery and bring benefits to the 'old' industries still suffering from the depression.[341] The reasoning was that although 'growth was increasingly dependent on the buoyancy of the domestic market', Britain's productive capacity remained interlocked with the international economy because of the structure of the British economy which had been created in the nineteenth and twentieth centuries;[342] British economic policy thus had to design measures that would contribute to the restoration of overseas trade as a stimulus to economic growth in Britain. One characteristic component of Britain's economic structure had lost its significance in the crisis; namely, the connection between British financial and monetary policy and Britain's function in the world economy. Instead, a second component, the structural

339. On the composition of British exports see Lewis, *Economic Survey*, p. 78; Kahn, *Great Britain in the World Economy*, pp. 126f.; Philips/Maddock, *Growth of the British Economy*, p. 116. E.A.C.(S.C.)21. 18th report, tab. 9; Howson/Winch, *Economic Advisory Council*, pp. 127, 133. On 'sheltered industries': H. Clay, *The Post-War Unemployment Problem*, 1929, p. 93.

340. G.P. (35)58, §162, Cab. 27–584; cf. McKibbin, 'Economic Policy,' pp. 96ff.; Howson, Winch, *Economic Advisory Council*, ch. 5.

341. Baldwin, 10 July 1935, HofC.; N. Chamberlain, 14 Febr. 1935, HofC, vol. 297, cols. 2205ff.. The fourth point on Chamberlain's list of priorities for the 1935 election campaign covered foreign trade: hopes for expansion and employment were directed to overseas trade (Cab. 27–591).

342. W. Ashworth, *An Economic History of England, 1870-1939*, and A.E. Kahn, *Great Britain in the World Economy*, are still the best surveys. Economist, 24 Dec. 1938, 'Home Markets vs. Export', pp. 647f., stresses the growing importance of the home markets as a factor making for growth; cf. Pollard, *Development*, pp. 188f.

weaknesses of industrial production in Britain and their effects on the competitiveness of exports and the balance of payments, gained in significance the more Britain had to face international problems;[343] the more events called for 'real' rearmament, the more one of these problems grew as imports increased. The government and its economic advisers (CEI; Leith-Ross) felt that the second phase required British policy to supplement its stimuli towards internal recovery with agreement with foreign countries in order to avoid another setback (see below). The second phase could be entered into as soon as important foreign countries succeeded in overcoming the 'crisis' and became interested in a revival of world trade.

In view of the high level of Britain's import requirements – primarily raw materials and foodstuffs, but also semi-finished and finished goods – British foreign economic policy had to ensure that her export industries, old and new, contributed to the balance of payments, despite its relative decline in importance in the creation of domestic wealth. The decline in invisible earnings[344] from services to world trade (shipping, banking, etc.) and the suspension of interest payments on public loans and foreign investments (e.g. Argentina) not only made it necessary to repatriate capital in order to redress the balance of payments (instead of exporting capital) but also attracted the government's attention, confronted as it was with the task of 'maintaining Britain's credit' as the fourth arm of her defences.

In the period 1919–29 Britain had been able to resume the export of capital, arranging foreign loans. She also repurchased part of the foreign (dollar) securities sold during the war to defend the pound. In the depression and its aftermath, conditions had changed profoundly; foreign lending was restricted to the Dominions, and an embargo on foreign loans operated.[345] Although the British government and the Bank of England were in favour of, and presented, plans for 'recycling' international credits (by ob-

---

343. McKibbin, *Economic Policy*, pp. 102ff.

344. Alford, *Depression and Recovery?*, tab. 6; H.W. Richardson, *Recovery*, pp. 56ff., Phillips, Maddock, *Growth*, pp. 133ff.; Kahn, *Great Britain*, p. 146; Pollard, *Development*, pp. 191f. Whereas 'invisible incomes' had paid for 30% (before 1913) resp. 25% (in the 1920s) of Britain's import, Britain had to repatriate capital after 1932.

345. In the crisis of 1931 Britain attempted to induce the U.S.A. to 'finance' world trade; on the Kindersley-, Henderson- and other British projects see R.W. Oliver, *International Economic Co-operation and World Bank*, London 1975, pp. 56ff.; Kindleberger, *World in Depression*, pp. 205ff., 212 ff. See note 330 on the embargo on foreign loans and the resumption of foreign lending — albeit on the basis of 'tied loans' — to the Dominions (in 1934).

taining credit in wealthy countries for use in less wealthy), and thereby setting world trade in motion, the government hesitated to respond to suggestions from the banking community and its own economic advisers to revoke the 1932 embargo on foreign loans, although proposals to this effect justified this as a means of promoting exports. The demands on Britain's financial resources on behalf of rearmament and the problem of paying for imports in the event of war cast their shadow[346] over the debate on whether 'home market versus exports' was the issue or whether export expansion had to supplement and sustain the internal recovery of the first phase of 1932–35.

The debate, of course, also covered Britain's demands on other leading countries, the central powers of 'currency units': France (still on the gold standard), the US (dollar), and Germany (mark zone). At a general level this catalogue of requests included a reduction of exchange restrictions and a commitment by Britain, the US and France to end competitive unilateral exchange depreciation as a means to gaining trade advantages. It was hoped that Germany might also exercise this restraint. Britain expected Germany to put an end to the contradictions of domestic inflation whilst at the same time retaining the Reichsmark on the gold standard. France was to be persuaded to devalue the franc and to abandon deflationary policies.[347] To ease their balance-of-payments problems, Britain wanted the US to adapt the pound–dollar rate to 'market' conditions.[348]

346. In time of war Britain had to finance not only raw material imports and food but arms and tools, too, from $-bloc countries (U.S.A. and Canada!); the flight of capital in 1931 and again in 1938 as well as the 'collective' memory, in the shape of the historical parts (i.e. World War I experiences) in the memoranda of the CID system and of the Treasury, haunted the officials in charge and gave a 'real' dimension to their insistence on finance as fourth arm of the defence system; their assertion of the need to husband Britain's credit standing was no mere pretension. Although Britain's trade deficits in 1936–1938 were on a similar level to 1929–31, the difference existed that in 1929 Britain's current account registered a surplus of £ 103 mill., whereas in 1937 and in 1938 Britain accumulated deficits of £ 56 resp. 54 mill. Simon, 5 July 1939, Cab. (39)36, Cab. 23–100; Hopkins-Memo., Note on the Financial Position, ibid.; Sayers, *Bank of England*, vol. 2, pp. 567ff. Hancock, Gowing, *British War Economy*; B. Collier, *The Defence of Britain*; Sayers, *Financial Policy 1939–1945*; N.D. Hall, *North American Supply*. See ch. II: Political System and Appeasement.

347. British views on Germany's monetary and financial policy: Pinsent, June 1936, C 5020/99/18, FO 371-19 933, pp. 410ff. On French monetary policy: J. Bouvier, 'Contrôle des changes et politiques économique extérieure de la S.F.I.O. en 1936,' *RI*, vol. 13(1978), pp. 111–115, and R. Girault, *Léon Blum*, ibid., pp. 91–109.

348. H. Clay, *Lord Norman*, pp. 421ff.; Oliver, *International Economic Cooperation*, pp. 85ff.; Gardner, *Sterling-Dollar Diplomacy*. On the Tripartite Agreement and Anglo-French-American negotiations in 1935-36: BT 11-735; Clay, *Lord Norman*, pp. 417ff.; Sayers, *Bank of England*, vol. 2, pp. 474ff.

The competitive and productive capacity of Britain's export industries provided the second point of reference. Changes in the pattern of demand within world trade[349] and shifts in the positions between creditor- and debtor-nations, accentuated by the problem of reparations and war debts after the First World War, had as early as the 1920s been used to explain structural unemployment and the fact that Britain had drawn very little benefit from the upturn of the 1925–29 period: 'History took its toll'. Before 1914 Britain had exported more than two-thirds of her manufactured goods to primary-producer countries, which in the 1920s and again during the World Depression, experienced a worsening of their terms of trade. This did not remain without its effects on Britain's export industries. There was also the problem that Britain, in comparison with the US and Germany, had directed her resources less effectively towards capital-intensive or highly specialised products. After the First World War Britain came off badly in the competition for this expanding world trade in manufactured goods.[350] In the 1920s individual 'modern' industries (cars, chemicals, heavy electrical goods and synthetic fibres) did, however, match at least their European competitors;[351] improvements in production methods gave Britain access to new markets. However, the shift to 'modern' sectors of industrial production did not occur to an extent which corresponded to Britain's leading position with regard to capital resources and skilled labour. The overwhelming problem was how to adapt the structure of the economy to changes in technology as well as demand and how to divert resources from declining industries into expanding sectors of the economy to ensure a profitable employment of the labour force.[352] The overvaluation of the pound – especially when compared with the competitive depreciation of currencies as a means to gain trade

349. E.A.C.(S.C.) 21, 18th report, 27 Sept. 1935, p. 4; All Souls conference, 11 and 12 July 1931, Jones- Mss., Class C, vol. 4, no. 73; Loveday, *Britain and World Trade*, London 1931; Balfour Committee on Industry and Trade, Survey of Overseas Markets, 1925; see note 321 of German original.

350. F. Blackaby, *British Share of World Trade in Manufactures*, 1965; A. Maizels, *Industrial Growth and World Trade*, Cambridge 1963; League of Nations Publications, Economic . . . Department, Industrialization and Foreign Trade, Geneva 1945; see note 322 of German original.

351. Loveday, All Souls Conference, 11 and 12 July 1931, minutes p. 3; R.S. Sayers, 'The Springs of Technical Progress in Britain, 1919–1939', *Economic Journal*, LX(1950); Kahn, *Great Britain*, p. 109.

352. S.R. Dennison, *The Location of British Industry and the Depressed Areas*, 1939; Aldcroft/ Richardson, *The British Economy 1870–1939*, ch. 8; F. Benham, *Great Britain under Protection*, London 1940.

advantages (see France) – and high interest rates in the 1920s, hampered the development of new industries, in particular when it came to making advances in export markets to compensate for the decline in 'old' export-intensive industries.[353] The rigid wage–cost structure provided a popular explanation for the setbacks suffered by British exporters. In combination with the effects of an over-valued pound, which worked to the detriment of the export indus-tries, contemporary criticism often culminated in the slogan: 'Too good and too expensive'. The change in direction in economic policy in 1931–32, which amounted to making 'employment for home consumption' the new priority, improved opportunities for domestic production to such an extent[354] that observers feared industry would not be particularly interested in an expansion of exports; these fears increased at the moment when rearmament set in and added a stimulus to the leading sector of the domestic economy, iron and steel,[355] which replaced the construction in-dustry[356] as multiplier of growth.

In public, the government repeated its view that it had done better than most other governments in promoting economic recovery, adding that the 'emergency' measures were of a transi-tory nature and that it felt obliged to work for a revival of interna-tional trade with a view to raising 'export-sensitive' employment. Import restrictions and protective measures alone were not enough[357] to create jobs for 1.5 million unemployed;[358] rather

353. Leith-Ross, C.P. 339(36), 7 Dec. 1936, §13, p. 12f.; Leith-Ross, *Money Talks*, pp. 228f. Clay accused Leith-Ross of over-estimating the current account deficit of £10 mill.; Leith-Ross got no support in 1931, and none in 1936/7 when he urged depreciation of the £ Sterling; Howson, *Monetary Management*, pp. 123ff.; Sayers, *Bank of England*, vol. 2, p. 474. On the situation in the 1920s see Moggridge, *Return to Gold*; Alford, *Depression and Recovery?*, pp. 16ff., 34f.; Pollard, *The Gold Standard*; see note 325 of German original.

354. *Foreign Policy Report*, 14 August 1935, vol. 11; cf. H.W. Richardson, *Economic Recovery*, chs. 2 and 4; British Association, *Britain in Recovery*.

355. E.A.C.(S.C.)21, 18th report, p. 6; *Economist*, 1 Dec. 1934 and 15 June 1935; A.F. Lucas, *Industrial Reconstruction and the Control of Competition*, 1937; *Foreign Policy Report*, 14 August 1935, vol. 11, pp. 144ff.; D.C. Burn, *The Economic History of Steelmaking, 1867–1939*, 1943; J.D. Scott, *Vickers A. History*, London 1962; Howson, *Monetary Management*, p. 138.

356. E.A.C.(S.C.)21, 18th report, July 1935, p. 6; 'Building' employed 1,425,000 in the first quarter 1935 (compared to 1,290,000 in 1929); iron & steel had 915,000 in 1934/5, compared to 1,019,000 in 1929 and 762,000 in 1932; the service industries/'tertiary sector' employed 350,000 persons more in 1934 than in 1929.

357. Whereas economic historians (Aldcroft, Howson, Richardson) see no evidence to substantiate any correlation between the introduction of a general tariff and 'Ottawa' and the process of economic recovery, the National Government and in particular the protectionists related Britain's favourable situation and recovery to protection and imperial preference.

358. The analyses of the CEI are well covered by Howson, Winch, *Economic Advisory Council*, p. 111. A remark by Chamberlain on the inevitability of unemployment was quoted by Labour

Britain had to reckon that other countries would retaliate against any continued or increased import restrictions affecting their products in the British market; in other words, they would attempt to reexport their own unemployment problems into Britain.[359] Working on the principle that countries wishing to export must allow imports[360] and calculating that the application of such a formula, if it remained limited to 'Ottawa' and the trade agreement countries, would not get British industries out of the depression, it was only a matter of timing as to when Britain had to attend to international trade. In this context, Britain had to keep in mind that no revival of international trade could last without relief through international lending and a relaxation of conditions governing the flow of investment capital. Conversely, the withdrawal of quota arrangements, exchange controls and other measures to curb balance-of-payments deficits, were dependent on prospects for improving world trade. In order to promote recovery into sustained growth it was seen as essential to find economic and financial methods and instruments suitable to the aims of the second phase and at the same time to allow for the reduction of excessive protection or for a partial abandonment of restrictive practices.[361] In reality British economic policy found it extraordinarily difficult, (1) to revise quota agreements even with the Dominions in a way favourable only to other members of the sterling bloc and the Trade Agreement Systems, (2) to drop her claims to equality of treatment by suspending rights under the 'most-favoured nation' clause in order to facilitate regional integration by means of multilateral tariff concessions (e.g. in the Danube area)[362] and (3)

---

politicians to support their charge that the 'National' government was 'unsocial' and then served as an explanation as to why the opposition distrusted rearmament policy.

359. Leith-Ross, C.P. 339(36), 7 Dec. 1936; P.E.P., Report on International Trade, 1937, p. 90; P.E.P., *Britain and World Trade*, 1937, p. 25; G.P. (35)10, pp. 7f., and G.P. (35)58, pp. 22f.; Sir George Schuster, 'Empire Trade before and after Ottawa', *Economist Supplement*, Nov. 1934.

360. This principle guided C. Hull's RTA policy; Junker, *Der unteilbare Weltmarkt*, p. 57, 68ff., 72ff.; see note 334f. British trade policy was handicapped by different evaluations of the £ : $-relationship after 1933; see note 332 of German original.

361. E.A.C.(S.C.)21, Committee on International Economic Policy, First Report, 11 Oct. 1932, p. (32)2; H. Morrison(Treasury), League of Nations, October 1936, M. MacDonald to Eden, 10 Oct. 1936, W 13 551/2/98, FO 411-19, no. 46, p. 107. Following the Tripartite Agreement, the British government expected 'free exchange countries' to start with gradual reduction of quota restrictions, etc.; 'other' countries (i.e. Germany) would then discover that they had to join the exchange stabilisation agreement in order to benefit from a return to international trade.

362. In 1931/32 the Dominions rejected proposals to dispense with treaty rights in order to facilitate the forming of preferential areas in central and southeast Europe; Britain opposed the

to protect domestic industries from imports with the help of temporary quotas and higher tariffs, but on condition that they became more competitive and supplied the home market cost-efficiently. It was also appreciated that the international capital markets had to provide borrowing facilities in order to reintegrate the agricultural and primary producer countries into world trade.[363] However, the government limited its own contribution to restoring 'confidence' and left it to 'market forces' to decide the credit worthiness of each individual 'potential' case, be it a foreign government or a private company, and to keep the rate of the pound steady on a 'realistic' basis in an attempt to offer a firm base for multilateral commercial transactions.[364] Proposals to revoke the embargo on foreign loans and, through the export of capital, to stimulate demand for British products, did not find the chancellor of the exchequer's ear until 1938.[365]

In the debate on ways of encouraging the process of economic recovery or protecting it from setbacks, 'vested interests' argued in favour of extending 'imperial preference' and installing preferential loan arrangements within the sterling bloc/Commonwealth, whilst the proponents of a liberal economy pointed to the importance of non-Empire markets for Britain and pointed towards outlets for European trade. The government concerned itself with a combination of proposals from both sets of ideas. Some imperialists who agreed with Amery recommended that Germany's (Japan's and Italy's) imperial demands for 'hinterlands' be respected, and this was likely to result in 'economic appeasement effects' either indirectly or because of the efforts made to propagate this view; 'economic appeasement effects' were even more likely to emerge from the

Ouchy convention of the Oslo partners, and in 1937 the Treasury rejected the Hodza plan and French plans, due to political reasons; BT 11–234; BT 11–375; BT 11–715; Arndt, *Lessons*, pp. 236f.; D. Kaiser, *Economic Diplomacy*. British policy was influenced by political calculations: The U.S.A. insisted on maintaining the most favoured nation clause; Germany aimed at establishing an informal empire by means of preferential arrangements, and France launched and supported Czech plans for 'uniting' the former parts of the Danubian/Habsburg Empire economically and politically to resist German penetration.

363. Macmillan report, Cmd. 3897(1931), §§316–319, on international lending; E.A.C.(S.C.)21, 18th report, §3, p. 4; Skidelsky, *Politicians and the Slump*, pp. 318ff.

364. Sayers, *Bank of England*, vol. 2, pp. 419ff.; Foreign Policy Reports, 31 July 1935, and 18 August 1935, vol., 11, pp. 132 and 149. The British government was never sure whether Roosevelt would devalue the $, for the President had authority to act in this direction; if Britain had to stop a run on the £ or to increase Bank rate, the one instrument of its economic policy — 'cheap money' — would be impeded.

365. Howson, *Monetary Management*, p. 143; Howson, Winch, *Economic Advisory Council*, pp. 109ff.; Sayers, *Bank of England*, vol. 2, pp. 491f.

internationalists' plea to restore the 'old trade channels' as well as London's role as the 'service centre of world trade'.

Anyone joining this debate had to be aware of three elements. Firstly, the share of capital goods in British total exports as opposed to consumer goods was expanding and rose from 24 per cent in 1934 to 26 per cent in 1935.[366] Secondly, the expansion took place in the markets of the sterling-bloc countries whose buying power had recovered well in comparison with other areas, albeit more slowly than in Britain. Thirdly, countries belonging to the sterling bloc could expect to benefit considerably from a world-wide rise in wholesale prices of industrial raw materials and food-stuffs. British industry – especially manufacturing engineering and iron and steel – could count on continuing market opportunities in these countries, save for the fact that these countries, including the Dominions, encouraged industrialisation and supported domestic industries through a variety of fiscal policies and subsidies and that the distant countries had 'local' cost advantages over their British competitors.[367] The different evaluation of these and some other background factors determined the debate as to whether pursuing the path taken successfully in 1931–32 would ensure sustained recovery or whether additional or alternative measures were needed to induce the employment of the British economy to full capacity. 'Internationalists' viewed the prolongation of the first recipe as an extension of the imperial preference system to the detriment of the 'rest of the world'.[368] A conflict of aims appeared on the horizon. The question which interests us is whether the 'internationally-minded' were, by criticising the influence of 'protectionists' and 'imperialists' on British foreign (and economic) policy, driven into positions and policy recommendations which amounted to economic appeasement.

The government's economic advisers, in particular members of

---

366. E.A.C.(S.C.)21, 18th report, §27/tab. 8, and §§28/29, tab. 10; cf. Lewis, *Economic Survey*, p. 78; H.W. Richardson, *Economic Recovery*, p. 263.

367. The wage level in the Dominions was reduced to a larger extent than in Britain; the Dominions devalued their currencies even more than Britain; E.A.C.(S.C.)21, 18th report, §37. The FBI complained of the Dominions' protection and industrialisation and expected the British government to force the hands of the Dominions by threatening import restrictions on Australian agricultural products if Australia did not alter her industrial policy or her prohibitive tariff rates; London was to press for 'secure' markets for British industrial exports to compensate for granting safe markets in Britain to the Dominions' primary products and foodstuffs.

368. The Empire Industries Association resp. the Empire Economic Union wanted to extend preferential treatment to imperial shipping, imperial loans, imperial communications, etc.; the Central Council of the National Union of Conservative and Unionist Associations adopted resolutions expressing the same ideas.

the Committee on Economic Information of the Economic Advisory Council[369] and the government's chief economic adviser, Sir Frederick Leith-Ross, may be regarded as representing the countervailing influences to a reliance on 'Ottawa' and cheap money as the best and most rewarding elements of a 'policy of sustained growth'. In a previous context it has already been mentioned that the economic appeasers (in the Foreign Office and among the 'attentive public') immediately took up the economic reports and forecasts and balance of payments analyses of the advisers, and presented their case to their superiors with a view to opening a new round in the contest of appeasement strategies. In what follows, only those aspects will be investigated which bear on the question of whether the experts aimed at economic appeasement or whether their arguments or their recommendations displayed tendencies which favoured economic appeasement.

7. The Committee on Economic Information

The Committee on Economic Information (CEI), where a number of distinguished British economists (Stamp, Keynes, Lewis, H. D. Henderson, Salter, Sir Ernest Simon, G. D. H. Cole) met with top Treasury officials (Phillips and Leith-Ross) and at regular intervals presented reports on the state of the economy to the cabinet, had from the very beginning stressed in its recommendations 'that the government should actively promote recovery at home and abroad by means of cheap money, public works and international monetary measures, designed to give debtor countries relief from the pressures which had led them to adopt "beggar-my-neighbour" trade policies'.[370] One consideration dominated their analyses of economic developments, which between 1935 and 1937 concentrated on aspects of the international economy: they forecast a further depression in 1937–38. In order to combat this slump – which was in fact caused in 1937 by the 'Roosevelt' recession[371] – they recommended that the government concentrate on two devices: (1) not simply to continue with the

---

369. Howson, Winch, *Economic Advisory Council*, pp. 119, 127ff., 135., 139. Leith-Ross worked with the CEI. Since the members of the CEI held different views and since their engagement varied, the report's emphasis changed, too.

370. Howson, Winch, p. 108.

371. The recession affected Britain in late 1937; foreign exchanges (deposits) were withdrawn; the rearmament boom, since April 1938, counteracted the trend. The depression helped to conclude Anglo-American Trade negotiations; Kottmann, *Reciprocity*, p. 205; Sayers, *Bank of*

policy of cheap money, but also to underpin this with public works programmes and (2) to use the scope for increasing international trade, however small the chances of 'liberalisation' might be. The actual development of the 1937–38 recession confirmed the accuracy of their forecast: 'We have far more to lose, and are more likely to lose, from a setback in our internal recovery than we are likely to gain in the field of foreign trade.'[372]

Whereas during the 1937–38 recession there was no fall in the real gross domestic product, British foreign trade showed a downward tendency.[373] Since their diagnosis was that Britain owed her recovery primarily to the buoyancy of the domestic economy, they did not expect the function of foreign trade to differ from the trend of economic development in the 1930s.

In July 1935 the experts forecast a crisis for 1937–38; they predicted that by this time the building boom would have ended, but were unable to identify any other leading sector which would be capable of giving a comparable impulse to the economy.[374] The unavoidable decline in the house-building trade would result in a fall in jobs by up to 500,000. For the British economy this would be almost as serious a blow as that dealt by the decline in the export sector between 1929 and 1933 which resulted in 600,000 people losing their jobs. The difference was, however, that in 1937–38 home-investment industries offered no prospect as a refuge.[375] A lack of demand in house-building meant that this leading sector would not react to a policy of cheap money a second time. If rearmament expenditure, because of the transitory nature of its albeit welcome impact, was not to be used for reviving the economy, no more than two options were left: firstly, the economic advisers recommended schemes for home investment – that is, the preparation of a programme of public works so as to have projects ready to speed up and mitigate the slump which was anticipated to follow a rearmament boom[376] and, secondly, measures

---

England, vol. 2, pp. 561ff.; L.J. Williams, *Britain in the World Economy*, pp. 78ff. On the recovery process see E.A.C.(S.C.)21, 18th report, §44, p. 20; Howson, Winch, p. 113; Oliver, *International Economic Co-operation*, p. 87f.

372. Phillips, 4 June 1935, T 175–88, 'Relations with USA'.; cf. Howson, *Monetary Management*, p. 119.

373. Kindleberger, *World in Depression*, pp. 278ff.; Howson, pp. 138f.

374. E.A.C.(S.C.)21, 18th report, pp. 1, 12, 14f.; Treasury comment on E.A.C, 12th report, 3 August 1934, FO 800–289, p. 254; G.P. (35), 2nd meeting, 4 Febr. 1935, Cab. 27–583; on building as leading sector: EAC, 18th report, §§45f., p. 21; Howson, Winch, pp. 134ff.

375. E.A.C.(S.C.)21, 18th report, §24, p. 14.

376. Ibid., §45, p. 21; the Phillips Committee's terms of reference were to investigate 'what

to stimulate the export industries. The second aspect coincided with worries in government circles about what was to happen to production capacities when the Four-Year Armaments Programme – decided upon between the summer of 1935 and March 1936 – ran out in 1939–40; healthy export industries would be needed to maintain employment once rearmament and the housing boom were over.[377]

Insofar as the government objected to basing its 'growth policy' on an alignment of public works and expenditure on rearmament, because it feared the disadvantageous consequences for Britain's credit-worthiness and her role in international trade, the question arises as to whether the economic advisers shared the basic views of economic appeasers; namely, to endeavour to achieve 'economic disarmament' and thus spare Britain the consequences of following Germany on the road to *Rüstungswirtschaftsautarkie*.[378] An effort to revive international trade and international lending and to reintegrate Germany into this system was regarded as the expedient which could still stop the momentum of Germany's excesses, thus forcing Britain and other countries, however unwillingly, to adapt their policy standards to the German model.

Economic appeasement in this context could take on different forms:

(1) Just as one wished to keep Britain's flexibility in economic policy, it could be assumed that other countries, especially Germany, had not yet decided once and for all on a policy strategy leading to a *kampfbereite Wehrwirtschaft* as the culmination of economic nationalism. Assuming that a certain degree of openness still existed in Germany, Britain could still hope to shape the course of events in the direction of her operative ideals, provided British offers to assist in the reversion of the German economy were so substantial that the productive capacity generated by expenditure on armaments was likely to be diverted towards exports and consumer goods production.

---

we can do to prevent excesses during the boom period into which we are entering and what precautions we can take in advance with a view to mitigating the slump which we must in reason anticipate will follow the boom', 13 March 1937; see Peden, *Treasury*, pp. 89ff.,; Howson, *Monetary Management*, p. 128.

377. See below on Leith-Ross; on Inskip see ch.II/6, 'Political System'; cf. Howson, *Monetary Management*, pp. 124, 129ff.

378. According to Petzina, 'Vierjahresplan und Rüstungspolitik ', in: Forstmeier, Volkmann, eds., *Wirtschaft und Rüstung*, p. 66, during the first three years rearmament did not yet involve 'controls' in the sense of 'militarising' the economy; this set in with the accumulation of bottlenecks, necessitating attempts at control in order to proceed with armaments expansion.

(2) Just as claims were made on behalf of the propriety and efficiency of the elements of one's own national economic policy to ensure 'domestic stability', one could grant the same to foreign governments (i.e. tolerate in principle their emergency measures to stimulate their economies) even if this implied a policy of keeping the country detached from the effects of changes in world trade and international finance. Adherence to this in the case of Germany was tantamount, on the one hand, to accepting that her special policy mix would do for Germany, but was no 'model' for export, and, on the other hand, to urging Britain to negotiate with Germany (as well as with the US and France) to agree on measures designed to serve common interests, such as a relaxation of the restrictions on the movement of goods and capital in an attempt to revive world trade. In February 1936, the CEI devoted a report on Germany (and the US) to this topic.[379]

The central idea was that the recovery, both world-wide and in individual countries, could only be consolidated if governments actively promoted the ability to exchange products manufactured in the depressed areas of their countries through international trade. This idea corresponds to the design of the economic appeasers to re-establish the Triangular Trade System and to abandon exchange restrictions and similar devices of state-controlled foreign trade.[380] Like the economic appeasers, the economic advisers held Britain, along with other powers, at least partly responsible for the turn in the development of the German economy before 1933 and even under the Hitler regime. The CEI justified its call that the British government take the lead by referring to evidence that Germany's economic (armament) policy was moving towards a point of no return. The interpretation of the situation amounted more or less to a recommendation to try economic appeasement. Although the CEI related the symptoms and causes for Germany's economic bottle-necks – her lack of foreign exchange and raw materials as well as her methods of foreign trade – to the political goals of the regime (i.e. its rearmament programme), they also traced the dominance of the arms economy (*Rüstungswirtschaft*) in Germany's economic policy back to the fact that other countries, partly because of their own 'security' interest, had burdened the German nation with reparations demands and from the beginning

379. E.A.C.(S.C.)21, 19th report, 10 Febr. 1936, §§91 and 93, Cab. 24–260.

380. ibid., §§78/79, p. 38, and §85, p. 40. The Economic Section referred to reports of the CEI; the members of the CEI cannot be regarded as economic appeasers; some of them were political opponents of fascism and the Third Reich.

of the 1929 crisis with the withdrawal of short-term capital without providing export outlets so as to enable her to earn foreign exchange. The economic appeasers had concluded from their line of argument that those who had been responsible for causing the difficulties must also take some responsibility for removing them as soon as they themselves had recovered sufficiently so to do, of course on the assumption that both economies remained interdependent. The CEI implicitly acknowledged this evaluation and then turned their attention to two aspects:

(1) Germany had imported foreign capital and not only paid for reparations but also for her imports; the countries of Central and Eastern Europe, on whose purchasing power the expansion of Germany's exports depended to a certain extent, had also lived on borrowed foreign capital.

(2) Just as German competitors had benefited from the overvaluation of the pound in the 1920s, the devaluation of the pound and the fiscal revolution in Britain had adversely affected German industry.

In order to mitigate the effect of these factors, it was necessary to re-establish the Triangular Trade System;[381] Germany had squared her deficit with the Dominions, South America and other sterling-bloc economies by means of a surplus with Britain and Scandinavian countries; the Nordic countries achieved an export surplus with Britain; Britain balanced her deficits through surpluses and/or balance-of-payments surpluses. The revival of this flow-pattern of trade between Germany, Britain, and Empire–Commonwealth and neighbouring European states of the *Reich der Mitte* was designed to release Germany from her unilateral economic dependence on her armament programme and at the same time to prepare the way for an expansion of world trade which offered improved conditions for British exports needed to cope with the predicted slump. British policy should take account of the problem the German government would have to face if she entered into the proposed bargain; that is, how to combat the rise in unemployment in the wake of a transitional period, in which the 'liberation' from the burden of armaments would have a stimulating effect.

The CEI report spotted a chance to delay the development within Germany before it came to the point of no-return: Germany apparently had begun to modify her methods of public finance in the 'right' direction. The Committee indicated that

---

381. E.A.C.(S.C.)21, 19th report, §79; on trade relations between Britain and the Empire and between Germany and the countries of '*Mitteleuropa*' see note 268 of German original. On Germany's dissatisfaction with barter trade see ibid., notes 198, 199.

Germany was consolidating her debts through long-term securities, thereby removing from the money market those means which would otherwise lead to an oversupply of short-term assets and push up prices. A by-product of these changes, which gave rise to hopes that Germany was prepared to devalue the Reichsmark, might be that German industry would in future not have to rely so heavily on export subsidies, clearing agreements and barter trade arrangements; the CEI realised, as did the economic appeasers, that German officials in charge were dissatisfied with the results of the country's 'barter trade' policy and thus might welcome an offer to return to multilateral trade. With a view to closing the gap between the price levels of countries which had maintained their gold parity and of those with devalued currencies and mindful of the fact that maintaining an overvalued currency in the face of a strong trend in the opposite direction required a series of restrictive measures, the CEI suggested that Britain should respond to Schacht's 'kite flying'. He should be asked to devalue the mark and to allow the resumption of normal relations with the West in exchange for the West's assistance. Anxious to avoid competitive exchange-rate depreciation, the CEI suggested arranging a bank credit for Germany with a view to giving support to the mark during the difficult transition period; it was a scheme similar to Britain's 40-million pound credit granted to France in February 1936 (negotiations for which had started in the spring of 1935) and to the announcement of the Tripartite Trade Agreement of 25 September 1936 which had accompanied the devaluation of the franc. Thus the CEI's report on the world-economic situation more or less directly provided the ammunition for anyone wishing to recommend action that would draw Germany back into an international economic order;[382] guessing that German interests pointed in that direction, it seemed worthwhile to invite German participation in talks and test Berlin's 'internationalism'. Just like the economic appeasers, the CEI report suggested arranging for stand-by credits as an effective means of assisting Germany in the process of readjustment.

International developments and comments on the various reports between 1935 and 1937 led the foreign secretary, Eden, and Chamberlain, the chancellor of the exchequer, to ask interdepartmental committees to review the economic policy which Britain had been pursuing since 1931–32 in the light of the situation of

382. E.A.C.(S.C.)21, 19th report, §§84ff., p. 40.

1936–37 (Leith-Ross Committee) and to report on proposals for counter-cyclical public investment (Phillips Committee) with particular regard to iron and steel and to postponing public works schemes (other than expenditure on rearmament) with a view to using the ideas of these Committees during the prospective recession.[383] The passages of the CEI report which related to foreign affairs were made part of the debate on foreign policy. The findings that the expansion of overseas trade was stimulating recovery (with imports growing faster than exports) and that commodity prices were rising all over the world (in 1936–37),[384] led the CEI, in its reports of December 1936 and February 1937, to recommend taking advantage of these tendencies. It also reminded the government of its statement 'that before there could be stabilisation [of currencies] there would have to be a world-wide rise in wholesale prices'. Since a world-wide commodity boom was developing from mid-1936 onwards, the members of the CEI recommended considering a revision of recent economic policy which had been based on protection for the home-market and preferential tariffs for the Dominions: 'full recovery, both in the Empire and the rest of the world, cannot be expected without some resumption of trade along its old channels'.[385] Whether intentionally or by chance, these statements became an integral part of intra- and interdepartmental debates about economic appeasement initiatives.

8. Leith-Ross, Chief Economic Adviser to HM Government

The recommendations contained in the CEI's reports of December 1936 and February 1937 corresponded with the thinking of the chief economic adviser and special representative at international

383. Jebb, 7 Jan. 1937, FO 371–21 215, pp. 6ff.; Ashton-Gwatkin, 12 Jan. 1937, ibid.; (Jebb) Eden-Memo., 'Economics and Foreign Policy', 17 March 1937; on the genesis and background factors of this memorandum: Jebb, 17 March 1937, FO 371–21 215, pp. 178ff.; Chamberlain to Eden, 7 April 1937, and 30 April 1937, ibid., pp. 203f., 280, agreed to the appointment of an Interdepartmental Committee; cf. T 188–175 and 176. The economic appeasers discovered favourable circumstances, e.g. the Schacht-Blum/Delbos talks, the activities of Dominion representatives in London (Bruce-McDougall resp. Massey and Pearson), and economic facts mentioned in the CEI reports (= internal revival in Britain, improved purchasing power in Europe).

384. E.A.C.(S.C.)21, 25th and 26th reports; Jebb minutes, 9 Jan. 1937, FO 371–21 215, pp. 5ff.; CTP (37)11, 7 June 1937, §§4 and 34; cf. Howson, Winch, *Economic Advisory Council*, pp. 137f.;Kindleberger, *World in Depression*, pp. 245f., 263f.

385. Howson, Winch, p. 139; cf. Oliver, *International Economic Co-operation*, pp. 85ff.

meetings; Leith-Ross argued determinedly for measures to strengthen or relieve foreign trade[386] in his report on the balance of payments which had been requested by the prime minister, Baldwin, in December 1936. He did so again in the report of the Committee on Trade Policy of June 1937, which he had chaired. Driven by his growing concern over great price rises in the wake of a domestic boom fuelled further by (expected) expenditure on rearmament, Leith-Ross emphasised the need to take precautions against a slump that might follow a short-lived boom; inflation would handicap Britain's export industries and thus check developments in a field that was to supplement the process of recovery. Leith-Ross reminded the heads of government of their promise not to increase import barriers (quotas and/or tariffs); confronted with an adverse balance of payments, because imports were rising faster than exports, the pressure of radical protectionist interests favouring a raising rather than the abolition of restrictions was noticeable. According to Leith-Ross, this development gave no excuse for a new round of protectionism; this recommendation that British industry should not receive any further protection had been made as early as the summer of 1934.[387]

There are numerous differences of emphases and contradictions in the statements of the economic advisers, which can be explained partly by the 'movement of events'. One example is the Committee on Trade Policy's statement of June 1937 that the question (brought up by the CEI in February 1936) of Britain's constructive attitude towards German devaluation was purely academic;[388] this was because Germany did not react to British initiatives, launched by Eden in the House of Commons on 5 November 1936, to join the Tripartite Trade Agreement; the CEI, however, could refer in early 1936 to Schacht's soundings in the City (in November 1935) on how Britain might view the devaluation of the mark.[389] These contradictions warn against identifying statements

---

386. Leith-Ross, 'Balance of Payments', 7 Dec. 1936, C.P. 339(36), Cab. 24–265, pp. 276–284; Leith-Ross memo. on Export Trade (1 Dec. 1936–23 Jan. 1937), T 160–686, F 14 884; the Cabinet approved of the Leith-Ross memo., 20 Jan. 1937, Cab. 2(37) 6, Cab. 23–87, pp. 69ff.; Leith-Ross, *Money Talks*, pp. 228ff.

387. Howson, Winch, *Economic Advisory Council*, pp. 132ff.

388. Howson, Winch, p. 144; although directors of the Reichsbank had discussed devaluation of the Reichsmark with Ashton-Gwatkin, Pinsent, Governor Norman, the Hitler government did not respond to Eden's appeal — 5 Nov. 1936, HofC — to enter (negotiations on) the Tripartite Agreement. See above notes 189, and below notes 561f.

389. Schacht had suggested a British initiative in monetary matters with a view to expanding world trade and offered 'technical' proposals on British steps in case of currency stabilisation and devaluation of the Reichsmark; Phipps to FO, 6 Nov. 1935, C 7493/635/18, FO 371–18 873,

in the reviews of the more important advisers to the government with government policy. They also call for a more detailed analysis of the connection between 'cyclical trends, evaluations of economic interests and economic appeasement. This will be undertaken by using the example of Leith-Ross, who had been cast by the economic appeasers in the role of promoting their ideas[390] at the Anglo-German level and on the international stage.

Leith-Ross, it is true, performed for Britain on both platforms, and his diplomacy in international economics may be linked with economic appeasement on a number of occasions. First of all, it was he who negotiated the Trade and Payments Agreements of 1 November 1934,[391] which placed export earnings in sterling at Germany's disposal, thus making German imports of essential raw materials from the Empire–sterling-bloc countries possible. Similar to the economic appeasers, he dismissed economic sanctions against Germany as ineffectual and hence useless as a political weapon. He advised maintaining commercial relations with Germany for as long as possible without, however, extending credit commitments.[392] On this count, Leith-Ross was satisfied with the position of the Bank of England and the Treasury that the embargo on foreign loans accorded control over the activities of the banks:

> As regards banking or acceptance credits, the position is more difficult to watch as this market is already overburdened with a mass of frozen German debts (Standstill or other). Anyway, there is not likely to be any disposition there to provide funds for war purposes either of Germany, or for that matter, of Italy.[393]

---

pp. 29f.; Phipps to FO, 10 Dec. 1935, C 8205/635/18, FO 371-18 873, pp. 291ff.

390. Leith-Ross regarded the Schacht-Blum/Delbos talk in August 1936 as a starting point; Leith-Ross, *Money Talks*, pp. 232ff.; T 172-1801; Ministerial Meeting, 14 Oct. 1936, Cab. 21-545. The Dominions did not want 'colonial appeasement' and opposed talks with Schacht; see notes 283 and 385 of German original, and pp. 405ff. of German original (on the raw materials question).

391. In so far as the payments agreements symbolised appeasement and paralleled the Naval Agreement, Leith-Ross as the British representative in these talks could be called 'economic appeaser'; Leith-Ross, *Money Talks*, ch. 14; Wendt, *Economic Appeasement*, p. 290. Leith-Ross rejected 'financial sanctions' since they would harm British interests without exercising real pressure on Germany; Britain's investments and deposits in Germany were regularly reported on in the Advisory Committee on Trade Questions in Time of War, Committee on Economic Pressure, CID 1118–B; 1128–B; 1175–B; 1177–B; CID meeting 11 July 1935, Cab. 2–6/1, pp. 207ff.; Report, 16 May 1933, Cab. 47–8.

392. C.P. 218(210) 34, p. 1, Cab. 24–250.

393. Norman to W. Fisher, 18 July 1935, C 5574/635/18, FO 371-18 871, p. 173. Cf. Wendt, *Economic Appeasement*, pp. 342ff., and note 3 of German original.

Together with the CEI and the economic appeasers, he took account of the fact that – just as other governments – the German rulers were entitled to believe that they had come down in favour of sensible policy options, both available and effective, to combat the slump and to protect the domestic economy from disruptive external influences; all countries had to adapt imports to their ability to pay for them.[394] He advised British industrialists to follow the German example and to create sector-specific export organisations in order to be equipped for entering talks on market-sharing agreements with German and Japanese competitors as well as to prepare themselves for joint ventures in third countries.[395] He recommended that heavy-engineering industries imitate the German method of arranging for an export subsidy fund in order to improve their negotiating position with German competitors.[396]

Leith-Ross ventured to forecast that competition with Germany over exploring and maintaining export markets held prospects that were more favourable to Britain:[397] the financial strength of her merchants and commercial classes, the efficiency of London's capital markets, both for long-term credits and for lending, in promoting international trade, would, in his view, present a strong counterbalance to recent German business methods, which were based on compensation (barter trade and clearing). However, this was true only if Britain organised and mobilised her advantages more efficiently. Comparing the stakes in the international economy, Leith-Ross expected certain tendencies to impinge on Germany's interests; for example, the barter-trade method would lose its attraction as soon as the demand for raw materials began to improve world-wide and stimulated a rise of commodity prices, as happened from the second half of 1936. In other cases – for example, export cartels, methods of financing exports, and so on – British industries should be encouraged to copy the German example and then make Germany refrain from cut-throat competition

---

394. C.P. 339(36), §§9–10, pp. 11f. Leith-Ross recognised the connection between German practises and methods of export subsidies and the 'over' valuation of the Reichsmark; he rejected suggestions to subsidise British industries and their exports, which had to face German competition; §13, p. 13.

395. C.P. 339(36), §§20–21, p. 15. FBI-Memo., Jan. 1939, §8 'International Industrial Agreements'; cf. Wendt, *Economic Appeasement*, p. 493, 522ff. See note 372 of German original for more details.

396. C.P. 339(36), §23, p. 15.

397. C.P. 339(36), §3, p. 3. *Der deutsche Volkswirt*, 4 March 1938, argued that compared with British and American competitors German export trade was at a disadvantage. See note 374 of German original.

by agreeing on an 'orderly market' and market-sharing arrangements.[398]

Up to a point it is possible to compare Leith-Ross's recommendations on economic policy to Hankey's advice in matters of security policy. Hankey was able to argue that efforts to normalise relations with Germany should continue for as long as possible, because he was convinced of Britain's greater staying-power, provided the powers-that-be insured a more efficient mobilisation and organisation of Britain's resourcefulness. Leith-Ross similarly represented economic appeasement tendencies in the arena of foreign economic policy. He maintained that the British government, given Britain's 'position of strength', had an excuse to sound out Germany's interest in 'working agreements'. In contrast to the sense of desperation which provided the impetus for a preventive economic diplomacy among the economic appeasers, Leith-Ross's motivation for advocating similar measures resulted from an assessment of Britain's strengths. In 1931–32 Leith-Ross had isolated himself in the decision-making process with his rejection of exchange controls[399] and his preference for a return to the gold standard. In 1936–37 he aimed at the coordination of government measures for the second phase of recovery, starting from the proposition that governments should not rely too much on efforts to generate a domestic boom. Resembling the perspective of economic appeasers, he pointed to the essence of politics: 'political actors' intending to bring about certain effects must take the responsibility for their actions (i.e. redress the situation) if things turned out badly. Leith-Ross charged British policy with a series of sins both through ommission and commission. Britain too had deprived Germany of foreign investments, licenses, patents and other sources of 'external' revenue; thus Germany was forced to expand her exports to pay for necessary imports as well as repaying foreign debts. Most countries reacted to Germany's export drive by creating a network of restrictions; Britain was late in joining the club, but acted drastically to curb Germany's surplus in their bilateral trade.[400] Leith-Ross criticised Britain's foreign economic

---

398. The FBI favoured international cartels as a means to assure remunerative price levels and organise 'old' industrialised countries to counteract low cost competitors; tariffs were regarded as insufficient protection. Glenday, 'Germany's Foreign Trade Policy', FBI/C/2/1936.

399. Cf. Howson, *Monetary Management*, p. 78.

400. Leith-Ross, 'The Position of Germany', 25 Febr. 1938, C 1828/541/18, FO 371–21 701. Leith-Ross' analysis considers the repercussions of the Treaty of Versailles, of reparations and of the 'fiscal revolution' in Britain 1931/32 on British–German trade and on Germany's foreign economic policy; see note 377 of German original.

policy for shifting her own problems onto countries with weaker financial and economic resources through devaluation, 'Ottawa' and the fiscal revolution; Britain's own policy resulted in forcing Germany and others to adopt even harsher protective measures than Britain:

> The German buying in Europe is, in fact, the counterpart to our own Ottawa and trade agreement policies, and it seems to have the same result in strengthening political as well as trade relationships . . . We cannot afford to revise that policy [Ottawa] drastically, but any modifications which would tend to increase our trade with the Continent would probably have a beneficial effect politically, as well as in the trade field.[401]

The consequence of this view was to consider 'the actual shift in foreign trade as a practical reaction to the construction of exclusive economic areas in other parts of the world'.

Like Ashton-Gwatkin, Lothian[402] and other economic appeasers, Leith-Ross related Germany's drive to dominate a *Mitteleuropa* economy to Britain's turn towards an 'imperial economy' during the World Depression. If Britain wished to prevent the transformation of economic supremacy into political hegemony, then (in 1936–37) she must either reverse the decisions of 1931–32 or (in 1938) make sure that her own sphere of economic influence did not lack the ability to compete with Germany in mobilising resources for defending her empire.[403]

Both Leith-Ross and the economic appeasers held that it was up to Britain to help increase the purchasing power of third countries (i.e. her 'good customers'), through removing or at least relaxing import restrictions; powers to curb import surpluses were at the disposal of governments, but it was extremely difficult to expand exports once a temporary domestic boom had accelerated the rate at which prices were rising and had disturbed the cost-efficiency structure of export industries. In view of the economic conditions prevailing in 1936–37, Leith-Ross underlined the necessity of taking account of the redundancies likely to result from expanding productive capacities which depended on specific demands; that is, armaments. How was employment to be main-

---

401. Leith-Ross, 25 Febr. 1938, C 1828/541/18.

402. Lothian to Smuts, 16 March 1937, GD 40–17, vol. 333, pp. 880ff., coined the notion 'a sort of Ottawa economic Mitteleuropa'.

403. Lothian's efforts since mid-1937 concentrated on improved Anglo-American relations and cooperation between the Commonwealth and North America.

tained once those demands had spent their force? He strongly advised encouraging exports and developing the export side of industry rather than heeding those who took the adverse balance of payments as an excuse to prolong and complete the fiscal revolution of 1931–32.[404] He pointed out that British exports could not expect further expansion in the direction of markets belonging to the 'Ottawa'–Trade Agreements–sterling-bloc areas, but had to turn to the 'rest of the world'.[405] The Dominions, as he realised, were already establishing trade links with Europe. Like the economic appeasers, he recommended that the government re-establish old trade channels, albeit without any abrupt change;[406] it was not a question of Britain returning to 'free trade pure and simple'. He also asked that the government, together with the European creditor states and the US, attempt to initiate a sustained European recovery. Britain's contribution should consist of a pledge to dispense with the idea of extending the imperial preference system, should the bolder proposals for transforming 'Ottawa' into a 'lower customs union' come up against insurmountable difficulties.[407] Both for him and the economic appeasers, tactical aspects also played a role: as the Ottawa Agreements were due for renegotiation in 1937 anyway, Britain should endeavour to bring the Dominions to accept her original ideas; this would also distract from criticisms which Germany and Japan as well as the US and France had made of Britain;[408] the Dominions might agree to reduce their demands on Britain for preferential treatment if they were given assistance in obtaining access to alternative European markets.

As the expansion of Germany's arms production would in any case force Britain to follow her down the road of inflation, Leith-Ross's policy was propelled by his growing concern about this fatal

404. Leith-Ross, C.P. 339(36), §§9ff. Instead of restricting imports of competitive foreign products, Britain was to improve the export performance of her industries (§10); imports would be a welcome corrective to boom conditions (rise of prices and profits) accompanying 'real' rearmament; s. ch. II 'Political system'.

405. C.P. 339(36), §11, p. 12; §2, p. 6. Leith-Ross expected the consolidation of economic recovery from trading with 'other countries'; he recognised that the Dominions and British colonies were searching for markets in Europe. Cf. CTP (37)11, §5; E.A.C.(S.C.)21, 25th report, §53, 26th report, §17.

406. C.P. 339(36), §11; C.P. 341(36), 18 Dec. 1936 = W 2380/5/50, 'Survey of Economic Situation,' FO 371-21 215; E.A.C.(S.C.)21, 26th report, 19 Febr. 1937 = C.P. 77(37), 1 March 1937, 'Economic Policy and the Maintenance of Trade Activity', §17; CTP (37) 11, §5(7 June 1937).

407. C.P. 339(36), pp. 3ff. Because of the agreement on these points, Jebb and Ashton-Gwatkin wanted Leith-Ross appointed to enter talks with Berlin.

408. CTP (37) 11, §§6–7.

threat to the British economy. This was as effective a motivation for finding a settlement with Germany as the economic appeasers had with their escalation theory. He shared their opinion that the tendencies of the Import Duties Advisory Committee to comply with further applications to limit imports[409] would threaten Britain with the unholy alliance of protectionism and militarism, nourished, albeit unwillingly, by increasing expenditure on rearmament.[410] Great Britain was confronted by the threat of following the pattern of Germany's development: in the event that Britain could not help but concentrate her economy on rearmament, no one could any longer discount the danger that one branch of industry after another, starting with the 'food and defence' campaign, would stress its national significance and demand protectionist measures and preferential treatment. Once rearmament and nationalist economic protectionism interlocked, nothing could stop the 'emergency measure' from becoming a 'system'. In economic terms, this process would repeat and complete the disastrous mistakes of allocating capital and labour resources into declining industries. It would consolidate outdated structures, as had happened during the First World War and in the immediate postwar period; rearmament and protectionism would distort British industry, handicapped and disadvantaged as it was by price levels, costs of production, and so on.[411]

Leith-Ross's plea to beware of treading the path of protectionism and to avoid the misuse of rearmament for the promotion of the policy objectives of whole-hearted protectionists was at the same time an appeal to regard only that policy as sound economic policy which would allow economic forces to operate and enable normal relations to be resumed with other countries.[412] Overseas trade and export expansion would always be important for Britain. Leith-Ross was strongly influenced by the idea that Britain's economic growth was tied to the international economy, however

409. IDAC report 1937, BT 13–154, E 49705; the recommendations of the IDAC affected various commercial links with Germany; CTP (37) 11, §§4 and 34; Leith-Ross, C.P. 339(36), §§10ff., pp. 3f.; (Jebb) Eden-Memo., 17 March 1937, W 6363/5/50, FO 371–21 215, p. 187; on the IDAC and the working agreement initiative in early 1936 see FO 371 – 19 884, p. 46, and FO 371–19 885, pp. 273, 297, C 979 and C 998/4/18.

410. Jebb, 11 June 1937, W 11 812/393/18, FO 371–21 247, p. 69f.; cf. Leith-Ross, C.P. 339(36), pp. 9f.; the criticism was directed against the Empire Industries Association and the food & defence lobbyists.

411. C.P. 339(36), pp. 9ff.; (Jebb) Eden-Memo., 'Economics and Foreign Policy', 17 March 1937, FO 371–21 215, p. 190.

412. C.P. 339(36), §§7ff., p. 10; cf. Jebb minute, 9 Jan. 1937, on W 363/5/50, p. 7; CTP (37) 11, §§4 and 34; FO 371–21 216, pp. 444ff.

important the home market had become.[413] He therefore regarded it as necessary to criticise the complacency of 'new light industries' and other branches of the home market which began to rely on the developing armaments economy instead of taking a long-term view and to anticipate the task of developing their export side and to compete for overseas markets.[414] In a similar way to the economic appeasers, his thinking combined elements of an economic appeasement strategy with an interest in preserving the socio-political culture of Britain. On the one hand, the argument on behalf of the export industries and overseas trade and his demand for a resumption of international lending in order to promote a European recovery implied a key role for Germany and thus the necessity of meeting Germany halfway; on the other, the goal of not allowing the demands of 'security through rearmament' to determine the economic development and structure of the economy can be traced back to socio-political motives. In any case, in the debates of 1936–37 Leith-Ross pursued the idea that the structure of the British economy had to respond to the world economy. British economic policy therefore had to encourage the export-mindedness of competitive industries more clearly and more forcefully than the leading representatives of the Treasury and the economists of the CEI were doing.[415] Although he accepted the necessity of rearming quickly, he insisted that this must not impinge on Britain's essential interest in pursuing a 'sound' economic policy. There *was* a way of combining the aims of rearmament and of respecting the role of export industries (old and new), and Leith-Ross did not hesitate to press on with this solution: the British government should rather contemplate a long-term adverse balance of payments of some 10 million pounds, resulting from increased imports, including weapons, than commit the capacities of industries exclusively to the production of armaments, capacities which were just as important for the future of the export economy as for armaments. This applied above all to heavy engineering, light mechanical industries and iron and steel, which would otherwise find their chances for future growth prejudiced.[416]

413. C.P. 339(36), §6, p. 2; §9, p. 3; §1, p. 6.

414. C.P. 339(36), §4, p. 8. The Political and Economic Planning Group recommended in its draft of a self-government of Industry bill encouraging the export of capital goods and reorganising the production and distribution of agricultural products; Foreign Policy Report, 14 August 1935, vol. 11, p. 151.

415. C.P. 339(36), p. 13, §12.

416. C.P. 339(36), p. 13, §12, and p. 10, §7. Leith-Ross refers to the example of an agreement between Inskip and British machine tool producers on reducing an order of the

There are several indications which support the view that Leith-Ross's considerations were motivated by political–ideological views of the domestic situation:

(1) His growing concern over the lack of competitiveness of British export industries due to an excessively high price structure is reminiscent of discussions which took place between 1917 and 1920 as to how Britain could curb rising prices and exaggerated expectations that had resulted from the 'war economy'. Leith-Ross's line of argument also reflects the experience of the deflationary policies of the 1920s which were influenced by considerations for Britain's position in the world economy. He knew that the chances of attaining an internal equilibrium by deflation were limited, but he also took it for granted that countenancing relatively high prices, exacerbated by the effects of an armament programme on industry, would cause lasting damage to the export side of British industry.

(2) We can point to certain 'conservative' tendencies in his thinking on financial policy; they can by implication be derived from his positive references to the German system which, in his view, favoured the interests of the export industries and controlled profits, dividends and labour costs with a view to balancing the interests of export trade, the home-market (agricultural self-sufficiency) and armaments.[417] This favourable reference to the way in which Germany coped with the problem does not imply that he recommended imitating Germany's restrictive practices. But his warning against entering the vicious circle of rising prices, rising wages, rising costs and a depreciation of the pound is telling if contrasted with his concern over developments in Britain that might further handicap Britain's export performance.[418]

Leith-Ross, unlike the CEI reports, had the impact of armament programmes on British industry very much on his mind. His conclusions in respect of trade policy, however, followed the same line as the CEI's recommendations. He also referred to public statements of individual ministers directed as warnings to industry in

---

volume of £8 mill. by £2,5 mill. and import tools up to that amount, Cab. 21– 429, 431/32. On the machine tool industries and the problem of imports, even from Germany, in order to avoid bottlenecks in arms production, see Postan, pp. 12ff., 17ff.; Hillmann, in: *Survey of International Affairs, 1939–46*, pp. 451ff.

417. On the complex of German rearmament and German foreign trade: Volkmann, in Forstmeier, Volkmann, eds., *Wirtschaft und Rüstung*, pp. 84ff., 87ff.

418. C.P. 339(36), p. 15, §21, and p. 10, §5. Leith-Ross, 19 March 1937, C 2304/270/18, FO 371–20 735, pp. 81ff. On the social-conservative implications of the Cunliffe Committee report 1919 see my Habilitationsschrift; cf. Brown, in: Pollard, ed., *The Gold Standard*, p. 64.

order to demonstrate that his arguments actually conformed to the policy goals of the National government, although they criticised the influence of the protectionists on governmental activities. For example, he quoted the president of the Board of Trade, Sir Walter Runciman, favourably who had argued, 'Let our industries see to it that when the time comes (when the present lively home demand will begin to fall) they have not lost their export connections. I strongly commend to industrialists the long view that export trade should be maintained and expanded'.[419] Nonetheless, Runciman's department steadfastly resisted proposals by the Committee on Trade Policy and the initiatives of the economic appeasers to stimulate world trade; in the question of armaments the Board adhered to the 'business as usual' doctrine. Whilst the CEI recommended that the government postpone investments of a non-urgent character in order to have public works programmes ready for operation, as soon as the forecast recession in 1937–38 would set in, and for the bottle-necks which would follow the scaling down of the armaments programme, Leith-Ross saw in exports the decisive factor which would induce economic growth. In this context it is necessary to remember[420] that in the budget debates of 1935 and in the election manifesto of the autumn of 1935 the government had maintained that henceforth overseas trade and exports offered greater prospects for expansion than home employment and production for the domestic market.

Taking stock of the material on which the preceding analysis has concentrated, it is tempting to classify Leith-Ross as a supporter of economic appeasement. Comparing his views with the frame of reference within which the economic appeasers had developed their strategy, it is obvious that both wanted Britain to adhere to her traditional way of life and socio-political culture; the driving concern of Leith-Ross was to repel early steps towards the unholy alignment of protectionism and militarism. The main difference to the economic appeasers is that Leith-Ross in fact based his proposals on the principle that British politics must aim at pushing Germany to adapt to British standards and that Britain should not be allowed to slide into the direction of the Germany model. Contrary

419. C.P. 339(36), p. 11, §8; Leith-Ross quotes a statement by Runciman to the Iron & Steel Exchange (London); Runciman supported Leith-Ross' memoranda in Cabinet, but saw no need to act on the recommendations.

420. N. Chamberlain, 14 Febr. 1935, HofC, vol. 297, cols. 2205ff.; Baldwin, 10 July 1935, HofC. Government Policy Committee, 21 and 22 Oct. 1935, Cab. 27–591; C.P. 26(36), 12 Febr. 1936; Cabinet meetings on 25 Febr., and 2 March 1936, Cab. 23–83; N. Chamberlain, 19 Febr. 1938, Cab. 23–92. See ch. II Political System.

to the economic appeasers, he did not find it difficult to agree with the general reservations of the cabinet and the Foreign Office with regard to economic appeasement initiatives; that is, with the primacy of the 'political' approach. It was 'political' reasoning that led Leith-Ross to recommend the continuation of diplomatic relations with the Third Reich. The idea was that political endeavours, aimed at a European settlement, would spare Britain the need to accelerate her 'economics of rearmament'. He viewed Germany with the eyes of a politician: 'The only thing seems to be to let the Germans stew in their home-made juice . . . If they want to get help, they must purge themselves of their present diseased mentality'.[421] He even proposed to lecture Germany publicly and to pillory Germany's armament policy as the cause of her economic misery. He demanded a change of course in Germany as a prerequisite of any economic assistance from Britain. The economic appeasers, who had great hopes that Leith-Ross would propagate the views which had been developed collectively and laid down in the report of the Committee on Trade Policy[422] in his talks in Germany as well as a member of the Economic Committee of the League of Nations, were disenchanted with this 'change' of emphasis towards the 'political' approach and away from the action-related programme based on economic analysis.

The economic appeasers went on pronouncing that Germany's rulers also preferred a solution to her economic difficulties which avoided war. They saw them as ready to respond positively to offers of a solution to the problem; for example, through a devaluation of the mark, a removal of exchange restrictions and a creation of export outlets.[423] The economic appeasers would have had the government take the lead in the sphere of international economic politics, whereas Leith-Ross was more concerned to declare Britain's general interest in high-level talks with Germany. However, Germany would have to give proof of her good-will in the political

421. Leith-Ross, *Money Talks*, p. 235. Leith-Ross wanted to keep in touch with Germany for political reasons and with a view to warning Britain against moving into another crisis; to him economic appeasement was not the only avenue towards delaying the 'catastrophe'; Leith-Ross to Phipps, 4 Febr. 1937, Phipps-Mss., 3/4, p. 65.

422. Jebb and Ashton-Gwatkin took care to prevent N. Chamberlain from noticing that the recommendations presented to him by Eden and the FO were indeed the result of joint efforts by Leith-Ross and the Economic Section of the FO; minutes, 17 March 1937, FO 371–21 215, p. 179. For reasons of their own, the heads of the Treasury had advised Chamberlain to appoint a Committee on Trade Policy; cf. Howson, Winch, *Economic Advisory Council*, p. 144.

423. (Jebb) Eden-Memo., 17 March 1937, FO 371–21 215, pp. 187f. German export offensives were taken to mean that Germany was attempting to maintain contact with surrounding countries.

arena before she was to receive concrete offers of economic appeasement. The economic appeasers were forced to adapt their arguments in internal government consultations to the prevailing terms of the debate; that is, to offer versions of how Britain could win time and use it. Their aim remained, however, to make a contribution towards détente and towards 'economic disarmament' through the correction of economic nationalism in Germany *and* Britain:[424]

> We have to welcome peace at short term, counting every year gained for peace as a real achievement. Later we hope to rely more certainly on the pacifying influence of our armed strength . . . During this year or two of intermezzo [up to Germany being capable of war . . . we should endeavour] in the economic sphere . . . to improve the chances for peace in the years that are to follow.

The paths of the economic appeasers and Leith-Ross diverged in a second respect. In the summer of 1937 the economic appeasers believed (wrongly) that German governmental circles perceived signs which indicated the failure of the country's economic policy; they interpreted this sense of desperation as providing the impetus for a high-level rethinking concerning the primacy of rearmament; they thought that Germany might, for reasons of her own, stop the fateful escalation from culminating in the final stage.

Seen in this perspective, it was judged to be dangerous and to run contrary to British interests to adopt Leith-Ross's recommendation to declare Germany's armament policy to be the only cause of her current economic predicament, as this would lead the Germans to rally behind the Hitler regime.[425] German propaganda would interpret Leith-Ross's arguments to mean that Germany (like Italy and Japan) should abandon rearmament, whilst the US, Great Britain, France and Russia were not required to make similar moves; the (tactical) essence of appeasement as preventive diplomacy was to avoid the diplomatic errors committed before

424. (Jebb) Eden-Memo., W 6363/5/50, FO 371-21 215, pp. 183ff., 187f.; Jebb, 9 Jan. 1937, W 373/5/50, ibid., p. 5f.; Jebb, 11 July 1937, W 13 982/393/98, FO 371-21 247, p. 179; cf. Jones, *Diary with Letters*, p. 221 (Morton plan).

425. Jebb minute on Leith-Ross memorandum, 11 July 1937, FO 371-21 247, p. 179; Leith-Ross to Stoppani (Economic Relations Section, League of Nations, Geneva), 19 May 1937, W 9680/393/80; Leith-Ross to Vansittart, 29 July 1937, FO 371-21 247, pp. 199–201. Jebb wanted to hold back Leith-Ross' letter to the League; the League's report — Committee for the Study of the Problem of Raw Material, LN, II.B, Economic & Financial, 1937, A. 27, II. B, 8 Sept. 1937, pp. 7 and 23 (§4) — had Leith-Ross' points of view, but without mentioning Germany as the offender.

1933; that is, to repeat France's policy of securing the position for the 'haves' and postponing concessions to the 'have-nots' *ad calendas graecas*. To proceed now along the lines of the example of France's security policy of the 1920s/early-1930s would provoke the danger that extremists in Germany (and Japan) could successfully advocate taking advantage of Britain's period of weakness; this was the time when rearmament was only just starting; they would embark upon a 'forward strategy' which would harm Britain. However, if Britain took up the recommendations of the Interdepartmental Committee on Trade Policy (i.e. the Leith-Ross Committee) to promote a liberalisation of import policies and thereby of world trade, there was reason to hope that the moderates in Germany (and Japan and Italy) would be assisted in their struggle against a further slide towards an autarkic arms economy.[426] If Britain set a good example, there was a fair chance that France would follow and begin to relax her import restrictions; in this way there was a chance that a liberalisation of world trade would be conducted in earnest. The more relaxed atmosphere in the economic arena would also make steps towards détente in the political arena more probable; in their opinion a political truce could in turn promote international lending and other measures to stimulate and sustain world trade and world-wide economic growth.

Whilst Jebb and Ashton-Gwatkin urged their government to adopt the proposals formulated together with Leith-Ross in the report of the Committee on Trade Policy,[427] Leith-Ross – in matters of tactics and procedure – commenced his retreat to the position of the Foreign Office and the majority in the cabinet which insisted on the priority of political confidence-building measures. He was under the spell of the disappointing experience of his visit to Berlin (the Conference of the International Chamber of Commerce in June 1937) and the assertiveness he discovered in statements of the National Socialist leadership.[428] He blamed Germany's economic difficulties on her armaments policy and

426. Jebb, 11 June 1937, W 11 812/393/98, FO 371–21 247, pp. 66ff.; cf. Lothian's report on his meeting with Schacht, 5 May 1937, GD 40–17, vol. 204; Conwell-Evans to Th. Jones, 10 June 1937, Jones-Mss., Class E, vol. 1, no. 32.

427. F.P. (36)12, 11 June 1937; F.P. (36)13, 16 June 1937, Cab. 27–627. Jebb and Ashton-Gwatkin regretted the fact that the government, in instructing its representative (Leith-Ross) at the Raw Material Committee, had watered down the recommendations of the Committee, chaired by Leith-Ross – Ashton-Gwatkin minutes on the redrafted instructions, 12 June 1937, W 11 815/393/98, FO 371–21 247, pp. 78ff.; Eden, 20 Sept. 1937, League of Nations, Official Journal, Special Supplement, no. 169(1937); cf. T 160–692, F 15 225.

428. Leith-Ross to Vansittart, 29 July 1937, FO 371–21 247, pp. 199ff.; Leith-Ross, 'The Position of Germany', 25 Febr. 1938, C 1828/541/18, FO 371–21 701.

therefore demanded a change of attitude and of political priorities in Germany before Britain could consider the appropriateness of advancing any offers that would come out of the intra-governmental debate on the terms for a European settlement. He wanted Germany to become aware of the fact that it had gambled away the legitimacy of her grievances by her own actions and verbal attacks. The world should hear that Britain had come round to the view that from now on Germany's rearmament and not the measures of the 'have' powers were seen to have caused her raw-material and exchange problems. If this fact were laid out in a document of the League of Nations or through a statement from the British government it could help to foster intragovernmental criticism within Germany of the excessive policy of financing rearmament, and might even bring Hitler to his senses; this policy might work on condition that the criticism would be accompanied by offers to help those countries which changed their armaments policy. Only when some kind of a political truce had been achieved – that is, once Germany had corrected (reduced) her armament policy – would the set of conditions prevail which, according to Leith-Ross, allowed for the provision of aid for a 'sound' economic reconstruction from outside.[429]

The difference between the economic appeasers and Leith-Ross concerns their views as to which groups in Germany should be identified as 'moderates' or critics of official Nazi-German policy. Whilst the economic appeasers regarded Schacht and Göring as being the pillars of the 'moderates', Leith-Ross seems to have become more strongly orientated towards the 'resistance' and the Goerdeler Circle. These groups advised him to call a spade a spade; only thereafter would the prospect of a moderation of National Socialist policies present itself.[430] The continuation of appeasement policies for which, as far as Leith-Ross was concerned, there

429. Whereas Leith-Ross felt encouraged by Hitler's speech of 30 January and looked forward to meeting Schacht at Badenweiler (2 Febr. 1937), he returned from Berlin in July 1937 with negative impressions (T 188–170 and 171); in February 1938 he thought that Hitler did not wish any conference where German 'natural claims shall be coupled with political business.' Hence, Leith-Ross came out more decisively with the argument that Germany had to prove 'good will' first; Britain might offer assistance to any German return to 'sound' economics. See the references in note 425.

430. Leith-Ross, *Money Talks*, pp. 244f.; Leith-Ross, report, 9 July 1937, C5139/71/62, FO 433–4, no. 38, p. 112; report on talk with Goerdeler on 2 April 1938, C 3448/541/18, FO 371–21 702; Brüning expressed the view that there were people in Germany willing to bring about changes in the political system, if the Hitler regime were forced by economic pressure from outside to alter its economic policy. Cf. Wendt, *Economic Appeasement*, pp. 468f.; H.J. Schröder, in: Knapp, *Die USA und Deutschland*, p. 129.

was no alternative, had to be accompanied by clear statements from the British government that, in view of the lack of trust in the policies of the German leaders, it was up to Germany to take the first step towards restoring political confidence:

> But what sort of a reception could we expect from Germany for such a scheme [a common fund *à la* Van Zeeland report] in present circumstances?. . . I regard a scheme of this kind as the sort of plan which may some day be practicable. . . but I think it will have to wait until the general political settlement is at least in sight . . . I disagree with some who think you can solve political difficulties by removing economic thorns from the flesh. Politics in international affairs govern actions at the expense of economics, and often of reason.[431]

If one agreed with Neville Chamberlain, Leith-Ross and Vansittart in assuming that 'political ambitions lie at the root of the economic difficulties in Europe', then one also had to insist on certain rules of the game. The first of these was to make the Hitler regime agree to regard economic demands not as 'natural claims' but as the object of international conferences; there had to be a *quid pro quo* which linked economic claims with political business; it was only on the basis of a mutual willingness to negotiate and to compromise that British economic concessions could be contemplated in exchange for 'settlements intended to defuse political conflict' (*Dämpfungsabkommen*).

The 'Political Approach' versus 'Economic Appeasement'

The opinion that politics in international affairs govern state action, often to the detriment of the economy and common sense, and that Britain had to make efforts to improve political cooperation between nations, characterises the policies of the British government after the First World War. This disposition is not only a constant factor in Britain's relations with Europe, but also in Anglo-Japanese[432] and Anglo-American relations.[433] This opinion lent itself to tactical purposes. One could indicate that the cause of

---

431. Leith Ross, *Money Talks*, p. 247. Chamberlain expressed this position to Morgenthau, March 1937, FRUS, 1937, vol. 1, p. 101. Leith-Ross stresses the agreement between his views and the position of the FO: Leith-Ross, *Money Talks*, pp. 235ff.

432. Drummond, *Economic Policy*, pp. 132, 134ff.

433. Kottmann, *Reciprocity*, pp. 143ff.; Offner, *Appeasement*, pp. 178ff., on Chamberlain's talks with N. Davis, *Morgenthau*; see ch. I/U.S.A. of German original, and M. Fry, *North Atlantic Triangle*, on the 1921–23 period and D. Reynolds, *The Creation of the Anglo-American Alliance*, on the 1937–41 period.

international tensions lay not in the economic sphere but in the 'wrong' policies of other countries (France, the US, Japan, the Balkan States, etc.). Meanwhile, Britain evaded requests to mobilise her resources in favour of economic reconstruction or a stabilisation of the political systems of former or future allies. In this way Britain had tried, in the aftermath of the First World War, to shake off the role forced upon her during the Great War of the 'milk-cow' of the Allies;[434] this argument also served to demand that the US become actively involved in securing peace in Europe and/or the Far East, thus relieving Britain of her role as the world's policeman. Referring to disruptive political factors as the main cause of the disarray in international politics, Britain was provided with an excuse to stand up to American pressure for currency stabilisation and trade negotiations: providing that the US relieved Britain of the *political* burden of maintaining world peace, Britain promised her cooperation in economic affairs. The British governments did not deny that economic problems both strained and determined the policies of individual countries as well as international relations; however, they saw economic problems as a disruptive element rather than the main cause. In their opinion it was necessary to convince other countries to pull their weight in order to achieve international stability.

In Britain's European policy the withdrawal of the US from 'alliance politics' in the security arena and the consequences of the Franco–German antagonism impinged on British interests.[435] These background factors constituted the scenario for the continuing debate between 'economic appeasement' and 'political approach' strategies.

British foreign policy after the First World War was confronted with the lasting problem of how to maintain the advantageous position of France, seen as indispensable for Britain's own security, and yet still promote the interest in a European recovery which was necessarily bound up with the return of Germany to her key position in the economy of Central Europe. The Dawes Plan and the Locarno Pact, once they had been signed, came close to Britain's practical vision of a working European peace system.[436] The political rapprochement, negotiated and guaranteed by Brit-

---

434. G. Schmidt, *Politische Tradition* (1971).

435. G. Schmidt, ed., *Konstellationen internationaler Politik 1924–1932. Politische und wirtschaftliche Faktoren in den Beziehungen zwischen Westeuropa und den Vereinigten Staaten*, Bochum 1983.

436. The characteristic document is a FO memorandum 'on the Foreign Policy of HMG. . .', send to Austen Chamberlain 10 April 1926, AC 38/4/2 = DBFP, Ser. Ia, vol. 1, pp.

ain, between Germany and France kept a European recovery going which had been sponsored and facilitated by the flow of credits from the US. Britain's policy in the period between the Armistice and the Dawes and Locarno agreements had been determined by her policy of voluntary disarmament and attempts to side-step her economic problems with an imperial solution; there were also disarmament and economic problems in Germany, America's school-masterly economic policy and French assertiveness. The futility of Britain's attempts at conciliation had been demonstrated to the British governments in 1921–23 which subsequently resigned themselves to wait and see. From both phases British policy had learnt the lesson that a relapse into an era of precarious truce had to be avoided. Thus Britain had to provide 'security' for France so that French governments would be willing to be taken in tow by British détente policies.[437] Secondly, Britain had to avoid another slide by Germany into 'chaos', as happened in the first postwar years, because 'uncertainty' about the state of the German economy was always likely to cause both political trouble and economic mischief. Considering the nature of Germany's and France's position, Britain had to reckon with two sets of problems: Germany's willingness to cooperate on the question of a liberalisation of world trade bore comparison with France's willingness to cooperate in matters of security and foreign policy. Conversely, France's protectionist stance in economic policy was just as annoying as Germany's quest for 'parity' in security affairs. The combinations of the two sets varied in the period from 1924–25 to 1929–32; and just as Britain had vainly attempted to solve the dilemma in the 1920s, she felt bound to continue efforts under changed circumstances of the 1930s.

Already in the Dawes–Locarno epoch 'politics' had been given precedence over 'economics' in British foreign relations: without political stability any economic arrangement was thought to be in danger. This was and remained the dominating perspective of Britain's perception of the Great Depression and its consequences. It could be shown in detail that British foreign policy in 1930–32 began to forge links between 'political truce' and 'econ-

---

846ff. The 'Locarno' – Dawes – linkage is a point of reference to the economic appeasers; Lothian, *The Peace Aspect of Reconstruction*, August 1935, GD 40–17, vol. 113, pp. 128ff.

437. Wigram, 'Review of British-French Differences,' 8 Jan. 1932, FO 800–292; Wigram, 'France' (ms. of a lecture), ibid. A. Chamberlain urged this policy in debate on security policy, against the position of Churchill; J. Jacobson, *Locarno Diplomacy*, pp. 18ff.; Gilbert, *Winston Churchill*, vol. 5, pp. 124ff.

omic relief actions' and that this pattern anticipated the basic structure of British foreign policy towards the Third Reich.[438] This is not, however, our concern in this study; instead, we must direct our attention towards the set of conditions which make up the competing relationship between the 'political approach' and 'economic appeasement'. Such an analysis will serve to illustrate and determine the importance of economic appeasement strategies in British foreign policy in the 1930s.

The continuing controversy between political-truce/political-approach and economic appeasement, from the Dawes–Locarno era through the World Depression (1930–33) to the period from 1933 to 1937, manifested itself in the question of whether confidence, progressively destroyed by the triumph of nationalist influences on economic and foreign policy since 1928–29, could be re-established better and more lastingly through successes in the (dis-)armament field or through economic disarmament. Heads at the Foreign Office (before 1932) and the majority in the cabinet before 1934 were inclined to think that advances in the question of disarmament in the sense of curbing the instruments of national prestige and militarism, would allow economic problems to be dealt with.[439] However, after 1934–35 they concentrated their attention on the fact that Germany was using her rearmament as an economic and diplomatic weapon.[440] In order to mitigate this effect, they wanted to limit its growth; that is, weaken Germany's capacity to threaten.[441] The economic appeasers, on the other hand, tried to shift the discussion of the German question to the economic level in both phases.[442] They perceived the political problems predominantly as a consequence of an economic crisis

438. See ch. I/§4 of German original. Parallels exist in British policy towards Japan: Louis, *British Strategy*, pp. 214ff. With regard to American policy in the Far East: Junker, *Der unteilbare Weltmarkt*, pp. 117ff., 200, maintains that an American policy based on Hull's principles might have succeeded (before 1937) in 'keeping' or reintegrating Japan into an international economy.

439. Leeper, 31 Jan. 1933, FO 371-17 318, pp. 115ff., 128ff.; H. Smith, Sargent, and Vansittart asserted this idea: minutes on Selby Memo., W 894/278/50, 1 and 26 Febr. 1933, FO 371-17 318, pp. 133ff. See above on 'Sargent chain'; cf. Gilbert, *Roots*, pp. 130ff. The Government and the FO obviously hold the view that Britain could improve her economic position on her own if an international conference failed; the consequences of a prolonged depression on the political–territorial 'order' did not impress the 'political' appeasers to such an extent that they were prepared to bow to the 'economic appeasement strategy'/escalation theory.

440. See ch. II 'Political System'. The FO interpreted Germany's trade agreements with neighbouring countries as a success due to the demonstration of the military power of the Third Reich.

441. See ch. II/§4.

442. Wellesley, 8 May 1931, FO 800-283, p. 329; Wellesley- Memo., 1 Dec. 1930, pp.

resulting from the inherent problems of 'modern' industrial societies and developed their escalation theory, according to which
economic nationalism led to a state economy and from there
eventually to autarky and a war economy. They reproached their
opponents for fixing attention on the 'political' aspects of international relations, although, with the transition to protective tariffs
and to changes in the power hierarchy of the international system,[443]
the conditions for operating foreign policy on the old basis of the
balance of power had changed for good.

During the World Depression the economic appeasers founded
their demand for a shift in Britain's foreign policy towards economic endeavours on the argument that peace was threatened
primarily by economic realities. They thought that the constraints
on weapons production and military expenditure in general –
because of the effects of the slump on socio-political priorities –
would at least postpone the danger of military confrontation in the
near future.[444] Once Germany began to defy her obligations under
Part V of the Versailles Treaty and accelerated rearmament, the
economic appeasers claimed that their strategy should have precedence by pointing out that economic and financial policy decisions, taken by governments to combat the slump, had in fact
spread disarray in international politics. The first signs of an arms
race were a symptom of economic tension, they said, not its cause.
In both phases they were of the opinion that 'economic war' was
the precursor of military war because economic conflict prepared
the soil for armed conflict.[445] Consequently, 'economic disarmament will be the principal question of the immediate future'.[446] In
keeping with their views, they had to intensify their efforts once
they discovered that not only Germany's development was deter-

29ff.; Wellesley minute on Selby-Memo., W 894/278/50, 20 Febr. 1933, FO 371– 17 318, pp.
132ff.; Ashton-Gwatkin, minute on C 8070/635/18, FO 371–18 873, pp. 130f. (23 Dec. 1935).
Van Zeeland warned in his speech at the League of Nations on 4 July 1936 against concentrating on political matters and methods instead of attempting to revive international trade, since
national economies had recovered (in 1936) and there was a chance of restoring and restructuring the world economy; see above on the Van Zeeland Committee.

443. Ashton-Gwatkin, W 238/238/50, FO 371–17 318, p. 95. The following analysis concentrates on the dispute and terms of debate within the FO and in interdepartmental meetings; this
chapter is to illustrate and underpin my general criticism on interpretations of 'economic
appeasement' (MacDonald, Wendt, Gilbert).

444. Wellesley-Memo., W 2306/441/50, 1 Dec. 1930, esp. pp. 1 and 23; Vansittart, June
1933, see note 38, Part IV of German original.

445. Wellesley-Memo., pp. 3 and 23; Wellesley, 6 Febr. 1933, FO 371– 17 318, pp. 133f.;
Ashton-Gwatkin/Jebb, 31 Jan. 1936, C 807/4/18, FO 371–19 884, p. 46.

446. Wellesley-Memo., p. 32; cf. BT 11–60; J.H. Richardson, *Economic Disarmament. A
Study on International Cooperation*, London 1931 (reprint 1977).

mined by economic difficulties, armaments and political adventurism,[447] but that the British government had also been placed under pressure by a downturn in the economic recovery as well as by criticism of the Opposition.[448] Faced with the impact of real forces on output and employment and with criticism of its performance, the government had to make up its mind whether it should, given Britain's dependence on foreign trade, help create international stability and facilitate access to export markets or whether the best way forward was to assist the economy in working for full employment and adopt 'public works', including rearmament orders. When in the spring and summer of 1935 the government rejected both Lloyd George's plan to 'conquer prosperity' and the Defence Requirement Committee's proposals to produce a programme of public works based on armaments orders for an active employment policy, it had by implication opted in favour of promoting international trade[449] as a supplement, of course, to the policy instrument of cheap money.

The proponents[450] of various appeasement initiatives (of November 1934/February 1935, November 1935/February 1936, November 1936/February 1937 and of May/June 1937) also let themselves be guided by the principles which were expressed by Runciman, Leith-Ross and Neville Chamberlain. These were that a *Rüstungskonjunktur* (an upswing in the economy through armament production) would stimulate those sectors of the economy whose overcapacities had already burdened Britain with chronic unemployment. By harnessing new industries to the rearmament process (e.g. heavy engineering and light mechanical industries) to the same degree, they would be diverted from developing export industries on which they would have to rely once expenditure on rearmament came to an end, probably in three to five years' time.

477. Minutes on C 8070/635/18, Dec. 1935, FO 371–18 873, pp. 137ff.; the debate was about (1) whether talks on economic issues would lead to a defusion of political tensions, or whether talks had to start with political subjects/proposals (Air Pact, arms reduction-limitation talks); (2) whether Britain could afford to propose economic bargains or if she had to consider the priority of national economic measures (and the 'vested interests' of 1931/33).

448. Ashton-Gwatkin/Selby memorandum, Jan. 1933, FO 371–17 318, pp. 120ff. Sir Arthur Balfour (Lord Riverdale), 7 Jan. 1933, *Times Trade and Engineering Supplement*.

449. See Ch. II/§§1 and 6.

450. This refers to Leith-Ross, Ashton-Gwatkin, Runciman, s. above. N. Chamberlain, 19 Febr. 1938, Cab. 23–92.-Jebb, 7 July 1936, FO 371–19 933, pp. 302ff., defended the Hall scheme and the proposals of H. Butler (ILO) by stressing the need to see Britain through the next 2–3 years (1935/6–1938/9), i.e. to safeguard Britain's future position in world trade whilst seeing through 'rearmament'. Chamberlain, Simon, Inskip, Runciman, Hankey shared the reasoning and the motives, but linked the opening of 'economic' venues to Germany's obliging on political (security) issues.

The economic appeasement strategy implied accordingly that rearmament should not trespass on the territory of a reasonably balanced economy. This could be achieved if Britain filled in the gaps by importing arms and, above all, if she relentlessly pursued her efforts to reach a negotiated settlement with Germany, particularly in the economic sphere.[451] Offers of economic appeasement were to induce Germany to direct her economy towards other areas than rearmament, above all towards export markets and consumer goods production, and thus to prevent Germany from ever increasing her (presumed) advantage in arms production. If this strategy succeeded, Britain would be spared the alternative of having to close the gap by accelerating her own rearmament disproportionately to her 'sound' economic intentions. Since they felt that, under the banner of rearmament, Germany was moving towards a point where the structure of the economy would be completely determined by the needs of armament production, they held that time was running out and that Britain must act soon if she expected to influence Germany's development.[452] Estimating that it was necessary to maintain Germany's interest in 'trade and peace', the economic appeasers felt a sense of desperation over the shortsightedness of the views of their superiors in the Foreign Office; namely, that Germany should stew in the juice of her economic difficulties caused by her own expenditure on armaments. They equally disagreed with the attitude of the Treasury that Britain should not be burdened with the expense of readjustment aid to Germany:[453]

> But if reason is still to influence our decisions to the slightest degree, it would pay us to make certain sacrifices with a view to re-establishing international trade and counterbalancing the effects of autarky . . . it is only because the connection between any economic action on our part and the avoidance of war is not clear that it is possible to hold the view [of the Board of Trade] that such action *whatever its nature* would merely be Danegeld.[454]

---

451. To Jebb and Ashton-Gwatkin their suggestions of 'economic appeasement' were 'part and parcel of a general settlement which would include an arms agreement', 25 March 1936, FO 371-19 932, pp. 294f.

452. Eden to Runciman, 17 July 1936, C 5197/99/18, FO 371-19 934; this letter comprises the ideas put forward by the Economic Section, H. Butler, the Hall study group, and partly by Kirkpatrick and Pinsent (Berlin Embassy); Jebb, 16 June 1936, FO 371-19 933, pp. 197ff.

453. Waley to Pinsent, 19 June 1936; Wigram, 25 June 1936, FO 371-19 933, pp. 270f.

454. Jebb/Ashton-Gwatkin, 24 June 1936, FO 371-19 933, pp. 427f.; Ashton-Gwatkin/Jebb,

If Britain really wanted to negotiate arms limitations, then, so the economic appeasers urged, it made no sense to treat the issue as a matter of 'security' and 'equal treatment'; the failures since 1932 (or 1927) in this area should have been lesson enough, as should have been the deadlock in the 'political' approaches to attain German participation on a reform of the League of Nations or a 'New Locarno'. In their view everything depended on offering Germany real alternatives; that is, export outlets. This alone would help to restructure the German economy in the direction of trade overseas and away from arms production.[455]

But if British foreign policy decided to orientate itself towards the ends of the economic appeasers, it was not only necessary to oust the pro-French faction within the Foreign Office and the cabinet. This did occur to a certain extent, although the pro-French faction was able to make an increasingly strong case; it also had to permeate British economic, financial and foreign economic policies, and this was quite a different and much more formidable task. It had always proved difficult to coordinate the policy instruments and points of view of the Treasury, the Board of Trade, the Foreign Office and the Bank of England – for example, in the reparations and debt question[456] – particularly since 1928–29 and during the slump, when policy conflicts coincided with disputes over jurisdiction and when the policy options of some departments impinged on the interests and even the 'international' activities of other departments which were no longer primarily 'home service' departments. The 'new' policies and policy instruments of 1931–32 generated new problems, while the receding of 'old issues' by no

---

31 Jan. 1936, C 807/4/18, FO 371–19 884, p. 2; Eden to Runciman, 17 July 1936, C 5197/99/18, p. 2.

455. H. Butler, C 2140/99/18, FO 371–19 932; Cranborne, 17 March 1936, FO 800–296, p. 141; Jebb, 16 June 1936, on Pinsent report upon German rearmament, C 4074/99/18, FO 371–19 933, pp. 197ff. In his letter to Chamberlain Eden pointed to the fact that 'political negotiations' with Germany had made no headway; Britain had to suffer setbacks in the 'New Locarno' talks; perhaps the suggestions on economic appeasement might lead to a modus vivendi? Eden to N. Chamberlain, 17 March 1937, W 6363/5/50, FO 371–21 215, p. 183. Problems in communication with France, the resistance of Dominions against colonial appeasement, delaying tactics by the economic departments, vicissitudes in the Spanish Civil War (which led to the postponement of Neurath's talks in London 1937) worked together to interrupt the decision-making process.

456. Minutes on C 865/49/18, Jan./Febr. 1928, FO 371–12 876, pp. 6ff.; C 88/49/18, early Jan. 1928, FO 371–12 875, pp. 90ff.; Interdepartmental Meeting, C 478/49/18, 9 Jan. 1928; Interdepartmental Meeting, 22 March 1928, C 2338/49/18, FO 371–12 876, pp. 133ff.; C 7416/49/18, minutes on C.P. 281(28), Sept./Oct. 1928, FO 371–12 878, pp. 109ff.; Sargent, 10 Dec. 1931, C 92/172/62, comment on the Treasury's criticism of his memorandum on 'Changing Conditions of British Foreign Policy'.

means put an end to problems of coordination. The 'settlement' of the reparations question, for which the Treasury had had prime responsibility, for example, did not mean that the task of coordinating 'politics' (Foreign Office) and 'economics' (Treasury, Board of Trade, Bank of England, etc.) was similarly at an end. However, the positions on, and stakes in, issues shifted, with the first attempt being made to establish a managed economy, and particularly a managed currency: the agenda of the Treasury grew larger, both in the domestic and the overseas sphere.[457] The Foreign Office was the main loser. During and after the war it had lost mainly to the prime minister, albeit not at one stroke and not without compensations; during and especially after the Great Depression it suffered at the expense of the economic departments. The Treasury, the Board of Trade and the Ministry of Agriculture began not only to organise domestic economic activities with their own methods of steering, control and regulation, but also began to determine the substance of negotiations with foreign countries.[458] Add to this the fact that foreign policy was burdened by exchange restrictions, compensatory trade agreements and tariff wars. Economic departments claimed 'economics', and for that matter foreign economic policy, for themselves, especially as they had to deal with the reactions of the 'business community' to world events and to the sins of omission and commission of British governmental policies. A special continuity problem arose in respect of Germany. On the one hand, one could presuppose that economic bonds as well as problems would continue and hence survive a change of regime, however much economic events or crises had caused changes in the regime or changes in policy directions. On the other hand, on a political level it was open to dispute as to whether Hitler merely continued what had been introduced under Brüning, Schleicher and von Papen, of whether he represented another spell of the 'incorrigible German urge for power', and of whether he, in particular in his economic policies, trod the path paved by his predecessors. Or had he gone from bad to worse by interlocking common 'emergency measures' with a dangerous ideology?

It can be established in general terms that the continuity thesis influenced the perspective of the Foreign Office as to how Britain

457. The field of competence and the functions of the Treasury were extended, thanks to the management of the Exchange Equalisation Fund, embargo on foreign loans, the revolution in fiscal policy, and then financing rearmament; cf. Clay, *Lord Norman*, pp. 402ff.

458. The FO and Foreign Secretaries Simon and Eden complained about Ministers such as Elliot who supported 'nationalist' economic demands of the protectionists and food & defence lobbyists.

should perceive the German problem. This thesis had re-emerged in 1928 under the slogan of 'old Adam' and was partly related to the rediscovery of the 1907 Crowe memorandum.

In the economic departments the prevailing impression was that the actions of the Hitler regime were only differentiated by degrees from the 'emergency measures' of its predecessors. The implication for practical politics was that Britain had to accommodate to Germany's catalogue of crisis management, as she had to tolerate French or American measures of combating the slump and rearrange positions in the world economy; to do so would help Britain to deny Paris, Berlin and Washington the 'right' to dispute Britain's fiscal revolution. To do otherwise would result in the unwanted situation that Britain would be faced with the demand that he who gives advice – that is, he who wants to prescribe a specific economic and financial policy to Germany (or France!) – must also offer help. In the first phase of the World Depression, for example, the British ambassador in Berlin recommended that the then Labour government should assist the Brüning 'experiment' from outside by impressing upon the US that she should not only continue her capital investments in Germany but should also go on with foreign lending. Working from the premise[459] that the crisis in Germany was primarily connected with the state of public finance, Germany appeared to be the only European country in which financial means could be a positive influence on the situation. The 'only' problem was that 'power blocs' which mattered in German politics – heavy industry and the president of the Reichsbank, Hans Luther – wished to implement a reduction in wages to stimulate the economy before considering calling in foreign capital to assist a further recovery. Britain, who would benefit most if Germany were prevented from sliding into a crisis, should, in Rowe–Dutton's opinion, assist the 'moderate' Brüning government against the nationalists in its political choice between a reduction in wages and an inflow of foreign loans:

> The German movement to reduce wages and prices is quite largely dictated by theories of internal purchasing power – i.e. the same total wages bill spread over more and cheaper goods. Consequently, it would lose a great deal of its force if internal purchasing power were artificially

---

459. Rowe-Dutton to Leith-Ross, 22 May 1930, C 4190/52/18, FO 371–14 357, p. 362; Rowe-Dutton to Leith-Ross, 27 June 1930, ibid., pp. 374f., 376; cf. T 188–39. For details see note 437 of German original, and G. Schmidt, 'Dissolving international politics?', in: G. Schmidt, ed., *Konstellationen internationaler Politik*.

increased–e.g. by the inflow of any considerable volume of foreign loans.[460]

If London saved the German government from provoking a political 'crisis' by following a policy that was known to comply with the demands of heavy industry through capital aid from abroad – as an alternative to wage cuts – Britain could hope to protect herself from having to use wage cuts as a last resort in her own economic policies at a later stage. In this sense it seems permissible to assert that 'tariff reform' was to serve as a 'socially acceptable means to circumvent drastic wage cuts' with a view to reducing the cost–price level and ensure competitiveness of production for exports. Investments in Germany, next to those in the Empire, were, so to speak, a method of helping Germany directly, and Britain indirectly, out of the depths of economic crisis and to avoid being confronted with drastic alternatives in domestic politics. But it was a long way to bring such notions of 'international solidarity' home to the players on a political stage on which all too many problems were piling up.

One of these was the problem of whether Germany or Britain would have to implement wage and price cuts if 'capital imports' from abroad failed to materialise or were not authorised. It must be remembered that both Britain and Germany, the leading trade nations before the war, were falling behind in the export league table in the 1920s.[461] Industrialists related the problem of competitiveness to the 'high' wage levels. Sir Arthur Balfour expressed his worries to the prime minister, Ramsay MacDonald, in June 1930 that Germany was able to underbid Britain on the world market because of wage cuts and to obtain contracts to the detriment of an overburdened British industry.[462]

When in the year following these deliberations Britain actually

---

460. Luther in his conversation with Rowe-Dutton: Rowe-Dutton to Leith-Ross, 27 June 1930, FO 371–14 357, pp. 380ff.; cf. Clarke, *Central Bank Cooperation*, pp. 177ff., on Luther's appeal to fund short-term American claims.

461. The crisis strategy of the Brüning government aimed at increasing German exports and the competitiveness of German industry with a view to inducing Britain and the U.S.A. to take the initiative on reparations; see note 438 of German original and references in note 460 above.

462. Skidelsky, *Politicians and the Slump*, pp. 329ff., sketches the internal British debate. Sir Arthur Balfour, chairman of the Committee on Industry and Trade, representative of the Association of Chambers of Commerce to the International Chamber of Commerce, and a Sheffield steel magnate, visited Berlin on many occasions; Balfour was an adversary of Keynes and E. Bevin in 1929/32. Butler to Selby, 9 June 1930, C 4615/140/18 ; 15 July 1931, C 5426/9/18, FO 371–15 210, pp. 256 ff.

entered a financial crisis, the external dimension of the problem and foreign policy considerations towards Germany played no role in the response to it.[463] Nevertheless, the preferred options touched upon the German scenario. As J. D. Heyl points out: 'The question was whether Brüning could convince the Young Plan nations that the devaluation of the pound rendered the payment of reparations impossible before the economy of Germany collapsed and Germany exploded into revolution'.[464] With the devaluation of the pound and import restrictions, which affected Germany in particular, the British government opted for measures which appeared to be viable internally because they reflected a common explanation of the causes of the British financial crisis.

A closer analysis of British 'crisis management' would show that in the Great Depression not only the 'objective' conditions relating to the interdependence of Dawes–Locarno disappeared, but also that attempts failed to improve the position of the Foreign Office in the decision-making process through a strengthening of its 'economic' clout. Economic problems were decided upon without paying heed to the requests of the Foreign Office for 'proper' consultation. The advocates of an 'economic appeasement strategy' had, insofar as they 'inherited' this state of affairs, settled in 1931–32 not only for fighting against the opposition inside the Foreign Office to the policy recommendations submitted to successive foreign secretaries, but they also had to try to counterbalance the weakening Foreign Office's position. The question is therefore whether the economic appeasers found support in the economic departments or whether the Treasury, the Board of Trade and Ministry of Agriculture aligned their foreign policy to the vested interests which had to a certain extent achieved their material and positional gains during the crisis against the advice of the Foreign Office. These circumstances provide a further warning not to overestimate the effect of economic appeasement strategies on British foreign policy and to distinguish between the impact of economic interest considerations and other 'economic factors' on foreign policy, on the one hand, and economic-appeasement-orientated attempts to guide Britain's search for a European settlement, on the other. It makes little sense to maintain that the March

463. J.D. Heyl, 'Economic Policy and Political Leadership in the German Depression 1930-1936', Washington University Ph.D. 1971, pp. 46ff.

464. Heyl, p. 46; cf. Ch.W. Chappius, 'Anglo-German Relations 1929–1933: A Study of the Role of Great Britain in the Achievement of the Aims of German Foreign Policy', University of Notre Dame Ph.D. 1966, pp. 235ff.

crises of 1935, 1936 and 1938 were episodes in the history of British foreign policy which can be written in terms of economic appeasement.[465]

It is true that economic appeasement aimed at engaging Germany on British proposals 'to collaborate as far as possible in a new period of European tranquility and economic reconstruction'.[466] But there can also be little doubt that the economic departments took apart the set of proposals presented by the economic appeasers. As a result their ideas were watered down before they were passed on for testing in diplomatic talks with France and Germany.[467] It is quite another affair whether the economic departments, in laying down the guidelines for negotiations with Germany on 'real' economic topics, were influenced by economic appeasement motives of their own. Wendt's book is particularly good on these negotiations.[468] Above all, the policy recommendations of the 'economic appeasers' – in our terminology – remain isolated moves. Not one of the influential economic interest groups or political power blocs adopted the concept and subscribed to their particular action-related programme. In this respect economic appeasement strategies, whose origins and connections with the 'liberal tradition' have already been shown, shared the fate of other liberal political movements. Their chances to influence developments did not even benefit from the fact that liberal forces in the US (Cordell Hull) and in the Dominions (in Canada under MacKenzie King) also demanded 'economic disarmament' and wished to lay the 'economic foundations of peace' and pressed the British government to join their efforts. In order to make an impact economic appeasement strategies would have had to implement not only a revision of the priorities of economic policy agreed between the Treasury, the Board of Trade and the Ministry of

465. Wendt, *Economic Appeasement*, pp. 331, 290, 525, 497, 480ff. Important industrialists, e.g. Weir, Sir Noel Birch (Vickers), Sir Charles Craven (Vickers-Armstrong), Sir A. Duncan, Sir James Lithgow (Shipping), Sir George Beharrell, Lord MacGowan (ICI), are dealt with only at random. Furthermore, industrialists who favoured talking to Germany (on a bilateral basis) and maintaining economic links with the Third Reich, did not think much of the projects of economic appeasers (e.g. Hoare's Geneva speech); the economic departments reacted in similar manner to the suggestions of the FO deriving from the Economic Section; see above, Phipps to Eden, 5 March 1936, C 1556/99/18, FO 371–19 931, pp. 210f.

466. Ashton-Gwatkin, 4 March 1936, FO 371–19 889, pp. 18f.; cf. F.P. (36)5, §12 (13 July 1936), Cab. 27–626; see above on Sargent chain; see ch. I of German original on Cabinet Committee on Germany.

467. See below note 531; the economic appeasers regarded the pursuit of Hoare's Geneva speech as a road leading to an all-in-settlement, see notes' 282 and 286.

468. On the payments agreements and commercial relations between Britain, the Empire/Dominions and Germany see the excellent survey in Wendt, *Economic appeasement*.

Agriculture, but would also have had to convince the higher levels of the Foreign Office and the cabinet of the necessity to commit Britain to a foreign policy prepared and able to fill 'deficits' in international politics with economic substance and to provide the necessary instruments.

9. Terms and Points of Debate in the Controversy between 'Political Approach' and 'Economic Appeasement'

The political forces of all shades in Britain agreed almost unanimously that 'encircling' Germany and engaging her in an arms race could not be regarded as a responsible answer to the heightened nationalism which had developed during the Great Depression. In their view the ambitions of the 'have-not' powers involved both economic and territorial issues. Their political stance and their historical experience favoured the idea that self-determination and liberal democracy constituted an integral part of this; thanks to this belief as well as to the inclination not to stir up a hornets' nest, British policy and public opinion did not encourage 'territorial revision'; that is, redrawing the political map of Europe to suit Pan-German ambitions. Rather, they, welcomed plans for circumventing the 'territorial revision' issue. The unanimous approval for Hoare's speech at Geneva on 11 September 1935 reflected the hope that the political calculation might succeed: Britain would save the world from a course of events similar to the one before 1914 by trying to divert the danger of the politics of power and prestige towards 'reasonable' economic solutions: 'The pressure for that most difficult thing – the transfer of territory – will lessen in proportion as security for raw materials and markets for all nations can be obtained for all nations in other ways'.[469] It was easy to subscribe to this ideal; it was a different matter to force the government's hand to find someone to pay the bill, as sacrifices had to be made if peaceful revision was to operate.

One of the questions was as to whether the shift in the level of discussion acceptable to the political forces in Britain was also acceptable to the other nations. If the 'have-not' powers rejected out of hand the problems identified by Britain and insisted on playing the game according to the rules of power politics, Britain

---

469. Lothian, 'The Peace Aspect of Reconstruction', August 1935, GD 40–17, vol. 113, p. 133; cf. Hoare, Lord Templewood, *Troubled Years*, pp. 155 ff.; Cross, *Hoare*, pp. 213ff.; Middlemas, Barnes, *Baldwin*, pp. 855ff.; Earl of Avon, *Facing the Dictators*, pp. 260ff.

would be faced with the dilemma of whether a policy of détente (or, respectively of defence) should be conducted in the political or economic arena. This question, which had become acute as early as 1931 with regard to Japan, will only be pursued with reference to Germany here. The social and political consequences of the depression in Germany – that is, the 'nationalist' turn which had started before Hitler's seizure of power, but had become a concern to the British political elites once National Socialism was in power – brought about a change in the European constellation. Mindful of the socio-economic origins of Hitler's dictatorship, certain government circles, interest groups and advisers adhered to the maxim that one must fight economic problems with economic means. This procedure, they hoped, would bring about a relaxation of the political situation. The state of the German economy was therefore to be regarded as a problem of British policy. It had to be treated on two levels and in two directions:

(1) The Foreign Office and the cabinet were to address themselves to the political side-effects and consequences of Germany's economic development.

(2) The economic departments were to seek ways and means of keeping or directing the development of Britain's economy at its own pace and of doing so in a way different from the methods chosen by Germany.

The intragovernmental debate was fought over whether Germany's relapse into power politics could be traced back to worldwide economic causes or whether the socio-economic (domestic) difficulties, which might push a militant regime into war, resulted from the 'wrong' policies adopted by Germany's rulers. In the first case, there was still some hope that the dangers to peace could be counteracted primarily in the economic sphere with economic means; in the second case, 'security policy' had first call on resources to provide the platform for economic initiatives.[470] The British decision-makers' resolve to opt for the second solution meant that they saw Germany's policies as the root of the evil and did not consider economic concessions to be suitable to the task of avoiding dangers emanating from Germany. In short, it is a different matter whether economic concessions, offered in the context of bargaining for economic agreements, are to be judged as 'factually' or intentionally 'appeasing' Germany.

---

470. N. Chamberlain to Ida, 3 Nov. 1934, NC 18/1/894.

The few successes in the area of economic settlement also speak for the supremacy of the 'political approach'. In the opinion of the Treasury and the Board of Trade, delaying tactics in negotiations over debt and payments agreement, accompanied by the threat of retaliation and political counter-measures,[471] had paid off to the extent that Germany had met British demands. This had rendered a settlement possible[472] which was satisfactory insofar as Britain also attained some of her objectives. British negotiators saw no reason to doubt that they had gambled away their reputation of successfully driving a 'hard' bargain. Happy with the 'economic' results of their bargaining, they also saw their calculations confirmed, that political priorities – that is, the expectation of sizable political relief – would justify concluding an economic compromise and would, above all, secure domestic support.[473] As Britain had more often than not to face challenges on different fronts (Germany, Italy, Japan as well as France and the US in the economic sphere), she had to address herself to the more 'acute' problem and to think of solving at least the economic disputes with her second-rank rivals. This approach can be seen even more clearly in the talks with the US on the Trade Agreement; here the economic disparity was such that the British government could hope for very few advantages for British exports in the economic area.[474] As Chamberlain put it:

The reason why I have been prepared [*pace* Amery and Page Croft] to

471. Perowne-minute, 6 July 1934, FO 371–17 684, p. 92: 'The moral of all is that the Germans . . . admit no argument but force . . . it surely behoves us in our dealing with Germany to take a firm line in defence of British interests'; Vansittart claimed a success by the FO over the Treasury and the Board of Trade and a 'climb down' by Germany.

472. Leith-Ross to Phipps, 23 Oct. 1934, and Leith-Ross-memorandum, 20 Oct. 1934, in Phipps-Mss., 3/4, pp. 48-55.; Dew-note, 6 July 1934, C 4699/1/18, FO 371–17 684, pp. 92ff., on debt negotiations since 1933. According to Wendt, *Economic Appeasement*, pp. 128ff., the Payments Agreement was satisfactory to most of British interested parties concerned. In principle, the Government steered the same course in payments negotiations and in negotiations on international cartels; 20 March 1935, Cab. 23–81, pp. 237ff. (re Iron & Steel Federation).

473. It seems likely that Britain's stance in payments negotiations was influenced by the state of the debate on whether Britain had rather to appease Japan or Germany; 'We cannot provide simultaneously for hostilities with Japan and Germany, and the latter is the problem to which we must now address ourselves', Feiling, *Chamberlain*, p. 253; Cab. 23–79, pp. 216ff. (27 June 1934) and pp. 277ff. (11 July 1934); in November Chamberlain thought the Japanese were bluffing and he wanted to call the bluff; Davis to Hull (on conversation with Chamberlain), 21 Nov. 1934, FRUS, 1934, vol. 1, pp. 358f.; cf. D.C. Watt, *Personalities*, p. 98. Drummond, *Economic Policy*, pp. 134, 136ff., makes similar points in his analysis of British-Japanese negotiations.

474. Kottmann, *Reciprocity*, pp. 204ff.

go a long way to get this [Anglo-American Trade] treaty is. . . because I
reckoned it would help to educate American opinion to act more and
more with us, and because I felt sure it would frighten the totalitarians.
Coming at this moment, it looks just like *an* answer to the Berlin–
Rome–Tokyo axis.[475]

British policy towards the US, as well as Germany, Japan or
France, clearly shows that economic concessions would only be
granted by Britain if the other side promised to ease (or, even
better, actually alleviated) Britain's political position. Although
Britain was critical of 'the [French] habit of mixing up politics with
finance' (and later in the 1930s, with trade),[476] she stuck to her line
that a political 'profit' should be gained in all those instances where
neither economic compromises for their own sake were at issue
nor where Britain's economic bargaining position gave rise to
hopes for a balanced result (as in trade relations with America).

The following conditions are essential for this procedural stance:[477]
British policy assumed that economic sanctions against Germany
would, firstly, remain inefficient and, secondly, would be more
likely to damage Britain's economic interests and, above all, thirdly,
would never in the short term exert a moderating influence on the
German regime. Logically, however, the reverse also had to be
valid; that is, economic assistance or concessions would not immediately and favourably affect the attitude and conduct of the
powers-that-be. As long as these dispositions prevailed, the aim of
obtaining concessions in the political arena[478] could only be
achieved in the first instance through a range of political–diplomatic pressures (rearmament and arms limitation, 'deterrence',
'encirclement', etc.). In addition, British politicians did not forget
their experience that – as Neville Chamberlain had said – politics

475. The quote is from Feiling, *Chamberlain*, p. 308; cf. Kottmann, *Reciprocity*, pp. 173ff.,
205ff., 214; Drummond, *Economic Policy*, p. 114. For other instances (in the 1920s and 1929/32)
see note 378 of German original.
476. The British lamented the 'French habit of mixing up politics with finance', see ch. I of
German original; Rowe-Dutton to FO, 10 February 1930, FO 371–14 365, p. 91. G. Schwar-
zenberger, *Machtpolitik*, Tübingen 1955, p. 328f., rightly asserts that 'politics' had the upper
hand on economics in the inter-war period.
477. Leith-Ross memo., Sept. 1934, C.P. 218(34), p. 1; 25 Sept. 1934, Cab. 23–79, pp.
392–400, and 3 Oct. 1934, Cab. 23–80, pp. 6ff. The CID-committee on Trade Questions in
Time of War provided up-to-date informations.
478. Any definition of economic appeasement should include reference to its aim of
attaining political effects; in detail, one would have to investigate in each instance whether
business transactions between members of divergent 'political regimes' were motivated by
and/or gave consideration to the political consequences, or were mainly interested in achieving
an economic pay-off.

was more often than not pursued in international crises to the detriment of economic interests and points of view. Knowing from experience that political divergencies rather prevented the adoption of sound economic arrangements or plans, they doubted whether political tensions could be relaxed through economic conciliatoriness, especially if the opposite side was prone to use its political–military power for extorting concessions. Even the 'economic appeasers' such as Lothian, though still vacillating in 1936–37, and Leith-Ross by mid-1937, were captivated by this idea; when they discovered Germany's ubiquitous 'political' will to practise power politics, they renounced economic appeasement, but not appeasement in general.[479]

In the political arena there was no lack of opportunities[480] to test Germany's reaction to British offers and to find out the precise details of their common interest in normalisation. These opportunities were used, some of them leading to agreements, while others led to continuing negotiations: the toleration of Germany's secret rearmament, the Naval Agreement, the Air Pact, a 'New Locarno', localising the Spanish Civil War conflict, a colonial settlement. In the economic arena, on the other hand, the only opportunities which arose were singular events, none of which were likely to create spill-over effects into politics. This was so essentially because departments and interest groups, affected by the terms of settlement at one level, insisted on bargaining anew on another. The preference for a political approach therefore reflected the conveniences of the domestic political bargaining processes. The concessions in the economic arena connected with economic appeasement strategies could be implemented at home only on condition that the deal offered the prospect of compensating for sacrifices through generally acceptable gains in the political arena:

> we feel that any sacrifice which Lancashire [the textile industry] might be called upon to make to the interests of an agreement [with Japan

479. Lothian, 10 Dec. 1932, Liberal Meeting, GD 40–17, vol. 435, pp. 554 and 556: 'The war and the desperate economic nationalism to which it gave rise have created such economic obstructions that it is impossible for the economic process to function . . . Every one of these causes of catastrophe is political . . . You have only to move, by political action, the political interferences in the way . . . (and the economic system is, G.S.) free working.' On Leith-Ross see above notes 425 and 429.

480. Legalisation of 'secret' German rearmament; Naval Agreement; Air Pact project (= New Locarno); regional security schemes (Belgium); localisation' of Spanish Civil War; colonial settlement.

concerning the relaxation of restrictions on Japanese textile exports to the colonies; the author] would be more than compensated by the larger advantages which we contemplate. It is hardly necessary, for instance, for us to draw attention to the discouraging effect on any aggressive intention on the part of either Italy or Germany which would be produced by any Anglo-Japanese agreement.[481]

The cabinet and the Foreign Office and, at times, also some economic appeasers (Lothian, Jones et. al.) held the view that economic cooperation was to enter the stage 'in return for', and subsequent to a general political settlement: 'Approach to an economic settlement should be through a preliminary political settlement';[482] political considerations had to retain the upper hand over the prospect of achieving a trade agreement advantageous to both sides. Precisely because political and economic interests/ commitments were, to all intents and purposes, inseparably intertwined in Germany's rearmament since 1932, the well-positioned members of the British government made any offer of economic appeasement conditional on Germany making the first move; she was to begin to moderate her political, military and foreign economic aims before economic concessions that had been alluded to in negotiations could be implemented or given a concrete form.[483]

These considerations were accompanied by the view that the World Depression – at critical junctures, unduly influenced by politics as it was –[484] had changed the world political situation to such an extent that the re-establishment of 'trust', considered to be essential, might still not be achieved, even if economic measures appeared to offer the chance for a 'restoration of confidence'. Britain's concern was based on the experience that political pressures and ambitions could at any time disturb the process of consolidation which they hoped to initiate through 'economic appeasement'. All deliberations on economic measures to stimulate a world-wide recovery, which were also considered vital for a continuation of the recovery process in Britain, had to overcome the handicap that all efforts would be in vain, if trust had not been built up beforehand in political relationships. It was not so much the

481. CTP (37) 11, 7 June 1937, §58, FO 371-21 247.

482. C 979/4/18, Febr. 1936, FO 371-19 885, p, 276. In his comments on the Compensation Brokers Ltd. project Ashton-Gwatkin acknowledged this position, cf. Wendt, *Economic Appeasement*, p. 409; on Lothian see Butler, p. 213.

483. In the financial crisis of 1931, the Foreign office advised the Brüning Government to moderate its tone and its foreign policy; see G. Schmidt, *Dissolving International Politics?*, p. 378.

484. N. Chamberlain, 6 Dec. 1931, quoted in Feiling, *N. Chamberlain*, p. 201.

worry of an economic recession or even economic breakdown in Britain itself but rather the fear of 'revolution' in Europe (1931–32)[485] and of war (from 1935–36 onwards) that informed the perception of events and influenced action programmes for British policies. Thus only 'political' solutions could conquer the factors which caused disturbances and break through the vicious circle of economic and political causes of war that might end in a 'real' war. Just as the 'politicisation of economic relations', embracing the reparations and debt question, had disrupted international economic transactions and led to the crisis of 1929–32, so (economic) nationalism, culminating in the trend towards *Rüstungswirtschaft* as a symbol of a 'politicised' economic system, would end up in the catastrophe of total war in which entire societies would be pitted against one another.[486]

As we have demonstrated, it was precisely this reciprocal relationship of politically motivated rearmament and economic difficulties that motivated the economic appeasers to urge advances in the economic arena. Yet British policy did not opt for this strategy. On the contrary, it decided to adopt the political approach on the grounds that this would not only meet Britain's security needs and be in line with the expectations of public opinion in Britain, but would also correspond with the views of Germany's leaders who professed being interested in political achievements. The main impetus for following the 'political approach' was the belief of the decision-makers that the National Socialist leaders were not interested in international economic agreements nor in Britain's economic offers. Had not even Schacht looked askance at proposals for lowering 'tariff walls' as mere rhetoric and emphasised instead, 'Possession of raw materials has become a political factor, just as the voluntary change of the money standard has become a political instrument'.[487] Germany's disinterest was partly based on the im-

---

485. All Souls conference, 11 and 12 July 1931, Jones-Mss., Class C, vol. 4, no. 73, esp. pp. 9ff. (Salter). The conference was attended by Loveday, H.D. Henderson, A. Salter, B. Blackett, Sir John Brook, John Hilton, W. Eady, R.R. Enfield, E.H.M. Lloyd, J.J. Mallon, F. Wise, W.M. Citrine, Th. Jones. The only chance of finding a way out of the cul-de-sac was — according to Salter — if the U.S.A. helped to solve the debt-reparations embroglio and thus carried the world out of the mess that had been caused by American economic policies.

486. The notion 'politisation' is based on E.L. Morse, 'Crisis Diplomacy', *World Politics*, 24(1972), pp. 127ff. Schacht's statements that he had a mandate to talk economic matters, but that Hitler reserved political aspects to himself, undermined the strategy of the economic appeasers and played into the hands of the champions of a 'political approach.' Furthermore, Schacht's launching of colonial questions in 1936 reminded the British of Schacht's interference in 1929 and in 1933; see note 460 of German original, and pp. 405ff.

487. Schacht, 'Germany's Colonial Demands', *Foreign Affairs*, 15(1937), pp. 230-233: ' . . .

pression that Britain could not help but insist on political assurances; to Berlin it was a question of tackling the issues of status, political leverage and 'parity' head on. Whatever representatives of the Reichsbank, German economic circles or military spokesmen might say and tell their British counterparts, official British policies were dominated by the idea that the Hitler regime 'would prefer to talk politics'. Thus Britain was thought to have no choice but to attempt to set up talks with Germany on political subjects.[488]

The expectation that a political initiative, which aimed at a negotiated European Settlement, could also be advantageous for the Western powers and not only for Germany, was rooted in a 'typical' political concept first presented by Hoare in the cabinet;[489] concerned with 'public opinion' as a constraint on Britain's international manoeuvrability, the idea occurred of trying to bring the German people to put pressure on Hitler's policy. If Britain signalled a readiness to settle accounts with regard to many of Germany's 'legitimate grievances', but not at the same time amounting to an increase in Germany's strength in 'real' terms, Germany's leaders would find it difficult to mobilise the people of Germany for a course of conflict (i.e. war) to achieve the 'rest'. On paper this was a shrewd concept, reflecting all the experiences of British politicians as to the ways and means of steering the country through the rough passages of domestic and inter-imperial troublespots. The (implied) lesson was that it was worthwhile aiming at negotiated settlements as long as Britain's concessions on points of prestige did not mean a comparable gain in power in real terms for the adversary. This notion constitutes one of the most important motivations behind Britain's appeasement policy, which, as a 'preventive diplomacy', intended to seize the initiative in order to dissolve the Franco-German 'antagonism' and force both countries to fall into line with Britain's view of a European settlement.

---

possession of raw materials has become a political factor, just as the voluntary change of the money standard has become a political instrument.'

488. The view that Germany's difficulties in getting raw materials was the consequence of exchange problems and that these in their turn were due to 'wrong' political priorities did much to label the issue 'political' and obscure the considerations of the economic appeasers. On the 'colonial appeasement' problems see note 460f. of German original and pp. 405ff.

489. Hoare, 9 March 1934, Cab. 23–78, p. 286; Hoare also relied on the deterrent function of the disparity between the rearmament of France and her partners on the one hand and Germany on the other; remnants of this thinking can be seen in Cadogan's comments in 1938, cf. Lammers, *From Whitehall after Munich*, p. 848. The hope that internal problems might induce Hitler to caution, influenced Chamberlain: N. Chamberlain to Ida, 18 Jan. 1937, NC 18/1/991; see ch. II, 'Political System'.

The political calculation behind this finds a parallel in the premise with which the economic appeasers operated. Whereas the latter maintained that economic offers would help to upvalue the position of the 'moderates' in Germany and would further Germany's willingness to compromise, the political approach pretended that it would be possible to bring the German people into play and that this, accompanied by the measures suggested, would restrain Germany's ruling classes from adventurism.

10. The Controversial Positions

Both the advocates of the political approach[490] and the economic appeasers[491] urged the government and heads of the Foreign Office to dispense with the tactic of 'keeping Germany guessing' and to mount a diplomatic offensive. Both founded their strategies on the argument that socio-economic developments in Germany as well as in France offered little time in which to find and strengthen partners in both countries who were willing to or, more importantly, capable of, compromise.

If Britain wanted to make her interests in the defence of peace felt in international politics, she had to come up with firm proposals. Both sides argued that it would be better to do 'something' than to remain idle or to protest against Germany's *coups de force*. In view of public opinion in Britain and France, on whose reluctance to face the 'German peril' Hitler speculated, and considering that Germany could instrumentalise her growing military strength to bring pressure to bear on her neighbours, it appeared to be fatal to risk a waiting-game any longer. Should Britain adhere strictly to the formula 'to be strong before dealing with Germany'[492] and in addition measure strength in terms of progress with her rearmament programmes (i.e. defer meaningful 'preventive diplomacy' – as the majority in the Cabinet and the top officials in the Foreign

490. Wigram/Sargent-Memo., 21 Nov. 1935, 'Britain, France and Germany', §§27 and 31; O'Malley (Southern Section, FO), G (36)6, 24 Febr. 1936, Cab. 27–599; Strang, 31 Jan. 1936, on C 585/4/18, FO 371–19 884, p. 225; Cranborne and Stanhope — 29 Febr. and 4 March 1936, p. 228 — agreed with Strang's comment.

491. Ashton-Gwatkin, 'Germany's Economic Position', C 400/99/18, FO 371–19 931; Ashton-Gwatkin/Jebb, 'Economic Aspect of the European Security Problem', C 807/4/18, 31 Jan. 1936, FO 371–19 884.

492. Chamberlain conversation with Flandin, 29 Jan. 1936, Cab. 23–83, pp. 42f.; cf. Eden, 13 Jan. 1937, Cab. 23–87: Eden suggested that British rearmament would mitigate German foreign policy, via the impact of the military on the Nazi leadership.

Office argued – this would simply allow Germany to use her current strength to present demand after demand and to achieve her aims through the mere threat of violence.[493] In the event of the government submitting to this reasoning, it still had to choose the platform and the point of departure for appeasement efforts and, therefore, had to choose between a political approach and economic appeasement.

The economic appeasers became the principal adversaries and opponents of the Vansittartists at the Foreign Office.[494] Since Britain neither could nor wanted to accept further commitments in the security arena, and since she had nothing to offer for a bargaining on security issues – except to the detriment of (potential) 'allies' – they wanted to make it obvious and press the alternative that the only starting point and issue of material substance for driving a bargain lay in the economic arena: 'We cannot take political initiative in the shape of further commitments. All the more need, therefore, for economic initiative. Surely this will go a long way to meet criticisms of His Majesty's government at home'.[495] In this context the economic appeasers also thought of steps which both Vansittart and the advocates of the political approach in the Foreign Office and in the cabinet *office* (Sargent, Cranborne and Hankey) had rejected. They emphasised that the political and economic approaches had to be treated with equal urgency, which in fact meant that offers of economic appeasement should not be shelved solely on the grounds that one ought to wait for political solutions.[496] The chance to avoid Anglo-German tensions erupting into a Second World War was, in their opinion, essentially dependent on whether (1), when Germany was weigh-

493. Ashton-Gwatkin/Jebb, 31.1.1936, C 807, p. 6; Jebb, 2 July 1936, FO 371–19 933, p. 334; Wigram/Sargent-Memo., §§27 and 31.

494. The Economic Section succeeded — in early 1936, in June/July 1936, in Dec. 1936 and in March 1937 — in convincing Eden of the need to approach the Treasury and the Board of Trade to start talks on the economic aspects of foreign policy, on the basis of the suggestions of the Economic Relations Section of the FO; the outcome of the labours of the Committee on Germany and the Committee on International Trade was disappointing to the economic appeasers; they did not 'register' that Germany crossed the internal debate in Britain both in March 1936 and in mid-1937(by postponing the Neurath visit).

495. Leeper, 26 June 1936, on Hall-Memorandum, FO 371–19 933, p. 323; Eden minuted 'I agree'. H. Butler and the authors of the Hall-Memorandum argued in the same manner as Leeper; Eden to Runciman, 17 July 1936, C 5197/99/18, FO 371–19 934, p. 5; Eden to N. Chamberlain, 17 March 1937, W 6363/5/50, FO 371–21 215.

496. Minutes of internal FO meeting, 10 Febr. 1936, C 979/4/18, FO 371–19 885, p. 276; Ashton-Gwatkin's review of reactions to his suggestions by his superiors and other sections in the FO, 16 March 1936, FO 371–19 892, pp. 202ff.; Vansittart minute on Ashton-Gwatkin/Jebb memorandum of 31 Jan. 1936, C 807/4/18, 1 Febr. 1936, FO 371–19 884, p. 45; Jebb, 25 March 1936, C 2140/99/18. FO 371–19'932, p. 294A.

ing up the pros and cons, Britain played any significant role and (2) whether Britain formulated her policy with a view to its impact on the struggle for power within Germany. As long as the so-called moderate forces – above all Schacht[497] and then Göring – acted as some kind of counterbalance to the autarkists and war-mongers,[498] there was still hope. But Britain had to take the initiative in the economic sphere, because this was the danger zone, where the internal power struggle in Germany would be decided. Reflation in Germany pointed to collapse and to a subsequent German over-reaction, unless export expansion offered an alternative;[499] if goods were not allowed to cross frontiers, armies would force their way across. Germany would not idly allow economic difficulties to come down on her; rather Germany would move to a pre-emptive attack, even if it had to be against a British–French–Russian coalition. The only reason the economic appeasers did not resign themselves to the logical inevitability of the development described by their escalation theory was the hope that the 'sounder elements' would retain sufficient control in Germany. After all, Germany was the country of economic efficiency and model organisation, so why not hope for the best and signal to the 'moderate' elements in Germany that their preference for bringing Germany back into the world economy met with response in Britain? They were to be encouraged to defend their influence in the domestic power struggles by referring to pertinent British statements and activities.[500]

The economic appeasers gained their impetus through a variety of experiences, which at times also helped to create a positive reaction to their proposals. Learning by experience, they realised that initiatives limited to (political) security topics could neither

497. The view that the appointment of Göring to head the *Vierjahresplan* rather established Schacht's position was presented to the economic appeasers by Ritter, their envied opposite number in the Wilhelmstraße; in fact, Schacht and Göring became opponents. Furthermore, Schacht publicly disavowed the principles dear to the concept of economic appeasement: Schacht ridiculed the notions 'open door', lowering tariff walls' etc.; see note 495, Cf. MacDonald 'Moderates', and Wendt, *Appeasement 1938*, on British views of Schacht and Göring.

498. See above note 93. R. MacDonald told Eden in reply to Eden's letter to Runciman, 17 July 1936, that his policy since 1931 had been to prevent 'outbreak of War': R. MacDonald to Eden, 24 July 1936, C 5568/99/18, and C 5920/99/18, FO 371–19 934. Jebb/Ashton-Gwatkin 24 June 1936, FO 371–19 933, pp. 319ff., and 427ff.

499. Ashton-Gwatkin/Jebb, C 807/4/18, 31 Jan. 1936, FO 371–19 884, pp. 44ff.; id., FO 371–19 888, pp. 75ff.; Ashton-Gwatkin, 25 June 1936, FO 371–19 933, pp. 273ff.

500. Ashton-Gwatkin conversation with Vansittart, 30 June 1936, C 4758/99/18, FO 371–19 933, p. 332; cf. Ashton-Gwatkin, 25 June 1936, FO 4501/99/18, FO 371–19 933, p. 373; cf. Ashton-Gwatkin, 20 Nov. 1934, minute on C 7540/1/18, FO 371–17 689, p. 225 (re Payments Agreement).

induce France to board the British ship nor interest Germany in waiting for Britain's 'working agreement' proposals before launching unilateral 'revisionist' coups. While preparing the diplomacy to prevent the one-sided remilitarisation of the Rhineland, the existing list of political offers was extended to include suggestions of the economic appeasers. They stressed that there was little left of the illusion that Germany could be frightened by gestures of 'Allied unity',[501] if one took the experience with the initiatives of November 1934/February 1935 until the autumn of 1935 at all seriously. The strained Anglo-French relations and the breakdown of the Stresa Front made it advisable to extend 'preventive diplomacy' to a wider range of topics than just security negotiations to avoid a 'Locarno' crisis.[502] The negotiations over the London communiqué of 3 February 1935, which had contained no economic topics, had been abortive.[503] On the other hand, there was no denying the fact that in late 1935 Germany was confronted with economic problems in general and with economic-social difficulties in the Rhineland in particular: representatives on the spot were unanimous in reporting that Germany was planning to resolve some of her problems by attempting to win a prestigious victory in external affairs.[504] This analysis helped to turn attention to economic aspects and economic offers. British diplomacy in

501. The 'Stresa' front concept guided the 'early move' initiative in 1934/35 with a view to 'legalising' German rearmament and getting something in return; Sargent-Memo., 5 Dec. 1934, §3, Cab. 21–417; Cabinet meetings, 12 and 19 Dec. 1934, Cab. 23–80, pp. 323 and 354; Phipps-Memo., 24–26. Nov. 1934, C 8014/20/18, = Annex 4 to G.R. (34)4, Cab. 27–572.

502. Wigram/Sargent-Memo., 'Britain, France, and Germany', 21 Nov. 1935, §§27 and 31. Germany benefitted from the Abyssinian crisis since it extended her economic and political influence in central and south eastern Europe, partly at the expense of Italy; economic appeasement at this stage resembled an attempt to prevent a Locarno crisis by granting Germany that influence which Berlin had recently acquired in the *Mitteleuropa* region; 3 Jan. 1936, minutes on C 585/4/18, FO 371–19 884, p. 225. See note 473 of German original.

503. Wigram/Sargent — Memo. of 21 Nov. 1935 — concluded that the Anglo-French Agreement of 3 Febr. 1935 was no longer to serve as a platform but had to give way to a working agreement method which included economic issues; see ch. I of German original, and Emmerson, *Rhineland Crisis*, ch. 2: 'Anglo-French Anticipation 1935/36'.

504. Eden (Febr. 1934), in: Earl of Avon, *Facing the Dictators*, pp. 60ff., esp. 70; Wigram/Sargent-Memo., §7; Eden, accompanying letter to C.P. 42(36), 11 Febr. 1936, Cab. 27–599; Ashton-Gwatkin, C 400/99/18, FO 371–19 931, pp. 35ff.; Ashton-Gwatkin/Jebb, C 807/4/18, FO 371–19 884, pp. 46f.; Breen/Kirkpatrick (Berlin Embassy), comment on Wigram/Sargent-Memo., late Nov. 1935, Phipps-Mss. 5/6. The French, via the meetings between Flandin, de Margerie, Comert, Léger and Hoare resp. Eden in Paris, Geneva and London, and the British representatives based in Cologne, Bavaria and Berlin had passed on continuous information since early 1935 and more specifically since November 1935 on 'local' pressures upon Berlin to come to a decision on the demilitarised zone; e.g. Phipps to FO, 20 Jan. 1936, C 470/4/18, FO 371–19 883; C 884, and C 940/4/18, FO 371–19 885.

early 1936 did not, however, integrate any of the proposed offers to Germany which belonged to the catalogue of economic measures and methods but favoured political objects (the Air Pact).[505] The reasons for this can be found in the evaluation of the international constellation, on the one hand, and in the domestic political constraints on British foreign policy, on the other.

One of the unspoken assumptions of British foreign policy between the wars was that approaches towards Germany should not damage the relationship with France. Complying with this rule, the economic appeasers stressed that initiatives supported by political offers had in the past provoked precisely this danger; this implied that economic matters offered the only starting point. The argument that economic arrangements, especially if they referred to French, German and British positions and interests, could smooth the way to a political settlement, was, however, contrasted with the argument that the strategic–political balance in Europe had to be redressed by mutual consensus before an economic settlement could be discussed directly in a second round of negotiations. It turned out that for the initiators of the 'working agreement'[506] the perspective that France should reduce, if not liquidate, her connections with Eastern Europe was more important than the idea of tackling the problem of an economic reorganisation of Europe through negotiations with Germany and France. In contrast to those who pointed to Germany's economic weakness and called for taking advantage of this godsend[507] either by applying financial sanctions or by severing essential commercial links between Germany and her suppliers of primary products, the plan of the British

505. Ashton-Gwatkin, 16 March 1936, FO 371–19 892, pp. 202ff., regretted that the FO and the Cabinet had once again, before 7 March 1936, taken a resolution on the 'political approach'; in the aftermath of the crisis he asserted the ideas which *The Times* leader 'A Chance to Rebuild' of 9 March 1936 had introduced into public debate. In official statements, the British government stressed that a debate on whether appeasement should start in the economic or in the political sphere was idle; practically, the government almost always came down in favour of the political approach. The public statements were addressed to the U.S.A. and to domestic 'middle opinion'.

506. Cranborne, 17 March 1936, FO 800–296, pp. 140f., for the following; on Simon, Hankey, Chatfield see ch. II of German original, and see above note 135.

507. During the Rhineland crisis Vansittart, Waley, Phipps, took the visit of Staus (director of the Reichsbank) to Paris as an indication of Germany's demand/need for credit facilities; Flandin and Léger and the pro-French faction in British politics (Lord Camrose, W. Steed, Churchill, Boothby, A. Chamberlain) maintained that financial sanctions would have an impact on Germany; Waley to FO, 13 March 1936, C 1883/99/18; Phipps to Sargent, 1 April 1936, C 2619/99/18, FO 371–19 932, pp. 238ff. Ashton-Gwatkin and Sargent derived contrary conclusions from the 'facts' presented in the report of the A.T.B. (CID committee): Sargent, FO 371–19 892, pp. 205f; Ashton-Gwatkin, ibid., p. 202, and 17 March 1936, C 1883/4/18, FO 371–19 932, p. 239.

government from March 1936 considered 'positive' economic actions (a world economic conference), but only in third place behind temporary security measures (staff talks) and negotiations over a 'New Locarno' supplemented by German non-aggression pacts with her neighbours to the East, as a substitute for an 'Eastern Locarno'. This sequence reflects above all the relative positions of power within the ruling bloc. Although the economic appeasers had – in comparison with their influence in the pre-crisis scenario – made some headway in the period of crisis management, mainly because of the intervention of influential outsiders with the foreign secretary, Anthony Eden, [508] on balance they had lost an equal amount of support. Stanhope, Cranborne and Sargent at the Foreign Office, who had indicated their agreement before the crisis that a new round of negotiations should include economic matters, withdrew during the crisis to the position that political questions and aspects were rightly given priority.[509] They did not perceive the lesson of the Rhineland crisis to be that one should try an economic settlement after political offers had failed; that is, to use the Air Pact as a lever in order to make the change in the Rhine Zone status part of a comprehensive settlement. They objected to the 'preferential area' concept of Ashton-Gwatkin as this would strengthen German hegemony and encourage her inclination towards unilateralism. Rather, they wanted to pursue their political approach consistently to its end. By that they meant that Britain should not take on or increase any political–military commitments which she could or would not discharge or whose implications were unpredictable. In straightforward terms they aimed at relieving Britain of those burdens which she was unable and hesitant to throw off in the Locarno negotiations of 1925; if a decade later Britain now got rid of this embarrassment, she could concentrate properly on her West European security arrangements.[510]

508. In order to demonstrate that they were not alone when they advised turning to 'economic appeasement', Jebb and Ashton-Gwatkin enumerated and elaborated on statements by H. Butler, Van Zeeland, and French voices recommending a return to Briand's Plan for Europe and the Comité d'Etudes (founded in 1930). Ashton-Gwatkin quoted a French government pronouncement (23 June 1936) on the revival of the Committee of Inquiry into European Union in his survey of events: 31 August 1936, FO 371–19 934, p. 188; cf. Eden's letter to Runciman: FO 371–19 934, pp. 1ff. cf. T 160–761, F 14 735/1–5 (22 May 1936 to 2 Dec. 1938); and T 160–770, F 15 583; T 160–762, F 14 735/03/1–4.

509. Cranborne, 17 March 1936, C 2086/4/18, FO 371–19 891, pp. 234ff. = FO 800–296, pp. 139ff; Cranborne, 27 March 1936, FO 371–19 892, pp. 210f.; Sargent, 20 March 1936, C 2134/4/18, FO 371–19 895, pp. 10f.; Stanhope, 20 March 1936, FO 371–19 892, p. 207.

510. Sargent, 20 March 1936, C 2134/4/18, FO 371–19 895, pp. 10f. See ch. I of German

A further implication was that France should rest content with her role as a West European/North African colonial power, whereas Germany should be recognised as the main economic power in Central Europe. They somehow anticipated and then accepted remilitarisation as a fact, which meant that the platform in the West which might have been employed as a deterrent had disappeared and with it the chance to contest Germany's economic superiority. However, before Britain could fully accept the *fait accompli* and its repercussions, she had to consider the political matters separately from the economic questions; in their opinion a West European political solution[511] was to have first charge on Britain's list of priorities. In a second phase, foreign policy was to concentrate entirely on the economic aspects. To their mind this was the logical sequence; if Britain's top priority was an arms limitation agreement (either as a general settlement or specific – Air Pact – arrangement in addition to the Naval Agreement), she also had to search for an outlet for German capacities, freed by the transition from armaments production to consumer and export goods. A convenient solution could be Germany's economic expansion into central Eastern Europe. Assuming that Britain's interests pointed to a solution along these lines, it was not expedient to raise the economic issue first. Rather Britain should attempt to use this concession of giving Germany a 'free hand' in central Eastern Europe, as a bait in the first phase of political negotiations.[512] Assuming that Berlin wanted Britain's support, Britain could press Germany into a political *quid pro quo*, even if the outcome was a foregone conclusion. For that reason the general proviso prevailed that aid or economic concessions to Germany were sheer folly, if they preceded a political solution.[513] Thus the 'political' heads of the Foreign Office returned to Vansittart's camp and parted company with the economic appeasers. Vansittart had indicated in

---

original for details; Sargent, Cranborne, Stanhope, insisted that Britain's foreign policy should not strengthen Germany; they accused Ashton-Gwatkin of tipping the balance – a preferential area in *Mitteleuropa* would establish the predominance of the German economy and undermine any chance of arranging for a system of collective security; Vansittart, minutes on C 2134/4/18, FO 371-19 895.

511. Cranborne, 17 March 1936, FO 371-19 891, p. 235; id., 27 March 1936, FO 371-19 892, p. 210.

512. Cranborne, C 2086/4/18, 17 March 1936, p. 3.

513. Phipps, 7 March 1936, C 1558/4/18, FO 371-19 888, pp. 75ff.; see above notes 486ff. Most of Germany's 'grievances' were considered to be of a political nature; Cabinet meeting, 29 Jan. 1936, Cab. 23-83, debate on report of the Interdepartmental Committee on Freedom of Access to Colonial Raw Materials, 7 Jan. 1936, W 195/195/98 = C.P. 15(36); cf. Pinsent to Waley, 15 June 1936, C 4487/99/18, FO 371-19 933, pp. 268f.

consultations before the crisis that if Britain declared her willingness to respect Germany's zone of influence, created by barter-trade and clearing settlements, this would cause a political landslide: 'An economic solution cannot precede a political solution, of which it is only a part, and the easier and less dangerous part to boot'.[514]

In these debates the dispute was revived whether Britain should regard an economically strong or weak Germany as the greater threat. The question was whether German expansionism was merely the result of a hunger for power – a political and mass-psychological problem – and whether it could be countered by encircling the 'tiger', or whether it had been caused by economic conditions.[515] The economic appeasers were certain that the danger of an explosion in Germany would continue in any case[516] and that there was, therefore, only one answer to the German problem; namely, to create a peaceful outlet, such as export opportunities, in good time.[517] Their dictum was that 'a reasonable, fat Germany with a political settlement [is preferable to a] desperately lean one with the continuance of the present state of political strain and uncertainty'.[518]

Their judgement relied on the assumption that economic recovery in Germany was impossible in her current position.[519] Against the historical argument that Germany had been strong and prosperous in 1913–14, but had, nevertheless, thrown her resources into armaments for a hegemonic war, the economic appeasers held that Britain had to pay the price for a weak Germany; namely, the loss of trading opportunities and political uncertainty. Their critics countered that the procedure of the economic appeasers simply meant assisting the development of German ambitions; the only result would be the broadening of Germany's bases for recruiting manpower, raw materials and foodstuffs, without the prospect of

---

514. Vansittart, 11 Febr. 1936, C.P. 42(36), §34, Cab. 27–599.

515. Ashton-Gwatkin/Jebb, 31 Jan. 1936, C 807/4/18, FO 371–19 884, p. 46, insisted on their interpretation that economic problems had caused 'national socialism' and claimed that Germany's present position was not simply due to the political priorities of the Nazi leadership.

516. FO 371–19 884, pp. 44ff.; FO 371–19 888, pp. 75ff. The economic appeasers applied their frame of reference which they established in 1930–1933 to the 'German case' since autumn 1934 consistently.

517. Jebb, 16 March 1936, refutes Phipps' advise, C 1558/4/18, FO 371–19 888, pp. 76f.; cf. Ashton-Gwatkin/Jebb, C 807/4/18.

518. Ashton-Gwatkin, 20 Febr. 1935, minute on C 1266/635/18, FO 371–18 869, p. 150; the opposite view is formulated by Nixon, Export Credits Guarantee Department, 16 Jan. 1935, C 794/635/18.

519. Ashton-Gwatkin, 20 Febr. 1935.

British trade regaining its good customers.[520] The economic appeasers warned of the dangers which – analogous to the Japanese and Italian case – would originate from a heavily armed Germany saddled with economic problems.[521] The linkage between rearmament and economic pressures on policy increasingly interested government circles. The government shared the view that Germany's economic situation would make itself felt in her foreign policy and that Britain therefore had to enter the ring to combat the effects of a slump which were occasioning Germany to upset international politics. For a while Eden adhered to the advice of economic appeasers to bring about a change in the tendency of German policy through offers of economic and financial help.[522] He added:

> The poverty of Nazi-Germany . . . may be expected to have the same effects as in Italy, and to encourage a dictator to lead his people on some foreign venture as the only means. . . to distract their attention from the failure of his policy at home. Our purpose being to avoid war, it should follow that we should be wise to do everything in our power to assist Germany's economic recovery, thereby easing the strain upon the German rulers, and making an outbreak less likely.[523]

Nevertheless, this consideration was accompanied by the proviso that economic measures would only be taken 'in return for, and subsequent to, a general political settlement'.[524] This political reservation detracted from the central argument of the economic

520. Vansittart minutes, 1 Dec. 1935, VNST 2/24, pp. 9–10, on Wigram/Sargent-Memo., 21 Nov. 1935; cf. Phipps, 10 March 1936, statement to the Cabinet Committee on Germany (the scheduled meeting did not take place because of the 7 March 1936 crisis intervening), Phipps-Mss. 5/6, pp. 15f.; Board of Trade, 26 Febr. 1936, G (36)7, Cab. 27–599; Runciman, 17 Febr. 1936, 1st meeting of Cabinet Committee on Germany.

521. Ashton-Gwatkin, 23 Dec. 1935, FO 371–18 873, p. 130; Ashton-Gwatkin, 1 Jan. 1936, C 400/99/18, FO 371–19 931, p. 35.

522. Earl of Avon, *Facing the Dictators*, pp. 323ff. Ashton-Gwatkin suggested testing the chances for a rapprochement in the economic arena at the level of meetings between Schacht and Governor Norman, 16 March 1936, minute on C 2213/4/18, FO 371–19 892, pp. 203f.

523. Eden, introductory letter to C.P. 42(36); quoted in Earl of Avon, *Facing the Dictators*, p. 323. Reports on a 'slump' in Germany lead one rather automatically to think of forthcoming troublemaking by German foreign policy: minutes on C 8070/635/18, FO 371–18 873, Berlin Embassy to FO, 3 Dec. 1935, Memorandum of the Commercial Secretariat to Department of Overseas Trade, 26 Nov. 1935, 'Economic Condition in Germany'; see ch. I of German original. Phipps had been asked to assess the repercussions of domestic conditions in Germany on Hitler's foreign policy, e.g. Sargent to Phipps, 28 Oct. 1933, C 9498/319/18, FO 371–16 728, pp. 295ff. In 1930 Sargent had argued to the contrary: 'The more the Germans get involved in internal wrangles the less danger there is of their adopting a forward foreign policy', 20 Febr. 1930, C 1284/140/18, FO 371–14 361, p. 239.

524. Eden, 18 March 1936, FO 371–19 892, pp. 206f.

appeasers that economic assistance constituted the only alternative to war: 'The danger point will come when the economic misery of Germany has reached such a point that war will be a preferable alternative.'[525]

The result of the proviso was that Britain should avoid anything that would strengthen Germany – as long as there had been no change in the conduct, attitude and disposition of the German rulers.[526] The consequence was, therefore, to proceed by applying delaying tactics to the proposed contacts on the economic level – between Leith-Ross and Schacht, Schacht and Norman – and to plan negotiations on economic matters only after 'political' topics on the agenda had been prepared; the visits were restricted to gathering information on German views and on the scale of the economic crisis in Germany; they were to listen and not to offer. The Foreign Office and the cabinet wanted to settle the matter of a 'New Locarno' before giving an economic appeasement project the go-ahead.[527] Since the British government could at no time ascertain a readiness to compromise on the German side with the hard-core of British political counter-demands (peaceful-change method, arms limitation), the proposals of the economic appeasers were put into cold storage. The economic appeasers now felt the more compelled to adapt their argument to the official position since they had always regarded a German *quid pro quo* as an obvious component of a bargain.[528] However, contrary to the advocates of a political approach, they saw more than just one reason for tackling the German problem, even if the solution would not be totally favourable to Britain.[529] In their opinion Germany's difficult economic situation could not be explained exclusively by 'unsound' economic policies of the National Socialist regime, but rather that the regime itself was a product of the Great Depress-

525. Th. Jones to Flexner, 22 Febr. 1936, Jones-Mss., Class S, vol. 1, no. 134; cf. Wigram/Sargent-Memo., 21 Nov. 1935, §7; Ashton-Gwatkin/Jebb, 31 Jan. 1936, C 807/4/18; see above note 504.

526. Vansittart, 1 Dec. 1935, VNST 2/24, pp. 9–10; Phipps, 10 March 1936, see above note 520.

527. Vansittart to Eden, 5 Nov. 1936, FO 371–19 930; Vansittart, 31 Dec. 1936, 'The World Situation and British Rearmament'; see ch. II of German original. Massigli (Quai d'Orsay) shared Vansittart's stance, he further demanded that the alignment with the Soviet Union should not be endangered and that the soundings on 'New Locarno' should not revive or return to the Four Power Pact concept of 1933; cf. R. Girault, 'Léon Blum', pp. 106f.

528. Jebb, 25 March 1936, minute on C 2140/99/18, FO 371–19 932, p. 294a. Lothian, too, stated that political appeasement had to flank the economic soundings, s. Butler, *Lothian*, p. 213.

529. Ashton-Gwatkin/Jebb, 31 Jan. 1936, C 807/4/18, p. 1; see below note 579.

ion; the only way to remove the threat to peace posed by Germany would be to reduce the economic causes to which British policies had also contributed. As we have shown in preceding sections, the economic appeasers asked for 'advance payments', such as the removal of trade barriers, contribution to currency stabilisation, the resumption of foreign lending, access to colonial raw material markets; these were to serve both as a contribution to economic recovery and as an influence on the political power structure in Germany. The concessions were regularly defamed as Danegeld. Within the framework of this polemic, the consistency and plausibility of arguments in favour of economic appeasement initiatives were not examined seriously any further. Stamped as pro-German propaganda during the crises,[530] they would again be upgraded between the crises as matters for interdepartmental consultations when talks over arms limitation agreements or political settlements stagnated.[531]

In internal government consultations the opponents of economic appeasement could afford to speak with a forked tongue. The reasons formulated, in particular by Vansittart, for a strategy of waiting and testing Germany's readiness for political compromise did not correspond with the information contained in reports which he used in a different context for different aims and in a more pressing manner:

(1) If it was correct that Hitler had caused the crises of 1936 and 1938 against the advice of the military, as Vansittart learnt from French, German and British sources, it was dishonest to justify delaying tactics on the grounds that German policies were under the influence of the military: 'We risk nothing by [being cautious], for the German General Staff is not going to take on any major adventure on insufficient supplies, and we shall therefore have automatically the necessary time for testing'.[532]

(2) Whilst in the Defence Committee Vansittart justified an acceleration of British rearmament on the grounds that the Ger-

---

530. Wigram, 25 June 1936, on C 4501/99/18, FO 371–19 933, pp. 270f.; cf. Vansittart's comment on Butler's proposals, C 2847/99/18, FO 371–19 932. The economic appeasers had contacts with Jäckh and Schacht; in some instances the economic appeasers based their proposals on information on and demands forwarded by Schacht, e.g. C 7493/635/18 (Schacht, 6 Nov. 1935) and C 8205/635/18, FO 371–18 873, pp. 29f, and 291ff. (re British support in case of a devaluation of the Reichsmark).

531. Eden to Runciman, 17 July 1936, C 5197/99/18, FO 371–19 934, pp. 5ff.; Eden to Chamberlain, 17 March 1937, W 6363/5/50.

532. Vansittart, 27 March 1936, FO 371–19 892, p. 211a; cf. Eden, Cabinet meeting, 13 Jan. 1937, Cab. 23–87.

man threat of war could occur earlier (from 1937 onwards) than anticipated in the armament programme (i.e. 1939), he held that 'Germany will not be ready for another eighteen months for an explosion that would be really dangerous to us nationally'[533] when he was trying to push the economic appeasers' plea for action aside.

If the foreign secretary and the government were content that Vansittart blocked the proposals of the economic appeasers with a somewhat dishonest argument, they can hardly be regarded as having had a great interest in economic appeasement as a peace strategy. And the argument that there was time to test Germany's intentions in the political arena, served to weaken the strongest argument for economic appeasement.

The economic appeasers, who wanted both to divert Germany from the path towards establishing an autarkic armaments economy (Four-Year Plan)[534] and to remove the need for Britain to adapt to the pace of German armament, insisted that it was decisive to do 'something' quickly.[535] They constantly had recourse to the formula that one could indeed make economic negotiations subject to political solutions, but that this did not change the fact that British efforts to maintain peace also had to take account of the fears of economic survival in Germany.[536]

By stressing that negotiations in political (security) matters needed time, the economic appeasers had only to convince the other policy-makers that the autonomy of the arms process al-

533. Vansittart, 27 March 1936.

534. Jebb/Ashton-Gwatkin, 24 June 1936, C 4757/99/18, FO 371–19 933, pp.319ff.; id., pp.427ff.; id., 371–19 934, p.5f.; Pinsent to Waley, 15 June 1936, C 4487/99/18, and Torr-Minute, 23 June 1936, FO 371–19 933, pp.263f.;270.

535. Jebb, 2 July1936 : 'If we do nothing, we are in for war'; FO 371–19 933, p.334(a); cf. Ashton-Gwatkin/Jebb, 31 Jan.1936, C 807/4/18; see note 494. The economic appeasers were in favour of British rearmament and subscribed to its deterrent function; but contrary to Vansittart they did not think of rearmament as a means in itself. The 'logic' of their escalation theory demanded 'action now', i.e. especially during the period of rearmament. The economic appeasers asserted the need to pay attention to collective economic security — Jebb, 15 April 1937, 'The Raw Materials Enquiry and the Open Door', W 7323/393/98, FO 433–4, pp.124, 121ff. (§§18–19); this is to be viewed in the context of their system of economic order and 'sanctions', see above notes 213f.

536. Ashton-Gwatkin to Kirkpatrick (Berlin), 20 March 1936, C 1558/4/18, FO 371–19 888; Ashton-Gwatkin, 16 March 1936, FO 371–19 892, pp.202ff. Eden told the Cabinet on 29 May 1936 (Cab. 23–84, p.251) of Schacht's saying that Germany would explode (:start war) if no access to raw materials was granted. Eden linked exchange difficulties and German forward policy on many occasions, e.g. 24 July 1934, FO 371–17 684, p.38(a); Sargent expected that Hitler would make a diversion in foreign affairs if the economic situation worsened; instead of blood-bath in Germany similar to the Röhm-Putsch, Hitler would now launch a foreign adventure; 28 August 1935, FO 371–18 858, p.392. See above notes 523, 498.

lowed no such time to ensure the consideration of their economic approach. When, in the summer of 1936, Eden agreed with the arguments put forward by Ashton-Gwatkin, Jebb, Bruce, Butler and others in the internal debates at the Foreign Office, thus threatening to isolate Vansittart, the latter sought to block further discussion by dismissing the approach of the economic appeasers as academic.[537] According to him no-one, not even in the City, was currently considering economic settlements with Germany. In the end, he used the fact that he and his partisans in the ministries were able to control and block approaches aiming at a 'diplomacy' of economic experts. Vansittart, who on the occasion of his talks in Berlin with French diplomats had staked his reputation on the precedence of political questions (i.e. 'New Locarno') stood in the way of the economic appeasers who wanted to weigh up the chances of an economic settlement through talks between Leith-Ross and Schacht.[538] As Vansittart put it:

> I want to get on with the political arrangements . . . before we embark on this other sea . . . In this respect we have a lever: do not let us compromise it by premature gestures . . . a political settlement . . . would have to precede the necessary and eventual economic one . . . Do not let us spoil that effect by going off at half-cock . . . else we shall fail politically later in the autumn. If the Germans are uncomfortable economically, let us keep them guessing for a month or two.[539]

The hypothesis that the Reich's economic difficulties were the result of self-inflicted political errors played a decisive role in the assertion that a political solution should precede all economic considerations and that Britain must first become strong (rearmed) before she could engage in bargaining procedures. Therefore Britain had to avoid anything that might help the Hitler regime during its rearmament process.[540] Only under such circumstances

537. Vansittart, 27 March 1936, FO 371–19 892, p.212.

538. Ashton-Gwatkin had been asked during his stay in Berlin to arrange for a meeting between Schacht and Leith-Ross; 24 July 1936, C 5685/99/18, FO 371–19 934; 5 August 1936, C 5770/99/18, ibid. Ashton-Gwatkin asked Leith-Ross to include Berlin into his forthcoming trip to Europe; as an architect of the Payments Agreement, he would be welcome in Berlin; Newton (Berlin Embassy) agreed to the suggestion, 25 August 1936, C 6145/99/18. The Board of Trade did not oppose Leith-Ross's talks in Berlin, 31 August 1936, FO 371–19 934, p. 190. On his return from Geneva, Leith-Ross went to Berlin, Lord Gladwyn, *Memoirs*, p.64.

539. Vansittart, 3 Sept.1936, on C 6145/99/18, FO 371–19 934, pp.185f.

540. The speeches of Baldwin, Chamberlain, Halifax, Eden, in winter 1936/37 (see above note 284) stressed this point. Vansittart, Collier, Waley, made the same case in the debate on the 'working agreement' initiative whey they disputed the views of the economic appeasers; Vansittart, 3 Febr. 1936, on C 585/4/18, FO 371–19 884, pp. 227f.; Collier, C 8523/55/18, FO

would Germany recognise her economic weakness as a problem and be prepared to consider the conditions which Britain would attach to any form of economic aid. It almost seemed as if Vansittart still held the opinion prevalent in the years between 1931 and 1934 that 'the more trouble the Germans meet, the better; . . . and the less satisfaction they obtain, the better; *at such moments they come to us, cap in hand, as they have always done*; it is only when things are going well for them and when they have obtained that they become truculent'.[541] The economic and societal transformation arising from Britain's own process of accelerated rearmament was not as important for those who supported a political approach as it was for the economic appeasers, whose economic approach was motivated by this growing concern.

Nor was a change in priorities effected by the warning that the more the Germans got involved in internal wrangles and difficulties, the less hope there was that they would adopt a conciliatory attitude to negotiations and, above all, that a delay would cause a shift in the German power-structure which would have an adverse effect on relations with Britain. Eden and Vansittart and the cabinet were calculating that Britain must remain in the background and should, as the stronger partner in economic matters, leave the first move to the more disadvantaged; that is, Germany. For them Germany's economic difficulties provided the leverage which Britain could exploit should Germany threaten to slam the door on a negotiated political settlement or even actually slam it.[542] The readiness indicated by Schacht in August 1936 to interest Hitler in a political compromise, should the Western powers make concessions in the economic sphere and satisfy Germany's colonial 'legitimate grievances', was transformed by the advocates of the political approach to mean as the first noticeable sign 'that the Germans are beginning to need foreign economic assistance and may be prepared to make concessions in other spheres'.[543]

371–18 852, pp.144ff.; Waley (Treasury) to Eden, 8 March 1936, C 2213/99/18, FO 371–19 932; Waley to Sir Horace Wilson, C 2140/99/18, ibid.

541. Wigram, 3 May 1934, on C 2726/29/18, FO 371–17 706, p.350; Vansittart, 5 May 1934, ibid., p.351.

542. Eden, 18 Oct. 1936, minute on C 6681/99/18, FO 371–19 949.

543. Baxter/Cadogan minutes, 1 Sept. 1936, on C 6156/99/18, Clerk (Paris) to FO, 28 August 1936, on the Blum/Delbos-Schacht meeting, FO 371–19 934. In these talks Schacht offered to compensate an alignment of currencies and access to raw materials with consideration to French positions in the field of arms limitation. The British were under the impression that France did not fully inform London; Eden was disappointed with his meeting with Blum in October 1936, for details see note 511 of German original. Leith-Ross' report on Schacht's version of German-French talks differed from the informations Blum had supplied to Eden.

The economic appeasers for their part seized upon Schacht's warning to Leith-Ross that it would be a serious mistake 'to suppose that economic difficulties would be an effective means of political pressure on Germany. It would strengthen the hands of the wild men, who would then work for some explosion'.[544] They therefore urged using the opportunity provided by Schacht's initiative and the Blum government's (apparent) responsiveness to start talks on a 'New Locarno' linked with economic topics, partly with a view to convincing the US government of France's interest in a peaceful settlement.[545] Internal government consultations in London favoured a waiting-game, in the expectation that the West's counter-demands had a greater chance of success if one let Germany 'come'.[546] Whilst the economic appeasers recommended a move to influence decisions on the future direction in Germany against the implementation of the Four-Year Plan, official British policy reserved its appeasement effort for testing the German attitude towards a political European settlement. They waited until the end of 1937 when Germany condescended to give a – negative – answer to the series of British reminders![547]

In the first half of 1937 the Cabinet Committee on Foreign Policy (German Affairs) turned its attention to Schacht's suggestion for tripartite British–French–German talks, but arranged the procedural order in such a way that Britain was first of all to decide for herself and then communicate to France the political desiderata, with which Germany would be asked to comply.[548] Since

544. Leith-Ross to Chamberlain, 4 Febr.1937, Phipps-Mss. 3/4, p.68; cf. FO 371–20 725, pp.238ff. (C 958/78/18).

545. Economic Section, comment on Leith-Ross report, 8 Febr. 1937, FO 371–20 725, pp.224ff. The French had offered talks on New Locarno and economic issues with a view to improve the chances of getting access to American financial markets. Blum's speech in Lyon on 24 January 1937 renewed the French government's interest in the subject matters of the Blum-Schacht talk; although Blum went into details, Goebbels — in conversation with the French ambassador — did not respond. The British regarded Hitler's speech of 30 Jan. 1937 and Schacht's reminder to start trilateral talks as rather encouraging; the mistrust in French intentions induced London to test Schacht's interest in 'economic appeasement.'

546. Wigram and Vansittart had insisted on this proviso when they talked over Ashton-Gwatkin's and Jebb's proposals before officially addressing the Board of Trade and the Treasury with the set of ideas forming the economic appeasement strategy (see above), 30 June 1936, C 4758/99/18, FO 371–19 933, p. 332, pp. 273ff.

547. Emmerson, *Rhineland Crisis*, p. 236.

548. Eden-Memo. 'The Colonial Question. Dr. Schacht's Proposals for Conversations between the United Kingdom, France and Germany', FO 371–20 735, pp. 194ff. The story takes off with the visit paid by Emile Labeyrie (Governor, Banque de France) to Berlin in early August 1936. Schacht's visit to Paris in late August 1936 is recorded in DDF, 2e ser., vol. 3, pp. 307ff., and for the follow-up see DDF, vol. 5, p. 754, 793, 806ff.; vol. 6, 640ff. The second stage of negotiations is determined by the issue whether Schacht was in a position to talk on the

the suggestion for talks had come from the Germans, it was left to Schacht to present Germany's economic counter-demands: 'The next step . . . is for the French and UK governments to outline the political questions on which satisfactory assurances would have to be obtained from Germany before progress can be made on economic issues'.[549]

The decision on this procedure offered two convenient results: (1) the response to Schacht's proposals need not disturb Anglo-French relations; (2) it would ensure that domestic British discussions over 'colonial appeasement', 'colonial versus economic appeasement' and the main points of an 'economic appeasement' bargain (revision of 'Ottawa'?) would not be subjected to the time-table of German politics.[550] The economic appeasers once again lamented the dilatoriness of British policy and the reluctance to initiate something instead of having to react to external developments: 'Whether we discuss relations . . . with Germany . . . Japan or even relations with America, no attempt seems to be made by HM government, to think out what we want and to evaluate a practical programme for its attainment (including the concessions which we are prepared to make for its attainment) and then to initiate action to carry it through'.[551] The time-consuming interdepartmental consultations in Britain and the inherent problems of a colonial deal between Britain and France concerning Cameroon and Togo coincided in such a way that the cabinet was spared having to come to a decision on the ticklish problems of a reorientation of foreign economic policy. Events in other areas of international politics (i.e. the Spanish Civil War), which caused the ministerial visit from Germany by von Neurath to be postponed, allowed the matter to be dropped. One gets the impression that the adjournment of a concrete decision on the question of an economic appeasement move was a great relief to the British government. At the time of an Imperial Conference and the overdue decision on whether Britain (and the Dominions) should open formal official trade agreement negotiations with the US, the

---

political concessions which Germany was expected to contribute; Eden-Memo., §10; for details see note 516f. of German original and pp. 405ff.

549. N. Chamberlain, 'Outline of Programme to be communicated to French Government', 2 April 1937, F.P. (36)23, §3, FO 371–20 735, p. 107.

550. The economic appeasers on the one hand and the champions of a colonial deal on the other had their eyes on the forthcoming Imperial Economic Conference. The Imperial Group, organised by Amery and Sandys, opposed colonial appeasement and any revision of 'Ottawa' and protectionism.

551. Leith-Ross to Ashton-Gwatkin, 25 Febr. 1937, T 188–175.

British government was preoccupied in the economic arena; the economic appeasers hoped in vain that precisely this accumulation of problems might lead the cabinet to combine the issues at stake and fall back on recommendations similar to the Sargent Chain, the first of a series of plans for a comprehensive settlement. The government gained relief from oppositional political pressure by Liberals and Labour when it decided to promote the establishment of the Van Zeeland Committee.[552] Claiming the Committee to be a success of British efforts, the British government maintained that it actively supported a 'liberalisation' of world trade and was thereby able to repel American criticisms.

The internal British discussions following Schacht's initiative evolved time and again along the same pattern: Should Britain play into the hands of the German 'moderates' in order to find out how much authority was left to them to effect a real change in Germany's foreign policy?[553] But to raise this issue in fact meant voicing the concern of those who adhered to the priority of the political approach. None other than Lothian pointed to this problem. Returning from one of his missions, he reported to Neville Chamberlain in quite telling terms: 'I put your positive question to Hitler, who said that Schacht was authorised to discuss economic questions, but that before he could trench on political issues he would have to get authority from himself'.[554] The economic appeasers could take some comfort from the observation that their proposals would, as Leeper put it, 'go a long way to meet criticism on His Majesty's government at home'.[555] They were also able to establish that leading members of the cabinet (Baldwin, Eden, Halifax and Neville Chamberlain in the winter of 1936/37) argued along their lines in public speeches, albeit mainly to counter Opposition criticism of the government's inactivity in international economic policy. When it came to decision-making, however, the economic appeasers had to give in to the accumulated objections from the economic departments:[556] 'Mr Cham-

---

552. The British Government claimed the establishment of the Van Zeeland Committee to be a result of its own efforts; referring to this achievement, London refuted American and domestic criticism of Britain's lack of interest in restoring international trade; Leith-Ross papers, T 188-218/221; Leith-Ross, *Money Talks*, pp. 236ff.

553. Schacht told Leith-Ross on their second meeting in May 1937 that he had no authority to talk 'political' issues.

554. Lothian to N. Chamberlain, 11 May 1937, GD 40–17, vol. 203.

555. Leeper, 26 June 1936, FO 371–19 933, p. 323; cf. minutes on C 5197/99/18, FO 371–19 934, pp. 1ff.; Leeper — and Jebb — had worked with the Hall study group.

556. Ashton-Gwatkin, 31 August 1936, FO 371–19 934, p. 189. When confronted with economic arguments in the inter-departmental official and informal preparatory meetings, the

berlain took the line that for the United Kingdom to be called upon to take the initiative in improving the commercial, monetary and financial situation of other countries, particularly Germany, is a proposal full of danger'.[557]

It was precisely the economic departments – Board of Trade, Treasury and Ministry of Agriculture – which emphasised time and again that a political settlement had to precede bargaining on 'economic settlements'.[558] They openly admitted why they rejected the plans of the economic appeasers: to accept them would mean that they had to sacrifice the policies sanctioned by the elections of 1931 and 1935; proposing 'economic foundations of peace' that collided with Britain's 'new economic policy' would only cause political difficulties at home without guaranteeing the prospect of an advantage or success in foreign policy.[559] 'The subjects raised [in connection with the Committee on Trade Policy] are of great importance, and some of them of great difficulty. Since they nearly all involve a certain sacrifice on our part in return for an uncertain reciprocal sacrifice by them, they are not likely to be very popular'.[560] They added that Germany would not abandon her mischievous economic devices that had altered her economic structure; they disputed as a mere fiction the suggestion that Germany wanted to return to a multilateral world-trade system.[561] Since both in Germany and in Britain vested

---

Economic Section could made no headway; whilst they based their 'theory' on the political consequences to be expected of Germany's development, the representatives of the Board of Trade (Q. Hill) and the Treasury (Waley) pointed to the political situation and the facts of political life in Britain since 1931/33; C 998/4/18, FO 371–19 885, p. 276; see notes 482, 505 above and note 562 below.

557. Chamberlain's statement is quoted in Ashton-Gwatkin's note, 31 August 1936, FO–371 19 934, p. 189; cf. Chamberlain to Morgenthau, 20 March 1937, FRUS, 1937, vol. 1, p. 101; M. Blum, ed., *Morgenthau-Diaries*, pp. 463ff.; Leith-Ross, *Money Talks*, p. 247; N. Chamberlain, 2 April 1937, F.P. (36) 23 = C 2618/270/18, FO 371–20 735, pp. 107ff.; Foreign Policy Committee, 8th meeting, 6 April 1937, Cab. 27–626.

558. Runciman, 17 Febr. 1936, Cab. 27–599. The Treasury's position is clearly stated in its memorandum. 'Foreign Loans. The Case against Germany', 19 June 1933, C 5584/62/18, FO 371–16 696, p. 274; this position stands in the 1930s; see note 525 of German original.

559. Runciman to Eden, 23 July 1936, C 5567/99/18, FO 371–19 934. The 'sacrifices' expected of Britain by the economic appeasers comprised: renunciation of additional tariffs; no retaliatory duties in case of a devaluation of the Reichsmark; abandoning quota regulations; open door (with regard to access to colonial raw materials); reduction of tariffs and revision of Ottawa (lower tariff union); assisting the stabilisation of French currency in the hope of France's return to a liberal foreign economic policy; Leith-Ross to W. Fisher/N. Chamberlain, 2 April 1937, T 188–175; Leith-Ross to Ashton-Gwatkin, 25 Febr. 1937, T 188–175.

560. N. Chamberlain, 26 March 1937, comment on Eden-Memo., T 188–175; Runciman, too, saw no reason why Britain should deviate from its successful methods of stimulating economic recovery; there had been no sin and hence no need for the National Government to repent.

561. Pinsent to Waley, FO 371–19 933, p. 266; see above notes 189f., 388.

interests of different persuasions opposed a change of course, the Board of Trade and the Treasury saw little point in considering the start of a new era of economic cooperation between Germany and Britain.[562] The economic departments not only advocated letting the matters raised by the economic appeasers lie for the time being,[563] but also argued in favour of the alternative; that is, to act on political topics first. In this case their departments would not be burdened with the responsibility of having to make sacrifices, inherent in any compromise solution, plausible to their own 'constituencies':

> The impression exists abroad that we are in a better position than other countries to make sacrifices, but despite much lip service to more liberal trade, we refuse to do anything [which is also the standard thesis of economic appeasers] . . . On the other hand, we must be sure that, in return we get some adequate return either in the economic or political field . . . I fear that concessions on the economic side will be wasted unless they are linked up with a more positive programme on the political side'.[564]

Some of the British representatives, like Leith-Ross, whom the economic appeasers liked to view as a 'middleman' of their ideas between the British government and the German 'moderates' also advised the cabinet 'always [to] express . . . our readiness to help Germany, but state as clearly as possible the conditions which would have to be satisfied before help was forthcoming'.[565] They maintained that their 'sources' in Germany also asked the British to link their readiness to help Germany out of her economic difficulties to the condition that the Hitler regime first change its policy.[566] Leith-Ross in fact advocated that a package deal as proposed by the

---

562. Board of Trade to FO, 23 July 1937, C 5567/99/18, FO 371–19 934; Torr minute, 18 August 1936, on C 5920/99/18, ibid., pp. 143f.; the FBI hold similar views, see Phipps to FO/Eden, C 5928/99/18, FO 371–19 934, p. 145. Leith-Ross pointed to domestic opposition to the ideas of the Economic Section; Leith-Ross, 17 July 1937, FO 371–21 216, pp. 485–488; Waley referred to public opinion in Britain which would not take to neglecting the interests of British foreign trade in order to improve Germany's standard of living; Waley to FO, 19 June 1936, C 4501/99/18, FO 371–19 933.

563. Runciman to Eden, C 5567/99/18, and FO (Vansittart) minutes, 15 Sept. 1936, FO 371–19 934.

564. Leith-Ross to W. Fisher/N. Chamberlain, 2 April 1937, T 188–175.

565. Leith-Ross report on Raw Materials' Enquiry and session of the International Chamber of Commerce in Berlin, C 5139/71/62, 9 July 1937, FO 433–4, no. 38; cf. T 188–177.; Leith-Ross to Ashton-Gwatkin, 25 Febr. 1937, T 188–175.

566. Leith-Ross, *Money Talks*, pp. 244f.; Jebb, 14 July 1937, C 5138/165/18, FO 371–20 733, pp. 270ff. (to my knowledge this is the first occasion on which Göring was given

economic appeasers should be put forward. Yet he wanted to demand forcefully that Germany pay tribute to Britain's precondition of arrangements of this type: 'You could not devise any definite programme for restoration of freedom without having first a political settlement'.[567]

The insistence on a political settlement had a great deal to do with Leith-Ross's political preoccupations. Germany should, as it were, accept and practise the standards which Leith-Ross wanted to introduce in Britain against the advocates of protectionism and rearmament; namely, a balance between armaments, export production and agricultural activities. He also wished 'to reassure capital' and show a readiness to cooperate with other countries to relax or even remove trade restrictions. The dictum that help for Germany from abroad could only be effective if the political direction was 'safe' at the same time, was to commit Britain to a programme of 'sound' economics: 'Progress upon [political questions] is the essential condition of progress on financial and economic questions. But even if there were an improvement in the political atmosphere, there would still be a number of things which would have to be done by the Germans before we could help Germany much financially'.[568]

Influential members of the cabinet, above all Neville Chamberlain, shared the readiness of the economic appeasers to interpret declarations from Schacht, Göring and occasionally Hitler as invitations to start general discussions. They paid more attention, however, to whether the objects for such negotiations accorded to the maxim that the responsibility for failure never be laid at Britain's door. This resulted in reservations about substantiating any of the 'economic' or 'colonial appeasement' offers in detail: 'Our objective should be to set out the political guarantees which we want from Germany as part of any general settlement; and if the discussions have to break down, we want the breakdown to be due

---

preference as head of the German moderates and as the 'address' of British soundings; (this refers to Jebb).

567. Leith-Ross, 9 July 1937, FO 433–4, no. 38, pp. 111f.; cf. Leith-Ross report on his talks with Schacht and Puhl on 6 July 1937, C 4897/78/18, FO 371–20 728, pp. 299ff.

568. Leith-Ross to Eden, 19 March 1937, C 2304/270/18, FO 371–20 735, p. 82. Chamberlain integrated Leith-Ross's formulae into his memorandum to the Cabinet on the terms of trilateral talks, F.P. (36)23, p. 3 (see notes 549 and 557). As to German concessions, Leith-Ross gave some thought to devaluating the Reichsmark: Leith-Ross report on talk with Schacht/Puhl, see note 567). Pinsent had asserted in his analysis that the German exchange restrictions had contributed decisively to the altered structure of the German economy; Pinsent, 15 June 1936, C 4487/99/18; C 2872/99/18.

to Germany's refusal to accept our reasonable requirements in the political field'.[569]

The economic departments built up a solid defence against any successful take-off of economic appeasement initiatives.[570] They did so by posing the question of whether the economic appeasers could offer any German reciprocity to British businessmen worth the sacrifices on Britain's part. Furthermore, even the politicians, who sometimes seemed convinced by the logic of the economic appeasers' argument, raised the objection that 'merely to decide that our general economic policy should be to help rather than to hinder German trade is not striking enough to make a difference to the course of European history, though it may be all that is permissible in the way of practical politics'.[571]

The economic departments, if they did not use their veto, diluted the measures suggested by the economic appeasers; this was one of the reasons why Britain's offers proved unattractive.[572] Generally the Treasury raised biting criticisms of the amateurish nature of their opponents' 'comprehensive schemes'; the Board of Trade rejected them by pointing out that Britain had no need to offer Danegeld.[573] The departments primarily responsible for 'economics' – imperial, foreign and domestic – moreover sought to prevent the Foreign Office, and not just the economic appeasers, from using opportunities to initiate foreign economic policy under the primacy of strategic political interests. Even the request not to disrupt Foreign Office policies by 'petty-minded' external economic measures serving the interest of particular branches or regions remained generally without response.[574] Attempts by the Foreign Office to include economic matters in its own sphere of

569. N. Chamberlain, 2 April 1937, F.P. (36) 23.

570. N. Chamberlain, 25 Febr. 1936 C.P. 60(36); Runciman, 25 Febr. 1936, C.P. 61(36), Cab. 24–260; Cabinet meeting, 25 Febr. 1936, Cab. 23–83, pp. 183ff.; the IDAC had advised an increase of duties on leatherware imports; the FO asked for a dispense, at least during the working agreement initiative; C 979/4/18, FO 371–19 885, pp. 273, 276; cf. FO 371–19 884, p. 46 (Ashton-Gwatkin and Jebb minutes); Wigram, 25 June 1936, on C 4501/99/18, FO 371–19 933, pp. 270ff.

571. Wigram, 14 March 1936, FO 371–19 888, pp. 75f. (minute on Pinsent's statement on the proposals of the FO before 6 March 1936, Cab. 27–599).

572. Apart from the cooperation leading to the Tripartite Agreement, the British government did not meet the expectations of the economic appeasers; modifications of agricultural quotas, of protecting iron & steel industries, or of measures against Japanese competition in the Colonies were ruled out.

573. Runciman to Eden, 23 July 1936; Runciman, 17 Febr. 1936; Board of Trade, 26 Febr. 1936, G (36)7.

574. Eden, 17 Febr. 1936, Cabinet Committee on Germany, 1st meeting, Cab. 27–599; CTP (37) 11, §58, 7 June 1937, FO 371–21 247; see above note 409.

responsibility because of their 'international' implications or repercussions on relations with specific states were immediately
countered by the Treasury and the Board of Trade, which insisted
that the Foreign Office should limit itself to its sphere of responsibility and, if at all, deal with specialised economic questions affecting individual countries;[575] this occurred independently of whether
the Foreign Office's inquiries were drafted by the appeasers or by
Vansittart and his group. The economic departments for their part
employed political arguments and references to political events[576]
in order to counteract claims by the Foreign Office that it would
and must be allowed to present in the cabinet the basic principles
of economic policy in relation to the US, the Dominions and
Germany and, therefore, must be able to participate in the 'decision-making process' on economic issues.

The economic appeasers had to cope with the additional handicap that, in order to secure their main aim, they had to defend
bastions of free-trade ideology, even if modified, and thereby challenged the stalwarts of the 1931–32 change of direction. By
consciously introducing the arguments of those nations who held
British governments at least partly responsible for the 'triumph' of
'economic nationalism' in Great Britain into interdepartmental
consultations, they provoked the reproach that they spoke more in
the interests of the US or Germany or the opposition parties than
in the national interest. The view that 'on the Foreign Office . . .
devolves the responsibility . . . of helping to suppress economic
nationalism whether in foreign countries or in our own departments at home',[577] revived the Treasury's and Board of Trade's
mistrust of all demands to negotiate a general economic settlement
with Germany, the US and France; 'bad' experiences in the 1920s

575. Eden memorandum, 6 May 1937, 'Economics and Foreign Policy', W. 9040/5/50, FO
371–21 215; FO memo., 'The Economic Aspects of Foreign Policy', 28 May 1937, W 11
034/5/50 = E (37)28 (draft of Eden's speech at the Imperial Economic Conference); Board of
Trade (Overton) reaction on Eden's memo., 'Economics and Foreign Policy' asked for the FO
to be restricted to advising on individual cases. In response, the FO demanded that the
Treasury's and the Bank of England's (Lord Norman's) economic and financial diplomacy be
restricted to exchanges of information; e.g. Sargent and Vansittart minutes on C 7493/635/18,
Nov. 1935, FO 371–18 873, pp. 25ff.; but even Halifax' instructions to Ashton-Gwatkin (at the
end of 1938) — cf. Wendt, *Economic Appeasement*, p. 551 — demonstrate the will to 'political'
control on economic foreign diplomacy. This presumption caused difficulties in managing and
operating Anglo-American relationships in the interwar period!
576. The effort to establish a sort of general staff within the FO failed; the Economic
Section was of a different nature; see above, notes 56ff.
577. Craigie minute, 6 Febr. 1933, on Selby memorandum, W 890/278/50, FO 371–318,
p. 131; Craigie disputed Vansittart's, H. Smith's, Sargent's and Leeper's advise for concentrating
on disarmament.

and at the London World Economic Conference of 1933 had in a way helped to shape the aversion of the economic departments to 'internationally'-minded criticisms.

Furthermore, the essence of the strategies of economic appeasement, which was to approach Germany 'with proposals to collaborate as far as possible in a new period of European tranquillity and economic reconstruction', was undermined from the start. This was because one started off from the opposite direction by pin-pointing specific questions which were to serve as footholds for contacts. The economic appeasers by contrast preferred to discuss a package deal. Such a deal, they thought, provided the only opportunity for both sides to bear the 'disadvantages of sacrifices'.[578] This applied, for example, to their favoured project of re-establishing the Triangular Trade System; such a move involved, on the one hand, the removal of protective measures taken to stabilise internal economic trends and hence threatened, at least temporarily, to increase unemployment in specific industries and/or areas.[579] On the other hand, it was to open up the prospect for a revival of overseas trade and hence to make the reactivation of unused capacities possible. This dilemma was experienced by quite different societies; if the 'competition in separate action' was to be turned into 'cooperative competition', it should be obvious that any plan could only work if the process began in parallel on many fronts.

With the decision to start off with specific aspects, the choice of a suitable 'candidate' for action was moreover left to those who were pressing the cabinet for positive action *vis-à-vis* Germany in the economic sphere. Above all, agreement on a particular 'candidate' for action was seldom achieved. On some occasions individual representatives of the Board of Trade and the Economic Section of the Foreign Office preferred to pursue the idea of a customs union between the British Empire, Germany and France. The Treasury, on the other hand, favoured making an offer of British assistance

578. Ashton-Gwatkin, 4 March 1936, FO 371–19 889, pp. 18f.; cf. F.P. (36) 5, §12, 13 July 1936, Cab. 27–626. The proposal to pursue Hoare's Geneva speech aimed at an 'all-in-settlement' similar to the 'Sargent chain'.

579. Eden to Runciman, 17 July 1936, C 5197/99/18, p. 2, FO 371–19 934; Jebb, 24 June 1936, FO 371–19 933, p. 320; Bruce/Stanhope conversation, 10 June 1936, FO 371–19 933, p. 325; Ashton-Gwatkin/Vansittart conversation, 30 June 1936, C 4758, FO 371–19 933, pp. 331f.; Ashton-Gwatkin/Jebb, 31 Jan. 1936, C 807/4/18, FO 371–19 884, p. 46. The sense of these recommendations was to tackle the German problem even if this implied some 'sacrifices' for Britain; they argued that Britain's long-term economic interests would be safeguarded and the defusion of political tensions would pay off economically.

with the devaluation of the Reichsmark a test case.[580] The Economic Section at the Foreign Office expected more from an explicit renunciation of Britain's most-favoured-nation treatment of German neighbouring states in order to smooth the path for a preferential area under German leadership in Central and South-Eastern Europe.[581] In view of these disagreements, the economic appeasers in the Foreign Office and representatives of the economic departments came to an understanding in their preliminary meetings (i.e. before going into interdepartmental meetings) that the time for specifically orientated advances in the economic sphere was not yet ripe.[582] What remained was to acknowledge the achievement of the Payments and Trade Agreements with Germany from 13 April to 3 May 1933 and 10 August to 1 November 1934 which had resulted from 'hard' bargaining between experts. The economic appeasers pointed to them as a contribution to the economic recovery of both Germany and Britain.[583]

Undeniably, then, British policy, in particular economic foreign policy, was subject to economic influences. Yet, as the sections above have sought to demonstrate, the influence of trade and finance on a foreign policy which was effectively one of appeasement – the latter being defined either as 'preventive diplomacy', or in terms of the ultimate repercussions of foreign policy – was not in itself synonymous with economic appeasement. The economic appeasers were neither successful in putting into practice their strategies on questions of diplomatic crisis-management – they had instead to concede precedence to 'politically' motivated

580. N. Chamberlain, 5 Oct. 1936, Mansion House speech, proclaimed that Britain would not retaliate if Germany devalued the Reichsmark, and he referred to British assistance to French devaluation in Sept. 1936; cf. H. Morrison, 5 Oct. 1936, presented this view at the League of Nations annual session; Economic Relations section. report, 6 Nov. 1936, C 7953/7746/62, FO 433–3, no. 22, p. 149.

581. The British government waived its most-favoured nations' claims in the instance of the Polish-Austrian Trade Treaty; this was an exception to the rule. Ashton-Gwatkin considered a deal on the basis that Britain would acknowledge Germany's preferential area in Central and South East Europe in exchange for Germany's acknowledgment of Britain's predominance in the Sterling bloc area and in North-East Europe (Finland, Poland, the Baltic countries, Denmark) — 17 Jan. 1936, C 397/8/18, FO 371–19 917, pp. 147ff.; cf. Ashton-Gwatkin, 23 Dec. 1935, FO 371–18 873, pp. 129f. On Germany's preferential agreement policies since Brüning and U.S. counter-actions see H.J. Schröder, in: Knapp, ed., *Deutschland und die U.S.A.*, pp. 145ff. Waley (to Pinsent, 19 June 1936, FO 371–19 933, pp. 276ff.) rejected such 'pro-German' proposals.

582. Ashton-Gwatkin report on informal meeting between Wigram, Jebb, Ashton-Gwatkin, Q. Hill and Waley on the economic appeasers' set of proposals, 17 Jan. 1936, C 397/8/18, FO 371–19 917, pp. 147ff.; see above note 189.

583. Ashton-Gwatkin, 15 August 1936, minute on C 5920/99/18, FO 371–19 934, p. 144 (a); cf. Wendt, *Economic Appeasement*, pp. 290ff.

alternatives – nor were they in any position to win over the economic departments to their ideas, or indeed to prevail on the custodians of economic interests to demand of their economic and political clientèle at home and in the Empire and Commonwealth the kinds of 'sacrifices' which would produce political effects on Germany. Whenever British policy responded to *political* influences and considerations with some declaration of international intent bearing the hallmark of the economic appeasers – as in Hoare's Geneva speech of September 1935, the Tripartite Agreement of September 1936, and the Van Zeeland Committee of 1937–38 – or whenever the economic appeasers attempted to capitalise on such announcements, in other words to put international declarations into concrete practice as British policy, they were confronted with a situation in which, firstly, their efforts were obstructed by procrastination and 'stonewalling' in the upper echelons of the Foreign Office and in which, secondly, the economic departments continued to insist on offers of 'political securities' before negotiations could begin on an economic arrangement whose ultimate goal was to influence German (foreign) policy. While economic factors may be identified in appeasement policy, they are not synonymous with the mobilisation of British economic substance and influence in any attempt to further a strategy of economic appeasement.

II

The Political System
and Foreign Policy

British foreign and defence policies between the wars were guided
by two interrelated principles endorsed in 1919 at the time of
peace-making and consolidated in the 1920s by diplomacy and
economic and financial policy.

The first affected the scope of Britain's foreign policy: in view of
Russia's and Germany's diminished status as 'great powers' – the
one weakened by civil war and revolutionary disorganisation, the
other by enforced disarmament – the British government took the
risk of reducing the British military and armaments potential to a
level calculated on the assumption that there would be no renewed
involvement in a European war during the next ten years. The Ten
Years' Rule was prepared by the Finance Committee of the
cabinet in August 1919, tightened up by the Geddes Committee in
1922 and modified by the chancellor of the exchequer, Winston
Churchill, to read 'that at any given date there will be no major war
for ten years from that date' (July 1928). It cloaked the policy of
unilateral 'arms limitation' in a strategy apparently (!) based on
rational calculation. In reality this decision was taken under the
pressure of financial worries. The cabinet filed away the comments
they themselves had requested from their military advisers without
serious discussion, disregarding the long-term effects on the British
armaments industry.[1] The general principle that 'it should be
assumed for framing revised Estimates, that the British Empire will

---

1. These long-term effects were spelled out by Balfour in his report to the Committee of
Imperial Defence, 236th Meeting, 5 July 1928. R. Higham, *Armed Forces in Peacetime, Britain
1918–1940. A Case Study*, London 1962, provided the first useful survey.

not be engaged in any great war during the next ten years, and that no expeditionary force is required for this purpose'[2] was further based on the foreign policy premise that – thanks to the terms of Part V of the Peace Treaty – France was militarily superior to Germany and that Great Britain had to cooperate to maintain this relative advantage. However, the idea that France's military power had to remain greater than Germany's – since Britain's security was thus assured – was at odds with the readiness expressed by Britain to guarantee assistance to her French partner – subject to American cooperation – in the event of a German war of revanche. For it was hard to imagine that Britain, under the aegis of the Ten Years' Rule, could maintain the military forces necessary for a 'continental commitment'.[3] The Locarno Pact[4], agreed as a substitute for the failed Mutual Assistance Pact, was based on the same contradiction – Locarno was considered to be a 'treaty of peace, not war'; so that even the foreign secretary, Austen Chamberlain, answered the chiefs of staff's question – as to whether military arrangements were necessary to fulfil the guarantee – in the negative.[5] The fact that Britain had promised assistance without fully intending to enter into obligations became obvious in 1936 during the Rhineland crisis when the Prime Minister, Stanley Baldwin, reproached France that she had 'caught [Britain] at a disadvantage'. His argument was that France knew, firstly, that Britain had signed Locarno on the assumption that – given the favourable relation of French military strength over Germany – her commitments presented no risk in case of Germany's repudiation of the Treaties of Versailles and Locarno, and that, secondly, Britain, as a democratic country, had been delayed in commencing rearmament (after 1933–34). He further argued that France had nevertheless confronted Britain, the guaranteeing power, with the dilemma either of supporting risky military sanctions, relying on France's continuing superiority and on the known internal differences in Germany, or

2. The quote and its context are presented in my 'Effizienz und Flexibilität politisch-sozialer Systeme. Die deutsche und die englische Politik 1918/19', *VZG*, 25 (1977), p. 179; cf. N. Gibbs, *Grand Strategy*, vol. I: *Rearmament Policy*, London 1976, ch. 1.

3. M. Howard, *The Continental Commitment: The Dilemma of British Defence Policy in the Era of the Two World Wars*, London 1972, pp. 78ff. The introduction of the notion 'Field Force' in the autumn of 1934 as a substitute to 'Expeditionary Force' marks the difference between the pre-war politics of 1906–1914 and 1935–1940.

4. J. Jacobson, *Locarno Diplomacy. Germany and the West 1925–1929*, Princeton 1972, pp. 23ff.

5. J.Th. Emmerson, *The Rhineland Crisis, 7 March 1936. A Study in Multilateral Diplomacy*, London 1977, p. 24.

of acquiescing to any breach of the Treaty.[6] The British solution of striving for a 'New Locarno' by renouncing the limitations on German sovereignty (demilitarised zone) no longer acceptable to Berlin, had been blocked both by France and Germany.[7]

The second directive formulated in 1919 was intended to protect British room for manoeuvre in domestic politics. According to this dictum, Britain could rather afford to take risks over defence abroad than chance a conflict with 'labour'[8] which might provoke a crisis of the whole system by overextending the resources of Britain's economy and society.

This central principle also corresponded to a specific set of circumstances in Britain; namely, the unrest and protest which took place during the transition from a war to a peacetime economy and the need for the government to set priorities in checking inflation caused by the cost of the war. By deciding to reduce the military budget after the war to a level comparable to what had emerged in Russia after the successful revolution and in Germany after the lost war and enforced disarmament, British policy at least gave itself the opportunity of steering an exemplary course of domestic reform which would serve to integrate and legitimise the socio-political system: 'In the postwar years we had to choose between . . . a policy of disarmament, social reform and latterly financial rehabilitation and . . . a heavy expenditure on armaments. Under a powerful impulse for development every government of every party elected for the former'.[9]

These two basic directives of British policy were not called into question until the beginning of the 1930s. In 1933–34 Britain still sought to maintain the substance of France's military superiority in negotiations over (French) *sécurité* and (German) equal treat-

---

6. St. Baldwin, 11 March 1936, Cab. 23–83, p. 295; cf. K. Middlemas, J. Barnes, *Baldwin. A Biography*, London 1969, pp. 763ff.

7. The story is outlined in ch. I of the German original of this book.

8. The notion '*labour*' has been defined in the Introduction. Its meaning comprises both the claims and needs actually advanced and pronounced by the Labour Party and the unions *and* the perception and image of the danger/risks involved in the self-generating process of inflation, profiteering, control etc., which form the subject and focus of this chapter. The governments' pronouncements in favour of 'taking risks for peace', i.e. arms limitation and/or limited rearmament, are popularised variants of the 'risk formula', Hankey, who invented the formula in 1919, repeated the saying in the 1930s, e.g. Hankey's draft of the 1935 Statement Relating to Defence, Cab. 21–407, p. 5, but at the same time he deplored its bearing on 'official mind' as well as on the capacities of industry for arms production.

9. St. Baldwin, 9 March 1936, Parl. Deb., House of Commons, ser. 5, vol. 309, col. 1832.

ment. However, when, after the autumn of 1934, she tried to take the initiative, there was a shift in emphasis towards the needs of British security and defence policy. The shift was justified in statements pronouncing that efforts should aim at keeping the 'peace' (i.e. Britain's and the 'general' interest) instead of defending the status quo (i.e. France's insistence on preserving the 'integrity' of the Treaty of Versailles).[10] The British government, aware of the dangerous aspects of its risk theory in the altered context of international conflicts in the Far East and in Europe, sought to replace it with a strategy of peaceful 'preventive diplomacy'. The government tried to secure an agreement on arms limitation, designed to enable Britain to make up for existing deficiencies – that is, make good the shortages resulting from the Ten Years' Rule epoch – whilst deterring Germany from pressing her claims to rearmament too far. This was not just a problem of diplomacy, it was central to the deep cleavages of political life, for it raised the question of whether the domestic political circumstances permitted a revision of or even a *volte-face* from the premise of the primacy of socio-political palliatives in favour of an emphasis on armament expenditure, which addressed itself to external threats. Were the Great Depression and its aftermath suitable for a shift in emphasis from social to armament spending, contrary to decisions taken in 1918–20 under similar domestic political circumstances? By consenting to the chiefs of staff's demand for the abrogation of the Ten Years' Rule only on condition that, firstly, hopes of disarmament negotiations in Geneva would not thereby be torpedoed[11] and that, secondly, the economic crisis would be taken into consideration, the cabinet reinforced the tenet that avoidance of domestic political risks must take precedence over security risks abroad.[12]

Despite mounting concern over the 'German peril' and despite rearmament on an increasing scale, the perception of domestic (economic and socio-) political risks nevertheless continued to shape the decision-making process on defence and foreign policy.[13] Until the spring of 1938 the outcome of debates on the

10. R. MacDonald, 11 Dec. 1934, Cab. 27–572.

11. P. Dennis, *Decision by Default. Peacetime Conscription and British Defence 1919–1939*, London 1972, pp. 28ff.; St. Roskill, *Hankey. Man of Secrets*, vol. 3: *1931–1963*, London 1974, pp. 86ff.

12. N. Gibbs, *Rearmament Policy*, pp. 77ff., 99ff. In contrast to the situation in 1918/20 when the unions caused concerns about industrial unrest, there was no fear of 'revolution' in 1931; nevertheless, '1931', i.e. the repetition of 1931, stands for 'crisis at home' and had an enormous impact on the state of the 'official mind' and decision-making in the 1930s; we return to this matter in due course.

13. It is significant that Simon as Foreign Secretary in 1931 until 1935 advocated 'rearma-

relative importance of appeasement and rearmament in the dual strategy was determined by the argument that there was still time to defer the decision on the increase of public finances and the use of production capacities for an arms build-up which would be appropriate to her 'continental commitments'. The advocates of delay also advanced foreign-policy arguments to support them; they maintained that hopes for a relaxation of the international situation were still justified.[14] With this argument, Neville Chamberlain, Simon, Inskip and the Treasury successfully opposed the warnings of the Foreign Office and the military. Those departments responsible for foreign and defence policy stressed that they could fulfil the tasks delegated to them only within limits because of the dilemma of financing armaments. The Foreign Office was expected to reduce 'external' threats through diplomatic efforts and 'deterrence' strategies – but how could this be achieved if progress depended on the fact that Italy, Japan and Germany were only likely to feel restrained by demonstrations of 'real' military strength? The Foreign Office and the chiefs of staff pointed out that because of the fundamental differences between Britain and Germany (and Britain *vis-à-vis* Japan and Italy) in the style, methods and aims of their foreign policy, they could not count on their efforts solely to achieve 'appeasement' having any success, unless they were accompanied by accelerated arms programmes keeping pace with those of their 'adversaries'. The call from the Foreign Office and the Defence Services (chiefs of staff) to change course because of ever-growing risks abroad did not, however, aim at a reorientation of foreign policy (in favour of an alliance policy) but rather at a suspension of the pre-eminent status accorded to considerations of financial and socio-political issues. This call aroused only limited response, even in the winter of 1937/38. The combination of economic, social, politico-strategical considerations and conditions which held sway relatively unchanged from the 1920s to the 1930s, delayed the process initiated by the Foreign Office and the military which aimed at directing public

---

ment', but as Home Secretary and Chancellor of the Exchequer (1935–1939) had a hand in limiting arms expenditure, both out of financial and economic and social considerations; on this, see M. Postan, *British War Production*, London 1952, p. 17. A similar ambiguity is characteristic for N. Chamberlain and most of his colleagues in charge of domestic, economic and social 'affairs'.

14. This is evident from the debates in September to November 1937 on Halifax' visit to Germany and on the Statement relating to Defence; cf. B.-J. Wendt, *Economic Appeasement*, pp. 439ff., 453ff.; K. Middlemas, *Diplomacy of Illusion*, pp. 132ff.; N. Gibbs, *Rearmament Policy*, pp. 249ff.; D. Dilks, ed., *The Diaries of Sir Alexander Cadogan 1938–1945*, London 1971.

attention to the dangerous changes in the international environment and at establishing a willingness to risk a break with domestic
political 'doctrines'.

The arrears in defence – even in relation to the limited standards
of the programmes of the 1920s which British governments had
risked after 1919 for the reasons outlined above – provides the
point of reference for the interpretation of foreign policy in the
1930s, the so-called appeasement policy:[15] 'Since neither the
arms nor the arms manufacturing capacity existed, Britain was
forced to limit its projected role on the Continent . . . Limited
expenditures implied limited commitments . . . Appeasement was
the result . . . of the economic currents and fiscal policies of the
post-1919 period'.[16]

In British eyes Germany's return to power politics meant that
the Anglo-German (power) relationship had become the decisive
factor in the development of international politics and, more
importantly, that (re-)armament would henceforth play a central
role in domestic politics.[17] The assumption (November 1933)[18]
that Germany needed five years before the level of her armaments
became a threat to Britain, served as a rough guideline to define
the time span in which Britain had to make good her 'deficiencies'.[19]
A further reason for the concentration on armaments in British
politics was that British decision-makers saw possibilities of establishing contacts in this field for negotiations with the Third Reich.
They supposed that the Germans 'would prefer to talk politics' so
that Britain had to seek talks on political matters: 'To the Nazis
national prestige was the predominant issue and economic con-

15. The 'preventive diplomacy' - aspect of appeasement policy and the reasoning behind the
emphasis on arms talks within the context of Anglo-French-German relations are analysed in
ch. 1 of the German original.

16. F. Coghlan, 'Armaments, Economic Policy and Appeasement. Background to British
Foreign Policy 1931–1937', *History*, 57(1972), p. 216.

17. This was due to the awareness that German rearmament surpassed British estimates of
Germany's rate of increase; consequently, Britain would have to expand her own capacities for
arms production in order to keep even with Germany's progress. The difficult problems of
assessing Gemany's 'real' achievements are evaluated by R. Overy, 'The German Pre-War
Aircraft Production Plans, November 1936–April 1939', *EHR* 90 (1975), pp. 778–797. Cf.
Gibbs, *Rearmament Policy*, pp. 170ff.

18. (Hankey) Defence Requirements Committee, meetings 15 Nov. 1933, Cab. 23–77, and
19 and 22 March 1934, Cab. 23–78; Report of the DRC, 28 Febr. 1934, C.P. 64(34), Cab.
24–247. The proposition corresponds to von Bülow's assessment in 1931 and 1932 that
Germany could and should agree to a five-year 'truce', for Germany would have no money to
spend on expansion programmes (for details, see note 16 of German original).

19. The Interim Report of the DRC, No. 25, 24 July 1935, Cab. 16–112, fixed January 1939
as target date; this decision had regard to the capacities of British industry (for further details see
note 38 of German original).

siderations took second place'.[20] Boundary changes and other territorial solutions to the German problem were not seriously considered before autumn 1937.[21] Moreover, concentrating on diplomatic efforts aiming at arms talks had the advantage that both in the event of successful negotiations with Germany and in the event of a failure, a settlement of domestic political differences of opinion on conceptions of who the enemy was, on armaments measures and on the readiness to face the war risk could be achieved.

By adopting the armaments question as the medium of the 'political approach' strategy the British government did, however, expose its actions to domestic and foreign political uncertainty. It had to demonstrate to the advocates of disarmament, and (after 1934) of non-rearmament,[22] that it would undertake everything to find a fair solution to the problem of security, on the one hand, and to Germany's military equality, on the other. In contrast to this, the National government had to prove to critics within its own ranks that it had correctly assessed the 'German peril' and had taken adequate security precautions.[23] In order to find its way between both positions, the British government concentrated its efforts on those areas of foreign and armaments policy which presented the best prospect of linking the defensive aspects of its armament programme with its function as deterrent. Since this theme – (partial) arms limitation agreements – was also favoured partly by Germany (Naval Agreement) and partly by France (Air Pact) as a starting point for negotiations, the way forward for British foreign policy appeared to be staked out both by domestic political conditions and by international circumstances. Armaments policy defined both the credibility and scope of the peace strategy; conversely, the continued efforts to secure peace by sounding out the possibility of arms limitation treaties constituted the basis for the management of the armaments question in domestic politics. Foreign policy conducted on the basis that Germany would agree

20. R.A.C. Parker, 'Großbritannien und Deutschland 1936–37', in O. Hauser, ed., *Welpolitik 1933–1939*, Göttingen 1973, pp. 73ff.; M. Gilbert, *Roots*, p. 158 (Refers to Leith-Ross).

21. Meeting of Study Group, All Souls College, 18 and 19 Dec. 1937, H. Nicolson-Papers; cf. N. Nicolson, ed., *Harold Nicolson, Diaries and Letters, 1930–1939*, London 1966, entries 22 Dec. 1937 and 22 March 1938. The Government discussed the same problem in the context of Halifax's visit to Germany; Inskip 'briefed' the All Souls Study Group.

22. The proponents of 'collective security', 'pooled security' and related concepts presumed that Britain could contribute her Navy to the 'pool', i.e. 'give a lead' without any need to join or accelerate the arms race.

23. The first public occasion was the parliamentary debate of 30 July 1934 on the program for expanding the RAF.

to arms limitation within the framework of a 'European appease-ment' or of bilateral agreements ('colonial appeasement') had at least as much significance for the domestic political management of the armaments question as domestic British mobilisation in favour of rearmament had for facilitating the foreign-policy task of deterring aggressors from an attack on the 'island of stability and common sense'.

Two aspects of the outlined theme have always been recog-nised; they emerged in fact, in the discussions that went on at the time:

(1) The armaments question as a constraint on foreign policy (in the Rhineland crisis, in the *Anschluss* question, in the Munich crisis): The divergent interpretations range from the thesis that the British armed forces would not have been capable of action[24] to the assertion that British foreign policy had been forced into acquiescence and into employing ruses as long as it could not rely on a sufficient military back up.[25] The fear that the pitiful condition of the British armed forces would become obvious as soon as Britain took part in military sanctions against Germany – be it as part of an international (League of Nations) formation, or in response to her treaty obligations (Locarno) – constituted the decisive impulse for the policy of pursuing peace talks and using all available possibilities for negotiations,[26] even if the result could only be to ratify *faits accomplis*. The pressing need for appeasement could thus be blamed on the long years of domestic political neglect of security and armaments issues. From the point of view of the proponents of appeasement initiatives,[27] Britain could not

24. 'The real question to my mind is whether we can yet afford to be strong with anybody . . . Somebody might call our bluff and we should then be exposed . . . We have nothing with which to fight – literally nothing – and will not have anything for two years'. *The Ironside Diaries*, ed. R. Macleod and D. Kelly, London 1962, 26 and 27 June 1937; cf. Lord Ismay, 'Note on the question of whether it would be to our military advantage to fight Germany now or to postpone the issue', 20 Sept. 1938, Cab. 21–544. A detailed statement on the situation in March 1936 was presented in COS-Report = CID 1224 B, 16 March 1936; cf. N. Gibbs, *Rearmament Policy*, pp. 244ff.; B. Bond, *British Military Policy between the Two World Wars*, Oxford 1980, chs. 8 and 9.

25. The Foreign Office, but Neville Chamberlain, too, claimed they were proceeding on this basis: 'Our object is to try to restrain [the Nazi element, G.S.]. Anything that shows that we are determined to press on with our rearmament and that it is proceeding vigorously will have a steadying influence'. Eden-Statement, 13 Jan. 1937, quoted in: Earl of Avon, *Facing the Dictators*, London 1962, p. 480.

26. Cabinet Meetings of 9 and 12 March 1936, Cab. 23–83, pp. 236ff. and 298; cf. Earl of Avon, *Facing the Dictators*, pp. 343ff.

27. Wigram/Sargent-Ashton-Gwatkin Memorandum, 'Britain, France, and Germany', 21 Nov. 1935, FO 371–19 931, and Phipps Mss., vol. V/5.; Simon-Memorandum, 29 Nov. 1934, G.R.(34)3, Cab. 27–572.

pursue waiting tactics. To make British political initiatives (peace moves) dependent on considerable advances in rearmament[28] would only mean that German demands would be consolidated to such an extent as to make a compromise solution completely impossible.[29] Likewise, the question was asked, 'Does our rearmament make any real progress?'[30] How would Britain then stand in the face of a hardened German attitude? Advocates of 'preventive diplomacy' therefore stressed the need to initiate moves towards negotiations as long as the objects desired by Germany (Rhineland, Austria and Sudetenland) still retained bargaining value.[31] They argued that the main danger in the next two to three years (1936–38) lay in the possibility that Germany could bring her military power to bear as a means of diplomatic pressure whilst none of the opponents would be prepared to call Germany's bluff: thus it seemed more sensible to attempt a negotiated solution *before* the crises materialised.[32] For example, if one wanted the Rhine Zone status to disappear peacefully[33] then one had to try to come to an agreement with Germany without delay. In other words, to postpone efforts for détente until Britain felt able to operate from a position of military strength was to steer directly towards an Anglo-German war. Apart from that, the British government would never achieve the necessary political support at home for an expansion of armaments if it did not exhibit a readiness for a compromise with Germany.[34] Thus the appeasers not only claimed that concessions to the Hitler regime were expedient and necessary but that their recommendation of preventive diplomacy would also achieve the internal political mobilisation which Britain needed to regain her place amongst the great powers.

(2) The armaments question as a problem of 'capabilities': At what stage of the economic recovery was it feasible for Britain to

---

28. Neville Chamberlain conceded to Flandin the need 'to be strong before dealing with Germany', 29 Jan. 1936, Cab. 23–83, pp. 42f. Inside the Foreign Office, Vansittart and Collier advocated 'waiting games' with regard to talks with Hitler's Germany and succeeded in convincing Eden to follow their advice.

29. Wigram/Sargent-Memorandum, §12.

30. Wigram, Minute 10 Jan. 1936, to C 157/4/18, FO 371–19 883.

31. C.P. 295 (34), Cab. 23–80, pp. 319ff.; cf. Minutes ref. to C 157/4/18, FO 371–19 883, pp. 114ff.

32. Sargent, 30 Nov. 1935, note on C 7931/55/18, FO 371–18 851, pp. 175ff.

33. Report on a meeting of Foreign Office officials, on 14 Febr. 1936, FO 371–19 885, pp. 273ff. The concept of a 'working agreement', which results from this point of view, is analysed in ch. 1 of the German original.

34. Wigram/Sargent Memo., 21 Nov. 1935, §§12 and 33; Eden to Phipps (Berlin), 24 Febr. 1936, C 750/4/18, FO 371–19 884, p. 8.

embark on armaments expenditure to the extent actually demanded by the threatening situation abroad? The answer to this question depends on an assessment of the point at which German rearmament posed a threat to Britain's security and to peace in Europe and of what defence measures Britain ought primarily to have taken to thwart Hitler's successful disruption of the Peace Settlement of Versailles.

The discussion of these aspects is in no way at an end at this point. In this chapter, however, they will be subordinated to the attempt to understand foreign (appeasement) policy as a function of the socio-political system.

My own interpretation starts from the premise that appeasement policy was bound to *armaments policy* in three ways:

(1) Appeasement policy sought to normalise relations with Germany through arms limitation agreements.

(2) Appeasement policy wanted Germany to recognise the danger of encirclement whilst Britain would be spared the dilemma of bloc and alliance policies through the deterrent function of the rearmament process.

(3) Appeasement policy sought to prevent Britain prematurely siding with the Franco-Russian Pact and thus participating in encirclement policies,[35] since in that eventuality German–Japanese collaboration was feared; that is, a situation which would place the British socio-political system under enormous strain.[36] In British eyes, Germany and Japan were more than a match for the Franco-Russian powers. In order to produce a balance favourable to the League of Nations powers, Britain would have had to mobilise her resources to a greater extent than if she had tried to conserve her power through appeasement towards one of her opponents and/or through arms limitation agreements with both.

Each British initiative under every one of the three aspects of armaments policy effected the socio-political system. The problem was, of course, how to tackle the armaments question taking both the 'allies' or 'enemies' and at the same time the British taxpayers into account.

---

35. Cabinet Meeting, 8 April 1935, Cab. 23–81, pp. 299ff.; Baldwin's Statement to Defence Deputation, 29 July 1936, Cab. 21–438.

36. Lord Lothian in particular warned that none of Britain's European 'allies' would assist Britain if Germany and Japan joined forces or if Japan launched an attack on the British Empire; left in the lurch, Britain would be forced to strain her resources in a two-front war. Lothian incriminated the 'Balkan troubles' as a 'local affair' that should not bother Britain, the Dominions and the United States; Lothian-Memorandum, 11 May 1937, GD 40–17, vol. 203, pp. 264ff. (for further implications see ch. I: 'Economic Appeasement').

Foreign policy in general requires the mobilisation of domestic resources and forces and particularly their readiness to give moral support for those goals defined as being in the national interest. Foreign policy in the 1930s in particular demanded the capability both to mobilise financial, economic and social resources and to manage the domestic political situation in such a way that the emergence of international ideological blocs would not be anticipated in or predetermined by political conflicts at home[37] (in the sense of the 'rather Hitler than Blum' slogan in France). The generally accepted hypothesis that armaments policy provides the connection between domestic and foreign policy acquires a specific meaning in the 1930s. In the epoch in which armaments policy became the focus of national and international attention, both domestic and foreign policy were stripped of their relative autonomy; by virtue of the pivotal function it performed, armaments policy remained dominant. Since armaments policy integrates domestic and foreign policy issues, but is itself embedded in specific constellations of the socio-political system, it is necessary to analyse British foreign policy in the 1930s in the context of the socio-political system.

For the British power élites, changes in the international situation between 1930 and 1933 signified that the focal point of British foreign policy had to be shifted. Until then British policy had relied mainly on 'diplomacy' in its endeavours to influence and, as far as possible, regulate relations between foreign powers. Henceforward, the task was to balance the shift in power which had occurred in the international system since 1932–33 as a result of Germany's self-assertiveness, accompanied by her turn to rearmament. This was to be done by Britain mobilising her internal reserves to the same degree, albeit in another way, as Germany who, by changing her domestic political system, had effected the changes in the European order.

The Hitler government has just announced an initial programme for unemployment relief involving the expenditure of very large sums.

---

37. If one shares the assumption made at the time by 'centre-left' intellectuals (Lord Allen of Hurtwood) that the 'Diehards' were likely to consolidate their position within the Conservative Party and that consequently the National Government would have to spend its energies on battling the 'Right', thus immobilising her 'social policy', then it makes sense to interpret the postponement of launching 'rearmament' in 1933–35 as an attempt to avoid agitation on the lines of 'rearmament and class politics'. Baldwin, when trying to explain his famous Statement to the House in November 1934 to the Defence Deputation on 29 July 1936, imitates the reasoning of Lord Allen (for details, see note 36 of German original).

Such commitments must, for social and political reasons, form a first charge on Germany's available resources; and so long as this does not increase too rapidly, she will have not much to spare for rearmament or other forms of external adventures.[38]

The prevailing opinion in government circles was that in the long term neither France[39] nor the Soviet Union[40] would be in a position to mobilise sufficient domestic forces to defend peace in Europe against National Socialist Germany. This led the disposition of British politics away from a course of unilateral arms limitation (from 1919–21 until 1932–34) to a policy which sought to combine 'deterrence through rearmament' and a 'willingness to compromise': 'Our object is to try to restrain [the Nazi element] ... Anything that shows that we are determined to press on with our armament and that it is proceeding vigorously will have a steadying influence'.[41]

British security–armaments–peace policy took its particular stamp from the perception that Britain had responded to the general demand for world-wide disarmament in order to secure world peace in 1919, thus almost voluntarily assuming a similar status to Germany and that she must now conversely keep step with Germany's rearmament[42] precisely because Britain considered military intervention a disproportionate reaction to German violations of the Treaty of Versailles. Concentrating on rearming a specific sector of the armed forces within a specific time limit[43] was both to lessen Britain's vulnerability and to enable her foreign policy to break the deadlock in arms talks. Expansion in one decisive sector

38. Vansittart-Memo., 'A prosperous Germany?', 15 June 1933, C 5456/62/18, FO 371–16 696, pp. 239ff. The German decision that financial restraints should not be imposed on rearmament was passed in spring 1933, whereas the British (nominal) equivalent dates from July 1935. H.W. Richardson, *Economic Recovery*, p. 215, and A. Milward, *The German Economy*, p. 16, provide comparative data on the development of defence expenditures (as share of the GNP).

39. COS 698 = FP (36)57, March 1938, Cab. 27–627; N. Chamberlain-Diary, 15 March 1936, 29 April 1937, 19 February 1938. On Hankey's views see *Pownall-Diaries*, ed. B. Bond, vol. 1, London 1972, p. 85, and St. Roskill, *Hankey*, vol. 3, p. 308.

40. G. Niedhart, 'Der Bündniswert der Sowjetunion im Urteil Großbritanniens 1936–39', *MGM*, 10(1971), pp. 55–67. On Churchill's assessments (and doubts) see Hankey's report to Baldwin and D. Cooper, 21 April 1936, Cab. 21–435, and M. Gilbert, *Winston Churchill*, vol. 5: *1922–1939*, London 1976, pp. 723ff.

41. Eden, 13 Jan. 1937, in Earl of Avon, *Facing the Dictators*, p. 480.

42. The first instalment of this 'convergence' — concept is the Cabinet's decision, in November 1934 and March 1935, to attain 'parity' with the German Air Force.

43. C.P. 116(35), 'Air Parity in Western Europe', Cab. 24–255; Cabinet Meetings of 15, 21 and 31 May 1935, Cab. 23–81; Simon-Diary, 2 May 1935. The Admiralty aimed at a similar solution with a view to Japan, but Neville Chamberlain preferred air parity (in relation to Germany) and criticised the Two-Power-Standard planning of the Royal Navy.

would hide the backwardness of British rearmament in general and would feign a position of strength in an area where the opponent was precisely considered to be vulnerable. According to British calculations it was sufficient to demonstrate a willingness to keep up with the main opponent in key sectors of rearmament (parity formula) to achieve a deterring effect; that is, to force an encounter at the negotiating table rather than on the battlefield.

This calculation was less of a gamble than it might appear, provided, of course, that one shares at least some of the assumptions:

(1) 'Deterrence' is a psychological category; demonstrating a commitment to 'parity' was thus more decisive than the actual level of development of the weapons system. The British assumed that Hitler was bluffing; although the cabinet panicked when the production data of the German Air Force were disclosed, it felt that the immediate threat of a direct attack had been successfully countered by the decision to accelerate and/or expand the building programme: 'I am pretty satisfied that if only we can keep out of war for a few years, we shall have an air force of such striking power that no one will care to run risks with it'.[44]

Trust in the 'rationality' of their own strategy of deterrence survived even the outbreak of war in 1939. Chamberlain remained convinced that Germany would come to realise that she could not win the war; a settlement with Germany (not Hitler!) could be reached if Britain continued to demonstrate her ability to establish a countervailing power and maintain her specific strengths; that is, her superior financial resources and survival capacity, the united home front and lines of communication with the Dominions and the US.[45]

(2) The British government's deterrence strategy took account of the direct Anglo-German 'arms race' in the one sector only. For Britain the Royal Air Force functioned virtually as an ally with which to impress Hitler at the negotiating table. This quasi-ally was thought to count for more than possible allies: 'In the absence of any powerful ally, and until our armaments are completed, we

44. N. Chamberlain, 9 Febr. 1936, quoted in K. Feiling, *The Life of Neville Chamberlain*, pp. 313f.; cf. N. Chamberlain, 23 July 1939, quoted in D. Dilks, '"The Unnecessary War". Military Advise and Foreign Policy in Great Britain, 1931–1939', in A. Preston, ed., *General Staffs and Diplomacy before the Second World War*, London 1978, p. 127; G.C. Peden, *British Rearmament and the Treasury, 1932–39*, Edinburgh 1979, pp. 118f., 121.

45. K.A.C. Parker, 'Britain, France, and Scandinavia 1939/40', *History*, 61 (1976), pp. 370, 374; M. Cowling, *Hitler*, pp. 355ff.; Dirksen to Weizsäcker, 16 Dec. 1938, *ADAP*, 4, No. 281, p. 306.

must adjust our foreign policy to our circumstances'.[46]

British security policy was not attuned to the interests of allies or to a balance in the sense of the 'old' balance of power doctrine: 'This sort of contributions which Britain might possibly make would primarily be measures to ensure *British* security, but which could and would be represented [*sic*] as constituting contributions to European and French security'. Rather, British security policy was to calm the British public alarmed by the bomber psychosis ('the bombers always get through'): 'I recognise and indeed insisted on the need for such a recasting of our air programme as would show its truly formidable character and thus act as a deterrent'.[47] At the same time the expansion of the Royal Air Force was to deter the German leadership from seriously misusing Britain's readiness to negotiate: 'My conclusion is that the further we proceed in rearmament, the more effective will be any intimation we make to the Germans on the lines you suggested. They are just seeing how far they can exploit our weakness'.[48]

(3) Calculations motivated by domestic political concerns were decisive for the hopes placed in the policy of deterrence. British politicians transferred their own visions of horror, which anticipated the suffering and great devastation a bomber offensive could bring about, to the German home front. The RAF expansion programme was to suggest to the German leaders that Britain could retaliate with a bomber attack demoralising the German populace. Mindful of the destabilising effect of such a shock on the regime, the British 'dual strategy' indulged in the illusion that Hitler feared the reprisal just as much as Baldwin or Chamberlain. Had not Hitler himself in a number of speeches referred to the horrors of war and/or his willingness for peace? Perhaps the consideration that the Hitler movement had spread the *Dolchstoss* legend also played a role. In any case, it was seen as an indication that the Hitler regime would carefully weigh up whether the 'home front' could withstand the psychological burdens before starting a war.[49] Should the 'lessons' which Hitler had drawn from the First World War prove to be relevant for German foreign

46. N. Chamberlain, 16 Jan. 1938, quoted in K. Feiling, *Life*, p. 324; cf. N. Chamberlain, 25 April 1937, ibid., p. 292; N. Chamberlain to Eden, 10 Sept. 1937, PREM. I/210.

47. Sargent-Memo., 'The Problem of German Rearmament', 5 Dec. 1934, §16, Cab. 21–417; this memo. forms the basis of G.R. (34)4, 8 Dec. 1934, Cab. 27–572, debated in Cabinet 13 Dec. 1934, Cab. 23–81. — N. Chamberlain, 26 May 1935, quoted in N. Gibbs, *Rearmament Policy*, p. 175; cf. Simon-Diary, 2 May 1935.

48. N. Chamberlain to Simon, 23 Sept. 1936, Simon-Mss.

49. Hoare started the debate in Cabinet on such 'speculative elements' in March 1934, 9

policy, then strategic bombing appeared to be the most effective deterrent that Britain could mobilise.

The 'rational' calculation had just two drawbacks: firstly, Britain had the required type of aircraft only after the building programme had been debated in 1938 and begun in 1939; secondly, the dilemma with which British politicians saw themselves faced – namely, that because of the democratic structure, readiness to enter into a conflict could mean loss of power – did not apply in the case of the National Socialist leadership.[50]

The concentration of armaments policy on the deterrent role of the RAF – whose strategic function was of limited value if one saw it in the context of the concrete German threat to peace[51] – can be explained by two further considerations: firstly, in this area a considerable force could be established with a relatively moderate increase in expenditure (compared with an expansion of the Royal Navy or the production of munitions for the Field Force); secondly, 'voluntary' agreements between the government and industry provided the basis for an expansion of weapon production without – in the first stages at least – interfering with industry's control over the economy.[52] Moreover, the RAF guaranteed a great degree of independence as an instrument of British foreign policy.

However one analyses or judges the component of 'deterrence' in the British 'dual strategy', its centrality in armaments policy points to one specific interpretation. Anticipating the situation in 1940, the British government planned rearmament on the basis of Britain having to fight a war against Germany alone if need be: 'We should concentrate upon home invulnerability against air attack within the first ten weeks of war'.[53] Concentration on the expansion of the RAF as an instrument of a deterrence-cum-appeasement strategy resulted in Britain specialising in defence against a German air strike (on Britain as armourer and financier of the Western Alliance) whilst it could otherwise only hope that France

March 1934, Cab. 23–78, p. 286, although the 'deterrent'–aspect was not yet advanced as an argument.

50. On the contrary, Hitler intended to exploit the weaknesses of 'Western democracies' and overruled his Chiefs of Staff, who pointed to the relative strength of the armed forces of France and her allies and Germany's disadvantages.

51. It is well-known that the German Air Force was (at first, anyhow) not shaped with a view to attack Britain; on the other hand, the RAF was not (yet) equipped to launch bomber offensives against Germany, and would have to rely on bases in Belgium/Northern France anyway.

52. See part 6 of this chapter.

53. All Souls Meeting, 18 and 19 Dec. 1937, Nicolson-Mss.; cf. Gibbs, *Rearmament Policy*, pp. 634ff.

would be able to stop the German armies thanks to the Maginot Line.[54] In fact, Britain depended to a large degree on France and Belgium defending certain positions from a German attack which could, on the one hand, be used by the German armed forces to pose a serious threat to Britain and which, on the other hand, would provide bases for British retaliatory actions.[55] Yet the government delayed until 1938[56] the opening of binding joint Staff talks with Belgium and France.[57] 'The object of Staff talks . . . was not so much to reassure the French as to place ourselves in the best position to be able to discharge our treaty obligations.'[58] But it should be noted that neither Baldwin's Statement on the Rhine as Britain's front line of defence (July 1934) nor the reminders on Britain's obligations under the Treaties of Versailles and Locarno had any bearing on the stages of rearmament, from the requirement programmes of 1932–35 to the Four-Year Plan of 1936 or the decisions in 1938 and March 1939. The decisive element here was that the British government was not prepared to allow France a say in domestic British disputes either by including her in Staff talks or adopting coordinated armaments measures.[59] The politicians and chiefs of staff ought actually to have approved talks on the coordination of mutual cooperation long before 1938 since Britain's defence policy was based on the premise, firstly, of never taking part in a European conflict which involved France except on her side and, secondly, that she was dependent on the assistance of the French Navy in the event of an armed conflict with Germany and Japan.[60] However, they resisted these talks because they rejected the 1914–18 war 'model'. In this context the 'time-winning' component functioned to protect British policy from the consequences of the assumptions already mentioned. For the

54. Trenchard was most outspoken on this aspect: 28 July 1936 (Defence Deputation), Cab. 21–438; COS 513, 'Appreciation of the situation in the event of war against Germany in 1939', 26 Oct. 1936, Cab. 53–29; cf. C.P. 296(37); Pownall-Diaries, vol. 1, p. 238; G. Peden, *Treasury*, p. 126 (re Ismay, Sept. 1936); Gibbs, *Rearmament Policy*, pp. 635ff.

55. M. Howard, *Continental Commitment*, pp. 116ff.; Gibbs, pp. 115, 170ff., 634ff.; Ch. Webster, N. Frankland, *United Kingdom Policy, Foreign, Strategic and Economic*, London 1950, pp. 65ff., 91ff.; M. Gilbert, *Churchill*, vol. 5, pp. 768ff.

56. On the motives and characteristics of this aversion see notes 56/57 of German original.

57. 'This contact between the General Staffs cannot give rise in respect of either Government to any political undertaking, nor to any obligation regarding the organisation of national defence', CID, 3 April 1936, Conclusions, p. 3, FO 371-19 901.

58. N. Gibbs, *Rearmament Policy*, p. 635.

59. CID 1224 B, 1 April 1936; Cabinet Meeting 1 April 1936, Cab. 23–83, p. 404; C.P. 218(36) = COS 511, 1 Sept. 1936, FO 371-19 912, pp. 49f.; C.P. 6(35), §7, Cab. 23–81, p. 37; Cabinet 12 Dec. 1934, Cab. 23–80, pp. 321ff.

60. Gibbs, pp. 168ff., 607ff., 632.

majority of cabinet ministers and the chiefs of staff maintained that it was the task of foreign policy to preserve Britain from the effects of premature involvement in alliances and treaties (except the very carefully restricted 'Locarno' Pact) which might threaten the very existence of Britain.[61] Everybody expected Britain to be the 'saviour in the last resort', but who would save Britain: France, Russia, or someone else, and if so, at what costs (if it were the US)? As the cabinet, for example on the occasion of the preparations for Anglo-French ministerial meetings in February 1935, even rejected proposals for a strengthening of 'Locarno' or for specific guarantees in relation to Belgium with one eye on public opinion which classed such declarations of intent as 'quixotic interference',[62] it prepared itself to devise 'escape routes' from obligations and to defend ever new variants of time-winning tactics against criticism at home and abroad. These tactics were generally aimed at improving Britain's defence in the event of an attack in the West or a first strike on Britain. The 'grand strategy' and the armaments programmes were explicitly designed to protect Britain: defence policy contributed only indirectly to achieving a balance of power by the fact that efforts to re-arm were to deter Germany from striving for world domination.[63] In other words, since security, foreign and armaments policy did not contemplate military capability for a war in Central or Eastern Europe – which might have been triggered off by France's treaty commitments – Britain's range of action did not improve in this respect, despite progress made with rearmament between 1935 and 1939.[64] The alternative of concluding military conventions similar to those made prior to the First World War in order to continue playing a world role and protecting world economic interests without having to foot the bill for corresponding military and financial measures, existed only in theory. Prior to the First World War, Britain had recognised that she needed allies if she wanted to prevent Germany's rise to world-power status. The domestic political 'frame of mind' in Great Britain in the 1930s was different.[65] It was in-

61. This applies especially to the project of an Air Pact; see Roskill, *Hankey*, vol. 3., pp. 156ff., (and pages 114ff. of the German original of this book).

62. C.P. 6(35), §8e, 9 Jan. 1935.

63. See the quote in note 214 of this chapter. Simon, at the First Meeting of the British Commonwealth Prime Ministers, 30 April 1935, P.M. (35), p. 4 Cab. 32–125. Similar statements: Committee on Foreign Policy, 27 March 1939, Cab. 27–624; N. Chamberlain, 20 March 1939, Cab. 23–98.

64. Gibbs, *Rearmament Policy*, p. 647.

65. On the attitudes of 'the public' to staff talks and related matters see Earl of Avon,

fluenced and formed not only by memories of or aversions to 'bloc politics' but also by reservations about the 'internationalistic' alignment of the financial and economic policies of the 1920s. All of this resulted in foreign policy actions which can be described as isolationist insofar as they went against the idea of an 'alliance' which had prevailed before the First World War.

Such an interpretation is also borne out by the characteristic features of 'appeasement'; that is, Britain's efforts to conduct negotiations not primarily with 'allies' but instead with those powers which forced the arms question on her.[66] Through arms limitation agreements with Germany and Japan – 'gentlemen's agreements' relating to an exchange of information on production plans and data – one could hope to keep the pace and cost of armaments measures within limits; that is, to keep rearmament below the threshold which would place the system under serious strain: 'If we could not make terms with Germany, then we must face rearmament on our own part on an ever-increasing scale'[67] The impression that official foreign policy was pro-German and anti-French can thus be largely explained. These labels, however, miss the specific way causes and effects worked; namely, the dependence of foreign policy on domestic political conditions which manifested themselves in the armaments debates.

The manner and direction which the mobilisation of Britain's rivals took created the framework within which the armaments debate was conducted in Britain. The threat from Japan and Germany arose from the fact that both powers channelled their economic resources into ever-increasing rearmament destined for militant expansionism. The fact that both challengers used economic as well as military means and methods for a strategy of attrition prevented Britain from attempting, in the traditional sense,[68] to defer – temporarily – some of her commitments in

---

Facing the Dictators, pp. 360ff.; Pownall-Diaries, vol. I, pp. 107ff.; on the 'pacifism' of the military see D.C. Watt, *Too Serious a Business. European Armed Forces and the Approach to the Second World War*, London 1975.

66. In general 'isolationists', such as Republicans in the United States (before the 1950s), or Gladstonian Liberals, aim to achieve disarmament and search for agreement with their adversary rather than 'potential' partners. These observations form part of the notion 'isolationism' as it is used in this study.

67. Simon, 1 Febr. 1935, Anglo-French Meeting, A.F. (B) 35, Cab. 21–413. The aspects which went along with increased rearmament are summarised in the notions 'inflation spiral' and 'labour'; see Introduction, and note 8 to this chapter.

68. J. Frankel, 'The Intellectual Framework of British Foreign Policy', in K. Kaiser, R. Morgan, eds., *Britain and West Germany. Changing Societies and the Future of Foreign Policy*,

world politics and to differentiate between those areas of interest which she was prepared to defend with military means and those in which she would limit herself to the use of economic means. In view of the doubt as to whether economic means (sanctions) would be effective against a regime which could force a reduced standard of living upon its population to pursue prestige and power politics abroad, and given the pressure of the World Depression and the adverse balance of payments situation in the 1930s, Britain's powers-that-be regarded an effort to narrow the gap in the military field as their only choice. Before 1937 the use of economic pressure and influence had played almost no role in their calculations, apart from the special case of sanctions against Italy in the Abyssinian conflict, which was occasioned by domestic politics. Above all, they resisted any temptation to bolster 'resistance' in Central and South-Eastern Europe to German penetration and feared getting involved in these 'Balkan' affairs.[69]

The interrelationship between the conduct of foreign policy, on the one hand, and the socio-political structures, 'operative ideals' and historical experiences and conditioning of a society on the other, primarily determines the extent to which social interests and resources are mobilised for foreign relations. In the 1930s, this always took effect in the context of interpretations of events in Germany (and Japan); that is, the question of the extent to which German (and Japanese) measures for overcoming the World Depression and for the so-called national renewal had to be seen as 'reconstruction' or as preparation for violent expansion. The different evaluations by the various power élites of the degree of British efforts necessary to meet the progress of Britain's competitors also determined their interpretation of relevant events in Germany as well as in France, Russia, Japan and the US. The internal controversies over the possibilities and the limits of British efforts in matters of foreign and defence policy reflected aims, wishes and conjectures which already determined the debates on the correct formulation of Britain's 'national interests'; that is to say, events abroad were not viewed on their own merit.[70] It was

Oxford 1971, pp. 81–103, esp. pp. 95ff.; cf. G. Schmidt, *Der europäische Imperialismus*, München 1985; G. Schmidt, 'Britische Strategie und Außenpolitik. Wahlchancen und Determinanten britischer Sicherheitspolitik im Zeitalter der neuen Weltmächte 1897–1929', *MGM*, 9(1971), pp. 197–218.

69. Eden, 3 June 1937, Imperial Conference, FO 371–21 139; cf. Simon-Diary, 22 May 1938.

70. Seen in this context, it appears quite correct for M. Cowling to term the volumes in his series on British politics and policies in the age of 'mass culture': Impact of Labour – Impact of

only when German troops entered Prague in March 1939, thereby shattering the illusions which had characterised defence and armament policy debates in Britain over a long period, that the dispute as to how Britain should prepare herself to counter the Third Reich's aggressiveness was stripped of its concern with aspects that mattered only in a 'British' context. Public opinion tended to view Germany as having so far profited in her actions from the fact that she had been able to confront her opponents with risks which they were not prepared to take. Domestic political opinion was almost unanimously agreed that after 'Prague'[71] only one strategy was viable for opposing Hitler's power politics, which had effectively played on the 'mass psychology' of Western democracies. This strategy aimed to place German leaders under psychological pressure by establishing a countervailing power by means of rearmament *and* alliances, which was to deter any further *coups de main*.

Two related observations constitute the starting point for further analysis:

(1) British political circles in the 1930s had observed the precarious domestic political and, in particular, economic situation in Germany with special interest even before Hitler came to power. In the light of their observations, they posed the question as to whether German leaders would try to solve these problems by adapting a policy of a 'flight forward' and whether other countries, primarily Britain, might not, for as long as possible, be able to take the risk of assisting the 'moderates' in Germany with offers of negotiations (readiness to compromise).[72] Germany's rearmament provided the criterion for this peace strategy: Britain conceded that German rearmament was unavoidable; the important question was, however, whether it could be kept within limits which did not yet involve risks to the leading Western powers[73] or whether German rearmament, begun as an economic recovery measure,[74]

Hitler – Impact of Inflation (not yet published).

71. Gibbs, *Rearmament Policy*, pp. 647f.; J.A.S. Grenville, 'Contemporary Trends in the Study of the British Appeasement Policies of the 1930s', *Internationales Jahrbuch*, vol. 17 (1976), pp. 236–247, and M. Cowling, *Hitler*, pp. 301ff., and 379, suggest that N. Chamberlain because of this change became isolated even within his Cabinet.

72. On the 'Moderates–Extremists' topic see ch. I, 'Economic Appeasement'.

73. Air Staff-Memo., 'Rearmament of Germany: Proposed terms of limitation', 16 Jan. 1935, Cab. 21–417. Neville Chamberlain in particular stressed this device in the debates preceding Anglo-French negotiations, 1 to 3 Febr. 1935, in order to avoid that Britain had to adjust her rate of arms production according to any new information on Germany's output.

74. Baldwin, 28 Nov. 1934, Parl. Deb., House of Commons; Simon-Diary, 28 Nov. 1934.

would lead to structural change threatening an explosion in the foreseeable future. Should such a situation develop it would be necessary for Britain to resort to 'deficit spending' and to mobilise her industrial and manpower resources for an embryonic war economy which would essentially mean ruining the international financial standing so central to her prosperity.[75]

(2) The political actors in Britain – the government, the opposition, political circles, heads of associations and journalists – knew that Britain was affected as much as other countries by the basic tenet that, in times of international conflict, controversies in foreign policy would perforce turn into controversies in domestic policy. This was particularly so since the massed threat posed by Germany and Japan demanded a foreign policy which evidenced both a will and a capacity to use 'power' of all sorts. Since British policy did not have effective economic and ideological means of power at its disposal to counter German and Japanese threats, the armaments question acquired a central significance. With this, there automatically arose not only the problems of distribution of burdens and the priorities of public spending but also questions concerning the social and economic order. Linking the armaments question to problems of economic regulation, public procurement and spending priorities was bound to turn foreign affairs into a problem area affecting domestic politics as a whole. The diverging interests of large organised social groups (parties, associations, TUC, FBI) affected the controversies over international issues and the very nature of these disputes greatly curtailed the autonomy of foreign policy. Since government and opposition (before 1938–39) classified the financial and socio-political dangers connected with full-scale rearmament as a greater risk to Britain's 'security' than those dangers threatened by shifts in the international system, the power élites limited themselves to formulating those economic and socio-political interests and demands in the 'foreign policy' controversies which they regarded as being affected in different ways by the 'crises' with which Britain was confronted from abroad.

Armaments questions not only effected changes in the structure of the demands of and distribution between social groups and caused shifts in economic interests but also influenced the way in which these changes were perceived; they further conditioned

75. R.V.N. Hopkins, 'Note on the Financial Position', 15 July 1939, C.P. 149(39), Cab. 23–100; Simon, 14 March 1938, Cab. 23–92; Pownall-Diaries, vol. 1, pp. 76ff.. The problem of capital expenditure for defence purposes was on the agenda of the Cabinet and the CID since July 1935, see below.

the programmes of action which were derived from the changes with regard to the structure and function of the socio-political system, on the one hand, and foreign relations on the other. The proposals revealed the social roots of foreign and domestic policy strategies and thereby raised the question of how much stress the British political system could stand. Since armaments questions make specific 'security' policies necessary, they affect the economic structure, economic interests and the system's capability to cope with altered circumstances at home and abroad. In order to manage the various problems of adjusting manpower, industrial and financial resources to the requirements both of the domestic and the international situations, the government asked rather for the voluntary cooperation of the interests concerned. Hence not only ex-officio participants in the decision-making process join in the struggle over policy but also the attentive public, especially those pressure groups and debating circles relevant to foreign relations. For this very reason the debate on rearmament, designed to mobilise resources for specific foreign purposes, brings about increased politicisation and mobilisation. The issue at stake was how far the country at large (i.e. organised interests of all shades)[76] was willing to follow the government's lead in the 'security arena', acknowledging that in order to defend 'Britain's way of life' against the 'fascist' challenger, they had to comply with the government's 'rearmament' programme, whatever the differences with past and future policies.

The dominance of the armaments question in British politics after 1933–34 meant that the internal political system, with its characteristic tendencies towards 'consensus' and 'non-interference',[77] became the key factor in a foreign policy which was overshadowed by armaments policy.

The course and outcome of the domestic political debate on armaments policy was essentially determined by the fact that the Conservatives, who dominated the government, acknowledged the necessity of rearmament whilst at the same time distancing them-

---

76. I have also read a number of daily newspapers, periodicals, and printed material issued by political parties, associations, chambers of commerce, including letters to the editor in the local press, etc.; scanned the private papers of politicians and major industrialists; and interviewed ex-ministers, military personnel and higher civil servants. Only a very small part of the information derived from these efforts has found its way into the present book, but it has, of course, heavily influenced my understanding of the period and shaped the formulation of my questions and answers.

77. 'Search for agreement' (*innenpolitische Zustimmung*) refers to deliberations as to a 'fair' distribution of tax burdens to meet defence expenditure; 'commands at non-interference' refers to regards for industry's and labour's aversions towards control, conscription, etc.

selves from the position they had held prior to the First World War when they had advocated intervention in order to restore the European balance of power against Germany's drive for hegemony.[78] In the 1930s, 'left-wing' parties,[79] by contrast with their pre-1914 stance, presented themselves not only as supporters of the 'rule of law' but also as advocates of collective interventionism. They demanded that the government pursue a 'policy of strength' ('give a lead') and a policy of economic and if necessary military sanctions to deter and restrain aggressors. Yet they refused the government the means which were necessary if Britain as the leading power in the system of collective security was to pursue a strategy of 'power and strength'.[80] The fear that the National government might misuse the armed forces for imperialist policies was one pretext for refusing increases on armament expenditure; the second pretext was that Britain, as a leading naval power, contributed a central share towards collective security and thus did not need any massive rearmament. The misgivings of the Conservatives and their resultant hesitancy in the armaments question was influenced by the fear that a further war would deplete the resources that had underpinned the liberal state and the 'deferential' political culture in Britain.[81] At the level of tactics, their concern was compounded by the idea advocated by Hankey, Baldwin, Neville Chamberlain, Simon and others, that time was on Britain's side: 'It was hoped that, if war could be postponed, some new development might occur postponing it still further, and it was believed that Japan, by attacking in the Far East this year, while Germany was still unready in Europe, had weakened the German–Italian–Japanese bloc'.[82] This mentality of hoping always for the best was bound up with the missionary vision of Britain as an island of peace and a place of rational decision-making which had to pursue a cautious, wait-and-see approach. It was an approach based on the hope that even a

78. The stance of Conservatives in the 1930s has been termed a 'conservative blend of pacifism'; W. McElwee, *Britain's Locust Years*, London 1962, p. 228.

79. The notion 'pooled security' and the views on the foreign policies of the powers are summarised in Labour Party, Advisory Committee on International Questions, 'The Labour Party's Policy and the Service Estimates', Memo. 441A, Jan. 1934. Similar views were held by the League of Nations Union, the Next Five Years Group, and other centre-left movements.

80. H. Nicolson, *Why Britain is At War*, 1939, p. 129; Lord Percy of Newcastle, *Some Memoirs*, London 1958, p. 188. On the foreign policy of the Labour Party see S. Davis, 'The British Labour Party and British Foreign Policy 1931–1939', Ph.D., London School of Economics, 1950; J.F. Naylor, *Labour's International Policy. The Labour Party in the 1930s*, London 1969.

81. On this see ch. I and note 83/ch. 4 of German original.

82. All Souls Meeting, 19 Dec. 1937, morning session, Nicolson-Mss.

dictatorship would become more moderate – particularly if it could overcome the causes that had given rise to it (economic crises) and show successes in foreign policy (e.g. equal treatment).

The tactic of 'wait and see', which relied upon long-term effects, was designed not only to check the actual conflict but also to remove the root causes of a possible catastrophic confrontation.[83] This strategy implied a deliberate renunciation of any attempt to apply the standards of one's own system to other regimes to change or even overthrow them, at least as long as the dynamic of those systems did not openly lead towards world conflict. This indifference towards political systems based on different ideologies can be seen as a transfer into the sphere of foreign affairs of concepts developed from domestic political experience where a strategy of yielding to the 'legitimate grievances' advanced by the opponents of the status quo had helped to wear down criticism and had preserved the integrative capacity of the system as a whole. To that extent appeasement is an extension to foreign relations of domestic political strategies of self-preservation and the conservative 'national' regime in Britain constitutes an opposite pole to the aggressive power politics of the National Socialist regime.

The imminent formation of blocs among the members of the League of Nations, on the one hand, and the aggressive 'fascist' powers, on the other, induced the British government to keep the country out of this ideological confrontation. It wished to prevent the international cooperation of domestic political forces from prejudicing the necessary efforts to achieve a minimal consensus between government and opposition parties on the national interest. Direct or indirect collaboration of the Right[84] with Germany against the Left with France and Russia as protagonists of the *paix une et indivisible* theory of the League of Nations movement would limit Britain's room for manoeuvre in her security, armaments and foreign policy. In order to ward off this danger, the British governments of MacDonald and Baldwin followed the principle of denying the labour movement the chance of accusing the government of

83. N. Chamberlain, Simon, Eden and Hankey were influenced by the idea that economic bottlenecks and financial constraints were not only on their minds, but already did or would have some bearing on Hitler and his entourage; see my analysis of 'economic appeasement' and references in note 85 of German original.

84. Historical writings on the 1930s have not yet raised a whole range of important questions, e.g. the influence of the pro-German resp. pro-French 'Rights' in British politics or to the consequences of the view that 'Rightist' French governments were either prone to interference/preventive war or to collaboration with Germany (see note 86 of German original).

missing opportunities to secure peace and turning this into credible propaganda.[85] It was feared that otherwise 'revolutionary' agitation or – in reaction to it – a lurch to the Right could also occur in Britain.

In the context of British politics, the turn towards 'full-scale' rearmament passed for an admission that peace could now only be saved through power-politics:

> Rearmament will cost a terrible lot of money and will be a new stimulus to the opposition to turn the National government out. . .The loss of credit which the British government will suffer in the eyes of the public if there is no international agreement which can be called a disarmament convention will be something tremendous . . .I feel in my bones that we are digging the grave of the elder statesmanship if we can't do better than that [rearmament as the answer to international crises].[86]

The government saw itself confronted with the indictment that, even if it had not desired this development, it was at least partly caused by its inefficiency. Thus it could only expect agreement on armaments projects[87] if rearmament was paralleled by public efforts to achieve détente: 'In the event of the British Government agreeing to take the initiative outlined above [peaceful revision, etc.] no opposition need to be offered to the policy of the government during this transitional period'.[88] Besides, the slow recovery from the world economic crisis – accompanied by orthodox economic views which ruled out public works and public borrowing for rearmament and thus accentuated the question of covering the costs through increased taxation – together with permanent structural unemployment made the cabinet cautious about using dangers abroad as grounds for forced rearmament.[89] Whilst at the

85. Simon-Diary, 21 March 1935; cf. F.S. Northedge, *The Troubled Giant. Britain among the Great Powers 1916–1939*, New York 1966, pp. 385ff.

86. Simon, 23 Dec. 1933, Baldwin-Mss., vol. 121, p. 132. This statement tries to rebut Labour's charges; the best example is Attlee's speech on the 1935 White Paper on Defence, Parl. Deb., ser. 5, vol. 299, col. 46: 'This policy of the old men, this moving backwards to an anarchic world brought us to the war of 1914–1918, and will bring us to a far more terrible war unless the policy is entirely changed'.

87. Hankey to R. MacDonald, 14 Jan. 1935, Cab. 21–422 A.

88. Next Five Years' Group, 'Programme of Priorities', §5 International relations. Th. Jones, Lothian, Leeper pressed these views on Baldwin, Eden. Foreign Office-Meeting, 14 Febr. 1936, C 998/4/18, FO 371–19 885, p. 236; Eden, 5 Febr. 1936, Cab. 23–83, p. 58; Nicolson-Diary, 13 Febr. 1936, p. 236.

89. Aspects of electioneering were involved, both in the minds of Baldwin and the leaders of the Opposition and in actual fact (see notes 91–93 of German original); Hankey, 'Disarmament and Rearmament', Cab. 21–34, p. 13; D.C.M. (32), 55th meeting.

beginning the British government could excuse Germany's rearmament as an attempt to stimulate her domestic economy, it had good reason to refrain from justifying its own rearmament as a measure of economic expansion.[90] Even the argument that Britain's 'deficiencies' could not remain concealed from the other powers or that British trade relations and prospects for diplomatic negotiations would worsen if she were seen as a nation without power and influence,[91] did not help to boost the rearmament campaign. The politicians were hoping for peace ('in our time') too much to think of playing on the argument that armaments orders mean employment; they would rather keep the Defence Services in short supply in order to make sure that armaments could win back her discretion and scope of action in foreign policy only by eliminating the 'deficiencies' in her weapon arsenal and in the productive capacity of her armaments industry.[92]

Against these arguments, which were based on domestic and economic considerations, the military, supported by top civil servants at the Foreign Office, championed the theory that Britain could win back her discretion and scope of action in foreign policy only by eliminating the 'deficiencies' in her weapon arsenal and in the productive capacity of her armaments industry.[92]

British policy was, therefore, confronted with the following conflict of objectives. The increasing frequency of international crises called for a forced expansion of defence potential to protect Britain's interest in a global balance of power which was threatened by Japan, Italy and the Third Reich (it is important to note in this context that these actual aggressions occurred in the sequence

90. Simon, Diary, 28 Nov. 1934; Baldwin, 28 Nov. 1934, Parl. Deb., HofC; Baldwin to Defence Deputation, 29 July 1936, Cab. 21–438; Baldwin, 12 Nov. 1936, Parl. Deb., HofC, ser. 5, vol. 317, col. 1133ff.; Middlemas/Barnes, *Baldwin*, pp. 745ff., 969ff. N. Chamberlain thought in terms of increasing expenditure on armaments by about £120 million (to be spent in four to five years) with a view to reducing unemployment (N. Chamberlain, Diary, 2 August 1935, NC 2–23A) but the election platform put the emphasis on trade and exports. From 1936/37 onwards and especially with the recession of 1937/38 government propaganda linked rearmament and employment. Shipbuilding orders were always styled as providing work to derelict areas. In economic terms, 'rearmament' carried the recovery into 1936/37. Nonetheless, this evidence should not blind us to the fact that the Government did not embark on rearmament as an instrument of stimulating growth.

91. Hankey, 'Disarmament and Rearmament', p. 9, Cab. 21–434; D.C.M. (32), 51st Meeting.

92. Vansittart's comment on Hankey's draft of the Statement relating to Defence, 3 Jan. 1935, Cab. 21–407, re §§15ff. and 26–28. These views were pronounced by Simon, Eden, N. Chamberlain; see N. Chamberlain to Simon, 23 Sept. 1936, Simon-Mss.; but in fact Chamberlain and later Simon had a hand in cutting the proposals of the Defence Requirements Committee and its follow-up bodies.

listed). The domestic political circumstances, however, demanded a circumspect security, armaments and foreign policy:[93] 'In my draft I have begun by pitching it rather high about our peace policy, which I describe as our first line of defence . . . I am nervous lest we should irretrievably damage the prospects of the National Government by going too fast on this question [rearmament]'.[94] Against the background of a structural economic crisis and the ensuing social distress, every acceleration of rearmament threatened a polarisation of society.[95] In the political scenario of 1934–37 not only the left-wing Opposition but also influential Conservative fringe groups were using mass-circulation newspapers to proclaim that the dictum 'Watch on the Tyne' – the symbol of unemployment and structural economic crisis – was more important than the 'Watch on the Rhine' (*Wacht am Rhein*), which, in Baldwin's words, was the new front line of Britain's defence policy, having had to be moved to this point because of improvements in weapon technology. The strained domestic political situation thus called into question the very relation of means to ends which primarily had to be used to justify rearmament. Enforced armaments policy appeared to be synonymous with a latent self-blockade of the British socio-political system. The benefit which it was hoped rearmament would bring – freedom of manoeuvre as a global power – was called into question by considerations relating to domestic circumstances. Britain's political leadership opted for a gradual expansion of armaments, orientated at domestic political considerations rather than for the proposals of the committees in which the military and leading Foreign Office figures were dominant: 'But its [Interim Report] contents will be hair-raising to ministers – in fact it suggests we should be ready for war by 1 January 1939 instead of 1942 and say that we can't do it out of income – obviously – and must proceed to a loan. With the election coming on next winter they'll hate this talk'.[96]

The community of interest between the Foreign Office and the military, however, turned out to be fragile. The discrepancy between existing instruments of deterrence and the deterioration of the international situation – evident from 1936 onwards – produced further a conflict of objectives. The military advisers (chiefs of

93. For references to the 'no more war'-mood, on trade revival and peace-slogans and their impact on politicians see notes 98–100 of German original.

94. Hankey to W. Fisher, 10 Jan. 1935, Cab. 21–407.

95. This is what the notion of 'labour' is all about; Baldwin, Inskip, N. Chamberlain, K. Wood et al. based their defence policy views on these assumptions. On Baldwin see notes 87, 98–100 of German original, on N. Chamberlain's NDC-project see below.

96. Pownall-Diaries, 22 July 1935, vol. 1, p. 76.

staff) put forward principles which were at odds with the operational concepts of the Foreign Office. Whilst between 1936 and 1938 the chiefs of staff argued increasingly for keeping the road to détente with Germany open, the Foreign Office pursued an initiative to compensate for the deficiencies in the defence preparations and strengthening the trust between Britain and her French partner through Staff talks, exchanges of information and specific armaments measures. Prior to the Anschluss crisis the chiefs of staff's argument, which tended towards 'appeasement' and was influenced by their mistrust of France, was a decisive factor in British foreign policy.[97]

1. Variations of the Risk Theory[98]

The decision against forced rearmament highlights the fact that the views which were dominant at the introduction of the Ten Years' Rule remained important even under the altered international circumstances of the 1930s. Whilst the Ten Years' Rule as such was annulled in 1932, with effect from 1934, and attempts were made to repair the damage it inflicted, both the primacy of 'economic recovery' – firstly from the effects of the First World War during the 1920s and then from the effects of the World Depression in the 1930s – and even more the policy of gestures and the psychological appeasement strategies at home, still retained their importance. Rearmament (until March 1938) was limited by the precept that the future of the economy must not be impaired by directing resources (capital and workforce) to sectors where concentration would only lead to accumulating 'overcapacities' instead of restoring growth in leading sectors; this was the meaning of the formula 'business as usual'.[99] On account of this regard to the structure of British industry and to conditions of sustained growth the government's guideline of July 1935[100] was never fully implemented. This guideline had pronounced that the Defence

97. Gibbs, *Rearmament Policy*, p. 628; D. Dilks, *Unnecessary War*, pp. 118–121; Howard, *Commitment*, pp. 94ff., 116f.; P. Dennis, *Decision*, pp. 116ff.
98. See my definition of the notion 'labour'.
99. Inskip, 11 Nov. 1936, Parl. Deb., HofC; Simon-Diary, 24 March 1938; cf. Gibbs, *Rearmament Policy*, pp. 301ff.; R. Meyers, *Britische Sicherheitspolitik 1934–1938. Studien zum außen- und sicherheitspolitischen Entscheidungsprozeß*, Düsseldorf 1976, ch. 5.3
100. DRC 25, 24 July 1935, Cab. 16–112; Pownall-Diaries, vol. 1, pp. 70–77; R.P. Shay, *British Rearmament in the Thirties: Politics and Profits*, Princeton 1977, pp. 55ff.; W.K. Hancock, M.M. Gowing, *British War Economy*, London 1949, pp. 62f., 68, 70.

Requirements Committee could assume that, compared with the urgency of obtaining security as soon as possible, financial considerations were of secondary importance. 'Security policy' was still subject to the directive that Britain could rather afford to take risks over the defence issue than run the risk of dividing the country along class lines. This maxim put into practice the crucial lesson drawn from political experience since the turn of the century; namely, that trade unions had learnt how to exert pressure through industrial action in key industries (mining, railways, shipping). Governments in any case preferred 'willing co-operation' to 'industrial conscription' but hesitated in enforcing accelerated rearmament because they feared granting concessions to labour in related-issue areas. In the 1930s, by contrast with the periods 1912–14 or 1918–20, trade unions did not adopt a totally oppositional role towards the government. They did, however, harbour deep-rooted mistrust towards national rearmament in general – because of the danger of 'industrial conscription', 'dilution' – and towards Conservative-National governments in particular, following the debacle of the 1926 General Strike and the myths surrounding the collapse of the second Labour government and the founding of the National government in 1931. Against this backdrop, the rearmament campaign, justified on foreign-policy grounds, seemed risky even when individual, influential union leaders (Bevin and Citrine) made it known that, in their opinion, 'collective security' demanded considerable efforts for rearmament in Britain, regardless of which government was in power. This degree of agreement on the principle of 'real' rearmament, however, meant that neither the conflict over the correct course of British foreign policy nor the dispute over the prerequisites and accompanying circumstances[101] of the rearmament process – namely, the mobilisation of the workforce (industrial conscription) and general military conscription – were settled conclusively.[102] Baldwin's pledge when introducing the Statement relating to defence in March 1936, that the government would never introduce conscription in peacetime,[103] was meant to allay misgivings at the start of the process of

101 The unions made public statements on their demands, which clearly went beyond the realm of industrial relations; they asked especially for conscription of wealth, for nationalisation (of the Bank of England and heavy industries) and for close relations with the Soviet Union.

102. On the problems of 'rationing' skilled labour see DRC, 3rd Report, 21 Nov. 1935, C.P. 26(36), Cab. 24–259; C.P. 57(36); Cabinet Minutes 10(36); Brown-Memo., 'Defence Programme: Labour Issues Involved', 26 March 1936, C.P. 96(36), Cab. 24–261 and Cab. Minutes 25(36)1, Cab. 23–83; Committee on Man-power, Cab. 21–433; on Swinton's views see Middlemas, Barnes, *Baldwin*, pp. 1025ff.; on the disputes between the War Office and the Ministry of Labour see Dennis, *Decision*, pp. 77ff.

103. Baldwin, 1 April 1936, Parl. Deb., HofC, ser. 5, vol. 310, col. 1992; Statement relating

'real' rearmament. To Baldwin, Neville Chamberlain, Weir and Brown (Ministry of Labour), industrial peace was an essential prerequisite to any progress in rearmament.

The Treasury's efforts to prevent profiteering by offering armaments firms target prices (i.e. allowing for basic costs plus a fixed profit) and distributing the burdens of expenditure on armaments according to the principle of 'equality of sacrifice' served the same purpose, although, in practice, firms, particularly in the aircraft industry,[104] managed to circumvent these limits. The government's (i.e. the Treasury's) attempt to limit profits in those industries awarded armaments orders[105] was primarily undertaken so as to pre-empt the demand for a 'conscription of wealth' and deny the working class in case of 'legitimate grievance' to ask for higher wages by striking or threatening to strike. Mindful of the experience of the First World War the government itself was always aware that actions aimed at securing 'dilution might well lead to serious labour unrest and concessions to labour [were] apt to damage the position of the export trade'.[106]

In order to avoid the development towards a command economy and an 'industrial' policy geared towards armament production, the government aimed at balancing social and economic aspects in the handling of its armaments policy. To this end it attempted firstly to deter those industries and companies vital for the implementation of the armaments programmes from exploiting the situation by threatening business organisations and captains of industry which firmly believed in industrial self-government with 'control'. Secondly, in order to placate labour, it approached the problem from the opposite end by warning industry against any provocative price rises which would spark off the 'spiral of inflation'. By anticipating the fears of industry and labour ('control' or 'dilution' and 'conscription', respectively) and by restricting the rate of armaments production, the government tried to avoid the need for political negotiations; that is, the granting of participatory rights.

---

to Defence, Cmd. 5107(1936), §49, p. 16; cf. Shay, *Rearmament*, pp. 272ff.; Gibbs, pp. 310ff.; Dennis, *Decision*, pp. 71ff.

104. Statement Relating to Defence, Cmd. 5107, §59, 61. On 'profiteering' see the controversy between Shay, pp. 272ff., and Peden, *Treasury*; M.M. Postan, *War Production*, pp. 43ff. The different views inside the Government and the Conservative Party on this issue were expressed on occasion of the Defence Deputation, 28 and 29 July 1936, Cab. 21–438 (for details see note 109 of German original).

105. Statement, 13 May 1937, T 172–1856; cf. N. Chamberlain, 25 April 1937, quoted in K. Feiling, *Life*, p. 292. These statements are the *locus classicus* of the notion of the inflation spiral.

106. Inskip, 30 Oct. 1936, C.P. 297(36), Cab. 24–265.

To avoid the dangers of 'power-sharing', the government employed strategies of persuasion. To the same end it offered an assurance to employers that 'control' would not be implemented as long as industry complied with its own undertaking to fulfil government orders cooperatively and to set up an efficient armaments production. The government conducted business negotiations with individual firms (the car industry), with leading organisations within specific industries (aircraft construction) and with the Federation of British Industries[107] relating to issues such as the supply of skilled labour, armaments orders for regions hit by unemployment, profit levels, and so on. Somewhat late in the day,[108] in fact only in the spring of 1938,[109] the government entered negotiations with the trades unions on limited wage increases as compensation for an agreement on the organised reallocation of manpower. In its initial talks with the Federation of British Industries and the trade unions in October 1935, the government, however, concentrated on allaying fears on both sides concerning a regulatory economic policy in order to increase their readiness to cooperate.

In the case of organised labour, the close organisational links between party and trade union movement[110] and the Opposition parties' (!) attitude to the National government in general and to armaments policy in particular, provided the government with an excuse for pursuing an indirect approach; that is, for pretending that labour's 'interests' would be considered on account of government's commitment to avoid 'another 1931' and 'another 1917–18'. The general directive on averting the danger of taking risks on domestic issues was thought to signify a genuine approach to labour's legitimate grievances (i.e. pretend that the government took care of labour's interest); this line of argument necessitated no direct exchanges of opinion or negotiations between the government and the TUC (before March 1938). The argument that an invitation to talks between the government and the trade

---

107. See part 6 of this chapter.

108. Baldwin's preliminary talks with Citrine and Hicks (13 Sept. 1935) had no follow-up; on the reaction of Bevin and on Baldwin's reasoning after the 1935 election see A. Bullock, *The Life and Times of Ernest Bevin*, vol. 1, London 1960; Lord Citrine, *Men and Work*, London 1964, pp. 352ff.; A.W. Baldwin, *My Father. The True Story*, London 1955, pp. 344ff.; Baldwin's reply to the Defence Deputation, 29 July 1936, Cab. 21–438 (see notes 113–114 of German original).

109. Shay, *Rearmament*, pp. 207ff.; K. Middlemas, *Politics in Industrial Society*, London 1979, pp. 216ff.

110. Naylor, *Labour's International Policy*, pp. 150ff.; C.F. Brand, *The British Labour Party – A Short History*, Stanford 1965, pp. 198ff. Davis stresses the aspect of the unions' fighting against 'bolshevic' attempts at penetrating these organisations at home and against 'fascism' abroad; this was an aspect that appealed to Baldwin when he met Citrine and Hicks.

unions would have signalled an emergency and that the public would have become alarmed by the international situation threw a screen around its decision to make it possible to implement the armaments policy by way of 'gestures' and other ways of heading off those whose interests were involved. Had it come to official negotiations, the government would also have had to reckon with the trade unions demanding foreign policy concessions. Possible concessions in the event that the trade unions were asked to support industrial mobilisation[111] were no secret; they were clearly stated and made public at TUC conferences, at the annual conferences of individual unions and in meetings with representatives of the government: they included efforts to secure an agreement on arms limitation and on an Air Pact and, above all, to improve relations with the Soviet Union.

During the 1920s the maxim according to which an external threat was to be tolerated in preference to internal dangers, had served to relieve debates on how to rid the country of debts incurred in the First World War from the burden of a polemic which held that arms expenditure always lent itself to the same end – that of class politics. In the 1930s, the same maxim caused dubious risks to be taken in foreign policy. The successful implementation of the 'risk theory' in the 1930s required a strategy of creating a democratic consensus in the face of differently motivated and articulated opposition from the Labour Party and the trade unions, and also from business organisations, the peace movements and those 'derelict areas' dependent on armaments orders. This meant primarily that the government had to take trends in public opinion into account and try to borrow those slogans from the main opposition (Labour) which struck a chord with the electorate. Stealing a march on the Labour Party and the League of Nations movement in the Abyssinian Crisis, the National government, which had always rejected 'irrevocable decisions' on the Franco-German problem, maintaining that an intervention, though permitted under the terms of the League of Nations and Locarno Treaties, would disrupt the implementation of the armament programmes,[112] even went so far as to throw the warnings of the chiefs of staff and the armed-service departments overboard. Con-

111. Cabinet meeting 4 Dec. 1935, Cab. 51(35)3, Cab. 23–82, pp. 363ff.
112. It is essential to keep in mind that 1936 was in any case regarded as the critical year in the process of rearmament, since it was then that the passing from 're-equipment' to 'rearmament' was due, the Japanese would gain an advantage, etc. This subject is dealt with in ch. 1 of German original.

sequently, the chiefs of staff reacted to the imminent threat from Germany by maintaining that Britain could not afford military action unless measures taken during the Abyssinian Crisis were withdrawn.[113] In other words, whilst in the 'German question' public opinion and the level of rearmament restricted actions, Italian aggression led to pressures of public opinion going in a totally wrong direction from the point of view of military strategy and armaments policy.[114]

Baldwin's manoeuvre has often been labelled a trick to win the 1935 General Election by professing to favour a system of collective security. This move was initially supplemented by the cabinet's change of mind towards sanctions (2 December 1935) but then unmasked as make-believe by the Hoare–Laval Pact. It was also a prelude to those actions taken at the end of February 1936 when the prime minister, Stanley Baldwin, and the foreign secretary, Anthony Eden, in the cabinet staked everything on an intensification of sanctions against Italy with a view to compensating, on the one hand, for the blow of December 1935 and, on the other, creating a favourable climate for the publication of the Statement on Defence. Baldwin, only too conscious that his position had been badly affected and that the next election would be fought under the spell of the 'confidence trick', openly advocated in the cabinet on 26 February 1936 that Eden should become active in Geneva.[115] Europe should know whether economic sanctions worked and whether the European nations were prepared to cooperate in a system of collective security. Only if the government could prevent reports from Geneva saying that Britain had given way under pressure from the French could the armaments programme be set in motion. Without labour (i.e. without the unions), it would be impossible to realise the programme; however, labour demanded sanctions against Italy. Baldwin added a statement characteristic of British foreign policy in relation to the German question: thanks to labour's cooperation Britain would have nothing to fear in three to five years time; that is to say, the target years of the armaments policy. It was felt that France should accept this fact as her best security and, for the time being, refrain

113. COS 442, 12 March 1936; it was on the Cabinet's agenda on 18 March 1936, and again on 29 April 1936, Cab. 23–84; for details see Gibbs, *Rearmament*, pp. 218ff., and A. Marder, 'The Royal Navy and the Ethiopian Crisis of 1935–36', AHR, 75/5 (1970), pp. 1327–1356.

114. Cabinet Meetings of 29 April and 11 May 1936, Cab. 23–84, and Cab. 21–436.

115. Baldwin, 26 Febr. 1936, Cab.23–83 (for more details, see note 121 of German original).

from demanding any British declaration that she would honour the obligations of Locarno.[116] It is quite another matter whether the Baldwin government really worked to achieve labour's consent to national defence and to reassure France to the extent that France could afford to abandon the need for retaining her traditional options.

Baldwin's argument illustrates the thesis that Britain could afford to take risks in her foreign policy rather than risk a conflict with labour, which would restrict her room for manoeuvre. The primacy of domestic 'appeasement' tactics and the inherent assumption that such a course would automatically benefit France's security led to serious complications in her relationship with that country. According to Baldwin's and Eden's calculations, Britain was expected to take the initiative in the League of Nations to thwart France's efforts to end the dispute with Italy, who was the second guaranteeing power of the Locarno Pact and who could act as a bulwark against the *Anschluss* of Austria to the German Reich. The planned initiative,[117] which would definitely split the Locarno powers and alienate Italy from Britain, was generally interpreted as giving Hitler the go-ahead to attack the Locarno Pact. However, the British quest for sanctions against Italy never got off the ground because Flandin's hint of an imminent coup in the Rhineland changed the terms of debate between the Allies and within the British government.

The fact that Baldwin declared his support for collective security as a concession to public opinion, with the aim of improving the chances for the adoption of the Five-Year Armament Programme, plays a decisive role in my interpretation of British foreign policy. In practice the government allowed for the foreign policy risk, and whilst a great deal of fuss was made about the Italian affair, it remained silent on threats facing the Locarno security system, thereby playing into Germany's hands.[118] The government did, however, try to avoid exposing its armaments policy to criticisms; thus it did not for example explicitly refer to the German threat as a justification for the armaments programme but to the world-wide

116. Baldwin, ibid.; Baldwin, 5 and 9 March 1936, Cab. 23–83; cf. O'Malley (FO), 24 Febr. 1936, C 1028/14/18, FO 371–19 885, pp. 321ff.; Middlemas, Barnes, *Baldwin*, pp. 814, 918.
117. Emmerson, *Rhineland Crisis*, pp. 54f.; Earl of Avon, *Facing the Dictators*, pp. 337ff.
118. The Cabinet Committee on Germany and the Foreign Office 'laboured' with working agreement-offers to Germany in order to prevent the Locarno Crisis, and attempted to calm down the press; the agitation against Italy, especially in the press and on the 'left' (League of Nations Union, Labour Party), which was engendered by reports on gas bombing in Ethiopia, carried the Government and impaired British relations with France during the March 1936–Crisis.

build up of arms production, whilst stressing the connection between the expansion of armaments and the task of the collective
defence of peace as it had done during the election campaign in
spite of Italy calling the British government's bluff where its drive
to 'give the lead' was concerned.

In order to circumvent the dilemma of rearmament, influential
circles in the government took refuge in the first stages of armaments debates, in the concept of collective security.[119] Parallel
with this manoeuvre, a bid was made to rescue the disarmament
conference[120] and/or to bring about a minimum consensus between Germany and France on arms limitation.[121] Behind these
efforts lay the unmistakable aim of lessening the strain on the
domestic political front.[122] MacDonald and Neville Chamberlain in
particular steered the debate towards discussions of whether some
sort of arrangement under the heading of 'collective security' or of
mutual guarantees within the framework of regional security
agreements could help to reduce Britain's financial obligation.
Consideration was given to whether it would be cheaper[123] to
agree on security schemes with other powers (France) – for
example concerning Belgium – thus entering into political commitments, than to adopt as the basis of security and armaments
policies the recommendations of the (Hankey) Defence Requirements Committee, which were modelled on a national–imperial
strategy; the latter option would cost approximately an extra
£76,000 over five years.[124] Chamberlain's and MacDonald's[125]
calculations differentiated between specific agreements (e.g. with

119. Thomas, 19 March 1934, Cab. 23–78, p. 290, and 3 May 1934, Ministerial Committee
on Defence Requirements. Thomas refused to think of any continental commitment and any
idea of an Expeditionary Force. The CID introduced the notion 'Field Force' with a view to
counteracting the bad moral effect of the BEF–CID, 266th meeting, 22 Nov. 1934, Cab. 2–6/1.

120. K. Wood, 19 March 1934, Cab. 23–78, p. 290; Steel-Maitland, 28 March 1934, Central
Council Minutes, National Union of Conservative and National Associations (for details see
note 127 of German original).

121. R. MacDonald, 19 March 1934, Cab. 23–78, p. 291.

122. A series of by-elections, the Peace Ballot campaign and the terms of debate in the press
reminded the Government of the priority to restore cuts in social policy as a first charge on its
agenda.

123. N. Chamberlain, Diary, 3 Febr. 1935, NC 2–22, reports on a meeting with Flandin (on
the dangers of disorderly devaluation by the Gold bloc), in which he raised his ideas on a 'limited
liability scheme of international police force'.

124. Cab. 21–406; cf. Gibbs, pp. 110ff.; Peden, *Treasury*, pp. 68f.

125. N. Chamberlain and R. MacDonald agreed on the principles of rationing and coordination in defence expenditures, but differed in their preferences for the RAF (Chamberlain) and
the Navy (MacDonald); N. Chamberlain–R. MacDonald, 19 March 1934, Cab. 23–78; Hankey
to MacDonald, 6 March 1934, PREM. I–153; Cab. 21–384; D. Marquand, *Ramsey MacDonald*,
London 1977, p. 760; Meyers, *Sicherheitspolitik*, pp. 211ff.

France and central Eastern Europe), which were regarded as an 'overcommitment', and 'general security schemes'. Neville Chamberlain felt that obligations towards allies were too demanding; for him unilateral declarations guaranteeing the 'status' of specific countries in important areas (e.g. Belgium)[126] or participation in international forces,[127] conditional on and as an adjunct to arms limitation conventions, deserved to take precedence:

> If we could only get security by material guarantees it might be found that our share of some general scheme came to less than the figures suggested in this report.

> Some commitments were unavoidable whatever our policy, but we might find a security commitment the less expensive of the two.[128]

The mistrust of France[129] and the collective aversion of the cabinet towards any return to the formation of 'blocs' and encirclement, together with other circumstances,[130] meant that those advocating an armaments policy centred on vital British interests had a stronger influence on the decision-making process[131] than the Foreign Office, which recommended linking rearmament and joint consultation with France, the chancellor (Neville Chamberlain), or the prime minister (MacDonald) with their occasional experiments with collective security schemes.

The maxim that taking risks over domestic issues presented a greater threat than the danger of 'unpreparedness' in the defence arena was applied in a second area, namely that of finance,[132]

126. N. Chamberlain, 19 March 1934, Cab. 23–78, pp. 284, 289, 291; Feiling, *Life*, pp. 251ff.; Simon to MacDonald, 11 July 1934, and Simon-Diary, 11 July 1934, Simon-Mss.; Marquand, *MacDonald*, pp. 758f.; Dennis, *Decision*, pp. 40ff.

127. N. Chamberlain-Diary, 3 Febr. 1935, NC 2–22.

128. N. Chamberlain, March 1934, Cab. 23–78.

129. Baldwin warned against the tendency to deny France her claims for guarantees as an essential element of an arms convention, 19 March 1934, Cab. 23–78.

130. The *Röhmputsch*, for instance, served as an argument that the military had asserted their influence and that they would use that influence to calm down German foreign policy. It was this among other things which prevented N. Chamberlain from getting a decision on his Belgium scheme.

131. Cabinet meeting, 22 March 1934, Cab. 23–78, p. 332; cf. Gibbs, pp. 615ff. Some Cabinet Ministers offered the idea that by granting Germany 'limited rearmament', French pressures to meet Germany's violations of Treaties jointly could be undermined.

132. S. Howson, *Monetary Management*, p. 120; Hancock, Gowing, *War Economy*, p. 63. Readers are reminded that 'finance' forms part of the 'labour'-notion; henceforth, 'finance' is not to be seen simply as a problem of raising revenue and deciding on priorities of public spending, but is imbued with the socio-political processes of sharing out/distributing 'material means' as well as chances of participating in decision-making.

where it was received with considerable approbation. The problem of finance was twofold:

(1) As long as the Treasury maintained the principle that each generation must be prepared to pay off the debts they accrued in their lifetime[133] – that is, that armaments expenditure should be met through taxation (since most of it, by its very nature, produced no monetary return) – it was a matter of apportioning the share of contributions from direct and indirect tax sources 'fairly'. This conflict affected both the Labour Party and the trade unions as representatives both of their own and 'consumers' ' interests, and the Conservatives, representing not only those classes hit by increased inheritance and estate taxes but also industrial and financial circles, which were to redirect part of their income derived from the armament economy back into the state coffers through a National Defence Contribution.[134]

(2) As soon as it became clear that Britain could not compete successfully in the arms race on a 'balanced-budget' basis with competitors who engaged in conscious deficit spending, Britain also had to have recourse to public borrowing. The increase in the National Debt, however, gave rise to fears of inflation,[135] with all its adverse socio-political implications. The coalition government's view was that inflation in the 1930s to an even greater extent than during the war and postwar inflation (1916–20) was – to paraphrase Lenin's words – the grave-digger of the 'bourgeois capitalist' social and economic order. This was so not because of the consequences for those living on fixed incomes (pensioners, civil servants) but rather because of the causal link between rising prices and 'profiteering', on the one hand, and between a rising cost of living and legitimate action by workers for higher wages on the other.[136] 'Inflation' was considered as much of a threat to the social order as unemployment. The 'injustices' caused by both inflation and unemployment would arouse protest movements which would inevitably be directed against the system and thus erode the basis on which

133. D.C.M. (32), 25 June 1934, 50th meeting, Cab. 16–110; cf. Shay, *Rearmament*, p. 42; Gibbs, pp. 178ff.

134. On Chamberlain's National Defence Contribution (NDC)-project see Shay, pp. 147ff.; Feiling, *Life*, pp. 292ff; Meyers, *Sicherheitspolitik*, pp. 211ff.

135. The relationship between rearmament and inflation is analysed by H.W. Richardson, *Economic Recovery*, pp. 284ff., 233, 55. The repercussions on foreign trade, balance of payments, stability of the £ were part of the standard arguments of N. Chamberlain, Inskip, Baldwin, Simon against Britain joining an arms race. The gist of the argument is in Phillipps' Memo., 31 Dec. 1936, T 175–94 (quotations in Howson, pp. 122ff).

136. N. Chamberlain to Hilda, 25 April 1937, NC 18/1/1003; cf. Feiling, *Life*, p. 292.

reform politics ('Liberal socialism', 'Tory democracy') could thrive. In other words, every government, except a government of the party of the working class would be seen as unrepresentative and forfeit its claim to be capable of governing. Borrowing for defence purposes might thus fuel inflation and threaten the socio-political fabric before the country was directly attacked by Germany: 'We are rapidly drifting into chaos and are in danger of undermining ourselves before the Boche feels it desirable to move'.[137] The need to break the deadlock from time to time by attempts at 'social appeasement' was stressed on many occasions:

> All the elements of danger are here . . . (increasing cost of living . . .a genuine feeling that things are not shared out) and I can see that we might easily run, in no time, into a series of crippling strikes . . . I don't say that N[ational] D[efence] C[ontribution] will prevent all this, but I feel sure that it enormously diminishes the danger. It will make the workmen feel that this government is not in league with their employers to 'soak' them while running off with enormous profits themselves . . . Industrial unrest is only just round the corner . . .but this [i.e. NDC] may help and keep it there.[138]

The National government, therefore, tried to keep rearmament within the limits defined by the first problem area. The government could rely on mobilising enough support for its rearmament programme and for the necessary increases in taxation by spreading the burden of tax in a balanced way.[139] Whilst the government (Treasury) could hope to maintain control over this part of the process, it feared that the inflationary spiral set in motion by a substantial 'defence loan' would lead from one measure of 'control' to another and eventually to an undesirable centrally planned economy.

Before the Treasury saw itself confronted with these problems, it had taken the opportunity in the preceding phase of the armaments debate of pushing back the limits of what could be 'allowed for' even further. Neville Chamberlain and the Treasury supported the argument that Britain must, for the time being, tolerate 'dangers of unpreparedness' until the country had had the time and opportunity 'to recuperate and improve its financial situation'.[140]

137. W. Fisher, 1 June 1937, T 161–783, F 48431/02/1; cf. N. Chamberlain, *Diary*, 25 Oct. 1936; cf. Peden, *Treasury*, pp. 80ff.
138. N. Chamberlain to Hilda, 25 April 1937, NC 18/1/1003.
139. B.E.V. Sabine, *British Budgets in Peace and War, 1932–1945*, London 1970, provides a fair summary of the facts and arguments put forward in the debates on the Estimates.
140. N. Chamberlain, 15 Febr. 1933, Cab. 23–75.

By complying with this policy statement the government in fact (for all practical purposes) reaffirmed the lines of reasoning which had held sway on the eve of the Ten Years' Rule, between 1932–33 and 1935–36.[141] In the decisions taken on the defence requirements for 1934–35, which went a long way to meeting the targets first established during the 1920s for the peacetime strength of the three armed forces, the Treasury introduced the proviso that neither the chancellor of the exchequer nor his successor could be bound 'to find the additional sums mentioned in this Report within five years or in the particular years to which they are allotted'.[142]

Later on, when it came to 'real' rearmament, the Treasury used its powerful position within the decision-making process to enforce its version of cost–benefit evaluation. Despite the warning that if the Treasury's recommendation of cuts in the Defence Requirement Committee's estimate from £40 million to £20 million (spread over five years) were enforced,[143] the Army would be totally incapable of serious military action before 1938, the Treasury made sure that the allocation of financial and economic resources favoured the RAF; in effect, the Treasury rejected the aspect of 'continental commitments' and paved the way for the triumph of the doctrine of 'limited liability'.[144] Neville Chamberlain successfully supported his objection that the country simply could not afford an extensive preparation for international crises[145] by asserting that public opinion was in no mood to accept 'full-scale' rearmament schedules. In his criticisms of the armed services' plans and of the recommendations of the Defence Requirements Committee, the chancellor of the exchequer stressed that the government should avoid offending public opinion and offered his own ideas on how to reformulate plans for security in a way acceptable to the country. He warned the cabinet that if it decided

141. The Government used figures comparing the shares of defence to national expenditure in the early 1930s to 1913/14 as evidence that the charges of the Opposition against its 'war-mongering' were irrelevant. On the development of expenditure on defence see H.W. Richardson, *Economic Recovery*, p. 215.

142. Cabinet meeting, 18 July 1934, Cab. 29(34)5, Cab. 23–79, p. 311; Cabinet meeting, 31 July 1934, and C.P. 205(34), §50, Cab. 23–79.

143. The figures are increases on the regular estimates; for details see Gibbs, ch. 4; Roskill, *Hankey*, vol. 3, pp. 107ff.

144. Cabinet meeting, 31 July 1934, Cab. 23–79, pp. 357, 359. The total increases of £76,8 mill. (according to the DRC-Report) were cut to £50,3 mill.; the largest reduction affected the Army. On the 'New Standard' programme of the Royal Navy see Peden, pp. 113ff., Shay, pp. 82ff., and Gibbs, pp. 285ff., 318ff., 378ff.

145. Gibbs, p. 125.

to work for the 'balanced' programme of the Hankey Committee against the Treasury's advice, then it would have to renounce promised tax cuts; even if the state of the armed forces and the international situation were explained to the electorate,[146] there was no doubt in Chamberlain's mind that the government would be voted out. On the face of it this was a powerful argument in favour of prolonging the process of 're-equipment' rather than launching rearmament.

The financial provisos imposed a constraint on British rearmament but did not guarantee that the cabinet adopted the Treasury's recommendations in each specific case. Thus Neville Chamberlain was overruled when it came to providing the finance for speeding-up the programme for the expansion of the RAF as an instrument of deterrence. Although Chamberlain had engaged in what his opponents termed a 'window-dressing' exercise over the expansion of the RAF, his reservations were that:[147]

(1) The process of economic recovery could not yet be considered complete.

(2) According to information from the Air Ministry – that is, the very body that was to place additional orders intended to bring forward the target year – industry did not have the ability to produce in two years the number of aircraft which, according to the preceding plan, should have been the output over a five-year period.

(3) Each additional expenditure commitment required increased revenue; he reminded his colleagues that decisions taken so far added up to a total of £36.5 million and that it was therefore no good increasing expenditure without at the same time tapping sources for new or increased taxation since the budget had to be balanced.

These reservations could not, however, invalidate the *domestic* argument that the government could win the imminent debate in the House of Commons (at the end of November 1934) only if it publicly undertook 'something' towards the build-up of the RAF as the mainstay of Britain's defence.[148] It is significant that in this respect the intragovernmental controversy ignored Chamberlain's

146. G.C. Peden, 'Sir Warren Fisher and British Rearmament Against Germany', *EHR*, 94(1979), pp. 29–47; Dennis, *Decision*, pp. 44f.; Shay, *Rearmament*, pp. 41ff.
147. Cabinet Meeting, 26 Nov. 1934, Cab. 23–80, pp. 237ff; cf. Middlemas, Barnes, *Baldwin*, pp. 786ff.
148. Cabinet meeting, 26 Nov. 1934, Cab. 23–80, pp. 233ff., 237ff.; Gibbs, pp. 134ff.; Gilbert, *Churchill*, vol. 5, pp. 585ff.

objection that there was nothing in the information concerning the development of the German Air Force which justified advancing the target date for attaining the RAF's state of readiness from 1939 to 1937.[149] The fact that domestic political arguments – used successfully on one occasion by Neville Chamberlain against the 'balanced' programme of the experts and, on another, against the chancellor of the exchequer – could decide the outcome of internal debates on rearmament arising from the dual pressure of Germany and Japan is remarkable. It illustrates the thesis that in 1934–35 security policy still considered maintaining the domestic status quo to be more important than reacting to shifts in the distribution of power in the international arena. The feeling that Britain's economic and socio-political stability was a key factor in the maintenance of her power abroad, caused rearmament to be measured against considerations of whether or not it would further heighten political controversies at home.

The uncertainty and/or hesitancy in identifying Germany as the potential enemy towards whose activities defence planning would have to be orientated, had helped to delay rearmament in 1933–34. The feeling that Britain could herself become the object of a first strike by the German Air Force rather than simply being threatened indirectly by German expansion in the East,[150] however, led to a breakthrough in defence planning to a situation in which the problems of each armed service were dealt with separately. The solutions to these problems were varied, as the Naval Agreement of June 1935 and the Air Parity Programmes were to show. At the end of July 1935 the cabinet instructed its Defence Committees to work out programmes for the rearmament of the armed services on the basis that 'financial considerations [were] to be of secondary importance to the earliest possible security'.[151] This development had its parallel in a shift of emphasis whereby there was no longer any stipulation to compensate for the effects

---

149. N. Chamberlain, 26 Nov. 1934, Cab. 23–80, pp. 237f. On British estimates of the expansion of the German *Luftwaffe* see Sir John Slessor, *The Central Blue*, London 1956, pp. 174ff.; Webster, Frankland, *Strategic Bombing*, pp. 65ff.; Gibbs, pp. 135ff.

150. The Hankey Committee-Report identified Germany as the main threat; but N. Chamberlain and Hoare disputed whether it should be left to 'officials' to lead the way; they launched a debate on whether to oppose Germany or Japan; Cabinet meeting 19 March 1934, Cab. 23–78, pp. 282ff. Other factors retarding an implementation of the recommendations of the Hankey Committee in November 1933 and March 1934 were the superior strength of Germany's neighbours and the intent to distinguish between Germany's 'bad' methods and her legitimate grievances; Germany, it was pointed out, did not yet have capacities for military ventures.

151. On the decision of 29 July 1935 see Gibbs, p. 180, and further pp. 99ff.

of the Ten Years' Rule; that is, to reach targets established years ago. The maxim was now that, considering the rearmament of all countries and Germany's in particular, British defence planning must aim at readiness for war by the target dates. Whilst the 're-equipment' programmes[152] had kept within the limit set for armaments expenditure as long as the disarmament question dominated domestic politics, the rearmament programmes were a sign of adapting to the tempo forced by Germany.[153] Nevertheless, even they remained bound up in the struggle between the principles of budgetary policy and defence policy. In 1936 the Treasury partially relaxed restraints and the armed-service departments were able to increase their level of spending:[154] 'By 1937 the defence departments were getting out of hand . . . so that less important items threatened to hold up more important ones'.[155] Against a background of concern at the move towards financing the increased pace of rearmament programmes from borrowing, the conflict between budgetary and defence aims was resolved in 1937–38 in favour of Neville Chamberlain, Simon and Inskip, who resolved that the strategic aims and the armaments programmes had to accommodate themselves to the limits of available finance.[156] Here the 'limited liability' doctrine and, above all, the idea of 'financial stability' as the fourth arm of the defence forces made a breakthrough.[157] Only with the coming of the Sudeten crisis (from about April 1938 onwards) and after 'Munich'[158] was this argument no longer decisive, although the Treasury continued to maintain it. In consequence, the expansion programmes of the armed services were judged on their merits instead of having to conform to rigid financial limits. However, certain restrictive conditions, on the one hand the government's reservations over the transition to a war economy ('control and conscription of industry and labour'), mistrust expressed by industry of state intervention and the structural problems of British industry,[159] and, on the other hand, reser-

152. Cab. 23–79, p. 52.

153. The DPR-Committee recommended a total of from £394m. to £417m. (covering a five-year period); Cab. 21–422 A; the DPR-Committee deliberated 21 Nov. 1935 to 9 March 1936; cf. Howson, pp. 120ff.; Peden, *Treasury*, pp. 74ff.; Gibbs, pp. 254ff.

154. Shay, *Rearmament*, pp. 144, 159; Gibbs, pp. 276ff.; Middlemas, *Diplomacy of Illusions*; pp. 116ff.; Postan, *War Production*, pp. 25ff.

155. Peden, *Fisher*, p. 43.

156. Simon-Memo., C.P. 165(37), 25 June 1937, Cab. 24–270; cf. Howson, pp. 121ff.; Gibbs, pp. 276f.

157. Gibbs, pp. 291ff.; Meyers, *Sicherheitspolitik*, ch. 5.3.

158. Middlemas, *Illusion*, pp. 216ff.; Gibbs, p. 296.

159. Postan, *War Production*, pp. 1ff., 12ff.; Hancock/Gowing, pp. 136ff.

vations about entering upon 'alliance politics' continued to have their effect until a further change of direction in March/April 1939.[160]

The government's attitude of not wishing to burden the debate on its rearmament policy with additional controversies over foreign policy preferences and 'commitments' has to be seen against the backdrop of its financial worries. The increasing frequency of crises and unexpected complications[161] more than once caused the rescheduling of target years to earlier dates and changes in the rearmaments programmes, particularly for the Air Force.[162] The result was 'confusion' insofar as no one, at least no one outside the government, could assess the total cost. It had to be anticipated that public discussions would exaggerate the volume of expenditure and that the opposition would question the government's 'will for peace' but also, conversely, that the increased expenditure would be presented as a demonstration of intentions to defend peace (by the Right and pro-British influences in France). With regard to public relations, the government had to face the problem of whether assurances of its will to 'search for a general European settlement' (the covering formula for negotiations with Germany) would retain their credibility if the estimated total became known.[163] Moreover, there was the problem that a specification of the rearmament programme for the following four years in the order of between £1 billion and £1.5 billion[164] was bound to raise doubts in industry and the trades unions as to whether the government would be able to keep its promise[165] that armaments would bring neither cuts in social services nor interference in the production of export and consumer goods.

For a while the problem was partly solved when the Treasury began to apply the 'cost-rationing' principle to defence spending.

160. Dennis, *Decision*, chs. 10–11; Middlemas, *Illusion*, chs. 6–8; Gibbs, pp. 420ff., 502ff., 508ff., 583ff.; C. Barnett, *The Collapse of British Power*, London 1972, pp. 550ff.

161. The about-turns in Britain's relations with Italy, involving the strategic function of the Mediterranean, are covered in Eden's memoirs: Earl of Avon, *Facing the Dictators*, pp. 479ff.; cf. D.C. Watt, 'Britain, France and the Italian Problem 1937–1939', in: *Les Relations Franco-Britanniques de 1935 à 1939*, Paris 1975, pp. 277–294.

162. R. Higham, *Armed Forces in Peacetime*; Roskill, *Hankey*, vol. 3, pp. 260ff.; Slessor, *Central Blue*, pp. 174ff., 204ff.; Peden, *Treasury*, pp. 128ff.

163. N. Chamberlain insisted on a formal Cabinet resolution which pledged Ministers to give no hint of the cost of the rearmament programme; 25 February 1936, Cab. 23–83, pp. 157ff. The heads of expenditure and the methods of financing are explained by Shay, pp. 74ff., and Gibbs, pp. 265ff.

164. Howson, pp. 120ff.

165. C.P. 36(36), 12 Febr. 1936, Cab. 24–259; Cabinet meetings on 25 February and 2 March 1936, Cab. 23–83, pp. 157ff., 206ff.

It aimed at reducing the total cost of the Five-Year Rearmament Scheme in a different way to the procedure adopted in 1934, by defining the cost–benefit effect of the armed forces indirectly rather than directly; that is, by taking into account its contribution to protecting Britain against 'first strike' operations of an enemy as well as to providing room for manoeuvre for British policy. In order to employ Britain's resources in the best way, top priority was given to those sections of the Defence Programme which held out the prospect of effectively deterring the enemy from an attack on Britain and keeping open the Empire's lines of communication. The requirements of the Cinderella of the defence forces, the Army, were deferred once more because their implementation was said to lead to the dislocation of industry without guaranteeing British security. As those defence services which had preserved their industries during the 'drought' of the 1920s [166] – namely, the Royal Navy and RAF, were the successful bidders in the phase of rearmament, it was hoped that armaments orders would not grievously disrupt the economy. Considerations which sought to balance the extension of the capacity of the armaments industries with the normal functions of an economy dependent on imports were more than a match for defence schemes which aimed at a balanced expansion of all three forces but which in the eyes of the Treasury and industry were seen as too expensive and as absorbing too many resources.[167]

2. The Priorities of Armaments Policy, 'Isolationism' and Appeasement

The British policy principle of taking risks over defence issues rather than over domestic ones reflected the intention to shield the British polity from the influence of external political factors as far as possible.[168] This applied particularly to the armaments de-

166. Pownall-Diaries, vol. 1, p. 76; cf. Postan, *War Production*; R. Higham, *Armed Forces* (for further details see note 168 of German original).

167. N. Chamberlain 'hired' Lord Weir as an ally in his refutation of the arguments advanced by Vansittart, Hankey, Fisher and the Chiefs of Staff and in his controversies with Duff Cooper on the role of the Army; Chamberlain-Diary, 19 Jan. 1936, NC 2–22; C.P. 227(36), C.P. 334 and C.P. 337(36), Cab. 24–265; cf. Dennis, *Decision*, pp. 88ff.; Roskill, *Hankey*, vol. 3, pp. 290ff.; Pownall-Diaries, vol. 1, p. 99 (27 Jan. 1936).

168. Simon, 30 April 1935, Imperial Conference, P.M. (35), 1st meeting, p. 4, Cab. 32–125; complementary to this attitude is that the Government gave the leaders of the Opposition advance notice of the Statements Relating to Defence and outlined its appreciation

bate, which the government did not want to be disturbed by additional external political factors. The directive, formulated by Baldwin,[169] demanded that the British government concern itself primarily with those aspects likely to facilitate the process of restoring the armed services at home. On the other hand, any new obligation, even if it only extended or defined existing commitments (Locarno), would give rise to the suspicion that rearmament was to serve specific foreign policy objectives and not just the general goal of supporting the credibility of Britain's peace policy and of providing British foreign policy with a powerful deterrent. In order to avoid burdening the decision on the expansion programme or its implementation, in particular of the RAF as an instrument of deterrence,[170] with the stigma of a desire to use force[171] in specific circumstances, British foreign policy appeared to be compelled to play down all occasions on which she would have to show her colours. This appeared to be even more urgent as the discussions within the cabinet showed that Britain could defend her interests in the Low Countries (i.e. Belgium) only by joining a tripartite alliance which included France. In view of France's efforts to achieve security by the encirclement of Germany – through an Eastern Locarno and the Franco-Soviet Pact – and in view of her attempts to evade British pressure,[172] the British government thought that any statement which implied an obligation to military action[173] would seriously damage the domestic political situation. The government was primarily concerned to free itself from the dead weight of bloc politics linked with the arms race; that is, the nightmare of 'prewar diplomacy'. In order to defuse domestic debates over rearmament programmes it sought to keep quiet about political commitments abroad – Belgium, Staff talks – and at the same time directed its armaments policy at 'what [is] necessary for our own defences'.[174]

---

of international relations: in this manner, the government tried to channel the demand for joining a public debate with the leaders of the Opposition on these issues.

169. Baldwin, 27 June 1934, Cab., 23–78, p. 223; Baldwin, 11 July 1934, Cab. 23–79, p. 278.

170. On the bomber offensive (Trenchard doctrine) see B.D. Powers, *Strategy without Sliderule: British Air Strategy 1914–1939*, London 1976.

171. Baldwin, see note 169; cf. Gibbs, pp. 111ff; for details see ch. 1 of German original and notes 66, 233.

172. Cabinet meeting, 6 June 1934, Cab. 23–79, pp. 154ff.; on the Anglo-French meetings in February 1935 and the Anglo-German Naval Agreement of June 1935 see ch. 1 of German original.

173. MacDonald 27 June 1934, and Baldwin, July 1934, Cab. 23–79, pp. 219 and 278.

174. Inskip, 30 August 1938, Cab. 23–94; cf. notes 47 and 64 of this chapter; N. Chamberlain, 20 June 1934, 'Note on the Finance of Defence'; D.C.M. (32), 50th and 51st meeting,

The government could reckon with least resistance to rearmament in public opinion by concentrating on the build-up of the Royal Navy as a traditional mainforce and, in particular, on the expansion of the RAF.[175] The Army, which would have been the appropriate force in the context of alliance policies, remained the Cinderella of the armed forces precisely because of the political mood at home, memories of the bloc policy before 1914 and aversions to the French nurtured by ex-servicemen.[176] Moreover, the implementation of the first expansion programme was slowed down so as not to arouse public indignation. (A justification for this postponement was provided by Germany's apparent domestic difficulties assumed in connection with the Röhm Putsch, which were thought to have reduced the tempo of German rearmament.)[177] Bringing the armaments question to a satisfactory conclusion in the domestic arena and avoiding definitive statements, however desirable, in the arena of foreign affairs,[178] remained unchallenged priorities until March 1939.

This very approach was taken by MacDonald, Baldwin and Neville Chamberlain in inter-allied negotiations too. They maintained that Britain had to retain her sovereignty to decide in each individual case. They also determinedly rejected the principle of collective security[179] and resisted proposals to tighten existing treaties;[180] for example, to remove the intermediate stage of calling upon the Council of the League of Nations[181] in the event of a

Cab. 16–111; Hankey, 'Disarmament and Rearmament', p. 8, Cab 21–434.

175. The 'window-dressing' aspect of the expansion of the RAF was heavily criticised by the Admiralty, see Chatfield to Fisher, 16 July 1934, Cab. 21–434; Roskill, Hankey, vol. 3, p. 119; Pownall-Diaries, vol. 1, pp. 44ff., 100; Postan, *War Production*, p. 12.

176. D.C.M. (32), 51 and 52th Meetings, Cab. 21–434. The British Legion influenced the attitude of MPs in the March Crisis of 1936, e.g. G. Braithwaite, *Hendon Gazette*, 10 April 1936, p. 7; Rickards, *Craven Herald*, 20 March 1936, p. 7.

177. See note 130 of this chapter; cf. Gibbs, pp. 114, 116ff.

178. Baldwin, 11 July 1934, Cab. 23–79, p. 278.

179. Cab. 23–76, pp. 116ff.

180. Anglo-French Negotiations, Ministerial Meeting, 1 Febr. 1935, A.F. (35) (B), p. 11; COS 364 = CID 1161–B, 8 Febr. 1935, §21, pp. 14ff.; Briefing for Stresa Conference, C.P. 79(35), §20, p. 7, Cab. 24–254; Cabinet Meeting, 16 Oct. 1935, Cab. 23–82, p. 271; on the imminent Locarno Crisis see Emmerson, pp. 54f., and Earl of Avon, *Facing the Dictators*, pp. 332–337ff.; Hankey reminded — and Cabinet Ministers gladly took the point — that 'Locarno' was no alliance and that Austen Chamberlain himself had explained this difference to the House of Commons at the time; see Baldwin, 11 March 1936, Cab. 23–83, p. 295.

181. Britain had introduced the differentiation between 'flagrant' and 'non-flagrant' treaty violations and insisted, in view of a series of 'harmless' treaty violations (e.g. building of barracks in the demilitarized zone), on consultation procedures and on convening the Council of the League of Nations; Cabinet meetings in October 1933, Cab. 23–77, pp. 50, 57, 62ff.; Cabinet meeting, 5 March 1936, Cab. 23–83, pp. 227ff., 231, 235; Cranborne (FO) to Cecil, 8 March 1936, C 1618/4/18, and C 1631/4/18, FO 371–19 889.

breach of contract. Instead, the British side tried to dodge the issue with formulas about a permanent settlement based on non-aggression pacts extended through 'pacts of mutual assistance to reinforce the security of the parties concerned'.[182] The issue was that she could be obliged to offer 'additional commitments at our expense'; that is, guarantees of military assistance to those powers (France and Belgium) who would have to give up positions which guaranteed their own security[183] in the negotiations with Germany which were being advocated by Britain. With an eye to public opinion (and published opinion), which spoke out against automatic commitments to assistance, but also under pressure from it, the British side[184] as a rule attached provisos to its verbal concessions to its foreign partners, whether Staff talks or standard formulas of French policy such as 'regime of security', and so on, were concerned.[185]

Amongst British decision-makers the question was not so much whether Britain could yet stand a fight to the finish in Europe (this question was clearly answered in the negative) but rather the careful consideration of whether or not the British government should reveal the formative conditions which defined the scope for its actions – the state of armaments and an 'isolationist' public opinion – to the power (France) with which Britain's fate was felt to be bound up.[186] The majority in the cabinet and the chiefs of staff wanted to avoid holding talks with the friendly powers on the priorities of armaments production and the most effective deployment of the existing forces;[187] they only contemplated an exchange of technical information and did not consider anything which came near to integrated Staff planning.[188] Instead of compensating France for the loss of elements of her security with

182. C.P. 79(36), 16 March 1936, Cab. 23–83, pp. 303ff.

183. C.P. 19(35), 24 Jan. 1935, §7, p. 2, Cab. 21–413; Hankey, 1 Febr. 1935, A.F. (B) (35), p. 17, Cab. 21–413.

184. Earl of Avon, *Facing the Dictators*, pp. 360ff.; Middlemas, Barnes, *Baldwin*, pp. 920ff. Simon, K. Wood referred to the state of 'public opinion' in Cabinet debates, and Baldwin and Chamberlain asked their French counterparts to live with that fact of life. 'Pro-French' politicians and opinion-leaders, such as Lord Camrose, W. Steed, A. Chamberlain, Boothby, Churchill did not succeed in convincing the British Government of the advantages of granting France its request for guarantees in order to win consent from French diplomacy for British attempts at mediation.

185. G.R. (34)5, 14 Dec. 1934, §19; C.P. 295(34), 11 Dec. 1934; C.P. 6(35), 9 Jan. 1935; C.P. 19(35), 24 Jan. 1935, Cab. 21–413. For the events in 1936 see notes 182 and 184; cf. Gibbs, pp. 143ff., 607ff.

186. Baldwin, N. Chamberlain, Monsell, Swinton, D. Cooper in Cabinet meetings on 11, 12 and 16 March 1936, Cab. 23–83, pp. 236, 298ff., and Cab. 27–603 (Locarno Committee of the Cabinet).

187. Meeting of Ministers, 30 March 1936, Cab. 27–603, re 'letter of intent' on Staff talks.

188. Cabinet meetings 1, 8 and 22 April 1936, Cab. 23–83 resp. Cab. 23–84.

strategic Staff talks and thereby complying with the demands of the French military,[189] the British government suppressed preparatory talks about possible consultation procedures and particularly about common Anglo-French actions in the next predicted crisis. Being convinced, firstly, that Britain could at present offer no effective help and, secondly, that every fighting engagement in European conflicts would disrupt rearmament, the British government withdrew to the standpoint that it had already secured the mandate for rearmament! This effectively meant that the government claimed to make a positive contribution to Britain's security, and also to that of her ally, simply by embarking upon rearmament.[190] This argument suggested that rearmament would encounter difficulties in domestic politics if it was conducted as part of bloc/alliance policies (Staff talks).[191] The gist of all this was that the decision on the direction of rearmament had to be reserved for the domestic British political process: 'This sort of contribution which Great Britain might possibly make would primarily be measured to ensure *British* security, but which would and could be represented[!] as constituting contribution to European and French security'.[192]

The catch phrase 'a mandate to rearm' was supposed to bridge the gap between the fact that the British arsenal was 'empty' and the hope that things would improve for Britain, and therefore her partners, within a few years. Only in the last resort did Britain wish to inform France that, for example, the RAF could inflict no damage on Germany 'at present' but that it would definitely be able to do so in two years' time. Diplomacy's task of shielding rearmament thus meant dissuading the other powers from actions which could involve Britain in conflicts prematurely; that is, before the completion of the rearmament programme, which was spread over several years. On the other hand, this also meant consoling friendly countries by claiming that British rearmament contributed to building up a 'sense of confidence' and therefore would soon compensate for the diplomatic losses (non-implementation of Part V of the Treaty of

189. P. Renouvin, 'Les relations franco-anglaises, 1935–1939. Esquisse provisoire', *Les Relations franco-britanniques de 1935 à 1939*, CNRS, Paris 1975, p. 28.

190. Cabinet Meeting, 12 Dec. 1934, Cab. 23–80, p. 322; Cabinet Meetings, 26 Febr. and 9 March 1936, Cab. 23–83.

191. Rumours on French proneness (in 1933/34) to 'preventive war actions', the pro-Italian tendency in French politics during the Abyssinian crisis and a number of incidents nourished mistrust of France and formed the background of agitation against a return to pre-war diplomacy/staff talks; not only the Labour Party, but conservative backbenchers and Ministers responded to or contributed to this atmosphere.

192. Sargent–Memo., 5 Dec. 1934, §16, Cab. 21–417 and Cab. 27–572; Simon-Memo., G.R. (34)4, 8 Dec. 1934; Cabinet meeting, 13 Dec. 1934, Cab. 23–81.

Versailles and of the central provisions of the Locarno Pact, etc.):

> the action they [the French] proposed would result not only in letting loose another great war in Europe. They [the French] might succeed in smashing Germany with the aid of Russia, but it would probably only result in Germany going Bolshevik . . .it seemed very unfriendly [of the French] to put us in the present dilemma. People would take a long time to forget it . . . . The French ought to welcome our coming rearmament rather than expose us to the present embarrassments.[193]

The counter-argument, that in a few years France and the other powers would be comparatively less well placed and, more importantly, that the system of collective security would have collapsed,[194] only appeared to reinforce the British leadership's view that because of the present distribution of power, Britain could influence a new settlement of the European order less at present than in a few years' time.

In government circles, the view prevailed that the limited armaments expenditure in the years between 1920 and 1934 had restricted Britain's room for manoeuvre in international politics. This meant, therefore, that Britain had to win time in order to compensate for these 'deficiences' and to rearm[195] in the hope of winning back her freedom of movement in respect both of potential enemies (Germany, Japan and Italy) and her armed allies (e.g. France)[196] and at the same time deter the offensive policies of the former. However, the deterrent function of British rearmament in the end remained unconvincing. The formula that a 'deterrent' was being developed served more to avoid having to take action in crises than to indicate to partners and opponents alike the point at which they would have to reckon with Britain's active intervention.[197] Britain also partly lacked the technical prerequisites – the range of bombers capable of action did not correspond with the premises of the Trenchard Doctrine[198] –

---

193. Baldwin, 11 March 1936, Cab. 23–83, p. 295.

194. Flandin put this argument to Chamberlain and Baldwin, 12 and 13 March 1936, Cab. 27–603. A. Chamberlain, W. Steed, P. Einzig, W. Churchill et al. stressed the same view publicly and in informal meetings.

195. The thesis that 'appeasement' was about 'winning time for rearmament' is a standard argument of most interpretations, e.g. W. R. Rock, *Appeasement on Trial: British Foreign Policy and its Critics 1938/39*, Hamden 1966, and W. R. Rock, *British Appeasement in the Thirties*, London 1977, pp. 89f.; H. Herzfeld, 'Zur Problematik der Appeasement-Politik', *Aus Politik und Zeitgeschichte*, 17 April 1963, pp. 3–24.

196. This is one of the main motives behind Hankey's efforts as the self-appointed coordinator of British defense policy in 1932–36.

197. C.P. 79(36), 16 March 1936, Cab. 23–83, pp. 303ff.

198. Slessor, *Central Blue*, pp. 204ff.; Watt, *Too Serious a Business*, pp. 76f.; Gibbs, ch. 15;

and she partly neglected precisely that part of the armed forces, namely the Field Force, which the Allies valued most.[199] From 1936 onwards, there are an increasing number of statements made by the chiefs of staff according to which neither the state of British armaments nor the capacity of the arms industry permitted action against a great power. To act as if Britain was committed to an alliance would, according to these statements, increase the danger for her because a closer alignment with France would automatically bring the German–Japanese (and possibly Italian) counter-alliance into being.[200] This indicates that the rearmament policy accentuated 'isolationist' implications rather more sharply than the political authorities may have desired: 'Disarming ourselves in advance, by ourselves, by way of an example has not increased our negotiating power in the Disarmament discussions at Geneva'.[201] The belated admission that Britain's limited scope of action resulted from her own weaknesses[202] eventually led to the repeal of the 'business as usual' rule and to a new attempt to free rearmament from domestic political restrictions; this, however, only happened in the early summer of 1938.[203]

Until then the process of rearmament, which was visibly to support the dual functions of providing 'confidence' among allies and 'deterrence' against potential aggressors, was so slow that the scope of British foreign policy remained circumscribed by these 'deficiences'. The decisions between 1933 and 1935–36 on the question of rearmament effectively meant little more than closing the gap between existing capacities and target figures drawn up in the 1920s. From the British point of view it was, therefore, unavoidable that the rearmament process would have to pass through a critical phase. This phase was expected in 1936,[204] firstly because the restructuring of the existing armed forces would impair their deployment capability and effectiveness and, secondly, because in the Far East,[205] Japan would conclude the modernisation of her armed forces by 1936 and thereby gain a lead over

---

Webster, Frankland, pp. 91ff.

199. Dennis, *Decision*, pp. 173ff.; M. Howard, *Commitment*, pp. 34ff., 126ff.; P.M. Kennedy, 'The Tradition of Appeasement in British Foreign Policy 1865–1939', *British Journal of International Studies*, 2(1976), pp. 195–215.

200. See ch. 1 of German original, esp. parts 4 and 11; cf. Gibbs, p. 313.

201. Simon, 28 Nov. 1934, Parl. Deb., HofC.; Statement Relating to Defence 1935, Cmd-4827, §6, p. 4.

202. Simon, 30 April 1935, Cab. 32–125; Simon to N. Chamberlain, 23 Sept. 1936, Simon-Mss.; cf. Shay, *Rearmament*, pp. 263ff., 291f.; J.A.S. Grenville, *Trends*, p. 235ff.

203. Middlemas, *Illusions*, pp. 216ff.; Gibbs, pp. 314.

204. COS 364 = CID 1161 B, 8 Febr. 1935, §16, Cab. 21–413; cf. Gibbs, p. 178.

205. CID 1151–B, Annex, and CID 1181–B, Annex I.

Britain. Eventually, therefore, Britain as an imperial power would be faced with the necessity of easing the situation in Europe, at least for the time being, in order to avoid having to abandon the imperial strategy and thus having to revise the fundamental assumptions of her armaments programme.[206] Such a revision would have burdened the relationships within the power structure (*Herrschaftssynthese*) with considerable strains. If only for this reason, it appeared advisable to postpone the date of opting for one strategy or another by employing appeasement and pacification tactics, thereby keeping out of domestic debates the question of which war – and/or combination of war theatres – armament measures should anticipate. Should it be in the West, in the Far East, in the Mediterranean or in Central and Eastern Europe? By defining rearmament as a deterrent against Germany and Japan and as a psychological support for friendly powers, and by pursuing the search for general appeasement, the British hoped to spare themselves the need to respond to pressures from abroad.[207] The aim of their peace strategy and armaments measures was to defend the sinews of the British Empire – that is, the international sea routes – and to protect London and the Midlands against air raids. The terms of debate indicate to what extent British politics was marked by strongly 'isolationist' tendencies which aimed at securing relative autonomy for actions in foreign affairs. The central question was how Britain could create a situation which would deter other powers from attacking her. The answer that the RAF provided an effective deterrent[208] was based on the assessment that the government would find the support and understanding of public opinion for this sector. Neville Chamberlain, supported by Baldwin,[209] became spokesman for this view: in his proposals, which were based on financial considerations and domestic (party) political views, he justified the decision for a strong air force by arguing that 'the public would object to large sums being spent on the Army'.[210]

By neglecting the Army, the British government gave a clear

206. COS 364 = CID 1161–B, and CID–meeting, 22 Nov. 1934, Cab. 2–6/1, pp. 155ff.; see ch. 'Strategien' in the German original.

207. Cabinet meeting, 26 Febr. 1936, Cab. 23–83, pp. 179ff.; for further details see ch. 1 of German original.

208. D.C.M. (32), 50th meeting, Cab. 16–110.

209. D.C.M. (32), 52nd meeting, and Simon, 55th meeting; Hankey 'Disarmament and Rearmament', p. 10, Cab. 21–434; Middlemas, Barnes, *Baldwin*, pp. 787ff., 796ff.

210. D.C.M. (32), 51st meeting; see C.P. 26 (36), Cab. 24–259; Pownall-Diaries, vol. 1, p. 99 (27 Jan. 1936).

indication that apart from satisfying Britain's primary needs for security, she would not make provisions for fulfilling her treaty obligations as a member of the League of Nations, a party to the Locarno Treaty or even comply with the idea of a collective security system. The resolution not to consider possible preventive actions by France against Germany[211] which was brought about by the chiefs of staff at the beginning of the rearmament process (June/July 1934) points to a lack of confidence in France as an important reason for the 'isolationism' of armaments and foreign policy. The second premise of British foreign policy was that armament measures could not simultaneously allay British fears of a German air attack and Japanese naval operations and serve the interests of the French partner who had close links with central Eastern Europe.[212] Neville Chamberlain even advocated an appeasement policy towards Japan (1933/34) in order to limit armament expenditure overall and to concentrate any additional expenditure on the threat posed by Germany.[213] The political consequence he drew from these two premises was that: 'The real hope for Europe [is] that, while the United Kingdom should make preparations as were necessary to defend *herself*, she should still pursue a policy of a settlement in which Germany could take an equal share'.[214] This view only allowed concessions to be made to France's 'quest for security' which did not stretch Britain's commitments beyond the point[215] where they were likely to disrupt the 'home front'. Some of the driving forces behind the rearmament campaign (e.g. Hankey)[216] used this statement to justify their project of pulling France into an armaments convention. Furthermore, they maintained that exploratory talks in Berlin served European peace and thereby both British and French interests. Britain therefore owed France no compensation for the concessions the latter had to make in respect of her own security doctrine.[217] French concessions should, however, provide the basis for an arms limitation agreement with Germany. Britain thought

---

211. Webster, Frankland, p. 88; Gibbs, pp. 646ff.; for details see ch. 1 of German original.

212. Hankey's draft of 1935 Statement relating to Defence, Cab. 21–434 and Cab. 21–407.

213. Middlemas, *Illusion*, pp. 47ff., 116ff.; Barnett, *Collapse*, pp. 444ff.; Gibbs, pp. 444ff.; Dennis, *Decision*, pp. 96f., 108ff.

214. Simon, 30 April 1935, P.M. (35), p. 4, Cab. 32–125; see note 63 of this chapter.

215. See above on staff talks.

216. On Hankey's activities see ch. 1 of German original.

217. Anglo-French Negotiations, 1 Febr. 1935, A.F. (B), p. 17, Cab. 21–413. The point had already been raised in October/November 1933, see Cab. 23–76, pp. 126ff.; Eden to Baldwin, 3 June 1934, Baldwin-Mss., vol. 122, pp. 101f.

that with the end of the Barthou/Tardieu era (1934) the time was ripe to move France towards these concessions which entailed a so-called realistic handling of the German question.[218]

The proposition that British foreign and defence policy tends towards isolationism is thus based on the following facts:

(1) Britain tended to pursue a policy of retaining a 'free hand', although the idea of a 'security community' with France should have pointed to different patterns of behaviour; namely, Staff talks, armaments cooperation based on a division of labour, and so on.

(2) She also tended to structure defence measures according to British capacities and essential British interests.[219] The notion that Britain could not afford a loss similar to that incurred during the First World War led to a 'cheap' and at the same time popular strategy.[220] The result of these tendencies is to be found in the concept of 'limited liability'.[221] This concept was shared also by those forces who did not support the priorities set by Liddell Hart and Neville Chamberlain for the different sectors of the armed forces. The cabinet wanted to avoid at almost any cost the risk of an offensive foreign policy; that is, any policy which transcended narrowly defined 'British interests'; it favoured instead 'preventive diplomacy' (i.e. early moves towards a negotiated settlement – appeasement). Thus the room for manoeuvre in foreign policy was so restricted that Britain could not and did not want to risk war before 1939, that being the target year for the completion of the armaments process. The consequences of this were acts of conciliation (time-winning tactics) in order to shield this process of armament.

(3) In the Naval Agreement[222] (and in efforts for an Air Pact)[223]

218. Simon report on his talks with Laval, C.P. 19(35), §3, Cab. 21–413; R 318/1/67, 12 Jan. 1935 (Simon-Laval, in Geneva), Cab. 21–413; Simon-Diary, 13 and 14 Jan. 1935; Simon to King George V, 14 Jan. 1935

219. On this concept see K. Hildebrand, '"British Interests" und "Pax Britannica"'; G. Niedhart, 'Friede als nationales Interesse: Großbritannien in der Vorgeschichte des Zweiten Weltkriegs', *NPL*, 17(1972), pp. 451–470.

220. Readers should remember that 'policy on the cheap' is a structural (traditional) element of Britain's expansion overseas and has figured prominently in many theories of (British) imperialism. In his criticism of Cooper's and the War Office's memoranda on the 'Role of the Army' N. Chamberlain charged the WO with having neglected this operative ideal; C.P. 334(36), Cab. 24–265; it was Basil Liddell-Hart, who made 'limited liability' a household word in defence debates during the mid-1930s; he based his thinking on this 'British tradition'.

221. Liddell-Hart, *Memoirs*, vol. 2, pp. 196ff.; B. Bond, *Liddell Hart. A Study of Military Thought*, London 1977; Gibbs, ch. 12; Watt, *Too Serious a Business*, pp. 70ff.

222. Earl of Avon, *Facing the Dictators*, pp. 230ff.; Middlemas, Barnes, *Baldwin*, pp. 827ff.; C.P. 23(35), 25 Jan. 1935, Summary of Conclusions, §40a.

223. Roskill, *Hankey*, vol. 3, pp. 156ff.; Pownall-Diaries, 16 Dec. 1935, p. 94.

the calculation that for once relations with Germany should be conducted without waiting for France (and without prior consultation with that ally) also played a role. More important, however, was the fact that the Admiralty was interested in maintaining its global strategy; this meant finding temporary relief on one front because of domestic political–financial limits described above.[224]

3. Rearmament Debate and Foreign Policy

The problem of 'isolationism' sketched here is not the only important element for an analysis of foreign policy in the 1930s; the resulting consequences both for the formation of public opinion and for the decision-making process are just as important. The fact that the dispute over the aims, political prerequisites and scale of rearmament became the focus of the domestic political controversy meant to all intents and purposes that the concentration on economic–financial, socio-political, structural and psychological implications of rearmament clouded the perception of the political scene abroad and of foreign policy problems in the strict sense. In the European crises of the 1930s, questions of international conflict as such were much less of an issue for the British power élites than the connection between issues of psychological appeasement tactics at home with the rearmament process and the 'search for general European agreement'. Concentration on domestic aspects of rearmament – namely, the burden on industry and the danger of socio-political immobility – meant that individual crises abroad were not discussed primarily as foreign-policy problems and that the specific aspects of each of these crises were, rather, excluded from the continuing political debate on rearmament.

This was especially true for the 'opposition from the Left', although (or perhaps because) they advocated different principles in foreign policy to the parties in government. It is significant that prior to the March crises the opposition from the Left – the Labour Party, the trade unions, Liberals, LNU, Council of Action for Peace and Reconstruction – had shelved attempts to develop a definite policy statement on the challenges posed by Germany. They evaluated the predicted attack on the Treaty of Versailles primarily under the aspect of how the government's chances to

224. Simon-Diary, 30 June 1935; cf. Baldwin, 4 March 1936, Parl. Deb., HofC, vol. 309, cols. 1376f.

'sell' its rearmaments programme at home would be affected by the shift of power in Europe. The terms of debate between the government and the Opposition were almost exclusively determined by the rearmament question. When the government – Baldwin and Eden – on 9 March 1936 informed the Opposition leaders in advance of the content of the government's statement on the foreign-policy crisis, the opposition groups could only listen to the government's views; even in the further course of the crises (prior to 'Munich') the main policy bodies of the opposition reached no decision as to what reactions to German actions they should demand of the government. The government's assurance that it would not exploit the crisis for a rearmament campaign ensured that the European crises did not dominate the domestic process of forming public opinion making it subject to some sort of 'primacy of foreign policy'.[225] This renunciation of the opportunity to stress the external security dilemma in the hope of shoring up the government's position at home is one of the points where the difference between the British regime (*Herrschaftssynthese*) and the power structure of the Third Reich clearly reveals itself.

The 'opposition from the Right', conversely, whose leading representatives were often not present in London during the early days of the March crisis, pressed for forced rearmament and, above all, for alliance policies; that is, Staff talks with France. 'Real' Staff talks would have shifted the emphasis of the debates on security, foreign and armaments policy from the sphere of domestic politics to international relations. The government and the 'opposition from the Left' therefore took care that this expansion and relocation of the focal point of the terms of debate did not actually take place. The government resisted the demand to use the crises in order to steamroller the Labour Opposition by exploiting the government's clear parliamentary majority to introduce large-scale rearmament. Indeed, the government did not try to accelerate and increase the armaments programme at the peaks of crises abroad.[226] At this stage, the government did not encourage or favour either

225. The speculation on who would be appointed Minister for the Coordination of Defence, on the competence of that Department or Minister, etc. served as a welcome distraction; the unanimous view that Winston Churchill should not be considered is an indication of the fact that the primary and immediate concern was not with improving Britain's performance on the European scenario.

226. For reasons of foreign policy, too, the government wanted to avoid a turn to 'dramatics'; the Foreign Office wanted to get on with its working agreement approach to Germany, C 998/4/18, 15 Febr. 1936, FO 371–19 885, p. 276.

talks on trade restrictions or attacks on German militarism, although it criticised the Opposition's turning a blind eye on the general increase of armaments all over the world and in Europe in particular. Of course, the introductions to the Statements Relating to Defence in the annual budget debates due in March/April each year, addressed themselves specifically to the 'German peril',[227] and yet the fact that the crises in Europe provoked by Germany happened during this period induced the government to play down the danger rather than to use the crises as an occasion for extending the programmes beyond the fixed targets.[228]

The political authorities justified the resulting gradual pace of rearmament by saying that labour, especially the trade unions, had to agree with the essential elements of an expansion of armaments; for example, the mobilisation and rationing of skilled workers.[229] Such an agreement could only be expected, however, if the government first furnished proof that, on the one hand, it was adopting a course of collective security and, on the other hand, was making efforts for 'peaceful change' in international politics.[230] The regard paid to the labour factor in the decision-making process took an intermediate form in that the party and government leadership saw themselves obliged to bring representatives of an active minority within the government's parties into the cabinet (Percy and Eden) who sympathised with the Left's tenets (collective security, industrial reconstruction, social reform) and who in this way were thought to help to capture industrial constituencies for government parties.[231]

Whilst the government increasingly spoke of the principle of collective security, but in practice – with a view to the level of armaments – qualified its stance in the League of Nations with a number of provisos,[232] it went beyond the goals demanded by the

227. Even Vansittart, who reminded the Cabinet of the 'structural' components of *Drohpolitik* in Germany's drive to world power, did not press for altering the terms of the programme in order to fit the new set of conditions in Europe.

228. See note 334 of this chapter.

229. C.P. 57(36), Cab. 24–260; Cab. 10(36), Cab. 23–83.

230. Cab. 51(35), 4 Dec. 1935, Cab. 23–82, pp. 363ff.

231. Baldwin's reply to the Defence Deputation (29 July 1936, Cab. 21–438) was very similar to arguments advanced in the centre-left circles and the press. Lord Wakehurst (Captain V. Loder), Lord Crathorne (Sir Thomas Dugdale), and McEwen stressed in interviews with the author that Baldwin, as well as Kingsley Wood and N. Chamberlain, had the impact of rearmament on electoral chances in industrial (!) constituencies very much in mind, i.e. were reluctant to force the issue.

232. These provisos were : cooperation with the United States; a guarantee that economic sanctions would not provoke military actions. Th. Jones, Percy, Eden, Baldwin, who argued in favour of having regard to the interests and positions of the unions and the Labour Party, insisted

Left with regard to 'peaceful change' and readiness to negotiate with Germany (though more in principle than concretely). Tactical considerations moved the government even to declare publicly its readiness to find a procedure of revision which would accommodate German demands whilst at the same time persuading opponents of appeasement actions not to object:

> Whatever [Hitler's] motives may have been [concerning threats in an interview with François-Ponçet in November 1935], I still feel that we should persevere in our attempt to resume discussions; if it only be to put the onus on Hitler for rejecting our advances, and to show the British public that we have made every possible attempt to come to terms with Germany before proceeding to rearm.[233]

> It was pointed out that, even if Germany declined the terms offered, the approach would have been worth taking, as putting us right with our own public opinion.[234]

In order to succeed with this manoeuvre the British government not only had to gain the diplomatic initiative – that is, manoeuvre Hitler publicly into the role of saying No to sensible offers and thus playing the villain of the piece – but also accompany its search for agreement with an effective amount of propaganda. But this stood in need of the government being united on its course and on the objects of the 'bargaining procedure'; however, it was never able to come to a definite conclusion before Hitler thwarted each phase of consultations by his unilateral *coups de main*. The reason for this was that some members of the cabinet (MacDonald, Simon, Kingsley Wood) and their advisors (e.g. Hankey) worked on the assumption that even if Britain could not trust the sincerity of Germany's protestations of peace, she 'must assume it for our own sake'.[235] The policy of 'as if', which preferred prompt contacts with Berlin to forcing the pace of rearmament or to negotiations on mutual assistance with partners in the League of Nations, was

---

on sticking to these provisos, although the Labour Party and unions wanted to teach the 'smaller' dictator a lesson.

233. Sargent, 23 Nov. 1935, on C 7818/55/18 (Phipps' report on François-Ponçet's interview with Hitler, to Foreign Office, 22 Nov. 1935), FO 371–18 851, p. 143.

234. All Souls Meeting, 19 Dec. 1937, Nicolson-Mss.

235. K. Wood to Eden, 22 May 1936, FO 371–19 906; R. MacDonald to Eden, 22 May 1936, ibid, p. 66. Lloyd George's caricature of the 'appeasers' (Simon, Inskip, Wood, Brown, Ormsby-Gore) illustrates the point: Th. Jones, *Diary with Letters*, p. 247. (On the related aspects of the 'as-if'-notion see notes 25, 48, 85, 232 of German original).

opposed by others who based their view on the 'experience' that Germany would only show readiness to compromise and negotiate if Britain (and France) made the limits of her 'fair play' diplomacy clear with 'stiff language' and the resolution to enter the arms race if necessary. The results of the government's internal debates were varied. In 1935 the view prevailed that if one wanted to coordinate the guidelines on foreign and defence policy (Statements Relating to Defence) with the requirements of domestic politics, one had to give a clear warning of the 'German peril'.[236] It did not escape the cabinet's notice that Hitler was conducting a policy of interference in British politics through his interviews with Lothian, Allen and others which were reported in *The Times*. Hitler tried to provide opponents of British 'official' policy with arguments and thus attempted to put pressure on the British government's defence policy. The government, therefore, had no choice but to point to Germany's rearmament, which contradicted her declamations of peace:

> In general the cabinet are chiefly concerned with the reaction about the Estimates and very little about the German tantrum. It had however . . . been . . . realised that any addition to the Estimates was bound to create a storm and that this must at any rate be faced and surmounted on account of our own growing needs. In a word, what we said via Baldwin to the Germans in November [1934] we are now saying via the White Paper to our own people [March 1935].[237]

In 1936, by contrast, the overwhelming tendency was to eliminate 'tough' passages contained in the White Paper so as not to prejudice the main desire of general negotiations with Germany.[238] According to this argument, public opinion expected Britain to make a 'real effort' to bring Germany into contact with Europe (or to maintain her contact with Europe). If that was not done it was felt that the National government would lose still more ground to the 'no more war' maincurrent and to the Labour Party who fought for collective security without rearmament and opposed rearmament programmes. The British government was faced with the alternative of making concessions to Germany either at the expense of continental allies (Rhineland status/France) or at the

236. Hankey to Phipps, 8 March 1935, Phipps-Mss., vol. 3/4, pp. 42ff. Hankey tried in vain to eliminate §5 of the Statement Relating to Defence in order to make sure that Simon's and Eden's visit to Berlin occurred as scheduled.

237. Sargent to Phipps, 7 March 1935, Phipps-Mss., vol. 2/10.

238. C 998/4/18, 15 Febr. 1936, FO 371-19 885, p. 276.

expense of the protectionists and imperialists (revision of Ottawa, 'economic appeasement' or 'colonial appeasement'): 'Van's memorandum gave up the demilitarised zone as a lost cause and strongly urged the handing back of colonies as well'.[239] But Vansittart himself wanted to go on record with a warning that 'our first object . . . [is] to prove to our own people that we have made every effort to secure peace, but not at the expense of other people. That will be highly important, if it comes to a show-down'.[240] The government had to defend itself against accusations from the 'opposition from the Left' that it was betraying the League of Nations as well as accusations from the 'opposition from the Right' that it was betraying British security interests with its lax armaments policy. It also had to settle disputes between the armed forces about their share of the defence budget and could, therefore, only hope to strengthen its domestic political position by concentrating on the armaments question – the dual policy of flexible foreign policy and 'arms limitation talks' (with Germany).

The dispute between the government and the Opposition on the relationship of defence, armaments and foreign policy was dominated on both sides by orthodox views rooted in domestic politics. Both camps presupposed that armament expenditure inevitably implied stagnation in social policy and that the mountain of debts could not be increased further without overburdening the taxpayer and thereby prejudicing the competitiveness of the British economy still further. Speeches from both the government and Opposition on defence and armaments matters thus addressed themselves to the context of domestic British politics; they remained colourless and shapeless on foreign policy aims or measures against the Third Reich. The rhetorical currency consisted of phrases like 'keeping faith with the League of Nations' (collective security) or assurances of a 'search for a general European settlement'; they allayed fears at home but were actually meaningless when it came to creating a 'sense of confidence' as regards the Allies.

The statements, geared to domestic controversies, contributed little to establishing a consensus with foreign powers! The government's 'deterrent' argument lacked concrete foundations just as much as the Opposition's theory that even in the conditions of international politics in the 1930s, British foreign policy could operate successfully with its existing means of force (the Royal

239. Pownall-Diaries, 3 March 1936, p. 103.
240. Vansittart, 3 Febr. 1936, FO 371–19 884.

Navy) and 'no more arms'. The Opposition rejected government policy by maintaining that Britain could rely on her world-wide standing and take the initiative and lead collective actions against the pre-Munich aggressors: Japan (1931–35) and Italy (1935–36). They were, however, loath to demand such a leading role against Germany in the March crises of 1935, 1936 and 1938.[241]

In the crises with Germany (Saar Question and Rhineland) the forces which wanted to capitalise on Britain's prestige asserted themselves in the government and its parliamentary majority. The international policing actions which they advocated were to protect Britain from having to provide assistance within alliances. For them it was decisive that British troops on a ('preventive') peace mission could polish up Britain's international reputation and, more importantly, impress public opinion at home. The longer the cabinet delayed the discussion on the organisation of collective security (international armed forces and General Staff) the more readily cabinet ministers turned to proposals that Britain should provide the main contingent for international policing actions with a view to enhancing the chances of an orderly implementation of a negotiated settlement. This was influenced by the fact that corresponding initiatives had been suggested to Britain not only by the French but also by some Germans. Faced with the choice of dispatching troops on a so-called peace mission to the Saar (1935) and the Rhineland (1936) or sending them to support French retaliatory actions, the cabinet opted for the first alternative. This corresponded with the state of the armed forces; their symbolic function was greater than their fighting strength.[242]

This readiness to make symbolic use of existing defence forces with the intention of shaping international constellations in a way favourable to Britain had an important function in foreign policy.[243]

Primarily, however, it served to protect the government from criticisms that it was inactive.[244] It very quickly became fairly

241. Naylor, *Labour's International Policy*, pp. 150ff.; S. Davis, *British Labour*.

242. N. Chamberlain and the CIGS made the point: 16 March 1936, Cab. 27–603; Pownall-Diaries, 16 March 1936, p. 106; on the Saar issue 1934/35 see Saar Committee, 3 Dec. 1934, Cab. 27–573; Baldwin, 3 Dec. 1934, in Jones, *Diary with Letters*, p. 139; Simon-Diary, 9 Dec. 1934; Hailsham, 28 Nov. 1934, Cab. 23–80, pp. 251f; Hailsham, 22 Nov. 1934, Cab. 27–572. In both instances, the Chiefs of Staff were reluctant to act (see Gibbs, p. 245) while the CIGS preferred 'symbolic' action (16 March 1936).

243. Britain (re)gained a say in international crisis management (see ch. 1 of German original).

244. Baldwin, 3 Dec. 1934, in Jones, *Diary with Letters*, p. 139; N. Chamberlain, 16 March

obvious that the peace missions – which in any case went beyond the stage of declarations only in the Saar crisis – had failed to achieve a 'general European appeasement'. The government and Opposition, however, appeared to learn nothing from the crises and continued to react in similar ways, albeit with different symbols and gestures. On the question of whether a more substantial contribution had to be made to relax tensions and secure stable conditions for peace, the differences within the government and Opposition were greater than the distance between them.

The Rhineland crisis clearly shows that the dominance of domestic political considerations hindered British policy-makers in adapting the terms of debate to the requirements of international relations. On the one hand, there is no doubt that the British government recognised the demilitarised zone as the key to power in Europe;[245] nevertheless, it was prepared to hand over, albeit as part of a bargain, what Hitler was threatening to take by force. Amongst the numerous reasons for Britain's attempt to prevent a *coup de force* with offers of a negotiated settlement and, failing this, to accept the *fait accompli*, issues connected with the armaments debate appear to have been decisive. Once the government had decided to step up rearmament in the summer of 1935[246] and consequently established contacts with the FBI and TUC on the eve of the election campaign, one date assumed considerable significance – 9 March 1936 – when the House of Commons was due to debate the White Paper on Defence. Leading cabinet ministers and civil servants concentrated their attention on the finance and coordination of defence expenditure. Although signs of a Locarno crisis were unmistakable, the domestic political circumstances played a decisive role in the armaments issue, particularly in Britain's handling of the Abyssinian crisis, and in the presentation of the first real British rearmament programme, both of which called for the focusing of attention on a renewal of the dual strategy of a 'peace offensive' ('preventive diplomacy') coupled with the deterrence of potential aggressors: 'The feeling

---

1936, Cab. 27–603.

245. Eden-Memo., C.P. 42(36) = G(36)3, 14 Febr. 1936, §5; War Office/CID 1211–B, 27 Jan. 1936; Air Ministry/CID 1210–B, 24 Jan. 1936; CID meeting, 30 Jan. 1936, Cab. 2–6/1, p. 243. Cabinet meeting, 14 Jan. 1935, Cab. 23–81, p. 28; Hankey–Vansittart correspondence, 8 to 18 Jan. 1936, FO 371-19 883. On 'background factors', e.g. erosion of support to France's strategic point of view, see note 242 and ch. 1 of German original; cf. Emmerson, *Rhineland Crisis*, ch. 2.

246. The directive of July 1935 is quoted in Gibbs, p. 180; it was reinforced by the Cabinet, meeting 11 Dec. 1935, Cab. 54(35)7, Cab. 23–82, pp. 428ff.

of the Committee [on Germany] at its first meeting seemed rather to be that some diplomatic approach to Germany would greatly assist in the preparation of the Defence Programme next month'.[247]

The way in which overseas crises were dealt with in the armaments debate therefore had major implications for Britain's reaction to events abroad. By treating the core issues of international conflicts out of their context – particularly in the period leading up to these conflicts – both the government and the Opposition rendered themselves to a certain extent unacceptable as partners in an alliance or coalition.[248] Staff talks with Great Britain and Belgium were essential for France's strategy, and yet Britain rejected them, although for her part she wanted to rely on France.[249] The assertion that Britain's armaments programme already provided vital security for the Allies[250] in fact only meant that Britain wanted to be autonomous in her decisions about the level, disposition and direction of her defence provisions. The most remarkable by-product of this was that Britain did not intensify her efforts for an understanding with potential allies but orientated her policies towards her potential opponents. She did this partly by adapting to the pace of their rearmament (by aiming at parity for the RAF, envisaged as the main strike force) and partly by exploring possibilities for arms limitation agreements, if necessary restricted to specific areas and without binding herself to prior agreements with France. Britain's attempts to make contact with Germany indicated her desire to avoid forced rearmament in all three sectors of the armed services. This was done not simply to free resources for defence expenditure thought necessary to combat Japan;[251] it also aimed at maintaining flexibility in British policy and avoiding the choice of priorities between armaments, exports and consumer goods industries; that is, of using state interventionism in the service of a prewar economy. The trend was to agree arms limitations with Germany alone if necessary and to put pressure on France either to accept the *faits accomplis* of such armaments agreements or to join in the British drive to limit German rearmament to a level still acceptable to the Western powers.[252] In the

---

247. Eden to Phipps, 24 Febr. 1936, C 750/4/18, p. 2, FO 371–19 884.
248. A case in point is Britain's reaction in March 1935, Simon-Diary, 21 March 1935.
249. Britain still 'would fight to the last French soldier' (Dennis, *Decision*, ch. 4) but in contrast to pre-World War I diplomacy did try hard to avoid moral entanglements.
250. C.P. 19(35), §7, Cab. 21–413; Cabinet meeting, 26 Febr. 1936, Cab. 23–83, pp. 178ff.
251. COS 364 = CID 1161–B, 8 Febr. 1935, §§16 and 17, Cab. 21–413.
252. Simon-Memo., G.R. (34)3, 29 Nov. 1934, §6, Cab. 27–572; Hankey-Memo., 14 Febr.

same way as the parity formula for the RAF, this tendency signalled that Britain's calculations conceded a level of rearmament to Germany which was based on Britain's need for security but did not necessarily consider the French or Belgian point of view. This element also helps to confirm the theory that British foreign, defence and armaments policy amounted to 'isolationism' (in the sense of 'going it alone', defined above).

4. Peace Strategy at Home and Abroad

The reasons detailed above for 'isolationism' necessitate a closer analysis of the impact of the socio-political system on British foreign policy. The analysis of appeasement and rearmament policy is aimed at those factors of the socio-political system which influenced Britain's attitude abroad: the working of the constitution, the structure of the decision-making process, the historical traditions and those experiences of the ruling classes which determined their behaviour, the economic system or the relationship of economy and polity and the operative ideals, fundamental socio-political and socio-cultural values. The analysis of these factors provides the starting point for the eventual filtering out of the methods and goals of British foreign policy. The example of the March crisis of 1936, in which the domestic preconditions come to light with especial clarity, will be used to show appeasement policy as a crisis strategy essentially determined by domestic politics. The intention is to present an explanatory model of British foreign policy which is set against the backdrop of the political and social system. It is self-evident that the analysis can only deal with selected aspects.

Three selected arguments which direct attention to the questions sketched out above will be considered more closely in what follows:

(1) It was not possible to build a consensus on security policy before the events of spring 1939.[253]

(2) The conjecture of the German Embassy in London[254] that a

1935, CID 1162–B, §§50 and 53; Hankey, 1 Febr. 1935, A.F.(B) (35), pp. 7ff., 16f., Cab. 21–413. Hankey and the Chiefs of Staff got a hearing for their plea in favour of 'normalisation', they refuted Vansittart's 'sign-on-the-dotted line' proposal. N. Chamberlain proceeded on lines similar to Hankey and the Chiefs of Staff; see notes, 50, 298 and 338 in ch. I of German original.

253. 'Prague', nor 'Munich', is the turning point, see note 28 (Introduction of German original), and Gibbs, pp. 647f.

254. Hoesch to Auswärtiges Amt, 21 March 1936, GD, ser. C., vol. 5, No. 178, p. 236; cf.

government under Churchill or Austen Chamberlain (as prime minister) would have pursued a different course in the crises.

(3) Finally, Churchill's criticism of the so-called MacDonald–Baldwin regime, that it was 'decided only to be undecided. . .all powerful to be impotent. . .it would go on preparing more months and years. . .for the locusts to eat',[255] addressed the central issue of whether the link between the cautious acceleration of rearmament and gestures of willingness to come to an understanding with the 'dictators' (Germany, Italy and/or Japan) had been necessary because of conditions of the socio-political system.

Although Churchill argued that the necessity of changing direction and expanding arms production had to be explained to the public, he thought that this depended on Baldwin taking the initiative ('to tell the people the truth'): 'The only thing that could have saved the public from being stampeded by the unholy combination of muddle-headed pacifists and panic-mongers with astute political wire-pullers was a whole-hearted counter-campaign led by the government itself'.[256] This was not simply an acknowledgement that the opinions advocated by opponents of the government found only limited response, but can also be seen as anticipating the answer to the question raised above. The answer would be that Britain, as a democratically ruled country, had the government (Baldwin–MacDonald) which she 'deserved',[257] in the sense of Baldwin's answer to the Defence Deputation (July 1936). Explaining why he ruled out mobilising the public towards rearmament specifically intended to meet the 'German peril',[258] he went on: 'I think the one line whereby you can get people to sit up in this country, [is] if they think dictators are likely to attack them . . . but I have never seen the clear line by which you can approach people to scare them but not scare them into fits'.[259]

It has sometimes been argued in defence of appeasement policy that a country which rejected politicians who were tainted as 'strike breakers' (Churchill) would not allow anyone to determine foreign policy – even in the face of dictatorships – who advocated

Emmerson, *Rhineland Crisis*, pp. 160ff.

255. W. Churchill, 12 Dec. 1936, Parl. Deb.. HofC, ser. 5, vol. 317, col. 1107.

256. L.S. Amery, *My Political Life*, vol. 3, London 1955, p. 159; Baldwin's reply to the Defence Deputation (29 July 1936) contains his 'case' against Churchill's charges (see note 255).

257. R. Tawney, in Jones, *Diary with Letters*, p. 103; on the issues involved see notes 251–253 of German original.

258. See note 226 of this chapter.

259. Baldwin, 29 July 1936, Cab. 21–438.

'nipping this development in the bud' and furthermore, postulated a primacy of armaments and foreign policy. Even if one rejects this line of argument because of its polemical construction, one cannot overlook that this way of thinking was indeed used in the battle for political influence on the decision-makers. Some appeasers (Jones, Horace Wilson) claimed the right to advise in foreign affairs – in opposition to the foreign secretary, Anthony Eden, who was inexperienced in domestic politics – because they themselves had been successful as conciliators in strikes on a national scale. Since foreign policy was concerned with even more important matters (namely, preventing a war), they maintained that the experience they had gained in avoiding domestic political conflicts was the best qualification to contribute towards overcoming international differences.[260] In practice, however, Foreign Office experts successfully rejected any attempts of the Joness and Horace Wilsons to run a special mission between Baldwin or Chamberlain, on the one hand, and Hitler, on the other, by pointing out that negotiating conditions were not comparable. Although they had the prime minister's sympathy and were allowed to pursue explorations, their views on how to go about 'official business' as an alternative to the diplomatic service did not prevail because of the multitude of reservations made against the fallacious analogy between domestic and foreign politics.

However, their political strategy did influence the British government's attitude towards foreign affairs insofar as their missionary vision was reflected in the government's view that Britain should act as mediator to free Germany from isolation and re-establish the 'comity of nations'. This was regarded as a functional equivalent to the self-evident precept that the 'striking' side should be re-integrated by reasonable offers into the economic and social order. The 'appeasers' appealed to Baldwin that he should seek to keep the possibility for further negotiations open up to the very last moment in foreign affairs as had been done in the General Strike:[261]

in the latter part of the nineteenth and the first part of the twentieth

---

260. Jones, printed diary, 16 June 1936, pp. 196–198; it is marked 'omit' and was not published in *A Diary with Letters*, p. 244; Jones-Mss., ser. P, vol. 2, No. 137, pp. 1–3; Jones to Flexner, 24 Febr. 1938. Jones-Mss., Class S. vol. 2, 33. On Jones' activities see note 257. The claim has a tradition of its own; Lloyd George's criticism of Grey in his war memoirs contrasts the collaboration of the two in many crises 1911–1914.

261. It is another matter whether Baldwin's and the Government's policy in 1925/26 fits the views of Jones's.

century the 'have-nots' of most countries steadily improved their position through a series of strikes and negotiations, and the 'haves', whether through a sense of justice, or through fear of revolution in the event of refusal, yielded ground rather than put the issue to the test of force. This process eventually produced on both sides a willingness to submit disputes to various forms of conciliation and arbitration, and ended by creating something like a regular system of 'peaceful change' ... [If this were applied to international relations] ... the dissatisfied Powers [might] realise the possibility of remedying grievances by peaceful negotiation (preceded no doubt in the first instance by threats of force) [and] some regular procedure of 'peaceful change' might gradually be established.[262]

The message was that the experiences of socio-political conflict regulation at home, undertaken as peaceful change of existing power relations (reforms), was transferable to international conflicts between oversatisfied and dissatisfied powers.

The decisive difference between the two situations was, however, that governments could allow 'social appeasers' the opportunity to test their ideas on the eve of a strike whilst at the same time preparing to defend public interests in the event of being challenged by the party willing to go on strike. In the field of foreign policy, however, there was no guarantee that the government could successfully threaten counter-actions should negotiations fail. This was the decision-makers' view and is the one which matters for this analysis. The alternatives to particular courses of action and the attendant risks were different in the two arenas. Contrary to the tenet that the country preferred taking risks abroad to taking them at home, the risks involved in state action in the arena of European security were such as to make the dangers incomparably greater on the eve of a crisis abroad than on the eve of a domestic one. The readiness and willingness to 'break' the General Strike was correspondingly much more pronounced than the willingness to risk war. Since military impotence constituted the main argument for the inevitability of a negotiated solution, it was sufficient for the opponents of the appeasers' (e.g. Jones') advice to ask what would happen if Germany rejected the procedure of peaceful change. This immediately revealed the weaknesses of the conclusions drawn from the domestic analogy and helped to introduce the reservation that Britain could only become

---

262. E.H. Carr, *The Twenty Years' Crisis 1919–1939*, London 1939, p. 272; cf. N. Thompson, *The Anti-Appeasers*, Oxford 1971, pp. 30f.

involved in a negotiated settlement when British rearmament had reached a level that would give her a position of strength. The advance of the appeasers,[263] who used this analogy in the arena of foreign policy, could thus be blocked.

Historical tradition and the experience which determined the behaviour of the ruling élites constitute a second area in which the impact of domestic political structures on foreign policy can be gauged. The starting point for such an analysis must be the recognition that British society was shaped by conventions and institutions whose function in regulating conflicts increased proportionately as social policy became more complex in the wake of socio-economic changes within an industrial society which was also regionally differentiated. Over and above the frequently treated subject of foreign-policy traditions, in the strict sense,[264] one question relating to these conventions and traditions deserves particular attention in the analysis of foreign affairs: the question, that is, of whether characteristics of political culture or political style stimulated or hindered the progress and success of British foreign affairs.[265] There already exist a range of explanatory models. It is claimed that either:

(1) The concept of 'fair play' and sympathy for the 'underdog' worked in favour of Germany in foreign policy.

(2) The recruitment of politicians from law and business[266] reinforced the cult of 'dealing with questions as they arise'; that is, of arguing on the basis of topical statements and narrowly defined precedences. Neville Chamberlain talked of this as 'trying to get criticism focused on the points on which I have something to give away'.[267]

263. In the following context 'appeaser' refers to 'pro-German' attitudes and to the proponents of high-level Anglo-German diplomacy (Hitler–Baldwin 'summit' meeting).

264. The varieties of the balance of power-doctrine are demonstrated by M. Wight in H. Butterfield, ed., *Diplomatic Investigations*, pp. 149 ff., and by E.B. Haas, in J.N. Rosenau, ed., *International Politics and Foreign Policy*, New York 1961, pp. 318–329. On the concept 'Concert of Europe' see C. Holbroad, *The Concert of Europe. A Study in British and German International Theory 1815–1914*, London 1970; C. Howard, *Britain and the Casus Belli 1822–1902*, London 1974. On the views of 'internationalists' and fore-runners of the League of Nations movement: A.J.P. Taylor, *The Troublemakers. Dissent over Foreign Policy 1792–1939*, London 1964[2]; P. Brock, *Pacifism in Europe to 1914*, Princeton 1972.

265. J. Joll, *1914: The Unspoken Assumptions*, London 1968; J. Joll, ed., *Britain and Europe*, Introduction, pp. 4, 8ff.; F.S. Northedge, *Troubled Giant*, pp. 619f.; Frankel, 'Intellectual Framework', in Kaiser, Morgan, *Britain and West Germany*, pp. 96ff.; A. Wolfers, *Britain and France Between Two Wars. Conflicting Strategies of Peace Since Versailles*, New York 1940, 1963, p. 274.

266. Runciman to Simon, 1 August 1938, Simon-Mss.; Runciman refers to the working agreement method and claims that Britain, in contrast to France, never wanted to be too clever.

267. N. Chamberlain to Hilda, 21 March 1936, NC 18/1/952.

(3) The superimposition of conclusions drawn from experience of the market, in which different 'factions' always seek and find the lowest common denominator of agreement, onto foreign-policy relations with Hitler, who considered economics and politics as two separate worlds with antithetical standards, caused misunderstandings in Anglo-German politics.

In the context of this study's argument two factors in the relationship between political culture and foreign policy have to be emphasised:

(1) Having concluded from its domestic experience that political opponents were unlikely to maintain their grievances to the point at which no compromise could be reached, the government carried that conclusion over into the sphere of foreign affairs.[268] British politics appeared to be concerned primarily with mastering the problems of adjustment to the socio-economic changes taking place both at home and abroad; it did so, however, in a way which obstructed experiment and innovation.[269] The British government understood its role of mediator in the great social conflicts as one of presenting the trade unions with those of the employers' claims which it thought reasonable and the employers with what it considered the legitimate grievances of the workers. Only in cases of emergency would it supplement the negotiating package by offering temporary assistance (subsidies) and/or guarantees that it would force the contracting parties to keep to the letter and spirit of the agreement. The British government also operated in the same way in the sphere of foreign policy, which was conducted along the lines of inducing opposing parties to recognise those demands made by the other side which Britain considered legitimate.

However, this was done without Britain herself being prepared to make any 'material' commitment to removing the causes of old tensions between Germany and France by restructuring either the European security system or the world economy.

(2) The British socio-political system owed its relative stability and continuity to the 'skill' of its political élites in generating *ad hoc*

268. 'Sense of confidence' and other formulas are evidence of such transfers from domestic to international politics; certain topoi, e.g. repair dikes to stem the flood (instead of building new 'defence' systems), reflect a habit of thinking and preferred options; Baldwin, 29 Oct. 1936, Parl. Deb., and Eden, 12 Jan. 1937, address to the international press, present this set of topoi. Th. C. Schelling, *The Strategy of Conflict*, 1960, pp. 3ff., seems to be the 'theoretical' reflection of the 'British experience' (for further details see note 260 of German original).

269. D.A. Kavanagh, 'Crisis Management and Incremental Adaptation in British Politics: The 1931 Crisis of the British Party System', in G. Almond et al., eds., *Crisis, Choice, and Change*, Boston 1973, pp. 152–223; I. Kramnick, ed., *Is Britain 'Dying'?*, Ithaca 1979.

solutions and short-term definitions of goals and in finding the 'right' tone in crises.[270] There was no compulsion on the British élites after Lloyd George to be unremittingly successful – they merely could not afford to make blatant errors. It was enough that their image met the expectations of a mass society. Disputes were thus spared the sharpness of fundamental controversies and limited to displays of rhetorical muscle. This contributed, on the other hand, to a situation where 'pragmatism' could remain the philosophy of the British political system even at a time when the two-party system was in danger of being overlaid and permeated by the conflicts of a class society.[271] 'Unspoken assumptions' relevant here originated in the British case from a political élite which was relatively homogeneous and exerted its influence without being opposed by a counter-élite. Office-holders, prominent individuals within the upper echelons of the large 'state-like' interest groups and those engaged in shaping public opinion were all recruited from the same socio-cultural milieu. Their common approach to politics was formed and influenced in Parliament and also in the debating clubs which copied the parliamentary style. This guaranteed the existence of models of political behaviour which ran across the whole spectrum of the political parties.[272] Against this background the perpetuation and reproduction of 'pragmatism' appears as the central socio-psychological perspective from which the basic general attitudes of British politics and foreign policy in particular, must be seen: '[The notion of pragmatism] implies a lack of ideological preoccupation and concentration upon the concrete details of the environment . . . the cult of the implicit, a tendency to avoid harsh and precise formulation, hence the inclination to meet difficulties not by immediate action but by postponing unpleasant decisions, to blur grand choices, to avoid dilemmas, to be reactive rather than active'.[273]

---

270. This is shown in the tributes paid to Baldwin, e.g. Shinwell, *The Times*, 20 April 1936; H. Morrison and Grenfell, 9 resp. 6 Dec. 1935, Parl. Deb., HofC; A.W. Baldwin, *My Father*, pp. 293, 302; G.M. Young, *Stanley Baldwin*, London 1952, p. 103; Middlemas, Barnes, *Baldwin*, p. 1078. To Bevin, Attlee, Dalton, Greenwood and other Labour leaders, Baldwin was the 'trickster', 'hypocrite', etc.

271. For this same reason, that of the 'high politics' metaphor, M. Cowling's studies must be seen as fundamentally suited to writing on 'modern' British history.

272. Frankel, 'Intellectual Framework', in Kaiser, Morgan, pp. 82ff.; C. Barnett, *Collapse*, pp. 91ff., 120ff.

273. Frankel, pp. 83ff.; K. Rohe, review article, *The Round Table*, vol. 61(1971), p. 131: 'political pragmatism as a philosophy has its narrowly defined historical place in being the proper philosophy of those who can afford to be content with a minimum of slow change — the *beati possidentes*'.

A further characteristic influence of political culture on British foreign policy is that – as already stated – it transferred an approach which had proved appropriate and successful in the sphere of domestic politics to the arena of foreign affairs. Indeed, the political principle of differentiating [274] between the 'methods' employed in enforcing a claim – which were thought to merit condemnation – and a certain sympathy for the substance of that claim, belongs to the pragmatic philosophy of the socio-political system. In a manner which reflects their handling of domestic political crises, those responsible had already written off the various objects of irredentist aspirations (the Rhineland, Sudentenland, the *Anschluss*) before the foreign policy crises occurred. [275] Hitler's actions above all disturbed British politicians because they thwarted British expectations of obtaining concessions from Germany in exchange for British involvement in helping Germany to achieve her goals, which included the restoration of full military sovereignty and the return of the Saar, German Austria and the Sudentenland to their 'home' in the Reich. Just as the British government used numerous pretexts in its foreign policy to avoid facing the fact that the historical origins of the Rhineland's neutral status, the proscription of *Anschluss* and other moral–legal commitments constituted them as test cases of Anglo-French solidarity, so also it operated at home with a distinction between the defence of legitimate interests, on the one hand – the position of the employer being considered inviolable within a liberal economy – and, on the other, an understanding that it could not guarantee to optimise the interests of one side alone but had rather to attempt to afford redress to the other side (labour), whose grievances were equally 'legitimate'. This it had to do in order to maintain the system as such by gradually adjusting basic structures to altered power relations and changed interest structures. French stubborness and imprudence gave rise to a degree of circumspection in the Conservative government's attitude towards its French ally; in substance, however, its politics were always determined by the two countries' basic common interest in security. In the same way, the government criticised and voiced annoyance at the employers' resistance to reform, while at the same time continuing to resist pressures from labour

274. N. Chamberlain, 26 Nov. 1937, in N. Gibbs, p. 647; cf. Bismarck to Dieckhoff, 13 Febr. 1936, GD, ser. C., vol. 4, No. 562, pp. 1135–1139.
275. It is important to note that 'writing off' did not extend to the basic tenets or 'principles' of the British power elites and that on the other hand the claims and demands of the labour movement were of a pragmatic sort and favourable to 'bargaining procedures'.

to force 'industry' (e.g. the coal or cotton industries) into structural changes which take account of their criticisms. One further factor which demonstrated the impact of political culture on foreign policy should be emphasised here since it illustrates how domestic political considerations, elements of political morals, collective knowledge or fears and prejudices constitute factors much more relevant to policy-making than specific political constellations and events abroad. In those foreign policy situations in which active opposition appeared to offer prospects of success,[276] fears tended to be expressed that such action might cause Germany (or Italy) to turn 'Bolshevik' or that Bolshevik Russia might benefit from such a conflict. In a Russian Bolshevik sphere of influence, Britain's opportunities to exert influence and protect her interests would, it was claimed, be seriously impaired. This line of argument was underpinned by ideas which were put forward quite independently of the respective international crises – in 1919, 1923, 1931, 1935, 1936, and 1938 – by important decision-makers such as Churchill, in opposition to the majority of the government, in 1919, and by Baldwin and Neville Chamberlain in the 1930s, in response to criticisms from Churchill. Anti-socialist attitudes were linked here with a set of ideas which saw 'Bolshevism' as associated either with chaos, unprofitable economic management, falling efficiency and standards of living or with dictatorship, state-controlled trade, administrative prescription of ideologies and doctrines, and so on, and which demanded that it be perceived and combated as a principle antagonistic to the normative ideals of British politics.[277] This set of ideas also included the expectation that a 'tough' internationalist political line on the German question would release uncontrollable social unrest not only in Germany but also in Great Britain and France in their capacity as intervening powers.[278] A further argument mobilised here was the contention that 'punitive action' would only hasten the gathering of forces in Germany under Nationalist banners.[279] Finally, doubts were cast over the capacity

276. Baldwin, 11 March 1936, Cab. 23–83, p. 295; cf. Middlemas, Barnes, *Baldwin*, pp. 918, 814.

277. Londonderry to Page-Croft, 3 July 1936, and 28 Sept. 1937, Croft-Mss., vol. 1/15. For Londonderry, but not necessarily for Baldwin, Chamberlain and other critics of the Franco-Russian Pact, this view prejudged the search for agreement, even alliance, with Germany (i.e. the Third Reich!).

278. G. Schmidt, 'Wozu noch "politische Geschichte"?,' *Aus Politik und Zeitgeschichte*, B 17/75, pp. 38ff. (on the 1918/19 period). This, of course, has to do with 'lessons' drawn from 'revolution and wars of intervention'.

279. This argument played a crucial role in internal debates and in Anglo-French talks before the March crises actually 'happened'; see ch. 1 notes 59–60; cf. H. Nicolson, 12 March 1936,

of British troops to play the role of international peace-keeper if they marched into German territory against Germany's will. The role of these ideas in giving a continuity to political activity serves to clarify the importance in foreign-policy matters of domestic political perspectives and collective experience as against the inherent significance of particular international configurations of circumstances. The same set of ideas was continuously used to judge quite different situations in Germany, as well as to assess the correspondingly varied impact of the German question on British politics in the crisis years of 1918–19, 1923, 1931–32 and 1935–39; the roots of this continuity may be traced to points as distant as domestic disputes on British policy towards the French revolution.[280] 'Political morals' constitute a third set of factors relevant to our considerations here. It must be emphasised in this context that the reputation and prestige of foreign policy were particularly undermined by the double standards of the foreign-policy lobby groups and national agitation leagues. In cases where treaties were seen to offer welcome support to the aims of groups such as the Navy League,[281] the National Farmers' Union,[282] the Federation of British Industries,[283] the British Empire Association and others, they put pressure on the British government to defend those agreements and to champion the principle that they should only be revised by mutual consent. However, in cases where it was felt that agreements and treaties limited the flexibility of British policy – where, in other words, they failed to advance the interests of these groups – the government was exhorted to withdraw from or revoke naval treaties, trade agreements, and so on, and, if necessary, to do so unilaterally. This 'double standard' shows itself even more clearly in the fact that Churchill, Austen Chamberlain

---

quoted in Thompson, *Anti-Appeasers*, p. 108; Middlemas, *Illusion*, ch. 8.

280. G. Schmidt, *Politische Tradition und wirtschaftliche Faktoren in der britischen Friedens-strategie 1917–1919*; M. Gilbert, *Roots*; H. J. Nelson, *Land and Power. British and Allied Policy on Germany's Frontiers 1916–1919*, London 1963; E.L. Presseisen, *Amiens and Munich: Comparisons in Appeasement*, Den Haag 1978; D.G. Boadle, *Winston Churchill and the German Question in British Foreign Policy 1918–1922*, Den Haag 1973, pp. 20ff.

281. The *Navy League Quarterly* has many leaders and articles which presume Britain's 'legitimate' right to change the status quo of Treaties unilaterally; they do not acknowledge 'rules and laws' as compromises agreed to by British Governments.

282. The agrarian lobby requested the Government to cancel treaties with the Argentine, Denmark, etc., if these countries did not take up revisions asked for in the interest of Britain under the slogan 'Food and Defence'.

283. The dissatisfaction of the Federation of British Industries with the Trade and Clearing Agreements, including those with Germany (1934), should be seen as occurring on a different level but the FBI, too, claimed the right for Britain to change the rules of the game unilaterally.

and other critics on the Right assessed the motives underlying Japan's and/or Italy's territorial expansion sympathetically, even conceding the necessity for these aggressors to retain their 'spheres of influence' ('hinterland') or defining their activities as civilising missions;[284] German policy, meanwhile, was measured by other standards.

By contrast, Lothian and Amery recommended 'tolerance' of German expansion but expressed desires to put a spoke in Japan's and/or Italy's wheel. In the specific crises of 1935–36, these two had no qualms about publicly exonerating one aggressor in order to mobilise its support in the crises created by another. The 'double standard' obvious in these cases seems to have contributed decisively to an attitude of reticence within official policy towards using the principle of *pacta sunt servanda* (honouring contractual commitments) as the yardstick for its actions abroad during foreign-policy crises. The government which had given its legal advisers a decisive role in international negotiations in the 1920s, continued to rely on their support, together with that of the Crown lawyers, in the 1930s. Thanks to such people as Hurst or Malkin, Britain's treaty obligations were worded loosely enough for her to retain some discretion as to how they should be fulfilled; thus it remained unlikely that the issue in international law of *pacta sunt servanda* would ever become a serious problem. The armaments situation, which motivated the strategy of turning a blind eye to one aggressor while keeping an eagle eye on the other also, of course, influenced government policy decisions not to undertake any obligations which might force Britain to back up strong words with corresponding punitive actions for the maintenance or restoration of the rule of international law. Some cabinet ministers even showed themselves to be prepared to sacrifice the system of international law when they advocated – as the prime minister, MacDonald, did at the end of 1934[285] – that it was more important to maintain peace than to protect the status quo, since the latter

---

284. L.S. Amery, *The Forward View*, London 1936; L.S. Amery, *Political Life*, vol. 3, pp. 202ff. N. Thompson, *Anti-Appeasers*, makes the point with regard to A. Chamberlain and W. Churchill. Lothian, Th. Jones, Ashton-Gwatkin, Hankey, Swinton, Cranborne likened *Mitteleuropa* to 'Monroe spheres', see ch. 1 of this book.

285. R. MacDonald, 11 Dec. 1934, Cab. 27–572. MacDonald had been a critic of the Peace Treaties. In the 1930s, *The Times* and *The Observer* played the Treaty of Versailles off as a mere 'truce' against 'Locarno' (as a stepping stone to peaceful order). MacDonald's device was accompanied by another distinction, i.e. between 'local disputes' and 'challenges to peace', which served the same purpose; MacDonald's Guildhall Speech in November 1934 is an illustration of this approach. Another example is the argument put forward to justify the Naval Agreement of June 1935 (see note 276 of German original).

(as the 'Versailles System') had, in his view, been discredited.

It is worth looking more closely at this strategy of avoiding crises since it constitutes an important thread in the pattern of British foreign policy. It may be viewed as a component of the British tendency to 'isolationism' if only because it was explicitly elaborated as a counterpart to prewar diplomacy (before 1914) and because it had to defend its position[286] in the continual dispute with those interventionist–internationalistic opinions and pressure groups which maintained that Britain could have prevented the outbreak of the First World War if she had expressed her willingness to intervene in the event of a German attempt to seize world power more clearly than the Asquith–Grey government had done. Proponents of the latter argument – Wickham Steed, Lord Camrose, Churchill, Boothby, Duff Cooper, Vansittart and Collier – maintained that Britain could best prevent the outbreak of a Second World War if she unequivocally proclaimed her commitment to alliance treaties and obligations to intervene under international law (according to Articles 10 and 16 of the League of Nations Treaty). Since these demands would have committed Britain to a 'partnership' with specific allies (France, Belgium, Italy, and to a certain extent Russia and nations in 'New Europe')[287] and would clearly have aimed to circumscribe the boundaries of the Third Reich, they constituted the antithesis of 'appeasement'. Supporters of this line, who at first (before the *Anschluss* crisis) had relatively little influence, collaborated with the advocates of a 'tough line' within the French government (parties) and sought to push London into the threefold role of protector of international law, judge and enforcement agency operating within an international framework. Insofar as 'appeasement' can be seen as the result of British foreign crisis management, it can essentially be interpreted as a reaction which rejected the role definition advanced by the 'interventionists'. The notion of the 'honouring contractual commitments' (*pacta sunt servanda*) thus offers a useful point of entry into the study of appeasement.

In the autumn of 1934, during the first phase of the 'dual policy', with the beginning of rearmament (the expansion of the RAF) and

286. This was of special concern to Simon and Runciman, who resigned from the War Cabinet in 1916; Simon-Diary, 22 May 1938. The attitude is not tied to personal experience or to politicians with similar backgrounds, see All Souls Meeting, 18 and 19 Dec. 1937, 3rd meeting, Nicolson-Mss.; cf. Middlemas, *Illusion*, ch. 8.

287. G. Schmidt, *Politische Tradition*; K.G. Calder, *Britain and the Origins of the New Europe 1914–1918*, Cambridge 1976.

the first comprehensive appeasement initiative, the foreign secretary, Simon, issued a declaration which was to cover a large part of British foreign policy in the following years.[288] His assumption was that it would only ever be possible to influence the 'manner and form' of changes in the status quo in Europe; in other words, all that could be done was to ensure that a revision of the Treaty of Versailles did not lead to any conflict. Since the victorious European powers were neither willing nor in a position to prevent German breaches of the Treaty, they therefore had to find ways and means of resolving those of Germany's grievances which public opinion in Britain and France thought legitimate: 'as an early attempt to come to terms with Germany can only work towards rendering it less likely that this dangerous question . . . will be raised in an aggressive and threatening manner'.[289] The practical consequences of Simon's maxim are many and varied. They entail:

(1) A refusal to reaffirm existing obligations in a way which might exert a deterrent influence on a particular power (Germany) which was attempting, by gradual or violent means, to undermine the status of any given region.[290]

(2) A reluctance to collaborate with other guarantor powers (Italy and France) or with the prospective victims of a (German) repudiation of the Treaty, in the organisation of counter-measures, that it considered premature.

(3) A tendency to evade direct discussion of threats to the status quo, which arose out of Britain's own contemplation of the possibility of relinquishing core elements within the treaties (100,000-man army, demilitarised zone, etc.) and her simultaneous reluctance either to discuss how this was compatible with the principle of honouring contractual obligations or to enter into a debate with France[291] on the substitute solutions which Britain might propose

---

288. Simon, 19 Nov. 1934, G.R. (34)3, Cab. 27–572; C.P. 295(34), Report of the Ministerial Committee on German Rearmament, 12 Dec. 1934, Cab. 23–80, pp. 318ff. The same line of argument is recorded in Sargent/Wigram-Memo., 'Britain, France and Germany', 21 Nov. 1935, §17, and Eden to Phipps, 24 Febr. 1936, C 750/4/18, FO 371–19 884 (see further note 279 of German original).

289. Sargent/Wigram-Memo., §17.

290. The refusal 'to put teeth into Locarno' was confirmed in 1935 before the Anglo-French Negotiations on 1–3 Febr. 1935 and once again in January/February 1936. Foreign Secretary Simon had raised the question in October 1933 from a 'pro-French' stand point, but could not carry the Cabinet with him. Instead of listing all the copious evidence, see notes 280ff. of German original. I rather refer to Emmerson, pp. 63ff., and R.J. Young, *In Command of France. French Foreign Policy and Military Planning, 1933–1940*, Harvard 1978, who have worked parallel on the same archives.

to France in the event of Germany refusing to offer France any equivalent benefits in exchange.

(4) As an addition to point (3), manoeuvres using exploratory talks with the likely 'contract breakers' to bring about a negotiated agreement rather than unilateral action. By pretending to explore opportunities for a peaceful solution in the interests of France, or even as her representative, Britain was able to dismiss as politically damaging any proposals that Germany should be warned against treaty violations.[292] By pointing to the difficulties involved in drawing Germany into talks, British policy-makers at the same time aimed to circumvent the delicate problem of deciding whether and when France was to be informed of how slim the British regarded chances of maintaining the status quo.

(5) A self-confident trust in British negotiating skills; British diplomacy knowingly took the risk of the German side questioning the status quo during negotiations, in the hope that this very questioning would offer an opportunity to discuss the 'essential requirements' laid down by the Western powers and thereby to link (a) changes of the status quo with (b) German concessions (arms limitations, non-aggression pacts with neighbouring states in Central and Eastern Europe) within the framework of a comprehensive settlement.[293] The ultimate goal of British 'preventive diplomacy', (i.e. appeasement offensives), was to transform moments of 'crisis' into opportunities for a comprehensive solution.

A detailed analysis from this perspective once again reveals the intimate connections between British domestic and foreign policy; they are evidenced in particular by the application in both spheres of a methodological principle according to which the dilemma of having to take sides could be avoided by prevailing upon opposing factions to make reciprocal concessions in order to bring about 'peaceful change'. An assessment of the domestic situation which could reveal the respective resoluteness or irresoluteness of the opponents (Germany and France) was considered a vital

291. The alternative was debated between Vansittart and Eden, and between Hankey and Vansittart as well as within the Foreign Office and between London and Paris — Cabinet Committee on Germany, 17 Febr. 1936, Cab. 27–599; Vansittart to Eden, 20 Jan. 1936, C 418/4/18, FO 371–19 883, pp. 168ff.; C 1028/4/18, 24 Febr. 1936, FO 371–19 885, pp. 318ff.

292. Cabinet meeting 5 March 1936, Cab. 23–83, p. 235; FO/AM/WO-Memo., 'The Air Pact', 2 Mar 1936, G (36)6, §§4–5, Cab. 27–599. These memoranda stressed that Laval had conceded to Hoare that it was up to London to test the Air Pact-project as a stepping stone to a 'New Locarno' — Hoare/Laval meeting, 11 Sept. 1935, C 6516/55/18, Cab. 21–417.

293. C 998/4/18, 15 Febr. 1936, FO 371–19 885, pp. 273ff.; C.P. 42(36), 11 Febr. 1936, Cab. 27–599; G (36)4, 14 Febr. 1936, §8, Cab. 27–599.

element in this process. Thus, for example, it was the objective of the British peace offensive in the Locarno crisis to sidestep the embarrassing question of how the government in London stood in relation to its treaty commitments.[294] Inevitably, the government responded to the thwarting of British plans by a German *coup de force* by attempting in the first instance to define the situation which had now arisen – undesirable as it was – as a case which remained outside the ambit of 'alliance rules'. The first statement[295] prepared by Eden, presented to the House of Commons on 9 March 1936 before his departure for consultations with the Locarno partners in Paris, was still entirely orientated towards resolving the crisis at the negotiating table by integrating it into a more comprehensive framework, even if Eden did add that Britain felt obliged because of 'Locarno' to hurry to the aid of the country under attack. In cabinet discussions the already balanced statement was further amended under the influence of Simon so as to underline the preliminary character of this exploratory exchange of opinions. Eden and Halifax were not to agree to any decision which could prejudice the discussions of the Council of the League of Nations. Over and above this, the British negotiators were instructed at least to put forward the view that a meeting to examine Hitler's constructive proposals had to remain possible.[296] Even when London was forced to acknowledge that France had reacted more decisively than might have been expected before the onset of the crisis, the cabinet decided that Britain's course was to be seen initially as correct, and that it was to be adhered to.[297] The cabinet could not, however, protect British policy from the influence of two conflicting pressures.

(1) British policy had to 'appease' France; that is, insist that her reactions kept to the approach which Britain had predicted before 7 March 1936. For France this meant renouncing unilateral action and accepting instead the delays which resulted from using the

---

294. Baldwin and MacDonald, 5 and 11 March 1936, Cab. 23–83, pp. 232ff., 285ff.; cf. Gibbs, pp. 227ff.

295. Eden/FO-Memo., 'Germany and the New Locarno Treaty', 8 March 1936, §§27ff., Cab. 24–261; Cabinet meeting, 9 March 1936, Cab. 23–83, pp. 244ff.; Jones, *Diary with Letters*, pp. 177ff.

296. Cabinet meeting, 9 March 1936, Cab. 23–83, pp. 244ff.; Earl of Avon, *Facing the Dictators*, pp. 360ff.; Middlemas, Barnes, *Baldwin*, pp. 920ff.

297. DDF, 2e ser., vol. 1, Nos. 163, 184; G (36)3, 17 Febr. 1936, §4, Cab. 27–599. The Cabinet had expected 'non-flagrant' violations and, accordingly, proceedings involving the Council of the League of Nations; Cabinet meetings 11 and 17, 18 March 1936, Cab. 23–83, pp. 285ff., 343ff.

official channels of the League of Nations procedure.[298] If Britain was to succeed in this context, the case had to be classified as 'non-flagrant'; this meant differentiating between the remilitarisation of German territory and an act of aggression which would have involved a violation of the borders of a foreign territory.[299] In order to allay French doubts, Britain considered both offering direct promises of help, and applying pressure on Germany not to aggravate the situation further but to be satisfied with the success she had already obtained through her use of surprise tactics. The measures taken by Britain in both these latter areas were designed above all to prevent the problem of Britain's treaty commitments becoming too acute; the details of those measures are well known and need not be repeated here.[300]

(2) Britain was not forced to inform France of the views and motives which had led her to opt for concessions before 7 March 1936. The restrictive conditions which those motives imposed were more significant for Britain now that the event they had hitherto only feared had taken place. As in the Munich crisis, the British reaction had been determined long before the event. That is to say, neither Britain nor France was in a military position (however favourable the situation might have been)[301] to risk a war.[302] Furthermore, in view of the poor state of her armed services, Britain could at best provide token forces, and would in so doing endanger other British spheres of interest.[303] Britain had to

298. Cabinet meeting, 5 March 1936, Cab. 23–83, pp. 227ff.; Wigram and Sargent had listed French statements before 7 March 1936, which were interpreted to mean that 'immediate action' would only be called forth in case of an attack on France and/or Belgium, i.e. crossing of frontiers; C 1405/4/18, FO 371-19 887.

299. Cranborne to Cecil (League of Nations Union), 8 March 1936, C 1618 and C 1631/4/18, FO 371-19 889. The international lawyers, Bennett and Malkin, advised that the League procedure was obligatory in case of non-flagrant violation; C 1994/4/18, 14 March 1936, FO 371-19 893, pp. 199ff. Malkin had made clear at an earlier stage (30 Jan. 1936, C 1064/4/18, FO 371-19 885, pp. 347ff.) that France would be justified to ask the League for sanctions if the Council of the League laboured in vain; Britain would then have to obey the Council's resolution on measures of assistance to the aggrieved parties.

300. 'Diary of Events, March to November 1936', Cab. 21–545; Emmerson, pp. 177ff. Berlin did nothing to comply with Britain's suggestions/requests to contribute to defusing the conflict either by accepting symbolic international police forces in the (former) Rhine Zone, desisting from building defence walls, or at least withdrawing some of the re-entry forces.

301. Cabinet Committee on Locarno Crisis, 1st and 2nd meeting, 13 March 1936, Cab. 27–603; Pownall-Diaries, vol. 1., pp. 105f. (9 March 1936); C.P. 81(36), 12 March 1936; cf. Gibbs, pp. 69f., 111, 227ff., 246ff., 250ff.; Emmerson, pp. 184ff., 237ff.

302. Chamberlain-Flandin meeting 13 March 1936, report in Cab. 27–603; BD, 2nd ser., vol. 16, No. 115; P.-E. Flandin, *Politique Française 1919–1940*, Paris 1947, pp. 207f.; CID 1224–B, 1 April 1936=C 2608/4/18, FO 371-19 889. The Berlin Embassy (Phipps) reported on the strength of the German forces on 11 March 1936, C 1687/4/18, FO 371-19 889.

303. WO-Memo., 8 March 1936, FO 371-19 888, p. 38; D. Cooper's interview with

do more than claim that she herself was not ready for action; she also had to warn France of the burden she might have to shoulder, were she to consider retaliation. If Britain were to endorse France's belief that she was strong enough to teach Germany a lesson alone, then Britain would eventually be forced to participate in retaliatory action with forces hardly capable of action. Since Britain either did not – or perhaps did not wish – to believe in[304] in the potential success of French retaliatory action, it was important at least not to encourage France to act.[305] It was this which led Britain to divert discussions onto questions of principle, including not only the problem of France's unreliability in affairs which did not directly affect her security[306] but also the lack of cooperation between the military and the Foreign Ministry in France,[307] the provocative features of Laval's policy in the Abyssinian crisis[308] and the alarming impression gained by the British military from comments of French participants during Staff talks on the state of the French armed forces,[309] especially the Air Force. Moreover, Britain's assessment of the concrete situation pointed her towards similar conclusions. Before the beginning of the Rhineland crisis on 7 March 1936, the British cabinet, in discussion about the domestic political situation in France and of the mood of French public opinion during the Abyssinian crisis, had expressed doubts as to whether the government in Paris wanted to risk action in the Rhineland crisis at all. The cabinet presumed either that Paris had approached Britain only in her capacity as

---

Hoesch, the German Ambassador, 8 March 1936, GD, ser. C, vol. 5, No. 33, p. 57; COS 442, 12 March 1936, debated in Cabinet on 18 March 1936; C.P. 81(36); the FO draw attention to a possible German-Japanese line-up, 29 April 1936, Cab. 23–84.

304. See above on the 'bolshevic' complex.

305. Chamberlain–Flandin meeting, 15 March 1936, Cab. 23–83, pp. 303ff; and Committee meeting, 13 March 1936, Cab. 27–603.

306. Earl of Avon, *Facing the Dictators*, pp. 337ff.; Pownall-Diaries, vol. 1, p. 85. The Staff talks in October and December 1935 and the diplomatic exchanges with the French left a disastrous impression on the British delegations; furthermore, the British wondered whether French governments, in view of the 'pacifist' mood in the country (outside Paris), really would intervene to forestall the *Anschluss*; against this background the British asked what useful purpose the demilitarised zone would and could serve; Sargent-Memo., C 796/4/18, 10 Febr. 1936, FO 371–19 884, p. 25; O'Malley, G (36)6, 24 Febr. 1936, Cab. 27–599; Eden-Memo., G (36)3, 14 Febr. 1936, §§3 and 4, Cab. 27–599.

307. Wigram, 16 Jan. 1936, C 291/4/18, FO 371–19 883; cf. Earl of Avon, *Facing the Dictators*, pp. 274f., 280ff.; Roskill, *Hankey*, vol. 3, pp. 182ff.; Pownall-Diaries, vol. 1, p. 85 (14 Oct. 1935); see ch. 1, note 320 of German original.

308. Cab. 47(35)1, 16 Oct. 1935, Cab. 23–82, p. 271; Middlemas, Barnes, *Baldwin*, pp. 861ff.; A. Marder, *Royal Navy*.

309. Emmerson, p. 109; R. Young, *In Command of France*, pp. 110ff.; Slessor, *Central Blue*, pp. 157, 230ff.

guarantor power, to provide an alibi for her own passivity[310] or that she had intended to take advantage of the crisis to replace Locarno with an alliance with Britain.[311] Although these questions were raised in the cabinet on 5 March when Flandin's request was being considered, cabinet discussions were then overtaken by the events of 7 March. By asking these questions, the cabinet had wanted to induce its French partners to withdraw their request. In so doing, France would have been subordinating the question of Britain's 'legal' obligations to honour its treaty to political considerations: Was this the opportune moment to teach Hitler a lesson, and what were the chances of success?[312]

Once the impending threat had become a reality, Britain emphasised these aspects of the situation even more. The reasons for so doing may be traced back to the continuing course of the discussion on domestic politics, which was not interrupted by the turn of events abroad but went on unchanged. Most importantly, debates before 7 March had created an atmosphere in which the demilitarised zone could already be entered in the books as a loss.[313] Britain's opting for 'bargaining procedures' is a symptom of the precedence she gave to 'political' aims over lawful, legally enforceable obligations. The famous leader in *The Times* of 9 March 1936, 'A Chance to Re-build', was characteristic of the dominant mood.[314] A cabinet minister, who considered resignation during the crisis, paints the following telling picture:

> The Government has sapped its own morale for some months past in its tentative thinking about a future settlement with Hitler. Ministers both in London and Paris had got into the habit of treating the neutralisation of the Rhineland as expendable for such a purpose . . . there was still less heart in public opinion. This was the only sort of situation where a statesman can ever be justified in pleading that the unreadiness of public opinion has made right action impossible, for here right action had to be decided in a matter of hours and, once the governments concerned had got themselves involved in conservations and explanations, any right action became impossible.
>
> . . . to go to war with Germany for walking into their own backyard . . .

310. MacDonald, 5 March 1936, Cab. 23–83, pp. 227f., 236ff.
311. G (36)3, §4; Sargent, 18 March 1936, on C 1912/4/18, FO 371–19 892, pp. 292ff.
312. Baldwin and MacDonald, 5 March 1936, Cab. 23–83, pp. 227ff., 231ff.
313. C.P. 42(36), 11 Febr. 1936, Cab. 27–599; C 998/4/18, 15 Febr. 1936, FO 371–19 885; Cab. 23–83, pp. 39ff., 58f., 78f.; Pownall-Diaries, vol. 1, p. 103 (3 March 1936).
314. FO internal meeting, 7 March 1936, in I. Colvin, *Vansittart in Office*, London 1965, p. 79; Pownall-Diaries, vol. I, pp. 104ff.; Jones, *Diary with Letters*, pp. 179ff.; Nicolson-Diaries, vol. I (paperback ed.), pp. 242f.

at a time moreover when you were actually discussing with them the dates and conditions of the right to resume occupation, was not the sort of thing people could understand. So that moment which . . . offered that last effective chance of securing peace without war went by.[315]

Reports of the chiefs of staff[316] on the military situation in March 1936 together with reports on the mood in the constituencies[317] helped to consolidate the view within the cabinet that Germany could not be banished by force from an area whose return to German sovereignty had already been contemplated.[318]

Cabinet decision-makers declared themselves to be at one with the War Office[319] in the view that Britain could hardly enter into a conflict simply because Germany had chosen a 'form and procedure' (*sic!*) which Britain considered wrong, whilst she agreed with Germany on the substantive issue. Germany's unilateral action should not, they maintained, obscure the fact that most of the proposals in the memorandum submitted by Germany at the time of the reoccupation, were identical to ideas which Britain advocated. In contrast to previous situations of a similar nature, Britain should in this case not allow the path to negotiations over non-aggression pacts, over an Air Pact, over Germany's return to the League of Nations, and so on, to be blocked by French demands. The War Office even agreed to allow Germany equal treatment by permitting her to build fortifications in the Rhineland, on the basis of an assumption that France was unlikely to demolish the Maginot Line. With this the War Office not only disavowed its own assessment of the strategic value of a demilitarised Rhineland, which it had declared in January 1936 to be a necessary obstacle to a German *Drang nach Osten*, but also distanced itself from a demand which France regarded as 'essential' to her defence and foreign policy. France regarded the building of German fortifications in the West as a sign that Germany had no desire for negotiations over a 'New Locarno' and that the remaining Locarno powers, including Britain, had no other choice than to turn Locarno into a West

315. Percy, *Some Memoirs*, p. 184.

316. Hankey report on COS meeting, 12 March 1936, in Locarno Committee, Cab. 27–603, 13 March 1936; COS 442, FO 371-19 899, p. 46.

317. N. Chamberlain, 13 March 1936, Cab. 27–603; the reports on the Meetings of Government backbenchers' Foreign Affairs Committee are kept in PREM. 1-194; on this aspect see below.

318. Ministerial Meeting, 13 March 1936, Cab. 27–603.

319. WO, 8 March 1936, FO 371-19 888, pp. 37ff.; Cooper-Hoesch meeting, 9 March 1936, GD, ser. C, vol. 5, No. 33; Richard Law reported similar views from the 'City'; Law to Sargent, 9 March 1936, C 1643/4/18, FO 371-19 889.

European alliance without – and thereby against – Germany. The consensus within the cabinet, by contrast, was that Britain could not accept that the building of German fortifications of itself implied that the time had come for the serious discussion of reprisals.[320] In April 1936 the cabinet accordingly rejected France's request for Britain to concede that the 'conciliation' phase had failed and for her to impose sanctions in response to the German fortifications.[321] The British maxim according to which the maintenance of peace was considered more important than preserving the status quo – which gave precedence, in other words, to political calculations over the letter of the law – led British policy in this and other crises not only to renege on its pledges and allow treaty violations, thereby sacrificing elements of its security policies, but also subsequently to put up with further unilateral German action, to the detriment of Britain's French ally. Since British offers of compensation to France turned out to be no more than hollow gestures without even symbolic value, Britain's attempt at a trade-off between 'politics and law' clearly ended in Germany's favour. The 'alliance' of British forces, which had demanded action to protect international law, broke asunder over differences of opinion. While some (the Labour Party, the League of Nations Union) demanded that the government's first move should be to take stronger measures against the Italian aggressor and only later to move against Hitler, others (Churchill, Austen Chamberlain and Percy) – including the French government – argued for the suspension of sanctions against the Italian law-breakers and the concentration of the Locarno and League of Nations Powers on the more serious threat from Germany. To a great extent, these cleavages may be considered responsible for a situation in which formative experiences within British political life could continue to exert an influence, untouched by the 'harsh realities' created by Germany.

5. System of Government and Foreign Policy

The weaknesses of British foreign policy in the 1930s have been

320. Chamberlain-Flandin meeting, 15 March 1936, Cab. 27–603; Flandin, *Politique*, pp. 207ff.; Cabinet meeting, 12 March 1936, Cab. 23–83, pp. 298ff.; DDF, vol. 1, Nos. 316, 317, 345, 363, 409f.

321. Cabinet meeting, 8 April 1936, Cab. 23–83, p. 442. On the state of German fortifications in the West at that time see Emmerson, *Rhineland Crisis*, pp. 234ff.

seen, both by apologists for and critics of the National government, as being connected with the system of government. The critics' task has been simple; they have merely had to point out how the government neglected to use its majority in Parliament to develop purposeful and energetic policies, and in particular how it failed to provide leadership in defence policy. Two interpretations, which are concerned with specific phases, events and power élites, are commonly put forward in this context:

(1) Commentators closely involved in government policy-making, as well as historians who have adopted the same views, recognise the commitment to a prioritisation of domestic political consensus asserted by MacDonald and Baldwin as given and therefore in a way think that a trend towards 'isolationism' was inevitable: 'I wonder if we could have kept out of the German War had a government like this been in power. I think definitely at any rate that much of the loathsome slaughter and material waste would have been saved'.[322] They credit the National government with a foreign policy which enabled Britain – in contrast to the pre-1914 situation – to take united action when this could no longer be deferred.[323] In an attempt to defend the government against the criticism that it had failed to recognise that the internal dynamics of the Hitler regime were driving Germany towards aggression, these commentators offer an interpretation which may be seen as at least minimally tinged with cynicism: the government, it is claimed, was making provision for a situation in which it would have failed to prevent a second 'Anglo-German' world war, by laying the foundations for Britain to enter such a war with a clear conscience and a united domestic front – as it would do, for example, if Germany were to reject reasonable offers and insist on territorial gains and rights of domination instead of 'equality of opportunities'. This legitimising ideology should not, however, deflect our attention from the principal goal underlying British policy: the tendency of British appeasement policy stubbornly to persist in offering Britain's services as negotiator, both before and immediately after Hitler's successes in the March crises, in order to incorporate Germany into the 'comity of nations', must be seen as an attempt to pursue peace policies as an alternative to Britain's pre-1914 diplomacy – an attempt motivated by domestic political

322. Runciman to Simon, 13 July 1934; in August/September 1938, Simon and N. Chamberlain exchanged similar views, Simon-Mss.

323. Amery, *Political Life*, vol. 3, p. 223; Earl of Kilmuir, *Political Adventure*, London 1964, pp. 48f.

experiences and expectations: 'our own policy is quite clear. We must keep out of troubles in Central Europe at all costs. July twenty years ago stands out as an awful warning'.[324]

However, to conclude from the 'honourable' nature of the government's subjective intentions that Britain's internal unity is to be seen as a great achievement of government policy, which compensates for its other oversights, would be to distort the picture of the domestic political scene. For what characterised the contemporary climate at home was precisely the fact that both the 'opposition from the Right' and the 'opposition from the Left' appeared consistently more inclined to contemplate conflict with the Third Reich than the government;[325] thus the unity which ensued after the outbreak of war may be seen as forced on the government by the Opposition, rather than the other way around. In contrast to the prewar situation of 1914, neither the military[326] nor the government felt any need either to alert Britain to the risks of 'impending war', nor to advocate steering a course towards conflict. Arguments which seek to justify government policy in the terms outlined above are correct only in as much as the governments of MacDonald, Baldwin and Chamberlain reflected the mood and spirit of the interwar period;[327] foreign policy and strategy, orientated as they were to domestic political considerations, underwent a process of change from appeasement to the anti-Hitler coalition which reflected similar changes in public opinion.

(2) If we turn now to changes in the public mood after 1945 (i.e. after the Labour Party's victory in the general election), it might appear possible to view that change as just retribution of the National government's shortcomings in the spheres of economic and social policy. The Conservatives' election defeat might be interpreted in this scheme of things as a natural counterpart to the

324. Simon to R. MacDonald, 27 July 1934 (after the murder of Dollfuß), Simon-Mss. and FO 800–291.

325. A. Chamberlain, Churchill, R. Boothby wanted to back up the French resolution in 1936, and argued for calling Hitler's bluff; they referred to rumours of military opposition to Hitler's coup and asserted that this was the moment to stand up to German coups de main. The Left took refuge in the argument that Britain and France should persuade the League to take action against Italy first. During the Spanish Civil War the opposition on the Right and on the Left 'neutralised' one another even more; they began to close ranks on the eve of 'Munich', but actually worked together to the same end only after 'Prague'.

326. D.C. Watt, *Too Serious a Business*, pp. 28ff., 116ff. The Service Ministers, with the exception of Hailsham and D. Cooper, supported a 'search for agreement' against a 'politics of despair'. On Eyres-Monsell and Swinton see note 318 of German original.

327. *History of the Times*, vol. 4, p. 484; Gibbs, p. 806.

failure of appeasement policies towards the Third Reich; thus, in the end, the same faults would appear to have dogged government policy throughout the period. By drawing out further the lines of criticism advanced from both the left-wing and the right-wing of the contemporary Opposition, it would then be possible to trace government failure back to weaknesses in the *Herrschaftssynthese*[328] of the interwar period.

However, no interpretation can simply be restricted to discussions of the governing circles, but must also, given the competitive nature of processes of democratic opinion-formation, include within its purview a study of the policies of the groups who opposed government domestic and foreign policy. The aim of such an analysis cannot, however, simply be one of 'shifting responsibility' by reproducing the government propaganda concerning the Opposition, which presented them as the 'guilty men', who, while their strong language was prejudicing all foreign powers against England, were arguing at the same time for withholding all effective weapons from Britain.[329] Extending our investigation to those groups who shaped the 'terms of debate' serves rather as a means of analysing the impact of the socio-political system on foreign policy. The British socio-political system presented the competing parties with an alternative: they could either fight over the same pool of potential public support – thus 'lapsing' into a process of mutual accommodation[330] – or drift apart on fundamental issues as these were raised by specific events, which occurred for instance after the Labour government crisis of 1931. Within this framework it might be possible to judge any government simply to be as good as the Opposition's challenges and *vice versa*. However, more decisive for our analysis of the 1930s is an observation of the similarities between the ways in which government and Opposition contributed to the identification of problems and to developing the means by which they were tackled.

An unusual party-political situation was created by the fact that the government had an outsize majority, which was confused in its goals; it was opposed by an heterogeneous, low-profile Opposi-

---

328. This criticism was voiced long before '1945' and was no monopoly of members of the opposition. Hankey, for instance, compared the management of the Unemployment Assistance Board affair in late 1934/early 1935 to the disastrous handling of the Air Pact idea, which he never stopped criticising; Hankey Diary, 10 Febr. 1935, in Roskill, *Hankey*, vol. 3, p. 159.

329. Q. Hogg, *The Left was never Right*; this is the polemic return to Simon Haxey, *Tory MP*; and 'Cato', *Guilty Men*.

330. This was the predominant interpretation at least at the time, e.g. Ivor Jennings, L. Keir; it is manifested in the term 'Baldwin-MacDonaldism'.

tion, which was blinkered in relation to the questions of defence, particularly where the German question was concerned. This created a constellation in which *ad hoc* associations – for example, amongst well-known journalists – not only played a part in setting the terms of debate but also undermined the government's diplomatic monopoly by embarking on self-appointed missions to establish direct contacts with the state and government leaders of other countries and to draw up catalogues of themes for bilateral or international negotiation.[331] They thereby filled a vacuum in public political debates on important foreign and domestic political questions which the National government, the governing parties and the Labour Opposition had themselves created. It can then be said in general terms that just as electoral considerations prevented the alternating parties in government – Conservative and Labour – from formulating a concrete programme of action to organise capitalism at home,[332] they were also shadow-boxing in the arena of foreign policy. Discussions of decisive problems were suppressed; in terms of foreign policy, those problems included the necessity of containing the 'German threat', or achieving 'concession and compromise all-round'; at home, they involved the question of structural improvements in the industrial sector or the implementation of strong measures for the restoration of world trade. Instead, a series of half-way measures was introduced. Debates on foreign policy were bland and full of verbiage; although speeches revealed which countries were classed by whom as aggressive states or as peaceful democracies, they did not make clear how Britain was to face the problems of foreign policy. Their use of nondescript terms which could be interpreted freely by any listener is of course explicable in terms of the limitations placed on Britain's scope for action, on the one hand by the armaments deficit, as well as her decision on the target date for the rearmament process and her doctrine of 'limited liability', and, on the other hand, by domestic priorities. These contributed also to the government's ready acceptance of the Opposition's interest in

---

331. Lothian, Allen, Lansbury scheduled their visits to Berlin, Washington parallel to Anglo-French ministerial conferences or to Imperial Conferences; *The Times* or debates in the House of Lords offered them a forum; sometimes they suggested that the recent visitors had more first-hand knowledge on Hitler or Roosevelt than speakers from the front benches.

332. J. Stevenson, 'Myth and Reality. Britain in the 1930s,' in A. Sked and Ch. Cook, eds., *Crisis and Controversy*, London 1976, p. 105; cf. D.A. Kavanagh, 'Crisis Management,' p. 220. The problems raised by Lloyd George, the Macmillan Group et al. were reduced to administrable affairs and were then dealt with as if they were indeed specific questions; see Cab. 27–583/84 or the Unemployment Assistance Board affair in 1935.

conducting the armaments controversy on the level of principles alone.

Before 1914 both the government and Opposition had clearly stated the reasons for either rearming certain branches of the armed forces against Germany or for choosing instead to oppose Germany by diplomatic means alone, thereby placing it on a level with France or Russia. Debates between 'official' representatives of the government and the Opposition in the 1930s, by contrast, avoided identifying the enemy clearly. Thus these debates took the form of discussion of whether British armaments policy should be more strongly aligned to the principle of collective security or to national and imperial needs for defence. The Left were convinced apologists for the former view – which included the bold theory that British rearmament was more or less unnecessary since the members of the League of Nations as a collective already greatly outnumbered the aggressor and since also, in the form of the Royal Navy, Britain supplied the pool of collective security with an unrivalled instrument for the imposition of sanctions. The government, on the other hand, was not able, nor did it have any desire, either to adhere to the principle of collective security, since in so doing it would have had to ignore the warnings of its military advisers or publicly to commit itself to taking 'national interests' as the yardstick of its armaments policy. In the 1935 election campaign ministers avoided 'discussions of this dangerous topic'; that is, of rearmament and the League.[333]

Despite the crises to which German action had given rise, the government and the Opposition studiously avoided defining the 'enemy' more clearly, on adapting armaments measures to the potential theatre of war by making any public declarations on the nature of their 'strategy'.[334] The prime example of this ostrich-like policy[335] was the Peace Ballot campaign of 1934–35. Immediately after the launching of the campaign, the League of Nations Union side-stepped the specific issues involved by focusing on the general question of sanctions. The campaign's initiators feared that a

---

333. J.C. Robertson, 'The British General Election of 1935', *JCH*, 9(1974), p. 162.

334. The French Ambassador Corbin quite correctly assessed that the debate on the 1936 Statement Relating to Defence followed its course just as if nothing had happened on 7 March 1936; Corbin, 12 March 1936, DDF, vol. 1, No. 409, p. 529 (for other aspects see note 326 of German original).

335. A. Livingstone, *The Peace Ballot. The Official History*, 1935; cf. Naylor, *Labour's International Policy*, pp. 65ff. Dennis, *Decision*, p. 35, correctly relates the 'new' notion 'Field Force' (instead of Expeditionary Force) to the Peace Ballot. CID, 226th meeting, 22 Nov. 1934, Cab. 2–6/1.

fatal majority would vote against the fulfilment of international law obligations if concrete issues were raised – the question, for example, of whether Britain intended to honour her Locarno obligations or whether she should help France if Germany reneged on her treaty obligations.[336] The same approach was adopted, though in less drastic form, by leading figures in the government and the political parties, as well as within the leadership of the Labour Party, the International Committee of the Labour Party, the Liberal Party and action groups such as the Council for Action for Peace and Reconstruction and the Next-Five-Years Group.[337] None of these could pluck up enough courage before the advent of crisis to strive for an internal understanding over the action to be taken in an emergency, despite the fact that they were able to predict imminent conflict on the basis of the information to which they had access, and that they had also concluded that indecision on Britain's part would work in favour of the Hitler regime and to the detriment of their allies, France and members of the League of Nations. Neither the government nor the Opposition were in a position to 'give a lead'; in other words, to offer the kind of systematic formulation of the situation which might both have acted as a guideline for their supporters and at the same time allowed the politicians to retain a certain flexibility in domestic and foreign policy. Even if we admit that it is not the responsibility of foreign policy or diplomacy to declare its position publicly, it remains important to establish whether the politicians were in any position to make decisions when the situation so demanded. In the following, then, it will be necessary first to analyse the functions and conditions of the decision-making process.

The first question which arises in an analysis of the impact of the system of government on British foreign policy is that of whether and how the organisation of governmental activities influenced the external representation of 'British interests'. Once it has become clear that the political side of the government's work was con-

---

336. An opinion poll on behalf of the 'Ilford Recorder' induced the initiators of the Peace Ballot campaign to take refuge in abstract questions; Lord Robert Cecil, *A Great Experiment. An Autobiography*, London 1941.

337. Cecil styled the Air Pact as part of a general peace scheme, once he realized the extent of opposition to granting France a 'favour'; Cecil to Mrs B. Williams, Edinburgh League of Nations Union Branch, 14 Febr. 1935, Cecil-Mss. On 3 March 1936 the International Sub-Committee of the National Executive Council of the Labour Party had the question on its agenda: 'What should Great Britain do if the demilitarised zone is flagrantly violated by Germany?' But the meeting then concentrated on how to rescue the League and quell Mussolini, the 'smaller dictator'.

ducted through the committee system, it is possible for analysis to concentrate on this aspect of its activities.[338] We might ask, for example, whether the process of consensus-formation during committee proceedings (in the CID, the DRC, the Ministerial Committee on Disarmament, etc.)[339] allowed the cabinet, as the organ of collective responsibility, to control the foreign policy of the different departments responsible for foreign affairs. Did it increase the efficiency of the government's performance? Did it facilitate the flexibility of British policy in international affairs? The answer to all three questions is No. Having discussed the same problems for the umpteenth time, heads of departments, experts and ministers in the numerous committees, sub-committees and endless new *ad hoc* special committees seldom identified anything more than the lowest common denominator of agreement amongst their diverse opinions. The ambiguous compromises which they formulated and put forward either represented vain attempts to unify and placate opposing interests within Britain and/or between Britain and other countries, or else registered a consensus whose actual basis was a reduction of the range of proposals discussed to hollow platitudes. In neither instance did the process of opinion-formation within the government expand the range of decisions which it might later take on the basis of its assessment of the state, or its interpretation of the international situation. As a rule, the framework of Britain's foreign policy crisis decisions was marked out by decision already taken during hypothetical discussions of the implications of particular events in committee. Within established government structures, it was more or less impossible for new information arising from and about other powers involved in any crisis to be used to bring about either a renewed questioning of positions adopted in previous committee consultations, or a relaxation of entrenched government attitudes. Reports of internal disagreements within the German leadership or of signs of the French government's resolve to insist on the fulfilment of Britain's legal obligations produced no new considerations from the British side; instead, they were played down in numerous ways.[340] In those instances in which British initiatives

338. K.C. Wheare, *Government by Committee*, Oxford 1955. My set of questions is influenced by the concept of 'bureaucratic politics' (R. Neustadt; G.T. Allison).

339. Ch. 'Strategien' provides the material for the study of government by committee.

340. Schacht's appeals to the Foreign Office under Eden or N. Chamberlain's or Vansittart's reaction to messages from the 'German Opposition' as well as visits of Cabinet Ministers to Paris or of French Ministers to London even in the early stage of crises did not induce a new process, but were simply 'taken in', i.e. denied any 'real news value'.

were undertaken in an attempt to set international politics in motion, the compromises reached in the committees proved to be more durable and to carry greater weight than cries for help from British delegates asking the government to take steps to lead international negotiations out of impasse. As the beginning of this present chapter shows, the main reason for Britain's limited flexibility was the failure of individual interest groups or lobbies to persuade their domestic opponents to accept their evaluation of international and German politics as the only correct diagnosis and prognosis of events.

The constant pressure on top-level representatives of departments to discuss both potential and existing conflicts in the committees further strengthened tendencies towards a stagnation in policy. On the one hand, it forced experts in the departments into defending old positions; rather than rethinking the situation on the basis of newly received information, they tended to make their interpretations with their own previous arguments, in an attempt not to appear indecisive and inconsistent. On the other hand, the participation of the same circle of people in the elaboration of proposals for cabinet and interdepartmental discussions led to a situation in which fundamental questions were shelved; discussions focused instead from the outset on specific selected issues, which could be taken care of by concrete administrative decisions. There was in any case no time for attending to the fundamental aspects of any problem or for entering into 'endless' clarificatory debates; moreover, a cabinet which delegated the task of producing reports to committees had no interest in listening to long discussions of this kind. The discrepancy between the plans of action produced by committees of 'officials' and the decisions arrived at by cabinet ministers who were operating under political pressures of various different kinds led moreover to a growth in the importance of the cabinet committees.[341]

In these ministerial committees the recommendations and conclusions presented by departments on the basis of the information to which they had access, carried far less weight than political calculations, wishful thinking, considerations of domestic political reactions or conjectures on the 'psychology' of foreign opponents, which, for example, presented Mussolini and Hitler as 'mad dogs'

---

341. To mention but a few of these: Ministerial Committee on Disarmament (1932–34); Ministerial Committee on German Rearmament (21 Nov.–14 Dec. 1934); Committee on Germany, later Committee on Foreign Policy (1936–39); Locarno Committee; and of course, the CID and its numerous Sub-Committees.

from whom one had to expect the worst. Any more cautious deliberation on the possibility of calling the dictator's 'bluff' could not expect to receive an adequate hearing. Quite the reverse: anyone who could claim to have met Hitler or Mussolini in the recent past and to know the present state of his (Hitler's) mind was likely to be taken for an 'expert', at least by some cabinet ministers. This led to a situation in which the advice of outsiders sometimes carried considerably more weight with influential cabinet ministers[342] than the opinions of the departments which were presented by the permament secretaries or integrated into the committee reports. This peculiarity can be explained, on the one hand, by the fact that the politicians, especially Baldwin, but also Simon and Kingsley Wood,[343] considered themselves more able to assess public opinion than the civil servants (in some cases this meant that they trusted the editors of leading newspapers, such as Dawson of *The Times*, more than leading civil servants at the Foreign Office). On the other hand, leading civil servants were unable to present the particular sort of information and impressions which members of the cabinet valued as much as they valued domestic public opinion; namely, a picture of the leadership of the Third Reich based on 'fresh' impressions of non-official 'rapporteurs'. Outsiders such as Toynbee, Thomas Jones, Lothian and others, whose visits to Berlin took place with the knowledge and partly with the consent of the prime minister and foreign secretary (Baldwin and Simon), or journalists who, like Ward Price were 'sought after' by Hitler, Göring and Schacht amongst others, were able to arouse the interest of the 'strong men' in the cabinet by casually introducing proposals and models which appeared at first glance to offer solutions to the problems debated in cabinet.[344] The fact that the 'desk officers' and heads of divisions in the Foreign

342. The preference for outsiders' advice signals the distrust among Cabinet Ministers of the Foreign Office (Vansittart); Vansittart's lengthy memoranda, his habit of taking a long weekend, poor administrative performance etc. were a constant nuisance to both his superiors and his opposite numbers in other departments.

343. Earl of Avon, *Facing the Dictators*, p. 446; Earl of Kilmuir, *Adventure*, pp. 48f.; Viscount Swinton, *I Remember*, London 1948, p. 266. The higher civil servants respected the fact that politicians were better trained to gauge public opinion, especially with regard to the speeding up of rearmament. W. Fisher to Chatfield, 11 July 1934, Baldwin-Mss., vol. 131/94.

344. N. Chamberlain's interest in the concept of international police action was renewed in March 1936: Ward Price sent the contents of his interview with Hitler and Göring to Baldwin, Eden, Halifax and Hankey; Phipps and R. Hankey reported the message to the Foreign Office, C 1827/4/ resp. C 1892/4/18, 13 March 1936, FO 371–19 891. N. Chamberlain insisted that the proposal be considered both in Cabinet and in the Locarno Committee (2nd to 4th meeting Cab. 27–603). Earl of Avon, *Facing the Dictators*, pp. 362f.; Emmerson, p. 187; Ward Price, *I Know These Dictators*, London 1937, pp. 128ff.; Flandin, p. 209.

Office did not elaborate similar solutions in advance but instead took obvious trouble to point to the pitfalls which such proposals contained, diminished the usefulness of 'official' advisers in the eyes of the inner cabinet.

The evidence which we have at our disposal to identify those figures who filtered the mass of divergent pieces of information into a credible conceptual framework, and who found an attentive audience amongst the upper echelons of the leadership, does not appear to point to the leading civil servants.[345] Although the cabinet continued to delegate to the committees the task of processing the endless flow of information and making it more accessible to the cabinet, this in no way implied that the analysis contained in the reports would also be binding for the decision-makers. Only central figures firmly established in the 'web of government', such as Hankey[346] and Warren Fisher,[347] who had direct access to the levers of power and had built up a wide but nevertheless finely spun network of specialist information and connections, could, through their omnipresence or indispensibility, ensure or insist that their preparatory work would be recognised in the cabinet as the basis for discussions. Consequently, in foreign affairs, the Foreign Office met with substantial competition from top civil servants from other governmental offices as well as from unofficial advisers. Additionally, senior members in the Foreign Office themselves did not operate in unison; the various specialists – O'Malley in the Southern Department, Wigram and Sargent in the Central Department and Collier in the Northern Department – were divided in their recommendations, variously favouring concessions to Germany or delaying tactics through appeasement or a policy of encirclement. They also totally disagreed on whether the states of 'New Europe' were bound to fall under Germany's spell (*Mitteleuropa*) or had the will

345. It is, for example, very difficult to decide whether Eden's draft of the Government's statement on the 7 March 1936 event owes more to the internal Foreign Office meeting or to his presence at Lord Lothian's Blickling party; the thrust of his statement has elements of both the official advice and the influential network. Jones, *Diary with Letters*, pp. 179ff.; I. Colvin, *Vansittart*, p. 79.

346. Hankey used his influential position as Secretary to the Cabinet and the CID and the willingness of R. MacDonald and Baldwin to have him act as informal coordinator of defence; moreover, his copious correspondence with Dominion politicians and British Ambassadors (and/or their staff) over the years placed him in the centre of things. With 'rearmament' proceeding, his was a first address for captains of industry, too.

347. Warren Fisher, Permanent Secretary to the Treasury and Head of the Civil Service from 1919, is often regarded as the incarnation of 'Treasury control'. Peden, *Treasury*, pp. 52ff., correctly stresses that Fisher's influence was declining rapidly after 1935.

and the resources to stand up to Germany's *Drang nach Osten* and should therefore be encouraged by the Western powers (i.e. France and Britain) to strive for independence.[348] Each of them in turn enjoyed the patronage of different parliamentary state secretaries (Stanhope and Cranborne) or under-secretaries in charge of the Foreign Office (Vansittart, Cadogan and Strang), who competed among themselves for influence over the foreign secretaries (Simon, Hoare, Eden and Halifax).

Whilst the task of civil service heads of department was to concentrate on and specialise in specific political configurations and 'case studies', potential crisis areas only assumed significance for the cabinet (whose attention was addressed at any one time to numerous fields of conflict at home and abroad) when a crisis was actually imminent. By this stage, psychological calculations – such as the question of whether the British and French peoples would regard retaliation as legitimate, or whether Hitler might perhaps have come down on the idea of extreme advisers, and so on – often played a more decisive role in the decision-making process than information contributed by leading civil servants in the departments on the origin and significance of the crisis. Indeed, on the basis of their experience in domestic politics, cabinet ministers declared themselves to be far more skilled in judging these psychological issues than their expert advisers. It was precisely this reliance on improvised decision-making and 'common sense' psychologies in phases of severe crises which fostered a climate of inertia and inflexibility in British foreign policy, whose proponents were consistently unwilling to change their own patterns of behaviour or to countenance any shift in positions they had adopted towards allies (France) or opponents (Germany). Explanations for the rigidity of the basic structure of British foreign policy during the period in question are thus to be found in the frame of reference adopted by the politicians: in their according primary importance to recovery and financial stability; in their perceptions of deficiencies in armaments levels (which were not finally brought into line with other powers and with planned targets for rearmament until around 1938) and finally in the prejudices they still nursed with regard to France, Germany and the US.[349]

---

348. O'Malley, G (36)6, 24 Febr. 1936, Cab. 27–599; Collier, C 8523/55/18, 22 Nov. 1935, FO 371-18 856, pp. 151ff. Similar differences occurred both in Cabinet and within the Foreign Office in relation to the Far East; the studies of Ch. Thorne, A. Trotter, R. Louis, S.L. Endicott, J.R. Leutze et al. reveal many insights into Britain's Far Eastern 'strategy and diplomacy'.

349. Accordingly, I have selected these items to form part of the German original (especially pp. 154–179).

Despite Britain's pledge that she would be able to mediate successfully between Germany and France if they would only put her formulas for compromise to the test of reality, the British government was in fact far too preoccupied with the problem of reaching interdepartmental consensus to be able to assume a flexible role as a mediator in foreign policy. As soon as negotiations reached the point at which it was no longer sufficient for Britain to group together French concessions to Germany and German concessions to France, and to present these as a compromise solution, but where she herself had to make concessions at her own expense in order to find a way out of deadlock, it became obvious that British delegates could not and would not renegotiate compromise formulas at the international negotiating table, since those formulas had been established in the course of tough interdepartmental negotiations and were in general based on the understanding that Britain should offer 'good-will' but no sacrifices. The process of give-and-take which characterised 'government by committee' showed clear similarities with the forms of conflict encountered by the British in diplomatic negotiations. In the British context, each different department – the Foreign Office, the War Office, Admiralty, Air Ministry, Treasury and the Board of Trade – exaggerated the positions and demands they brought with them to negotiations, in order to ensure that their minimum demands survived the process of adjustment which accompanied discussion to be incorporated into instructions issued to the British negotiating delegation. The government's representatives therefore preferred to make it clear to the international forum from the very beginning that they considered any revision of conclusions arrived at in the domestic context too risky, if it took place on the basis of, or as a consequence of, international influences. For the British in the 1930s, the 'last word' in international negotiations and conferences was commonly spoken before diplomatic talks involving an international or bilateral bargaining process even began.[350] As our analysis of 'economic appeasement' projects (such as the raw-materials question) has demonstrated in detail above, decisions on matters of principle were hardly ever allowed to be renegotiated in diplomatic negotiations.

350. Anglo-French Negotiations, 1–3 Febr. 1935, Cab. 21–413, Cab. 29–146, and C 893/53/18, 1 Febr. 1935. The events in 1934 are covered in Eden's memoirs (Earl of Avon, *Facing the Dictators*, pp. 87ff.), and N. Rostow, *Anglo-French Relations, 1934–1936*, London 1984. Anglo-French relations in 1938 are best analysed in the studies of K. Robbins; K. Middlemas; and A.P. Adamthwaite.

The function of Britain's stereotypical opening gambit at Anglo-French conferences, in which leaders of the British delegation delivered statements on British public opinion and/or the state of armaments and the economic-financial situation, was to draw the attention of her negotiating partners to domestic constraints on Britain's foreign policy, and thus to mark out from the very beginning the narrow limits within which Britain would tolerate concessions to the interests of foreign allies. Any concessions which were in fact made consisted either in the kind of 'face-saving' verbiage which allowed allies, in particular France, to justify their wooing of Britain as a principal ally to public opinion at home, or in formulas for concrete action which the British knew to be unlikely to materialise in the short term. Much water would have to flow under Westminster Bridge before the British government was faced with the unpleasant task of answering for and elucidating its postures abroad[351] to public opinion at home in Britain.

The above may be taken as evidence to support the hypothesis that British foreign policy was directed by the desire to achieve results which could be 'sold' to the British public, rather than results which would be acceptable to other governments and their electorates, and which would therefore correspond more closely to Britain's self-adopted role as mediator. The seriousness of this claim becomes evident when we consider that it was Britain's explicit intention to assume a dominant role in her security alliance with France from 1934 to 1935, in an attempt to shake off the ballast of what she considered to be France's misdirected *idées fixes* on a European settlement; her aim was to sensitise France to the predominant mood in Great Britain by demonstrating the success of the British method of 'peaceful change' in achieving a normalisation of relations with the Third Reich. Yet British attempts to adumbrate areas of shared language to the rulers of Germany were rejected – and both in form and content more or less by return of post, by the National Socialist government. However, instead of acknowledging this as a clear rejection of its policies, the British government turned its attention to demonstrating to a British public its own consistency and continuity as well as its awareness of dangers and its peaceful intentions. In this way, it was able to avoid entering into public debates on fundamental issues relating to the system and dynamics of Britain's 'fascist' and 'militarist' opponent:

---

351. See ch. 1 of German original.

The role structures that make issues in the foreign and domestic areas ... [are different]. Unlike their domestic counterparts, foreign-policy issues necessarily include the occupants of roles that are not part of the system ... the foreigners who provide the consent of those in the environment who are affected (by the rearrangement of the objects or the restructuring of the values) inevitably become parties to the interaction whereby the issue is resolved ... To achieve consensus within a system over foreign policy is not to guarantee the cessation of controversy, as it is with domestic issues. If the foreigners towards whom the policy is directed resist, then the external environment will not be altered to conform to the internal consensus and the differences will probably reappear, reopening the issue.[352]

This 'standard' problem of foreign policy was further complicated in the 1930s, as the 'international environment' constituted two different sets of counterparts, the one – that is, the fascist challenge – offering no acceptable alternative to the restructuring of domestic consent but having to be considered with regard to conflict resolution 'abroad', whereas the other – 'Western democracies' – demanded British solidarity but did not alleviate the problems of attaining domestic consensus. Neither Germany nor France, neither the US nor Japan, made any single proposal to Britain which the British government felt able to introduce to its advantage into domestic British debates. For her part, Britain – as we have seen above – never took account in outlining her own proposals of the difficulties which her actions (or non-actions) caused for other governments, but focused instead on her own perceptions of the issues at stake. Britain's perception of German and French policy always shaped British political reactions in advance; accordingly, British policy during the crises was designed to shift French and German policy back into line with British expectations of the likely reactions of Germany or France in times of crisis.[353]

A second set of issues raised by the British decision-making process relates to the contradiction between the relatively 'secure' position, of which the government was assured by virtue of its large parliamentary majority, and the government's own insecurity, or rather its irresolution, in armaments and foreign policy. The government was always forced to take account of a widespread

---

352. J.N. Rosenau, 'Foreign Policy as an Issue-Area', in J.N. Rosenau, ed., *Domestic Sources of Foreign Policy*, 1967, p. 39.

353. See my remarks on British assumptions concerning 'non-flagrant' treaty violations, on the distinctions between 'Locarno' and 'Versailles', etc.

mood against rearmament in the country,[354] since the distribution of parliamentary seats did not reflect the number and distribution of votes cast in the election.[355] The leaders of the coalition parties therefore had to reckon with continual and direct challenges to their authority; thus they chose to implement tactical measures designed to realise, at least gradually, their version of what was necessary in the 'national interest' in foreign, defence and armaments policy. It was not sufficient that resolutions be passed on important principles on armaments in the cabinet, then ratified in Parliament; the government also had to find ways of implementing those directives with a minimum of friction. There were thus compelling reasons for it to take account of the public opinion trends articulated in by-elections, opinion polls and in the constituencies.

Central figures in the government (Baldwin, Eden,[356] Simon and MacDonald[357]) and important advisers at the Foreign office (Sargent, Wigram, Stanhope, Ashton-Gwatkin and Cranborne), as well as advisers to the prime minister (Jones) and to the king argued vigorously in this context for the observation of the golden rules. They maintained (1) that the mood articulated by labour in the country had to be taken into account and (2) that 'the policy of reconditioning the defence services [had to] be accompanied by some attempt at an arrangement in the political sphere with Germany, although [Eden] could not at the moment specify when and in what circumstances'.[358]

Whilst these advisers stressed that people were ready to accept a defence programme so long as they were convinced that HMG was seeking peace, top officials in the Foreign Office (Vansittart and Collier), who advocated structuring foreign policy *vis-à-vis* Germany around the dual strategy of maintaining the balance of

354. Hodsoll to Hankey, 3 Dec. 1934, Cab. 21–389; Cabinet meeting, 4 Dec. 1935, Cab. 23–82, pp. 363ff.; on Peace Ballot and related matters see above.

355. In November 1935, the Government parties won 431 seats and cast 11.5 mill. votes; the parties of opposition gained 175(176) seats and 9.95 mill. votes. The Liberals (Simon) claimed that they influenced about 5–6 mill. voters in favour of the National Government. The fact that the Government did not come forward with a 'Vote for Rearmament', as N. Chamberlain called it, is due to Baldwin's and Simon's estimates as to how industrial constituencies would respond. The Liberals, Simon, Runciman and Brown, held ministries (Home Office and later Treasury, Trade, Labour) that were important in the process of rearmament.

356. Baldwin, 26 Febr. 1936, Cab. 23–83, pp. 179ff.; H. Nicolson, R. Law, Emrys–Evans, Thomas, H. Kerr and other 'friends' of Eden set to campaign for the dual strategy; Nicolson-Diary, vol. 1, p. 236 (13 Febr. 1936).

357. Cabinet Committee on Germany, 17 Febr. 1936, Cab. 27–599; MacDonald to Baldwin, 14 Febr. 1936, PREM. 1–192; D. Marquand, *MacDonald*, p. 760.

358. Eden, 5 Febr. 1936, Cab. 23–83, p. 58.

power while accelerating rearmament, showed a marked preference for the first argument outline above.[359] In contrast to their
predecessors at the Foreign Office before 1914, they shared the
assumption of their contemporary opponents that the consequences of a political split at home would never be mitigated by
the benefits of joining forces with foreign powers. At the same
time, they felt that consensus in foreign policy was only possible
on the basis of Russia's present and future participation in the
League of Nations. Thus they concluded that Britain was obliged
to oppose Germany's attempts to satisfy her hunger for land in the
East. Since Britain needed the support of the Left (Liberals, trade
unions, the Labour Party) for rearmament and since, on the other
hand, that support was dependent on the government deciding on
one of its two foreign policy options – collective security (with
the inclusion of Russia) versus the 'appeasement' of Germany –
they advised the government to risk a break with the Right rather
than with the Left[360] should it be forced to make a choice
between the groups supporting a League of Nations policy (in
which Russia was included as an ally) and adherents to a positive
policy *vis-à-vis* Germany. The government's call for domestic political measures to be taken against the 'fascists' was similarly
designed to demonstrate that it was not hostile to labour.[361] In
terms of their policy recommendations, Vansittart and Collier took
sides against the hard core of the governing Conservative Party,
whose recruitment area comprised safe constituencies in the
south-east and south-west of England and in the London region:
fear of German air-raids led these latter members of parliament to
move to the forefront of the 'rearmament' campaign, from
whence they propagated the enlargement of the RAF and the
expansion of the Royal Navy; some also began a recruitment
campaign for the Army.[362] As advocates of protective tariffs and a

---

359. Vansittart to CI. Wigram (King George V), 7 Nov. 1935, VNST 2/27; Collier, C.
14471/42/18 (Oct. 1938), FO 371-21 659; Vansittart established contacts with H. Dalton,
Labour's shadow minister on foreign affairs, and the Soviet Ambassador I. Maisky.

360. Vansittart's preference for 'colonial appeasement' — if appeasement there had to be —
was in contradiction to the views of the 'Imperial Group'. On Collier's views see D.N.
Lammers, 'From Whitehall after Munich: The Foreign Office and the Future Course of British
Policy', *HJ*, 16(1973), pp. 842ff.

361. Vansittart, 17 Oct. 1936, C 7296/576/18; Vansittart and Collier, of course, did not
identify the 'Right' and Mosley's fascists.

362. Baldwin, too, reminded the Defence Deputation that they had 'safe' constituencies, whereas
he as Party Leader had to have regard to industrial constituencies and their worries as well. On the
recruitment campaign in favour of the Army see Amery, *Political Life*, vol. 3.; E. Beddington-
Behrens, *Look Back — Look Forward*, London 1963, pp. 107ff.; Dennis, *Decision*, pp. 75ff.

'new, imperial economic policy', these MPs not only joined Vansittart and Collier in opposing all attempts at economic appeasement – albeit for different reasons and in pursuit of different interests – they also resisted any advances towards socio-economic reform.[363]

The demands from these various different quarters that labour's interests be taken into account in the decision-making process, were only ever mediated to government indirectly. Proposals were put forward, on the grounds of the high costs involved, for a return to the pre-1914 practice of informing the Opposition directly of armaments expenditure levels and of involving them in regular secret consultations, following the precedents set by Balfour (1911–15) and Haldane (1924) in the Committee of Imperial Defence. It was even suggested that party leaders be invited to three-party meetings in which participants would take stock of the effects of the Ten Years' Rule, for which all three parties had to answer: yet none of these proposals was ever implemented.[364] Attempts to develop foreign policy along 'bipartisanship' lines, and thus to apportion a share of governmental responsibility more or less directly to the Opposition, were widely viewed as inopportune. Informal 'official' contacts with the Opposition appeared to offer poor prospects for success, since the opinions represented were too diverse.[365] Since the Opposition's slogan, 'Not a single penny for this government's rearmament programme' signalled a fundamental distrust on their part of official foreign policy, the prospects for cooperation appeared non-existent. The government further feared that the disclosure of tripartite consultations would alarm public opinion. On the basis of these arguments the cabinet continually rejected suggestions that it take the Opposition into its confidence (see its discussions of 19 March 34, 8 May 1935, 6 July 1936) in view of the seriousness of the international situation.[366] Official contacts between the government and the

363. Members of the Imperial Group advocated rearmament and along with it industrial mobilisation, but rejected proposals, form the Melchett Group, from Macmillan's 'Middle Way' group et al., directed to 'planning'; 'planning' bears many similarities to the model of *Soziale Marktwirtschaft*.

364. The Cabinet did not take to Hoare's proposal, 19 March 1934, Cab. 23–78, pp. 282ff. Hoare could also have mentioned the recent example of tripartite meetings concerning the India Bill. At another stage, in Cabinet on 6 July 1936, Cab. 23–84, the position remained unchanged.

365. Cabinet meeting, 14 Jan. 1935, Cab. 23–81, p. 34.

366. Baldwin told the Defence Deputation (29 July 1936) that only a few union leaders (Citrine, Hicks) were aware of the dangers abroad; so long as the general public disputed the 'facts' of world politics, i.e. blamed the British Government for international tensions, it would

Opposition remained limited to the advance disclosure to the Opposition of government statements and White Papers on Defence or reports on the state and progress of international bilateral negotiations – a procedure, which belongs to the everyday conventions of the parliamentary system of government. The most important practical reason why no course of direct cooperation was pursued lay, however, in the cabinet's awareness of its own inability to develop a clear line in its armament and defence policy. Advance agreement on the guidelines to be laid down in security and defence policy was considered to be a prerequisite for government consultations with the Opposition parties; in the absence of such agreement, the government feared that joint invitations to leaders of the Opposition might induce the Lloyd Georges, Churchills and Labour leaders to close ranks and force the hands of the Ramsay MacDonald/Baldwin/Neville Chamberlain/Simon 'team'.[367]

In its use of the committee system, the government had created a means of responding to the need for coordination and, at the same time, of regulating, if not actively reducing conflict; there are, however, indications that the government-by-committee system did not adequately fulfil the function for which it was designed; namely, the coordination of the views of departments and the preliminary clarification of options. Particularly in the area of armaments, defence and foreign policy, committee participants had continual grounds for complaint[368] that the infinite committee and sub-committee meetings served no other purpose than to waste time. The committees' reports were often modified in a relatively arbitrary fashion during their passage through the next level of the hierarchy – usually the cabinet; as the history of the Defence Requirements Committee's reports illustrates, this undermined any balance of opinions achieved in committee.[369] In other cases, the conclusions of committee work contained information of only limited value, since they were formulated on the basis of unclear instructions and dubious assumptions on the productive capacity of the German armaments industry, the British economy, and so on. The multitude of plans[370] which were drawn

---

make no sense to turn to bipartisanship in foreign politics.

367. Cab. 23–79, pp. 51ff.; Cabinet meeting, 14 Jan. 1935, Cab. 23–81, p. 34. The one exception was Churchill's membership in the Air Defence Research Sub-Committee of the CID since 1935.

368. Roskill, *Hankey*, vol. 3, p. 110; Pownall-Diaries, vol. 1, pp. 73f. (27 May and 6 June 1935); Jones, *Diary with Letters*, p. 176; Vansittart, 17 July 1935, VNST 2/28.

369. Dennis, *Decision*, pp. 35ff.; Gibbs, pp. 99ff.; Roskill, *Hankey*, vol. 3, pp. 87ff., 103ff.

370. With regard to the expansion of the RAF see Gibbs, ch. IV/3a; Higham, *Armed Forces*,

up by the cabinet only to be revoked, enlarged or transformed through a shift in emphasis into the precise opposite of the original, speak volumes for the lack of coordination and political leadership in British government. Scarcely had decisions on mass armaments production been taken (let alone implemented) than new arms programmes, with entirely different emphases, were being put forward. The reasons for this were numerous: in part they lay in the nature of the industry itself, since, for example, the aircraft required had by this time not reached the production stage; in part they arose out of a discrepancy between resources and productive capacity, on the one hand, and a divergence between the requirements of armed forces engaged on several different fronts, on the other.[371] Finally, the decision-makers themselves contributed to this general lack of coordination.

In attempting, through negotiations, to eliminate the possibility of enemy action as a 'principal variable' in considerations of the armaments programme, Britain could certainly sustain hopes that the scale of the problem of intragovernmental coordination might be reduced. However, the problem of the relationship between the stated priorities of the armed forces and the capacity of the armaments industry[372] was left unresolved by such negotiations. The dilemma which this posed presented itself in different forms and on different levels:

(1) The more 'essentials' were added to current lists of priorities by the three services, and the less willing (indeed, the less able) they were to coordinate their needs for supplies with the other forces which were in competition for a portion of the total defence budget, the more their demands were likely to conflict with the position of the economic departments (Treasury, Board of Trade, Ministry of Labour) and the economic associations. The latter expressed their fear that an uncoordinated deluge of orders of

pp. 170ff.; Webster, Frankland, pp. 65ff.

371. The Army had the most divergent tasks: anti-aircraft defence; imperial policing; coast defence; Field Force, but the least continuity in testing and ordering weaponry; further, it had to bear heavy cuts on its 'planning targets'. The Royal Navy had a strong lobby and a continuity in building programmes, but it took time to complete new orders, and to cope with challenges on three war theatres (Pacific, Atlantic/North Sea and Mediterranean). The RAF in theory had a prime target and a (fancy) strategy ('bomber offensive'), but was most exposed to changes in technology and 'types'. Prestige conflicts, on the Fleet Air Arm, on the Navy's 'transport assistance' to the Field Force etc., impaired the progress of rearmament and caused inefficiency in running the supply departments of the Service Ministries.

372. Postan, *War Economy*, pp. 3ff., 7ff., 12ff., 69ff.; Gibbs, p. 287ff.; H.C. Hillmann, 'Comparative Strength of the Great Powers', in *Survey of International Affairs 1939–1946. The World in March 1939*, London/ New York 1952.

this kind would cause prices and costs to rise, increase wages and inflation[373] and lead directly to a situation paraphrased, in one statement, as 'risks with labour'. Since the production capacity of the armament industries was in any case not capable of accommodating the potential volume of orders – neglected as it had been during the era of the Ten Years' Rule – inflation emanating from the armaments industry was likely to spread to civilian industries supplying armaments firms and, from there, sooner or later, to the whole economy. Quite apart from the other consequences this would entail, the state was likely as a result to feel obliged to demand ever increasing rights of economic control; it would, for example, have to ration raw materials, machine tools, skilled labour, and so on, in accordance with the priorities of the armaments economy – and thereby assume direct responsibility in peacetime for economic processes, the management of which it had only gradually accepted in the First World War, and then more out of necessity than a willingness to plan the economy. It was above all the government's reluctance to intervene in and regulate the labour market – that is, to manage mobile contingents of skilled workers[374] – or to introduce measures designed to 'dilute' trade union practices, which demonstrated the influence of the experiences of the First World War and of the transition period 1918–21.

> If . . .it is decided that the maximum speed must be applied to the programme, then a warning must be given that labour difficulties are probable. If the speed is such that the whole handling of the labour side of the situation can be left to the industries themselves, it will, from the point of view of the absence of labour troubles, be the best solution. The more the government are directly involved, the more they will be put into the position of solving the employer's difficulties by buying off the trade unions.[375]

(2) The relative limitations on the productive capacity of the armaments industry offered a welcome springboard for the arguments of those within government who wished to limit Britain's

373. This is the essence of the notion 'labour': C.P. 297(36), 30 Oct. 1936, Cab. 24–265; cf. Peden, *Treasury*, pp. 85ff.; Shay, *Rearmament*, pp. 244f.

374. Baldwin, 1 April 1936, HofC, vol. 310, col. 1992. Brown Memo., 'Defence Programme: Labour Issues Involved', C.P. 96(36), 26 March 1936; Brown, C.P. 36(36), 21 Febr. 1936, Cab. 24–260.

375. H. Wolfe Memo., (Ministry of Labour), 9 March 1936, ML 25–79. N. Chamberlain (as Minister of National Service 1917) and Lord Weir (Director of Munitions for Scotland, 1915/7) had experienced workers' and the unions' resistance to 'dilution', 'rationing' etc.

commitments for reasons of domestic as well as foreign policy. It allowed them to influence the struggle over the setting of priorities for armaments targets according to their own strategic concerns. In the end this proved particularly disadvantageous for the Army. Bad management at the War Office and, in particular, deficiencies in its procedures for allocating contracts, produced an institutional framework within which the Royal Navy and the RAF (the interests of the latter being served by the climate of mass psychosis in Britain) were constantly to be given precedence over the Army in the apportioning of the defence budget. Pointing to the threat of a decline in exports, as well as to the strains already visible within the (skilled) employment market, and so on, Neville Chamberlain repeatedly blocked the ratification of the priorities set in the course of War Office negotiations in 1934, at the end of 1936, and in 1937–38.[376] He proved particularly obstructive in cases where productive capacities were to be used for such forces as the Territorial Army (as reserve for the British Field Force), which ranked very poorly in terms of cost-effectiveness. The supplies necessary to replenish the armed forces on the Continent through reserve units (seventeen divisions of the Territorial Army) would, in his opinion, not only overload capacity but would also represent a bad investment compared with what the RAF and Royal Navy could offer for Britain's defence against an attacker.[377]

In this context, the *Coordination of Defence* should have played a key role[378] in building up a cheap and popular defence force and in subjecting armaments measures to the principles of cost-effectiveness.[379] In fact, the debate on rearmament was conducted in the context of discussions on a possible ministry of defence which were usually accompanied by strong criticisms of the committee system created and defended by Hankey.[380] Within the government, repeated suggestions were made proposing the 'coordina-

376. N. Chamberlain, C.P. 326 and C.P. 337(36), Cab. 24–265; cf. Feiling, *Life*, pp. 313ff.; Peden, *Treasury*, pp. 124ff., 171ff.; Gibbs, pp. 110ff., 261ff.; Dennis, *Decision*, pp. 88ff.

377. Chamberlain, 9 Febr. 1936, in Feiling, *Life*, pp. 313f.; Cabinet meeting, 25 Febr. 1936, Cab. 23–83, on D.P.R. Report, 12 Febr, 1936, C.P. 26(36), Cab. 24–259.

378. R. MacDonald and N. Chamberlain joined forces to achieve coordination of defence measures and cost-rationing; Marquand, *MacDonald*, p. 760; Peden, *Treasury*, pp. 38ff., 86ff. 'Fighting Forces', 'Army, Navy and Air Force Gazette' amongst other 'service' journals were in favour of a Ministry of Defence mostly because of cost-efficiency.

379. C.P. 205(34), Cab. 23–79, pp. 357ff.; see note 210 of this chapter.

380. Hankey defended the CID-system and tried to retain a hand in formulating Government Statements relating to Defence; he opposed a Ministry of Defence as well as a Ministry of Economic Coordination. After the outbreak of World War II, Hankey was held responsible for deficiencies in the defense system, especially on the supply side; Salisbury to Swinton, 18 Jan.

tion of executive action and monthly progress reports to the cabinet on the execution of the reconditioning programmes'.[381] Such cooperation became essential for example after the ratification of the Defence Requirements Committee's report which left the ministries and committees of the Committee of Imperial Defence devoid of either instructions or 'terms of reference';[382] yet the coordination group[383] which had been created in March 1936 under Inskip, in the context of the Defence White Paper and the Rhineland crisis, limited its activities to pilot work in the area of procurement and supplies, and never succeeded in using coordination procedures to make better use of industrial capacity; in other words, to raise levels of production. In this sense, it never represented an effective alternative to a ministry of munitions.[384] Moreover the original brief of the group, which had to establish a strategic, politically acceptable basis for the armaments programme, to assess the value of potential allies and to make out the limits of Britain's willingness to make concessions to aggressors, was never fulfilled. The cabinet was neither prepared to delegate its responsibilities nor to discharge them itself. Between 1936 and 1938 the minister for the coordination of defence functioned as an extension of the Treasury; he was responsible for apportioning the defence budget to the armed services, and consistently favoured 'home defence' and 'imperial defence' to the detriment of the 'continental commitment'.[385] In the spring of 1938 he did, however, play a decisive role in the reorientation of armaments policy, and indeed to a large extent opposed the proposals put forward by the Treasury and by the prime minister, Neville Chamberlain.

1940, Swinton Mss., vol. 174/3/1. Hankey to MacDonald, 16 Jan. 1933, Cab. 21–384; Pownall-Diaries, vol. 1, pp. 98ff., 101ff.; Roskill, *Hankey*, vol. 3, pp. 52ff., 67ff., 98ff., 103ff., 202ff. Cf.F. Johnson, *Defence by Committee. The British Committee of Imperial Defence, 1885–1959*, London 1960.

381. Cab. 23–83, p. 146; N. Chamberlain, C.P.28(36), 11 Febr. 1936. Cab. 24–260.

382. Hodsoll to Hankey, 5 Oct. 1934, Cab. 21–434.

383. Thanks to Shay, *Rearmament*, pp. 215ff., to M. Gilbert, *Churchill*, vol. 5, pp. 761ff., and to the Pownall-Diaries, vol. 1, pp. 73ff., 98ff., Inskip today has a better 'press' than at the time.

384. The Minister for the Coordination of Defence, who was regarded as a candidate to succeed Baldwin as Prime Minister and later as an alternative to Chamberlain (he declined to take the 'job'), received limited power and started with virtually no staff. There existed no 'strategies' to guide the work of coordination; he was no overlord to the Chiefs of Staff or to the 3 Service Ministers.

385. Inskip, 29 April 1936, Cab. 23–84, and 23 Nov. 1936, Cab. 21–438. Inskip himself started serious deliberations and talks on 'strategy' once he discovered the discrepancy between the Foreign Office's and the War Office's assumptions as to the likelihood of Britain's involvement in a continental war and the state of Britain's armed forces; FO to Army Council, 25 April 1936, Cab. 21–441.

The National government proved, then, ultimately incapable of creating a common platform for its foreign and armaments policy. The party leaders in the coalition – who created an organisational and institutional framework for their own collaboration with the founding of the General Purposes Committee[386] in 1935 – did not succeed, even temporarily, either in coordinating party political activities to improve the National government's image or, more crucially, in outlining a set of governmental priorities and informing the national population of the principal elements of government policy. The major questions of domestic and foreign policy were only ever briefly aired in the meetings of the party leaders. Within this framework it became more difficult than ever to reconcile the opposing views held by the departments responsible for foreign and defence policy, or, more particularly, to allay the mutual distrust which characterised relations between the Foreign Office and the War Office. Each side accused the other of not knowing what they were talking about and maintained that it would have to take a hand in running the affairs of the other department if Britain's 'national interests' were not to suffer. Thus the Foreign Office criticised the armed-service departments, and in particular the War Office, for not having fought resolutely enough for the maintainence of defence preparedness; in other words, for having largely ignored warning signals from the Foreign Office. Conversely, the armed-service ministries accused the Foreign Office of having missed the opportunity of a settlement with Germany.[387]

Changes in the coalitions between departments on the question of defence and, in particular, variations in the priorities of the three armed-service ministries and the Committee of Imperial Defence, may be seen as an expression of their mutual incapacity to find common ground. Although it is possible to identify a degree of concurrence between the Foreign Office, the Dominion Office and the armed-service ministries in their annual reports on the situation between 1930 and 1936, those reports carry no reference to financial considerations. By contrast, the Treasury developed strategic concepts which certainly took account of the 'sinews of war' by stressing finance as the fourth arm of defence, but which were at the same time based on a different assessment of British involvement at the centres of world politics from that of the

386. 30 Jan. 1935, Cab. 23–81, pp. 83ff.
387. See ch. 'Strategies'. Vansittart, 17 Nov. 1936, C 7904/G, VNST 2/29; cf. Howard, *Commitment*, pp. 94, 117ff.; Gibbs, p. 628; Dennis, *Decision*, pp. 115ff. On the views of Swinton, Eyres-Monsell see note 318.

Foreign Office or the armed-service departments. Neville Chamberlain nonetheless continued to maintain that such policy decisions as had been made in recent years on the insistence of the Treasury – which included the identification of Germany (rather than Japan) as the main enemy as well as the according of priority status to the 'air deterrent' – had pointed in the right direction. It was on this basis that he argued for this ministry to be accorded a dominant role in future decision-making.[388] Thus struggles for control of coordination were conducted between the Treasury (which reasserted and consolidated its bid for leadership, or for a supervisory role),[389] Hankey[390] (through his key within the network of committees, and as closest advisor to the prime minister on the armaments question) and the Foreign Office.

The three service ministries and the chiefs of staff opposed all forms of coordination which departed from principles of past practice.[391] They particularly opposed any attempts to use financial controls to decide issues of strategy, resisted the Treasury's attempts to take part in departmental discussions and took offence at its efforts to prejudice the decisions of the cabinet;[392] all of this seemed to them an interference in and disturbance of their work as responsible advisers to the prime minister and the cabinet in matters of defence. Prime Ministers MacDonald and Baldwin, whose own interest in the survival of the government and in the performance of government parties at elections led them to look for the cheapest way to build up a credible deterrent, were neither in any position to guarantee a speedy passage through cabinet for the preliminary reports prepared by the special committees they themselves chaired, nor even to safeguard their work against the effects of domestic political manoeuverings in the course of future

388. Chamberlain, 11 Febr. 1936, C.P. 28(36), Cab. 24–260. Hankey and Montgomery-Massingberd (CIGS) disputed the Treasury's claim to coordination; they made a plea for the deployment of a British Expeditionary Force at the expense of another expansion programme for the RAF; Hankey to W. Fisher/Chiefs of Staff, 13 and 14 Febr. 1936, and Montgomery-Massingberd to Hankey, 17 Febr. 1936, Cab. 21–424.

389. The Treasury Control was reinforced with regard to the establishment of shadow-factories, Cab. 23–82, pp. 428ff. On the instruments and the problems of treasury control in general see Peden, *Treasury*; Duff Cooper (Lord Norwich), *Old Men Forget*, London 1954, pp. 219ff.; Percy, *Memoirs*, pp. 146ff.; F. Ashton-Gwatkin, *The British Foreign Service*, New York 1946, pp. 26f.; D.C. Watt, *Personalities and Policies. Studies in the Formulation of British Foreign Policy in the Twentieth Century*, London 1965, Essay 5.

390. Hankey to MacDonald, 3 May 1935, Cab. 21–406; see note 380.

391. COS-Memo, C.P. 36(36), 10 Febr. 1936, Cab. 24–260.

392. Hankey did much to coordinate the collective resistance of the COS to the intrusion of the Treasury; Hankey to Ellington/Chatfield/Montgomery-Massingberd, Febr.–April 1934, Cab. 21–382 and Cab. 21–384; he renewed his efforts in early 1936.

discussions.[393] They in fact anticipated that they would be judged 'historically' by whether Britain was equipped for the defence of the rule of international law and forms of peaceful conflict resolution, and yet at the same time, they showed indifference towards foreign and armaments policy risks. MacDonald's angry response to his military advisers when they demanded, not without some reproachfulness, that he follow developments in this important sphere with more interest and energy was: 'Well it won't be the first time the services will have entered into a war unprepared'.[394] By the summer of 1935, MacDonald's colleagues were no longer prepared to stand this kind of talk on the advantages of 'unpreparedness', yet the new resolve in rearmament policy was no substitute for the decision which still needed to be made on a coordination of efforts to achieve a situation in which Britain could afford to meet the realities of the European situation.

6. Public Opinion

MacDonald's 'indifference' is one indication of the way in which the government defined its policy with regard to other sources of social 'authority', in particular public opinion. The government perceived the example of the Peace Ballot campaign or the debacle of the Hoare–Laval crisis – when the uproar from party supporters and the press had forced the government to change its course[395] – as evidence of a need to take greater account of the domestic political background of foreign policy decisions and strategies than was commonly necessary. That perception was reaffirmed by its experience of similar constraints on the flexibility of French policy.[396]

The British reaction to Hitler's weekend coups of 1935–36 was

393. In 1934, Baldwin and MacDonald were distracted by the House of Commons inquiry committee on India; from July 1935 to January 1936, the Cabinet, Hankey and the COS were preoccupied with the Abyssinian affair and its many effects on the beginning of 'real rearmament'. At the same time, N. Chamberlain and Weir were establishing their positions for the ensuing debates.

394. Pownall-Diaries, vol. 1, p. 77 (29 July 1935, i.e. on the eve of the decision to fix 1 Jan. 1939 the target date for defence preparedness).

395. On the 'revolt' of the 'public' against the Hoare-Laval agreement see J.A. Cross, *Sir Samuel Hoare. A Political Biography*, London 1977, chs. 5 and 6; Jones, *Diary with Letters*, p. 161; Simon-Diary, 18 and 19 Dec. 1935; Feiling, *Life*, pp. 273ff.; Earl of Birkenhead, *The Life of Lord Halifax*, London 1965, 348ff.; Middlemas, Barnes, *Baldwin*, pp. 882ff.

396. The imminent elections (in April 1936); French soundings in Berlin (in late 1934 and in autumn 1935); Laval's vicissitudes in the Abyssinian conflict and many other instances were

influenced by a number of factors:

(1) The governments of MacDonald and Baldwin had suffered a relatively sharp decline in public credibility and, indeed, in their own self-confidence.[397]

(2) In backstage conflicts over foreign policy, there had been a number of interventions by the 'middle-men' of public opinion, who collaborated with the representatives of whichever foreign power was closest to their own opinion: while the Churchill/ Boothby, Austen Chamberlain, Lord Camrose/Wickham Steed groups had cooperated with the French delegation under Flandin, for their part, Lothian, Dawson and Jones had entered consultations with the US special envoy, Norman Davis, and the high commissioners of the Dominions.

(3) In the Hoare–Laval crisis and in the Locarno crisis, backbenchers (and through them the respective constituency organisations) had become involved in 'high politics'. The intervention of these groups[398] strengthened those forces in the government who argued for a limitation of British involvement in the settlement of the crisis to diplomatic measures alone. The reason the backbenchers were so effective was that, by referring to the July crisis of 1914 as a negative example, they touched a nerve in numerous cabinet ministers who believed that Britain had a mission to set an example of 'patience' and 'sanity' to the world.[399]

Baldwin, Halifax, Simon and Runciman surrounded the British negotiating strategy with something of a halo, by styling London an island of common sense which was favourably distinguishable from

---

directly related to the confusing games of parliamentary politics in France (for details, see note 391 of German original).

397. Baldwin, 26 Febr. 1936, Cab. 23–83, p. 181, admitted to this; cf. Jones, *Diary with Letters*, p. 175; Middlemas, Barnes, *Baldwin*, pp. 896ff.

398. Reports on the two meetings of the Foreign Affairs Committee on 12 and 17 March 1936 are deposited in Prem. 1–194; N. Chamberlain, 13 March 1936, Cab. 27–603; Rickards, *Craven Herald*, 20 March 1936, p. 7, claims that 'we humble folk of little experience' succeeded in turning the tables on the 'big guns' (Churchill, A. Chamberlain, Winterton, Boothby), who had dominated the first meeting; having done their homework, i.e. tested opinion in their constituencies over the weekend, the backbenchers gained a say in the second meeting. The British Legion (Ex-Servicemen) made a pro-German impact in Rickards' and other constituencies. Other pro-German MPs (Sandeman Allen, A.R. Wise, Lord Mansfield, V. Raikes) established links with French politicians, who shared their imperialist, anti-bolshevic points of view.

399. The main speakers on that occasion were Lady Astor, Col. Gretton, Richards (see note 398). Simon to MacDonald, 27 July 1934, and Runciman to Simon 13 July 1934, Simon-Mss; on Baldwin see A.W. Baldwin, *My Father*, p. 88; Baldwin-Flandin meeting, 14 March 1936, in Flandin, *Politique*, pp. 207ff.; Hoesch to Auswärtiges Amt, 10 March 1936, E 506 547ff., and 21 March 1936, E 508 053ff.; GD, ser. C., vol. 5, No. 178.

the 'mad dogs' in Berlin and Rome and the fickle heroes who wielded the sceptre in France.[400] This representation of British foreign policy both slotted neatly into the framework of demands outlined by the backbenchers and at the same time offered them access to channels of influence. On the basis of popular comparisons between Hitler's latest action and the July crisis, the government was able to formulate the general rule that every last opportunity should be taken to commence new – or to advance existing – negotiations. Simon and Kingsley Wood convinced the government not only to scale down Staff talks but also to refuse to specify the point at which Britain would side with France and seek to prevent further gains by Germany.[401] They supported their arguments with reference to negative public opinion regarding retaliatory measures and were helped by the fact that their opinion coincided with that of the party constituency grass-roots.

The British governments' readiness to formulate its foreign policy on the basis of its perception of public opinion thus led it to impose a certain self-inflicted blockade on the decision-making process.[402] The mutual interaction between the convictions of cabinet members and tendencies within public opinion created and reinforced a widespread conviction that the German demands were actually legitimate.[403] (In any case, apart from the absence of any moral legitimation for a controlled engagement with Germany, Britain did not at this stage have the means of power at its disposal to risk retaliatory action.) A problem whose significance had been played down by the government, both internally and in public, could not suddenly be reclassed as a question of national survival should it develop in a critical way: 'To go to war with Germany for walking into their own backyard . . . at a time moreover when you were actually discussing with them the dates and conditions of the right to resume occupation, was not the sort of thing people could understand. So that moment which . . . offered the last effective chance of securing peace without war, went by'.[404]

400. Simon to J.A. Spender, 10 Oct. 1938, Simon-Mss.; this letter is a reckoning up of the faults of French foreign policy. N. Chamberlain, Simon, Baldwin knew the difference between having Laval, Flandin, Herriot, Reynaud in London or watching them acting in Paris.

401. See notes 285, 286, 293.

402. Percy, *Memoirs*, p. 184 (see quote above); cf. Nicolson-Diaries, vol. 1, p. 236; on the working agreement approach see ch. 1 of German original.

403. Pownall-Diaries, vol. 1, p. 105 (9 March 1936); Nicolson-Diaries, 11 March 1936, p. 242; WO-Memo., 8 March 1936, FO 371–19 888, pp. 37ff.; Dieckhoff note, 12 March 1936, *Akten der Reichskanzlei* 47, vol. 2; GD, serv. C, vol. 5, No. 33, p. 57.

404. Halifax, *Fullness of Days*, p. 197.

These factors did not, of course, prevent the government from justifying Britain's passive behaviour in the crises of the 1930s by reference to the state of public opinion at the time. The use of the public opinion argument to veto forceful measures against Germany was of course ultimately rooted in the British politicians' habit of invoking their democratic parliamentary obligations as an expedient pretence to ward off disagreeable demands from other governments. By declaring that it must reserve its right to an independent decision on the *casus belli* – except in characteristically narrowly defined cases of vital and self-evident alliance interests – the government of the 1930s gave its allies to understand that its foreign policy was formulated in relation to its relative freedom of manoeuvre (or lack of it) in domestic politics, on the one hand, and to the state of government credibility at home, on the other. This policy of 'non-committal' could then serve as a facade behind which the government hid its preferences and prejudices from public opinion at home, thus evading public discussions of its moral commitments (as it had also done before 1914). Manoeuvrings of this kind became possible at any point when the views of the Opposition corresponded more closely to those of the government than did the opinions of sections of the governing parties themselves. Britain's proclamations were, however, also in some cases genuine, to the extent that they expressed a real resolve to remain open to developments on both sides; that is, in this instance in Germany as well as France. Britain neither wanted to give up hope of a moderation of the national-revolutionary regime in Germany, nor did she have sufficient trust in the reliability of her French ally to be prepared to allow London to risk a decision against Germany. Britain's emphasis on her own purported need to satisfy public opinion at home, which she claimed to be decidedly opposed to the redefinitions of Britain's treaty obligations desired by France, functioned as a rhetorical ploy to ward off any requests from France which threatened to undermine British policy. Elucidations of the current state of public opinion by the British served as a standard weapon in critical phases of negotiations to guard themselves against making 'irrevocable decisions at this stage' (the decision, for example, 'to put teeth into Locarno', discussed in the course of Staff talks).[405] In domestic debates, too, the same argument rarely failed to achieve its effect: the notion that public opinion in Britain favoured bringing Ger-

405. Meeting of Ministers, 13 March 1936, Cab. 27–603.

many back into the League of Nations was, as a rule, used successfully in the cabinet to avert any attempt to gain recognition for
France's increased need for security by implementing proposals
advocating British concessions to France in arms and defence
policy.[406]

In its courting of domestic public opinion the British government vacillated perpetually between two simultaneous impera-
tives: on the one hand, it could not give the impression that it
regarded German proposals as worthless; if it rejected them out of
hand, Germany would be able to take advantage of the situation for
propaganda purposes, and mobilise an 'opposition' to the government in Britain. Ministers had to arrange things so that blame could
be shifted on to Germany; for instance, by making it clear that
German aversion to mutual assistance agreements within the
framework of a regional pact of the Locarno type should not hinder
other partners from making such an agreement. In using arguments of this kind to open the door to demonstrations of good-will
towards the French, the government was at the same time protecting itself against French endeavours to exploit offers of good-
will, since it was always able to refer to the unwillingness of public
opinion to sanction any course of action which blocked efforts to
reach agreement with Germany. The insinuation here was that
closer coordination with French policy or even an alliance would
damage the atmosphere for negotiations *à trois*.[407] Thus Britain
took back with her left hand what she had offered with her right.

The ambivalence of British foreign policy in the interwar period
exposed it to the caricatures of contemporary critics, one of whom
compared the government's behaviour abroad with a company of
actors who refused either dress rehearsals or contingency plans in
case of failure: Do you know your part? – I will be alright on the
night.[408]

This caricature captures some of the crucial aspects of British
foreign policy; in particular, that pragmatism which consists in
splitting problems into their component parts and then suppressing
any residual fear that the series of piecemeal solutions proposed

406. Cabinet meeting, 14 Jan. 1935, Cab. 23–81, pp. 21f., 30. In 1936, the Foreign Policy
Committee debated for months on the reform of the League of Nations and 'New Locarno'
with a view to normalizing relations with Hitler's Germany and postponing the 'difficult
decision' of facing up to Germany's intransigence and thereby 'mending' the French alliance.

407. C.P. 79(35) (Briefing for Stresa Conference), Cab. 24–254, pp. 45ff.; Simon-Diary, 21
March 1935. Eden, draft memo., 8 March 1936; *The Times*, 9 March 1936, Leader 'A Chance to
Rebuild'; Jones, *Diary with Letters*, pp. 179ff.

408. *Round Table*, 'The Locarno Treaties', Dec. 1925, vol. 16, pp. 1 and 12.

might be jeopardised by the interdependency between the various single elements of a given 'case'. This kind of pragmatism depends, secondly, on crossing bridges when one comes to them; since problems are seen as susceptible to change at any moment, it is considered prudent to 'wait upon events and see how they shape up'. Finally, the pragmatist operates on the premise that battles do not necessarily have to be won; for, in the final analysis, the most important consideration is assumed to be the question of whose nerve is the stronger, whose staying power the greater, or simply who enjoys the greatest degree of 'luck'. No less telling is the second element within British foreign policy to which the caricature alludes: the habit of performing for the public at home. It is this which explains how particular politicians involved in the British decision-making process – mainly Baldwin but also Kingsley Wood and Halifax – were both widely seen to have their finger on the pulse of public opinion[409] and were at the same time able to influence armaments and foreign policy to an extent which far surpassed their level of knowledge of, or their interest and competence in, foreign affairs.

Of course, it was not simply the case that public opinion served as an excuse for British behaviour in the decision-making process. One event in particular calls into question the dominant interpretation[410] of government action, according to which government is considered to be in a position to act totally independently of public opinion or of government parties in the elaboration of its foreign policy. Since, 'by coincidence', the crises initiated by the Third Reich came in February and March at a time when government and the Opposition were intensifying their efforts to stake out positions for the budget debate on defence estimates, exceptional and unaccustomed significance accrued to the constituency canvassing activities of backbenchers from the government and Opposition parties. By the same coincidence, discussions of foreign-policy crises were absorbed into the terms of debates on domestic British armaments policy. The annual meetings of the constituency organisations, which took place in the spring,[411]

---

409. Seen in this context, it made sense to propose that Baldwin became Foreign Secretary (*Manchester Guardian* in May/June 1935). In December 1935 Halifax pressed for the resignation of Hoare, referring to public opinion and 'revolt' at the 'grass-roots'. K. Wood exemplifies this 'conservative blend of pacifism'.

410. D.C. Watt, 'British Domestic Politics and the Onset of War. Notes for a Discussion', in *Les Relations Franco-Britanniques de 1935 à 1939*, Paris 1975, pp. 243, 254.

411. N. Chamberlain and Eden recognised the need to educate opinion at constituency-

offered both government and Opposition an opportunity to test the constituency response to their proposed approaches to the armaments debate, and to sound out reactions to the slogans they had formulated. In 1936 they were able, moreover, to explore the possibility not only of using the Abyssinian crisis, which had raised questions as to the relative efficacy of collective security policies which either did or did not involve rearmament, but also of using the present state of relations between the partners of the Locarno Treaty to settle the controversy over the Defence White Paper. Reports on the mood in the constituencies strengthened the government's view that it would encounter a positive response to decisions on rearmament if it accompanied its forays into the tax-payers' pockets with the announcement that it would continue to seek arms limitation and a settlement with Germany.

The reciprocal effects of stage-management from above and of constituency responses to the performance of the backbenchers on the armaments questions from below, generated an atmosphere in which the government on the eve of the March crises of 1935 and 1936 still felt able to concentrate on implementing the proposals outlined in its Defence White Papers without paying more than the minimum of attention to the intrusive influences of actual foreign-policy crises. By contrast, the 'middlemen' were propagating the view that the government's aim was to take the path of least resistance in the German–French quarrels and to work towards a settlement. The reciprocal influence of these two currents of opinion provoked a unanimous reaction from 'officials' at the height of the crisis; in their estimation, public opinion in Britain was likely to respond to German breaches of treaty by maintaining that they were only to have been expected, and that their content, if not their form, was perfectly comprehensible.[412] Consequently, they claimed, the crisis was unlikely to be able to be made to serve as a justification for increases in the existing rearmament programme.

The effects of appeasement are similarly visible in the conditions determining institutional structures and configurations. The

---

level; L. Caplin of the Central Office made a tour to constituency meetings and lectured on the lines of the 'dual strategy' (rearmament and appeasement); cf. *Southern Daily Echo*, 11 March 1936; Nicolson-Diaries, vol. 1, pp. 236ff. (13, 24 and 26 Febr. 1936). (On the FO's and the Government's attempts at guiding the 'quality' press see note 404 of German original).

412. FO internal meeting, 7 March 1936, in Colvin, *Vansittart*, p. 79; on N. Chamberlain see above (13 March 1936, Cab. 27–603); the gist of COS 442 was reported to the Cabinet by Hankey, 12 March 1936.

March crises came at a time when, firstly, both the British government and 'business' (banks and insurance companies) were having to make up their annual accounts, and draw up reports on the year's progress; at a time also when the mood of the Stock Exchange was, in general, cautious; and, thirdly, when the economic data made available through the presentation of annual financial reports by the banks, institutes and companies had fuelled expectations within state economic departments and the upper echelons of industry that an economic upswing might be attainable, as long as the process of recovery could be shielded from upheavals in the political arena. In the period during which the German side was preparing the spectacular displays of strength with which it hoped to deflect attention from its internal difficulties, the makers of public opinion – daily newspapers and, in particular, the economic magazines in Britain – continued to focus public attention on the rays of hope which glimmered on the economic horizon.

During the same period, members of parliament from the governing parties were apportioned the task, on the one hand, of justifying arms expenditure to the public as a part of foreign policy, and, on the other hand, of emphasising that rearmament measures should not be taken to indicate any change of priorities which might work to the detriment of social and economic policy.[413] Thus, in this context also, the link between official reticence in foreign policy with regard to intervention and the government's concern to hasten the progress of economic recovery was further reinforced.[414] Finally, the Treasury and the Board of Trade used the economic crisis in France as a lever to gain acceptance for the terms on which Britain was prepared to abide by specific political responsibilities. Neville Chamberlain, Runciman, Inskip and other members of the cabinet hoped to be able to compel France to adopt the same rules which they had prescribed for British policy, namely that she pursue a policy of appeasement, 'which will allow them [France] to give undivided attention to the reconstruction of their own distracted country'.[415] The end result of these various developments was the emergence of a coordinated foreign policy

413. Eden set the tone with his first address as Foreign Secretary to his constituency, *The Times*, 17 Jan. 1936. EAC, 19th report, 10 Febr. 1936, Cab. 24–260; *The Observer*, 5 Jan. 1936, p. 19: 'The Return to Prosperity. Survey of the Country. Reports from the Provinces'. *The Times* leader, 'A Chance to Rebuild', faced on the same page a report on the state of economic recovery.

414. The Government's formulae on peace and recovery were repeated by 'local agents' of the party, e.g. *Hanley Evening Sentinel*, 23 March 1936; *The History of the Times*, vol. 4, p. 484.

415. Inskip to A. Parker, 18 June 1937, Cab. 21–541.

worked out by the Western powers along the lines of a doctrine of non-intervention; that policy was presented by the Board of Trade and the Treasury as an effective realisation of the service ministries' tenet that France's attention should be drawn to the weaknesses of the French and British military position.[416] Neville Chamberlain, Inskip and Runciman[417] used both military and economic arguments to block any change in British policy on a counter-offensive which would increase defence obligations.

7. British Foreign Policy: its Room for Manoeuvre

From the above analyses, it should have become clear that the basic characteristics and principles of British foreign policy towards the dictators were mainly determined by domestic political constellations, within which the armaments question played a dominant role. The attachment of such a high level of significance to the armaments question has been explained above, firstly in terms of the state of competitive relations between the British socio-political system and the dynamic of the power structure of the Third Reich, which was threatening to undermine the status quo; secondly, reference has been made to the continuities between various aspects of the British approach – an approach which found its expression in the 'risk' theory (and its variations). Finally, evidence which shows British diplomatic initiatives and reactions to have been dominated by the view that internal as well as external conflicts could be best defused through arms negotiations, has been preferred as a justification for the attachment of particular significance in preceding pages to the armaments policy complex as an explanation for appeasement policy. It is necessary at this point to consider the two main elements of this interpretation – the continuity of the risk theory and the shifts in the German–British–French power structure within the framework of international crises – in relation to a number of additional factors. Together these constitute a complex of conditions within which

416. In March 1936, Baldwin and Chamberlain directed Flandin's attention to the facts mentioned in notes 3413–415 in March/April 1938 and on the eve of 'Munich' the Staff talks and high level ministerial meetings served the same purpose; cf. Middlemas, *Illusion*, ch. 6.

417. Runciman (to Hoare, 2 March 1936, R 2/50/1) rejected a return to balance of power politics, which he identified with interventionism; cf. *The History of The Times*, vol. 4, p. 892. Chatfield and Hankey shared Runciman's views on the importance of British naval power, economic recovery, and non-entanglement in Europe (although Hankey asked for providing military power).

both armaments policy and the 'economic appeasement' strategy become explicable. The explanatory models put forward in relation to both these aspects of British foreign policy are interrelated in numerous ways; the crucial position of armaments policy is the key to a situation in which the economic structure, the economic cycle and security measures (rearmament and diplomatic crisis management) all had effects one upon the other, as did arms limitation agreements, 'economic disarmament' and the economic aid which was to smooth the transition from an 'arms economy' to a normalised peacetime economy. In the following pages, attention will be focused on the connections between the various rationales underpinning British policy on Germany, economic development and armaments policy. Two points may help to structure our argument in advance:

(1) The survival of a policy which emphasised the primacy of strategies of pacification at home over foreign policy[418] depended on whether the government could maintain an economic situation and a social atmosphere (a reduction in class tensions) which would allow it to take foreign policy and defence requirements more into account in response to a heightening of tensions abroad or whether the economic cycle surveys of the country's needs would necessitate the continued pursuit of domestic appeasement manoeuvres, in order to reduce or avoid conflicts which might jeopardise the progress of economic recovery. Furthermore, the decision-makers were faced with the question of whether, in view of external risks and threats, there could come a time when domestic (economic) political difficulties could not longer serve as a valid pretext for restrictions on armaments policy and when British policy would have to be granted the opportunity to pursue a more active containment policy towards the German peril.

(2) Drawing on the analogy of the questions central to its own decision-making process, Britain based her assessments of her own room for manoeuvre in foreign policy in relation to Germany on possible answers to the question of 'how far Hitler's foreign policy [is, and is likely to be] influenced by the absence of an economic recovery in Germany'.[419]

We may draw two conclusions from the fact that British policy focused on an evaluation of the economic situation in Germany and on the reaction of the National Socialist regime to the des-

418. This has to be understood in the context of our definition of the 'risk theory' and the notion 'labour'.

419. Sargent to Phipps, 28 March 1933, C 9489/319/18, FO 371–16 728, p. 295.

perate situation which prevailed there. It indicates, firstly, that the British power élites themselves saw their own room for manoeuvre in foreign-policy matters as a function of socio-economic conditions. Secondly, this emphasis within British policy may begin to explain the government's attempts to forecast the potential effects of British (economic) foreign policy on developments in Germany, as well as its discussions of the advisability of attempting to influence trends within German economic policy from the outside; for example, by starting talks on the basis of an assumed mutual interest in relieving both governments of domestic problems through arms limitation: 'Generally speaking, Europe seems a little less uneasy and I can't help thinking that the precarious internal situation of Germany is impressing a certain restraining influence on Hitler. I have got a little scheme on hand for re-establishing a contact with Schacht which may – or may not – lead further in the same direction'.[420] Debates and prognoses of this kind seem best interpreted in terms of a view of economic appeasement as a structuring component of British foreign policy in the 1930s, as view discussed in Ch. I above.

However, the only conclusion which can justifiably be drawn from both the above points is that economic factors, economic structures in general and the World Depression in particular, were important in *setting the parameters* of British foreign policy. Relevant for an analysis of that relationship are the direct connections between the economic system and foreign policy; the effects of the relationship between the British government and industry on foreign and armaments policy; the influences and events which affected, on the one hand, economic policy and the formation of coalitions of interests and, on the other, political structures and which thus transformed foreign relations. An explanation of British foreign policy can only be attempted in the light of answers to the fundamental question of whether Britain possessed either the necessary resources or the political room for manoeuvre to be able to wield influence in the economic sphere, given that British diplomacy could not and was unlikely to be in a position to employ military means for some time to come. In other words, the central question is that of whether the 'isolationist' tendencies described in the context of armaments policy were paralleled within the framework of the economy and economic interests by a policy orientated towards a principle of 'British interests first' or whether

420. N. Chamberlain to Ida, 18 Jan. 1937, NC 18/1/991.

internationalist tendencies, more strongly entrenched in domestic social structure thanks to earlier state decisions in favour of 'free trade', were able to assert elements of cooperation in British economic foreign policy.

The extent of the British government's room to manoeuvre in its foreign policy continued to be determined in the 1930s by Britain's foreign economic (trade and financial) relationships, which still constituted a major part of economic life.[421] The following factors were also influential in shaping the parameters of British foreign policy:

(1) The Great Depression furthered the erosion of the influence of international regimes in the world's trade and monetary system which had begun with the First World War and which hit Britain particularly hard.

(2) Britain's response to the great slump, which can be characterised in terms of the keywords 'Ottawa', 'protectionism', 'cheap money policy' and 'Exchange Equalisation Account', weakened the already declining economic interest in strategically important spheres of influence in Central and South-East Europe still further.[422] Since Britain – with the consent of the Foreign Office – had neglected her instruments of power (armaments) in the 1920s in favour of trade policy considerations and domestic political aims, the change in British economic (foreign) policy in the 1930s (Britain's gradual renunciation of free trade) may be seen as even more of a handicap for her European policy. By placing further restrictions on Britain's scope for manoeuvre, it deprived her of the opportunity to make economic gestures abroad; for example, by renouncing the 'most-favoured nation' clause or by offering any kind of active material support:[423] 'There can, unfortunately, be no doubt in our minds that the very fact that we must claim the right

421. See ch. 'Economic Appeasement' and note 420.

422. One has to distinguish between trade and finance; Britain's economic presence in some countries was important, although these countries' share in Britain's foreign trade was indeed small. In general, Britain was on the defensive, and had hardly any reserves to play with, in contrast to Germany; FO memo., 'German Economic Penetration of Central Europe...', 17 August 1936, R 4969/1167/67, FO 433–3. The British were aware of that position in 1931/33 and not just since 1934 (Schacht's new economic policy) or 1936; see BT 11–176. The studies of D. Kaiser, B. J. Wendt, A. Teichova, M.L. Recker (on the 1920s) and E. Barker (on the World War II-period) cover the problems (see note 415 of German original).

423. Interdepartmental Committee on Multilateral Tariff Reduction Scheme, meetings of 10 and 17 August 1933, BT 11–213. On the 'tariff truce' concept and the London World Economic Conference see R.N. Kottmann, *Reciprocity and the North Atlantic Triangle 1932–1938*, Ithaca 1968, pp. 40ff.; C. Hull, *The Memoirs of Cordell Hull*, New York 1948, chs. 18 and 19; A.A. Offner, *American Appeasement: United States Foreign Policy and Germany 1933–1938*, Cambridge (Mass.) 1969, p. 37ff.

to make extensive exceptions even at the very moment that we put forward the scheme under consideration [Multilateral Tariff Reduction Scheme] for adoption in principle is likely to militate greatly against its acceptance'.[424]

What is more, even the Foreign Office perceived no vital interests for Britain in the formation of a 'New Europe' (apart from her interest in the Baltic States, as well as, to an extent in Poland and in Greece). Attempts to combat the prejudice according to which the overindebted, 'corrupt' countries were not worth a penny of the British tax-payer's money would anyhow not have been able to overcome the hurdle of the 'British interest first' premise. It was the unhappy duty of the Foreign Office to respond to questions from the Treasury and Board of Trade who demanded to know whether politicians interested in foreign affairs really believed that they could convince British interest groups that for the sake of more important 'political' considerations they had to make specific economic (or financial) sacrifices to save the Peace System of Versailles. The Foreign Office, which had been denied any say in the economic turnabout of 1931–32, was then left only with the alternative of clearing the ground in individual cases for economic concessions, with a view to facilitating or assisting British diplomatic action, or simply giving foreign governments (e.g. the Doumergue government in 1934) which were 'willing partners' of Britain, a chance to remain in power;[425] the Foreign Office did this through constant criticism of 'Ottawa',[426] the sterling bloc[427] and the Import Duties Advisory Committee.[428]

(3) The turnabout in economic and financial policy, and the mobilisation of pressure groups with 'vested interests'[429] in keeping the government on their side, deprived British policy of the

424. Interim Report, Interdepartmental Committee on MTR Scheme, 1 Dec. 1933, §8, W 13977/9642/50, BT 11–213, and meeting, 10 August 1933, minutes, p. 5.

425. Once again the Foreign Office succeeded in postponing and dispensing with retaliatory duties, but even with regard to France (in early 1934) the plea of the FO not to add fuel to tense relations with France but to think of common security interests could not stop the economic departments proceeding with the announcement of retaliation; Runciman, 16 Febr. 1934, HofC.

426. Vansittart memo., 21 Dec. 1936, 'World Situation and Rearmament', §26.

427. Vansittart, 26 Febr. 1933, VNST 1/14.

428. Eden memo., C.P. 42(36); Ashton-Gwatkin, 31 Jan. 1936, FO 371-19 884, (see ch. 'Economic Appeasement'); Cabinet meeting, 26 Febr. 1936, Cab. 23–83, pp. 183f. The Cabinet did not follow Eden's advice.

429. This refers to: Empire Industries Association; Food and Defence League; National Farmers' Union; Iron and Steel ·Federation; to MPs linked to the Federation of British Industries (Colville, Ramsden), but also to 'key' industrialists (Sir Hugo Hirst/General Electric; Sir Harry McGowan/ICI; Sir Herbert Austin/Morris Motors).

freedom of movement it needed, either to be able to adopt the alternative of economic appeasement in accordance with a view of German (Italian, Japanese) aggression and breaches of treaties largely as attempts to escape from internal economic difficulties or to be able to help those countries threatened by German expansion to achieve economic and political stability. This domestic political background to foreign policy particularly troubled the exponents of economic appeasement,[430] the advisers to the Treasury and the internationalist members of the Economic Advisory Council (Committee on Economic Information), who proposed an economic peace strategy which, in contrast to rearmament and the arms race, was to effect a relaxation of the world situation:

> we may be less awful sinners than some; but we are less sinful because we don't need to sin. We are, still, the richest country in the world and anything we do in the way of restriction hurts the rest of the world . . . more than all the restrictions imposed, say, by the Balkan countries put together. If we want to get rid of trade restrictions, we must be prepared to make some positive contribution. But neither we nor the Dominions show any readiness to reduce tariffs or preferences – even when there is a chance to get the United States tariffs reduced; the appetites of our agricultural protectionists become more and more difficult to restrain; and our financial people will not easily be persuaded to take a risk on currency or lending.[431]

The economic factors and structures which directly influenced policy decisions, in particular in respect of Anglo-German relations, are too numerous to be dealt with in anything but a cursory fashion here. The structural changes which followed the First World War and the World Depression altered trade and finance relations and added 'new' dimensions to the frictions between nations and governments.[432] The disturbance of the balance between demand and productive capacity caused social tensions in Britain and aggressive behaviour towards rival countries. The British policy of balancing the internal budget was implemented in an attempt to restore a 'sense of confidence' at home and therewith to revive economic development; abroad it served to maintain con-

---

430. Eden (Jebb) memo., 'Economics and Foreign Policy', 17 March 1937, W 6363/5/50, FO 371-21 215. It was argued that just a tariff competition had increased nationalist tendencies and disturbed international relations, so in reverse 'a modification of our protection . . . would contribute . . . to peace'. This reasoning resembled C. Hull's political 'philosophy'.

431. Leith-Ross to Jebb, 17 July 1937, W 14270/5/50, FO 371-21 216, pp. 485f.

432. G. Schmidt, ed., *Konstellationen internationaler Politik*.

fidence in sterling's primary function as a medium of world trade and of the world monetary system.[433] The development of a capital market was important above all in respect of armaments policy and supportive actions, motivated by security considerations, in the areas threatened by German expansionism. It also allowed the state to intervene on the domestic front to support 'unprofitable' projects, and act as protector against dysfunctional economic and political influences from abroad. The development of the wage–price structure as well as state intervention in the economy – which led to an increase in the proportion of official budget contribution to the national product, as well as in the priority and scope of armaments orders – not only affected Britain's competitiveness with the 'national economies' of political partners and rivals but also produced a structure of political demands which influenced British foreign policy. Questions of trade-agreement policy and of the representation of the interests of the various groups of creditors in the many debt negotiations (Clearing Agreements) influenced the decision-making process in more than one direction. Rather than adding to what is already a long list of factors of relevance to our discussions here, the following analysis will concentrate on a handful of the particular aspects of the relationship between foreign and economic policy which figure in discussions of diplomatic history within this present study.

Britain's realisation that she had to find ways of preventing Germany from isolating herself through an autarkic arms economy which would increase the danger of an arms race, reflects the impact of the World Depression on foreign policy. Any hope of implementing a 'sound' economic policy in Britain could be abandoned unless the government succeeded in binding Germany to an arms convention, or at least convincing her that she should disclose and abide by her armaments programmes for several years to come; if she did not, then Britain would be forced to abandon her pursuit of a sound financial policy.[434] It was considerations such as these which led important members of the cabinet (Neville Chamberlain, Simon and Inskip) to advocate their particular approach to

433. T 172–1775; cf. Howson, p. 92. On the relation between $ and £ during the 1930s see Sayers, *Bank of England*, vol. 2, pp. 452ff., 463ff.; Kottmann, *Reciprocity*, pp. 75ff.

434. Bruce, the Australian High Commissioner and an influential figure in the League of Nations at that time, advocated preventive military action to forestall German rearmament; this alternative found no favour with Whitehall. Hankey to MacDonald, 21 Oct. 1933, Cab. 21–382; cf. E. Robertson, *Hitler's Pre-War Policy and Military Plans 1933–1939*, London 1963, chs. 3 and 5.

foreign policy as the only way out of the contemporary dilemma both at the beginning of the rearmament phase (1935–36) and during the period of expansion in arms expenditure (1937–38).[435] In their view, the main task facing the government was the maintenance of the 'effective strength' of the socio-economic system; it had to take care that a balance was maintained between the primary interests of foreign policy (i.e. 'peace in our time') and the burden of armaments (i.e. the level of the forces in peace-time).[436] Thus the goal of 'diplomacy' had to be to work towards a reduction in the number of enemies (in other words, of countries whose attitude towards Britain necessitated procurements of armed forces) by striving for economic disarmament and arms conventions, or prevailing upon those countries to adopt policies of good neighbourliness. On the other hand, it was considered important not to allow foreign policy commitments (i.e. alliances and treaty obligations) to restrict Britain in using her resources in a flexible way; Britain's goal was to reserve her option to decelerate rearmament if British diplomacy succeeded in defusing tension in international politics. Instead of adapting to an arms build-up accompanied by a suspension of 'diplomacy', Britain was called upon to take precisely the opposite line: 'our foreign policy must largely be determined by the limits of our effective strength'.[437] By claiming to be able correctly to assess the proper level of effective strength (i.e. of economic and financial efficiency) as well as the degree of social tension which was politically acceptable, the economic departments were at the same time disputing the primary role accorded to the Foreign Office over other foreign policy decision-makers. Although it might be expected that it would be the Foreign Office which laid down guidelines for the kind of action to be taken to comply with British security interests, it was in fact the Treasury that claimed to determine British activities in international affairs, since only the Treasury was able to know what Britain could afford financially and economically. The control of the fourth arm of defence was regarded as a lever to this.

In 1933–34 Neville Chamberlain and the Treasury had left the government in no doubt that 'appeasement' was to prevail over a

---

435. See part 1 of this ch., and ch. 'Economic Appeasement', note 285, and notes 427–430 of German original; cf. Gibbs, pp. 287ff.

436. R. MacDonald to Baldwin, 14 Febr. 1936, Cab. 21–422 A.

437. Bridges, 19 July 1937, T 161/783 F 48431/02/2; Eden to Chamberlain, 9 Sept. 1937, PREM. 1–210.

'programme for war' in the Far East in policies towards Japan. From late 1936 until spring 1938, at the end of an initial period of buoyant spending on arms, the Treasury began not only to reintroduce financial rationing but also to demand the kind of 'active diplomacy' approach to peace conditions which would ensure that arms expenditure did not reach a level at which it might jeopardise sound budget financing and thereby the government's credit and, secondly, at which it might burden future governments with discharging of debts as well as with the long-term financing of the armaments expansion programmes on which it had decided in 1936–37.[438] Clearly, the government and its advisers did not regard arms expenditure as 'national waste', nor as a totally unprofitable use of capital, but rather recognised that the iron and steel industries, together with new industries affected by the expansion of the RAF, had taken over from the construction industry as the new leading sectors in the recovery process.[439] It did not, however, occur to them to use armaments expenditure as a deliberate means of accelerating the upward trend in the economy, initially at least; they hoped that the economic upswing itself would raise tax revenue levels and that their financial problems would thereby resolve themselves more or less of their own accord. The loss of credibility which the 'Treasury view' began to suffer as a result of the worsening international situation between 1932 and 1936 was offset by the continued prevalence of a view according to which Britain's success in overcoming the experiences of postwar crisis was to be traced to her insistence on always balancing budgets.

According to this precept of severe budgetary control, which was now reintroduced in the form of finance rationing[440] and supported by governments until 1938, the financing of special tasks through extraordinary (unbalanced) budgets could be countenanced only as a limited temporary measure. We have seen that the report of the DPR (July 1935) had asked for public borrowing for defence, but that the cabinet agreed only to dropping financial limitations; in 1935 Neville Chamberlain insisted that since supplementary estimates had been granted, no new demands (regarding anti-aircraft defence) were to be considered justified, and – in 1936 – he countered calls for 'more expenditure on arms' by

438. Feiling, *Life*, pp. 314ff.; Peden, *Treasury*, pp. 86ff.,; Howson, pp. 122ff.
439. R.S. Sayers, *A Hisory of Economic Change in England 1880–1939*, Cambridge 1967, p. 55; Howson, p. 120.
440. Postan, *War Economy*, pp. 25ff.; Middlemas, *Illusion*, pp. 116ff.; Gibbs, pp. 123ff.; Howson, pp. 92ff.

stressing his own present commitment to savings; in his view, the generative forces of the economy should not be absorbed in defence spending, neither should 'savings', which were a necessary priority of government, be made on account of arms expenditure alone; they should instead be implemented even after any decision to start 'real' rearmament. In 1935–36, during the period in which consultations were taking place on the Five-Year Plan, it was feared that if the government renounced stringent budgetary policies in favour of borrowing to finance rearmament, the floodgates would be opened to deficit spending in other spheres; for example, on job-creation projects to boost 'derelict or depressed areas'.[441] Since on the eve of the general election of 1935,[442] under pressure from the Treasury and other influences, the government had rejected Lloyd George's plans for a National Prosperity Loan as the financial basis for the National Development Board, it could hardly risk starting a campaign for a Defence Loan only a few months later.[443] Had it done so, the government would simply have fuelled existing accusations according to which the government and the armaments industry were to be seen as 'merchants of death'.[444]

Such 'atmospheric' influences did not remain without their effect on the cabinet. For financial and economic reasons the Treasury wanted to postpone a defence loan, at least for one year (until 1937) and to use tax increases to finance the proportion of the proposed Five-Year Armaments Programme (1936–37 and 1940–41) which had to be provided for in the 1936 budget.[445]

441. Hopkins memo., 7 Oct. 1935, T 172–1832. The General Purposes Committee, which had to scrutinise Lloyd George's 'Conquering Unemployment' (published in July 1935), did reflect on the possible repercussions if the Government were to favour deficit spending on armaments whilst rejecting that principle as an instrument of steering the economy. The measures it recommended were similar to the Trade Facilities Acts of the 1920s.

442. N. Chamberlain, Diary, 2 August 1935. Hankey, Baldwin were in favour of instrumentalising armaments orders (warships etc.) to provide employment to distressed areas; J.E. Wrench, *Geoffrey Dawson and Our Times*, London 1955, p. 321; Peden, *Treasury*, pp. 69, 72f. But this became neither the election platform nor did the measures themselves amount to deficit spending. Revenue was buoyant in 1936. The orders of the Admiralty and War Office were carefully selected; GP (35) 58, §152, p. 32.

443. General Purposes Committee, GP (35) 58, §§28–30ff., Cab. 27–583/584; GP (35) 11, WO/Treasury memo. on loan proposals; meetings on 4 and 26 Febr. 1935.

444. The Nye-Committee had repercussions on British politics. The Labour Party (e.g. 'For Socialism and Peace', 1934), Labour and Liberal (Samuel) frontbenchers and spokesmen for the 'left' (A. Bevan) contrasted the Government's reaction to '1931', i.e. financial orthodoxy and cuts in the social services, to defence spending and profiteering. The debates on the occasion of the Defence Estimates (1935–37) are to be viewed against the background of the then generally accepted 'theory' 'that the pool of public money is rather limited', and that expansion in one sector of the economy therefore necessitated cuts in others.

445. Hopkins memo., 7 Oct. 1935, T 172–1832. *Financial Times*, 22 April 1936, 'Defence

Despite warnings from within the Treasury's own ranks (from Warren Fisher)[446] that raising taxes instead of borrowing for defence would further confirm public opinion in its blindness towards the 'German peril' by helping to obscure the urgent need for rearmament, the government in 1936 reaffirmed its commitment to so-called sound budget policies.[447] In other words, the government opted to accept as standard procedure the rule established by McKenna[448] during the First World War, according to which not a single penny could be borrowed unless new tax provision was made at the same time to cover interest and a sinking fund.[449] The hope was that this would allow the government to adhere to its principle of borrowing only for investments which accelerated economic growth, whilst covering 'unproductive' spending by revenue expenditure; that is, through taxation. The normal annual expenditure on armaments was to be covered by income from taxes, whereas non-recurrent expenditure (ammunition production, etc.) was to be paid for out of a special extra budget.[450] The Treasury's aim here was in part also a didactic one, insofar as it saw its policies as a counter-example to notions of a Defence Loan as a 'comfortable Lloyd Georgian device for securing not only larger forces but also lower estimates, budget sur-

---

Plans make a spartan Budget. Chancellor and the loan question'.

446. W. Fisher, 2 Dec. 1935, T 171–324 and T 172–1832. Cf. Howson, p. 121; Peden, *Treasury*, pp. 40ff.; Shay, *Rearmament*, pp. 76ff.

447. Regular defence expenditure would rise from £170 mill. (1936) to £215 mill. (in the last year of the programme); the expansion programme for the 1936/37 to 1940/41 period amounted to £417 mill. extraordinary spending. Tax increases were due in the 1936/7 budget anyway to cover expenses on supplementary estimates for the RAF (£20 mill.).

448. U.K. Hicks, *The Finance of British Government 1920–1936*, Oxford 1938, pp. 316ff.

449. N. Chamberlain, 50th meeting D.C.M. (32), Cab. 16–110; Phillipps memo., 29 Nov. 1935, T 171–324; cf. Howson, pp. 121ff.

450. Shay, *Rearmament*, p. 76.

Defence expenditure (£mill.)

	from revenue	under Defence Loan Acts	defence exp. (at current price)	total gov't revenue	total gov't expenditure
1935/6	137	—	140.8	890	867
1936/7	186	—	183.0	921	907
1937/8	197	65	254.7	987	989
1938/9	272	128	473.2	1,036	1,145
1939/40	248	502	—	—	—

Source: Howson, p. 122
For further details see Gibbs, pp. 285, 290–292.

pluses and diminishing taxation'.[451] The Treasury further believed that the increasing costs of rearmament could, for the time being, be financed in the customary way; namely, by issuing Treasury Bills and other short-term securities which could later be turned into long-term debts 'as it seemed expedient'.[452] Although this was also a form of public borrowing, it differed from the practice of a Defence Loan in that it guaranteed that control of the size of the deficit remained in the hands of the Treasury, and in that it retained the principle of parliamentary control.

However, in view of the amount necessary for the expansion of the armaments programmes,[453] new standards eventually had to be applied in the allocation of the armaments budget: direct and indirect taxes, which had been increased since 1936,[454] were earmarked for the civil budget and the major part of armaments expenditure, whilst the remaining £417 million of the £1.5 billion allocated for the Five-Year programme of arms expansion was made subject to defrayment by defence loans.[455] As a consequence of this financing strategy, and although the amount defrayed by loans was repeatedly raised in line with the continual increase in the requirements of the armed services, ministers were also eventually to be requested by the chancellor of the exchequer (from mid-1938) to reduce civil expenditure in order to allow the Treasury to use a larger proportion of tax income for armaments. Since the maximum rate at which taxation was considered tolerable had already been raised, and as an uncontrolled expansion of borrowing had been declared undesirable – firstly because of its effects on interest levels, secondly in response to fears of the socio-political consequences of inflation, and thirdly in view of the need for a stable value for sterling – the only remaining course of action open to the government was to limit the growth of other government expenditure to an essential minimum,[456] or even to impose reductions on expenditure.

451. Hopkins-Memo., 7 Oct. 1935.

452. Peden, *Treasury*, pp. 74ff.

453. The 1934-programme had added £51 mill. (to be spent 1934/35 to 1938/39) to the normal annual defence budget of about £120 mill. The expansion programme of late 1935/early 1936 envisaged a total of £1,038,500,000, i.e. £417 mill. extraordinary expenditure in addition to the annual estimates; the 1937 (February) Budget (Defence) increased the total to £1,500 mill. H.W. Richardson, *Economic Recovery*, p. 215; Gibbs, pp. 279ff.; Shay, *Rearmament*, pp. 75ff.; Peden, *Treasury*, pp. 74–81.

454. The standard rate of income tax was increased by 3d to 4s9d in 1936, to 5s in 1937 and to 5s6d in 1938.

455. Roskill, *Hankey*, vol. 3, pp. 289ff.; Shay, pp. 162ff.

456. Gibbs, pp. 291ff.; Howson, p. 125.

Once it had become impossible to maintain the dual principle of balancing the budget and of financing normal annual defence expenditure from tax sources, armaments programmes were reassessed on the basis of two criteria: from now on they were not only to be judged in terms of strategic doctrines which were acceptable in the context of domestic politics ('limited liability') but also increasingly in terms of the perceived need to balance 'national resources' (i.e. to have regard to 'effective strength'). Provided that no significant challenge was posed to the government's assumption that Britain could only emerge victorious from a war against any great power if the conflict were a protracted one, then the government's position appeared unassailable: 'Nothing operates more strongly to deter a potential aggressor from attacking this country than our stability . . . But were other countries to detect in us signs of strain, this deterrence would at once be lost'.[457] If Britain was to deter aggressors from attacking the 'island of stability' or, in the event of a *Blitzkrieg*, to exploit her greater staying power to emerge victorious in the end, she had, on the one hand, to double her rearmament efforts now and in the future without, on the other hand, distorting the structure of production and heightening social tensions. The capacities which Britain did not harness for arms production but which she earmarked instead for 'ordinary civil and export production' were seen by the government as guaranteeing the credit-worthiness and stability of sterling. By buying arms overseas (in the US and Canada),[458] Britain would, it was assumed, be able to close the gap between the level of 'self-sufficiency' which was attainable on the basis of voluntary cooperation in the 'prewar' economy, and the levels of arms manufacture expected from the switch to a war economy should a change from international discord to actual war occur:

> Our real resources consist not of money, but of our manpower and productive capacity, our power to maintain credit and the general balance of trade. . . . This country is particularly dependent on imports . . . . The amount of money which we can borrow without inflation is mainly dependent upon two factors: the savings of the country as a whole which are available for investment, and the maintenance of confidence in our financial stability. But these savings would be reduced and confidence would at once be weakened by any substan-

457. Inskip, C.P. 316(37), 15 Dec. 1937, Cab. 24–273; this source is one of most often quoted documents in the writing on appeasement and rearmament.

458. H.D. Hall, *North American Supply*, London 1955; Baldwin–MacKenzie King meeting 1936, Cab. 21–440; on the same issues in 1938 see Shay, pp. 218ff.

tial disturbance of the general balance of trade.

> If we are to emerge victoriously from such a [long] war, it is essential that we should enter it with sufficient economic strength to enable us to make the fullest use of resources overseas, and to withstand the strain . . . the maintenance of our economic stability is an essential element in our defensive strength . . . a fourth arm of defence.[459]

Still suffering as it was from the residual effects of the Ten Years' Rule, and of armaments restrictions in the World Depression between 1930 and 1934, armaments policy presented a whole range of different financial problems. In the wake of drastic shrinkages in the armaments industries' capacity, it was not only armaments companies which had to be motivated through new orders to reactivate their productive capacities;[460] apparently unrelated sectors – from the car industry to factories with no clear link to arms production – also had to be won over, through strategically placed orders, if they were to take the risks involved in preparing for the event of war.[461] In contrast to the situation in re-equipment programmes, it was moreover only possible to accelerate rearmament, for which the ground had been prepared since July 1935,[462] by eradicating obstacles such as the lack of skilled workers[463] or shortfalls in the supply of machine tools.[464]

The issue at stake was the following: either the government was to carry the burden of the acceleration it thought necessary and compensate for its intervention in the economy with conversion aid, subsidies, grants, and so on, or it was to leave it to industry to develop plans for expansion in the event of war as well as for the

459. Bridges, 8 Dec. 1937, T 161/855/F 48431/01/1; Inskip, 15 Dec. 1937, C.P. 316(37), §7, Cab. 24–273.

460. Cabinet meeting, 2 March 1936, 'Industrial Production and Defence Requirements'; Cab. 10(36), 25 Febr. 1936, Cab. 23–83; Statement Relating to Defence, 1936, Cmd. 5107, §§51ff.; cf. Postan, *War Economy*, pp. 7ff., 43ff. On shadow factories see Cabinet meeting, 11 Dec. 1935, Cab. 23–82, pp. 428ff.; Principal Supply Officers Committee, Report, CID 1138–B, 31 May 1934, Cab. 2–6/1, pp. 139ff.; Gibbs, pp. 265ff.

461. Cmd. 5107, §§52–54.

462. Gibbs, p. 180.

463. Baldwin and Hankey thought of armaments orders as public works schemes which could provide employment to skilled labour; Wrench, *Dawson*, p. 321; Middlemas, Barnes, *Baldwin*, pp. 910ff.; Gibbs, pp. 291ff.; Hancock-Gowing, pp. 143ff. The problem of de-skilling work processes was raised by Inskip.

464. WO, Progress Report, DPR 126, 141, 169, Cab. 16–141; Defence Deputation, 2nd meeting, 23 Nov. 1936, Cab. 21–437; N. Chamberlain, 8 Oct. 1937, address at Conservative Party Conference; Weir and N. Chamberlain, 6 Febr. 1936, Interdepartmental Committee, Cab. 21–422 A; 'Rearmament Negotiations with the Machine Tool Industry', Cab. 21–429/432 (for further details see note 457 German original).

reallocation of productive capacities to the armaments sector during the period of rearmament. If the government opted for the first alternative, it would be faced with an enormous financial outlay, since it would not only have to induce the relevant firms to take on arms orders but would also have to share the costs of plant construction, research and development, raw materials, warehousing, and so on, since it would be the sole client of its contractors. In 1935–36, the government opted for the second alternative: it decided to rely on the willing cooperation of industry and trade associations to implement its armaments programmes: it promised the minimum possible government interference, in order to allow business to continue as usual, but at the same time offered long-term contracts and prospects of profits as incentives to industries to expand: 'A very considerable amount of sub-contract work is being undertaken by all the firms in our own aircraft industry as well as . . . by outside firms, but it must be understood that in arranging our programme it was considered essential to do everything possible to allow firms to carry on at the same time with their export and civil work and so create revenue for the country and themselves'.[465]

The government decided at an early stage (in autumn 1933) on selected areas of armaments expansion within which it aimed to create additional capacities by means of consultative agreements with industry – through Lord Weir, Lord Riverdale et al.; its terms included stimuli for the expansion of plant through medium-term contracts and guarantees that it would bear part of the costs for the expansion of plants.[466] The government's expectation that industries would undertake the necessary conversions themselves, having recognised the advantages of a rearmaments boom, certainly made its decision easier; yet the government also knew that it had to limit industry's exploitation of the boom for socio-political reasons.[467] The government was equally cautious on questions relating to the long-term consequences of rearmament for the export capabilities of British industry.[468] Neville Chamberlain

465. Air Ministry Memo., Oct. 1936, Cab. 21–437. The concept of 'willing cooperation' was bound to produce 'gaps' between programmes and output and henceforth disputes between the Service Ministries, which were criticised for failing to achieve 'preparedness for war', and the economic departments, which aimed to 'husband' the nation's resources.

466. Cmd 5107, §§52–54, 58; Postan, *War Economy*, pp. 7ff.; Shay, pp. 101ff., 204. The Treasury intended to introduce 'break clauses', in accordance with its interests in flexibility and diplomatic offensives. Pownall-Diaries, vol. 1, p. 111 (4 May 1936); Middlemas, *Illusion*, pp. 56ff.

467. Phillips-Memo., 31 Dec. 1936, T 175–94; L. Brownett (Deputy to Chief Industrial Adviser), note in view of Defence Deputation, July 1936, Cab. 21–437.

468. Cabinet meeting, Cab. 2(37)6, Cab. 23–87; Feiling, *Life*, pp. 292, 317ff.; Cmd. 5107, §§54–62; Postan, *War Production*, p. 11.

stated: 'We would have to substitute for [commercial work] work which would not only be less profitable in itself but which would mean that orders which would have to be cancelled would go elsewhere and in future we might not find it easy to regain the markets we had set aside'.[469] However desirable armaments exports might appear, the expansion of arms capacities was not to be allowed to go beyond the threshold at which attempts might be made to ease the strain of overcapacity on the state coffers by according precedence to arms exports over other exports.[470] Furthermore, the government feared that a rearmament boom might encourage British industry to concentrate its attention on a potentially lucrative domestic market and that, in the wake of subsequent inflation, industry would lose its long-term competitiveness. It was these and similar 'facts' which lay behind the common arguments according to which rearmament placed Britain in danger of setting back her trade and business by a number of years, thereby risking her financial stability.

The cabinet's preference for relying on the 'willing cooperation' of firms and industries can be understood against the following background: the capacity of the armaments industry, in the restricted sense of the term, was insufficient to fulfil the targets of the armed forces in peacetime; that is, the target set by the re-equipment programme for the period 1934–35 to 1938–39. It was therefore in the second phase of armaments policy, during the actual process of rearmament (from 1936 onwards) that a decision had to be taken as to how far the exigencies of a war economy could be anticipated in the prewar phase without distorting the economic structure and pushing the balance of payments into chronic deficit.[471] The government, defending itself against the much further-reaching proposals put forward by Churchill and other advocates of a ministry of supply[472] or a ministry of munitions,[473] was at pains to emphasise the difference between the implementa-

469. N. Chamberlain, 23 April 1936, HofC; Runciman, 2 March 1936, Cab. 23–83, pp. 202f.
470. Roskill, *Hankey*, vol. 3, pp. 72ff., 165ff.; D.C.M. (32), 15 Nov. 1934, Cab. 27–508; Inskip, 23 Nov. 1936, Cab. 21–438. (For further details on the problems of arms exports, private manufacture of armaments and the Royal Ordnance see note 462 of German original).
471. Inskip, 29 July 1936, Cab. 21–438; WO-Memo., 21 Nov. 1936, Cab. 21–437; Weir to Swinton, 22 August 1935, T 172–1830; Interdepartmental Committee, 6 Febr. 1936, Cab. 21–422: A. Weir warned against copying the German example of 'Wehrwirtschaft'. The critical decisions were to come with the expansion of the Army.
472. Inskip, 30 Oct. 1936, C.P. 297(36), Cab. 24–265.
473. W. Churchill, 28 and 29 July 1936, wanted enabling laws; a ministry of munitions should be able to command about 25 to 30 per cent of Britain's industrial capacity.

tion of programmes orientated towards 'maintaining a balanced economy' – the target years being 1939 (from July/November 1935) and 1937 (from November 1934/July 1935 for the RAF) – and Churchillian attempts to accelerate Britain's transition to a phase of preparation for a major war, which would involve the expansion of all three of the armed forces and would also necessitate 'war measures of compulsion on industry and labour'.[474] The government's desire to continue 'business as usual' effectively prevented the armed-service departments from making full use of the money granted them for contracts: 'British firms, being already choked with orders for the home and export trades, were unable to give prompt attention to government orders'.[475] The conflict between American industry and Roosevelt's New Deal had not escaped the government's notice; it wished to avoid being forced, through rhetorical invocations of a crisis in the international system, into a confrontation with the self-government doctrine of industry and the trade unions. Furthermore, Austen Chamberlain, Boothby, Hoare and other proponents of an acceleration of rearmament openly advocated allowing for 'profiteering' (in the event of war, by contrast, the government was to forbid 'any profit'). The cabinet was also interested in German industry retaining a degree of autonomy as against its 'total' subjection to the 'state party', since it felt that this would make Germany more receptive to appeasement politics; thus it would have been nonsense politically to set the British economy unnecessarily on the track of the 'arms/defence economy': 'the economy of the country could not and must not be stimulated and reshaped to suit the needs of rearmament'.[476] The ideological reservations which, until the beginning of 1938, were shared by a broad majority in the cabinet, were accompanied by concrete fears that the doctrine of 'business as usual' would be undermined too strongly should rearmament proceed (these reservations and fears were, however, vigorously contested by the military and armed-service ministries, which thought them unjustified). Since 'orthodox' views on trade and finance reasserted their position of dominance in 1936–37, and since also the government aversion to 'enabling laws' as a means of

474. N. Chamberlain, 23 April 1936, HofC, accused Churchill of wanting to introduce arbitrary control. Later, the Service Ministers challenged Chamberlain and Inskip; towards the end of 1937, Inskip changed sides, i.e. recognised the need to intervene in industrial production; Postan, pp. 25ff.; Shay, pp. 246ff.; Middlemas, *Illusion*, pp. 116ff.
475. Postan, *War Production*, pp. 69f.
476. N. Chamberlain in Postan, p. 11.

changing the structure of the economy and the mentality of industry and unions by an act of will remained predominant, the point at which progress on rearmament might allow Britain to adopt a policy of strength and counter-pressure was once more delayed. The feeling in 1936–37, not only that Britain was still struggling to overcome the teething troubles of an expanding armaments economy[477] but also that German rearmament was meeting with obstacles, and that by no means all of Germany's resources were channelled into arms production,[478] served as a form of tranquilliser to British authorities.

British industry – like American, and pre-1931–32 German industry – nursed deep-rooted prejudices against improvised state interventionism; they were the residues of government 'control' in the First World War, and the bitter experiences of the years between 1919 and 1934, the era of unilateral disarmament and of the close-down of productive capacity under the Ten Years' Rule. A period of persuasion was therefore necessary[479] before British industry would recognise any political imperative to abandon its reservations towards the government and its armaments programme. In this context it should be noted that the National government did in fact comply with important aspects of industry's demands, by implementing protective tariffs, by concluding the Ottawa Agreement, by leaving the gold standard and by pursuing a policy of cheap money. However, in other areas proposals for overcoming the economic crisis made by industrial interest groups were ignored. A further source of tension in the relationship between the government and industry was what industry saw as the government's failure to make even the most minute of gestures towards defusing differences of opinion over questions of trade agreement policy and industrial reorganisation between the government and the Federation of British Industries or the National Union of Manufacturers: 'The FBI wanted to establish industry's right to be consulted by government – yet it feared too close an involvement with government because it meant making

477. Brown-Memo., C.P. 36(36), 21 Febr. 1936, Cab. 24–260.

478. B.H. Klein, *Germany's Economic Preparation for War*, Cambridge (Mass.) 1959, pp. 78ff.; D. Petzina, 'Vierjahresplan und Rüstungspolitik', in F. Forstmeier and H.-E. Volkmann, eds., *Wirtschaft und Rüstung am Vorabend des Zweiten Weltkrieges*, pp. 65–80; L. Herbst, 'Die Krise des nationalsozialistischen Systems am Vorabend des 2. Weltkrieges und die forcierte Aufrüstung', *VZG*, 26(1978), pp. 362ff.

479. Grand Council, Federation of British Industries; R.B. Holland, *Capitalism in Crisis*, p. 9, was given permission to quote. Weir reported the industry's reservations to Interdepartmental Committee, 6 Febr. 1936, Cab. 21–422 A.

choices'.[480] Two factors played a role in this:

(1) The Federation of British Industries' attempt to gain recognition for its claim that it spoke for the whole of industry. The FBI had been founded with the help of, and as a result of pressure from, the First World War government, who at that time (in 1916) were seeking an ally to support their proposed reorganisation of the war economy. [481] The FBI was now demanding the right to participate in the decision-making process in order to protect industry from repeating the failures and mistakes of the war economy of 1914–18. In claiming a key role for itself as intermediary between government and industry, it aimed to demonstrate the success it had had in performing a representative function in the two decades since its foundation. This more or less amounted to a request from the FBI that it be consulted by the National government as the national umbrella organisation of industry in questions of national survival (armaments and economic policy).[482] However, not only the government but also a number of industries vital for the rearmament process, particularly the engineering trades, stated a preference for bilateral negotiations.[483] The government's tactics[484] of calling leading industrialists such as Lord Riverdale, Lord Weir and Sir Harry McGowan (ICI), to mention but a few, into its committees without previously consulting the FBI, and of commissioning from them enquiries into or recommendations on the organisation of industry or on cooperation between employers and trade unions (specifically in relation to the exigencies of war production) did not help to strengthen the influence of the organisation.

(2) The fact that former members of the Foreign Office, the

480. Holland, *Capitalism*, p. 10. Locock's statement, *The Times*, 26 April 1933, 'Disappointment in Industry. Income tax Burden'.

481. H.I. Schmidt, 'Wirtschaftspolitik and "economic reconstruction" 1914–1918', (Ms.).

482. Debate in the Grand Council of the FBI on the talks of the Presidents' Deputation to the Prime Minister and Chancellor of the Exchequer, Oct. 1935; letters from members to Nugent and Locock stress this request.

483. The government made arrangements with the construction, iron & steel, machine tool and aircraft industries.; Inskip was in charge of negotiations with these industries; S. Gibbs, p. 291.

484. Weir and Lord Riverdale were asked in 1933 to help with the establishment of shadow factories. Swinton asked Weir to advice the Air Ministry (1935). Weir was asked to join the Subcommittee on Defence Policy and Requirements (16 Dec. 1935, Cab. 21–422 A) and had the privilege of offering opinions and advice on all subjects related to organising industry for the purposes of rearmament. Weir was opposed to control, interference, a Ministry of Supply, etc.; he was a great help to Chamberlain in the controversies on the role of the Army; DPR 22th meeting, 11 June 1936, Cab. 16–136. Middlemas, Barnes, *Baldwin*, pp. 901ff.; Dennis, *Decision*, p. 60. The Weir-Mss. at Churchill College, Cambridge, provide a wealth of information.

Department of Overseas Trade and the Colonial Office (Nugent, Tennyson and Locock) occupied the higher echelons of the FBI bureaucracy, led its executive managers to define their own role in processes of internal opinion-formation as one of being, in part, interpreters of the 'political' standpoint of government departments, and, in part, a buffer against exaggerated demands put forward by individual member organisations to the government.

The domestic political situation induced government and industry to begin their cooperation on armament matters with a discussion on the theme which was likely to present the hardest test for them both, that of profiteering. Each side expected the other to give ground: industry wanted an assurance from the government[485] that the task of converting 'industry to purposes of defence if need be' and of accommodating it to the government's armaments programmes would be left, as far as possible, to 'industrial self-government'; the government for its part was to coordinate[486] the priorities of the three armed services at departmental level, in order to prevent competition arising over 'free' productive capacities – a development which was likely to affect the cost structure and, in particular, the employment market (in terms of competition for skilled workers). In return the FBI would ensure that the government's interest in reasonable price levels would be adequately considered by companies when they concluded contracts with the government.[487] Industry and government explicitly stated their concern 'to prevent exploitation in any practicable way' in

---

485. Baldwin, 13 Jan. 1936, DPR, Cab. 16–123 and Cab. 21–422A; Cmd. 5107, §§50ff.; Baldwin, 1 April 1936, HofC. One has to remember that British governments were reluctant to become 'employers'; this influenced the debates on nationalisation (coal industry); on the other hand, governments threatened industry with control if attempts to 'organise capitalism' were of no avail in distressed industries; many debates in trade associations and in the FBI and NCEO turned on the question of how serious the government's threats really were.

486. Note of a Meeting between the Prime Minister and the Chancellor of the Exchequer and Representatives of the Federation of British Industries, DRC 38, 17 Oct. 1935, Cab. 16–112, pp. 370–375; J.B. Webb to Sir Arthur Robinson (PSOC), 27 Oct. 1935, Cab. 21–434; Cmd. 5107, §57. A FBI delegation met Fisher, H. Wilson, Weir and H. Ellis on 31 Jan. 1936, FBI/S/Walker 113. The FBI had asked for the interview in order to learn the government's position; the FBI was alarmed about resolutions presented and debated at the 1935 Party Conference of the Conservatives. Further, the FBI was worried about the lack of coordination of orders on behalf of the Service Departments. On the latter problem see Peden, *Treasury*, pp. 85ff.; Gibbs, p. 276.

487. Cmd. 5107, §58. The Interdepartmental Committee (Hankey, Weir, Wilson, Fisher) recommended the establishment of a committee of officials to keep contact with the FBI resp. Trade Associations as to terms of contract, prices, profits, etc. Minutes, 6 Febr. 1936, Cab. 21–422 A; cf. Shay, pp. 99ff., 110ff., 124, 254ff. W.J. Reader, 'Imperial Chemicals Industries and the State 1926–1945', in B. Supple, B. Barry, eds., *Essays in British Business History*, 1977, p. 238. On contracts and finance see the 'official' history volume by W. Ashworth.

order to avoid the infamy of profiteering as it had occurred in the First World War.[488] The formulation of this gentleman's agreement was designed to counteract in advance the expected condemnation by Labour and the unions of the unholy alliance between state power and the armaments industry.[489] Industry wanted recognition of the principle that it would be capable of effectively organising the difficult transition to arms production and offered to honour 'non-interference' with an assurance that it would guarantee 'self-regulation' in profit-making, such that industries would not, for example, exploit the government's dependence on arms supplies to demand excessive prices. The FBI referred here to examples of price increases where, following the awarding of government contracts to companies already operating to full capacity, prices had peaked as a reaction to the increase in orders; the FBI maintained that it was better placed than the government to control levels of contract expenditure because of its more precise knowledge of how to spread contracts in a more balanced way. Thus 'self-regulation' was offered as a means of attaining the government's primary objective. In other words, the FBI was suggesting to the government that the state could most effectively control price levels through the coordination of its contracts,[490] whilst it, as the representative organ of industry, could distribute contracts more economically and satisfactorily than Whitehall.

The government sought a compromise with industry[491] primarily because it did not want to tackle the most difficult problems it faced; namely, that of the 'rationing' of skilled labour and the development of the relation between wages, costs and prices, either directly, or any earlier than necessary.[492] The dilemma was

488. Cabinet meeting, 25 Febr. 1936, Cab. 23–83, pp. 157ff.; Middlemas, Barnes, *Baldwin*, pp. 902ff; Shay, pp. 119f.

489. For this reason, N. Chamberlain rejected industry's demand for direct access to the Prime Minister; in the aftermath of 'Munich', Chamberlain constituted a panel of industrial advisers; its members were former Presidents of the FBI; FBI, Executive Committee, Minutes, 18 Nov. 1938, FBI/C/2/1938. The hearings of the Royal Commission on the Private Manufacture of Arms reminded all concerned of the experiences during the First World War (Roskill, *Hankey*, vol. 3, pp. 246ff.). The Labour Party demanded nationalisation of armaments industries. The 'Left' agitated against 'merchants of death'.

490. On the practice of 'coordination of supply' see Gibbs, pp. 780ff.; Postan, pp. 39ff., 104ff.

491. Baldwin, 9 March 1936, HofC, vol. 309, cols. 1843ff.; Baldwin, 1 April 1936, HofC, vol. 310, col. 1992; Cmd. 5107, §§54ff. Inskip was satisfied with the working arrangements between Service Ministries and central bodies of individual industries.

492. Brown, C.P. 96(36), 26 March 1936, Cab. 24–261; Cabinet meeting, 1 April 1936,

seen as an inevitable one, since the expansion of arms production could not be achieved without skilled labour[493] and, despite high unemployment, there was a shortage in this area comparable to the shortfall in the second essential requirement for an acceleration of production; that is, machine tools.[494] Should the government resort to requisitioning available skilled labour and rationing it between armaments production and production for export and civil trade (in view of the shortages in this sector of the workforce)? The government's basic principle according to which the conversion of industry to defence purposes was not to cause undue damage to exports was founded not only on its view that finance for armaments would otherwise be jeopardised[495] but also on the knowledge that the psychological barriers of the trade unions to compliance with any form of dilution could not simply be removed by legal means. In order to tackle this problem the government would have had to negotiate with the unions. It foresaw that it would have to honour the trade unions' cooperation with concessions in other areas;[496] after the disappointments suffered by the trade unions during, and in particular after, the First World War, all forms of 'dilution'[497] – 'industrial conscription', and so on – would only be acceptable if appropriate 'guarantees' were also offered. Apart from this the government also had to take account of the fact that negotiations with the unions were likely to produce a general atmosphere of alarm on the political scene (see above).

Industry was easier to deal with. The government was able to frighten industry by pointing out that it would have to reckon with massive intervention (e.g. inspection of its 'books') if it did not

---

Cab. 23–83; Brown, C.P. 297(36), 30 Oct. 1936, Cab. 24–265.

493. Weir estimated a demand for an additional 120,000 men: C.P. 57(36), Cab. 23–83, p. 159; Cabinet meetings, 2 March and 8 April 1936, Cab. 23–83, pp. 206ff., 452. The problem became even more serious in the autumn of 1937, see Gibbs, p. 289ff.; Barnett, *Collapse*, pp. 478ff., 500ff.

494. On the problems of 'tooling up' see W.C. Hornby, *Factories and Plant, War Production Series, History of the Second World War* (for further details see note 457 German originial).

495. Cabinet Meetings, 2 March and 8 April 1936; C.P. 96(36), 26 March 1936, Cab. 24–261; N. Chamberlain, 9 Febr. 1936, in Feiling, *Life*, p. 292; cf. Middlemas, *Illusion*, pp. 116ff., 216ff.; Postan, pp. 25ff.

496. Cabinet meeting, 4 Dec. 1935, Cab. 23–82, pp. 363ff.; Brown (Minister of Labour), N. Chamberlain and Weir stressed this point of view in Cabinet meetings; Baldwin assured Citrine 'privately' and the Labour Party publicly that the Government would not introduce military and industrial conscription in peacetime, except after an election which had decided on the issue; Baldwin, 29 July 1936, Cab. 21–438; cf. Cowling, *Hitler*, pp. 212ff.; Dennis, *Decision*.

497. Cracken to Inskip, 19 Febr. 1938, in Gibbs, p. 311; on the First World War see S. Hurwitz, *State Intervention in Great Britain. A Study of Economic Control and Social Response 1914–1919*, Oxford 1948, pp. 89ff.

support the government in examining cost structures as soon as any reasonable suspicion arose that price increases were not explicable in economic terms alone.[498] The choice facing the FBI was that of either seeing to it that 'everything was above board' or, if it failed to do so, of being ignored by the government, which would be under pressure from public outrage in the event of profiteering.[499] At his first meeting with delegates from the FBI at the beginning of the general election campaign in 1935, the prime minister issued a warning that the government did not wish to impose an organisation on industry but that it was in industry's own interest 'to play the game both as industrialists and as taxpayers . . . . If industrialists would play the game there would be no need to impose an organisation on industry'.[500] In a certain sense this pressure was welcomed by the FBI, since it could be used to improve its own position *vis-à-vis* the powerful branch organisations.[501] The FBI could not, however, guarantee that its influence was sufficient to ensure that the government need no longer worry about prices and inflation. Under the terms of an agreement on the distribution of responsibilities with the NCEO (National Confederation of Employers' Organisations) and branch organisations, the FBI was neither able to pronounce on questions of wages and 'labour' nor to express an opinion on the structural and organisational problems of individual industries. It was for this reason that government departments created their own channels of communication to individual sectors of industries.[502]

The relationship of mutual support between government and industry was not only established under pressure from the prime minister but was equally influenced by the decisive rejection by both parties of the domestic and foreign policy aims of labour – namely, the nationalisation of industry, in particular the armaments

498. Protocol of FBI-Prime Minister meeting (see note 486). Chamberlain emphasised the alternative, i.e. government control. The debate is to be seen against the background of controversies on planning and reorganisation of industry (cotton, iron & steel; coal), which were partly tied to the debate on tariffs and protectionism.

499. N. Chamberlain to FBI deputation (see note 486). The Treasury threatened to inspect the books of contract partners; the FBI and industry did not feel themselves to be in the stronger position *vis-à-vis* the government; industry was interested in cooperation; e.g. *Birmingham Chamber of Commerce Journal*, 15 March 1936, 'Industry's Part in Defence'; cf. Shay, pp. 94ff., 121ff.

500. Report on Meeting FBI-Prime Minister, 17 Oct. 1935.

501. Beharrell, one of the FBI delegates, favoured in internal FBI debates negotiations between government and individual industries. Beharrell and Weir held important positions in the NCEO; the FBI was restricted to trade and industry; the NCEO insisted on the demarcation and claimed its competence to speak on labour issues.

502. Gibbs, p. 291; W. Ashworth, *Contracts and Finance*.

industry,[503] and 'collective security including the Soviet Union'. Through mutual cooperation, they aimed to guarantee success for the policies of the National government and thereby avoid a reallocation of power in domestic politics by political means. The government's policy of linking its efforts to achieve 'general European appeasement' to gradual and flexible rearmament and to attempts to negotiate arms limitation conventions (1932–38) also found support amongst social groups outside industry.[504] The understanding between government and industry on what had become the central question of British policy[505] has, however, to be seen in the proper perspective. Just as the British political system, in contrast to its German equivalent, never sought to use armaments policy as a last refuge from domestic crisis, so the articulation of economic interests and the political function of trade and industry were different in British and German politics. In the following pages, our analysis will again select only one of the significant aspects of British policy in this context.

In the winter of 1935/36 the government conceded some influence on rearmament to industry by appointing Lord Weir[506] – who was a director of International Nickel of Canada, Shell and ICI, ex-president of the umbrella organisation of the employers federations and one of the three representatives of industry and commerce at the Ottawa Conference – to the cabinet sub-committee on defence policy and requirements. From this moment on, the attitude of British interest organisations towards the situation in Europe was closely linked to their attitude to the parliamentary Opposition as an alternative to the governing parties. Leading industrialists and bankers expressed fears that the Opposition might succeed in convincing public opinion that a readiness to negotiate with totalitarian regimes would achieve nothing.[507] They supported the conciliation policy of the National

503. Labour Party, 1934 Programme 'For Socialism and Peace'; Brand, *Labour*, pp. 171, 189; Naylor, *Labour's International Policy*, pp. 70ff., 190f.; Roskill, *Hankey*, vol. 3, pp. 165ff., 246ff. Hankey accepted an invitation to give evidence to the Royal Commission, as he saw in the hearings a platform to express his concerns about the establishment of a Ministry of Supply.

504. See Introduction to this book.

505. Government and industry agreed on 'willing cooperation' instead of 'compulsion'; as armaments production touched on problems of economic order, both sides wanted to circumvent matters of principle.

506. W.J. Reader, *Architect of Air Power*, London 1968, ch. 9. Hoare, a former Air Minister in Baldwin's governments, proposed Weir's cooptation to the DPR Committee, Cabinet meeting, 4 Dec. 1935, Cab. 23–82. pp. 363ff.

507. W.A. Lee (Mining Association of Great Britain) to Locock, 1 Nov. 1938, FBI/EA/ Glenday/File 340/R 18e, Memo. 'International crisis 1938. Points to be taken up with the

government – that is, appeasement within the framework of the Four-Powers diplomacy – in order to prevent the Labour Party and the Liberals gaining ground in domestic politics by popularising their foreign-policy concept of 'collective security including the Soviet Union'. They feared that the Left would be able to compensate for the setbacks it had suffered during the crisis of confidence and finance in 1931, by mobilising popular foreign policy slogans. If the National government's appeasement policy were shown to be based on an illusion, and if also the Left's warning against negotiating with totalitarian regimes, were to find popular resonance, then there would follow, they predicted, a dangerous internal crisis of confidence during which a government of the Left could come to power. Such a government, they suggested, would either pursue a foreign policy of confrontation with the dictators, or would involve Britain in conflicts through its alliance with the Soviet Union. In relation to domestic politics, they predicted that the Left – like the Popular Front government in France – would use its majority to force through Parliament the far-reaching 'socialist' experiments repeatedly discussed at Labour Party conferences, under the influence of the intellectual Left and the Cripps group.[508] The conclusion of this line of argument was that the consequences of such a policy would be just as 'disastrous' as they had been in France, both in terms of the government's scope for action at home and in terms of economic activity. It was in order to prevent what they saw as this undesirable development that the leaders of industry expressed their support for the government's 'appeasement' strategy. Through public relations campaigns of their own, they aimed to counter the Left's relatively unsophisticated propaganda against official foreign policy. The advantages of the government's policy of moderation for trade and industry and, therefore, for Britain could not, in industry's view, be emphasised strongly enough: 'If we take the course of abandoning everything [i.e. fall in line with the Left's call to institute a bloc of peace-loving democracies against totalitarian states] it is difficult to know

---

Government when plans to defence would be strengthened. This crisis in retrospect, Industry and foreign policy'. I refer to this clear-cut memorandum; although it obviously owes a lot to the situation 'after Munich', the structure of the argument is such as to cover the 1936–1938 period.

508. In this context, N. Chamberlain's statement is ominous: 'On this plan [rearmament and public works, G.S.] our weak point [unemployment, G.S.] would recede into the background and we should make all our play with the two "bogeys", Stafford Cripps at home and Hitler abroad': N. Chamberlain, Diary, 2 August 1935 (see also note 441).

how any form of trade relations can be maintained in certain areas of Europe and how war can be averted beyond a few weeks or months'.

The leaders of industry, having declared the policy of collective security a failure, emphasised the need for public admission of the risks involved in the policy of appeasement, since this could only increase the credibility of the government's approach. In conceding that conciliation procedures might fail, they believed they could protect themselves against accusations of blindness in face of the German threat; at the same time, the propagation of notions that it was necessary to continue negotiations with Germany, despite any setbacks experienced in appeasement policy, provided a basis for demanding rearmament measures appropriate for a strategy of deterrence. However, industry, like the government, recognised the danger of provoking accusations that the 'ruling classes' were using the crisis as a pretext for expenditure on 'luxuries' by pursuing an inflated armaments programme instead of expenditure on social reforms.

The recipe drawn up by the industrialists for the success of the government's dual policy thus involved a strategy of limited specific rearmament rather than an overall mobilisation of economic resources for an arms race. Foreign policy was accorded the task of consolidating what were considered to be essential relations with the great bloc of neutral countries, in particular the US; the government was, at the same time, exhorted to refrain from any action which might provoke an angry response from the Dominions (as would, for example, Labour's call for collective security including the Soviet Union), since it was hoped that in an emergency Britain would be able to count on help from those countries 'which show no disposition to succumb to German influence'. Alignment with the policy of these neutral countries served at least two useful purposes: firstly, that of countering the accusation that 'appeasement' meant submitting to Germany's will and, secondly, that of opening up a reservoir of strength, thus rendering unnecessary the anticipation of the war economy, for example through the establishment of a ministry of supply. Both arguments were aimed not only at Labour but also at the 'opposition from the Right' (Churchill), which maintained that the government's rearmament measures were inappropriate for the serious nature of the threat posed by Germany.

The interests of industry and the business community, on the one hand, and of the government, on the other, coincided in one further aspect: both sides agreed that the process of *economic recovery*, which had begun to consolidate itself in 1935, had to be shielded from the impact of foreign-policy crises for as long as possible. This goal was pursued by differentiating between military threats, to which Britain must react, and diplomatic crises where it was said that the satisfaction of legitimate German demands for revision had to be one component of a solution. The British readiness to minimise dangers and to rely on the hope that a negotiated settlement could or should be achieved was related to Britain's desire to safeguard the recovery process which had only recently begun.[509] Financial statements from the large banks, companies, and so on, which appeared at the end of the financial year in February–March in advance of the official budget, as well as economic reports in the London press and official surveys conducted by the economic ministries, all painted the same rosy picture of the coming year.[510] Cynical observers remarked that the Stock Exchange, which always acted as a barometer of moods, appeared to have decided to treat the dispute between the diplomats and politicians over the interpretation of treaty obligations merely as an example of 'how politicians always manage to delay that era of prosperity which is just around the corner. . .and how businessmen turn not their other cheek but their blind eye'.[511] Economic interests were protected by the government showing a willingness to negotiate with Hitler: 'If we could. . .get this trouble behind us and start Europe on a new basis we should . . . see a rapid expansion, for the undertone is firm and enterprise is just waiting for the restoration of confidence to go ahead'.[512] Indeed, it was the government's desire to protect the economy which was one of the principle motivating forces of economic appeasement.

According to Runciman and Neville Chamberlain, Weir and their industrial advisers,[513] the confidence which was a prerequisite for reactivating the economy and, thereby, for increasing state revenue, would be destroyed if decisions were taken to increase

509. Hankey to his son Robin (Berlin Embassy), 22 Dec. 1936. in Roskill, *Hankey*, vol. 3, p. 238; Eden, in *The Times*, 17 Jan. 1936, p. 9.

510. *The Observer*, 5 Jan. 1936; *The Times*, 29 Jan. 1936, and 9 March 1936; Central Office, Conservative and National Associations, Hints for Speakers, 30 Jan. 1936: 'Trade and Industrial Progress', 11 June 1936 'Progress in Trade and Industry'.

511. R. Law to Sargent, 24 March 1936, C 2381/4/18, FO 371–19 897.

512. N. Chamberlain to Hilda, 21 March 1936, NC 18/1/952.

513. Brownett-Memo., June 1936, note in preparation to Defence Deputation, Cab. 21–437.

productive capacities to war economy levels before conflict arose. Trade and industry would thereby suffer a setback from which they would only recover after generations, if at all.[514] When the Defence White Paper was approved on the eve of the Rhineland crisis (2–3 March 1936), the cabinet proclaimed that the 'plan of defence requirements must be carried out without restrictions on the programme of social services and that the general industries and trade of the country must be maintained as essential elements in the financing of the reconditioning of the [armed] services'.[515]

The cabinet's decision to include Weir, as 'contact man' with industry, in the decision-making process[516] was of crucial importance, since Weir in particular, as well as Treasury officials (Leith-Ross), championed the principle that the process of rearmament, which gained real momentum only in 1936, had to be guided by the demands of industry[517] and not by those of the armed-service departments. The chiefs of staff resented the inclusion of a businessman in the administration, since they detected defeatist elements in Weir's proposals which they felt should preferably be eradicated from consultations on defence planning and requirements.[518] The chiefs of staff, who were admitted as 'advisers' to the cabinet committee and its sub-committees, wanted representatives from trade, industry and finance to be called in only at the point at which decisions had to be implemented; they did not want to allow them rights of co-determination in the phase of decision-making on programmes which the services had evolved and elaborated.

---

514. Inskip, C.P. 297(36), 30 Oct. 1936, Cab. 24–265; Inskip, 14 March 1938, Cab. 23–92; see note 472; Feiling, *Life*, p. 314; Middlemas, *Illusion*, pp. 56ff.

515. Cabinet meeting, 2 March 1936, Cab. 23–83, pp. 206–208; DPRC, 25 Febr. 1936, C.P. 26(36), Cab. 23–83, pp. 157ff.

516. See note 506.

517. Weir, 2 Oct. 1935, Cab. 16–112; Interdepartmental Committee, 6 Febr. 1936, Cab. 21–422 A; (H. Wilson reported Weir's point of view).

518. Chatfield to Hankey, 14 Jan. 1936, Cab. 21–422A; N. Chamberlain Diary, 19 Jan. 1936, NC 2–22, regarded Weir as a welcome ally in his struggles with the Services and the FO.

Conclusion

In the wake of a World Depression which had transformed power relations in the international field and inaugurated a new phase of destabilisation in the world economic order, strategic (defence) and structural economic policies were of prime importance for Britain's political development. The coalition of interests and opinions grouped together by the National government reacted to the economic crisis by abandoning the policies which were the hallmarks of an epoch (the Gold Standard and free trade) without, however, outlining possible guidelines for a new interpretation of the *modus operandi* of a capitalist economic system. The measures taken by the National government signalled a departure from the policy aims laid down after 1919, according to which London was to be reconstituted as the clearing house of multinational liberal trade; instead, they marked an attempt to establish London as the leader of a relatively autonomous economic and monetary system (which would be orchestrated through Trade Agreements and the establishment of a sterling bloc).

Advantage was now taken of changes in international configurations of power by those political forces which, prior to the First World War and in the 1920s, had lost ground to representatives of financial and free-trade interests, and who now found themselves in a position to consolidate and follow through the successes they had achieved in successive bids for power inside and outside the market-place between 1930 and 1932. At the same time, the problems surrounding the 'risks for peace' concept, which had become common currency in the 1920s under the aegis of the Ten Years' Rule, were brought into sharp focus as the eruption of conflict at various crisis flashpoints around the world revealed the strategic inadvisability of Britain's 'overcommitments' within her international empire.

In this context, 'security' was defined not only in terms of precautionary measures to preserve the territorial integrity of Britain and the Commonwealth and Empire (through national and imperial defence), but also in terms of measures to ensure the continuation of self-government at home; here, the 'freedom of independent social development',[1] in other words of autonomous political organisation, untouched by intervention from abroad, was taken as a prerequisite for the maintenance of 'security'. Within the terms of this debate, defence, foreign and armaments policies were emphasised as means of guaranteeing British autonomy from Europe; indeed, Britain's isolation was furthered precisely by persistent efforts to restrain (appease) the more conflict-orientated great powers – both friends and enemies. The specific approach demanded by these isolationist tendencies within British policy, with their aim of retaining British autonomy in decision-making on foreign-policy matters, was founded on the premise that 'the real hope for Europe [was] that, while the United Kingdom should make preparations as were necessary to defend herself, she should still pursue a policy of a settlement in which Germany could take an equal share'.[2]

The explicit renunciation by leading figures in the cabinet of the pro-French alliance policies of the pre-1914 Liberal cabinet was grounded in a view of 'good' domestic policy as providing the soundest basis for foreign policy. The ultimate aim of British foreign policy was to avoid British involvement in international rivalries, in order to allow Britain to devote herself to peaceful economic development and domestic reforms.[3] Although it is questionable whether the Conservative–Liberal groups supporting this isolationist-non-interventionist tradition in the 1930s intended to implement its so-called reforms in social policy – a move which would have implied a change in direction similar to that of the Liberal–Social cabinet before 1914 – there are however common strands within the foreign policies of both governments: for both, it was a matter of priority to avoid British involvement in war,

---

1. R. Löwenthal, 'Freiheit der Eigenentwicklung', in: U. Scheuner, ed., *Außenpolitische Perspektiven des westdeutschen Staates*, vol. 1, München/Wien 1971, p. 11; K. Kaiser, M. Kreis, eds., *Sicherheitspolitik vor neuen Aufgaben*, Frankfurt 1976; F.X. Kaufmann, *Sicherheit als soziologisches und sozialpolitisches Problem*, Stuttgart 1973², pp. 59ff.

2. See the quotation ch. II/216, and II/192.

3. The hypothesis of G. Hollenberg, *Englisches Interesse am Kaiserreich*, Wiesbaden 1974, p. 85, is appropriate to the Campbell-Bannermann and Lloyd George wings in the Liberal Governments before 1914, but also fits the conditions of the 1930–37 period.

through the implementation of a peace strategy whose aims were, on the one hand, to achieve limited changes in the system of international relations and, on the other hand, to negotiate agreements on arms limitation which would obviate the necessity for more drastic forms of conflict resolution.

British room to manoeuvre in foreign policy was limited both by existing configurations of power in international politics, which faced Britain with the problems of tensions between intransigent rivals in areas adjacent to her own front door, and to doorways to the Empire (in Western Europe, the Mediterranean and the Near East, India and the Far East), and by the restrictive structures and historical strictures imposed on the National government itself, which had achieved consensus primarily by agreeing to withdraw from overcommitments in as many policy fields as possible. In consequence, British political strategy came to consist of a series of symbolic gestures designed, if not to replace 'policy' *per se*, then at least to maintain a situation in which resources remained available to be committed in future to any one of several different goals. The government's rearmament measures, for example, which functioned both as a gesture of reassurance to France and as a deterrent to Germany, offered the dual advantage both of shielding the domestic political decision-making process from 'outside influences' (Staff talks, joint planning and 'division of labour' in arms production) and of making evident Britain's availability as a 'mediator' in foreign relations. The symbolic gestures and strategies which characterised both Britain's domestic policy and her foreign relations with sympathetic states (France and the US) were finally also characteristic of Britain's policy towards Germany.

British appeasement policy in the 1930s cannot simply be seen as a reaction to problems created by Hitler's Germany but must also be seen in the context of British attempts to regain the initiative in attempts to achieve a general European settlement and thus to influence the future course of events in ways which would serve Britain's vital interests (*Lebensgesetze*). In the autumn of 1934 British diplomacy declared that the moment had come for Britain to liberate Europe from a situation already predicted for the mid-1930s by the political progenitors of the appeasers, which was seen to have arisen as a result of French weakness, on the one hand, and as a result of the re-emergence of Germany as a power factor, on the other. However, Britain was not prepared to use her role as self-proclaimed leader to initiate a policy of encirclement. On the contrary, London's policy was directed at maintaining

Britain's freedom of action in order to be able – in contrast to 1914 – to continue right up to the last moment to explore the possibility of a settlement, and thus to avoid another round of blood-letting. It was considered necessary to 'appease' Germany (even against the better judgement of many concerned), firstly because France was going through a period of weakness and, secondly and more importantly, because it was assumed that Britain, as in the First World War, would have to bear the main burden of responsibility for countering Germany's *Griff nach der Weltmacht* (bid for world power). British policy was directed firstly by the notion that, for a number of reasons, defence capacity could not be restored until the target year 1939–40 and, secondly, by the assumption that, once the arms gap had been closed, Britain would be able, and might indeed have to rely in an emergency on her own potential – that is, on her effective strengths in industry, economy and finance and on the 'morale' of the population.

For all the above reasons, an analysis of appeasement policies which aims to clarify the preconditions, the scope for movement and the reference points of British policy must necessarily focus on the domestic political context of rearmament, and on British policies of 'preventive diplomacy' towards the Third Reich.

1. Continuity in British Policy

In contrast to the numerous studies of British appeasement policy which limit their sphere of reference to the Munich crisis and the events immediately surrounding it, while at the same time attempting to establish the nature of the dynamic determining developments in domestic politics, this present study has focused on the period 1930–34 to 1937. The period 1930–37 has been assumed to offer a more appropriate basis for the identification of those structures which allowed notions of 'British interests' to be brought into association with policies of isolationism ('limited liability') and preservation of peace. German policy in the period left opportunities open for diplomatic initiatives from Britain which would allow her – 'in spite of all' – to avoid the decisions made increasingly necessary by mounting conflicts of Germany's making. Throughout this phase in British foreign policy, options remained open to Britain which might have had far-reaching consequences had they been pursued after the March crisis of 1938. Whilst between 1933 and 1935, for example, it was still possible to debate the alternative of appeasing either Germany or Japan without having to fear immediately noticeable consequences should any choice be made, it became necessary after 1937 for Britain to fight simultaneously on both fronts. Britain's strategic overcommitments and her relative weakness in comparison with other great powers, was 'objectively' clearer and more topical in 1938–39 than in the period between 1930 and 1937:

> The combination of these two factors (the unique nature of the British economy; the uniquely global nature of Britain's strategic vulnerability) and the massive contradiction between both of them, were basic elements in Britain's world position which no alternative in home government or change in financial policy could very much effect . . . it was not just a lack of will (which, in some cases, is incontestable) but an awful lack of means on the part of the British government which forced the adoption of a policy of appeasement.[4]

If all research on British foreign and defence policy points to this conclusion, then future analysis must surely focus on the question of continuity, since the policy characteristics outlined above are by no means confined to the decade investigated here. British foreign and world policy in the twentieth century has been consistently characterised by elements of inertia, by political constellations of enduring stability, by a number of long-lived collective delusions (the balance-of-power doctrine; the ideology of the 'concert of Europe' and of the League of Nations); it has been further marked by the general interest in peace which is characteristic of a world trade and financial power as well as by the effects of the relative decline in Britain's powers, position and influence brought about by the emergence of new centres of commerce, wealth and military strength. Rather than focusing on these more general factors, this present study has however concentrated on identifying continuities between specific problem areas, which have been seen to be decisive precisely because foreign policy relies on the mobilisation of specific domestic forces in defence of goals defined as constituting 'the national interest'. Alongside discussions of British attitudes towards other 'revolutionary' movements on the Continent,[5] our study has aimed to identify the particular areas which

---

4. D. Dilks, 'Unneccessary War', in: A. Preston, ed., *General Staffs and Diplomacy before the Second World War*, London 1978, p. 102.

5. G. Schmidt, *Politische Tradition*; P.M. Kennedy, 'The Tradition of Appeasement in British Foreign Policy 1865–1939', *BJIS*, 2(1976), pp. 195–215.

were most closely linked to the specific developments of the 1930s in an attempt to limit the necessity of tracing 'the roots of appeasement' too far into the past; in this more specific context – given the unification of political forces from the first postwar decade in a national coalition government after the crisis of 1931, which allowed them to elaborate joint definitions of the 'national interest' – these continuities become particularly easy to identify.

The configuration of problems which appears to have been most decisive, and to have taken the most consistent form during the period, seems to have emerged out of the domestic and foreign-policy requirements of the disarmament and rearmament process. If a plausible explanation for the British abandonment of the 'illusions' of 1920s disarmament policy seems to lie in British perceptions of the necessity to adapt to external pressures, questions still have however to be raised as to the relative similarity of the effects of economic, social and political or strategic determinants in the 1930s, compared with those of the preceding decade. Was it possible, Britain had to ask, to tackle the question of armaments in relation both to the Allies and to the domestic British public in the same way and at the same time? It was the combination of these two considerations which constituted the most consistent feature of policy-making from the 1920s through into the 1930s, and it was the prestructuring of strategic decisions on foreign and domestic policy which marked appeasement policy as the dominant unitary feature of foreign policy in the interwar era. The key concepts which to a large extent encapsulate the ideals operative during this period were first elaborated by Hankey in his 1919 statement on security policy, in which he claimed that Britain could consider herself in a position to take and sustain risks abroad which she could not countenance at home.[6] His maxim certainly contains much which is ideological and manipulatory; however, it may nonetheless be seen as the key to any interpretation of the policies of the 1930s and the interwar period as a whole. Analytically the 'dual-risk formula' allows appeasement to be understood in terms of problems of continuity, while at the same time avoiding presenting a distorted picture of the problem of appeasement in the 1930s, in which it appears to have as much or as little in common with the 'moralising internationalism' of the nineteenth century (C. Barnett) or with post-1945 indulgence towards the US as with 'Munich' and 'Prague', with 'Locarno', or with the British

6. The notion 'labour' is defined in ch. II, notes 8, 95, 135ff., 373ff., and Introduction, note 22.

'failure' either to contribute successfully to the stamping out of Bolshevism in 1917–19, or to placate Stalin in wartime. According to the latter view – which is rejected in our analysis here – appeasement is to be seen as a product of 'decline' whose origin lies either in the decadence of the ruling classes, or in a resignation which derives from perceptions of relative strength and comparative power. By accepting the risk formula as the key to British foreign policy of the 1920s and 1930s, we at the same time avoid the pitfalls of the reverse extreme of analysis, in which appeasement is assessed purely in terms of the policies of Chamberlain's government and of 'Munich'.

2. Three Phases of Appeasement Policy

Appeasement policy can be divided into several phases. In the first phase (1933–36) appeasement as 'preventive diplomacy' was intended to provide a prompt means of dealing with 'legitimate German grievances'. In practice, however, this meant tolerating and subsequently legalising the unilateral breaches of treaties through which Germany aimed to re-establish her *Wehrhoheit* (military sovereignty) and thus to gain recognition of her claims to 'equal treatment' on the international political scene. Although meeting such demands would have required a total reshaping of European–international power structures, to the detriment of the victors of the First World War, a regulated crisis settlement of any kind was considered the lesser evil in comparison with either pre-emptive action or encirclement. While official public statements from the Foreign Office did acknowledge the fact that Hitler's foreign policy was unlikely to remain restricted to demands for a revision of the Treaty of Versailles, but would instead challenge and gradually undermine the very principles on which the international system was founded, the effects of that acknowledgement were cancelled out by a peace strategy whose basis was the continuing assumption that Britain could afford to spend time searching for alternative ways of bridging the developing gulf between the foreign policies of democratic and totalitarian regimes in an unstable international system, using 'working agreements' to reach consensus in a number of different issue-areas simultaneously. The domestic consensus on appeasement was based on the view that the Hitler regime would only exclude the possibility of talks on British proposals for securing peace in Europe if Germany was denied 'normal' status as a partner in negotiations; the government won the support of public opinion and both Houses of Parliament by more or less consciously playing down the dangers of the Anglo-German situation. In choosing not to emphasise the security dilemma abroad, the government aimed to stabilise its standing at home, which had been severely undermined by events on the domestic scene. It is in contrasting the constitutive forces of domination (*Herrschaftssynthese*) in Britain to the power structure of the Third Reich – a contrast highlighted by the above examination of British approaches to appeasement – that the difference between the two systems of power can be thrown into sharpest relief.

In the second phase of appeasement policy (1936–37) the British government set itself the task of preventing the Hitler regime from directing its revisionist efforts towards an annulment of the territorial settlement specified in the Peace Treaty. Since it was economic motives and difficulties which had been diagnosed as the causes of Germany's aggressive foreign policy, it was considered necessary to interest Berlin in economic negotiations. The policy of 'compliance' implemented by the National Socialist regime in the phase between the March crises of 1936 and 1938, on the one hand, and the first signs of a world economic upswing between the summer of 1936 and the autumn of 1937, on the other, induced the British government to follow an economic approach: by encouraging various movements towards an effective liberalisation of economic relations, through which in turn it was hoped that success could be guaranteed in the sphere of economic disarmament, the government aimed also to influence politico-military tensions. Signs of a *volte-face* in German foreign policy, which followed, for example, Germany's successful breakthrough in the Rhineland crisis, were considered to evidence the increased necessity of an 'economic approach'. Not only did Britain fear that Germany's neighbouring states would now begin to compete to win approbation from Berlin; above all, it was feared that the returning of industrial areas to German military sovereignty would give added impetus to National Socialism's autarkic aspirations – to its attempts to instal a *Grossraum* economy in Central and South-Eastern Europe. Were this to happen, it would no longer be possible to count on Germany's readiness to negotiate. The British government thus attempted to pre-empt any such development in a dual propaganda and diplomacy, first embarked upon in response to Schacht's approach to the Blum government (which was interpreted as a sign that the 'moderates' – as opposed to Hitler –

acknowledged that Germany was facing serious difficulties). The government offer included the linking of a general European settlement (a 'New Locarno' which would exclude the USSR) to arms limitation, as well as an offer of support for the German economy, which would allow Germany to employ the capacities released from the arms economy (*Wehrwirtschaft*) in different ways; in other words, to open up her export potential. This was, then, a policy elaborated against the background of the recovery in world commerce since mid-1936.

Decisions at ministerial level as to whether concessions should be offered to Germany in matters relating to raw materials, to the colonial question, or to the revision of tariff and 'Ottawa' policies were, however, made dependent on the dual condition (1) that political considerations should take precedence over economic ones and (2) that Germany should make the first move in negotiations.

The use of economic means to achieve what was agreed to be a mutual political end (securing peace) was, then, certainly considered at various points; yet the exercise of economic power and influence continued to take second place to political interests. Overall, the notion of 'linkage' introduced by the British Treasury under Neville Chamberlain, and presented at the Lausanne conference of 1932 as a definition of the British standpoint, remained dominant throughout the 1930s:

> We have discussed compensation in the economic and political spheres. Of these, I think, we all agree that the economic is less important than the political sphere. What we want to see is a settlement at Lausanne which would give to Europe and the world an assurance that the countries here assembled intend to work for a real appeasement of the international atmosphere and to set aside such differences as they may have to collaborate in the reconstruction of Europe. It seems to us that the German Delegation must be prepared to give assurances in this sense.[7]

Economic compensation, classified more or less as a technical problem, was thus deemed acceptable as long as certain political demands were fulfilled: Germany was called upon not only to play a part in a general restoration of confidence but also to make economic concessions in return for the waiving of reparations payments (in 1932) or for measures to relieve her foreign cur-

---

7. Treasury Note, 29 June 1932, T 172–1787.

rency shortages (a question of particular significance in raw materials debates between 1935 and 1937). It was forces within the government hitherto commonly characterised as supporters of appeasement policy who argued with particular insistence for political and economic reciprocity. Mindful of the structural links between British and German trade and finance (banking) interests, Chamberlain, the Treasury and the Board of Trade claimed 'simply' to be applying the same standard used in respect of France or the US: thus they consistently opposed French government proposals for the forging of a 'democratic' front against Germany in the currency and (free) trade sector. This axiomatic reflection of a bloc politics in the sphere of foreign economic relations represented the analogy and complement to the British government's expression of massive reservations over joint security policy. More clearly even than in affairs of defence, British monetary and trade policy articulated both British dependence on decisions taken in the US (a dependence resulting from the pound–dollar relationship), and at the same time, the British belief that foreign policy had necessarily to be moulded to the requirements of domestic British consensus. Demands made at the time for France herself to take steps to find her own way out of self-induced crises may be read as demands that she follow the British example; *de facto* aid for self-help was meanwhile limited to moral support only. The government at the same time assumed Britain's purely verbal support for France to provide a basis for concrete reciprocal concessions, including the improvement of the British export facility, both directly and indirectly, through the phasing out of import restrictions. The French government's argument, on the other hand, was that the very nature of the situation demanded domestic French measures to combat inflation, to restore confidence in the franc and to reduce the deficit; any such measures, it claimed, would have to be supported by a trilateral (British-American-French) declaration on the defence of stable exchange rates in order effectively to combat speculation against the franc. The British government, by contrast, stood by their demand that the French government set in motion a series of measures to counteract rising prices at home, to replenish state revenue and to stabilise the budget situation; further steps towards liberalising trade policy would, it claimed, also widen opportunities for French exports:

A fixed relationship between the pound sterling and the US dollar, which is for practical purposes tied to gold, would result in a formal stabilisation of the pound in terms of gold: to carry out such a measure under present circumstances would be beyond the powers and contrary to the declared policy of His Majesty's government. For their part, therefore, His Majesty's government are disposed to attach less importance to any further declaration which might be made than to measures of internal policy which the French government may decide to adopt. His Majesty's government would find difficulty in agreeing that the remedies lie outside of the French government's own authority and responsibility.[8]

The British government used similar arguments as a basis for its rejection of the French plea for a loan to the French government, to be raised either in sterling in London, or in dollars in New York, and earmarked for the deficit created by decisions on armaments policy.

The projected scheme will considerably embarrass [the chancellor of the exchequer] by its effects on the London market. . . . It should be borne in mind that we have opened our market to French borrowing twice in the last 12 months on each occasion for £40 millions, the last operation having been approved by the chancellor quite recently notwithstanding that it was unwelcome. At the same time restrictions on foreign issues have been in force in this country for a number of years and the present is specially a time at which our savings should be safeguarded in view of the large impending demands for rearmament.[9]

The French case – which is significant also in other respects – demonstrates clearly how government forces dominant in economic policy matters (currency, monetary, finance and trade) successfully asserted their policy of protecting the autonomy of the process of consensus creation in Britain by limiting their definitions of any 'legitimate' articulation of interests to British considerations and by recommending other governments to rely on self-help or self-correction to resolve their problems at home.

The opportunities which the economic sector – traditionally characterised as it is by structures of interdependence – might have offered for a policy designed to defuse tensions in the Anglo-German 'security policy' arena, were thus blocked by economic

8. N. Chamberlain to Le Norcy (Financial Attaché, French Embassy), 19 Febr. 1937, T 177–34, p. 31.

9. Foreign Office to Clerk (Ambassador in France), 8 March 1937, T 177–34, p. 70. Blum had asked for an exchange option to be attached, i.e. for 'bonds to carry payment of so many francs in Paris or in London or in New York at fixed rates of exchange.'

departments and interest groups themselves, through their insistence that, if Britain's economic resources were not to run dry, it was necessary (1) for the settlement of political problems to be given priority, and (2) for 'Danegeld' to be refused to friend and foe alike. Their plea was for a linkage between a more flexible foreign policy (i.e. 'political appeasement') and limited rearmament – that is, economic measures which, though they were motivated by foreign policy considerations, should be guided by considerations as to Britain's 'effective strength'.[10]

In the third phase of appeasement (1938–39), which has not been specifically covered in this study, both the economic and political conditions determining British policy worsened; the former as a result of the 'minor' economic crisis of 1937–38, brought about by the 'Roosevelt' recession, the latter following the outbreak of war in China in July 1937. Earlier signs of a movement towards liberalisation in economic policies now gave way to a new round of tariff increases and a stepping-up of exchange controls; progressive rearmament was matched in the arena of international relations by militant posturing and other acts of aggression. The traditional precepts which had dominated decision-making, and ensured continuity between the 1920s and 1930s (in the arms industry, the notion of 'business as usual') were abandoned during this period for forms of economic resistance already formulated and practised by Britain's opponents abroad (the pre-emptive purchase method, for example). Direct negotiations between industrial groups in Britain and Germany (as well as Japan) now came to be valued as a means of relaxing tensions on the international scene. Since by now the process of rearmament had bound politics and economics inextricably together in both Britain and Germany – even if politics was said to be accorded primacy in the Third Reich – attempts to smooth a pathway towards peaceful coexistence between antagonistic political systems by reducing conflicts of interests in the economic sphere, no longer had even the remotest chances of success. Until 1936–37 it might have made sense to speculate on the possibility of working agreements, since it was not until this point that Schacht and the 'moderates' were finally dispensed with. It would, in other words, have been possible to attempt to reinforce the moderates' position within the power structure of the Third Reich by maintaining and renewing economic interdependencies. However, in view of the European crises engineered by Berlin, as well as the chequered

10. The definition of this notion is provided on pp. 346ff., 352ff., 262ff.

history of Anglo-German 'exploratory talks', there could no longer be any doubt that the Hitler regime had no inclination to respond to British offers of an economic settlement of interests by adopting less aggressive postures. The lifebelts thrown to the drowning man of Anglo-German relations in 1938–39 (proposals for industrial talks, for example, as emergency measures for the protection of 'peace as it stands') were by now unlikely to be politically effective in Britain, since they followed in the wake of events which had transformed 'appeasement' into a synonym for one-sided concessions to an aggressor to the detriment of third parties.

3. Relative Decline and the Focus of Foreign Policy

British attempts to transform Britain's role in world politics in accordance with the requirements of her relative loss of power and significance necessarily involved a preoccupation with domestic political problems. This was publicly recognised by Bonar Law in October 1922:

> we cannot act alone as the policeman of the world. The financial and social condition of this country makes that impossible . . . if [our French Allies] are not prepared to support us there, we shall not be able to bear the burden alone but shall have no alternative except to imitate the government of the United States and to restrict our attention to the safeguarding of the more immediate interests of the Empire.[11]

With the World Depression and the relapse into an era of nationalistic militant power-politics, the desired process of reproduction and regeneration was, however, increasingly threatened by events abroad over which Britain could have no influence, unless she and other key countries declared themselves capable of voluntary cooperation.[12] However decisive the economic–financial conditions or the structure of Britain's society and constitution may be seen to

11. Bonar Law, Letter to *The Times*, 7 Oct. 1922, cf. R. Blake, *The Unknown Prime Minister. The Life and Times of Andrew Bonar Law*, London 1955, p. 448.

12. On the problem and the stages of development see G. Schmidt, 'Wozu noch "politische Geschichte"?'; id., 'Politische Tradition und wirtschaftliche Faktoren in der britischen Friedensstrategie 1918/19, *VfZ*, 29(1981), pp. 131–188; id., 'Das Zusammenspiel sicherheitspolitischer, wirtschaftlicher und ideologischer Faktoren in der englischen Weltpolitik und die Restrukturierung der internationalen Politik', in: K. Rohe, ed., *Die Westmächte und das Dritte Reich. Klassische Großmachtrivalität oder Kampf zwischen Demokratie und Diktatur?*, Paderborn 1982, pp. 29–56.

have been in marking out the boundaries of British freedom to manoeuvre abroad, the demands made on British policy by events in the international arena must also be acknowledged as a crucial influence on the aims and means adopted by British foreign policy.

In mapping out the differences between, and the displacements which took place within, contemporary configurations of international relations, we may discern the following principal features in the development of British foreign policy: in the first instance, attempts to find the right balance between the priorities of domestic and foreign policy, as well as between world (Empire) and continental political interests, were made dependent on the extent to which factors affecting the international constellation of forces influenced Britain herself, or the degree to which British policy might be capable of influencing the behaviour of other countries. The reaction of other countries to British policy may be explained by the instability of an appeasement politics which was, firstly, constrained by the requirements of domestic policy (both in relation to foreign economic policy and to defence) and, secondly, by the 'disturbed' relations of countries more or less directly affected by the German or Japanese threat with Britain and the Empire and Commonwealth. The prevalence of the impression that appeasement policy was biased in favour of Germany may be traced to the British government's refusal – until 1938–39 – to grant Britain's 'partners in fate' (France and Belgium) the right to participate in controversial domestic British debates (through Staff talks and coordinated arms measures), as well as to its simultaneous attempts to negotiate with those powers which had initially forced the arms question upon British policy. And yet, whilst it seems likely that internal German policy discussions floated the question of an alliance with Britain in the period between 1935 and 1937, and put out feelers towards Britain as a result, British strategy discussions seem neither to have addressed the question of any settlement which might have worked to the detriment of third parties, nor to have applied the principle of *divide et impera* to any specific sphere of influence. Instead, debates in Britain tended to attempt to establish the price Britain and other 'haves' would have to pay in order to interest the Third Reich in a stable cross-European settlement.

A further source of appeasement policy's reputation for 'pro-German bias' was Britain's failure to draw the appropriate conclusions from the collapse of 'preventive diplomacy' (Britain's 'early move' tactics): a failure which had clearly indicated the unwillingness of the Hitler regime to make concessions in order to attain a goal which could be more readily secured by unilateral action. Since neither British strategy and armament policy, nor indeed French arms policy, were geared towards deterring 'week-end coups', and since, moreover, British policy identified Germany aggression as deriving from 'legitimate grievances', the results of appeasement tended always to constitute it – retrospectively – as a policy of 'giving way'. The manoeuvrings of appeasement were, however, tolerated at home, at least as long as it remained possible to subsume Germany's unilateral actions under the heading of the complex of guilt generated by the Treaty of Versailles.

The British foreign policy principle of keeping Britain out of the German–*Russian* struggle for power gained even greater import-ance under Baldwin's leadership, in particular from the point at which France incorporated the 'Russian factor' into her crumbling encirclement front through the conclusion of the Franco-Russian Pact. It was common knowledge that French politicians and the French military neither held the military strength of the Soviet Union in high esteem nor did they intend to mobilise the USSR armed forces, since the nature of Russia's relationship to France's Eastern allies, Poland and Rumania, still remained unclear. Britain, with her limited trust in the stability of the French political and social system in the event of an international trial of strength, concluded that the Russian factor should be activated only if such action did not appear to prejudice a settlement with the Third Reich. It was feared that any other, more far-reaching arrange-ment would move Germany and Japan more or less directly to collaborate against British interests, without Britain being able to count on any of her potential allies (France, Russia and/or the US) providing effective relief from this two-pronged threat.

Until 1934 it had been an established fact that Britain was the subordinate party in Anglo-French relations, and thus that France had no need to make concessions to Britain. With the later reversal in power relations, Britain assumed a similar stance towards France. Effective advances in British rearmament policy did not, however, suffice to convince France that changes in the system of inter-national relations, through a system of peaceful revision, which Britain considered indispensable, would indeed raise the threshhold of war; instead, she saw them as providing the spring-board from which the 'aggressive powers' would in future be able to launch attempts to enforce their 'order' on the Continent.

Anglo-American relations of the period were formed against the background of a single enduring problem: the question of how to structure relations between the world's two leading currencies – the dollar and the pound – in ways which would not involve disadvantageous encroachments on the relative autonomy of Britain's (foreign) economic and social policy. Relations became strained when dominant forces in the National government, in academic life and in industry, blamed the US both for the World Depression and its devastating impact on the political and economic situation all over the world and, at least partially, for the relative instability of the position from which Britain was called upon to respond to the rise of the dictators. When Britain accelerated her rearmament programme in the period between 1936 and 1938, she demanded help (burden-sharing) from the US to relieve the dual pressure of threats from Germany and Japan. Yet throughout this period the US, on the one hand, continued to underscore its disengagement from questions of security policy and, on the other, to step up pressure on Britain to participate in the restoration of a 'liberal', undivided world market. As a result, the impression spread through Britain's ruling classes that not only Germany and Japan but also the US (and in a different way, the Soviet Union) were likely immediately to make moves to supplant Britain as a world power should she be enticed into any international conflict. Already overstretched, Britain would in the last resort be forced to defend her scattered interests alone; why then, they argued, should Britain feel obliged to carry the 'general' burden, when no one, not even the 'rich' US, cared to share Britain's responsibilities in the normal run of events?

4. Economic Interests and Appeasement Policies

The focusing of British policy interest on economic appeasement may be explained, on the one hand, by the government's assumption that Germany and Britain shared mutual interests in the economic sphere and, on the other, by Britain's refusal to enter into additional commitments in defence policy (an area of long-standing controversy). In relation to defence, Britain felt herself to be at a disadvantage both in terms of armaments volume and in terms of her own 'strategical overextension'; thus there seemed to be no prospect that a policy which aimed to solve the German question through a European settlement would ever be successful. It seemed only natural to Britain – given what she perceived as the instability of the international situation – that she should attempt to identify openings for a British initiative to bridge the gap between Britain and Germany in the economic field. In reality, however, there was little chance that the effects of economic appeasement strategies – structures of interdependence arising out of economic cooperation – would spill over from the economy into the arena of security policy. There were two reasons for this: firstly, the 'politicisation' of economic questions in the system of the Third Reich and, secondly, the fact that British priorities were set by the representatives of vested interests, and that British economic resources were jealously protected by the economic departments against any moves to use them for foreign assistance and stabilisation.

This leads us to conclude that although economic factors certainly influenced appeasement policies, the importance of economic appeasement for British foreign policy should not be overestimated. The problem confronting any analysis is primarily that of determining whether it is possible to group the various different links between appeasement policies and economic factors (in relation, for example, to the business cycle, the economic climate, the economic doctrines, the relationship between government and industry, etc.) under the combined heading of 'economic appeasement', to form a coherent explanatory model; whereas British policy itself might be full of contradictory features, its interpretation – in terms, for example, of 'economic appeasement' – demands a model from which such ambiguities are absent. The interests of government and industry were compatible in two respects: firstly, each regarded the other as a guarantor of its own security and, secondly, they were in fundamental agreement where foreign policy was concerned. Thus it was that heads of the umbrella organisation of British industry, the FBI, agreed voluntarily to eradicate the kind of profiteering which had been rife in the First World War by lending their support to government arms contracts in return for an assurance from the government that it would leave the organisation of an arms economy as far as possible to 'industrial self-government'. The hope was that such a strategy might undermine the criticisms expected from representatives of labour, who were likely to take a dim view of this unholy alliance between armaments interests and state power.

The most significant point of consensus between the government and industry was their common belief that the process of economic recovery had to be shielded from the influence of crises abroad for as long as possible. The government's readiness to play down external international conflicts, rather than using them to force through rearmament measures, may be traced to its desire to further the process of economic upswing which, it said, was 'only just' in the process of beginning. If the war-economy measures, recommended by amongst others Churchill and some of the armed-service ministers, were to be adopted – if, in other words the productive capacity necessary in the event of war were to be generated at this stage – then, the government argued, it would be undermining the very confidence which was a prerequisite for economic revival, and thus for the augmentation of state revenue. What was more, the government claimed, trade and industry would be damaged to an extent where they would require generations to recover – if indeed they ever recovered at all.

The government's readiness to negotiate with the Hitler regime in order to 'legalise' the results of unilateral 'revisionism', and thus to protect Britain's own economic interests has been situated in most interpretations of British policy under the heading of 'economic appeasement'. In other analyses – for example, that of Einzig and Gilbert/Gott – the same concept is used to describe the British policy of attempting to appease the dictators through economic concessions – for example, by offering economic 'benefits' to the Third Reich – a policy which took little or no account of the positive or negative repercussions which such measures might have on the British economy. These two different usages of the concept are in some ways contradictory; implicit in both, however, is the notion that it was under the influence of certain trade and financial (banking) forces with interests in the German economy that the British government was moved to defend business connections with Germany. The same implicit analysis of official policy, within which an economic settlement with Germany appears as a useful investment, the putative benefits of which include a relaxation of internal political tension in the Third Reich and a moderation of German policies abroad, gained widespread credibility in government circles at the time.

Since the major part of Chapter 1 is devoted to a critique of analyses such as these, there is no need to repeat that critique here. It should however be borne in mind that the motive underlying arguments advocating a submission of the economies of Central and South-Eastern Europe to German influence, as a means of winning time to answer what was said to be Britain's pressing need to rearm, was a hope that Germany might become thoroughly absorbed in the many problems of *Mitteleuropa*, and thus that her

influence might remain confined, at least in the foreseeable future, within this limited sphere. Since, it was argued, Germany
would thus be preoccupied with the task of overcoming her
'Balkan troubles', in other words with attempting to gain control
over her mandated territories,[13] Britain would have time to shore
up the gaps which were the legacy of her defence (arms) and
economic policies of the 1920s. Since the forces behind such
arguments – among others, Hankey, Simon, Leith-Ross, and Cranborne – regarded the financial strength of Britain as a fourth arm of
defence and believed Britain to have the advantage over Germany
in this respect, they resolutely opposed suggestions from other
'economic appeasers' that exchange loans and other financial means
should be used to help Germany overcome her difficulties in the area
of raw materials and foreign currency (difficulties which Germany had
inflicted on herself, through her commitment to overrapid rearmament).

Treasury, Board of Trade, Ministry of Agriculture, as well as the
FBI and the NFU, were in any case vigorous defenders of the view
that Britain's interests had to be accorded primacy in any given
context. The compromise formulas agreed upon in attempts to
reconcile internal conflicts in the aims of government departments, as well as disagreements between other economic appeasers, contained no financial or economic concessions capable
of inducing a 'totalitarian' regime to liberalise its domestic policy
or to change its course in foreign policy.

In order to be effective, the concept of 'economic appeasement',
which at one stage (in 1936–37) achieved practical significance as an
economic peace strategy, was dependent on the functioning of a
political alliance between parts of the Liberal Opposition, the
Labour Party and the left wing of the Conservative Party, on the
one hand, and the political as well as the 'material' support of the
US and some of the Dominions, on the other; hence the attempts
on the part of certain of the economic appeasers (e.g. Lothian and
Jones) to extend their personal network of influence into a 'system
of interpenetrations'[14] within Britain, the US and the Dominions.
In respect of international politics, the champions of this strategy

13. The experiences Britain had to face in Palestine, as well as in India, Sudan and Egypt,
obviously led Hankey, Hoare, Simon, Cranborne, Swinton, et al. to view German 'imperialism'
as likely to be faced with similarly enervating problems as soon as German rulers had to run
'dependent' countries in one way or the other; cf. ch. I of my *Habilitationsschrift*, and ch. I of
German original.

14. J.N. Rosenau, 'Pre-theories and Theories of Foreign Policy', in: R.B. Farrel, ed.,
Approaches to Comparative and International Politics, Evanston 1966, p. 65.,

had two motives for activating the Dominions and/or the US; since these were, or were perceived to be 'liberal' regimes, the appeasers could use Britain's connections with them, firstly, to limit Britain's defence obligations in Europe (to the defence of France and Belgium) and, secondly, to build bridges to the democracies overseas. In terms of international economics, they hoped also to strengthen economic ties with these liberal democracies and thus to persuade them to pledge themselves to the basic principles of a free-market economy; it was on this basis and in view of the favourable development of economic trends in world trade in 1936–37 that the economic appeasers attempted to interest Germany in returning to world economic interdependencies, in the hope that the 'moderates' would then save Germany from finally committing herself to a disastrously autarkic war economy. For the proponents of what was known as 'escalation theory', the decisive question was that of whether Britain, the British Empire and the US – as the obvious targets of attack for a German economy geared to the aims of political ideologies – would be capable of using their relative economic and financial superiority to arrest the fatal chain reaction set in motion by events in Germany; that is, by the transition, firstly from economic nationalism to the militaristic orientation of protectionism, then to an economy dependent on the spoils of war. Ultimately, however, the exponents of Anglo-American cooperation – a strategy first conceived in the context of discussions of economic disarmament as an effective means of achieving peace – came to argue for it as an end in itself, once it had become clear (in the course of 1937) that, for Germany, political considerations, the exertion of power and territorial expansion were paramount. From this point onwards, the consolidation of Anglo-American trade and currency relations – a theme which was for various reasons immediately hived off by the heads of the relevant economic departments, and discussed separately from questions relating directly to German appeasement – was presented by the economic appeasers as a central prerequisite for the prestructuring of a defence pact against the Axis powers.

Thus having first attributed Germany's economic misery and the dangers arising from it to the erroneous policies of the victors of the First World War, and having therefore mistakenly supposed that the Western powers could change Germany's system by correcting their own foreign economic policy, the economic appeasers of the 1930s now began to recall the warnings of their intellectual forbears (Garvin and Milner) who had argued in 1919 that it was necessary first to provide for an Anglo-American partnership or a 'new economic imperial policy' before the risk could be taken of giving Germany equal treatment as a significant economic power. 'Economic appeasement' – as a policy 'strategy' – is thus to be seen not so much as the direct product of economic interests or of reactions to economic crises (such as changes in the balance of trade and payments) but rather as the expression of a specific calculation of the relationship between various economic variables. In effect, the economic appeasement strategy amounted to the offer of a mutually advantageous trade-off: in return for guarantees of access to raw materials, as well as of 'unconditional' access to credit facilities and export markets, the 'haves' demanded respect from the 'have-nots' for the standards and values of Anglo-Saxon 'capitalist' democracies and international regimes. There is an obvious analogy here to the pattern of domestic British social liberal reform policies for the stabilisation of the political system and the economic order – an analogy which was quite intentionally introduced into the foreign policy debate by a number of economic appeasers.

5. Domestic Considerations and Foreign Policy

In this study, appeasement policy has been portrayed as a crisis strategy essentially determined by domestic policy; appeasement policy was formulated on the basis of a faith in Britain's 'political strength', and presented as an opportunity to deter Germany from overstepping the limits of Britain's willingness to allow revision. Britain's 'political strength' – which was seen to have been historically proven by the respect shown, even by Hitler, for the resilience of British society during the First World War – depended, in the eyes of the British power élites, on the maintenance of the economic and social 'fabric'; this in turn necessitated a foreign policy of limited liability: 'Our foreign policy must largely be determined by the limits of our effective strength'.[15] A strengthening of Britain's economic and social system – which required both the safeguarding of financial efficiency and credit-worthiness, and the securing of political support at home – was seen as capable of fulfilling its envisaged function as a deterrent only as long as no signs of socio-political tension (along the lines of the 'rather Hitler

15. See ch. II (Political System), pp. 346ff. (notes 437ff.).

than Blum' debate in France) could be detected by Britain's foreign opponents. It was the primacy of British desires to deter aggressors from attacks on this 'island of stability' which, up to the spring of 1938, occasioned the dominance of the 'risk theory', which was the prime object of analysis in Chapter II.

The experts – the military as well as the Foreign Office – remained consistently dissatisfied with a political strategy which considered the principal function of British armaments policy to be that of deterring Britain's most obvious potential attacker by convincingly demonstrating that no decisive initial success could be counted upon were an onslaught on Britain to take place. The experts considered the guidelines along which appeasement policy operated too vague, and ill-fitted for the situation of 'real' danger in which Britain found herself. The politicians, on the other hand, expressed doubts as to whether changes in the strategy's priorities and in the arms programme would improve the effectiveness of Britain's deterrent or, indeed, the general situation of the defence of Britain, to an extent which would justify jeopardising the domestic political consensus and the cohesion of British society. The extent of Britain's efforts to defend her various security interests, as well as the direction and intensity of the rearmament process, were indeed primarily determined by desires to prevent the British economy for as long as possible from reaching the point at which inflation was likely to begin to spiral, since it was felt that this would have serious effects on Britain's political and social system. The extent of mobilisation of financial, industrial and labour resources for defence and foreign policy, was not, it was stressed, to be determined by threats from abroad, nor by related alliance and treaty obligations; instead, it was to reflect the fact that 'labour difficulties [were] probable' once efforts for rearmament developed their own dynamic in the production process. It was these fears of the possible effects of a reorganisation of the economic and social structure of Britain – fears made more palpable by memories of the improvised war-economy of 1916–18 – which motivated attempts to link a 'flexible foreign policy' (= non-alliance policy and 'preventive diplomacy') and 'limited rearmament'.

British foreign policy thus exhibited threefold links to armaments policy:

(1) In its explicit aim of exploring links with Germany through arms limitation agreements.

(2) In its attempts to use rearmament measures to convince the Third Reich that encirclement was a threat to be taken seriously,

while at the same time sparing Britain the trouble of resolving her own dilemmas in the area of bloc and alliance politics.

(3) In the expectation of the British government that, given the risk of war in Europe and the Far East, German–Japanese collaboration would ensue, were Britain prematurely to endorse a policy of encirclement, and in its fears that the mobilisation which would then become necessary might put the British political and social system under considerable strain.

It was the connections between these three aspects of 'security' policy, the mobilisation of financial, economic and social resources, and the existing constitution of domestic political forces, which allotted to armaments policy its 'hinge function' – its function as mediator between foreign policy, and the domestic political and social system. Whereas the numerous crises in world politics pointed Britain towards an acceleration in the procurement of her defence potential to protect her global interests against Japan, Italy and the Third Reich, the domestic constellation demanded that she pay primary regard to Britain's 'effective strength to survive as a 'polity'. Political tension – between the government and the Opposition (and their 'attentive publics')[16] as well as tensions within the power structure arising out of conflicts between desires for 'security through rearmament' and for 'security through the husbanding of resources' – cast doubt on the very means–ends relation which was of prime importance for the justification of rearmament: enforced rearmament was seen to be potentially synonymous with a self-inflicted blockade of the British socio-political system. The gain it was hoped rearmament would bring – namely, the re-establishment of British freedom to develop a more assertive foreign policy – was thought to be likely to be cancelled out by the effects of a 'war-like economy' on domestic politics. The basic view in Britain that foreign policy risks were preferable to a domestic political conflict with labour, since the latter placed greater restrictions on Britain's room to manoeuvre, continued to hold sway (albeit in different versions) from 1919, when it was first proposed in response to the special circumstances of that year, to the spring of 1938. Since the defence and armaments debate threatened to introduce yet another dimension to existing polarisations in British society – conducted as it was in the context of economic crisis, and overshadowed by the threat of an international build-up of ideological blocs – the government felt

16. G. Almond, 'A Comparative Study of Interest Groups and the Political Process', *APSR*, 52(1958), pp. 270–282.

obliged to take steps to prevent international cooperation be-tween various internal political forces from seriously endangering what it considered to be an essential domestic political consensus on 'national affairs'. Support for government security policy abroad – in other words, for steps towards the kind of reorganisation of the economy and society which arms production would necessitate – was only likely to be guaranteed if it was backed up by efforts to secure détente abroad (arms limitation talks) as well as efforts at home to limit profiteering, industrial conscription, dislocation, and so on.

The incapacity of the government to resolve this dilemma had serious consequences for the process of political decision-making: since a good degree of emphasis was placed in discussions on the domestic political aspects of rearmament – that is, the burden which it would place on industry and the social unrest which might be provoked by spiralling inflation – individual foreign political crises were never primarily discussed as foreign-policy problems; the government's concentration on the economic, financial, psychological and societal policy implications of rearmament dis-torted its view of current foreign-policy problems. It was not the specific aspects of any given 'crisis' that were debated in cabinet, or through the 'government by committee' system, but rather the links which it might be possible to make between the process of rearmament, the 'search for a general European appeasement' and psychological appeasement tactics at home.

6. Biding Time

A significant and complex role was played in appeasement policy by the notion of the 'time factor'. Its frequent invocation suggests not only a desire to postpone the outbreak of war and gain time for further armament measures; delaying tactics on Britain's part also allowed her to improve her defences against attack further west, or onslaughts on Britain herself. Defence and armaments policy was clearly designed to ensure Britain's own protection; the possibility of adapting and extending the British capacity to intervene in any war in Central and South-Eastern Europe, in which Britain might become implicated through political–strategic considerations, or as a result of her alliance obligations to her French ally, was never considered.

According to policy restraints and directives issued in relation to the question of rearmament, the radius of action covered by British policy towards Europe, the Mediterranean and the Far East, seems never to have been extended throughout the period between 1935 and 1939. The British strategy of biding time, in an attempt to make up for the effects of earlier voluntary arms limitation between 1920 and 1934, which had narrowed Britain's scope for action abroad, had a dual function. In the first instance, it could increase Britain's leverage not only in relation to potential enemies (Germany, Japan and Italy) but also to her armed allies (France); at the same time, it could deter the aggressive powers from challenging British essential interests. Since neither the standard of her armed forces nor the arms industry's capacities made it possible for Britain to risk conflict with any great power, and since, also, a greater emphasis on Britain's *de facto* partnership with France would have placed Britain in an increasingly dangerous position – an approach to France or Russia being likely to prompt a German–Japanese counter-move – the isolationist effects of 'security policy' became more clearly visible in the area of armaments policy than had been envisaged even by the political advocates of 'limited liability'. The notion of a 'mandate for rearmament', which had been crucial in structuring both domestic and foreign policy, appears here as a rhetorical means of obscuring the contradiction between the depleted state of the British arsenal, on the one hand, and the government's optimistic forecast that Britain's position was likely to improve within a matter of a few years, on the other. In the interim, attempts were to be made to dissuade foreign powers from taking any action which might involve Britain in premature conflict, and to make it possible for Britain to use diplomatic means to obscure the process whereby she was recouping strength and military power. At the same time, Britain hoped to be able to persuade France and Belgium that her rearmament measures would indeed allow her – 'soon' – to make good the diplomatic losses incurred through German breaches of the Treaty of Versailles.

A further attitude implicit in British time-winning tactics was the notion that Britain, as an island of peace and unruffled determination, had a mission to remain detached, to play the role of an observer. This attitude was in turn rooted in the British expectation that dictatorships were bound to mellow over time, above all if they were given help in eradicating the causes of their aggressive policies (which were seen to lie in economic crises) and if they saw their prestige enhanced by foreign-policy successes. In playing for time as it did, the government was speculating on the possibility of finding a long-term resolution to international conflicts – which it saw in turn to be achievable as long as current conflicts could be contained within acceptable limits, and help given in overcoming the 'roots of present discontent'. The British government thus consciously refrained from measuring other countries' regimes by the standards of its own system, or from expressing any desire to change, let alone to overthrow them, at least for as long as the 'dynamic' of those regimes' development did not openly steer towards world conflict. The most decisive aspect of British responses to Hitler is not, however, the failure of British foreign policy to take the 'one-party state' slogan, or Hitler's statements of his *Weltanschauung* seriously enough, and thus also to adopt an 'ideological' stance itself. It is much more important to emphasise that the roots of appeasement policy lie in political culture and, above all, in the process of domestic political socialisation through which British 'political élites' had become versed in particular attitudes of mind and modes of political action. Amongst the catalogue of principles operative in the domestic context was the notion that the ideological demands of any given system would be diminished by the workings of the 'time factor'. The challenge of National Socialism, on the one hand, to liberal democracy, and thus to its so-called pacificism in foreign and domestic social policy, and, on the other hand, to principles of international law which Britain saw as inalienable, was indeed recognised; however, it was never thought likely that the Hitler regime would systematically extend its domination through aggressive action; that is to say, that it would not continue to implement the peaceful strategy of a 'permanent Munich' (Hildebrand), thereby eradicating any hopes of 'normalisation' over time.

In what one might almost call the 'disinterest' shown by Britain towards the antagonistic ideological base of other systems, it is possible to detect a transference of experience gained in domestic policy to foreign affairs. That transference is particularly evident in the British government's adoption of the 'erosion' method typical of domestic crisis strategy, which was thought to protect the integrative role of the main constituents of the 'polity' by giving way to challenges to the status quo which were judged to contain legitimate grievances. To this extent, appeasement may be seen as an extension of a domestic political strategy of self-preservation into foreign affairs, and thus as the opposite of the aggressive power-politics of the National Socialist system.

Bibliography

At all stages of my research, I have been able to draw widely on microfilm and photocopied source material from German, French and Italian archives, collected by my colleagues in the research project of the *Institut für Politische Wissenschaft* in Berlin. However, as this wealth of information was used mainly in chapter I of the original German edition but is not part of this English translation, this source material has not been listed in the Bibliography. Readers should be aware, however, that the present study is not based exclusively on British source material. In the present Bibliography section V (Books and Articles) has been revised and considerably shortened in that many German publications have been deleted. A number of works in English which have appeared since the publication of the German original are now included, mainly in the relevant footnotes.

I. Unpublished Documents

I.1. Private Papers (Individuals and Organisations)

Attlee, Clement R., 1st Earl: Churchill College, Cambridge
Baldwin, Stanley, 1st Earl: Cambridge University Library
Balfour, Arthur James, 1st Earl: British Museum, London
R.D. Blumenfeld: Beaverbrook Library, London
Burgis, Lawrence: Churchill College, Cambridge
Cecil, Robert, 1st Viscount Cecil of Chelwood: British Museum London
Chamberlain, Sir Austen: Birmingham University Library
Chamberlain, Neville: Prof. Agnes Headlam-Morley; Birmingham University Library
Christie, M.G., Group-Captain: Churchill College, Cambridge
Churchill, Sir Winston S.: Martin Gilbert; Bodleian Library, Oxford
Conservative Research Centre: London
Croft, Sir Henry Page: Churchill College, Cambridge
Crookshank, 1st Viscount: Bodleian Library, Oxford
Dalton, Hugh: British Library of Political and Economic Science, London
Davidson, J.C.C., 1st Viscount: Beaverbrook Library, London

Derby, E.G.V.St., 17th Earl: Liverpool City Library

Federation of British Industries: Confederation of British Industries, London; now: University of Warwick

Fisher, H.A.L., Prof.: Bodleian Library, Oxford

Francis-Williams: Churchill College, Cambridge

Halifax, 1st Earl: City Library, York; Churchill College, Cambridge

Hammond, J.H.: Bodleian Library, Oxford

Hankey, Sir Maurice P.A.: Churchill College, Cambridge

Hannon, Sir Patrick: House of Lords Records Centre, London

Hardinge of Penhurst, 2nd Baron: Cambridge University Library

Hewins, W.A.S.: Sheffield University Library

Hoare, Sir Samuel, 1st Viscount Templewood: Cambridge University Library

Hodsoll, Sir John: Churchill College, Cambridge

Holt, Sir Richard: Liverpool City Library

Inskip, Sir Thomas, 1st Viscount Caldecote: Lord Caldecote; Churchill College, Cambridge

Jones, Thomas: National Library of Wales, Aberystwyth

Keyes, 1st Baron, Admiral of the Fleet: Churchill College, Cambridge

Kilmuir, Earl, David Maxwell Fyfe: Churchill College, Cambridge

Labour Party Library: London

Lansbury, George: British Library of Political and Economic Science, London

Liddell Hart, Captain Basil: States House, Medmenham, Marlow, Bucks.

Lloyd George, David, 1st Earl: Beaverbrook Library

Lloyd, George, 1st Baron: Churchill College, Cambridge

London Chamber of Commerce: London

Lothian, Marquess of (P. Kerr): Scottish Record Office, Edinburgh

MacDonald, James Ramsay: David Marquand

Margesson, H.D.R., 1st Viscount: Churchill College, Cambridge

Murray, Gilbert: Bodleian Library, Oxford

Nicolson, Sir Harold: Nigel Nicolson

Phipps, Sir Eric: Churchill College, Cambridge

Runciman, Sir Walter, 1st Viscount: Sir Stephen Runciman; Newcastle University Library

Simon, Sir John: Viscount Simon; now: Bodleian Library, Oxford

Sinclair, Sir Archibald, 1st Viscount Thurso: Churchill College, Cambridge

Steel-Maitland, Sir Arthur: Scottish Record Office, Edinburgh

Strachey, J.St.L.: Beaverbrook Library, London

Swinton, 1st Earl (Sir Philip Cunliffe-Lister): Churchill College, Cambridge

Vansittart, Sir Robert, 1st Baron: Churchill College, Cambridge

Wallace, Euan: Bodleian Library, Oxford

Weir, 1st Viscount: Churchill College, Cambridge

Young, Sir Edward Hilton, 1st Baron Kennet: Cambridge University
   Library

I.2. Public Record Office

The following lists the files kept at the Public Record Office, London and
Ashridge, which the author has examined since 1967. The titles are given
in shortened form.

Cab. 2	— 3/9	Committee of Imperial Defence, Minutes of Meetings, 1912–39
Cab. 3	— 3/6	CID-Memoranda, Home Defence, Series A 1914–37
Cab. 4	— 24ff.	Memoranda, Miscellaneous
Cab. 16	— 68	Demilitarised Zones
Cab. 16	— 109/112	Defence Requirements Sub-Committee of the CID
Cab. 16	— 123	Defence Policy and Requirements Committee of the Cabinet (1936)
Cab. 16	— 136	Defence Policy and Requirements Committee of the Cabinet (1936–39)
Cab. 16	— 153	Foreign Policy and Defence
Cab. 21	— 336	Imperial Conference: Foreign Policy and Defence
	368/369	Review of Imperial Defence (1929–33)
	371	Shipbuilding and Armaments Industry
	382	Germany: Armaments, Aims at Disarmament Conference
	383	(Polish corridor/revision of Eastern frontiers)
	384	Proposed Ministry of Defence
	386	Defence of Australia
	394	Proposed Eastern Locarno
	398	Imperial Defence (Hankey Mission 1935)
	403	General Purposes Committee
	404/405	London Naval Conference
	406	Defence Requirements Committee
	407	Statement on Defence (1935)
	413	Anglo-French Air Pacts
	414	New Zealand: Cooperation in Defence
	416	Fighting Services Estimates
	417	German Rearmament
	419	German Air Force
	411/412/420, 441	Abyssinian Crisis
	422 A	Defence Policy and Requirements

	424	Coordination of Defence
	429/32	Rearmament Negotiations with the Machine Tool Industry
	433	Committee on Man Power
	434	CID-Defence Requirements
	435	Hankey–Churchill Correspondence
	436	Defence Problems (Mediterranean)
	437/39	Defence Deputations (1936)
	440	Baldwin–MacKenzie King Negotiations
	441	Collective Security — Strategical Review of the Situation in Europe
	447	Distribution of Imports in War
	449	Food Supply in War
	450	Fighting Services
	544	Ismay Note, 20.9.1938
	545	Diary of Events, March to November 1936, Germany Reoccupation of the Rhineland
Cab. 23	— 49/96	Cabinet (Minutes & Conclusions) (1924/1938)
Cab. 24	— 212/281	Memoranda circulated in Cabinet (1930/1938)
Cab. 27	—	*Cabinet Committees*
	— 164	Geddes Committee (1922)
	— 275	Foreign Policy Committee on Security (1925)
	— 407	Fighting Services (1929/30)
	— 416	Economic Consequences of Disarmament (1930)
	— 424	European Federal Union (1930)
	— 435, 451, 462	Trade Policy (1930/31)
	— 445	Export of War Materials and War Ships (1930/31)
	— 448	Policy of Reduction and Limitation of Armaments (1931)
	— 449	Export Credits (1931)
	— 466, 488	Reparations and War Debts
	— 468	Employment Policy (1931/32)
	— 482	Far East Committee (1932)
	— 489	Commercial Negotiations with Foreign Countries (1932)
	— 504/511	Ministerial Committee on Disarmament Conference
	— 517	Trading in Arms (1934–35)
	— 518	Air Parity (1935)
	— 547	Economic Consultation and Co-operation

	— 548	British War Debt to USA
	— 550	Anglo-Soviet Relations (1933)
	— 551	Armaments, Private Industry
	— 553	Imperial Economic Co-operation (1933)
	— 572	German Rearmament
	— 573	Saar
	— 583/584	General Purposes Committee
	— 591/592	Government Policy Committee
	— 596	Japan. Political and Economic Relations (1935/36)
	— 599	Germany
	— 600	Coordination of Defence
	— 603	Germany and Locarno Treaty
	— 622/627	Foreign Policy (1936/39)
	— 646	Czechoslovakian Crisis (1938)
	— 648/657	Defence Programmes and their Acceleration (1938/39)
	— 662	Defence Preparedness (1939)
Cab. 29	—	*International Conferences*
	— 136	London Conference, 20.–23.7.1931
	— 138	Situation in the Danubian States (1932)
	— 139	Lausanne
	— 140/145	Economic and Monetary Conference 1933
	— 146	Anglo-French Conversations 1935
	— 159/161	Franco-British Staff Talks 1939, Economic Pressure (1938/39)
Cab. 32	—	*Imperial Conferences*
	— 77	1930 CID Committee on Foreign Policy and Defence
	— 117/121	Committee on Economic Consultation and Co-operation,
	— 125	Meetings of British Commonwealth Prime Ministers, 1935
	— 126	Economic Discussions between United Kingdom and Dominion Ministers, 1935
	— 127/130	Imperial Conference 1937
	136	Economic Questions
Cab. 47	— 1	CID, Trade Questions in Time of War, 1924–38
	— 8, 12	Economic Pressure on Germany
Cab. 53	— 1/11	Chiefs of Staff Committee, Meetings, 1929–39
	— 12 ff.	Memoranda of the COS, 1923ff.
Cab. 54	— 1	Deputy Chiefs of Staff, 1932–37
Cab. 55	— 1/2	Joint Planning Committee 1927–38
Cab. 58	—	*Economic Advisory Council*

	— 2	Council Meetings
	— 8/10	Committee on Civil Research
	— 14	Economic Situation
	— 17	Committee on Economic Information, Meetings (1931–39)
	— 18/23, 30	CEI-Memoranda
	— 145	Economic Outlook (1930)
	— 183	International Economic Policy (1932)
	— 182	Limits of Economic Policy (1932)
Cab. 63	—	Hankey Files
Cab. 65	— 1/2	Cabinet Conclusions/War Cabinet 1939

ECG		*Export Credits Guarantee Department*
2	— 1/5	Executive Committee, Minutes
1	— 15/18	Advisory Committee, Minutes of Meetings, 1932–39

Foreign Office

FO 371	—	*Countries and Areas:*
		Germany 1929–39
		France 1929–39
		USA 1929–39
		Russia 1933–39
		Italy 1934–38
		Japan 1933–37
FO 433	— 2/6	General Economic Affairs, League of Nations
FO 411	— 18/20	League of Nations
FO 800	—	*'Official' private correspondence of the Foreign Ministers and their closest advisers*
	218/219	R. MacDonald (1924)
	222/226	Reading
	227/228	Locker-Lampson, Cushendun, Ponsonby
	243	Crowe
	252/254	L. Oliphant
	256/263	A. Chamberlain
	266/268	N. Henderson
	272/279	O. Sargent
	280/284	A. Henderson
	285/291	Simon
	292	Wigram
	293/294	Cadogan
	295	Hoare
	296	Cranborne
	309/328	Halifax
	383/385	Drummond
FO 627		Dominions Information

PREM. 1	—	Prime Ministers File
BT 11	—	*Board of Trade, Commercial Department*
	— 60	League of Nations, Committee of Enquiry for European Union (1931/32)
	375	Possible desire for modification of quota policy in return for currency stabilisation with France (1935–37)
	735	Correspondence with Treasury regarding commercial agreements with Scandinavian and Baltic countries, 1937
	1045	Military advantages to Germany by Payments Agreement with the United Kingdom (1939)
	1077	Financial and economic assistance including a United Kingdom loan to counteract German penetration (1939)
	237	Arms Trade Control (1933–41)
	68, 70, 72, 91, 92–98, 100, 103 –109,	Commonwealth Trade/Ottawa Conference
	112, 123, 139, 147, 227, 623, 694, 755, 757, 777, 779, 780, 783–792	Imperial Conference 1937/USA–UK Trade Agreement Negotiations
	190, 228, 274	Customs/Foreign Trade and Finance Powers Bill 1934 (Clearing)
	95, 154, 298, 1475	Dumping
	59, 82, 90, 141, 146, 196, 274, 442, 855, 1018	Exchange Control/Conferences of the 1930s
	87, 202, 211, 234, 375, 715	Most Favoured Nations Clause, Negotiations after 'Ottawa'
	75, 82, 94, 196, 197, 202, 213, 217, 591	Tariffs
	122, 126, 213	Payments and Debts
	2017	Trading with the Enemy
	336	Exchange Position (Southeast Europe)
	223	Stabilisation (Central Europe)(1932/33)
	405, 407, 122	Soviet Union
	120, 226	Poland
BT 11	— 431, 555, 696,	Rumania

	903, 965, 1072, 1074	
	— 1077	Jugoslavia
	— 69, 223, 436, 551, 754, 913, 1057, 1189, 1321	Bulgaria
	— 138, 176, 228,407, 431, 433, 442, 731, 733, 735, 901, 1001, 1006, 1045, 1077	Germany (The primary sources relating to commercial and payments agreements which B.-J. Wendt has fully exploited are listed only selectively here.)
	— 59, 1242	Czechoslovakia
	— 66, 375, 508, 978, 1169	France
	— 58, 175, 953	Canada
	— 589, 591, 629, 755, 790, 937, 1223, 1224, 1437/38	USA
BT 13	—	*Establishment Division*
	— 118	Trade Facilities Act (1924)
	— 120	Imperial Economic Committee (1925)
	— 125	League of Nations Consultative Committee
	— 126	Overseas Trade (Credit & Insurance) (1928)
	— 127/130	Export Credits Guarantee Department (1929/30)
	— 146	Safeguarding of Industries Acts (1926–35)
	— 154	Import Duties Advisory Committee, Report 1937
BT 15	—	*Finance Department*
	— 144	CID financial aspects of remedying defects in the country's existing defence measures (1938)
BT 55	— 49	Board of Trade Committee Papers, Policy Committee, Sub-committee on Trade and Industry
BT 59	— 24	Overseas Trade Development Council
	— 28	DOT, Development Council, Minutes of Meetings, 1930–36
BT 60	— 56	Germany, Annual Report for 1939 (DOT 25 157)

BT 90	— 1/26	Department of Overseas Trade	
T 160	— 487/490	F 13017/ . . .	World Economic Conference 1933
	— 498	F 14558	Multilateral Tariff Reduction Scheme, 3.8.–7.12.1933
	— 521/22	F 12750/ . . .	Payments Agreement . . . 1934
	534/535, 559,652/653	F 13460/ . . .	Clearing
	— 537	F 13017/017/1–2	Tariff Truce, 26.4.1933/4.4.1934
	— 539	F 13771/01/1–3	Anglo-French Commercial Treaty, 10.8.1933–22.11.1934
	— 572	F 13373/1–2	France: Import duties and quotas and UK retaliatory measures, 21.3.1933–22.11.1934
	— 573	F 13460/011	German raw material imports from England on long credit 28.9.1934–16.5.1935
		F 13460/012	Renewal IG-Farben Credit Hambro's Bank, 27.10.1934–28.1.1935
	— 627	F 14308/01/1–2	French proposals for reducing quota restrictions in return for stabilisation of currencies, 17.9.1935–24.4.1936
	— 681/682	F 14601/1–5	Ottawa Revisions — negotiations with Canada, 12.6.1936–2.9.1937
	— 684	F 14739	French proposals regarding reduction of certain customs duties: abolition of quotas following devaluation of the Franc 1936, 29.9.1936–28.1.1937
	— 686	F 14884	Leith-Ross

			Memorandum on export trade, 1.12.1936–23.1.1937
— 692	F 15225		Foreign Secretary's Speech in Geneva. . .:economic memoranda, 27.8–9.9.1937
— 728	F 12743/1–5		Anglo-French commercial negotiations, 4.12.1931–27.4.1938
— 755	F 14239/01		Proposed commercial negotiations, reactions of the Colonies and Dominions, 1.6.1937–25.11.1938
— 755/56	F 14239/03		Trade Agreement, 24.2.–1.11.1938
— 750	F 14239/1–3, 19		USA, World Trade; policy and possibility of a commercial agreement with the UK, 3.5.1935–12.12.1936, 11.11.1938
T 160	— 761	F 14735/1–5	Proposed international action for reduction of tariff barriers, 22.5.1936–2.12.1938
	— 762	F 14735/03/1–4	Interdepartmental Committee on Van Zeeland Report and Report of Interdepartmental Committee on Trade Policy, 1937, 18.2.1936–25.6.1938
	— 769	F 15456	Measures of financial pressure in the event of war, with special reference to Germany and Japan, 12.3.–27.5.1938
	— 770	F 15583	Economic policy in the light of changes

		in the economic situation and the international political position since 1932: Interdepartmental Committee, 16.6.1937–1.2.1938
— 771	F 19429	Economic Advisory Council, Committee on Economic Information, 26th Report on problems of rearmament, 28.11.–21.12.1938

Treasury

T 170	—	*Bradbury Papers*
T 171	—	Chancellor of the Exchequer's office, Budget & Finance Bill Papers
	— 336/337	National Defence Contribution
T 172	— 1376/1383	Reparations/inter-allied debts 1918–32
	— 1498/1499	Debt negotiations: France 1925/27
	— 1504/1512	Inter-allied debt negotiations 1925–33
	— 1530	Empire Industries (1925–37)
	— 1670, 1695	Extension of Trade Facilities
	— 1694	Hague Conference 1929
	— 1713	Tariff Truce (1930)
	— 1718	Balfour Report on Conditions in Germany (1930)
	— 1745	A Plan for Empire Development (1931)
	— 1746/49, 1741	Financial Position (1931)
	— 1755	London Conference, July 1931
	— 1765	Trade Defence in Trade Depression
	— 1766	Inter-parliamentary Commercial Conference, Prague, 1931
	— 1775	£ Stabilisation (1931–35)
	— 1780/82	Danubian Countries, Four Power Conference (1932)
	— 1787/88	Lausanne
	— 1789	International Monetary Union (1932)
	— 1801	Germany (1932–38)
	— 1808	International Investment Trust
	— 1812	Locarno Obligations
	— 1811, 1815/16	Monetary and Economic Conference (1933)
	— 1819	Tariff Reduction Scheme (1933)

T 172	— 1827/28	Special Areas
	— 1831	Japan: Anglo-Japanese Relations concerning economic questions and the return of Japan to the League of Nations
	— 1832, 1853, 1855/1856	Defence Expenditure (1937)
	— 1836	M. Flandin's Financial Policy (1935)
	— 1837	Debate on Imperial Defence (1934)/ German Rearmament
	— 1838	Italy: Oil Sanctions and Abyssinian Dispute
	— 1853	Total Estimates for Defence Departments (1937)
	— 1855/56	National Defence Contribution (1937)
T 175	—	Sir R. *Hopkins Papers*
	— 27	Control of profits and prices in war (1928–33)
	— 28	Disarmament (1928–34)
	— 34	League of Nations Loans, 1929
	— 35	Imperial Defence, 1929
	— 37/43	Budget/Unemployment
	— 51	Economic Crisis 1931
	— 55	Rueff/Leith-Ross Negotiations 1931/32
	— 62	British Commercial Debts (1932)
	— 74	Financial Relations with France and USA (1933)
	— 76/79, 81/83	Anglo-American Debt and financial negotiations Reduction of Tariffs and Repayment of Debts
	— 94, 104	Financial policy (1936/39)
	— 96	Defence Loans Bill (1937)
	— 101	Development of the Air Force (1938)
	— 102	Profiteering on armaments orders
T 177	—	Sir Frederick *Phillips Papers*
	— 10	Stresa. International Conference on Economic, Agrarian and Financial Policy, 1932
	— 12/13	International Economic Conference 1933
	— 14	Russian Trade Negotiations 1932/33
	— 15, 26	Central Bank Convention, Cooperation (1936)
	— 19	International Finance Corporation
	— 20	Anglo-German Clearing Agreement, 1934
	— 25	Budgeting for Defence Expenditure (1936)
	— 27	Foreign Investments in the USA
	— 30	Compensation Brokers' Co.
	— 31, 32–34	France: Devaluation, balance of payments,

		import restrictions, 1935–37
	— 35	US–UK Trade Relations, 1937
	— 36	Interdepartmental Committee on Trade Policy (1937)
	— 37	Interdepartmental Committee on Public Capital Expenditure (1937)
	— 48	Notes on Exchange reserves (1939)
	— 51	Anglo-French financial relations 1939–41
T 188	—	*Leith-Ross Papers*
	— 21	European economic situation: discussions with French Treasury (1931)
	— 31	Young Plan . . .: Memoranda on growth of Germany's competitive power (1931/32)
	— 36–38	Danubian States: conference on economic reconstruction/four power conference (1932)
	— 39	Young Plan . . .: E. Rowe-Dutton on German economic position (1932)
	— 72	International trade depression: UK recovery policy
	— 79/99	Anglo-German Exchange Agreement/Negotiations 1934
	— 109	Visit of M. Flandin: General papers on Anglo-French financial and economic questions
	— 116	Exchange stabilisation (1935)
	— 144/46	French devaluation (1936)
	— 147	Dunlop: import of rubber and other materials for use by German company (1936)
	— 148	European economic situation: visit of M. Stoppani, Secretary, League of Nations Economic Committee (1936)
	— 162	China and the Far East: F.T.A. Ashton-Gwatkin on British policy (1937)
	— 165	Danube Basin: economic rehabilitation (1937)
	— 167	French devaluation: international currency situation (1937)
	— 170	German economic situation: memorandum to Lord Privy Seal from a German source (1937)
	— 171	International Chamber of Commerce: 9th Congress, Berlin (1937)
	— 175/176	Trade Policy Committee (1937)
	— 177	Raw Materials Committee: Reports
	— 218/221	Obstacles to growth of international trade

		(Van Zeeland Committee) (1938)
MAF	—	*Ministry of Agriculture, Fisheries and Food*
	— 38	Statistics and Economics
	— 39	Establishment and Finance
	— 40	Trade Relations and International
C.O.	—	*Colonial Office*
	— 532	Dominions, Correspondence
	— 852	Economics, Correspondence
D.O.	—	*Dominions Office*
	— 35	Correspondence (1932–38)

II. Parliamentary Papers

Cmd. 2084	Imperial Economic Conference 1923. Resolutions relating to Imperial Preference passed at the Imperial War Conference 1917, (1924), XVIII. 45
2768/69	Imperial Conference 1926. Summary of Proceedings, (1926), XI. 545, 607
3539	Preliminary Conference with a View to concerted Economic Action, Commercial Convention; 1929–30, XXXII. 89
3770	Final Act of the Second International Conference with a View to concerted Economic Action; 1930–31, XXXV. 469
3885	Second Session–Protocol; 1930–31, XXXV. 487
3595	European Federal Union (French Memorandum); 1929–1930, XXXII. 259
3717	Summary of the Proceedings of the Imperial Conference of 1930; 1930–31, XIV. 569
3904	Report on the Organisation of the Foreign Trade of the USSR; 1930–1931, XVII. 343
3947	Reports of an International Committee of experts respecting suspension of certain Intergovernmental Debts; 1930–31, XXXV. 393
4126	Final Act of the Lausanne Conference, 1931–32, XXVII. 931
4129	Further Documents relating to the Settlement reached at Lausanne; 1931–32; XXVII. 947
4131	Declaration issued by HMG in the UK and the French Government regarding Future European Co-operation, (1932), XXVII. 877
4202	Agreement between the UK and the USA respecting Payments (Debts); 1932–33, XXVII. 915

4203/4210/ 4211/4215/ 4216/4217	Further Notes to Cmd. 4202: Note from the Government of the UK to the Government of the USA relating to the British War Debt, 10th. November, 1932; 1931–32, XXVII. 829; XXVII. 919; XXVII. 923; XXVII. 937; XXVII. 943; XXVII. 947; XXVII. 951
4297/4319	Exchange of Notes between HMG in the UK and the Government of the German Reich regarding Commercial Relations, (1933), XXVII. 375; Further Notes, 1932–33, XXVII. 381
4342	Despatch to HM's Ambassador at Rome in regard to the Agreement of Understanding and Co-operation between France, Italy and the UK, (1933), XXVIII. 889
4403	Monetary and Economic Conference. Declaration by Delegations of the British Commonwealth, (07.11.1933), XXI. 499
4620	Papers respecting the German Transfer Moratorium, (22.06.1934), XXVII. 335
4640	Anglo-German Transfer Agreement and Letters Exchanged between the UK and Germany; 1933–34, XXVII. 349
4673	Anglo-German Exchange Agreement relating to Commercial Payments; 1933–34, XXVII. 355
4702	Anglo-German Exchange Agreement relating to Commercial Payments together with Notes Exchanged, (10.08.1934), XXVII. 361
5787	Anglo-German Payments (Amendment) Agreement, with Exchange of Letters . . . regarding negotiations for Mutual Trade Relations with Germany, (01.07.1938), XXXI. 203
5788	Anglo-German Transfer Agreement, (01.07.1938), XXXI. 231
5880	Transfer Agreement 1938–39, XXVIII. 137
4590	Exchange of Notes between the UK and France respecting Commercial Relations; 1933–34, XXVII. 275
4632/4639	Agreement between the UK and France relating to Trade and Commerce; 1933–1934, XXVII. 29
4798	France and UK (Mutual) Assistance; 1934–35, XXIV. 89
4827	Statement relating to Defence, (1935), XIII. 803
5143	Correspondence showing the course of certain Diplomatic Discussions toward securing an European Settlement, June 1934 to March 1936, XXVII. 59

5149	Correspondence with the Belgian and French Ambassadors relating to 'Text of Proposals drawn up by the Representatives of Belgium, France, the UK of Great Britain and Northern Ireland and Italy. London, March 19, 1936, Cmd. 5134', (01.04.1936), XXVIII. 57
5175	Correspondence with the German Government regarding the German Proposal for an European Settlement, (24.03.–06.05.1936), XXVIII. 63
5233	Exchange of Notes between Canada and Austria regarding Commercial Relations; 1935–36, XXVII. 553
5346	Agreement between the UK and Italy regarding Commercial Exchanges and Payments; 1936–37 (Cmd. 5307), XXIX. 483 — Similar Paper; 1936–37, XXIX. 455
5669	Exchange of Notes between HMG in the UK and the Italian Government modifying the Agreement of 6th. November, 1936, regarding Commercial Exchanges and Payments; 1937–38, XXXI. 371
5348	Declaration by HMG in the UK and the Italian Government regarding the Mediterranean; (02.01.1937), XXIV. 497
5374	Statement relating to Defence, (1937), XVII. 1123
5482	Imperial Conference 1937, (1937), XII. 1
5682	Statement relating to Defence, (1938), XVII. 1143
5882	Trade Agreement between the UK and the USA, (17.11.1938), XXVIII. 637
5944	Statement relating to Defence, (1939), XXI. 225
6128	Agreement between the Government of the UK and the Italian Government to facilitate Economic Collaboration, (27.10.1939), XXVIII. 313
Bill 152	Debts Clearing Offices and Import Restrictions Reprisals 1933–34 (152) i. 553 (20.06.1934).

III. Selected Documents and Reports

Akten zur Deutschen Auswärtigen Politik, 1918–1945, Series B (1925–1933), Göttingen 1966ff.;Series D (1937–1945), Baden-Baden 1950ff.

Documents on German Foreign Policy, 1918–1945, Series C (1933–1937), 1957ff.

Annual Conferences of the Labour Party, Reports, 1923–1939

Annual Conference Reports of the National Union of Conservative and Unionist Associations, 1923–1939

Annual Trades Union Congress, Report of Proceedings, 1930–1939

Documents Diplomatiques Belges 1920–1940, Brussels 1964ff.

Documents Diplomatiques Français 1932–1939, Series 1 (1932–1935), Paris 1964ff.; Series 2 (1936–1939), Paris 1963ff.

Documents on British Foreign Policy, 1919–1939, Series Ia/III, London 1947ff.

Documents on International Affairs 1924–1945, ed. Royal Institute of International Affairs

Documents on Canadian Foreign Policy 1917–1939, ed. W.A. Riddell, 1962

The Communist International 1919–1943, Documents, vol. 3, ed. Jane Degras, London 1965

Deutschland-England 1933–1939. Die Dokumente des deutschen Friedenswillens, ed. Fritz Berber, Essen 1940

Europäische Politik 1933–1938 im Spiegel der Prager Akten, ed. Friedrich Berber, Essen 1942

Les Evénements survenus en France de 1933 à 1945, report of Charles Serre, Paris 1951ff.

Foreign Relations of the United States. Diplomatic Papers, 1929–39, 1946ff.

Der Prozeß gegen die Hauptkriegsverbrecher vor dem Internationalen Militärgerichtshof Nürnberg, 14. Nov. 1945–1. Okt. 1946, Nürnberg 1947–49

Soviet Documents on Foreign Policy, ed. Jane Degras, vol. 3, London 1953

IV. Newspapers, Periodicals

Daily Papers

Birmingham Daily Mail
Birmingham Post
Daily Express
Daily Herald
Daily Mail
Daily Mirror
Daily Sketch
The Daily Telegraph
Daily Worker

Eastern Daily Press
Evening News
Evening Standard
Glasgow Herald
Liverpool Post
Manchester Guardian
Morning Post
News Chronicle
North Mail
Nottingham Guardian
The Scotsman

Sheffield Daily Telegraph
Sheffield Post
Star
Sussex Daily News
The Times
Western Daily Press
Western Mail
Western Morning News
Yorkshire Evening Post
Yorkshire Post

Sunday Papers

News of the World
The Observer
The People
Reynolds News

Sunday Chronicle
Sunday Dispatch
Sunday Express
Sunday Graphic

Sunday Pictorial
Sunday Referee
The Sunday Times

Periodicals

Anglo-German Review
Contemporary Review
Economist
English Review
Foreign Affairs
Fortnightly Review
Forward
Free Press
Headway
Home and Empire
Imp
International Affairs
International Review
John Bull

Labour
League of Nations
   Union News Sheet
Liberal Magazine
The Listener
London News
New Age
News Letter
New Outlook
News Review
New Statesman
Nineteenth Century
   and After
Peace News

Politica
Political Quarterly
Politics in Review
Punch
Quarterly Review
Reuter's Journal
Review of Reviews
Round Table
Saturday Review
Slavonic and Eastern
   Europe Review
Spectator
The Link
The Week

Military Journals

Aeroplane
Army, Navy and Air
   Force Gazette
Army Quarterly
British Flag and
   Christian Sentinel
British Legion Journal
Fighting Forces
Fleet
Flight
Frontiersman
Gunner

Journal of the Royal
   Air Force College
Naval League Quarterly
Naval Review
Royal Air Force Diary
Royal Air Force
   Quarterly
Royal Army Pay
   Corps Journal
The Air Annual of the
   British Empire
The Hawk

The Journal of the Royal
   Aeronautical Society
The Journal of the Royal
   Artillery
The Journal of the Royal
   Engineers
The Journal of the Royal
   United Services
   Institution
The Journal of the Society
   for Army Historical
   Research
United Services Gazette

Business and Economic Journals

Bankers Magazine
Birmingham Chamber
of Commerce Journal
Board of Trade Journal
British Empire Review
British Export Gazette
British Industries
British Trade Review
Chamber of Commerce
Journal
City Press
The Economist

Financial News
The Financial Times
Industrial News
International Export
Review
Investors' Chronicle and
Money Market
Review
Iron and Coal Trade
Review
London Commercial
Record
Mercantile Guardian

Midland Bank Monthly
Review
Mining Journal, Railway
& Commercial
Gazette
National Farmers' Union
Record
Oil News
Railway Review
Shipping World and
Shipbuilding Marine
Engineering News
Statist

V. Books and Articles

Adamthwaite, Antony P., *France and the Coming of the Second World War, 1936–1939*, London 1977

Addison, Paul, *The Road to 1945: British Politics and the Second World War*, London 1975

Aldcroft, Derek H., *The European Economy 1914–1970*, New York 1978
——, *From Versailles to Wall Street, 1919–1929*, Berkeley 1977
——, H.H.W. Richardson, *The British Economy 1870–1939*, New York 1970²

Allard, Sven, *Stalin und Hitler: die sowjetrussische Außenpolitik 1930–1941*, Bern/München 1977

Ambrose, S.E., *Rise to Globalism: American Foreign Policy since 1938*, New York 1977 (Penguin)

Amery, Leopold S., *My Political Life*, vol. 3, London 1955

Aster Sidney, *1939. The Making of the Second World War*, London 1973

Barnes, John/Keith Middlemas, *Baldwin. A Biography*, London 1969

Barnett, Correlli, *Britain and Her Army 1509–1970*, Harmondsworth 1974
——, *The Collapse of British Power*, London 1972

Bartlett, R., *Policy and Power. Two Centuries of American Foreign Relations*, New York 1963

Basch, Antonin, *The Danube Basin and the German Economic Sphere*, London 1944

Batowski, H., *Central Europe in the Policy of the Great Powers in the Period 1918–1939/41*, Warsaw 1970

Baumont, Maurice, *La Faillite de la paix, 1918–1939*, Paris 1961⁴

Bennett, Edward W., *German Rearmament and the West, 1932–1933*, Princeton, N.J. 1979
——, *Germany and the Diplomacy of the Financial Crisis 1931*, Cambridge,

Mass. 1962

Berend, I./G. Ranki, *Economic Development in East Central Europe in the 19th and 20th Century*, New York 1974

Birkenhead, Earl of, Frederick, *The Life of Lord Halifax*, London 1965

Blank, Stephen, *Industry and Government in Britain. The Federation of British Industries in Politics, 1945–1965*, Farnborough 1973

Blaxland, Gregory, *J.H. Thomas, A Life for Unity*, London 1964

Blum, John Morton, *From the Morgenthau Diaries. Years of Crisis 1928–1938*, Boston 1959

Bond, Brian (ed.), *Chief of Staff. The Diaries of Lieutenant-General Sir Henry Pownall*, vol. 1: *1933–1940*, London 1972

———, *Liddell Hart, A Study of his Military Thought*, London 1977

Bonnet, George, *Vingt ans de vie politique, 1918–1938. De Clemençeau à Daladier* (Coll. Les grandes études contemporaines), Paris 1969

Borg, Dorothy, *The United States and the Far Eastern Crisis of 1933–38*, Cambridge, Mass. 1964

Bracher, Karl Dietrich, *Deutschland zwischen Demokratie und Diktatur*, Bern 1964

———, *Die Krise Europas 1917–1975*, Frankfurt a.M. 1977

———, *Zeitgeschichtliche Kontroversen um Faschismus, Totalitarismus, Demokratie*, München 1976

Bruegel, J.W., *Czechoslovakia before Munich: The German Minority Problem and British Appeasement Policy*, Cambridge 1973

Brüning, Heinrich, *Briefe und Gespräche 1934–1945*, Stuttgart 1974

Bullock, Alan, *Hitler. A Study in Tyranny*, New York 1971

———, *The Life and Times of Ernest Bevin*, vol. 1, London 1960

Burridge, Trevor D., *British Labour and Hitler's War*, London 1976

Butler, J.R.M., *Lord Lothian (Philip Kerr), 1882–1940*, London 1960

Buxton, Neil K./Derek H. Aldcroft (eds.), *British Industry Between the Wars. Instability and Industrial Development 1919–1939*, London 1979

Cadogan, Sir Alexander, *The Diaries of Sir Alexander Cadogan*, ed. David Dilks, London 1971

Cairns, John C., 'A Nation of Shopkeepers in Search of a Suitable France 1919–1940', *American Historical Review*, 79 (1974), pp. 710–743

———, 'March 7, 1936 Again: The View from France', *International Journal*, 20 (1965), pp. 230–240

———, (ed.), *Contemporary France: Illusions, Conflict and Regeneration*, London 1978

Campbell, F.G., *Confrontation in Central Europe. Weimar, Germany and Czechoslovakia*, Chicago 1975

Carmi, Ozer, *La Grande-Bretagne et la Petite Entente*, Geneva 1972

Carr, Edward H., *German–Soviet Relations Between the Two World Wars, 1919–1939*, London 1951

———, *International Relations Between the Two Wars 1919–1939*, London 1947

_____, *The Twenty Years' Crisis, 1919–1939. An Introduction to the Study of International Relations*, London 1948[2]

Carr, William, *Arms, Autarky, and Aggression. A Study in German Foreign Policy, 1933–1939*, London 1972

Carroll, Berenice A., *Design for Total War. Arms and Economics in the Third Reich*, The Hague 1968

Challener, Richard D., *The French Theory of the Nation in Arms, 1866–1939*, New York 1955

Channon, Sir Henry: *Chips. The Diaries of Sir Henry Channon*, ed. R.R. James, London 1967

Chappius, Charles W., 'Anglo-German Relations 1929–1933: A Study of the Role of Great Britain in the Achievement of the Aims of German Foreign Policy', University of Notre Dame Ph.D., 1966

Chilston, Viscount, 'The Rearmament of Great Britain, France and Germany down to the Munich Agreement of 30 September 1938', *Survey of International Affairs*, 3 (1938), pp. 460–603, London 1953

Churchill, Randolph, *Lord Derby, King of Lancashire*, London 1959

Churchill, Winston S., *Arms and the Covenant*, London 1938

_____, *Step by Step, 1936–1939*, London 1959

_____, *The Second World War*, vol. 1: *The Gathering Storm*, Boston 1948

Cienciala, Anna M., *Poland and the Western Powers 1938–1939*, Toronto 1968

Citrine, Lord, *Men and Work*, London 1964

Clay, Sir Henry, *Lord Norman*, London 1957

Clifford, Nicholas R., *Retreat from China. British Policy in the Far East 1937–1941*, London 1967

Centre National de la Recherche Scientifique, Comité d'Histoire de la 2me Guerre Mondiale, *Les Relations Franco-Britanniques de 1935 à 1939*, Paris 1975

_____, *Les Relations Franco-Allemandes 1933–1939*, no. 563, Paris 1977

Cochran, Thomas Childs, *The Great Depression and World War II, 1929–1945*, Glenview 1968

Coghlan, F., 'Armaments, Economic Policy and Appeasement. Background to British Foreign Policy 1931–1937', *History*, 57 (1972), pp. 205–216

Collier, Basil, *The Defence of the United Kingdom*, London 1957

_____, *The Lion and the Eagle. British and Anglo-American Strategy 1900–1950*, New York 1972

Colvin, Ian, *None so Blind: A British Diplomatic View of the Origins of World War II*, New York 1965

_____, *The Chamberlain Cabinet*, London 1971

_____, *Vansittart in Office*, London 1965

Cooper, Alfred Duff, *Old Men Forget*, London 1954

Coote, Colin, *A Companion of Honour. The Story of Walter Elliot*, London 1965

_____, *Editorial — The Memoirs of Colin R. Coote*, London 1965

Costigliola, Frank C., *The Politics of Financial Stabilization. American Reconstruction Policy in Europe, 1924–1930*, Ann Arbor 1973

Cowling, Maurice, *The Impact of Hitler. British Politics and British Policy 1933–1940*, Cambridge 1975

——, *The Impact of Labour 1920–1924. The Beginning of Modern British Politics*, Cambridge 1971

Craig, Gordon A./Felix Gilbert (eds.), *The Diplomats 1919–1939*, Princeton, N.J. 1953

Croft, Baron Page-Croft, *My Life of Strife*, London 1948

Cross, Colin, *Philip Snowden*, London 1965

Cross, J.A., *Sir Samuel Hoare. A Political Biography*, London 1977

Crozier, Andrew, 'Prelude to Munich: British Foreign Policy and Germany 1935–38', *European Studies Review*, 6 (1976), pp. 357–381

Crozier, W.P., *Off the Record, Political Interviews 1933–1943*, ed. A.J.P. Taylor, London 1973

Dallek, Robert, *Franklin D. Roosevelt and American Foreign Policy 1932–1945*, New York 1979

Dalton, Hugh, *Memoirs. The Fateful Years, 1931–45*, London 1957

Davis, J.S., *The World Between the Wars, 1919–1939: An Economist's View*, Baltimore 1975

Davis, Samuel, 'The British Labour Party and British Foreign Policy 1931–1939', Ph.D., London School of Economics, 1950

Dennis, Peter, *Decision by Default. Peacetime Conscription and British Defence 1919–1939*, London 1972

——, /A. Preston (eds.), *Soldiers as Statesmen*, London 1976

——, *Swords and Covenants*, London 1975

Deutsch, Harold C., *Conspiracy Against Hitler in the Twilight War*, Minneapolis 1968

——, *Hitler and His Generals. The Hidden Crisis, January–June 1938*, Minneapolis 1973

Dilks, David N., 'Appeasement Revisited', *University of Leeds Review*, 15 (1972), no. 1

——, 'The Unnecessary War', Military Advice and Foreign Policy in Great Britain, 1931–1939', in A. Preston (ed.), *General Staffs and Diplomacy before the Second World War*, London 1978, pp. 98–132

Divine, Robert A., *Roosevelt and World War II*, Baltimore 1969

——, *The Illusion of Neutrality*, Chicago 1962

Doherty, Julian C., *Das Ende des Appeasement. Die britische Außenpolitik, die Achsenmächte und Osteuropa nach dem Münchener Abkommen*, Berlin 1973

Dorpalen, Andreas, *Europe in the Twentieth Century. A History*, New York 1968

Douglas, Roy, *In the Year of Munich*, London 1977

Dreifort, John, 'The French Popular Front and the Franco-Soviet Pact, 1936–37: A Dilemma in Foreign Policy', *JCH*, 9 (1976), pp. 217–236

Drummond, Ian M., *The Floating Pound and the Sterling Area, 1931–1939*,

Cambridge 1981

_____, *British Economic Policy and the Empire 1919–1939*, 1972

_____, *Imperial Economic Policy 1917–1939. Studies in Expansion and Protection*, London 1974

Dülffer, Jost, *Weimar, Hitler und die Marine. Reichspolitik und Flottenbau 1920–1939*, Düsseldorf 1973

Dunbabin, J.P.D., 'British Rearmament in the 1930s: A Chronology and Review', *HJ*, 18 (1975), pp. 587–609

Duroselle, Jean-Baptiste, *La Décadence 1932–1939*, Paris 1979

Eayrs, James, *In Defence of Canada. Appeasement and Rearmament*, Toronto 1965

Eden, Sir Anthony (Earl of Avon), *Facing the Dictators*, London 1962

Edwards, C., *Bruce of Melbourne, Man of Two Worlds*, London 1966

Einzig, Paul, *Appeasement Before, During and After the War*, London 1942

_____, *Bloodless Invasion: German Economic Penetration into the Danubian States and the Balkans*, London 1938

_____, *In the Centre of Things*, London 1960

_____, *The Fight for Financial Supremacy*, London 1932³

Ellsworth, P.T., *The International Economy*, New York 1964³

Emmerson, James Thomas, *The Rhineland Crisis, 7 March 1936. A Study in Multilateral Diplomacy*, London 1977

Endicott, S.L., *Diplomacy and Enterprise: British China Policy 1933–1937*, Manchester 1975

Feavearyear, Sir Albert, *The Pound Sterling*, Oxford 1963²

Federation of British Industries, *A New British Financial Policy, Industry's Plan*, London 1932

Feiling, Keith, *The Life of Neville Chamberlain*, London 1946

Ferrell, Robert H., *American Diplomacy in the Great Depression. Hoover–Stimson Foreign Policy, 1929–1933*, New Haven 1957

Fest, Joachim C, *Das Gesicht des Dritten Reichs — Profile einer totalitären Herrschaft*, München 1963, 1975³

Fisher, Allan G.B., 'Appeasement as a Means to Political Understanding and Peace', *Survey of International Affairs*, 1 (1937) pp. 56–109

Flandin, Pierre-Etienne, *Politique Française 1919–1940*, Paris 1947

Forndran, Erhard/Frank Golczewski/Dieter Riesenberger (eds.), *Innen- und Außenpolitik unter national-sozialistischer Bedrohung. Determinanten internationaler Beziehungen in historischen Fallstudien*, Opladen 1977

Forstmeier, Friedrich/Hans-Erich Volkmann (eds.), *Wirtschaft und Rüstung am Vorabend des Zweiten Weltkriegs*, Düsseldorf 1975

Francis, E.V., *Britain's Economic Strategy*, London 1939

Frankenstein, Robert: 'A propos des aspects financiers du réarmement français, 1935–39', *RHDMG* (1976), pp. 1–20

Freidel, Frank, *The New Deal and the American People*, Englewood Cliffs 1964

Fridenson, Patrick/Jean Lecuir, *La France et la Grande-Bretagne face aux problèmes aériens, 1935–1940*, Paris 1976

Funke, Manfred (ed.), *Totalitarismus — Ein Studienreader zur Herrschaftsanalyse moderner Diktaturen*, Düsseldorf 1977

————— (ed.), *Hitler, Deutschland und die Mächte. Materialien zur Außenpolitik des Dritten Reiches*, Düsseldorf 1976

—————, *Sanktionen und Kanonen. Hitler, Mussolini und der internationale Abessinienkonflikt, 1934–1936*, Düsseldorf 1970

Furnia, Arthur H., *The Diplomacy of Appeasement: Anglo-French Relations and the Prelude to World War II, 1931–1938*, Washington 1960

Gannon, Franklin Reid, *The British Press and Germany 1936–1939*, Oxford 1971

Gardner, Lloyd C., *Economic Aspects of New Deal Diplomacy*, Madison 1964

Gardner, Richard N., *Sterling–Dollar Diplomacy. Anglo-American Collaboration in the Reconstruction of Multilateral Trade*, New York 1956, 1969[2]

Gatzke, Hans W., *European Diplomacy Between Two Wars, 1919–39*, Chicago 1972

Gehl, Jürgen, *Austria, Germany and the Anschluß 1931–38*, London 1963

George, Margaret, *The Warped Vision. British Foreign Policy 1933–1939*, Pittsburgh 1965

Geyer, Dietrich/Boris Meissner (eds.), *Osteuropa-Handbuch: Sowjetunion — Außenpolitik*, 3 vols., Köln 1972–1975

Geyer, Michael, *Aufrüstung oder Sicherheit? Die Reichswehr und die Krise der Machtpolitik, 1924–1936*, Wiesbaden 1980

Gibbs, Norman H., *Grand Strategy*, vol 1: *Rearmament Policy*, London 1976

Gignoux, C.J., *L'Economie française entre les deux guerres*, Paris 1942

Gilbert, Martin (ed.), *Plough My Own Furrow. The Story of Lord Allen of Hurtwood*, London 1965

—————, *Sir Horace Rumbold*, London 1973

—————, *The Roots of Appeasement*, London 1967

—————, *Winston S. Churchill*, vol. 5: *1922–1939*, London 1976

—————, /Richard Gott, *The Appeasers*, London 1963, 1967[2]

Girault, René, 'Léon Blum: La dévaluation de 1936 et la conduite de la politique extérieure de la France', *Relations Internationales*, 13 (1978), pp. 91–109

Gladwyn, Lord, *The Memoirs of Lord Gladwyn*, London 1972

Glynn, S./J. Oxborrow, *Interwar Britain. A Social and Economic History*, London 1976

Gombin, R., *Les Socialistes et la guerre. La S.F.I.O. et la politique étrangère française entre les deux guerres mondiales*, Paris 1970

Gordon, Michael R., *Conflict and Consensus in Labour's Foreign Policy, 1914–1965*, Stanford 1969

Graebner, N.A. (ed.), *An Uncertain Tradition. American Secretaries of State in the 20th Century*, New York 1961

Graml, Hermann, *Europa zwischen den Kriegen*, München 1969

Graves, Robert/Alan Hodges, *The Long Week-End. A Social History of Great Britain, 1918–1939*, New York 1941

Haight, John McVicker, *American Aid to France, 1938–1940*, New York 1970

Hall, H. Duncan, *Commonwealth: A History of the British Commonwealth of Nations*, Cambridge 1971

———, *North American Supply*, London 1955

Hancock, W.K., *Smuts*, vol. 2: *The Fields of Force, 1919–1950*, Cambridge 1968

———, *Survey of British Commonwealth Affairs*, vol. 2: *Problems of Economic Policy, 1918/1939*, Oxford U.P. 1940 (1964)

———, /M.M. Gowing, *British War Economy*, London 1949

Haraszti, Eva H., *Treaty-Breakers or 'Realpolitiker'? The Anglo-German Naval Agreement of June 1935*, Boppard 1974

Hardach, Karl, *Wirtschaftsgeschichte Deutschlands im 20. Jahrhundert*, Göttingen 1976

Harvey, John (ed.), *The Diplomatic Diaries of Oliver Harvey 1937–1940*, London 1970

Hauser, Oswald, *England und das Dritte Reich*, vol. 1: *1933–1936*, Stuttgart 1972

———, (ed.), *Weltpolitik 1933–1939*, Göttingen 1973

Henke, Josef, *England in Hitlers politischem Kalkül 1935–1939*, Boppard 1973

Herbst, Ludolf, 'Die Krise des nationalsozialistischen Systems am Vorabend des 2. Weltkrieges und die forcierte Aufrüstung', *VZG*, 26 (1978), pp. 347–392

Herz, John H., 'Sinn und Sinnlosigkeit der Beschwichtigungspolitik. Zur Problematik des Appeasement-Begriffs', *PVS*, 5 (1964), pp. 370–389

Hertz, Frederick, *The Economic Problems of the Danubian States: A Study in Economic Nationalism*, London 1947

Herzfeld, Hans, 'Zur Problematik der Appeasement-Politik', *Aus Politik und Zeitgeschichte*, 17 April 1963, pp. 3–24

Heuston, R.F.V., *Lives of the Lord Chancellors 1885–1940*, Oxford 1964

Heyl, John D., 'Economic Policy and Political Leadership in the German Depression 1930–1936', Washington University Ph.D., 1971

Hicks, Ursula K., *The Finance of British Government 1920–1936*, Oxford 1938

Hiden, J., *Germany and Europe, 1919–1939*, London 1977

Higham, Robin, *Armed Forces in Peacetime, Britain 1918–1940. A Case Study*, London 1962

———, *The Military Intellectuals in Britain 1918–1939*, London 1966

Hildebrand, Klaus, *Deutsche Außenpolitik 1933–1945. Kalkül oder Dogma?*, Stuttgart 1971

———, 'Hitlers Ort in der Geschichte des Preußisch-Deutschen Nationalstaates', *HZ*, 217 (1973), pp. 584–632

————, *Vom Reich zum Weltreich. Hitler, NSDAP und koloniale Frage 1919–1945*, München 1969

————, 'Die Frankreichpolitik Hitlers bis 1936', *Francia*, 5 (1977), pp. 591–625

Hilger, Gustav/A.G. Meyer, *The Incompatible Allies: A Memoir History of German–Soviet Relations, 1918–1941*, New York 1953

Hill, C.J., 'Great Britain and the Saar Plebiscite of 13 January 1935', *JCH*, 9 (1974/2), pp. 121–142

Hill, Leonidas, *Die Weizsäcker-Papiere 1933–1950*, Berlin 1974

Hillgruber, Andreas, 'Grundzüge der nationalsozialistischen Außenpolitik 1933–1945, *Saeculum*, 24 (1973), pp. 328–345

————, *Hitlers Strategie. Politik und Kriegsführung 1940–1941*, Wiesbaden 1965²

————, *Kontinuität und Diskontinuität in der deutschen Außenpolitik von Bismarck bis Hitler*, Düsseldorf 1969

Hillmann, H.C., 'Comparative Strength of the Great Powers', in A. Toynbee/F.T. Ashton-Gwatkin (eds.), *Survey of International Affairs 1939–46. The World in March 1939*, London/New York 1952

Hoare, Samuel (Viscount Templewood), *Nine Troubled Years*, London 1954

Hodson, H.V., *Slump and Recovery 1929–1937*, Oxford 1938

Howard, Michael, *Studies in War and Peace*, London 1970

————, *The Continental Commitment: The Dilemma of British Defence Policy in the Era of the Two World Wars*, London 1972

————, *War in European History*, Oxford 1976

Howson, Susan, *Domestic Monetary Management in Britain 1919–1938*, Cambridge 1975

————, /D. Winch, *The Economic Advisory Council 1930–1939*, Cambridge 1977

Hüttenberger, Peter, 'Nationalsozialistische Polykratie', in H.A. Winkler (ed.), *Das nationalsozialistische Herrschaftssystem*, *GG*, 2 (1976), pp. 417–442

Hull, Cordell, *The Memoirs of Cordell Hull*, 2 vols., New York 1948

Ironside, Sir Edmund, *The Ironside Diaries, 1937–40*, ed. R. Macleod and D. Kelly, London 1962

Irving, David, *Die Tragödie der deutschen Luftwaffe. Aus den Akten und Erinnerungen von Feldmarschall Milch*, Frankfurt a.M. 1971³

Ismay, Lord, *The Memoirs of General the Lord Ismay*, London 1960

Jacobsen, Hans-Adolf, *Nationalsozialistische Außenpolitik 1933–1938*, Frankfurt, a.M. 1968

Jäckel, Eberhard, *Hitlers Weltanschauung. Entwurf einer Herrschaft*, Tübingen 1969

Jäger, Jörg, *Die wirtschaftliche Abhängigkeit des Dritten Reiches vom Ausland*, Berlin 1969

James, Robert Rhodes, *Churchill: A Study in Failure 1900–1939*, London 1970
————, *The British Revolution, British Politics 1880–1939*, 2 vols., London 1976/77
Jarausch, Konrad H., *The Four-Power Pact, 1933*, Madison 1965
Johnson, Franklyn, *Defence by Committee. The British Committee of Imperial Defence 1885–1959*, London 1960
Joll, James, *Europe since 1870. An International History*, London 1973
————, (ed.), *The Decline of the Third Republic*, London 1959
Jones, B., *The Russia Complex. The British Labour Party and the Soviet Union*, Manchester 1977
Jones, Thomas, *A Diary with Letters, 1931–50*, London 1954
Jordan, W.M., *Great Britain, France and the German Problem 1918–1939*, Oxford 1954, 1971 (repr.)
Junker, Detlef, *Der unteilbare Weltmarkt. Das ökonomische Interesse in der Außenpolitik der USA 1933–41*, Stuttgart 1975

Kahn, A.E., *Great Britain in the World Economy*, New York 1946
Kaiser, Karl/Roger Morgan (eds.), *Britain and West Germany: Changing Societies and the Future of Foreign Policy*, Oxford 1971
Kavanagh, Dennis A., 'Crisis Management and Incremental Adaptation in British Politics: The 1931 Crisis of the British Party System', in Almond/Flanagan/Mundt (eds.), *Crisis, Choice, and Change*, Boston 1973, pp. 152–223
Kemp, Tom, *The French Economy, 1919–39: The History of a Decline*, London 1972
Kendle, J., *The Round Table Movement and Imperial Union*, Oxford 1974
Kennedy, Paul M., 'The Tradition of Appeasement in British Foreign Policy 1865–1939', *British Journal of International Studies*, 2 (1976), pp. 195–215
————, '"Appeasement" and British defence policy in the inter-war years', *British Journal of International Studies*, 4 (1978), pp. 161–177
Kindleberger, Charles P., *The World in Depression, 1929–1939*, London 1973
Kirkpatrick, Sir Ivone, *The Inner Circle. Memoirs*, London 1959
Knipping, Franz, *Die amerikanische Rußlandpolitik in der Zeit des Hitler–Stalin-Paktes 1939–1941*, Tübingen 1974
Knorr, Klaus, *Power and Wealth. The Political Economy of International Power*, New York 1973
Komjathy, Anthony T., *The Crisis of France's East Central Diplomacy, 1933–38*, New York 1977
Kottmann, Richard N., *Reciprocity and the North Atlantic Triangle 1932–1938*, Ithaca 1968
Kreider, Carl, *The Anglo-American Trade Agreement: A Study of British and American Commercial Policy, 1934/1939*, Princeton, N.J. 1943

Lammers, Donald N., 'Fascism, Communism and the Foreign Office 1937–1939', *Journal of Contemporary History*, 6 (1971), pp. 66–86

———, 'From Whitehall after Munich: The Foreign Office and the Future Course of British Policy', *Historical Journal*, 16 (1973), pp. 831–856

———, *Explaining Munich: the Search for Motive in British Policy*, Stanford 1966

Langer, William L./S. Everett Gleason, *The Challenge to Isolation*, New York 1952

Lary, Hal B., et al., *The United States in the World Economy, Bureau of Foreign and Domestic Commerce* (Department of Commerce, Economic Series, no. 23), 1943

League of Nations, *The Course and Phases of the World Economic Depression*, rev. ed. 1931

———, *Commercial Policy in the Inter-War Period*, Geneva 1942

———, *International Currency. Experience and Lessons of the Inter-War Period*, Geneva 1944

Lecuir, Jean/Patrick Fridenson, 'L'organisation de la coopération aérienne franco-britannique (1935–mai 1940)', *Revue d'histoire de la Deuxième Guerre Mondiale*, no. 73 (1969), pp. 43–71

Lee, Bradford A., *Britain and the Sino-Japanese War 1937–39. A Study in the Dilemmas of British Decline*, Stanford 1973

Leffler, Melvyn P., *The Elusive Quest. America's Pursuit of European Stability and French Security, 1919–1933*, Chapel Hill, N.C. 1979

———, 'The Origins of Republican War Debt Policy, 1921–1923: A Case Study in the Application of the Open Door Interpretation', *JAH*, vol. 59 (1972/73), pp. 585–601

Leith-Ross, Sir Frederick, *Money Talks. Fifty Years of International Finance*, London 1968

Leutze, James R., *Bargaining for Supremacy. Anglo-American Naval Collaboration, 1937–1941*, Chapel Hill, N.C. 1977

Lewis, Cleona, *America's Stake in International Investments*, Washington 1938

Lewis, W.A., *Economic Survey, 1919–1939*, London 1949

L'Huillier, Fernand, *Dialogues Franco–Allemands, 1925–1933*, Strasbourg 1971

Liddell Hart, Basil, *Europe in Arms*, London 1937

———, *Memoirs*, 2 vols., London 1965, 1967

———, *The Defence of Britain*, London 1939

Louis, William Roger, *British Strategy in the Far East 1919–1939*, Oxford 1971

Lowe, Peter C., *Great Britain and the Origins of the Pacific War: A Study of British Policy in East Asia, 1937–1941*, Oxford 1977

Luza, Radomir, *Austro-German Relations in the Anschluß Era*, Princeton, N.J. 1975

MacDonald, Callum A., 'Economic Appeasement and the German "Moderates" 1937–1939', *Past & Present*, 56 (1972), pp. 105–135

———, *The U.S., Britain and Appeasement, 1936–1939*, London 1980

MacDonald, Malcolm, *People and Places*, London 1969

MacLachlan, D., *In the Chair, Barrington-Ward of 'The Times' 1927–1948*, London 1971

MacLeod, Ian, *Neville Chamberlain*, London 1961

MacLeod, R./D. Kelly (eds.), *The Ironside Diaries 1937–1940*, London 1962

MacMillan, Harold, *The Past Masters. Politics and Politicians 1906–1939*, London 1975

———, *Winds of Change*, London 1966

McMurry, Dean Scott, *Deutschland und die Sowjetunion 1933–1936. Ideologie, Machtpolitik und Wirtschaftsbeziehungen*, Köln/Wien 1979

Maier, Charles S., *Recasting Bourgeois Europe. Stabilization in France, Germany and Italy in the Decade after World War I*, Princeton, N.J. 1975

Manne, R., 'The British Decision for Alliance with Russia, May 1939', *Journal of Contemporary History*, 9 (1974), no. 3, pp. 3–26

Mansergh, Nicholas, *Das britische Commonwealth*, München 1969

———, (ed.), *Survey of British Commonwealth Affairs: Problems of External Policy, 1931–39*, London 1952

Marks, Sally, *The Illusion of Peace. International Relations in Europe 1918–1933*, London 1976

Marquand, David, *Ramsay MacDonald*, London 1977

Martin, Bernd, *Friedensinitiativen und Machtpolitik im Zweiten Weltkrieg 1939–1942*, Düsseldorf 1974

Marwick, Arthur, *Britain in the Century of Total War: War, Peace and Social Change, 1900–1967*, London 1968

———, *War and Social Change in the 20th Century. A Comparative Study of Britain, France, Germany, Russia and the United States*, London 1974

Mason, H.M., *The Rise of the Luftwaffe: Forging the Secret German Air Weapon, 1918–1940*, New York 1973

Mason, Timothy W., *Arbeiterklasse und Volksgemeinschaft — Dokumente und Materialien zur deutschen Arbeiterpolitik 1936–1940*, Opladen 1975

Massey, Vincent, *What's Past Is Prologue*, London 1963

Medlicott, William Norton, *Britain and Germany: The Search for Agreement 1930–37*, London 1969

———, *British Foreign Policy since Versailles 1919–1963*, London 1968[2]

———, *Contemporary England, 1914–1964*, London 1967

———, (ed.), *From Metternich to Hitler, Aspects of British and Foreign History, 1814–1939*, London 1963

———, *Neville Chamberlain*, London 1953

———, *The Economic Blockade*, London 1952

Metzmacher, Helmut, 'Deutsch–englische Ausgleichsbemühungen im Sommer 1939', *VZG*, 14 (1966), pp. 369–412

Meyers, Reinhard, *Britische Sicherheitspolitik 1934–1938. Studien zum außen- und sicherheitspolitischen Entscheidungsprozeß* (Bonner Schriften zur Politik und Zeitgeschichte, vol. 11), Düsseldorf 1976

Middlemas, Keith, *Diplomacy of Illusion. The British Government and Germany 1937–39*, London 1972

———, *Politics in Industrial Society*, London 1979

Minney, R.J. (ed.), *The Private Papers of Hore-Belisha*, London 1960

Mommsen, Hans/Dietmar Petzina/Bernd Weisbrod (eds.), *Industrielles System und politische Entwicklung in der Weimarer Republik*, Düsseldorf 1974

Monick, Emmanuel, *Pour mémoire*, Paris 1970

Monroe, Elizabeth, *Britain's Moment in the Middle East, 1914–1956*, London 1964

Mowat, Charles Loch, *Britain between the Wars, 1918–1940*, London 1964, 1976

Müller, Klaus Jürgen, *Das Heer und Hitler*, Stuttgart 1969

Naylor, John F., *Labour's International Policy. The Labour Party in the 1930s*, London 1969

Neal, Larry, 'The Economics and Finance of Bilateral Clearings Agreements: Germany, 1934–38', *EcHR*, 32 (1979), pp. 391–404

Néré, J., *The Foreign Policy of France 1915–1945*, London 1975

Newman, Michael, 'The Origins of Munich: British Policy in Danubian Europe, 1933–1937', *HJ*, 21 (1978), pp. 371–386

Newman, Simon, *March 1939: The British Guarantee to Poland*, London, Oxford 1976

Newman, William J., *The Balance of Power in the Interwar Years, 1919–1939*, New York 1968

Nicolson, Nigel (ed.), *Harold Nicolson — Diaries and Letters, 1930–1939*, London 1966

Niedhart, Gottfried, *Großbritannien und die Sowjetunion 1934–1939. Studien zur britischen Politik der Friedenssicherung zwischen den beiden Weltkriegen*, München 1972

Nolte, Ernst, *Three Faces of Fascism*, London 1966

Northedge, F.S., *The Troubled Giant. Britain Among the Great Powers 1916–1939*, New York 1966

Norwich, 1st Viscount, *Old Men Forget*, New York 1954

Nove, A., *An Economic History of the USSR*, London 1969

Offner, Arnold A., *American Appeasement: United States Foreign Policy and Germany 1933–1938*, Cambridge, Mass. 1969

Oliver, Robert W., *International Economic Co-operation and the World Bank*, London 1975

O'Neill, R.J., *The German Army and the Nazi Party 1933–1939*, Introduction by Sir Basil Liddell Hart, London 1966

Ovendale, Ritchie, *'Appeasement' and the English-Speaking World*, Cardiff 1975

Parker, R.A.C., 'Britain, France and Scandinavia 1939/1940', *History*, 61

(1979), pp. 369–387

———, 'Great Britain, France and the Ethiopian Crisis 1935–1936', *EHR*, 89 (April 1974), pp. 293–332

———, 'The British Government and the Coming of War with Germany 1939', in M.R.D. Foot (ed.), *War and Society. Historical Essays in Honour and Memory of J.R. Western*, London 1973

———, 'The First Capitulation. France and the Rhineland Crisis of 1936', *World Politics*, 8 (1955/56), pp. 355–373

Peden, George C., *British Rearmament and the Treasury, 1932–39*, Edinburgh 1979

———, 'Sir Warren Fisher and British Rearmament Against Germany', *EHR*, 44 (1979), pp. 29–47

Percy, Lord Eustace, *Some Memories*, London 1958

Petzina, Dietmar, *Autarkiepolitik im Dritten Reich*, Stuttgart 1968

———, *Die deutsche Wirtschaft in der Zwischenkriegszeit*, Wiesbaden 1977

Phillips, G.A./R.T. Maddock, *The Growth of the British Economy 1918–1968*, London 1973

Poidevin, Raymond/Jacques Bariéty, *Les relations franco–allemandes 1815–1975*, Paris 1977

Pollard, Sidney, *The Development of the British Economy, 1914–1967*, London 1970²

Postan, M.M., *British War Production*, London 1952

Potter, Jim, *The American Economy Between the World Wars*, New York 1974

Powers, Barry D., *Strategy without Sliderule: British Air Strategy 1914–1939*, London 1976

Pratt, Lawrence R., *East of Malta, West of Suez. Britain's Mediterranean Crisis, 1936–1939*, Cambridge 1975

———, 'The Anglo-American Naval Conversations of January 1938', *International Affairs*, 47/4 (1971), pp. 745–763

Presseisen, Ernst L., *Amiens and Munich: Comparisons in Appeasement*, The Hague 1978

Preston, A. (ed.), *General Staffs and Diplomacy before the Second World War*, London 1978

Price, Ward, *I Know These Dictators*, London 1937

Reader, W.J., *History of Imperial Chemical Industries*, vol. 1, London 1970

———, *Architect of Air Power*, London 1968

Remak, Joachim, *The Origins of the Second World War*, Englewood Cliffs (N.J.) 1976

Remer, C.F., *Foreign Investments in China*, New York 1933

Renouvin, Pierre, *Histoire des relations internationales*, vols. 7/8, Paris 1957, 1958

———, /Melanges Pierre Renouvin, *Etudes d'histoire des relations and internationales*, Paris 1975

Reynolds, D., *The Creation of the Anglo-American Alliance, 1913–1937. A*

Study in Competitive Co-operation, London 1981

Rich, Norman, *Hitler's War Aims*, 2 vols., New York 1974

Richardson, Harry W., *Economic Recovery in Britain, 1932–39*, London 1967

Richardson, J. Henry, *British Economic Foreign Policy*, London 1936

Riekhoff, H. von, *German–Polish Relations, 1919–1933*, Baltimore 1971

Robbins, Keith G., *Munich, 1938*, London 1968

Robertson, Esmonde, *Hitler's Pre-War Policy and Military Plans 1933–1939*, London 1963

Robertson, E.D. (ed.), *The Origins of the Second World War. Historical Interpretations*, London 1971

Rock, William R., *Appeasement on Trial: British Foreign Policy and its Critics 1938/39*, Hamden 1966

———, *British Appeasement in the 1930s*, London 1977

Rohe, Karl (ed.), *Die Westmächte und das Dritte Reich 1933–1939. Klassische Großmachtrivalität oder Kampf zwischen Demokratie und Diktatur?*, Paderborn 1982

Roskill, Stephen, *Hankey. Man of Secrets*, vol. 1: *1877–1918*; vol. 2: *1919–1931*; vol. 3: *1931–1963*, London 1970–74

———, *Naval Policy Between the Wars*, vol. 1: *The Period of Anglo-American Antagonism*, London 1968; vol. 2: *The Period of Reluctant Rearmament 1930–1939*, London 1976

Rostow, Nicholas, *Anglo-French Relations 1934–36*, London 1984

Rothschild, J., *East Central Europe Between the Two World Wars*, Washington 1975

Rowland, Benjamin M. (ed.), *Balance of Power or Hegemony: The Interwar Monetary System*, New York 1976

———, 'Commercial Conflict and Foreign Policy: A Study in Anglo-American Relations 1932–1938', Ph.D., Johns Hopkins School of Advanced International Studies, Washington 1975

Royal Institute of International Affairs, *Germany and the Rhineland*, London 1936

———, *Monetary Policy and the Depression*, London 1933

———, *The Future of Monetary Policy*, Oxford 1935

———, *Political and Strategic Interests of the United Kingdom (An Outline by a Study Group of the Royal Institute of International Affairs)*, London 1939

———, *The Problem of International Investment*, Oxford 1937

———, *Survey of World Affairs*, London 1931ff.

———, *The Balkan States*, vol. 1: *Economics*, Oxford 1936

———, *South-Eastern Europe — A Political and Economic Survey*, Oxford 1939

Russett, Bruce M., *Community and Contention. Britain and America in the Twentieth Century*, Cambridge 1963

Sabine, B.E.V., *British Budgets in Peace and War, 1932–1945*, London 1970

Salewski, Michael, *Die deutsche Seekriegsleitung 1935–1945*, vol. 1: *1935–1941*, München 1970

Sauvy, Alfred, *Histoire économique de la France entre les deux guerres*, vol. 2:

1931–1939, Paris 1967

Sayers, R.S., *The Bank of England 1891–1944*, 3 vols, Cambridge 1976

Segal, E., 'Sir John Simon and British Foreign Policy: The Diplomacy of Disarmament in the early 1930s', Ph.D., Berkeley 1969

Seton-Watson, R.W., *Britain and the Dictators*, Cambridge 1939

Shai, Aron, 'Was there a Far Eastern Munjch?', *Journal of Contemporary History*, 9 (1974), pp. 161–169

Shay, R.P., *British Rearmament in the Thirties: Politics and Profits*, Princeton, N.J. 1977

Skidelsky, Robert, *Oswald Mosley*, London 1974

———, *Politicians and the Slump. The Labour Government of 1929–1931*, London 1967

Slessor, Sir John, *Air Power and Armies*, London 1936

———, *The Central Blue*, London 1956

Spier, Eugen, *Focus. A Footnote to the History of the Thirties*, London 1963

Svennilson, Ingvar, *Growth and Stagnation in the European Economy*, Geneva 1954

Swinton, Earl of, *Sixty Years of Power*, London 1966

Swinton, Viscount (Philip Cunliffe-Lister), *I Remember*, London 1948

Schatz, Arthur W., 'The Anglo-American Trade Agreement and Cordell Hull's Search for Peace 1936–1938', *Journal of American History*, 57 (1970/71), pp. 85–103

Schmidt, Gustav, 'Politisches System und Appeasement-Politik, 1930–1937. Zur Scharnierfunktion der Rüstungspolitik für die Britische Innen- und Außenpolitik', *MGM*, 1979, pp. 37–53

———, (ed.), *Konstellationen Internationaler Politik 1924–1932. Politische und wirtschaftliche Faktoren in den Beziehungen zwischen Westeuropa und den Vereinigten Staaten*, Bochum 1983

———, 'Politische Tradition und wirtschaftliche Faktoren in der britischen Friedensstrategie 1917–1919. Grundzüge einer europäischen Nachkriegsordnung in der Sicht englischer und französischer Machteliten', Habil-Schrift, Münster 1971

Schmidt, Paul, *Statist auf Diplomatischer Bühne 1923–1945*, Frankfurt a.M. 1964

Schröder, Hans-Jürgen, 'Deutsche Südosteuropapolitik 1929–1936. Zur Kontinuität deutscher Außenpolitik in der Weltwirtschaftskrise', *Geschichte und Gesellschaft*, 2 (1976), pp. 5–32

———, *Deutschland und die Vereinigten Staaten 1933–1939. Zur Entwicklung des deutsch-amerikanischen Gegensatzes vor dem Zweiten Weltkrieg*, Wiesbaden 1970

———, 'Südosteuropa als Informal Empire Deutschlands 1933–1939. Das Beispiel Jugoslawiens', *Jahrbuch für Geschichte Osteuropas*, 23 (1975), pp. 70–96

Schwoerer, L.G., 'Lord Halifax's Visit to Germany: November 1937', *The Historian*, 32 (1970)

Stachura, P., *The Shaping of the Nazi State*, London 1978

Stanworth, Philip/A. Giddens (eds.), *Elites and Power in British Society*, London/New York 1974

Stevenson, John, *Social Conditions in Britain between the Wars*, Harmondsworth 1977

Tamchina, Rainer, 'Commonwealth and Appeasement: Die Politik der britischen Dominions', *Neue Politische Literatur*, 1972, pp. 471–489

──────, 'In Search of Common Causes: The Imperial Conference of 1937', *Journal of Imperial and Commonwealth History*, 1 (1972), pp. 79–105

Taylor, A.J.P., *Beaverbrook*, London 1972

──────, et al., *Churchill, Four Faces and the Man*, London 1969

──────, *English History 1914–1945*, Oxford 1965

──────, *The Origins of the Second World War*, London 1961

Teichova, Alice, *An Economic Background to Munich: International Business and Czechoslovakia, 1918–1938*, Cambridge 1974

Templewood, Lord, *Nine Troubled Years*, London 1954

Tennant, E.W.D., *True Account*, London 1957

Thomas, Georg, *Geschichte der deutschen Wehr- und Rüstungswirtschaft 1918–1943/45*, ed. W. Birkenfeld, Boppard 1966

Thompson, Neville, *The Anti-Appeasers. Conservative Opposition to Appeasement in the 1930s*, Oxford 1971

Thorne, Christopher, *The Approach of War 1938–39*, London 1967

──────, *The Limits of Foreign Policy. The West, the League and the Far Eastern Crisis of 1931–33*, (1972), London 1973 (paperback)

──────, *Allies of a Kind: USA, Britain and the War against Japan*, London 1978

The Times, *The History of 'The Times'*, vol. 4, part 2, 1952

Tournoux, Paul-Emile, *Haut Commandement, Gouvernement et Défense des frontières 1919–1939*, Paris 1960

Trotter, Ann, *Britain and East Asia 1933–1937*, London/New York/Cambridge 1975

Ulam, Adam B., *Expansion and Coexistence. The History of Soviet Foreign Policy 1917–1967*, London 1968

United Nations, *International Capital Movements during the Inter-War Period*, New York 1949

United States Air Force, *The German Air Force in World War II*, ed. USAF, Historical Division, Research Studies Institute, Air University, 1959ff.

Vansittart, Lord, *The Mist Procession*, London 1958

──────, *Lessons of My Life*, New York 1943

Varg, P.A., 'The Economic Side of Good Neighbourhood Policy: The Reciprocal Trade Program and South America', *Pacific Historical Review*, 45 (1976), pp. 47–71

Waites, Neville (ed.), *Troubled Neighbours. Franco-British Relations in the Twentieth Century*, London 1971

Waley, D., *British Public Opinion and the Abyssinian War, 1935–36*, London 1975

Watt, Donald C., 'Appeasement. The Rise of a Revisionist School?' *Political Quarterly*, 36 (1965), pp. 191–213

———, *Personalities and Policies. Studies in the Formulation of British Foreign Policy in the Twentieth Century*, London 1965

———, *Too Serious a Business. European Armed Forces and the Approach to the Second World War*, London 1975

———, *Succeeding John Bull. America in Britain's Place 1900–1975. A Study of the Anglo-American Relationship and World Politics in the Context of British and American Foreign-Policy Making in the Twentieth Century*, Cambridge 1984

Webster, Charles/Noble Frankland, *The Strategic Bombing Offensive*, vols. 1 and 2, London 1961

Wee, Hermann van der (ed.), *The Great Depression Revisited. Essays on the Economies of the Thirties*, The Hague 1972

Weinberg, Gerhard L., *The Foreign Policy of Hitler's Germany. Diplomatic Revolution in Europe, 1933–1936*, Chicago 1970

———, *The Foreign Policy of Hitler's Germany. Starting World War II, 1937–39*, Chicago 1980

Weingärtner, Thomas, *Stalin und der Aufstieg Hitlers: Die Deutschlandpolitik der Sowjetunion und der kommunistischen Internationale 1929–1934*, Berlin 1970

Wendt, Bernd-Jürgen, *Economic Appeasement. Handel und Finanz in der britischen Deutschlandpolitik 1933–1939*, Düsseldorf 1971

Wheeler-Bennett, John W., *Special Relationships: America in Peace and War*, London 1976

———, *John Anderson, Viscount Waverley*, London 1962

———, *Munich: Prologue to Tragedy*, London 1948

———, *The Nemesis of Power: The German Army in Politics*, London 1964²

Wiggershaus, Norbert T., *Der deutsch-englische Flottenvertrag vom 18. Juni 1935. England und die geheime deutsche Aufrüstung 1933–1935*, Bonn 1972

Williams, L.J., *Britain and the World Economy 1919–1970*, London 1971

Williams, W.A. (ed.), *From Colony to Empire. Essays in the History of American Foreign Relations*, New York 1972

Winkler, A.R. (ed.), *Twentieth-Century Britain. National Power and Social Welfare*, New York/London 1978.

Wolfers, Arnold, *Britain and France Between Two Wars. Conflicting Strategies of Peace Since Versailles*, New York 1940, 1963

Wollsten, Günter, *Vom Weimarer Revisionismus zu Hitler. Das Deutsche Reich und die Großmächte in der Anfangsphase der nationalsozialistischen Herrschaft in Deutschland*, Bonn 1973

Wood, Derek/Derek Dempster, *The Narrow Margin. The Battle of Britain and the Rise of Air Power 1930–1940*, New York 1961, 1970[3]

Woodruff, William, *America's Impact on the World. A Study of the Role of the United States in the World Economy 1750–1970*, London 1975

Woytinsky, W.S./E.S. Woytinsky, *World Commerce and Governments*, New York 1955

Wrench, J.E., *Geoffrey Dawson and our Times*, London 1955

Young, Kenneth, *Stanley Baldwin*, London 1976

Young, Robert J., *In Command of France. French Foreign Policy and Military Planning, 1933–1940*, Cambridge, Mass. 1978

Ziebura, Gilbert, et al., *Bestimmungsfaktoren der Außenpolitik in der 2. Hälfte des 20. Jahrhunderts*, Berlin 1974

———, *Weltwirtschaft und Weltpolitik 1922/24–1931. Zwischen Rekonstruktion und Zusammenbruch*, Frankfurt a.M. 1984

Index

References to 'Great Britain' ('England', 'United Kingdom'); 'Germany' ('Third Reich', 'Weimar Republic', 'Wilhelmine Germany'); 'appeaser'; and 'economic appeaser' are not included below. The index does refer, however, to names and topics mentioned in the footnotes.